LET'S

■ PAGES PACKED WITH ESSENTIAL INFORMATION

"Value-packed, unbeatable, accurate, and comprehensive."

—*The Los Angeles Times*

"The guides are aimed not only at young budget travelers but at the independent traveler; a sort of streetwise cookbook for traveling alone."

—*The New York Times*

"Unbeatable; good sight-seeing advice; up-to-date info on restaurants, hotels, and inns; a commitment to money-saving travel; and a wry style that brightens nearly every page."

—*The Washington Post*

■ THE BEST TRAVEL BARGAINS IN YOUR BUDGET

"All the dirt, dirt cheap."

—*People*

"Let's Go follows the creed that you don't have to toss your life's savings to the wind to travel—unless you want to."

—*The Salt Lake Tribune*

■ REAL ADVICE FOR REAL EXPERIENCES

"The writers seem to have experienced every rooster-packed bus and lunar-surfaced mattress about which they write."

—*The New York Times*

"[Let's Go's] devoted updaters really walk the walk (and thumb the ride, and trek the trail). Learn how to fish, haggle, find work—anywhere."

—*Food & Wine*

"A world-wise traveling companion—always ready with friendly advice and helpful hints, all sprinkled with a bit of wit."

—*The Philadelphia Inquirer*

■ A GUIDE WITH A SPIRIT AND A SOCIAL CONSCIENCE

"Lighthearted and sophisticated, informative and fun to read. [Let's Go] helps the novice traveler navigate like a knowledgeable old hand."

—*Atlanta Journal-Constitution*

"The serious mission at the book's core reveals itself in exhortations to respect the culture and the environment—and, if possible, to visit as a volunteer, a student, or a teacher rather than a tourist."

—*San Francisco Chronicle*

LET'S GO PUBLICATIONS

TRAVEL GUIDES

Australia 9th edition
Austria & Switzerland 12th edition
Brazil 1st edition
Britain 2008
California 10th edition
Central America 9th edition
Chile 2nd edition
China 5th edition
Costa Rica 3rd edition
Eastern Europe 13th edition
Ecuador 1st edition
Egypt 2nd edition
Europe 2008
France 2008
Germany 13th edition
Greece 9th edition
Hawaii 4th edition
India & Nepal 8th edition
Ireland 13th edition
Israel 4th edition
Italy 2008
Japan 1st edition
Mexico 22nd edition
New Zealand 8th edition
Peru 1st edition
Puerto Rico 3rd edition
Southeast Asia 9th edition
Spain & Portugal 2008
Thailand 3rd edition
USA 24th edition
Vietnam 2nd edition
Western Europe 2008

ROADTRIP GUIDE

Roadtripping USA 2nd edition

ADVENTURE GUIDES

Alaska 1st edition
Pacific Northwest 1st edition
Southwest USA 3rd edition

CITY GUIDES

Amsterdam 5th edition
Barcelona 3rd edition
Boston 4th edition
London 16th edition
New York City 16th edition
Paris 14th edition
Rome 12th edition
San Francisco 4th edition
Washington, D.C. 13th edition

POCKET CITY GUIDES

Amsterdam
Berlin
Boston
Chicago
London
New York City
Paris
San Francisco
Venice
Washington, D.C.

LET'S GO

NEW ZEALAND

GTON

WRITERS

ECO, JR.

LMES

RICHARD LONSDORF

MEGAN SMITH

THOMAS MACDONALD BARRON MAP EDITOR

RACHEL NOLAN MANAGING EDITOR

ST. MARTIN'S PRESS ✖ NEW YORK

HELPING LET'S GO. If you want to share your discoveries, suggestions, or corrections, please drop us a line. We read every piece of correspondence, whether a postcard, a 10-page email, or a coconut. **Address mail to:**

Let's Go: New Zealand
67 Mount Auburn St.
Cambridge, MA 02138
USA

Visit Let's Go at **http://www.letsgo.com,** or send email to:

feedback@letsgo.com
Subject: "Let's Go: New Zealand"

In addition to the invaluable travel advice our readers share with us, many are kind enough to offer their services as researchers or editors. Unfortunately, our charter enables us to employ only currently enrolled Harvard students.

HOW TO USE THIS BOOK

Kia Ora! Welcome to *Let's Go: New Zealand.* In addition to providing you with the most up-to-date information on where to eat, where to stay, where to go, and where not to go, we'll tell you how to find the world's cheapest skydive (**Taupo,** p. 194), where to go for world-class diving (**Poor Knights Islands,** p. 110), and how to fall 40m in a sack with two of your best friends (**Rotorua,** p. 156). Whatever adrenaline rush you crave, we have your fix. So buckle up.

DISCOVER. Discover New Zealand (p. 1) provides an overview of travel on both islands, including **suggested itineraries** for how to spend your time there.

ESSENTIALS. This section outlines the practical information you need in order to travel safely and easily in New Zealand (p. 9).

LIFE AND TIMES. This chapter details historical and cultural information helpful in gaining a deeper understanding of the Kiwi life and of just how ginormous their squid is (p. 41).

BEYOND TOURISM. Traveling to New Zealand can entail much more than a tour-bus and a few snapshots. To find out how you can volunteer, study, or get some much-needed cash as a short-term employee, check out our chapter on **Beyond Tourism** (p. 54).

THE GREAT OUTDOORS. This section is a resource for outdoor and adventure activities in New Zealand, including bungy jumping, kayaking, and tramping. The nine **Great Walks** and several other tramps are labeled throughout the book with a 🔊 (p. 67).

TRANSPORTATION INFO. Before continuing on the next leg of your journey, be sure to check the transportation section at the beginning of each town, which lists trip duration, departure frequency, and price. Unless otherwise listed, prices are based on one-way fares.

COVERAGE LAYOUT. Coverage begins in Auckland and moves from the northern tip of North Island to the southern end of South Island.

PRICE DIVERSITY. Our researchers list establishments in order of value from best to worst, with absolute favorites denoted by the *Let's Go* thumbs-up (📧). Since the cheapest price does not always mean the best value, we have incorporated a system of price ranges for food and accommodations; see p. XII.

PHONE CODES AND TELEPHONE NUMBERS. Area codes for each region appear opposite the name of the region and are denoted by the ☎ icon. Phone numbers in text are also preceded by the ☎ icon.

A NOTE TO OUR READERS. The information for this book was gathered by *Let's Go* researchers from January through March of 2007. Each listing is based on one researcher's opinion, formed during his or her visit at a particular time. Those traveling at other times may have different experiences since prices, dates, hours, and conditions are always subject to change. You are urged to check the facts presented in this book beforehand to avoid inconvenience and surprises.

CONTENTS

VIII

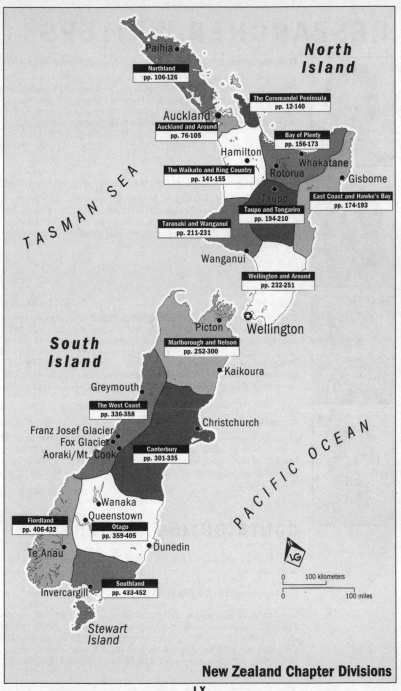

North Island

Paihia

Northland
pp. 106-126

The Coromandel Peninsula
pp. 12-140

Auckland

Auckland and Around
pp. 76-105

Hamilton

Bay of Plenty
pp. 156-173

Whakatane

The Waikato and King Country
pp. 141-155

Rotorua

Gisborne

Taupo

East Coast and Hawke's Bay
pp. 174-193

Taupo and Tongariro
pp. 194-210

Taranaki and Wanganui
pp. 211-231

Wanganui

TASMAN SEA

Wellington and Around
pp. 232-251

Picton

Wellington

South Island

Marlborough and Nelson
pp. 252-300

Kaikoura

Greymouth

The West Coast
pp. 336-358

Christchurch

Franz Josef Glacier
Fox Glacier
Aoraki/Mt. Cook

Canterbury
pp. 301-335

Wanaka
Queenstown

Fiordland
pp. 406-432

Otago
pp. 359-405

Te Anau

Dunedin

PACIFIC OCEAN

0   100 kilometers

0   100 miles

Southland
pp. 433-452

Invercargill

Stewart
Island

New Zealand Chapter Divisions

RESEARCHER-WRITERS

Mark Giangreco, Jr.　　　　　　　　　　*North of the North Island*

A Jacques Cousteau devotee, Mark gave up his position with National Public Radio to scour the sea bottom for New Zealand's magical sea life and follow in the wake of his favorite Frenchy. Despite initial computer snafus, this zealous zealander forged on adding spice to tame North Island fare with gracious wit and Italian recipes.

Lauren Holmes　　*South of the North Island including the Farewell Spit*

A three-time Italy researcher, Lauren faced new outdoor terrain during her time in New Zealand. Her travels led her through the sulfurous fumes of Rotorua and screaming down rivers in whitewater rafts. Through it all, her laid-back attitude allowed her to capture the thrilling side of New Zealand's udder.

Megan Smith　　　　　　　　　　*North of the South Island*

A dinosaur of a researcher, Megan charged into South Island's adventure heartland with bravada and fearlessness. Her high tolerance for adrenaline and penchant for spreading Monteith's love had her picking the brains of every tour operator between Wanaka and Picton as she plummeted over waterfalls on a rope, raft, or kayak. Her experience traveling and teaching in Australia's eastern outposts more than prepared this Midwesterner for her Kiwi crossover.

Richard Lonsdorf　　　　　　　　　　*South of the South Island*

An office warrior and first-time researcher, Richard headed straight from the symphonic clamor of Berlin to the wilds of New Zealand. Braving mud, dangerous keas, and less-than-satisfactory meat pies, Richard took on nature and small town Kiwi gossip with fabulous flair and humor.

CONTRIBUTING WRITERS

Max Morange graduated from Harvard College with a Bachelor's degree in English and American Literature and Language. His experience with WWOOF ranges from pressing olive oil in Tuscany to milking donkeys in the French Pyrenees.

Ann Robinson has made many contributions to *Let's Go: New Zealand*. She was a researcher-writer for the 2000 and 2002 guides and an editor for the 2001 guide. A recipient of a Fulbright scholarship, she received her Masters in History at Victoria University in Wellington, focusing on comparative US-New Zealand history.

ACKNOWLEDGMENTS

LET'S GO

TEAM NEW ZEALAND THANKS. Our sweet RWs, the entire Let's Go staff, and the good as gold Kiwis who helped us write this book.

LIZA THANKS. My awesomely epic RWs—Mark, Lauren, Megan, and Richard—for being the most bombproof group ever and for keeping me entertained in the empty 67 Mt. Auburn St. RaNo and Tom—there are no words. The rest of the ME team for helping me keep it together. My parents for paying my rent. The Qs for giving me shelter. And all the DOC offices in New Zealand, particularly the Nelson office.

RACHEL THANKS. Liza for going above and beyond the call of duty to wrap this book. The RWs for their laugh-out-loud marginalia. Tom for something. The ME team for highs and lows. My friends—especially Annie, Sophie, and Tish—for putting up with my senior spring absences. Molly, for emotional support and Amy for lending her. As always, my parents and grandma. Lastly, to Laura—who I am proud to call my sister.

TOM THANKS. Liza, you put together a great book, thanks for all the laughs. Rachel, thanks for never overwhelming RWs and for being sympathetic always. It was a pleasure as usual. Vicki and Jansen, thanks for all the typesetting work; your hard work is what gives us the final product. Thanks to the rest of the ME team for keeping us all sane and in business during the whole project. And thanks to all the RWs for your hard work.

Publishing Director
Jennifer Q. Wong
Editor-in-Chief
Silvia Gonzalez Killingsworth
Production Manager
Victoria Esquivel-Korsiak
Cartography Manager
Thomas MacDonald Barron
Editorial Managers
Anne Bensson, Calina Ciobanu, Rachel Nolan
Financial Manager
Sara Culver
Business and Marketing Manager
Julie Vodhanel
Personnel Manager
Victoria Norelid
Production Associate
Jansen A. S. Thurmer
Director of E-Commerce & IT
Patrick Carroll
Website Manager
Kathryne A. Bevilacqua
Office Coordinators
Juan L. Peña, Bradley J. Jones

Director of Advertising Sales
Hunter McDonald
Senior Advertising Associates
Daniel Lee

Editor
Liza Covington
Managing Editor
Rachel Nolan
Map Editor
Thomas MacDonald Barron
Typesetters
Jansen Thurmer & Victoria Esquivel-Korsiak

President
William Hauser
General Managers
Bob Rombauer, Jim McKellar

PRICE RANGES ❸ ❹
NEW ZEALAND ❺

①ﾠﾠ②

Our researchers list establishments in order of value from best to worst, and our favorites are denoted by the Let's Go thumbs-up (🖒). However, because the best value is not always the cheapest price, we have also incorporated a system of price ranges, based on a rough expectation of what you'll spend. For **accommodations,** we base our range on the cheapest price for which a single traveler can stay for one night. For **restaurants** and other dining establishments, we estimate the average amount a traveler will spend. The table tells you what you'll *typically* find in New Zealand at the corresponding price range; keep in mind that no system can allow for every individual establishment's quirks, and you'll typically get more for your money in larger cities.

ACCOMMODATIONS	RANGE	WHAT YOU'RE LIKELY TO FIND
①	under NZ$15	A basic budget hostel featuring running water, a bed, and shared restrooms and bath. Campers can expect basic, DOC-run cabins and powered tent sites.
②	NZ$16-25	A more upscale hostel with extra amenities like laundry, Internet access, and lounge areas. Possibly ensuite.
③	NZ$26-50	Similar to above, but with more amenities and usually in a quieter part of town. TV, private bath, and fridge are common; some also offer tourist services and/or breakfast. B&Bs often fall in this range.
④	NZ$51-99	A resort- or business-style accommodation. Excellent service, all the amenities, and a prime location.
⑤	above NZ$100	Expect a luxury resort or hotel with ocean views, all the amenities, and more (an on-site masseuse comes to mind).

FOOD	RANGE	WHAT YOU'RE LIKELY TO FIND
①	under NZ$7	A basic cafe, bakery, or street-corner stand. Don't expect an extensive menu or a guaranteed seat.
②	NZ$8-12	A typical lunch or cheap dinner at a local joint with seating. Menus often include pizza, burgers, and other quick options.
③	NZ$13-18	Typical dinner mains with a touch of class. Many establishments will offer ethnic options.
④	NZ$19-24	Full meals in a classy establishment. The menu will offer more sophisticated mains and more meat options.
⑤	over NZ$25	Your meal might cost more than your room, but there's a reason—it's something fabulous or famous, or both, and you'll probably need to wear something other than sandals and a t-shirt. Often includes fresh local fish cooked to perfection.

DISCOVER
NEW ZEALAND

Once visited only by the most intrepid explorers, modern-day New Zealand beckons to adventurous spirits with its vast wilderness. Created by the violent collision of continental plates and surrounded by daunting expanses of water, the island nation has never completely severed itself from its ancient beginnings. Known in Maori as *Aotearoa* ("the land of the long white cloud"), New Zealand's rich natural heritage is the foundation for its famous Kiwi pride and hospitality.

New Zealand's impressive ecological diversity draws visitors from around the globe each year. Developed in a spirit of integration and conservation, the tourism industry provides travelers with limitless opportunities to enjoy *Aotearoa*'s natural splendor, including a comprehensive network of tracks, nature reserves, and national parks. Not to be outdone by the nation's natural endowments, "adrenaline vendors" offer travelers the most exhilarating means by which to experience the country, from bungy jumping to adventure caving to heli-biking. Catering to those who choose to tramp through New Zealand's pristine countryside as well as to those who prefer to plummet toward it, Kiwis have created an atmosphere as thrilling as it is beautiful.

FACTS AND FIGURES

CAPITAL: Wellington

YEAR OF INDEPENDENCE: 1947

COMBINED LENGTH OF GREAT WALKS: 551km

YEAR RUGBY FOOTBALL UNION WAS ESTABLISHED: 1892

YEAR OF FIRST TELEVISED RUGBY MATCH: 1954

RATIO OF SHEEP TO PEOPLE AT LAMBING TIME: 35:1

AMOUNT OF LAMB CONSUMED ANNUALLY: Over 20kg per capita

WHEN TO GO

Most travelers to New Zealand visit during the sunny summer months (Nov.-Feb.), when temperatures are warmer, mountain peaks are accessible, and the tourist infrastructure is in high gear. High-season visitors can access the greatest variety of outdoors options but will also be faced with the largest crowds. Low season occurs during the dead of winter (May-Sept.), when many tours and activities, with the exception of skiing and snowboarding, shut down. The best combination of weather, availability, and crowd size occurs during the "shoulder" seasons (Mar.-Apr. and Oct.-Nov.), although in some popular areas such as Queenstown and Taupo the crowds continue year-round. Travelers from the Northern Hemisphere should remember that seasons reverse when crossing the equator.

For detailed **climate, holiday,** and **festival** charts for New Zealand, see the **Appendix,** p. 453, and **Life and Times,** p. 41.

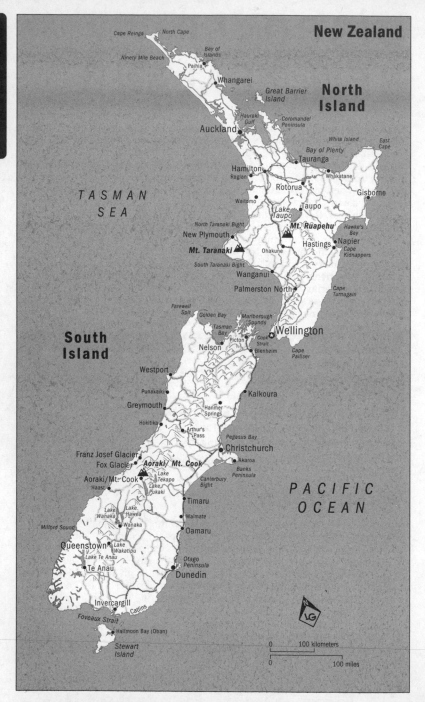

New Zealand

Cape Reinga   North Cape

Ninety Mile Beach   Bay of Islands

Paihia

Whangarei

North Island

Great Barrier Island

Hauraki Gulf   Coromandel Peninsula

Auckland

White Island   East Cape

Bay of Plenty

Hamilton   **Tauranga**

Raglan   Whakatane

Rotorua   Gisborne

Waitomo   Taupo

TASMAN SEA

Lake Taupo

North Taranaki Bight   **Mt. Ruapehu**

New Plymouth   Hawke's Bay

Mt. Taranaki   Ohakune   Hastings   Napier

Cape Kidnappers

South Taranaki Bight

Wanganui

Palmerston North

Cape Turnagain

Farewell Spit   Golden Bay   Marlborough Sounds

South Island

Tasman Bay   **Wellington**

Nelson   Picton

Cook Strait

Blenheim   Cape Palliser

Westport

Punakaiki   Kaikoura

Greymouth   Hanmer Springs

Hokitika   Arthur's Pass

Pegasus Bay

Franz Josef Glacier   **Christchurch**

Fox Glacier   Akaroa

Aoraki/ Mt. Cook   Banks Peninsula

Lake Tekapo   Canterbury Bight

Aoraki/Mt. Cook

Haast   Lake Pukaki

Timaru

PACIFIC OCEAN

Lake Hawea

Lake Wanaka   Walmate

Milford Sound   Wanaka   Oamaru

Queenstown   Lake Wakatipu

Lake Te Anau   Otago Peninsula

Te Anau   **Dunedin**

Invercargill   Catlins

Foveaux Strait

Halfmoon Bay (Oban)

Stewart Island

0   100 kilometers

0   100 miles

WHAT TO DO

The sheer number of activities available in New Zealand can be overwhelming. No matter how long you stay, there's always one more wave to surf, peak to summit, or reef to explore. The itineraries below should help to acquaint you with the endless possibilities and suggest how you might divide your time between them. For more specific regional attractions, see the **Highlights of the Region** box at the beginning of each chapter.

◪ LET'S GO PICKS

BEST PLACE TO BOOZE AND BOGEY: With holes replaced by goalposts and rugby-shaped golf balls, your score is almost guaranteed to remain sub-par at **Rippon's Winery GolfCross** (p. 400), even after sampling the many complimentary wines.

BEST PLACE TO TEMPT FATE: Get your thrills on a skydive over **Taupo** (p. 198) or **Franz Josef** and **Fox Glaciers** (p. 358).

BEST PLACE TO WORSHIP AT THE ALTAR OF RUGBY: Back the All Blacks, New Zealand's favorite sports team, at Christchurch's **The Holy Grail Sports Bar** (p. 315).

BEST HAND-CRANKED PASTA: For a rare taste of Italy's best export, hit family-run **Di Luca's** in hip Thames (p. 130).

BEST PLACE TO GET WRECKED: Dive into the **Mikhail Lermontov shipwreck,** one of the largest open wrecks in the world, in the Marlborough Sounds, (p. 271).

BEST PLACE TO BE BURIED ALIVE: Rent a shovel, dig a hole in the sand, and bask in your own personal hot spring at **Hot Water Beach** (p. 138).

BEST PLACE TO MEET THE LOCALS: Get up close and personal with New Zealand's most recognizable resident at **Waiau Downs Sheep Shearing and Farm Tour** outside of Tuatapere (p. 428).

BEST PLACE TO LAND THE BIG ONE: Reel in a chocolate marzipan fish at Wellington's see and be seen cafe, the **Chocolate Fish Cafe** (p. 239). For the real thing, head to **Lake Taupo** (p. 199), the self-proclaimed "trout fishing capital of the world."

MOST DIVERSE TRAMP: Cross through no fewer than four different eco-systems on the longest Great Walk, South Island's **Heaphy Track** (p. 295).

BEST BREW THRU: Fly in to **The Flying Fox** homestay on the Wanganui River on a zipline and stay for one of their organic home-brewed beers (p. 229).

THRILL SEEKERS

New Zealand's drug of choice is adrenaline, and Kiwis constantly overdose. The country has turned its natural surroundings into a true adventurer's wonderland—almost every town has its own bungy jumping, skydiving, jetboating, whitewater rafting, and kayaking operations. In the adventure capital of **Queenstown** (p. 373), two bungy companies outdo each other with ever higher and more death-defying jumps, while three jetboat operations compete for the most spins. North Island's energetic equivalent, **Taupo** (p. 194), lures budgeteers with one of the world's cheapest skydives. Meanwhile, in nearby **Rotorua** (p. 156), the Kiwi-conceived zorb allows travelers to roll down verdant hills in giant plastic balls.

However, not all of New Zealand's adventure activities involve such rash behavior; swimming with dolphins in **Kaikoura** (p. 266), admiring the **Franz Josef** and **Fox Glaciers** (p. 350 and p. 355), sea kayaking in the **Marlborough Sounds** (p. 252), and skiing or snowboarding down the craggy peaks of the **Tongariro** (p. 202), **Canterbury** (p. 321), and **Southern Lakes** ski fields (p. 373) are just a few of the limitless possibilities.

NEW ZEALAND TO THE EXTREME

As the land that brought you the very first sunrise (p. 183) and the world's first commercial bungy (p. 385), New Zealand is never one to avoid excitement. Located at the very extremes of the earth, New Zealand tests the limits of both mankind and Mother Nature. ·

1. **First to Summit Mt. Everest:** Sir Edmund Hillary (p. 52), of Auckland.

2. **World's Heaviest Insect:** The weta grasshopper weighs in at a whopping 71g.

3. **World's Longest Place Name:** Taumatawhakatangihangakoauau otamateapokaiwhenuakitanatahu Hill in Hawke's Bay.

4. **Most Socially Progressive Country in the World:** New Zealand was the first to grant women suffrage in 1893.

5. **World's Smallest Dolphins:** Hector's dolphins, the world's rarest, only live in New Zealand.

6. **Most Simultaneous Geyser-related Deaths:** Four tourists were killed in 1903 when the Waimangu (p. 168) exploded.

7. **Most Boats per Capita in the World:** The "City of Sails," Auckland (p. 78), deserves its title.

8. **First Person to Split the Atom:** Ernest Rutherford, of Nelson, did so in 1919.

9. **Southernmost Capital:** Wellington (p. 245), at 41°17'S.

10. **Most Sheep per Capita:** Sheep out-number Kiwis 15 to 1.

TRAMP AND PADDLE

Few places in the world combine such otherworldly landscapes with a solid infrastructure for exploring them. With about one-third of the country protected as wilderness areas and national parks by the Department of Conservation (DOC), you don't have to be Sir Edmund Hillary (the first person to successfully scale Everest, and a Kiwi no less) to enjoy New Zealand's world-renowned walking tracks. Nine designated **Great Walks** (3-5 days) satisfy trampers of all experience levels. The **Milford Track** ("the world's finest walk," p. 418), the **Kepler Track** (p. 412), and the **Routeburn Track** (p. 389) wander through the majestic fjords and ranges of **Fiordland National Park.** Golden shorelines along the **Abel Tasman Coastal Track** (p. 283), the **Heaphy Track** (p. 295), and the **Rakiura Track** (p. 447) unfold for sea kayakers and trampers. On North Island, the **Tongariro Northern Circuit** (p. 204) and the **Lake Waikaremoana Track** (p. 183) wind between volcanoes, passing eerie geothermal creations along the way. If your feet need a rest, you can paddle through ancient kauri forests in a canoe or raft on the **Whanganui River Journey** (p. 226). Additionally, there are dayhikes departing from virtually every town covered in this guide.

CULINARY DISCOVERIES

Before the arrival of European settlers or gawking tourists, the **Maori** revered the sublimity of the New Zealand landscape. They hunted ostrich-like moa birds, prospected for valuable *pounamu* (greenstone), and imbued the landscape with ancestral spirits. Today, Maori art and culture remain a vibrant part of Kiwi life. Travelers can witness this cultural heritage by attending a *hangi* (feast) in **Rotorua** (p. 163), **Christchurch** (p. 311), or **Queenstown** (p. 385). Other opportunities to discover Maori tradition include a visit to the **Museum of New Zealand Te Papa Tongarewa** in Wellington (p. 239) or a night's stay at a Maori *marae* "meeting grounds" in the rarely-touristed East Cape town of **Gisborne** (p. 174).

For a different taste of Kiwi culture, sample one of the country's many **wines** and **beers.** Vintages from the regions of **Hawke's Bay** (p. 189), **Blenheim** (p. 260), **Central Otago** (p. 385), and **Martinborough** (p. 248) have earned international recognition. Beermaking in New Zealand is a strongly regional affair: **Monteith's** in Greymouth (p. 345), **Speight's** in Dunedin (p. 364), and **Sunshine Brewing** in Gisborne (p. 177) are just some of the many Kiwi breweries who open their doors for **brewery tours.** For more foodie feasts, see **The Foodie Tour,** p. 7.

SEASIDE DELIGHTS

New Zealand is a nation of islands with over 18,000km of coastline. If there weren't water activities galore, something would be seriously wrong. Not for the faint of heart, South Island's chilly waters reward with rare animal sightings at the protected **Farewell Spit** (p. 290) and not-so-rare student sightings at Dunedin's **St. Clair Beach** (p. 365). Christchurch's summer retreat, **Sumner** (p. 317), has South Island's best surfing. Captured by the classic surf flick *The Endless Summer*, Raglan's **Manu Bay** (p. 147) with its endless lefthander is one of the world's most famous breaks. Other surfer-friendly beaches abound on North Island on the **Taranaki Coast** (p. 215) and remote **Northland** (p. 106). To escape the crowds, visit the electricity-free **Hauraki Gulf Islands** (p. 98), a short ferry ride from downtown Auckland. For a method to your beach-crazed madness, see **Go Coastal, p. 7.**

GET LOST

While it might seem that New Zealand has the best laid infrastructure in the world, there are still plenty of white spots on the map. The best way to discover off-the-beaten-path New Zealand is to rent or buy a car and get out there to find it. New Zealand has a glut of cheap cars for backpackers and the popularity of buy-backs (p. 27) is growing. With some planning, many remote areas are also accessible by bus. New Zealand's small towns offer a wealth of beaches, forests, and hillsides for casual exploration. In the **Marlborough Sounds** (p. 252), roaming travelers visit the homes of dolphins, seals, and penguins, and find comfortable dwellings in the area's many outstanding accommodations. The **Coromandel Peninsula** (p. 127) boasts unpaved roads winding past untouched kauri forests and relaxing ocean vistas. Small towns like **Papatowai** and **Curio Bay** in New Zealand's southernmost region, the **Catlins** (p. 437), astound with rugged cliffs and a stunning coastline.

BEST OF NEW ZEALAND (5 weeks)

Auckland (2 days)
New Zealand's cultural center has enough activities on land and in the air to get anyone's heart racing (p. 76).

Paihia (1 day)
The hotspot for water sports of all kinds in the Bay of Islands (p. 111).

Taupo (2 days)
New Zealand's largest lake is the high-adrenaline capital of North Island and home to the country's cheapest sky dive (p. 194).

START

Waitomo (1 day)
Irresistible tourist trap for spelunking, glowworms, and black water rafting (p. 151).

END

Tongariro National Park (3 days)
Home to the "best day hike in the world," the park dazzles with turquoise lakes and jagged mountains (p. 202).

Napier (1 day)
This Art Deco town calms frayed nerves with the perfect elixir—a bottle (or two) of New Zealand's famous Pinot Noir (p. 185).

West Coast (3 days)
Take time to explore the wild, white water of the untouristed Buller River (p. 336).

Aoraki/Mt. Cook (3 days)
Follow in the footsteps of world-class climbers on Australasia's largest peak (p. 332).

Marlborough Sounds (3 days)
The best luxury tramping in New Zealand, the Queen Charlotte Track offers five-star accommodations (p. 252).

Wanaka (2 days)
Frugal thrill seekers hit the slopes or take to the lake in the laidback alternative to Queenstown (p. 393).

Kaikoura (1 day)
Swim with New Zealand's mammals in the country's most populated marine reserve (p. 266).

Fiordland National Park (1 day)
The country's most famous park, Milford and Doubtful Sounds make for spectacular daytrips either by helicopter or by boat (p. 407).

Christchurch (4 days)
Enjoy buskers and Brits before heading to nearby Akaroa and the Banks Peninsula for natural entertainment (p. 301).

Slope Point (1 day)
A small lookout marks South Island's southernmost point on the Catlins' rugged coastline (p. 442).

Glenorchy (4 days)
Base your adventures from the gateway to all things tramping (p. 387).

Stewart Island (3 days)
Search for the elusive brown kiwi on an island with more birds than people (p. 443).

THE FOODIE TOUR (10 DAYS)

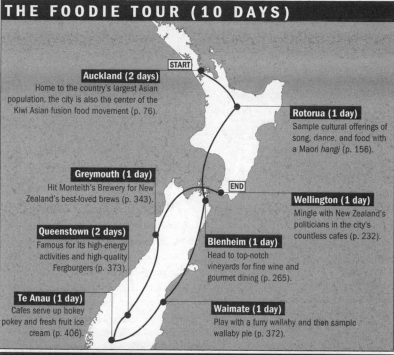

START

Auckland (2 days)
Home to the country's largest Asian population, the city is also the center of the Kiwi Asian fusion food movement (p. 76).

Rotorua (1 day)
Sample cultural offerings of song, dance, and food with a Maori *hangi* (p. 156).

Greymouth (1 day)
Hit Monteith's Brewery for New Zealand's best-loved brews (p. 343).

END

Wellington (1 day)
Mingle with New Zealand's politicians in the city's countless cafes (p. 232).

Queenstown (2 days)
Famous for its high-energy activities and high-quality Fergburgers (p. 373).

Blenheim (1 day)
Head to top-notch vineyards for fine wine and gourmet dining (p. 265).

Te Anau (1 day)
Cafes serve up hokey pokey and fresh fruit ice cream (p. 406).

Waimate (1 day)
Play with a furry wallaby and then sample wallaby pie (p. 372).

GO COASTAL (2 WEEKS)

END

Poor Knights Islands (3 days)
The protected marine reserve is a safe haven for rare sea life and adventurous scuba divers (p. 110).

START

Ahipara (2 days)
Escape the crowds and head to the far north for sand-dune surfing and dune-buggy tours (p. 120).

Coromandel (3 days)
A hippie haven with unpaved roads and remote beaches (p. 127).

Raglan (2 days)
Surf's up at the world's longest left-hand break (p. 146).

East Cape (2 days)
Well off the beaten track, the East Cape catches the first sunrise on its blustery headlands (p. 178).

Taranaki Coast Highway (2 days)
In the udder of New Zealand, family fun, golden sands, and friendly surf instructors await (p. 211).

WWW.LETSGO.COM
HERE TODAY, WHEREVER YOU'RE HEADED TOMORROW.

Whether you're planning your next adventure or are already far afield, letsgo.com will play companion to your wanderlust.

Peruse our articles and descriptions as you select the spots you're off to next. If we're making your decision harder, consult fellow travelers on our written and photo forums or search for anecdotal advice in our researchers' blogs.

If you're itching to leave, there's no need to shake that pesky travel bug. From embassy locations to passport laws, we keep track of all the essentials, so find out what you need to know fast, book that high-season hostel bed, and hit the road.

READY. SET. LET'S GO

ESSENTIALS

PLANNING YOUR TRIP

ENTRANCE REQUIREMENTS.
Passport (p. 10). Required for all visitors to New Zealand.
Visa (p. 11). Not generally required for citizens of Australia, Canada, Ireland, the US, or the UK.
Work Permit (p. 11). Required for all foreigners planning to work in New Zealand.

EMBASSIES AND CONSULATES

NEW ZEALAND CONSULAR SERVICES ABROAD

Australia: High Commission, Commonwealth Ave., Canberra ACT 2600 (☎02 6270 4211; www.nzembassy.com/australia).

Canada: High Commission, 99 Bank St., Ste. 727, Ottawa ON K1P 6G3 (☎613-238-5991; www.nzembassy.com/canada).

Ireland: Consulate General, 37 Leeson Park, Dublin 6 (☎01 660 4233; fax 660 4228; nzconsul@indigo.ie).

Japan: Embassy, 20-40 Kamiyama-cho, Shibuya-ku, Tokyo 150 0047 (☎03 3467 2271; www.nzembassy.com/japan).

UK: High Commission, New Zealand House, 80 Haymarket, London SW1Y 4TQ (☎020 7930 8422; www.nzembassy.com/uk).

US: Embassy, 37 Observatory Circle NW, Washington, D.C. 20008 (☎202-328-4800; www.nzemb.org). Consulate General, 12400 Wilshire Blvd., Ste. 1150, Los Angeles, CA 90025 (☎310-207-1605; www.nzcgla.com).

CONSULAR SERVICES IN NEW ZEALAND

Australia: High Commission, 72-76 Hobson St., Thorndon P.O. Box 4036, Wellington (☎04 473 6411; www.australia.org.nz). Consulate General, Price Waterhouse Coopers Tower, Level 7, 186-194 Quay St., Private Bag 92023, Auckland (☎09 921 8800).

Canada: High Commission, 61 Molesworth St., 3rd fl., Thorndon P.O. Box 12049, Wellington (☎04 473 9577; www.wellington.gc.ca).

Ireland: Consulate General, 18 Shortland St., Level 6, Auckland (☎09 977 2252; www.ireland.co.nz).

UK: High Commission, 44 Hill St., Thorndon P.O. Box 1812, Wellington (☎04 924 2888; www.britain.org.nz).

US: Consular Services, Citibank Bldg., 3rd fl., Private Bag 92022, Auckland (☎09 303 2724; fax 366 0870). Embassy, 29 Fitzherbert Terr., Thorndon P.O. Box 1190, Wellington (☎04 462 6000; www.usembassy.org.nz).

TOURIST OFFICES

The helpful **Tourism New Zealand** offices can provide information about any aspect of the country. Their website (www.newzealand.com) is easy to navigate. The main office in Wellington (☎04 917 5400) can help you locate your local office.

Australia: 1 Alfred St., Level 24, Ste. 3, Sydney NSW 2000 (☎02 8220 9000; fax 8220 9099).

Japan: World Trade Centre Bldg., 12th fl., 2-4-1 Hamamatsu-cho, Minato-ku, Tokyo 105-6112 (☎03 5400 1311; fax 03 5400 1312).

UK: New Zealand House, Haymarket, London SW1Y 4TQ (☎020 7930 1662; fax 020 7839 8929).

US: 501 Santa Monica Blvd., Ste. 300, Santa Monica, CA 90401 (☎310-395-7480; fax 395-5453). 222 East 41 St., Ste. 2510, New York, NY 10017 (☎212-661-7088; fax 832-7602).

DOCUMENTS AND FORMALITIES

PASSPORTS

REQUIREMENTS

Citizens of Australia, Canada, Ireland, the UK, and the US need valid passports to enter New Zealand and to re-enter their home countries. New Zealand does not allow entrance if the holder's passport expires in fewer than three months. Returning home with an expired passport is illegal, and may result in a fine.

NEW PASSPORTS

Citizens of Australia, Canada, Ireland, the UK, and the US can apply for a passport at any passport office or at select post offices and courts of law. Citizens of these countries may also download passport applications from the official website of their country's government or passport office. Any new passport or renewal application must be filed well in advance of departure, though most passport offices offer rush services for a steep fee; rushed passports still take two weeks to arrive.

PASSPORT MAINTENANCE

Photocopy the page of your passport with your photo, as well as your visas, traveler's check serial numbers, and any other important documents. Carry one set of copies in a safe place, apart from the originals, and leave another set at home. Consulates also recommend that you carry an expired passport or an official copy of your birth certificate in a part of your baggage separate from other documents.

If you lose your passport, immediately notify the local police and the nearest embassy or consulate of your home government. You will need to show ID and proof of citizenship. In some cases, a replacement may take weeks to process, and it may be valid only for a limited time. Any visas stamped in your old passport will be lost. In an emergency, ask for immediate temporary traveling papers that will permit you to re-enter your home country. More information regarding lost and stolen US passports is available at www.usembassy.org.nz.

VISAS AND WORK PERMITS

VISAS

As of January 2005, citizens of Australia, Canada, Ireland, Japan, the UK, and the US do not need a visa for entrance into New Zealand, just a valid passport. Citizens of Canada, Ireland, Japan, and the US need visas for stays over three months. Citizens of the UK need visas for stays over six months. Visas are available at most embassies and consulates and are valid for nine months out of an eighteen-month period. Double-check entrance requirements at the nearest embassy or consulate of New Zealand (**New Zealand Consular Services Abroad,** on p. 9) for up-to-date info before departure. US citizens can also consult http://travel.state.gov.

WORK PERMITS

Admission as a visitor does not include the right to work, which is authorized only by a work permit. Entering New Zealand to study requires a special visa or permit. For more information, see **Beyond Tourism,** p. 54.

IDENTIFICATION

When you travel, always carry at least two forms of identification on your person, including at least one photo ID—a passport and a driver's license or birth certificate is usually adequate. Never carry all of your IDs together; split them up in case of theft or loss, and keep photocopies of all of them in your luggage and at home.

STUDENT, TEACHER, AND YOUTH IDENTIFICATION

The **International Student Identity Card (ISIC),** the most widely accepted form of student ID, provides discounts on some sights, accommodations, food, and transport, access to a 24hr. emergency helpline, and insurance benefits for US cardholders. Cardholders receive some discounts on travel gear, entrance fees for museums and botanical gardens, and adventure activities. Applicants must be full-time secondary or post-secondary school students at least 12 years of age. Because of the proliferation of fake ISICs, some services (particularly airlines) require additional proof of student identity.

The **International Teacher Identity Card (ITIC)** offers teachers the same insurance coverage as the ISIC and similar but limited discounts. For travelers who are under 26 years old but are not students, the **International Youth Travel Card (IYTC)** also offers many of the same benefits as the ISIC.

Each of these identity cards costs US$25 or the equivalent. ISICs and ITICs are valid until the new year unless purchased between September and December, in which case they are valid until the beginning of the following new year. Thus, a card purchased in March 2008 will be valid until December 31, 2008, while a card purchased in November 2008 will be valid until December 31, 2009. IYTCs are valid for one year from the date of issue. To learn more about ISICs, ITICs, and IYTCs, go to www.myisic.com. Many student travel agencies (p. 21) issue the cards; for a list of issuing agencies or more information, see the **International Student Travel Confederation (ISTC)** website (www.istc.org). The **International Student Exchange Card (ISE Card)** is a similar card available to students, faculty, and youths aged 12-26. The card provides discounts, medical benefits, and access to a 24hr. helpline. An ISE Card costs US$25; call US ☎ 800-255-8000, or visit www.isecard.com.

CUSTOMS

Upon entering New Zealand, you must declare certain items from abroad and pay a duty on the value of those articles if they exceed the allowance established by New Zealand's customs service (NZ$700). Note that goods and gifts purchased at **duty-free** shops abroad are not exempt from duty or sales tax; duty-free merely means that you need not pay a tax in the country of purchase. Upon returning home, you must declare all articles acquired abroad and pay a duty on the value of articles in excess of your country's allowance. Be sure to keep receipts for all goods acquired abroad. Additionally, all camping gear and boots will be inspected for critters and seeds. For more information on customs, go to www.customs.govt.nz.

MONEY

CURRENCY AND EXCHANGE

New Zealand's unit of currency is the **New Zealand dollar (NZ$).** Coins come in denominations of 5¢, 10¢, 20¢, 50¢, $1, and $2; notes come in denominations of $5, $10, $20, $50, and $100. The currency chart below is based on April 2007 exchange rates between local currency and Australian dollars (AUS$), Canadian dollars (CDN$), European Union euro (EUR€), British pounds (UK£), and US dollars (US$). Check the currency converter on websites like www.xe.com or www.bloomberg.com, or a large newspaper for the latest exchange rates.

DOLLAR (NZ$)	
AUS$1 = NZ$1.12	NZ$1= AUS$0.89
CDN$1 = NZ$1.23	NZ$1= CDN$0.81
EUR€1= NZ$1.85	NZ$1= EUR€0.54
UK£1 = NZ$2.71	NZ$1= UK£0.37
US$1 = NZ$1.36	NZ$1= US$0.74

As a general rule, it's cheaper to convert money in New Zealand than at home. While currency exchange will probably be available in your arrival airport, it's wise to bring enough foreign currency to last the first 1-3 days of your trip. Typical bank hours in New Zealand are Monday through Friday 9:30am-4:30pm, and major banks include Bank of New Zealand (BNZ), Westpac Trust, Australia and New Zealand Banking Group (ANZ), and ASB Bank (ASB).

When changing money abroad, try to go only to banks or currency depots that have at most a 5% margin between their buy and sell prices. Since you lose money with every transaction, **convert large sums** (unless the currency is depreciating rapidly), but **no more than you'll need.**

If you use traveler's checks or bills, carry some in small denominations (the equivalent of US$50 or less) for times when you are forced to exchange money at disadvantageous rates, but bring a range of denominations since charges may be levied per check cashed.

TRAVELER'S CHECKS

Traveler's checks are one of the safest and least troublesome means of carrying funds. American Express and Visa are the most recognized brands. Many banks and agencies sell them for a small commission. Check issuers provide refunds if the checks are lost or stolen, and many provide additional services, such as toll-free refund hotlines abroad, emergency message services, and assistance with lost or stolen credit cards or passports. Traveler's checks are readily accepted in major cities in New Zealand. Ask about toll-free refund hotlines and the location of refund centers when purchasing checks, and always carry emergency cash.

American Express: Checks available with commission at select banks, at all AmEx offices, and online (www.americanexpress.com; US residents only). AmEx cardholders can also purchase checks by phone (☎800-721-9768). Checks available in Australian, British, Canadian, European, Japanese, and US currencies, among others. AmEx also offers the TravelFunds Card, a prepaid reloadable card. For purchase locations or more information, contact AmEx's service centers: in Australia ☎800 688 022; in New Zealand 050 855 5358, in the UK 0800 587 6023, in the US and Canada 800-221-7282, elsewhere, call the US collect at 801-964-6665.

Travelex/Thomas Cook: MasterCard and Visa traveler's checks available. For information about Thomas Cook MasterCard in the US and Canada call ☎800-223-7373; in the UK call 0800 622 101, elsewhere call the UK collect at +44 1733 31 89 50. For information about Interpayment Visa in the US and Canada call ☎800-732-1322, in the UK call 0800 515 884, elsewhere call the UK collect at +44 1733 31 89 49. For more information, visit www.travelex.com.

Visa: Checks available (generally with commission) at banks worldwide. For the location of the nearest office, call the Visa Travelers Cheque Global Refund and Assistance Center: in the UK ☎0800 51 5884, in the US 800-227-6811, elsewhere, call the UK collect at +44

20 7937 8091. Checks available in British, Canadian, European, Japanese, and US currencies, among others. Visa also offers TravelMoney, a prepaid debit card that can be reloaded online or by phone. For more information on Visa travel services, see http:/ /usa.visa.com/personal/using_visa/travel_with_visa.html.

CREDIT, DEBIT, AND ATM CARDS

Where they are accepted, credit cards often offer superior exchange rates—up to 5% better than the retail rate used by banks and other currency exchange establishments. Credit cards may also offer services such as insurance or emergency help, and are sometimes required to reserve hotel rooms or rental cars. **MasterCard** and **Visa** are the most frequently accepted; **American Express** cards work at some ATMs and at AmEx offices and major airports.

The use of ATM cards is widespread in New Zealand. Depending on the system that your home bank uses, you can most likely access your personal bank account from abroad. ATMs get the same wholesale exchange rate as credit cards, but there is often a limit on the amount of money you can withdraw per day (usually around US$500). There is typically also a surcharge of US$1-5 per withdrawal.

Debit cards are as convenient as credit cards but have a more immediate impact on your funds. A debit card can be used wherever its associated credit card company is accepted, yet the money is withdrawn directly from the holder's bank account. Debit cards often also function as ATM cards and can be used to withdraw cash from banks and ATMs.

The two major international money networks are **MasterCard/Cirrus** (for ATM locations US ☎800-424-7787; www.mastercard.com) and **Visa/PLUS** (for ATM locations US ☎800-843-7587; www.visa.com). Most ATMs charge a transaction fee paid to the bank that owns the ATM.

GETTING MONEY FROM HOME

If you run out of money while traveling, the easiest and cheapest solution is to have someone back home make a deposit to your bank account. Failing that, consider one of the following options.

WIRING MONEY

It is possible to arrange a **bank money transfer,** which means asking a bank back home to wire money to a bank in New Zealand. This is the cheapest way to transfer cash, but it's also the slowest, usually taking several days or more. Note that some banks may only release your funds in local currency, potentially sticking you with a poor exchange rate; inquire about this in advance. Money transfer services like **Western Union** are faster and more convenient than bank transfers—but also much pricier. Western Union has many locations worldwide. To find one, visit www.westernunion.com, or call in Australia ☎800 173 833, in Canada 800-325-6000, in New Zealand 0800 005 253, in the UK 0800 833 833, or in the US 800-325-6000. Money transfer services are also available to **American Express** cardholders and at select **Travelex** offices.

US STATE DEPARTMENT (US CITIZENS ONLY)

In serious emergencies only, the US State Department will forward money within hours to the nearest consular office, which will then disburse it for a US$30 fee. If you wish to use this service, you must contact the Overseas Citizens Service division of the US State Department (☎202-647-5225; toll-free 888-407-4747).

COSTS

The cost of your trip will vary, depending on where you go, how you travel, and where you stay. The biggest expenses will probably be your round-trip (return) airfare to New Zealand (see **Getting to New Zealand: By Plane,** p. 21). A bus pass (see **By Bus,** p. 24),

TOP 10 WAYS TO SAVE IN NEW ZEALAND

Just because expensive adventure activities seem to be the norm doesn't mean that there's no such thing as a budget traveler in New Zealand. Here are our top 10 tips to keep you from maxing out those credit cards:

1. Build **outdoors experiences** into your itinerary. It's almost a given that, in New Zealand, nature is often the best attraction in town.
2. Camping is a cheap, popular alternative to hostels.
3. Be on the lookout for **free days** at sights and museums.
4. Research adventure tour companies before you arrive and **book directly** through the company rather than a middle man.
5. Buy food at **markets, grocery stores,** or from **farmers** (New Zealand's got plenty) instead of the restaurant.
6. Find cheap(er) **Internet** at hostels.
7. If you'll be traveling for a long period of time, avoid huge car rental fees by considering **buybacks:** buying a car and selling it back upon departure.
8. Rent a **bike,** not a motorcycle.
9. Rent tramping gear instead of buying it, especially if the tramps begin and end in towns with rental outlets.
10. Visit during the **shoulder season** (Mar.-Apr. and Oct.-Nov.) to avoid the large crowds and prices of the high season.

car rental (see **By Car,** p. 26), or island-hopping pass (see **By Plane,** p. 23) is another pre-departure expense. Before you go, calculatie a reasonable budget.

STAYING ON A BUDGET

To give you a general idea, a bare-bones day in New Zealand (camping or sleeping in hostels, buying food at supermarkets) would cost about US$35 (NZ$47); a slightly more comfortable day (sleeping in hostels and the occasional budget hotel, eating one meal per day at a restaurant, going out at night) would cost about US$55 (NZ$75); for a luxurious day, the sky's the limit. Don't forget to factor in emergency reserve funds (at least US$200) when planning how much money you'll need.

TIPS FOR SAVING MONEY

Some simple ways include searching out opportunities for free entertainment, splitting accommodation and food costs with fellow travelers, and buying food in supermarkets rather than eating out. Bring a **sleep-sack** (p. 15) to save on sheet charges in hostels, and do your **laundry** in the sink (unless you're explicitly prohibited from doing so). Museums often have certain days once per month or week when admission is free; plan accordingly. If you are eligible, consider getting an ISIC or an IYTC; many sights and museums offer reduced admission to students and youths. Bikes are the most economical option for getting around quickly. Renting a bike is cheaper than renting a moped. Don't forget about walking.

TIPPING AND BARGAINING

Tipping is neither customary nor expected in New Zealand establishments. In restaurants, a gratuity is always included in the price of the meal. If the service provided is exceptional, you may consider offering a small tip, but it is by no means necessary or even common. Bargaining is basically nonexistent.

TAXES

A **departure tax** is levied in New Zealand at the airport for those over 12. Prices vary but are usually around NZ$25. The fee, not often included in your flight price, must be paid in New Zealand dollars. A 12.5% **Goods and Services Tax (GST)** is applied to all goods for sale and is usually included in display prices.

PACKING

Pack lightly: Lay out only what you absolutely need, then take half the clothes and twice the money. The online **Universal Packing List** (http://upl.codeq.info) will generate a customized list of suggested items based on your trip length, the expected climate, your planned activities, and other factors. If you plan to do a lot of hiking, also consult **Huts and Camping,** p. 35. Some frequent travelers keep a bag packed with all the essentials: passport, money belt, hat, socks, etc. Then, when they decide to leave, they know they haven't forgotten anything.

Luggage: If you plan to cover most of your itinerary by foot, a sturdy **internal frame backpack** is unbeatable (see p. 70.) Toting a suitcase or trunk is fine if you plan to live in 1 or 2 cities and explore from there, but it's not a great idea if you plan to move around. In addition to your main piece of luggage, a **daypack** (a small backpack or courier bag) is useful.

Clothing: Due to New Zealand's unpredictable weather patterns and occasionally fierce winds, a rain jacket and heavy sweater are necessities. (Gore-Tex® is both waterproof and breathable.) No matter when you are traveling, it's a good idea to bring a warm jacket, and sturdy shoes or hiking boots. Flip-flops or waterproof sandals are must-haves for hostel showers. While bars and pubs are often casual, nightclubs and some bars require neat dress including shoes (not sneakers) and pants other than jeans.

Sleepsack: Some hostels require that you either provide your own linen or rent sheets from them. Save cash by making your own sleepsack: fold a full-size sheet in half the long way, then sew it closed along the long side and one of the short sides.

Converters and Adapters: In New Zealand, electricity is 230V AC, enough to fry any 120V North American appliance. 220/240V electrical appliances won't work with a 120V current, either. Americans and Canadians should buy an adapter (which changes the shape of the plug; US$5) and a converter (which changes the voltage; US$20-30). Don't make the mistake of using only an adapter (unless appliance instructions explicitly state otherwise). Australians (who use 230V at home) won't need a converter, but will need a set of adapters to use anything electrical. For more on all things adaptable, check out http://kropla.com/electric.htm.

Toiletries: Condoms, deodorant, razors, tampons, and toothbrushes are widely available in New Zealand, but often slightly more expensive than those brought from home. **Contact lenses** are likely to be expensive and difficult to find, so bring enough extra pairs and solution for your entire trip. Also bring your glasses and a copy of your prescription in case you need emergency replacements.

First-Aid Kit: For a basic first-aid kit, pack bandages, a pain reliever, antibiotic cream, a thermometer, a multifunction pocketknife, tweezers, moleskin, decongestant, motion-sickness remedy, diarrhea or upset-stomach medication (Pepto Bismol® or Imodium®), an antihistamine, sunscreen, insect repellent, burn ointment, and a syringe for emergencies (get an explanatory letter from your doctor).

Film: Film and developing in New Zealand are reasonable (about $6-10 for a roll of 24 color exposures). Less serious photographers may want to bring a disposable camera or 2. Despite disclaimers, airport security X-rays can fog film, so buy a lead-lined pouch at a camera store or ask security to hand-inspect it. Always pack film in your carry-on luggage, since higher-intensity X-rays are used on checked luggage.

Other Useful Items: For safety purposes, you should bring a **money belt** and small **padlock.** Basic **outdoors equipment** (plastic water bottle, compass, waterproof matches, pocketknife, sunglasses, sunscreen, hat) may also prove useful. **Quick repairs** of torn garments can be done on the road with a needle and thread; also consider bringing electrical tape for patching tears. If you want to do laundry by hand, bring detergent, a small rubber ball to stop up the sink, and string for a clothesline. Other things you're liable to forget include: an umbrella, sealable **plastic bags** (for damp clothes, soap, food, shampoo, etc.), an **alarm clock,** safety pins, rubber bands, a flashlight, earplugs, and a small calculator. A **cell phone** can be a lifesaver (literally) on the road, (see p. 31).

Important Documents: Don't forget your passport, traveler's checks, ATM and/or credit cards, adequate ID, and photocopies of all of the aforementioned in case they are lost or stolen (p. 11). Also check that you have any of the following: a hosteling membership card (p. 33); driver's license (p. 11); travel insurance forms; ISIC (p. 11); bus pass (p. 24).

SAFETY AND HEALTH

GENERAL ADVICE

In any type of crisis situation, the most important thing to do is **stay calm.** Your country's embassy (p. 9) is usually your best resource when things go wrong; registering with your embassy upon arrival in the country is often a good idea. The government offices listed in the **Travel Advisories** box (p. 17) can provide information on the services they offer their citizens in case of emergencies abroad.

LOCAL LAWS AND POLICE

Travelers to New Zealand shouldn't encounter any outlandish laws, and police are trustworthy. You should remember, however, that when in New Zealand you are subject to local laws. A serious violation can result in a jail sentence.

DRUGS AND ALCOHOL

Remember that you are subject to the laws of the country in which you travel, not to those of your home country, and it is your responsibility to familiarize yourself with these laws. The legal **drinking age** in New Zealand is 18. New Zealand has recently cracked down on drunk driving, implementing policies against multiple offenders who can face up to two years in prison and a NZ$6000 fine. If you carry **prescription drugs** while you travel, it is vital to have a copy of the prescriptions and a note from a doctor readily accessible when entering and exiting the country.

SPECIFIC CONCERNS

NATURAL DISASTERS

EARTHQUAKES AND VOLCANOES. New Zealand is host to some active fault lines and thus has occasional earthquakes and volcanic activity. Most earthquakes are small, but if a strong quake does occur, it will last only a few minutes. Open a door to provide an escape route and protect yourself by moving beneath a sturdy doorway, table, or desk. In coastal or mountainous areas, tidal waves and landslides may follow quakes. Volcanic eruptions have happened in the past in New Zealand, but the level of recent volcanic activity has been mild.

TROPICAL CYCLONES. Tropical cyclones are severe tropical storms (equivalent to Atlantic hurricanes) with very high winds. They occur roughly from December to April, but New Zealand is only rarely in the path of a southbound storm. If there is a tropical cyclone, move inside, and stay away from windows.

FLOODS. New Zealand has experiences some torrential flooding nearly every summer, with one of the disastrous episodes in February 2004 and February 2007. Should you find yourself caught in the midst of severe flooding, your best strategy is to follow the instructions of the Ministry of Civil Defense and Emergency Management (☎04 473 7363; www.civildefence.govt.nz) regarding government-sanctioned evacuations and road closings.

TERRORISM

There are no known terrorist organizations or cells in New Zealand. After the September 11 attacks on the US, the country pledged itself against terrorism. Although there is low risk of any terrorist attack or activity in New Zealand, travelers should still stay alert for suspicious behavior throughout their stay, especially in crowded areas and on public transportation. The box on **Travel Advisories** (see below) lists offices to contact and websites to visit in order to get the most updated list of your home government's advisories on travel.

TRAVEL ADVISORIES. The following government offices provide travel information and advisories by telephone, by fax, or via the Web:

Australian Department of Foreign Affairs and Trade: ☎13 00 555135; www.dfat.gov.au.

Canadian Department of Foreign Affairs and International Trade (DFAIT): In Canada and the US ☎800-267-8376, elsewhere 613-944-4000; www.dfait-maeci.gc.ca. Ask for their free booklet, *Bon Voyage...But.*

New Zealand Ministry of Foreign Affairs: ☎04 439 8000; www.mft.govt.nz/travel/index.html.

United Kingdom Foreign and Commonwealth Office: ☎020 7008 0232; www.fco.gov.uk.

US Department of State: ☎202-647-5225; http://travel.state.gov.

PERSONAL SAFETY

EXPLORING AND TRAVELING

To avoid unwanted attention, try to blend in as much as possible. Familiarize yourself with your surroundings before setting out, and carry yourself with confidence. If you are traveling alone, be sure someone at home knows your itinerary, and never admit that you're by yourself. When walking at night, stick to busy, well-lit streets and avoid dark alleyways. If you feel uncomfortable, leave the area quickly.

There is no way to avoid all threatening situations you might encounter while traveling, but a **self-defense course** will give you ways to react to unwanted advances. **Impact, Prepare, and Model Mugging** can refer you to self-defense courses in the US (☎800-345-5425). Visit the website at www.impactsafety.org for nearby chapters. Workshops (2-3hr.) start at US$50; full courses (20hr.) run US$350-500.

If you are using a **car**, learn local driving signals and wear a seatbelt. Children under 40 lbs. should ride only in specially designed carseats, available for a small fee from most car rental agencies. Study route maps before you hit the road, and if you plan on spending a lot of time driving, consider bringing spare parts. If your car breaks down, wait for the police to assist you. For long drives in desolate areas, invest in a cellular phone and a roadside assistance program (p. 27). Park your vehicle in a garage or well-traveled area, and use a steering wheel locking device in larger cities. **Sleeping in your car** is one of the most dangerous (and often illegal) ways to get your rest. For info on the perils of **hitchhiking,** see p. 28.

POSSESSIONS AND VALUABLES

Never leave your belongings unattended: crime occurs in even the most demure-looking hostel or hotel. Bring your own padlock for hostel lockers, and don't store valuables in any locker. Be careful on **buses** and **trains;** some determined thieves wait for travelers to fall asleep. Carry your backpack in front of you where you can see it. When traveling with others, sleep in shifts. When alone, never stay in an empty train compartment, and use a lock to secure your pack to the luggage rack. Try to sleep on top bunks with your luggage stored above you (if not in bed with you), and keep important documents and other valuables on your person.

There are a few steps you can take to minimize the risk associated with traveling. First, **bring as little with you as possible.** Second, buy a combination **padlock** to secure your belongings in your pack, in a hostel, or in a train station locker. Third, **carry as little cash as possible.** Keep your traveler's checks and ATM/credit cards in a **money belt**—not a "fanny pack"—along with your passport and IDs. Fourth, **keep a small cash reserve separate from your primary stash.** This should be about US$50 stored in your pack, along with your traveler's check numbers and photocopies.

In large cities **con artists** often work in groups and may involve children. Beware of certain classics: sob stories that require money, rolls of bills "found" on the street, mustard spilled (or saliva spit) onto your shoulder to distract you while they snatch your bag. **Never let your passport and your bags out of your sight.** Beware of **pickpockets** in city crowds, especially on public transportation. Also, be alert in public telephone booths: if you must say your calling card number, do so very quietly; if you punch it in, make sure no one can look over your shoulder.

If you will be traveling with electronic devices, such as a laptop computer or a PDA, check whether your insurance covers loss, theft, or damage when you travel. If not, you might consider purchasing a low-cost separate insurance policy. **Safeware** (US ☎ 800-800-1492; www.safeware.com) specializes in covering computers, charging US$90 for 90-day comprehensive travel coverage up to US$4000.

PRE-DEPARTURE HEALTH

In your **passport,** write the names of people to be contacted in case of a medical emergency, and list allergies or medical conditions. Matching a prescription to a foreign equivalent is not always safe or possible, so if you take prescription drugs, consider carrying up-to-date, legible prescriptions or a statement from your doctor stating the medication's trade name, manufacturer, chemical name, and dosage. While traveling, be sure to keep all medication with you in your carry-on luggage. For tips on packing a basic **first-aid kit** and other health essentials, see p. 15.

IMMUNIZATIONS AND PRECAUTIONS

Travelers over two years old should make sure that the following vaccines are up to date: MMR (for measles, mumps, and rubella); DTaP or Td (for diphtheria, tetanus, and pertussis); IPV (for polio); Hib (for *haemophilus influenza* B); HepB (for Hepatitis B). For recommendations, consult the CDC (see below) in the US or the equivalent in your home country, and check with a doctor for guidance.

USEFUL ORGANIZATIONS AND PUBLICATIONS

The US **Centers for Disease Control and Prevention** (**CDC;** ☎ 877-394-8747; www.cdc.gov/travel) maintains an travelers' hotline and a website. The CDC's comprehensive booklet *Health Information for International Travel* (The Yellow Book), a biannual rundown of disease, immunization, and general health advice, is free online or US$29-40 via the Public Health Foundation (☎ 877-252-1200; www.phfg.org). Consult the government agency in your home country for consular information sheets on health, entry requirements, and other issues for various countries (see the listings in the box on **Travel Advisories,** p. 17). For quick information on health and other travel warnings, call the **Overseas Citizens Services** (☎ 888-407-4747 M-F 8am-8pm, after hours 202-647-4000, from overseas 317-472-2328), or contact a passport agency, embassy, or consulate abroad. For information on medical evacuation services and travel insurance firms, see the US government website at http://travel.state.gov/travel/abroad_health.html or the website of the **British Foreign and Commonwealth Office** (www.fco.gov.uk). For general health info, contact the **American Red Cross** (☎ 800-564-1234; www.redcross.org).

STAYING HEALTHY

Common sense is the simplest prescription for good health. Travelers often co
plain of their feet and their guts: drink lots of fluids and wear broken-in shoes.

ONCE IN NEW ZEALAND

ENVIRONMENTAL HAZARDS

Heat exhaustion and dehydration: One of the worst hazards for people in New Zealand is heat exhaustion, characterized by dehydration and salt deficiency. Heat exhaustion leads to nausea, excessive thirst, headache, and dizziness. Avoid it by drinking plenty of fluids, eating salty foods (e.g., crackers), abstaining from dehydrating beverages (e.g., alcohol and caffeinated beverages), and wearing sunscreen. Continuous heat stress can eventually lead to heatstroke, characterized by a rising temperature, headache, delirium, and cessation of sweating. Victims should be cooled off with wet towels.

Sunburn: Depleted ozone levels and unpolluted air make New Zealand a high-risk area for sunburn. Always wear sunscreen (SPF 30 is good) when spending excessive amounts of time outdoors. If you are planning on spending time near water or in the snow, you are at a higher risk of getting burned, even through clouds. If you get sunburned, drink a lot of fluids and apply an aloe-based lotion. Severe sunburns can lead to sun poisoning, a condition that affects the entire body, causing fever, chills, nausea, and vomiting. Sun poisoning should always be treated by a doctor.

Hypothermia and frostbite: In areas of New Zealand during the winter, travelers are at risk for hypothermia and frostbite. A rapid drop in body temperature is the clearest sign of overexposure to cold. Victims may also shiver, feel exhausted, have poor coordination or slurred speech, hallucinate, or suffer amnesia. **Do not let hypothermia victims fall asleep.** To avoid hypothermia, keep dry, wear layers, and stay out of the wind. When the temperature is below freezing, watch out for frostbite. If skin turns white or blue, waxy, and cold, do not rub the area. Drink warm beverages, stay dry, and slowly warm the area with dry fabric or steady body contact until a doctor can be found.

High altitude: The opportunities for mountaineering in New Zealand expose travelers to high-altitude settings. Allow your body a few days to adjust to less oxygen before exerting yourself. Note that alcohol and UV rays are stronger at high elevations.

INSECT-BORNE DISEASES

Many diseases are transmitted by insects—mainly mosquitoes, fleas, ticks, and lice. Be aware of insects in wet or forested areas, especially while hiking and camping; wear long pants and long sleeves and tuck your pants into your socks. Use insect repellents such as DEET and soak or spray your gear with permethrin (licensed in the US for use on clothing only). **Mosquitoes**—responsible for diseases including dengue fever—can be particularly dangerous in wet, swampy, or wooded areas. New Zealand is virtually free from **ticks.**

Dengue fever: An "urban viral infection," dengue fever is transmitted by *Aedes* mosquitoes, which bite during the day rather than at night. The incubation period is 3-14 days, usually 4-7 days. Early symptoms include a high fever, severe headache, swollen lymph nodes, and muscle aches. Many patients also suffer from nausea, vomiting, and a pink rash. If you experience these symptoms, see a doctor immediately, drink plenty of liquids, and take fever-reducing medication such as acetaminophen (Tylenol). **Never take aspirin to treat dengue fever.** There is no vaccine available for dengue fever.

Lymphatic filariasis: A roundworm infestation transmitted by mosquitoes. Infection causes enlargement of extremities and has no vaccine.

ESSENTIALS

FOOD- AND WATER-BORNE DISEASES

Prevention is the best cure: be sure that your food is properly cooked and the water you drink is clean. Culprits are raw shellfish, unpasteurized milk, and sauces containing raw eggs. Always wash your hands before eating or bring a quick-drying liquid hand cleaner. The tap water in New Zealand is clean and safe, but be careful of natural bodies of water that might be stagnant or unclean.

Traveler's diarrhea: Results from drinking fecally contaminated water or eating uncooked and contaminated foods. Symptoms include nausea, bloating, and urgency. Try quick-energy, non-sugary foods to keep your strength up. Over the counter anti-diarrheals (e.g., Imodium) may counteract problems. The most dangerous side effect is dehydration; drink 8 oz. of water with ½ tsp. of sugar or honey and a pinch of salt. If you develop a fever or your symptoms don't go away after 4-5 days, consult a doctor. Consult a doctor immediately for treatment of diarrhea in children.

OTHER INFECTIOUS DISEASES

AIDS and HIV: New Zealand does not screen incoming travelers for the HIV virus. For detailed information on Acquired Immune Deficiency Syndrome (AIDS) in New Zealand, call the CDC's 24hr. hotline at ☎800-342-2437, or contact the Joint United Nations Programme on HIV/AIDS (UNAIDS), 20, ave. Appia, CH-1211 Geneva 27, Switzerland (☎+41 22 791 3666; fax 22 791 4187). For more info once in New Zealand, contact the AIDS National Hotline (☎09 358 0099 or 0800 802 437), a 24hr. hotline that offers AIDS counseling. The hotline is sponsored by the New Zealand AIDS Foundation, P.O. Box 6663, Wellesley St., Auckland (☎09 303 3124; www.nzaf.org.nz).

Sexually transmitted diseases (STDs): Gonorrhea, chlamydia, genital warts, syphilis, herpes, and other STDs are easier to catch than HIV and can be just as deadly. Hepatitis B and C can also be transmitted sexually. Though condoms may protect you from some STDs, oral or even tactile contact can lead to transmission. If you think you may have contracted an STD, see a doctor immediately.

OTHER HEALTH CONCERNS

MEDICAL CARE ON THE ROAD

New Zealand offers a high standard of medical facilities, both public and private. These are not free; it is important to know that doctors often expect to be paid in cash immediately for their services. A foreigner's visit to most medical treatment centers costs about NZ$50-100. If your regular **insurance** policy does not cover travel abroad, you may wish to purchase additional coverage. Except for Medicare, most American health insurance plans cover members' medical emergencies during trips abroad; check with your insurance provider.

If you are concerned about obtaining medical assistance while traveling, you may wish to employ special support services. The *MedPass* from **GlobalCare, Inc.**, 6875 Shiloh Rd. East, Alpharetta, GA 30005, USA (☎800-860-1111; www.globalcare.net), provides 24hr. international medical assistance and evacuation resources. The **International Association for Medical Assistance to Travelers (IAMAT;** Canada ☎519-836-0102, US 716-754-4883; www.iamat.org) has free membership.

Those with medical conditions (such as diabetes, allergies to anti3biotics, epilepsy, or heart conditions) may want to obtain a **Medic Alert** membership (1st year US$40, annually thereafter US$25), which includes an ID tag and 24hr. collect call number. Contact the Medic Alert Foundation, 2323 Colorado Ave., Turlock, CA 95382, USA (☎888-633-4298, outside US 209-668-3333; www.medicalert.org).

WOMEN'S HEALTH

Women traveling in unsanitary conditions are vulnerable to **urinary tract infections** (including bladder and kidney). Over the counter medicines can sometimes alleviate symptoms, but if they persist, see a doctor. **Vaginal yeast infections** may flare up in hot and humid climates. Wearing loose-fitting trousers or a skirt and cotton underwear will help, as will over-the-counter remedies like Monostat or Gynelotrimin. Bring supplies from home if you are prone to infection, as they may be difficult to find on the road. **Tampons, pads,** and **contraceptive devices** are widely available, though your favorite brand may not be stocked—bring extras of anything you can't live without. **Abortion** is legal in New Zealand under some circumstances; contact the Family Planning Association for more information (☎ 04 384 4349; www.fpanz.org.nz).

GETTING TO NEW ZEALAND

BY PLANE

When it comes to airfare, a little effort can save you a lot. If your plans are flexible enough to deal with the restrictions, courier fares are the cheapest. Standby seats and tickets bought from consolidators are also good deals, but last-minute specials and charter flights often beat these fares. The key is to hunt around and to be flexible. Students and seniors should never pay full price for a ticket.

AIRFARES

Airfares to New Zealand peak during the summer season between December and February; holidays are also expensive. The cheapest times to travel are between April and September. Midweek (M-Th morning) round-trip flights run US$40-50 cheaper than weekend flights, but they are generally more crowded and less likely to permit frequent-flier upgrades. Not fixing a return date ("open-return") or arriving in and departing from different cities ("open-jaw") can be pricier than round-trip flights. Patching one-way flights together is the most expensive way to travel.

If New Zealand is only one stop on a more extensive globe-hop, consider a round-the-world (RTW) ticket. Tickets usually include at least five stops and are valid for about a year; prices range US$1200-5000. Try **Northwest Airlines/KLM** (US ☎ 800-447-4747; www.nwa.com) or **Star Alliance,** a consortium of 22 airlines including United Airlines (www.staralliance.com).

Fares for round-trip flights to Auckland and Christchurch from the US or Canadian east coast are US$1500-4000, US$1700-4000 depending on departure time; from the US or Canadian west coast, US$1000-4000/1200-4000; from the UK, UK£850-2000/900-2000; from Australia, AUS$125-500/125-500.

BUDGET AND STUDENT TRAVEL AGENCIES

While knowledgeable agents specializing in flights to New Zealand can make your life easy, they may not spend the time to find you the lowest possible fare, especially if paid on commission. Travelers holding **ISICs** and **IYTCs** (p. 11) qualify for big discounts from student travel agencies. Most flights from budget agencies are on major airlines, but in peak season some may sell seats on less reliable charters.

STA Travel, 5900 Wilshire Blvd., Ste. 900, Los Angeles, CA 90036, USA (24hr. reservations and info ☎ 800-781-4040; www.statravel.com). A student and youth travel organization with over 150 offices worldwide (check their website for a listing of all their offices), including US offices in Boston, Chicago, Los Angeles, New York, San Francisco,

Seattle, and Washington, D.C. Ticket booking, travel insurance, railpasses, and more. Walk-in offices are located throughout Australia (☎03 9349 4344), New Zealand (☎09 309 9723), and the UK (☎0870 1 600 599).

Travel CUTS (Canadian Universities Travel Services Limited), 187 College St., Toronto, ON M5T 1P7 (☎800-592-2887; www.travelcuts.com). Offices across Canada and the US including Los Angeles, New York, San Francisco, and Seattle.

USIT, 19-21 Aston Quay, Dublin 2 (☎01 602 1904; www.usit.ie), Ireland's leading student/budget travel agency, has 20 offices in Northern Ireland and the Republic.

FLIGHT PLANNING ON THE INTERNET. The Internet may be the budget traveler's dream when it comes to finding and booking bargain fares, but the array of options can be overwhelming. Many airline websites offer special last-minute deals. Check out the following websites for airfares to New Zealand: **Air Canada** (www.aircanada.com); **Air New Zealand** (www.airnz.co.nz); **Air Pacific** (www.airpacific.com); **American Airlines** (www.americanair.com); **British Airlines** (www.britishairlines.com); **Delta Airlines** (www.delta.com); **Qantas** (www.qantas.com); **United Airlines** (www.unitedairlines.com); **Virgin Blue Airlines** (www.virginblue.com). **STA** (www.sta-travel.com) and **StudentUniverse** (www.studentuniverse.com) provide quotes on student tickets, while **Orbitz** (www.orbitz.com), **Expedia** (www.expedia.com), and **Travelocity** (www.travelocity.com) offer full travel services. **ZUJI** (www.zuji.com) offers full travel services focusing on Asia and the Pacific, including New Zealand. **Priceline** (www.priceline.com) lets you specify a price, and obligates you to buy any ticket that meets or beats it; **Hotwire** (www.hotwire.com) offers bargain fares, but won't reveal the airline or flight times until you buy. Other websites that compile deals include www.bestfares.com, www.flights.com, www.lowestfare.com, www.onetravel.com, www.kayak.com, and www.travelzoo.com. Increasingly, there are online tools available to help sift through multiple offers: **SideStep** (www.sidestep.com; download required) and **Booking Buddy** (www.bookingbuddy.com) let you enter your trip information once and search multiple websites. **Air Traveler's Handbook** (www.faqs.org/faqs/travel/air/handbook) is a comprehensive listing of links to everything you need to know before you board a plane.

COMMERCIAL AIRLINES

The commercial airlines' lowest regular offer is the **APEX** (Advance Purchase Excursion) fare, which provides confirmed reservations and allows open-jaw tickets. Generally, reservations must be made seven to 21 days ahead of departure, with a seven- to 14-day minimum-stay and up to 90-day maximum-stay restrictions. These fares carry hefty cancellation and change penalties (fees rise in summer). Book peak-season APEX fares early. Use **Expedia** (www.expedia.com) or **Travelocity** (www.travelocity.com) to get an idea of the lowest published fares, then use the resources outlined here to try and beat them. **Low-season** (Apr.-Sept.) fares should be appreciably cheaper than the **high-season** (Dec.-Feb.) ones listed here.

TRAVELING FROM NORTH AMERICA

Standard commercial carriers like American and United will probably offer the most convenient flights, but they may not be the cheapest, unless you manage to grab a special promotion. You will probably find using one of the following ticket consolidators will get you a better deal. **Travel Avenue** (☎800-333-3335; www.travelavenue.com) searches for best available published fares and then uses several consolidators to attempt to beat that fare. Consolidators worth trying are **Rebel** (☎800-732-3588; www.rebeltours.com) and **Cheap Tickets** (www.cheaptickets.com). Consolidators on the web include **Flights.com** (www.flights.com) and **TravelHUB** (www.travelhub.com). Remember that these are just suggestions to get you started; *Let's Go* does not endorse any of these agencies. As always, be cautious, and research companies before you hand over your credit card number.

AIR COURIER FLIGHTS

Those who travel light should consider courier flights. Couriers help transport cargo on international flights by using their checked luggage space for freight. Generally, couriers must travel with carry-ons only and deal with complex flight restrictions. Most flights are round-trip only, with short fixed-length stays (usually 1 week) and a limit of one ticket per issue. Most of these flights also operate only out of major gateway cities, mostly in North America. Round-trip courier fares from the US to New Zealand run about US$400-1100. Most flights leave from Los Angeles, Miami, New York, or San Francisco in the US, and from Montreal, Toronto, or Vancouver in Canada. Generally, you must be over 18 (in some cases 21+) to travel as a courier. In summer, popular destinations usually require an advance reservation of about two weeks (you can usually book up to 2 months ahead). Super-discounted fares are common for last-minute flights (73-14 days ahead).

STANDBY FLIGHTS

Traveling standby requires considerable flexibility in arrival and departure dates and cities. Companies dealing in standby flights sell vouchers rather than tickets, along with the promise to get you to your destination (or near your destination) within a certain window of time (typically 1-5 days). Call in before your specific window of time to hear your flight options and the probability that you will be able to board each flight. You then decide which flights you want to try to make, show up at the appropriate airport at the appropriate time, present your voucher, and board if space is available. Vouchers are usually available for both one-way and round-trip travel. You may receive a monetary refund only if every available flight within your date range is full; if you opt not to take an available (but perhaps less convenient) flight, you can only get credit toward future travel. Carefully read agreements with any company offering standby flights, as fine print can leave you in the lurch. To check on a company's service record in the US, call the Better Business Bureau (☎ 703-276-0100).

TICKET CONSOLIDATORS

Ticket consolidators, or **"bucket shops,"** buy unsold tickets in bulk from commercial airlines and sell them at discounted rates. The best place to look is in the Sunday travel section of any major newspaper (such as *The New York Times*), where many bucket shops place tiny ads. Call quickly, as availability is typically extremely limited. Not all bucket shops are reliable, so insist on a receipt that gives full details of restrictions, refunds, and tickets, and pay by credit card (in spite of the 2-5% fee) so you can stop payment if you never receive your tickets. For more info, see www.travel-library.com/air-travel/consolidators.html.

GETTING AROUND NEW ZEALAND
BY PLANE

While domestic flights are more efficient, they deprive travelers of spectacular road-level scenery—arguably one of the best (and least expected) parts of traveling in New Zealand. The major domestic airline, **Air New Zealand** (NZ ☎ 0800 737

000, US 800-262-1234; www.airnz.com) provides connections between major towns and cities. Air New Zealand covers the country comprehensively; a number of smaller companies are also grouped under Air New Zealand Link. "Flightseeing" is another option. Smaller local companies in each area provide beautiful views from the air starting around NZ$130. See the **Sights** and **Outdoor Activities** listings in each town for more details.

Air New Zealand's **Smart Saver** fares offer travelers low prices with even deeper discounts for featured routes. Book a few weeks in advance to ensure a seat and guarantee low fares. These Smart Saver fares are available for all 25 of Air New Zealand's domestic destinations. For travelers planning to visit Australia as well as New Zealand, it might be economical to explore multi-leg passes such as the **Boomerang Pass,** valid for non-residents of New Zealand and Australia on Qantas Airlines. When coupled with an international ticket (e.g., from the US), the Boomerang provides open one-way tickets among a number of destinations in New Zealand, Australia, and the Southwest Pacific. Trips cost NZ$116-260, depending on where you want to go (min. 2; max. 10 segments). Even if just buying a ticket within New Zealand, ask about the special economy fares available. Some Air New Zealand flights feature fares discounted up to 50%, depending on the season (restrictions apply).

BY TRAIN

The phenomenal **TranzScenic** (☎0800 872 467; www.tranzscenic.co.nz) runs between major cities and towns, providing its passengers with spectacular views of New Zealand's ethereal landscape. Some trains have a "no-frills carriage" for backpackers with less luxurious seating, smaller windows, and cheaper fares. The **TranzMetro** (www.transmetro.co.nz) is a convenient commuter rail service that provides limited access to destinations around Wellington. **Rideline** (www.rideline.co.nz) has taken over TranzMetro service in the Auckland area.

BY FERRY

Interislander (www.interislander.co.nz) runs ferries between North and South Islands. Each run lasts 3hr. If you're in a hurry, hop on InterIslander's **Lynx** for a 2¼hr. ride across the Cook Strait. Both services carry vehicles. Economy fares are offered regularly during winter months (June-Aug.) as well as certain times of day.

BY BUS

Many budget travelers, especially backpackers, choose the bus (or coach, as Kiwis say) as their transport of choice, especially in more remote areas. Remember that bus schedules can be somewhat flexible, and many buses will leave if you are not at the stop when they arrive. Always reserve at least one day in advance (or earlier to take advantage of aggressive discount schemes), show up 15min. early, and do not be alarmed if buses are 20-40min. late. Visitors centers will have the most up-to-date information about bus schedules and fares, and many offer discounts if trips are booked through them. **InterCity** (☎09 913 6100; www.intercitycoach.co.nz) covers both islands extensively and offers both Flexi and Coach Passes. The Flexi Pass, well suited to meandering backpackers, allows travelers to purchase bus time in 5hr. increments (starting at 5hr. for NZ$55) valid on all InterCity buses. Coach Passes are less flexible but more scenic. Prices and tours range from local tours for around NZ$135 to extensive double island excursions ranging NZ$535-690. All buses can be booked in advance by phone, at travel centers, or at most visitors centers. In addition, cyclists and snow bunnies will be happy to know that buses carry **bikes, skis,** or **snowboards** for a nominal fee.

BACKPACKER BUSES

Many backpackers with too little time to explore New Zealand on their own opt to join up with one of the ubiquitous **backpacker buses.** Keep in mind that experiences vary greatly, refunds are forbidden, and tickets cannot be sold to other travelers. These tours have planned itineraries (including brief stops at sights and activities along their routes) and always stop for the night at pre-arranged destinations—eliminating the spontaneity that many backpackers treasure. But in return, you meet a busload of starry-eyed young travelers and benefit from knowledgeable tour guides. Trips range from one-week, one-island loops to more leisurely whole-country explorations. Accommodations are pre-booked by drivers with your input but are not included in the overall price; food is also at your own cost. Many backpacker buses also reserve spaces with various adventure companies, offering decent discounts on activities along the route. In addition to the New Zealand-based bus companies listed below, **Contiki Travel** (US ☎ 866-266-8454; www.contiki.com) offers comprehensive bus tour packages that include accommodations, transportation, and some meals. In New Zealand, their three- to 15-day tours start at US$210.

Kiwi Experience, 195-197 Parnell Rd., Auckland (☎ 09 366 9830; www.kiwiexperience.com). The most conspicuous of the backpacker buses, with countless green giants rolling through the country. Popular with North Americans and Europeans, especially Brits, Kiwi Experience caters to the adventure backpacker with planned activities such as hiking and mountain biking. Good for travelers in their late teens and early 20s. Prices range widely depending on discounts and locations, from 1-day jaunts for NZ$80 to month-long getaways for NZ$1700.

Magic Travellers Network, 132-138 Quay St., P.O. Box 949, Auckland (☎ 09 358 5600; www.magicbus.co.nz). A more subdued experience than the Kiwi bus, shuttling slightly older backpackers. Again, prices and routes vary, but Magic tends to be a bit cheaper than Kiwi, with trips ranging NZ$189-1110. Optional adventure activities include whale watching and skydiving. Magic has partnered with the New Zealand YHA to create **GoNZ** travel packages, which include transport on the Magic bus as well as accommodation in YHA hostels; see www.yha.org.nz for more information.

Stray Bus, 31 Beach Rd., Auckland (☎ 09 309 8772; www.straytravel.co.nz). Founded with independent travelers in mind, Stray Bus is the latest New Zealand backpacker bus line. Smaller buses cater to fewer party travelers than Kiwi or Magic. Each route has a moniker—"Tom" (NZ$240) visits North Island hot spots such as Raglan surf beach, Waitomo caves, and the Coromandel, while "Max" (NZ$980) does a whirlwind tour of both islands. Unlike some bus lines, Stray Bus guarantees nightly accommodations.

SHUTTLE BUSES

Local shuttle buses often supplement the service of the major bus lines (and occasionally offer lower prices on mainstream runs). These services use vans, often collect travelers from their respective accommodations, and usually travel to small towns not serviced by the main coach lines. However, there is a high turnover in shuttle companies and they can be less reliable and comfortable than buses. Two of the most etablished companies are **Atomic** (☎ 03 322 8883; www.atomictravel.co.nz) and **Westcoaster** (☎ 09 913 6100). Local visitors centers will often have current info on prices and schedules and can do bookings. During winter and in more remote locations, make sure to call ahead.

BY CAR

The most significant road difference for many travelers to New Zealand will be driving on the left-hand side of the road. Many roads in New Zealand outside major cities are narrow and only have two lanes. Some are unpaved and can prove hazardous for unprepared motorists. Road maintenance in New Zealand is generally good though drivers should remain cautious in more remote regions where it is less vigilant. Drivers heading through agricultural areas should also be wary of wandering livestock, which are often dangerous nuisances. Also, the birds in New Zealand will not necessarily get out of your way. Please be kind, and swerve.

As long as you have a current license from your own country, you probably won't need an **International Driving Permit (IDP)** while in New Zealand (p. 27).

RENTING

RENTAL AGENCIES

You can generally make reservations before you head to New Zealand by calling international offices in your home country. Sometimes the price and availability they give doesn't jive with what the local offices in your country will tell you. Try checking both numbers to make sure you get the best price.

To rent a car from most establishments in New Zealand, you need to be at least 21 years old. Some agencies require renters to be 25, and most charge those aged 21-24 an additional insurance fee. Policies and prices vary from agency to agency. Small local operations occasionally rent to people under 21, but be sure to ask about the insurance coverage and deductible, and always check the fine print. The major rental agencies in New Zealand are: **Avis** (NZ ☎ 09 526 2847 or 0800 655 111; www.avis.com); **Budget** (Auckland ☎ 09 976 2222, elsewhere 0800 283 438; www.budget.com); **Hertz** (NZ ☎ 0800 654 321; www.hertz.com).

COSTS AND INSURANCE

Rental car prices start at around NZ$50 a day from national companies, NZ$30 from local agencies such as **Darn Cheap Rentals** (☎ 0800 800 327; www.darncheaprentals.co.nz). **Omega Rental Cars** (☎ 0800 525 210; www.omegarentalcars.com) and **Ace Rentals** (☎ 0800 502 277; www.acerentals.co.nz) offer low rates, but be cautious—consider the reliability and reputation of all local agencies before committing. Expect to pay more for larger cars and for 4WD. Cars with **automatic transmission** will, surprisingly, sometimes cost less than manuals (stick shift).

Many rental packages offer unlimited kilometers, while others offer a set number of kilometers per day with a surcharge applied for each kilometer exceeding that limit. Return the car with a full tank of gas to avoid high fuel charges at the end. Be sure to ask whether the price includes **insurance** against theft and collision. Remember that if you are driving a conventional vehicle on an **unpaved road** in a rental car, you are almost never covered by insurance; ask about this before leaving the rental agency. Beware that cars rented on **Visa/Mastercard Gold** or **Platinum** credit cards in New Zealand might not carry the automatic insurance that they would in some other countries; check with your credit card company. **American Express** does not carry automatic insurance. Insurance plans almost always come with an **excess** (or deductible) of around NZ$900 for conventional vehicles; excess ranges up to around NZ$2500 for younger drivers and for 4WD. This means you pay for all damages up to that sum, unless they are the fault of another vehicle. The excess you will be quoted applies to collisions with other vehicles; collisions with non-vehicles, such as trees ("single-vehicle collisions"), will cost you even more. The excess can often be reduced or waived if you pay an additional charge.

National chains often allow one-way rentals, picking up in one city and dropping off in another. There is usually a minimum rental period of four days and sometimes an extra drop-off charge of several hundred dollars.

DRIVING PERMITS AND CAR INSURANCE

INTERNATIONAL DRIVING PERMIT (IDP). If you plan to drive a car while in New Zealand, you may do so for up to 12 months with a valid license from your home country or if you have an International Driving Permit (IDP). It may be a good idea to get one anyway, in case you're in a bind.

Your IDP, valid for one year, must be issued in your own country before you depart. An application for an IDP usually requires one or two photos, a current local license, an additional form of identification, and a fee. To apply, contact your home country's automobile association. Be careful when purchasing an IDP online or anywhere other than your home automobile association. Many vendors sell permits of questionable legitimacy for higher prices.

CAR INSURANCE. Most credit cards cover standard insurance. If you rent, lease, or borrow a car, you will need a **green card,** or **International Insurance Certificate,** to certify that you have liability insurance and that it applies abroad. Green cards can be obtained at car rental agencies, car dealers (for those leasing cars), and some travel agents. Rental agencies may require you to purchase theft insurance in countries that they consider to have a high risk of auto theft.

BUY-BACKS. Buying a car and selling it upon departure may be a smart option for longer stays. Buy-back outlets, such as **New Zealand Guaranteed Buy-Back Vehicle Associates,** 825 Dominion Rd. (☎09 620 6587), sell cars for NZ$2500-5000 for this purpose. You can buy a car for six months and only shell out NZ$2000. If you prefer to strike out on your own, Auckland has the best deals: check out one of its car auctions or the used car section of *The New Zealand Herald* (especially on W and Sa; www.nzherald.co.nz). The *Trade and Exchange*, published Thursday and Saturday, is a good place to look.

A car must have a **W.O.F.** (Warrant of Fitness, sometimes called a V.I.C.), which ensures that it is road safe. Make sure that your potential car has received one within the past month. For vehicles six years old or less, they are good for a year and cost NZ$40. A car must be **registered** (6 months around NZ$100, 1 year NZ$200). When there is a change of ownership, an **MR13A form** must be completed by the buyer and seller and turned in at a post office or shop. The buyer must also complete an **MR13B form** (NZ$9). Insurance is not necessary but highly recommended, as is Automobile Association membership (p. 39). The latter will get you emergency breakdown service, free service for simple problems, and free towing.

Before you buy your car, get it inspected. Vehicle inspection services can be found in the yellow pages and will do pre-purchase checks for NZ$100. You may want to check out **car fairs** in Auckland like **Sell It Yourself,** 1106 Great South Rd., Westfield. (☎09 270 3666. Open daily 8am-6pm.) **Car auctions** are another option. **Turners Car Auctions** (☎09 525 1920; www.turners.co.nz), Leonard and Penrose Rd., Penrose, Auckland, sells budget cars. Call for auction times. **Hammer Auctions,** 830 Great South Rd., Penrose, Auckland (☎09 579 2344; www.hammerauctions.co.nz), sells cars (M-Th 6pm, F 1pm, Sa 11am).

ON THE ROAD

New Zealand is a highly developed country with well-established infrastructure. State highways are abbreviated as SH; SH2 was recently renamed the Pacific Coast Highway, though most locals will understand what you're talking about.

DRIVING PRECAUTIONS. When traveling in the summer or in the desert, bring substantial amounts of water (a suggested 5L of **water** per person per day) for drinking and for the radiator. For long drives to unpopulated areas, register with police before beginning the trek, and again upon arrival at the destination. Check with the local automobile club for details. When traveling for long distances, make sure tires are in good repair and have enough air, and get good maps. A **compass** and a **car manual** can also be very useful. You should always carry a **spare tire** and **jack, jumper cables, extra oil, flares**, a **flashlight**, and **heavy blankets** (in case your car breaks down at night or in the winter). If you don't know how to **change a tire**, learn before heading out, especially if you are planning on traveling in deserted areas. Blowouts on dirt roads are exceedingly common. If you do have a breakdown, **stay with your car;** if you wander off, there's less likelihood trackers will find you.

Road conditions are generally very good, though unpaved roads in more remote regions can cause problems. Driving is particularly dangerous in the Otago and Southland regions where road conditions can be harrowing. Speed limits are strictly enforced with speed cameras and are set up at the traffic lights of many large towns to catch lead-footed offenders. The maximum speed limit on any open road is 100kph; 50kph in urban areas. The *New Zealand Road Code* (NZ$25), available at AA offices and bookstores, tells you all you need to know. **Gasoline** costs approximately NZ$1.45 per liter, though it is generally more expensive in smaller towns. When traveling, gas expenses can easily run NZ$15-20 per day. Members of worldwide Automobile Associations (see **IDP**, p. 27) can enjoy the agreement with the **New Zealand Automobile Association** (**AA;** ☎09 966 8800; www.aahost.co.nz) to obtain maps and services from AA offices in New Zealand.

BY THUMB

Let's Go never recommends hitchhiking as a safe means of transportation, and none of the information presented here is intended to do so.

Let's Go strongly urges you to consider the risks before you choose to hitchhike. Some visitors to New Zealand, particularly backpackers, rely on hitchhiking as a primary mode of transport and express satisfaction with its safety and convenience. Others, however, report that hitchhiking is much less safe than it used to be, especially for women traveling alone. A man and a woman are a safer combination when hitchhiking; two men may have a harder time finding a ride. No matter how safe or friendly New Zealanders may be, you should always think seriously before entrusting your life to a stranger, as you risk suffering an accident, theft, assault, or worse. Exercise caution if you elect to hitch: don't get into the back of a two-door car; when waiting for a ride, stand in a well-lit, public place; start early in the day and avoid hitchhiking at night; finally, never hitchhike alone. Even at the risk of offending the driver, **do not put your pack in the trunk;** you might not get it back. If you ever feel unsafe, don't hesitate to politely but firmly ask to be let off.

If you decide to hitch, it is reported to be easiest just beyond the end of a town's residential area, but before the open highway. Hitchhiking is illegal on highways. Hitchers report increasing their chances of getting a ride by choosing a spot on the side of the road with ample space for a car to pull over. They walk backwards with the traffic with their thumbs out and try to make eye contact

with the driver. They report that it is easier to be picked up if you hold a sign indicating your desired destination and they advise against accepting offers that will leave you in a small town, short of your goal.

KEEPING IN TOUCH

BY EMAIL AND INTERNET

High-speed Internet access in New Zealand is available widely. Internet cafes and free terminals are listed in the **Practical Information** section of cities.

Increasingly, travelers find that taking their laptop computers on the road with them can be a convenient option for staying connected. Laptop users can call an Internet service provider via a modem using long-distance phone cards specifically intended for such calls. They may also find Internet cafes that allow them to connect their laptops to the Internet. And most excitingly, travelers with wireless-enabled computers may be able to take advantage of an increasing number of Internet "hot spots," where they can get online for free or for a small fee. Newer computers can detect these hot spots automatically; otherwise, check out websites like www.jiwire.com. For information on insuring your laptop while traveling, see **Possessions and Valuables,** p. 17.

BY TELEPHONE

CALLING HOME FROM NEW ZEALAND

A **calling card** is probably your cheapest bet. Calls are billed collect or to your account. You can frequently call collect without even possessing a company's calling card just by calling their access number and following the instructions. To obtain a calling card from your national telecommunications service before leaving home, contact the appropriate company. To **call home with a calling card,** contact the operator for your service provider in New Zealand by dialing the appropriate toll-free access number.

You can usually also make **direct international calls** from pay phones, but if you aren't using a calling card, you may need to drop your coins as quickly as your words. Prepaid phone cards and occasionally major credit cards can be used for direct international calls, but they are generally less cost-efficient. Placing a **collect call** through an international operator is even more expensive, but may be necessary in case of an emergency.

PLACING INTERNATIONAL CALLS. To call New Zealand from home or to call home from New Zealand, dial:

1. The **international dialing prefix.** To call from **Australia,** dial 0011; **Canada** or the **US,** 011; **Ireland, New Zealand,** or the **UK,** 00.
2. The **country code** of the country you want to call. To call **Australia,** dial 61; **Canada** or the **US,** 1; **Ireland,** 353; **New Zealand,** 64; the **UK,** 44.
3. The **city/area code.** *Let's Go* lists the city/area codes for cities and towns in New Zealand opposite the city or town name, next to a ☎. If the first digit is a zero (e.g., 09 for Auckland), omit the zero when calling from abroad (e.g., dial 9 from Canada to reach Auckland).
4. The **local number.**

CALLING WITHIN NEW ZEALAND

National directory assistance: ☎018.
National operator assistance: ☎010.
International directory assistance: ☎0172.
International operator assistance: ☎0170.

EMERGENCIES	The emergency number in all of New Zealand is ☎111.

The simplest way to call within the country is to use a coin-operated phone. **Prepaid phone cards** (available at most convenience stores) and carry a certain amount of phone time depending on the card's denomination, usually save time and money in the long run. You can buy a NZ$5, NZ$10, NZ$20, or NZ$50 phone card. Any local call from a pay phone will cost you NZ$0.50. The computerized phone will tell you how money you have left on your card. Another kind of prepaid phone card comes with a Personal Identification Number (PIN) and a toll-free access number. Instead of inserting the card into the phone, you call the access number and follow the directions on the card. These cards can be used to make international as well as domestic calls. Phone rates typically tend to be highest in the morning, lower in the evening, and lowest on Sunday and late at night. Toll-free numbers in New Zealand start with ☎0800 or 0508.

CELLULAR PHONES

Prepaid cellular phones may be a good investment for travelers who are planning on staying mainly in populated areas of New Zealand. There is generally good coverage in the coastal areas, but sparsely populated or interior mountainous regions are largely without coverage. Prepaid phone packages often come with a set number of minutes (with restrictions on use such as nights and weekends), leaving the purchase of a physical phone up to you. One major phone company is **Vodafone** (☎09 368 4224; www.vodafone.com), which offers a prepaid phone package (NZ$40 for startup package at NZ$0.49 per min. anytime; phone not included). You can pick up a prepaid package from any Vodafone store around the country.

The international standard for cell phones is **GSM.** To make and receive calls in New Zealand you will need a **GSM-compatible phone** and a **SIM (Subscriber Identity Module) card,** a country-specific, thumbnail-sized chip that gives you a local phone number and plugs you into the local network. Many SIM cards are **prepaid,** meaning that they come with calling time included and you don't need to sign up for a monthly service plan. Incoming calls are frequently free. When you use up the prepaid time, you can buy additional cards or vouchers to get more. For more information on GSM phones, check out www.telestial.com, www.vodafone.com, www.roadpost.com, or www.planetomni.com. Companies like **Cellular Abroad** (www.cellularabroad.com) rent cell phones that work in a variety of destinations around the world, providing a simpler option.

 GSM PHONES. Just having a GSM phone doesn't mean you're necessarily good to go when you travel abroad. The majority of GSM phones sold in the US operate on a different **frequency** (1900) than international phones (900/1800) and will not work abroad. Tri-band phones work on all three frequencies (900/1800/1900) and will operate throughout most of the world. Some GSM phones are **SIM-locked** and only accept SIM cards from a single carrier. You'll need a **SIM-unlocked** phone to use a SIM card from a local carrier when you travel.

ESSENTIALS

TIME DIFFERENCES

New Zealand is 12hr. ahead of Greenwich Mean Time (GMT), and observes Daylight Saving Time. During Standard Time, New Zealand is 16hr. ahead of New York, and 11hr. ahead of London. During Daylight Saving Time, New Zealand is 18hr. ahead of New York, and 13hr. ahead of London. Daylight Saving Time in New Zealand runs from the first Sunday in October until the third Sunday in March.

BY MAIL

SENDING MAIL HOME FROM NEW ZEALAND

Airmail is the best way to send mail home. **Aerogrammes,** printed sheets that fold into envelopes and travel via airmail, are available at post offices or shops. They cost NZ$1.50 to send anywhere in the world from New Zealand. Write "airmail" on the front. Most post offices will charge exorbitant fees or simply refuse to send aerogrammes with enclosures. A regular 200g letter sent airmail from New Zealand will cost about NZ$2.50 to Australia and NZ$3 to the rest of the world. **Surface mail** is by far the cheapest and slowest way to send mail. It takes one to two months to cross the Atlantic and one to three to cross the Pacific. It's good for heavy items you won't need for a while.

SENDING MAIL TO NEW ZEALAND

In addition to the standard postage system, **Federal Express** (Australia ☎ 13 26 10, Canada and US 800-463-3339, Ireland 800 535 800, New Zealand 0800 733 339, UK 0800 123 800; www.fedex.com) handles express mail services from most countries to New Zealand. There are several ways to arrange pickup of letters sent to you while you are abroad. Mail can be sent via **Poste Restante** (General Delivery) to almost any city or town in New Zealand with a post office, and is quite reliable. Address Poste Restante letters like so:

> Elusive KIWI
> Poste Restante, CPO
> City, NEW ZEALAND

No zip or area code is necessary. The mail will go to a special desk in the central post office, unless you specify a post office by street address or postal code. It's best to use the largest post office, since mail may be sent there regardless. It is usually safer and quicker, though more expensive, to send mail express or registered. Bring your passport (or other photo ID) for pickup; there may be a small fee. If the clerks insist that there is nothing for you, have them check under your first name as well. *Let's Go* lists post offices or shops in the **Practical Information** section for each city and most towns. Post shops offer post office services in shops.

   American Express's travel offices throughout the world offer a free **Client Letter Service** (mail held up to 30 days and forwarded upon request) for cardholders who contact them in advance. Some offices will offer these services to non-cardholders (especially AmEx Travelers Cheque holders), but call ahead.

ACCOMMODATIONS

HOSTELS

Many hostels ("backpackers" in New Zealand) are laid out dorm-style, often with large single-sex rooms and bunk beds, although private rooms that sleep two to four are becoming more common. They sometimes have kitchens and utensils for your use, bike or moped rentals, storage areas, transportation to airports, breakfast and other meals, laundry facilities, and Internet access. There can be drawbacks: some hostels close during certain daytime "lockout" hours, have a curfew, don't accept reservations, impose a maximum stay, or, less frequently, require that you do chores. In New Zealand, a dorm bed in a hostel will average around NZ$15-25, and a private room around NZ$40-60.

> **A HOSTELER'S BILL OF RIGHTS.** There are certain standard features that we do not include in our hostel listings. Unless we state otherwise, you can expect that every hostel has no lockout, no curfew, free hot showers, some system of secure luggage storage, and no key deposit. Laundry and Internet are available in most hostels for a fee: usually around $5 for wash and dry, $2 per 20min. Internet, except when otherwise noted. Central heating is rare in New Zealand and is listed wherever found.

ESSENTIALS

HOSTELING ORGANIZATIONS

By far, the most common hosteling organization in New Zealand is **Budget Backpacker Hostels (BBH;** ☎03 379 3014; www.bbh.co.nz), offering many of the same services as YHA. Membership costs NZ$40 and can be purchased on the BBH website. Another option is **VIP Backpackers Resorts International (VIP;** ☎09 816 8903; www.vip.co.nz). Membership costs NZ$39 and can be purchased at any VIP hostel. **NOMADS World** (www.nomadsworld.com) has increased its Kiwi hostels . For an annual fee of AUS$34, the NOMADS Card entitles the cardholder to discounts on accommodations and transport. Membership can be purchased on the website.

Joining the youth hostel association in your own country (listed below) automatically grants you membership privileges in **Hostelling International (HI),** a federation of national hosteling associations affiliated with **Youth Hostels Association of New Zealand (YHANZ;** ☎03 379 9970; www.yha.org.nz). Non-HI members cannot stay at HI hostels in New Zealand. HI hostels are not the most prevalent type in New Zealand, but you will likely find them in larger cities. HI's umbrella organization's website (www.hihostels.com), which lists the web addresses and phone numbers of all national associations, can be a place to begin researching.

Australian Youth Hostels Association (AYHA), 422 Kent St., Sydney, NSW 200 (☎02 9261 1111; www.yha.com.au). AUS$52, under 18 AUS$19.

Hostelling International-Canada (HI-C), 205 Catherine St. #400, Ottawa, ON K2P 1C3 (☎613-237-7884; www.hihostels.ca). CDN$35, under 18 free.

An Óige (Irish Youth Hostel Association), 61 Mountjoy St., Dublin 7 (☎830 4555; www.irelandyha.org). EUR€20, under 18 EUR€10.

Hostelling International Northern Ireland (HINI), 22 Donegall Rd., Belfast BT12 5JN (☎02890 31 54 35; www.hini.org.uk). UK£15, under 25 UK£10.

Youth Hostels Association of New Zealand (YHANZ), Level 1, Moorhouse City, 166 Moorhouse Ave., P.O. Box 436, Christchurch (NZ only ☎0800 278 299 or 03 379 9970; www.yha.org.nz). NZ$40, under 18 free.

Scottish Youth Hostels Association (SYHA), 7 Glebe Cres., Stirling FK8 2JA (☎01786 89 14 00; www.syha.org.uk). UK£8, under 17 free.

Youth Hostels Association (England and Wales), Trevelyan House, Dimple Rd., Matlock, Derbyshire DE4 3YH (☎0870 770 8868; www.yha.org.uk). UK£16, under 26 UK£10.

Hostelling International-USA, 8401 Colesville Rd., Ste. 600, Silver Spring, MD 20910 (☎301-495-1240; www.hiayh.org). US$28, under 18 free.

> **BOOKING HOSTELS ONLINE.** One of the easiest ways to ensure a bed for the night is to reserve online. Click to the **Hostelworld** booking engine through **www.letsgo.com,** and you'll have access to bargain accommodations with no added commission.

OTHER TYPES OF ACCOMMODATIONS

HOTELS AND BED AND BREAKFASTS (B&BS)

Hotel singles in New Zealand cost about NZ$85 (US$60) per night, doubles NZ$115 (US$80). Nearly all hotel rooms are ensuite. Otherwise, you may have to share a hall bathroom. For a cozy alternative to hotel rooms, **B&Bs** (private homes with rooms available to travelers) range from acceptable to sublime. Hosts sometimes go out of their way to be accommodating by accepting travelers with pets or offering free, home-cooked meals. On the other hand, some B&Bs do not provide phones, TVs, or private baths, and often discourage children. Rooms in B&Bs generally cost NZ$75-125 for a single and NZ$110-200 for a double. For more information, check out the *New Zealand Bed and Breakfast Book* (US$30; www.bnb.co.nz), **InnFinder** (www.innfinder.com), **InnSite** (www.innsite.com), or **BedandBreakfast.com** (www.bedandbreakfast.com).

HOMESTAYS AND FARMSTAYS

Homestays and farmstays involve staying on a working farm or orchard, often alone or with a few other guests. These stays are usually arranged through the nearest town's tourist office, though some companies specialize in booking homestays and farmstays. Prices start around NZ$60 per person and include participation in farm activities and home-cooked meals; a few hostels also provide some aspects of a farmstay experience, especially in more rural areas. **TrueNZ Guides,** 64 Humffrey St., Blenheim (www.truenz.co.nz/farmstays), offers information on homestays and farmstays. For more information, see **Beyond Tourism,** p. 55.

HOME EXCHANGES AND HOSPITALITY CLUBS

Home exchange offers the traveler various types of homes (houses, apartments, condominiums, villas, even castles in some cases), plus the opportunity to live like a native and to cut down on accommodation fees. For more information, contact **HomeExchange.Com,** P.O. Box 787, Hermosa Beach, CA 90254 USA (☎800-877-8723; fax 310-798-3865; www.homeexchange.com), or **Intervac International Home Exchange** (NZ ☎04 934 4258; www.intervac.com). Hospitality clubs link their members with individuals or families abroad who are willing to host travelers for free or for a small fee to promote cultural exchange and general good karma. In exchange, members usually must be willing to host travelers in their own homes; a small membership fee may also be required. **GlobalFreeloaders.com** (www.globalfreeloaders.com) and **The Hospitality Club** (www.hospitalityclub.org) are good places to start. **Servas** (www.servas.org) is an established, more formal, peacebased organization, and requires a fee and an interview to join. As always, use common sense when planning to stay with or host someone you do not know.

LONG-TERM ACCOMMODATIONS

Travelers planning to stay in New Zealand for extended periods of time may find it cost-effective to rent an **apartment.** A basic one-bedroom (or studio) apartment in Auckland will range NZ$250-850 per month. Check out **RealENZ,** P.O. Box 9284, Auckland (☎0800 732 536, Auckland 09 353 2250; www.realenz.co.nz), for up-to-date listings of accommodations for rent plus agencies that can help you with the process. Besides the rent itself, prospective tenants usually are also required to front a security deposit (frequently one month's rent) and the last month's rent.

CAMPING

See **The Great Outdoors,** p. 64.

SPECIFIC CONCERNS

SUSTAINABLE TRAVEL

As the number of travelers on the road continues to rise, the detrimental effect they can have on natural environments becomes an increasing concern. With this in mind, *Let's Go* promotes the philosophy of **sustainable travel.** Through a sensitivity to issues of ecology and sustainability, today's travelers can be a powerful force in preserving and restoring the places they visit.

Ecotourism, a rising trend in sustainable travel, focuses on the conservation of natural habitats and using them to build up the economy without exploitation or overdevelopment. Travelers can make a difference by doing advance research and by supporting establishments that pay attention to their impact on their natural surroundings and strive to be environmentally friendly.

Ecotours New Zealand hooks you up with ecotourist guides (www.ecotours.co.nz). Also check out the ecotours offered by **Earthfoot** (www.earthfoot.org). Please see **Beyond Tourism,** p. 55 for more information.

 ECOTOURISM RESOURCES. For more information on environmentally responsible tourism, contact one of the organizations below:
The Centre for Environmentally Responsible Tourism (www.c-e-r-t.org).
Conservation International (www.conservation.org).
International Ecotourism Society, 733 15th St. NW, Washington, D.C. 20005, USA (☎202-347-9203; www.ecotourism.org).

RESPONSIBLE TRAVEL

The impact of tourist dollars on the destinations you visit should not be underestimated. The choices you make during your trip can have effects on local communities—for better or for worse. **Community-based tourism** aims to channel tourist dollars into the local economy by emphasizing tours and cultural programs that are run by members of the host community and that often benefit disadvantaged groups. An excellent resource for general information on community-based travel is *The Good Alternative Travel Guide* (UK£10), a project of **Tourism Concern** (☎020 7133 3330; www.tourismconcern.org.uk).

TRAVELING ALONE

There are many benefits to traveling alone, including greater interaction with locals. On the other hand, any solo traveler is a more vulnerable target for harassment and theft. As a lone traveler, try not to stand out as a tourist, look confident, and be careful in deserted or very crowded areas. Stay away from poorly lit areas. If questioned, never admit that you are traveling alone. Maintain regular contact with someone at home who knows your itinerary, and always research your desti-

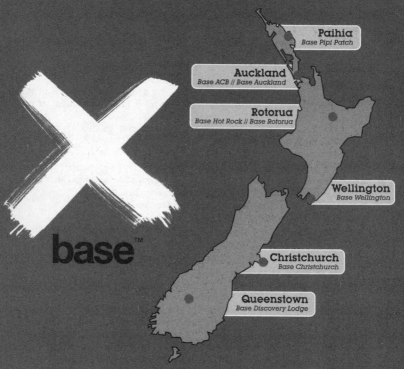

nation before traveling. For more tips, pick up *Traveling Solo* by Eleanor Berman (Globe Pequot Press, US$18), visit www.travelaloneandloveit.com, or subscribe to **Connecting: Solo Travel Network,** 689 Park Rd., Unit 6, Gibsons, BC V0N 1V7, Canada (☎604-886-9099; www.cstn.org; membership US$28-50).

WOMEN TRAVELERS

Women exploring on their own inevitably face some additional safety concerns, but it's easy to be adventurous without taking undue risks. If you are concerned, consider staying in hostels that offer single rooms that lock from the inside or in places with rooms for women only. Stick to centrally located accommodations and avoid solitary late-night treks or metro rides. Always carry extra money for a phone call, bus, or taxi. **Hitchhiking** is never safe for lone women, or even for two women traveling together. Look as if you know where you're going and approach older women or couples for directions if you're lost or uncomfortable. Wearing a conspicuous **wedding band** sometimes helps to prevent unwanted overtures.

Your best answer to verbal harassment is no answer at all; feigning deafness, sitting motionless, and staring straight ahead at nothing in particular will do a world of good. The extremely persistent can sometimes be dissuaded by a firm, loud, and very public "Go away!" Don't hesitate to seek out a police officer or a passerby if you are being harassed. Memorize the emergency numbers in places you visit, and consider carrying a whistle. A self-defense course will both prepare you for a potential attack and raise your level of awareness of your surroundings (p. 17).

GLBT TRAVELERS

Same-sex marriages were recently made legal and recognized by the government so same-sex couples have the same rights as heterosexual married couples. While not universally accepted, travelers of any sexual orientation should feel comfortable traveling in New Zealand, particularly in Auckland. Listed below are contact organizations, mail-order bookstores, and publishers that offer materials addressing some specific concerns. **Out and About** (www.planetout.com) offers a weekly newsletter and a comprehensive website addressing gay travel concerns. The online newspaper **365gay.com** also has a travel section (www.365gay.com/travel/travelchannel.htm).

Gay's the Word, 66 Marchmont St., London WC1N 1AB, UK (☎44 20 7278 7654; www.gaystheword.co.uk). The largest gay and lesbian bookshop in the UK.

Giovanni's Room, 1145 Pine St., Philadelphia, PA 19107, USA (☎215-923-2960; www.queerbooks.com). International feminist/gay bookstore with mail-order service.

International Lesbian and Gay Association (ILGA), 81 rue Marché-au-Charbon, B-1000 Brussels, Belgium (☎32 2 502 2471; www.ilga.org). Provides legal information.

ADDITIONAL RESOURCES: GLBT

Spartacus 2004-2005: International Gay Guide. Bruno Gmunder Verlag (US$33).

Damron Men's Travel Guide, Damron Accommodations Guide, Damron City Guide, and *Damron Women's Traveller.* Damron Travel Guides (US$18-24). For info, call ☎800-462-6654 or visit www.damron.com.

Ferrari Guides' Gay Travel A to Z, Ferrari Guides' Men's Travel in Your Pocket, Ferrari Guides' Women's Travel in Your Pocket, and *Ferrari Guides' Inn Places.* Ferrari Publications (US$16-20).

TRAVELERS WITH DISABILITIES

New Zealand is a very accessible destination for disabled travelers. All new buildings and sidewalks in New Zealand are required to provide wheelchair access. Those with disabilities should inform airlines and hotels of their disabilities when making reservations; some time may be needed to prepare. Call ahead to restaurants, museums, and other facilities to find out if they are wheelchair-accessible. **Guide dog owners** should inquire as to the quarantine policies of each destination.

USEFUL ORGANIZATIONS

Accessible Journeys, 35 West Sellers Ave., Ridley Park, PA 19078, USA (☎800-846-4537; www.disabilitytravel.com). Designs tours for wheelchair users and slow walkers.

Mobility International USA (MIUSA), P.O. Box 10767, Eugene, OR 97440, USA (☎541-343-1284; www.miusa.org). Provides a variety of books and other publications.

MINORITY TRAVELERS

Asian tourism is becoming increasingly common in New Zealand; prejudice against Asians in some areas is also growing. Minorities may find that they stand out, but are more likely to invite curiosity than harassment or violence.

DIETARY CONCERNS

Vegetarians and vegans will find ample dining options in New Zealand. The travel section of the The Vegetarian Resource Group's website, at www.vrg.org/travel, has a comprehensive list of organizations and websites that are geared toward vegetarians and vegans traveling abroad. For more info, visit your local health food store, and consult *The Vegetarian Traveler: Where to Stay if You're Vegetarian, Vegan, Environmentally Sensitive*, by Jed and Susan Civic (Larson Publications; US$16). Vegetarians will also find numerous resources on the web.

Travelers who keep kosher should contact synagogues in larger cities for information on kosher restaurants. Your own synagogue or college Hillel should have access to lists of Jewish institutions across the nation. If strict in observance, you may have to prepare your own food on the road. A good resource is the *Jewish Travel Guide*, edited by Michael Zaidner (Vallentine Mitchell; US$18). Travelers looking for halal restaurants may find www.zabihah.com a useful resource.

ADDITIONAL RESOURCES

Let's Go tries to cover all aspects of budget travel, but we can't put *everything* in our guides. Listed below are books and websites for additional info:

USEFUL PUBLICATIONS

101 Great Tramps in New Zealand, by Mark Pickering and Rodney Smith (1999), offers information on the Great Walks as well as lesser-known tramps (US$35).

AA New Zealand, published by AA New Zealand and available on their website, produces specific guides on accommodations, events, and food, as well as road atlases and street directories for major cities (NZ$10-30).

Cultural Studies in Aotearoa New Zealand, edited by Claudia Bell and Steve Matthewman, has essays on New Zealand culture (US$25).

WORLD WIDE WEB

Almost every aspect of budget travel is accessible via the web. In 10min., you can make a hostel reservation, get advice on travel hot spots from other travelers, or find out how much a bus from Christchurch to Queenstown costs. Listed here are some regional and travel-related sites to start off your surfing; other relevant websites are listed throughout the book. Because website turnover is high, use search engines (such as www.google.com) to strike out on your own.

 WWW.LETSGO.COM. *Let's Go's* website features a wealth of information and valuable advice at your fingertips. In addition to our online bookstore, we have great deals on everything from airfares to cell phones. Our resources section is full of information you'll need before you hit the road. Check back often to see constant updates, exciting new tips, and prize giveaways. See you soon!

THE ART OF TRAVEL

Backpacker's Ultimate Guide: www.bugpacific.com. Tips on packing, transportation, and where to go. Also tons of country-specific travel information.

BootsnAll.com: www.bootsnall.com. Numerous resources for independent travelers, from planning your trip to reporting on it when you get back.

Travel Intelligence: www.travelintelligence.net. A large collection of travel writing by distinguished travel writers.

INFORMATION ON NEW ZEALAND

Atevo Travel: www.atevo.com/guides/destinations. Detailed introductions, travel tips, and suggested itineraries.

CIA World Factbook: www.odci.gov/cia/publications/factbook/index.html. Tons of vital statistics on New Zealand's geography, government, economy, and people.

Tourism New Zealand: www.tourisminfo.govt.nz. Your first stop for up-to-date events, publications, and news.

LIFE AND TIMES

HISTORY AND CURRENT EVENTS

Don't be fooled by New Zealand's reserved demeanor on the world stage. Despite its relative brevity, the country's history is fast and tumultuous—better befitting its dramatic geological beginnings than its current reputation. In just 800 years, the islands have become fertile ground for not one, but two unique peoples and cultures: the Polynesian Maori and the white European Pakeha (although some take issue with the name). While it may seem that modern New Zealand follows the pattern of conquest, colonization, and eventual independence, the country and its peoples have a fiercely independent streak that continue to make it an intriguing study of struggle and resolution.

GEOGRAPHY

For nearly 680 million years, New Zealand was a land without people. Initially part of the large land mass Gondwana, 80 million years ago the islands pried loose from the continent and were swept away. The country rested upon its spiny mountain ranges—topped by glacier covered Aoraki/Mt. Cook (3794m) of South Island and the volcanic Mt. Ruapehu (2797m) of North Island—and waited. The ancient primordial landscape of kaori forests flourished despite geological instability and proved to be a fertile home to big game birds like the moa. However, it was the 18,000km of coast line with its golden shores and deep harbors that first drew attention from Polynesian canoes and European ships that carried New Zealand's future inhabitants.

ANCIENT MYTH

Maori legend has two separate tales that account for the dramatic creation of the islands. At the beginning of time, Papa (the earth) and Rangi (the sky) clung together in darkness. Forced to live in darkness, their children schemed to separate sky and earth and bring light into the world. The god Tane placed his shoulders against the sky and his feet agains the earth and finally drove a wedge between Papa and Rangi, flooding the world with light. Tane's brother, Tawhirimatea, was angered by his brother's inconsiderate act and joined his father in the sky, becoming the god of wind and storms. Distraught by their separation, Papa and Rangi wept due to their separation, their tears forming the rain, dew, and ever-present mists that blanket *Aotearoa*, the "land of the long white cloud."

The tale of the irreverent and mischievous Maui, one of the most beloved demigods of Polynesian myth, was developed to complement the early tale of Papa and Rangi. One day, Maui stowed away on his brothers' fishing trip and cast a hook made from his grandmother's jawbone and baited with blood from his own nose. Something tugged at the line. This fish, when brought to the surface, extended everywhere. To bring the fish into the boat, Maui recited a series of chants to make it lie still. His brothers, jealous of Maui's catch, hacked bits off the fish. When the sun rose, the fish's flesh turned solid, rough and mountainous due to the brother's mutilation. *Te ika a Maui* (Maui's fish) became the North Island of New Zealand, while *Te waka a Maui* (Maui's canoe) became South Island. *Te punga o te waka a Maui* (Maui's anchor) became tiny Stewart Island.

IMPORTANT EVENTS

c. 950-1300
Polynesian settlement.

1642
Abel Tasman makes the first European discovery of New Zealand.

1733
First sheep brought ashore by Captain Cook.

1769
Captain Cook circumnavigates New Zealand.

1820-1835
Musket Wars: intertribal conflict among Maori.

1835
Naturalist Charles Darwin, on his famed voyage of *The Beagle*, spends Christmas in the Bay of Islands.

1839
First brewery established at Thames.

1840
Maori chiefs sign the Treaty of Waitangi; British claim sovereignty over the whole of New Zealand.

TE AO MAORI (WELCOME TO THE MAORI WORLD)

While many Maori and Pakeha credit the great navigator Kupe with the discovery of New Zealand, research indicates that the beginnings of Maori settlement remain a mystery. It is known that the ancestors of the modern Maori came to New Zealand from the Polynesian Islands in about AD 1300. Led by the Great Fleet of seven canoes, the Maoris colonized the islands, eventually cutting all ties with their Polynesian ancestors. While tribal life was highly communal, the Maori were fiercely territorial, and intertribal warfare was both brutal and common. Tribes kept close watch over their hunting, fishing, and burial lands. This protective attitude toward their land was in full force hundreds of years later, when they first encountered Europeans.

THE EUROPEAN ARRIVAL

The first recorded European to lay eyes on New Zealand was Dutch explorer Abel Tasman. Sent on a mission to chart the southern waters and discover hidden treasures, Tasman laid anchor in South Island's Golden Bay in 1642. But he never set foot on land. Maori warriors who spotted the boat trumpeted a war cry, and the Dutch sailors mistook the call as one of welcome. The misunderstanding led to the death of four of his men and one Maori leader. Upon returning to Holland, Tasman's cartographer put the country on the world map for the first time, naming it *Nova Zeelandia* after a Dutch province.

The first group of Europeans who actually trod upon the uncharted land did not arrive until 1769 on the *Endeavour*, a British ship captained by the legendary explorer **James Cook**. In five missions in as many years, Cook mapped the entirety of the New Zealand shoreline, made friendly contact with several Maori tribes, and sent glowing reports of natural splendor and riches to mainland Europe. Although **timber** was an early cash crop, **sealers** and **whalers** were the first to establish outposts on the pristine land in the early 1800s. **Missionaries** also made an early appearance, but despite their efforts, Christianity failed to spread, as the Maori deemed the religion unsuitable for warriors. Heralding the start of heavier European settlement, independent **traders** soon arrived, seeking flax and novelty items in exchange for firearms, metal tools, and other European goods.

These increases in interaction lead to cultural clashes, although most often the clashes were between various Maori tribes. Traders brought European diseases, which killed an estimated 25% of the Maori population, while Western weapons escalated Maori violence and increased fatalities. The culmination of this intertribal warfare came in the form of the **Musket Wars** of 1820-1835, so named after the enormous change the deadly weapons brought to traditional war techniques.

THE FIRST TREATY

In 1830, New Zealand was still considered a small trading outpost. While its Australian neighbors had virtually eliminated aboriginal presence on the continent, the few hundred European settlers in New Zealand lived and worked closely with the country's Maori residents. By 1840, however, the number of European settlers had skyrocketed to just over 2000. The influx of Europeans led to increased tensions with Maori over land and hunting grounds. Encouraged by Maori chiefs, the first British resident, **James Busby,** and the colonial post in New South Wales, the British Colonial Office sent **Captain William Hobson** to initiate the transfer of sovereignty over land and government from Maori chiefs to the British in January of 1840. With the help of Busby and his secretary (neither of whom were lawyers), the infirm Hobson wrote the Treaty of Waitangi in just under four days and translated the document into Maori in one evening. On the morning of February 6, 1840, Hobson presented the document to a gathering of 200 Maori chiefs on Busby's front lawn along the banks of the Waitangi River. The contentious document called for a complete cession of sovereignty by each Maori chief to the Queen of England. In return, it promised the Maori full rights of British citizenship and guaranteed them the use of their lands. More than 40 Maori leaders signed the treaty, after which Captain William Hobson, in a gesture fitting the ceremonial moment, shook each Maori's hand, proclaiming: *"He iwi tahi tatou"* ("Now we are one people").

By September 1840, when the last signature was added to the Treaty, more than 500 signatures had been gathered, though the Treaty still lacked the support of a number of powerful and influential chiefs. Despite the lack of unanimous acceptance of British authority, in May of 1840, Hobson proclaimed full sovereignty over New Zealand. The name Waitangi means "weeping waters." Before long, the Maori leaders had reason to weep.

TIME OF TURBULANCE

As European settlement increased after 1840, the relationship between the Maori and settlers continued to deteriorate. The Maori began to suspect that they had given up more than they had intended by ceding some of their autonomy to the British. They responded by rebelling against British authority. In 1844, **Hone Heke,** one of the first chiefs to sign the treaty, cut down the flagpole at Kororareka near Russell (p. 116), which he saw as a symbol of British oppression of the Maori. The Russell incident marked the beginning of warfare between Heke's army and British-led forces, which lasted until 1846.

In 1852, the **Constitution Act** established a settler government with six provinces and a national parliament with a lower and an upper house. The act also granted suffrage to men over 25 with a property qualification. Though it was relatively low, Maori were almost entirely excluded because their land was often held under communal, not individual, titles.

As British governmental influence grew and Pakeha population soared, the Maori became increasingly disturbed to see the body that denied them representation gaining power. Maori tribal leaders urged tribes to unite under one common leader and began the Maori **King Movement.** Supporters of this policy sought to centralize Maori resources, naming **Te Wherowhero** of Waikato their king in 1858. The British gov-

1856
Britain declares New Zealand a self-governing colony.

1860s
New Zealand Wars: conflict between British and Maori.

1861
Gold discovered in Queenstown, starting a South Island gold rush.

1865
National capital moves from Auckland to Wellington.

1870
First rugby match played in New Zealand.

1886
Mt. Tarawera erupts over Rotorua.

1893
New Zealand becomes the first nation in the world to grant suffrage to women.

1898
The first car imported to New Zealand, a Benz brought over from Paris, requires an Act of Parliament before it can be driven.

1908
New Zealand native Sir Ernest Rutherford, the man who would split the atom, wins the Nobel Prize for Chemistry.

LIFE AND TIMES

1933
Elizabeth McCombs becomes the first woman elected to the House of Representatives.

1937
First commercial planting of Chinese gooseberries (a.k.a. kiwifruit).

1953
Sir Edmund Hillary, Kiwi climbing god, and Sherpa Norgay Tenzing become the first men to summit Mount Everest.

1960
First television broadcasts begin in New Zealand.

1978
Kiwi Naomi Jones becomes the first woman to sail single-handed around the world.

1982
The Warehouse (aka: The Red Shed), New Zealand's answer to Wal-Mart, opens its first store on Auckland's north shore.

1984
Labour Party wins election, pioneers a new free-trade economy.

ernment refused to recognize the Maori king, whom they viewed as a barrier to further settlement. When violence erupted once again in the Taranaki region in 1860, **Sir George Grey** blamed the King Movement instead of addressing the recurrent problem of land ownership. He decided to strike at Waikato, the movement's primary stronghold. The **New Zealand Wars** (also known as the **Maori Wars**) exploded across North Island as a result, with British forces gaining victory by 1870.

THE SOCIAL STATE

In 1865, the first Native Lands Act established a court to investigate Maori land ownership and distribute official land titles. Unfortunately, this act heavily favored new British arrivals in lieu of the communal Maori tribal system. In 1873, the second Native Lands Act continued to fracture Maori interests and further established that communal lands must split their shared titles among the owners. Disillusioned with the government, the Ngapuhi tribe sent the first of many delegations to England in 1882 to petition Queen Victoria. Although they were never given audience, Maori continued to send representatives to the Crown until the 1920s. By the end of the 19th century, an astounding 92% of New Zealand's land was out of Maori hands. Even while Maori struggled for their rights, the last decades of the 19th century ushered in an era of dramatic social reforms. Long removed from the global stage by of its remote location, New Zealand came to be known as one of the most socially progressive nations in the world, further encouraging emigration from mainland Europe. Throughout the country, factory conditions improved, conservation efforts increased, and Maori men were given the right to vote. In 1893, Pakeha and Maori women were the first in the world to receive the right to vote.

NEW ZEALAND ON THE WORLD STAGE

In 1907, New Zealand became a dominion of the British Empire, able to determine its own foreign policy. By virtue of their relationship with Britain, in 1915, the **Australia and New Zealand Army Corps (ANZAC)** were enlisted in World War I. Chosen to join the Dardanelles campaign, ANZAC fought at Gallipoli on April 25, 1915, attacking Turkish forces entrenched in the Dardanelles Strait. The battle was a military failure, leading to massive casualties, but winning great respect for the soldiers' bravery.

In 1935, the victory of the liberal **Labour Party** spurred the creation of the world's first universal social welfare system, including free healthcare and low-rent public housing. By the 1940s, New Zealand's main industries were booming and the country boasted one of the highest standards of living in the world. This prosperity came just in time to be disrupted by **World War II;** this time, with widespread fighting in the South Pacific, the disturbance was much closer to home. The **28th (Maori) Battalion,** in particular, won acclaim in battles fought from Crete to Africa and proved not only fierce in battle but creative and unorthodox in their tactics.

New Zealand was declared fully independent in 1947, but remained economically and politically tied to a number of nations. New Zealand protected itself by independently harnessing its energy resources and signing the **ANZUS Pact** for the mutual defense of Australia, New Zealand, and the US.

Domestically, the government replicated its international spirit of cooperation with attempts to ease tensions with the Maori. Adherence to traditional beliefs among the Maori had declined dramatically, though the traditional tensions over land and governmental power with Pakeha remained. In 1960, the **Waitangi Day Act** made a national "day of thanksgiving" in celebration of the bi-racial nature of the coalition created by the 1840 treaty. On February 6, 1974, it became a national public holiday. The 1975 **Treaty of Waitangi Act** established the Waitangi Tribunal to hear Maori claims against the Crown.

The **Closer Economic Relations Trade Agreement** of 1983 allowed free and unrestricted trade between New Zealand and Australia. With its foreign policy, New Zealand continued to retain an independent streak. In 1987, Labour Party Prime Minister David Lange took a stance in the midst of the Cold War and committed New Zealand to the **anti-nuclear movement** by barring all nuclear-capable vessels from New Zealand harbors. Although the anti-nuclear movement received criticism from several politicians within New Zealand, it did serve to distance New Zealand from traditional defense alliances with the United States. To better protect itself, the country became more involved with the **United Nations.** Kiwi troops were sent in large numbers to UN-sponsored missions across the globe, most visibly during the breakup of the former Yugoslavia.

NEW ZEALAND NOW

GOVERNMENT. Since the signing of the Treaty of Waitangi, New Zealand has continued to adapt its government to the country's changing needs without ever signing a written constitution. The **Constitution Act of 1986** serves as the guiding principles for the country's government. New Zealand is a constitutional monarchy with a single-house, popularly elected parliament. Queen Elizabeth II remains the Queen of New Zealand and the acting head of state while the Prime Minister, the head of parliament, is chosen from the leading political party. In 1993, the majority of New Zealanders voted in favor of a **mixed-member proportional representation (MMP)** system of government. Under the system, a 120-seat Parliament was established, with a predetermined number of general electorate seats, party list seats (to which the elected party selects members), and Maori seats. New Zealand citizens are accorded two votes, one for the parties and the second for a candidate. Citizens of Maori descent may choose whether to register either on the general or Maori roll.

In recent years, Kiwi politics have been defined by behind-the-scenes maneuvering, fragile power-sharing arrangements, and allegations of corruption. In November 1997, **Jenny Shipley** of the **National Party** seized party leadership

1985
Greenpeace vessel *Rainbow Warrior* is sunk in Auckland Harbour.

1987
Inventor of bungy, A.J. Hackett, bungy jumps off the Eiffel Tower in Paris.

1995
New Zealand's *Black Magic* yachting squad wins the America's Cup.

1997
Jenny Shipley becomes Prime Minister and the first female leader in New Zealand history.

1999
New Zealand lowers the drinking age to 18 from 20.

2001
DOC publishes ground-breaking biodiversity strategy to protect national parks, which make up more than 30% of the country.

2005
New Zealand becomes the first country in the world to have women in all the highest offices of the land.

2007
New Zealand fishermen catch a 450kg squid, the world's largest, off the coast of South Island.

LIFE AND TIMES

through a carefully constructed coup. She was sworn in as New Zealand's first female Prime Minister in December of that year. A primary focus of Shipley's government was to increase free-market competition and reduce government size. Shipley's term was thrown into disarray in August 1998 as her delicate coalition began to crack after she fired a leading cabinet member. Due to the fragile coalition between her own conservative National Party and the more liberal New Zealand First, Shipley was often embroiled in controversy, a possible factor in her subsequent electoral loss.

In November 1999, parliamentary elections restored the center-left Labour Party, led by **Helen Clark,** after nine years in the opposition. Labour Party success was credited in part to support from Maori citizens, following changes in the previously Maori-dominated **New Zealand First** party. As Prime Minister, Clark has allied herself with the left-wing Alliance Party (which in 2002 became the Progressive Party) but relies on support from the influential **Green Party** and **United Future.** In 2002, Clark began a push to replace Queen Elizabeth as the head of state and turn New Zealand into a republic. Although Clark has not yet succeeded in her bid, she remains a popular Prime Minister known for her careful coalition building, concern for social welfare, promotion of New Zealand arts, and stable economic growth. In 2005, New Zealand marked another first for women, becoming the first country in the world to have women in all the highest offices of the land including the Chief Justice of the Supreme Court. The tenuous balance between parties is sure to make for an exciting round of general elections, scheduled for 2008.

MAORI ISSUES. The recognition of Maori rights continues to be an issue of heated governmental debate. The legacy of the Treaty of Waitangi left a bitter taste in the mouths of many Maori leaders, but in recent years, Maori leaders have made up some lost ground. The **Office of Treaty Settlement** is the government organization responsible for mediating between Maori claims and the New Zealand Crown. In November 1998, the New Zealand Crown admitted in the **Ngai Tahu Deed of Settlement** that it had acted unfairly and in violation of the 1840 Treaty of Waitangi, loosening claims dating back to 1840 up for consideration in New Zealand courts. Since the new interpretation of the law, the Tainui and Ngai Tahu tribes won $170 million compensation packages. The Maori revival continuesl, receiving extra governmental funding to support and protect Maori language and culture, including the so-called "Sealord Deal" that allocated 20% of the nation's fish quota to Maori.

ECONOMICS AND TRADE. The turn of the century was a time of redefining trade relations and economic goals for New Zealand. Cooling relations with the US meant New Zealanders had to open their doors to other trade possibilities, including nearby Asia and Australia. PM Helen Clark has made great strides in creating stable trade ties to China and strongly supports Chinese entrance into the World Trade Organization (WTO). Dairy, wine, forest products, and tourism have replaced wool and meat as the primary exports of the island nation. The country continues to struggle to find a balanced way to protect its valuable natural resources while using them to support its citizens' comfortable lifestyle.

CULTURE

Largely shaped by its short, intense history as a peopled land, Kiwis pride themselves on their well-balanced culture. Best characterized by its most beloved sporting hero, **Sir Edmund Hillary,** the country honors its commitment to live simply on the margin between the tamed and untamed. In 1953, Hillary became the first man to climb Mt. Everest along with Sherpa Tenzing Norgay. After being knighted, he tall, gangly Hillary always preferred to be called Ed, rather than Sir, and returned to his life as beekeeper after his effort. Beyond this modest lifestyle, Hillary used his fame to support humanitarian causes Nepal and domestic conservation efforts. In 2007 at the age of 88, he returned to the New Zealand-managed Scott Base on the South Pole, which he established on his overland traverse of Antartica in 1958, in an effort to raise funds for the fledgling research camp.

PEOPLE

With only 4.1 million people, New Zealand has a lot of wide open spaces. Nearly three-quarters of the population live on North Island and half of those in Auckland alone. As a result, New Zealand has one of the highest percentages of foreign-born citizens in the world. Almost a quarter of the population is foreign born, mostly of British and Irish origin. While the large majority of the population is **Caucasian,** the **Maori** remain highly visible, making up 14% of the population. Asians are the fastest growing demographic at 9% of the population. Pacific Islanders are the other significant group on the islands. **Christianity** is the predominant religion; Anglican, Presbyterian, and Catholic denominations are the most common. Maori religions, such as **Ratana,** were first developed into cohesive groups during the missionary era of the late 19th and early 20th centuries in an effort to synthesize traditional Maori beliefs with the precepts of Christianity. Ratana has also become a strong political force and represents Maori issues in the New Zealand parliament.

MAORI ARTS AND CULTURE

New Zealand society is largely bicultural, comprised primarily of British, Pakeha, and Maori New Zealanders. The word *maori* was originally used to distinguish "ordinary people" from strange European explorers. In fact, many Maori did not self-identify as Maori until well into the 1830s. **Maoritanga,** loosely translated as "the ways of the Maori," serves as an umbrella term for the cultural traditions and organization of Maori life. Although many Maori now live off the traditional grounds in an urban environment, New Zealand has recently experienced a renaissance of *Maoritanga* as more Maori look to their rich heritage for identity.

BASIC CONCEPTS

The most fundamental idea of Maori custom is the notion of **tapu** and its lesser-known counterpart, **noa.** *Tapu,* roughly translated as "sacred" or "spiritual restriction," indicates the presence of supernatural power (whether good or evil) and commands respect and attention. Ignoring *tapu* is a great taboo—yes, that is the root of the English word—across New Zealand. *Noa* underscores the absence of such power and thus deserves no special caution. For example, a man has the *tapu* responsibility in a tribe to oversee ceremonial duties and give speeches at a *marae,* but he cannot look respectable without the help of the female's *noa* duties of preparing food and singing songs. Personal relationships within and between tribes also require an understanding of **mana.** Translated literally, the word means "prestige" or "respectability," but the meaning is more of an essence that grants seniority to a worthy individual. Traditionally, the amount of *mana* in an individual depends on his or her ancestry, experience, and seniority in a tribe. Nowadays, *mana* is instead often influenced more by one's success and achievements.

A MAORI TRIBAL STRUCTURE

In New Zealand, tribal association is not an official designation; there are over 40 recognized **iwi** in New Zealand. Within the *iwi* exist smaller regional communities called **hapu.** These communities were originally groups that owned land within the

teaching tradition to tots:

New Zealand's *Kohanga Reo* Schools and the Revitalization of Maori Language and Culture

It isn't unusual to meet a Kiwi bloke and fail to understand half the words that come out of his mouth. While the confusion is partly the accent, it is compounded by the Maori words that have slipped into everyday New Zealand speech. Newscasters open broadcasts with *kia ora* (hello), students return home to visit their *whanau* (family), and teenagers invite their crushes out for some *kai* (food). The prevalence of Maori language on signs, in publications, and on television makes it hard to believe that in 1960, *te reo Maori* (the Maori language) was pronounced a "relic of ancient Maori life"—a language that was going the way of Latin and Aramaic. Predictions were dire. Maori language was "dying."

In the 60s and 70s, *te reo* was spoken primarily by elders in Maori communities. English became the language of choice for young Maori, especially in urban areas. Fewer young adults were truly bilingual and speakers of *te reo* were aging. Maori communities were concerned that within the space of a few generations, knowledge of *te reo* would disappear. Out of this fear, the *kohanga reo* were born.

Kohanga reo, literally "language nests," are community nursery schools staffed primarily by Maori elders. English is checked at the door and everything from instruction to playtime to art and music is conducted entirely in *te reo*. The culture, values, and context of the *kohanga reo* mirror modern Maori life—contemporary, but mindful of the culture's traditional roots. In the centers, *te reo* is used to explore traditional Maori concepts like *mana* (prestige, power) and *aroha* (love) and to discuss popular culture essentials like the Internet, the X-Box, and Eminem.

Founded in 1981 by the Department of Maori Affairs, the *kohanga reo* program has expanded considerably in recent years. There are now more than 700 *kohanga reo* centers nationwide enrolling more than 13,000 children.

Recent government estimates indicate that 9% of students receiving early childhood education are enrolled in their local *kohanga reo*. The ramifications for *te reo* and Maori culture have been profound. In fact, the program has so successfully reintroduced and revitalized the language and it now serves as an exemplar for populations with fading languages across the world, from the Welsh to the Navajo.

In recent years, *kohanga reo* have broadened their mission beyond just childhood education. As more and more children became proficient in *te reo*, parents were frustrated by their own lack of fluency. Now nighttime, weekend, and longer immersion classes in *te reo* for parents and other adult members of the *tanga whenua* (community) are gathering large audiences. Such classes encourage the use of *te reo* in the *marae* (community meeting place) and in the home.

A visit to a *kohanga reo* is a fascinating and rewarding Kiwi experience.

"Fewer young adults were truly bilingual and speakers of *te reo* were aging."

The vibrancy of the atmosphere coupled with the children's facility in *te reo* testifies to this unique educational system's efficacy. Most *kohanga reo* are affiliated with local *marae* and trips can often be arranged—be sure to ask before visiting and to observe the proper protocol (when in doubt, just ask). While speaking in English is not appropriate during your visit, one way to engage is to learn a *waiata* (song) to share with the children, or just brush up on a few key phrases and gesture your way through the rest. Expect some incredulous stares—the children often cannot comprehend your inability to converse in *te reo*.

Ann Robinson was a researcher-writer for the 2000 and 2002 Let's Go: New Zealand guides and an editor for the 2001 guide. A recipient of the Fulbright scholarship, she received her Masters in History at Victoria University in Wellington, focusing on comparative US-New Zealand history.

A CLOSER LOOK

tribe. Today, each *hapu* seldom owns more land than a *marae* reserve. For this reason, the *hapu* generally has more significance for rural populations; city-dwellers generally tend to identify less with their *hapu*.

THE MARAE

The *marae* are the sacred grounds around a Maori **whare tupuna** (ancestral meeting house) and the site of the **powhiri** (formal welcome), receiving visitors into the community. The ceremony consists of four basic components. Upon arriving at the *marae*, a warrior from the village will greet visitors with a *haka* (see **Dance,** below), an elaborate set of body movements and a tongue-protruding facial gesture (it's exceedingly uncouth to return such a gesture). The **wero** (challenge) ends when a **teka** (peace offering) is offered and accepted. After this step, a female elder will issue the **karanga,** a chant of welcome and mourning for the visitors' great ancestors. As your group crosses the *marae,* pause and bow in respect for the ancestors of the tribe before congregating in front of the *whare.* In response to the chief's **whaikorero** (speech of welcoming), the designated chief of your group will deliver a brief speech in return (preferably in Maori as well, but protocol varies). To seal the bond of friendship, both chiefs press (but do not rub) noses together in the traditional greeting known as the **hongi.** After the *hongi,* the separate groups finally mingle and are called to dine in the *whare kai.* Shoes are not worn inside the *whare kai,* and pictures may not be permitted, depending on the tribe. After a **karakia** (prayer) is given, the **hangi** (dinner), is prepared—sweet potatoes, meat, and other goodies roasted in a pit of stones.

SONG AND DANCE

Tau marae orations are stylized tributes to the dead performed at traditional funeral ceremonies for important chiefs. Another important type of oratory is **karakia** (prayer), which were once strictly designated for **tohunga** (priests or specially learned men). *Karakia* imparted **mauri** (essence of its natural state) to objects. **Waiata** is the most common type of ceremonial song, customarily performed at *powhiri* and the conclusion of farewell speeches at **tangi** (funerals). In modern times, the two kinds of *waiata* that have survived—the *waiata tangi* (songs of mourning often composed by women), and the *waiata aroha* (love songs composed by women)—often dwell upon unrequited love and delinquent lovers.

The vigorous arm-waving, chanting, foot-stomping haka is an all-male dance once performed by armed warriors before battle to include the god of war. To see a modern *haka,* head to a *marae* or just check out the **All Blacks** (p. 52)—they perform the haka before each match. **Taparahi** are weaponless dances performed by both genders for a variety of reasons: to greet important guests, to honor the dead, or for sheer entertainment. In the **poi,** designed to increase suppleness in the wrists of warriors, women twirl balls on strings in a synchronized fashion.

CARVING

An early Maori art form, carving is still practiced today. The most common materials are bone, wood, and *pounamu* (greenstone). According to traditional Maori beliefs, it is the artist's responsibility to infuse certain qualities such as fear, power, and authority into his or her pieces in order to transform them from mere material objects to **taonga** (highly treasured, even sacred objects). Each object accumulates its own body of **korero** (stories) with every successive owner. A design particular to a tribe is passed down from generation to generation, distinguished by its repetition of certain stylistic features and motifs, such as **tiki** (human forms), **manaia** (bird men), and **taniwha** (sea spirits). Carvers create items large and small, decorating both towering meeting houses and tiny *tiki* pendants.

MOKO (FACIAL TATTOOING)

Moko has been one of the most famous Maori art forms since the days when 19th-century Europe was transfixed by portraits and photographs of New Zealand "savages" with full facial tattoos. While most tribes reserved the practice for males, *moko* sometimes served as a rite of passage for both males and females, as well as a marker of achievements and status. Men's *moko* began with a simple design for youths; more spiral flourishes were added as the wearer won prestige in battle. The intricacy of the *moko* was also indicative of the warrior's tolerance for pain. Thus, only older, highly distinguished warriors could sport full facial tattoos. Women's *moko* were simpler, surrounding only the lips and the tip of the nose.

Traditionally, *moko* was only executed by *tohunga ta moko*, experts trained extensively in using the sharp wooden adze and mallet to etch the design into the skin. They used a toothed chisel to fill in the ink dye (a mixture of burned kauri or totara resin and pigeon fat), all in complete silence. While the tattoo was healing, leaves of the karaka tree were placed on the skin and the *tohunga ta moko* declared the recipient *tapu*. During this time, sexual intimacy was prohibited and no one was permitted to view the *moko;* it was believed that the tattoo would fade if anyone saw it before it healed completely.

VISUAL ARTS AND LITERATURE

A number of prominent and critically acclaimed artists hail from New Zealand. **Frances Hodgkins** (1869-1947) and **Colin McCahon** (1919-1987) are two of the most famous 20th-century Kiwi painters. Hodgkins left New Zealand in 1913 for London, eventually becoming a leading figure in watercolor figurative painting, and then in oils. McCahon retained his Kiwi base and is considered one of the most important influences on indigenous modern art. In recent years, New Zealand has become renowned for its innovative and eco-friendly design practices, displayed by the modern cityscapes of Auckland, Wellington, and Christchurch.

New Zealand has its share of literary stars as well. **Katherine Mansfield** (1888-1923), a short-story writer, was another WWI expat in Britain. Her best-known collections are *The Garden Party* (1922) and *Bliss* (1920). Mansfield's childhood home in Wellington has been preserved as a museum (p. 240). **Dame Ngaio Marsh** (1895-1982), most famous for her mystery series featuring detective Roderick Alleyn, stayed firmly rooted in New Zealand as a member of the leading artistic group in Christchurch in the mid-1900s. Other notable New Zealand writers are nature poet extraordinaire **James K. Baxter** (1926-1972), and novelist **Janet Frame** (1924-2004), best known for her autobiographical *An Angel at My Table* (1985).

Maori writers have recently surged onto the literary scene. **Patricia Grace** (b. 1937), of Ngati Raukawa, Ngati Toa, and Te Ati Awa descent, is known for the bittersweet coming-of-age story *Mutuwhenua: The Moon Sleeps* (1978). **Witi Ihimaera** (b. 1944), whose recent book *The Whale Rider* (2003) was adapted for the screen, explored father-son relationships in *Tangi* (1973). Perhaps the best-known Maori author is **Keri Hulme** (b. 1947), a South Islander of Scottish, English, and Ngai Tahu descent. Her novel, *The Bone People*, won the 1985 Booker Prize. More recently, **Alan Duff** (b. 1950) earned the spotlight for his hit *Once Were Warriors* (1992) and its sequel *What Becomes of the Broken-Hearted* (1997).

MUSIC

Geographic isolation hasn't disconnected New Zealand from musical trends of the past. Kiwis embraced the 1970s punk movement, led by the influential Christchurch label **Flying Nun**. In the 1980s, **Split Enz** and its offshoot **Crowded House** enjoyed worldwide popularity as part of the New Wave movement. Alternative rock has also gained popularity, with student band **Zed's** popular album *Silencer* and hits from **Th'Dudes'**, including "Be Mine Tonight." The rock arena has featured Kiwi acts such as **The Feelers, Elemeno P,** and **Bleeders. Brooke Fraser,** the daughter of All Blacks (see **Rugby,** p. 52) legend Bernie Fraser, has made waves with her alt-rock folk style. Reggae-inspired groove groups such as **Fat Freddy's Drop** are perhaps the countries most popular performers and tour regularly with the ever present summer reggae festivals. A recent addition to the New Zealand music scene is Chinese-Maori **Bic Runga,** known for her hit song "Sway." Check out *The Fix*, a free glossy magazine, for info on the Auckland electronic scene. Down in Wellington, **DJ Mu** demonstrates his skills on the vinyl, while **Manuel Bundy** crisscrosses the country with rhythmically centered beats.

New Zealand's premier professional orchestra, the **New Zealand Symphony Orchestra,** enjoys an excellent reputation and travels over 20,000km a year to perform. Internationally renowned opera star and New Zealand native **Dame Kiri Te Kanawa** also performs for audiences worldwide.

FILM

New Zealand's native film industry was not fully established until the 1970s, but it has made a big impact both in Hollywood and Bollywood as a favorite site for filming. One notable figure from the early film scene was **Len Lye** (1901-1980), a kinetic sculptor and modern filmmaker of the 60s. The early 70s saw works mainly by independent filmmakers. A significant event in New Zealand film during this time, and a major benchmark for the representation of the Maori, was the release of *Tangata Whenua: The People of the Land* (1974), a six-part documentary series by Maori filmmaker Barry Barclay.

In 1978, the government created the New Zealand Film Commission, which encourages and supports the film industry. Since then, recent films made in New Zealand have become both popular and critical hits. One-sixth of the country viewed *Goodbye Pork Pie* (1981), directed by Geoff Murphy. A film every Kiwi will tell you to see is *Once Were Warriors* (1994), an adaptation of the Alan Duff novel, by prominent director Lee Tamahori. Jane Campion's *The Piano* (1993), filmed in New Zealand, broke box office records and won two Cannes Film Festival awards and a Best Supporting Actress Oscar for native New Zealander **Anna Paquin.** Kiwis claim the rough, tough, and buff *Gladiator* **Russell Crowe** and the equally rough, tough, and buff *Xena: Warrior Princess* **Lucy Lawless** as natives. Adopted Kiwi **Sam Neill** grew up on South Island before landing coveted roles in *The Hunt for Red October* (1990), *Jurassic Park* (1993), *Event Horizon* (1997), and *Jurassic Park III* (2001). Writer-director and Wellingtonian **Peter Jackson** first made a name for himself making horror films like the 1992 zombie-and-lawn-mower-psycho smash hit *Braindead* or *Dead Alive*. However, it is the *Lord of the Rings* trilogy, filmed entirely in New Zealand, which brought Tolkien fans and moviegoers to the edge of their seats. **Niki Caro's** *Whale Rider* (2003), based on the novel by Witi Ihimaera, moved audiences with its powerful story of a spiritually gifted Maori girl. As a result of the international success of the Tolkien trilogy and *Whale Rider*, New Zealand's Maori and Pakeha behind the scenes movie production has skyrocketed with Kiwis hired for stunts, special effects, and set building.

FOOD AND DRINK

In the tradition of the earliest inhabitants' dinners of roast moa and **kumara** (sweet potato), New Zealanders still maintain a largely meat-and-potatoes diet. While **vegetarian** and **vegan** options are becoming trendy (**kosher** fare is still rare), traditional New Zealand food tends to be meaty. The national dish is hot **meat pie** loaded with lamb or beef and gravy in flaky pastry. **Seafood** is always an abundant alternative; fresh fish, prawns, crayfish, shellfish, and more overrun coastal towns. Fruit-flavored **ice cream** with chunks of fruit is consumed in vast quantities, though **hokey pokey** (vanilla ice cream loaded with bits of toffee) is a national favorite. Not only does New Zealand proudly produce the ✄**most ice cream per capita** in the world, it also rivals the US for most ice cream consumed per capita.

In small towns, the tendency toward the basic can be seen in the Main St. triumvirate of fish 'n chip dives, cafes, and ever-present Chinese restaurants—all serving fried, greasy goodies. Ethnic restaurants, such as Thai, Malaysian, and Indian, are no longer few and far between. Middle Eastern **kebab** joints, usually a good deal, have proliferated recently. Keep in mind that ordering an **entree** will often get you an appetizer or starter in New Zealand; main courses are listed as **mains.**

While Kiwis serve excellent beer, with various national lagers and draughts (e.g., Steinlager, Speights, and Tui), it's the **wine** that takes the cake. The wines of the Marlborough and Hawke's Bay regions are world-famous, particularly the Sauvignon Blanc, Chardonnay, Riesling, Cabernet Sauvignon, and Pinot Noir varieties. New Zealand white wines are already challenging the French hold on the market, and red wines are improving annually. For non-alcoholic refreshment, try **Lemon and Paeroa (L&P),** a popular carbonated lemon drink that is "world-famous in New Zealand." For a more refined thirst-quencher, you can enjoy a British-style **Devonshire tea.** The late afternoon meal traditionally consists of tea, scones with Devonshire cream or jam, crumpets, and other delectables. A lighter Kiwi treat, often served for dessert, is the **pavlova,** a tribute to egg whites and kiwifruit. New Zealand offers a range of exotic fruits and veggies, including feijoas, nashi, persimmons, and of course kiwifruit. In 2000, the **golden kiwifruit,** a yellow, sweeter version of the traditional kiwi, was engineered for worldwide consumption.

SPORTS

New Zealand is a sports-crazed nation; almost half the population belongs to the **New Zealand Sports Assembly,** 150 national sporting associations. In addition to the multitude of outdoor sports, including skiing, rafting, swimming, hiking, and jetboating, Kiwis also hit the grass in organized sports like rugby, cricket, golf, tennis, and field hockey. New Zealand keeps certain sporting heroes close to its heart. While **Sir Edmund Hillary** is the most treasured Kiwi athlete, Olympic level track and field heroes have also won the affections of many Kiwis. **Jack Lovelock** was a 1500m gold medalist in the 1936 Berlin Olympics. In the 1960 Rome Olympics, **Peter Snell** and **Murray Halberg** took home the gold in the 800m and 5000m respectively. Though New Zealand's performance in the 2000 Sydney Olympics seemed less than stellar, **Rob Waddell** brought home a gold medal in the single scull. Several Kiwis carried the proverbial torch in Athens at the 2004 Olympics; **Hamish Carter** and **Bevan Docherty** brought home the gold and silver in the men's triathlon.

RUGBY. This country likes to sit on the sidelines, especially to watch rugby. When a big match is televised, all the locals will be glued to their TVs. Most people in New Zealand are die-hard **Rugby Union** fans. The **Super 12** tournament is a popular rugby event with the best players from Australia, New Zealand, and South Africa organized into 12 teams.

Kiwi pride swells enormously for the **All Blacks,** the national team whose season usually runs from late May to September. The team shines during the **Tri-Nations Games** that take place among the Australia, New Zealand, and South Africa teams from July to August. The All Blacks won the Tri-Nations in 2002, 2003, 2005, and 2006 and look to continue their winning ways in the abbreviated 2007 series. During the same months, the All Blacks also compete for the coveted **Bledisloe Cup,** which they won in 2003 and 2004. If anything, this obsession reached a fevered pitch following the All Blacks' 1987 victory in the **Rugby World Cup.** The All Blacks hope to recreate history for the 20th anniversary of their win in France in the fall of 2007. Despite their popularity, however, the team has garnered controversy. In 1960, the All Blacks made a protested tour of South Africa in which Maori players were excluded. Then, in 1981, the South African Springboks made a tour of New Zealand, prompting claims that New Zealand tacitly supported apartheid.

Be sure not to confuse Rugby Union with the less popular **Rugby League**, which features regional teams instead of national teams. The difference between the two can be confusing, but long ago the Rugby League split with Rugby Union over a disagreement about the "purity" of professional rugby play.

CRICKET. There are two types of cricket competition. The first is **test-match cricket**, which takes place between two teams in a six-hour match each day for five days. The second method is **one-day cricket,** typically played, as the name suggests, as a one-day series between pairs of teams or round-robin competitions between teams. A **World Cup** one-day competition is played between all the Test nations— the nine nations recognized by the International Cricket Council. New Zealand's next chance for World Cup glory will be in late 2007 in the Caribbean.

SAILING. In 1995 the Kiwi sailing team Black Magic swiped the America's Cup from the United States, marking only the second time in 145 years that the cup was not won by an American team. The 1996 mauling of the cup at the hands of a sledgehammer-wielding Maori rights activist drew international headlines to tense Maori-Pakeha relations. Fully restored, the cup made several countrywide tours.

In March 2000, **Team New Zealand,** determined to protect the Kiwi hold on the Cup, trounced their Italian opponent, Prada Challenge, with innovative racing techniques. With this decisive victory, New Zealand cemented its reputation as a top yachting nation, becoming the first country other than the US to defend the Cup. New Zealand's reign came to an end in 2003, as the Swiss snatched the prize. The presence of Kiwis on the Swiss team may have had a bit to do with this victory. While early races in the Louis Vuitton Cup look promising for Team New Zealand, the boat has yet to qualify for the challenger position in the 2007 America's Cup race, which will begin in late June 2007 in Valencia, Spain.

HOLIDAYS AND FESTIVALS

Kiwis celebrate all aspects of their culture, from independence to adventure.

2008 DATE	HOLIDAY NAME	2008 DATE	HOLIDAY NAME
February 6	Waitangi Day	June 2	Queen's Birthday
March 23	Easter	October 27	Labour Day
March 24	Easter Monday	December 25	Christmas
April 25	ANZAC Day	December 26	Boxing Day

DATE	FESTIVAL	LOCATION
January	World Buskers Festival	Christchurch
February	New Zealand Festival of Arts	Wellington
February	HERO Gay and Lesbian Festival	Auckland
March	Wild Foods Festival	Hokitika
April	Adventure Canterbury	Christchurch
May	International Comedy Festival	Wellington
June	National Fieldays	Hamilton
July	International Film Festival	Auckland
September	Wearable Art Awards	Nelson
October	International Jazz Festival	Wellington

LIFE AND TIMES

BEYOND TOURISM

A PHILOSOPHY FOR TRAVELERS

HIGHLIGHTS OF BEYOND TOURISM

PICK fruit to earn some dough (p. 56).

PROTECT endangered kaori forestland (p. 55).

HERD Kiwi sheep while living on an organic farm (p. 56).

One of the most rewarding ways to travel in New Zealand is to experience the country from the perspective of a student, worker, or community member. Opportunities to sample the natural flavor of Kiwi living are often overlooked by zealous explorers with grand plans to tackle the wilderness of Down Under, but adventure can be found in any number of academic, professional, or humanitarian pursuits. This chapter's purpose is to help you to reevaluate your perspective on travel and provide you with some ideas for further research.

Let's Go believes that the connection between travelers and their destinations is an important one. Many travelers care deeply about the communities and environments they explore, but even conscientious tourists can inadvertently damage natural wonders or offend locals. With this **Beyond Tourism** chapter, *Let's Go* hopes to promote a better understanding of New Zealand and enhance your experience there. You'll find Beyond Tourism information throughout the book in the form of special "Giving Back" sidebar features that highlight regional Beyond Tourism opportunities and in the **Practical Information** sections of some cities and towns.

There are several options for those who seek to participate in Beyond Tourism activities. New Zealand is eager to allow international visitors to share its knowledge and culture, making a concerted effort to promote opportunities online and overseas. Options for **volunteerism** abound, with both local and international organizations rejuvenating local communities and environments. **Studying** can be instructive, whether through direct enrollment in a local university or in an independent research project. In marine biology or environmental classes, you can get hands-on experiences unavailable in less exotic environments. **Working** is a way both to immerse yourself in the local culture and to finance your travels. Many travelers structure their trips around the work that they can do along the way—either odd jobs, or long-term stints. **Seasonal work** like fruit picking is very popular among backpackers, allowing them to extend their vacations almost indefinitely.

Begin your research with us, but as you find opportunities that interest you, keep exploring to find a perfect match. There's no use in taking an opportunity to go abroad and spending it on a program with which you are unhappy. Use the tips in this chapter to aid you in your research, and you'll be rewarded with an unbeatable adventure in New Zealand.

VOLUNTEERING

In New Zealand, travelers looking to do their part will find an enormous range of available projects, from kaori forest preservation, to endangered wildlife rescue, to community-based projects in underserved areas. Keep in mind, however, that most volunteer organizations require a minimum time commitment ranging from one week to three months. Read below for general volunteering suggestions as well as specific organization listings.

Depth of involvement varies depending on the individual program and your interest level; be sure to acquire the appropriate **visa** for your plans before committing to an organization (see **Visa Information for Extended Stays,** p. 57). Don't sign up for the first volunteer program you come across; research a wide variety of opportunities and weigh your options. Also keep in mind that volunteer work, particularly with wildlife or in environmental rehabilitation and protection, is not as glamorous as it might seem. Plan on a of repetitive, strenuous labor rather than days full of swimming with dolphins, comforting baby penguins, and swinging around the rainforest canopy. Cleaning and maintenance work comprise a significant part of many volunteer positions.

WHY PAY MONEY TO VOLUNTEER? Many volunteers are surprised to learn that some organizations require large fees or "donations." While this may seem ridiculous at first glance, such fees often keep the organization afloat, in addition to covering airfare, room, board, and administrative expenses for the volunteers. (Other organizations must rely on private donations and government subsidies.) If you're concerned about how a program spends its fees, request an annual report or finance account. A reputable organization won't refuse to inform you of how volunteer money is spent.

Pay-to-volunteer programs might be a good idea for young travelers who are looking for more support and structure (such as pre-arranged transportation and housing), or anyone who would rather not deal with the uncertainty implicit in creating a volunteer experience from scratch.

Those looking for longer, more intensive volunteer opportunities usually choose to go through a parent organization that takes care of logistical details and often provides a group environment and support system—for a fee. Some of these parent organizations provide comprehensive programs that arrange transportation, accommodation, food, cultural experiences, and even sightseeing for their volunteers. Travelers who bypass such programs, choosing instead to organize their own experiences, should plan to arrange accommodation, board, transportation, insurance, and other logistics themselves. This kind of independent experience is best suited to individuals not bothered by uncertainty and who don't mind investing extra time in preparation.

The best way to find opportunities that match your interests is to check local or national volunteer centers before departing. Government websites often list volunteer opportunities. National park services in particular are almost always in need of volunteers for wildlife preservation projects. Although these positions are usually geared toward locals, they are often open to travelers willing to make a minimum time commitment. New Zealand's **Department of Conservation (DOC)** is in nearly every town, and their website (www.doc.govt.nz) is a great resource for learning about ecological issues facing the country and opportunities to address them. For more information on volunteering abroad, check out *How to Live your Dream of Volunteering Overseas*, Penguin Books, by Joseph Collins et al.

CONSERVATION

A relatively isolated island nation, New Zealand is famed for its delicate, diverse ecology. These same natural resources are often exploited to provide jobs and a better standard of living for the country's human inhabitants. Many of the programs below promote a balanced usage of the New Zealand's natural wildlife, and opportunities range from coral monitoring to animal tagging.

BEYOND TOURISM

DOC Volunteers (www.doc.govt.nz). The Department of Conservation has many long- and short-term opportunities. Contact the local office of the area you wish to work in.

Eco-Adventure and Sustainable Living Programmes, Tararu Valley Sanctuary and Conservation Trust, P.O. Box 5, Thames 2815, NZ (☎07 868 8988; www.tararuvalley.org). Volunteers engage in projects aimed at protecting a section of the ancient Coromandel forest and teaching sustainable living practices. Programs range from 5 weeks to 2 years. Partial scholarships and academic credit available.

Greepeace (www.greenpeace.org). The international organization supports environmental, social, and political work on topics ranging from climate change to whaling.

New Zealand Dolphins (☎800-776-0188 or 978-461-0081; www.earthwatch.org/expeditions/wursig.html). Travelers monitor the behavior of dusky dolphins off the Kaikoura Peninsula and assess how tourism and fishing in the area are affecting their lifestyle. 2-week programs run Mar.-July and cost US$2750. Check the Earthwatch Institute website for other programs.

New Zealand Nature Program (☎04 569 9080; www.volunteer.org.nz/newzealand). Run by the Global Volunteer Network, this program provides several opportunities to assist with wildlife monitoring and research projects centered in Wellington. Programs last 2 weeks to 3 months. US$600-3600, not including airfare. Apply online.

New Zealand Trust for Nature Volunteers (www.conservationvolunteers.co.nz). Maintains a register of research-based ecology projects. Register online and search for volunteer opportunities.

AGRICULTURAL PROGRAMS

In a land where sheep outnumber the people that raise them, New Zealand's agricultural industry is always looking for helpers. These programs offer volunteers an exchange of labor for room and board in a number of different rural settings throughout the country. Programs vary widely depending on the region and season, but you should be able to find anything from kiwi picking to sheep shearing. For other agricultural opportunities, see **Working**, p. 59.

Farm Helpers in New Zealand, 31 Moerangi St., Palmerston North 4410 (☎06 355 0448; www.fhinz.co.nz). Publishes a booklet (NZ$25) with information on farms and families looking for those who will work in exchange for free room and board.

Permaculture in New Zealand (www.permaculture.org.nz) organizes native plantings and runs courses in the principles of permaculture—using natural, renewable resources to enrich local ecosystems. Courses and activities rotate frequently.

Willing Workers on Organic Farms (WWOOF), P.O. Box 1172, Nelson 7040 (☎03 544 9890; www.wwoof.co.nz). works to connect farmers and volunteers. With membership, WWOOF distributes a list of over 1000 farmers who offer room and board in exchange for 4-6hr. of work per day. Membership NZ$40, from overseas NZ$45. Couples discounts available.

COMMUNITY-BASED INITIATIVES

Although New Zealand is one of the most developed and integrated countries in the world, not all communities have benefited equally from recent economic upturn. The programs below allow travelers to interact with those communities and assist in the development of economic and social opportunities.

Community Net Aotearoa (www.community.net.nz). Lists information on different community programs as well as information on how to volunteer.

Habitat for Humanity New Zealand, 11 Marewa Rd., Auckland 1051 (☎09 529 4111; www.habitat.org). Long- or short-term volunteers help to build low-income housing. Programs start at US$1300, not including airfare.

Institute for Cultural Ecology, P.O. Box 991, Hilo, HI 96721, USA (☎808-557-1743; www.cultural-ecology.com). Offers programs in schools in Wellington and South Island. Projects include fighting drug abuse and working with inner-city students. Volunteer programs run 4-12 weeks and cost US$1895-3850, not including airfare.

International Cultural Youth Exchange, (www.icye.org). A database of cultural programs in New Zealand, including teaching healthy lifestyles to youth and working with the elderly. Long- and short-term programs available.

Volunteering Canterbury, Christchurch Community House, 141 Hereford St., Christchurch 8141 (☎03 366 2442; www.cvc.org.nz). Lists and arranges volunteer opportunities in Canterbury.

Volunteering New Zealand (www.volunteeringnz.org.nz). A database of different volunteer opportunities around the country.

STUDYING

VISA INFORMATION. See the New Zealand Immigration Service website (www.immigration.govt.nz) to find out how to apply for visas and work permits. Australian citizens and residents with a current Australian resident return visa do not need a visa or permit to work in New Zealand. A student visa is required for those intending to study in New Zealand for more than 3 months. The visa can be obtained from any New Zealand Embassy or High Commission with an admission letter from a New Zealand educational institution or program. Visit the Immigration Service website (www.immigration.govt.nz) for more information.

Study abroad programs in New Zealand range from informal culture courses to college-level classes, often given for credit. Unless you plan to complete your full degree there, most undergraduate programs require current enrollment in a university. In order to choose the program that best fits your needs, be sure to research costs, duration, and type of accommodation available, as well as what kind of students participate in the program, before making your decision. A good resource for finding programs that cater to your particular interests is **www.studyabroad.com,** which has links to different semester abroad programs based on a variety of criteria, including desired location and focus of study.

Students of conservation and natural resource management may be particularly drawn to New Zealand. Many of the university-level programs listed below involve field research and can often provide placements with the local Department of Conservation (www.doc.govt.nz).

While the easiest way to arrange to study abroad is likely through your own university, the following list of organizations can help to place you in programs if your school's options are limited.

AMERICAN PROGRAMS

American Field Service (AFS), 506 SW. 6th Ave., 2nd fl., Portland, OR 97204 (☎800-237-4636; http://usa.afs.org). AFS offers programs in New Zealand for US high school students and graduating high school seniors. Costs vary depending on program length and season.

Arcadia University for Education Abroad, 450 S. Easton Rd., Glenside, PA 19038 (☎866-927-2234; www.arcadia.edu/cea). Operates programs in at New Zealand state universities. Costs range from US$12,000 per semester to US$22,000 per year.

AustraLearn, 12050 N. Pecos St., Ste. 320, Westminster, CO 80234 (☎800-980-0033; www.australearn.org). Semester, summer, and full-year programs at New Zealand universities. About US$11,000 per semester. Scholarships available.

EcoQuest, 215 James Hall, University of New Hampshire, Durham, NH 02834 (☎603-862-2036; www.ecoquest.unh.edu). Offers summer and semester programs on ecology, biology, conservation, and sustainable management of land and sea. See website for prerequisites. 5- to 15-week program ranges US$5000-14,000.

Experiment in International Living, Kipling Rd., P.O. Box 676, Brattleboro, VT 05302 (☎802-257-7751; www.usexperiment.org). A 5-week summer program in New Zealand for high-school students. US$5600.

Institute for Study Abroad, Butler University (ISA), 1100 W. 42nd St., Ste. 305, Indianapolis, IN 46208 (☎800-858-0229 or 317-940-9336; www.ifsa-butler.org). Semester-long and full-year programs with the major New Zealand universities. ISA takes care of applications, visas, and housing, and provides personal guidance while abroad. Costs range from US$13,000 for a semester to US$24,000 for a full year. Some financial aid is available.

NEW ZEALAND PROGRAMS

Applying directly to a university in New Zealand may be cheaper, although transferring credits (and finding housing) may be difficult. New Zealand's eight state-funded universities all welcome international students. Unlike many countries, New Zealand's academic year begins in March and is divided into

three terms. The long vacation is from late November to early March. **Education New Zealand Trust,** P.O. Box 10500, Wellington (☎04 472 0788; www.mynzed.com), publishes an online directory of universities, colleges of education, polytechnic institutions, and secondary and English-language institutions. Other programs tailored to specific interests are listed below.

Massey University, (☎0800 627 739; www.maori.massey.ac.nz), has campuses in Auckland, Wellington, and Palmerston North. One of New Zealand's state-funded universities, Massey offers a complete course in Maori language and visual arts.

New Zealand Film and Television School, P.O. Box 27044, Marion Sq., Wellington (☎04 380 1250; www.filmschool.org.nz), enrolls students in a variety of film disciplines. The program aims to provide hands-on training for those looking to pursue a career in film or television.

New Zealand School of Food and Wine, 63 Victoria St., Christchurch (☎03 379 7501; www.foodandwine.co.nz). Due to rising interest in New Zealand's culinary specialties, the New Zealand School of Food and Wine is now offering a 16-week certification program in cookery and 3-month sommelier certification program.

WORKING

As with volunteering, working in New Zealand can be categorized into two groups. Long-term work offers the opportunity to become an active member of a Kiwi community. Short-term work often serves as a way to finance the next leg of a journey. New Zealand's focus on agriculture means there is always harvesting or farm work available. High-level permanent work may be difficult to find as obtaining legal work permits in New Zealand can be difficult, especially for US citizens. Before signing on with either long- or short-term work be sure to secure the

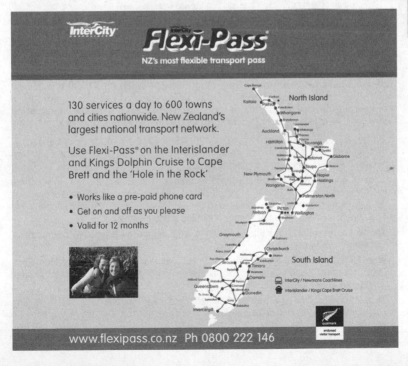

BEYOND TOURISM

proper work permit. For those considering working in New Zealand, *Live and Work Abroad in Australia and New Zealand* (Vacation Work Publications, by Dan Boothby and Susan Kelly) is an excellent resource.

Since many jobs, especially those that are short-term, advertise locally, it's impossible to compile all relevant listings. These listings will offer leads on job-hunting in the region or urban center, including what kind of work is generally available and how to contact local employment agencies. Hostels are great places to look for short-term opportunities, as employers will often post listings on the job board or even stop by to recruit willing backpackers.

VISA INFORMATION. See the New Zealand Immigration Service website (www.immigration.govt.nz) to find out how to apply for visas and work permits. Australian citizens and residents with a current Australian resident return visa do not need a visa or permit to work in New Zealand. The following visas are required for extended work:

Working Holiday Visa: For 18- to 30-year-old British, Canadian, Irish, Japanese, and US citizens. Valid for 1yr. Requirements include application and fee (varies depending on your country), a valid passport, a round-trip ticket out of the country, proof of medical coverage, and display of adequate funds (NZ$4200). Citizens of Canada may apply after arriving in New Zealand, but all others must apply from their home country.

Work Permit: To get a work permit, you often need to be sponsored by an employer who can demonstrate that you have skills that locals lack—not the easiest of tasks. Most permits must be obtained outside New Zealand, so if you think you meet these criteria, call the nearest New Zealand consulate or embassy to get more information, or visit the New Zealand Immigration Service website.

LONG-TERM WORK

If you're planning on spending a substantial amount of time (more than three months) working in New Zealand, search for a job well in advance. Remember that you'll have to find a niche that can't easily be filled by a local laborer, so work closely with potential employers to ensure that you will be cleared for a work permit. Be sure to read about long-term work eligibility on the Immigration Service website. Below is a list of resources for finding long-term work:

Bunac, P.O. Box 430, Southbury, CT 06488, USA (☎203-264-0901; www.bunac.org). Charges US$495 for organizing work permits, job placement, and travel through New Zealand for Brits and Americans aged 18-35.

Council on International Educational Exchange (www.ciee.org). The US$450 fee includes orientation, a 2-night stay in Auckland, airport pickup, a certificate of eligibility to get a work permit, pre-trip advice, and the New Zealand Work Abroad Handbook. For US citizens who have been at school within the last 6 months.

Jobstuff.co.nz (http://jobstuff.co.nz). A thorough database of employment opportunities in New Zealand.

Monster (http://workabroad.monster.com). The international arm of the well-known network, Monster has job listings, as well as tips on how to prepare an appropriate resume and cover letter for New Zealand employers.

New Zealand Herald (www.nzherald.co.nz/classifieds). The online classifieds section of the Auckland-based newspaper has a lengthy section devoted to an eclectic assortment of job listings.

seek.co.nz (www.seek.co.nz). Lists thousands of employment
around New Zealand cities.

Work Experience Down Under, 2330 Marinship Way, Ste. 250,
USA (☎415-339-2740; www.ccusa.com). The US$365 fee incl
work and travel insurance, 2 nights of accommodation, and access to a job search
center. Ages 18-30.

Working in New Zealand (www.workingin-newzealand.com). A listings database that
provides links to recruiting companies.

SHORT-TERM WORK

Traveling for long periods of time is expensive; many backpackers try their hand
at odd jobs for a few weeks to support their travel habit. New Zealand's climatic
diversity ensures that picking jobs are available nearly year-round, and the popularity of the work among young people has created a fruit-picking subculture.
Many hostels in picking areas cater specifically to workers, offering transportation to worksites and other amenities.

In cities and highly touristed areas, hostels often feature employment boards
and sometimes offer services to help lodgers find temporary work. One popular
option is to work several hours a day at a hostel in exchange for free or discounted
room and/or board. Most often, these short-term jobs are found by word of mouth,
or simply by asking owners of hostels or restaurants. Due to high turnover in the
tourism industry, establishments are eager for help, even if it is only temporary.

As for all jobs, travelers should visit a work site and try to speak with current
employees to get a feel for the conditions of employment before signing on for any
amount of time. The job listings at **www.backpackerboard.co.nz** are a good place to
look for general openings ranging from farmhand to au pair.

AGRICULTURAL WORK

One of the most popular short-term work options in New Zealand is **picking fruit.**
Pickers are paid by a piece-rate wage and can expect to earn about NZ$400 per
week. Some work is available year-round, but highest demand for pickers is from
January to May. The Hawke's Bay region on the North Island is the center of the
agricultural industry. Other opportunities can be found in Blenheim (p. 265),
Kerikeri (p. 117), Motueka (p. 286), Napier (p. 185), Tauranga (p. 164), and Takaka
(p. 288). Websites are a good place to start looking for work, but often your best
bet will be to keep an eye out for job boards around town. **Seasonal Work NZ**
(www.seasonalwork.co.nz) is a local search engine that has a variety of seasonal
listings. **AgriVenture** (www.agriventure.com) places job-seekers in farms throughout New Zealand for terms of more than four months.

TOURISM INDUSTRY

Other options for short-term work can be found at bars, cafes, and restaurants in
heavily touristed destinations. **Waitressing** or **bartending** usually pays NZ$14-16 per
hour; just remember that tipping is not customary in New Zealand. **Ski resorts** often
hire people for the winter season (July-Oct.), usually in restaurant positions or as
lift operators, but sometimes as ski instructors if you have demonstrated skill and
proficiency. Hourly pay may be supplemented by a lift pass, free food and drink,

getting to know ewe

WWOOFing it in New Zealand

After three months in New Zealand, I realized that the true ambassadors of New Zealand's green, eco-friendly image are its sheep. Sure, there are waterfalls, fjords, domesticated red deer, and the eerie embodiment of Tolkien's Middle Earth. However, when you take away the sheep, you've lost not only an important part of the country's heritage, but also a great portion of the animate bodies you'd otherwise meet on your travels. Thirty-eight million of these woolly buggers carpet New Zealand's two islands, and it doesn't take a statistician to figure out how important they are to their 4.5 million human companions. One way to linger with the sheep is to join **Worldwide Workers on Organic Farms (WWOOF)**. WWOOF is an organization that connects travelers and farms in need of help.

Several weeks into my own New Zealand odyssey, I was worn out from bushwhacking through national parks. I needed a day off from my trek across South Island, and I found my thoughts returning to that staple of Anglo heritage: the woolshed. A veteran of WWOOF in Europe, I relished the excitement of driving up to a hilltop sheep farm on the southeast coast of New Zealand. Within minutes of shaking the hand of my host, Rodger, I was clinging to the side grips of his ATV as we sped off into a pasture.

The job of a sheep farmer involves gathering together a herd of animals and was historically accomplished by men on horseback with sheep dogs keeping the flanks in line. On large sheep stations, the chore could take days.

Even with technological innovations like ATVs, no machine has yet replaced the sheep dog. As we cruised out over tufted tussocks, Rodger constantly called to the dogs in a series of commands and tongue clicks. The animals sprinted alongside the flock, molding and shaping the ranks of animals.

As we wove left and right, chasing down strays and guiding them into a tight group, Rodger predicted the movements of each beast. "Watch that one," he said, gesturing toward a ram that was looking around wildly from the edge of the pack. The dogs headed off the would-be fugitive just as it made a break for the open green. Rodger grinned and scanned the flock for more troublemakers. This man enjoyed his work; his enthusiasm was contagious.

Perhaps the greatest part of that day and of those that followed, however, was not the reality of being on the farm but instead the company Rodger and his family provided. When the sheep were all in, Rodger suggested a trip to the beach before heading home for dinner, and I wasn't one to argue. I also wasn't disappointed by the feast of roast lamb and fresh vegetables, which had been conspicuously absent from my diet in previous weeks.

"I found my thoughts returning to that staple of Anglo heritage: the woolshed."

Not all of WWOOFing is spent out in the fields riding on the back of ATVs—even in the course of a few days, I helped to feed the turkeys and work the garden. For a few days, I enjoyed a much-needed respite from exchanging gossip and advice with other backpackers; I finally felt able to connect with the land and culture I was visiting, if only a small piece.

As I continued to travel through New Zealand, I met WWOOFers who had babysat, worked in restaurants, and contributed their energy to farms in any number of ways. Far from an activity reserved for farming enthusiasts, WWOOFing is a cultural exchange as much as a work exchange, ideal for those—like me—fascinated with the mysteries of those iconic Kiwi sheep.

A DIFFERENT PATH

Max Morange earned his Bachelor's Degree in English and American Literature and Languages at Harvard College in Cambridge, MA. His experience with WWOOF ranges from pressing olive oil in Tuscany to milking donkeys in the French Pyrenees.

and discounts on ski-related gear. For example, the Mt. Ruapehu ski fields (p. 203) recruit 700 staff members every February. Hostels offer a more sedentary work option. Many travelers work as receptionists or housekeepers for four hours per day in exchange for room and board. Such work is informally arranged through hostel owners or other locals. **Changing Worlds,** 11 Doctors Ln., Chaldon, Surrey CR3 5AE, UK, is a service that places travelers in paid tourism and farming jobs or even unpaid work as deckhands on tall ships. Since most placements involve small pay, the fee covers the cost of placement and airfare to New Zealand from the UK. (☎44 01883 340 960; www.changingworlds.co.uk. UK£2630.)

TEACHING ENGLISH

New Zealand has become a popular destination for learning English. Teachers are often expected to provide proof of a TEFL certification. **Language Studies International** (☎09 303 3097 in Auckland; ☎03 377 7337 in Christchurch; www.lsi.edu) has locations in Auckland and Christchurch with frequent job openings.

INTERNSHIPS

The **Earthwise Living Foundation New Zealand (ELFNZ),** P.O. Box 108, Thames 2815, NZ (☎09 353 1558; www.elfnz.com), is a New Zealand-based organization that sponsors individualized internships in areas from photography to horse breeding. ELFNZ also sponsors a variety of eco-adventures aimed at getting people out into the wilderness with a focus on conservation projects and sustainable living. Programs start at NZ$3895 for six weeks.

FURTHER READING ON BEYOND TOURISM.

Alternatives to the Peace Corps: A Directory of Third World and U.S. Volunteer Opportunities, by Jennifer S. Willsea. Food First Books, 2003 (US$10).

Back Door Guide to Short-Term Job Adventures: Internships, Extraordinary Experiences, Seasonal Jobs, Volunteering, Working Abroad, by Michael Landes. Ten Speed Press, 2002 (US$22).

Green Volunteers: The World Guide to Voluntary Work in Nature, by Ausenda and McCloskey. Universe, 2003 (US$15).

International Job Finder: Where the Jobs Are Worldwide, by Daniel Lauber. Planning Communications, 2002 (US$20).

Invest Yourself: The Catalogue of Volunteer Opportunities. The Commission on Voluntary Service and Action (☎646-486-2446).

Work Abroad: The Complete Guide to Finding a Job Overseas, by Hubbs, Griffith, and Nolting. Transitions Abroad Publishing, 2002 (US$16).

Work Your Way Around the World, by Susan Griffith. Vacation-Work Publications, 2003 (US$18).

BEYOND TOURISM

THE GREAT OUTDOORS

Ringed by wild and churning waters, site of a major tectonic plate collision, and home to thousands of endemic plant and animal species, New Zealand overflows with geological and ecological splendor, enticing and enchanting those lucky enough to set foot upon its shores. New Zealand's landmass charted a singular evolutionary course following its separation from the ancient supercontinent Gondwanaland. It was this solitary development that created the towering crags and steaming pools that now draw millions of travelers to what feels like the very edge of the earth.

 LEAVE NO TRACE. *Let's Go* encourages travelers to embrace the "Leave No Trace" ethic, minimizing their impact on environments and protecting them for future generations. Trekkers and wilderness enthusiasts should set up camp on durable surfaces, use cooking stoves instead of campfires, bury human waste away from water supplies, and bag trash and carry it out with them. For more info, contact the **Leave No Trace Center for Outdoor Ethics,** P.O. Box 997, Boulder, CO 80306, USA (☎ 800-332-4100 or 303-442-8222; www.lnt.org).

THE LAND AND ENVIRONMENT

BEFORE HUMAN ARRIVAL

The ancient supercontinent of **Gondwanaland** combined modern-day South America, Africa, peninsular India, Antarctica, and Australia. The islands now known as New Zealand split from the supercontinent roughly 80 million years ago, much earlier than other present-day continents, making it an isolated ecological time capsule. With few natural predators, New Zealand's avian life evolved to occupy the ecological niches that mammals assumed elsewhere. They gained stronger legs, larger size, and many lost use of their wings. Two primary examples of these primordial birds—the **Haast eagle** *(Hapagornis)* and the **moa**—are now extinct. The giant Haast was the world's largest eagle and dominated South Island's food chain, and the moa was found on both North and South Island and was New Zealand's chief grazing bird. The Giant Moa towered above the 11 other species of moa, standing nearly 3m tall. The country's most recognizable bird, the thin-beaked **kiwi** also flourished on pre-human New Zealand.

FLORA

Before 1800, 70% of New Zealand's landscape was covered in the Gondwanian lowland forests, wetlands, and grasslands. Today, only 15% of the ancient forest remains. Despite this depletion, New Zealand is still home to a host of unique native plant life, nearly 2700 species. The most famous among these species are the towering **kauri forests,** which are among the oldest in the world. Although colonial loggers harvest 90% of the valuable original kauri forests to support the building of modern New Zealand, the kauri forests remain an invaluable asset to Northland's tourist industry (p. 106). The kauri are just one of a large family of **podocarps,** a class of conifers that includes other native trees such as the **totara, rimu, miro, matai,** and **kahikatea.** Such podocarps dominate many of New Zealand's forested regions, forming many-layered forest canopies across North Island. Endless **southern beech forests** are more common on South Island; the famous *Nothofagus* genus can trace its roots to the forests that blanketed Gondwanaland. One hundred ninety-three different species of ferns have also left an indelible imprint on New Zealand's flora. The **mamaku tree fern** can grow up to 20m in height; the **ponga tree fern,** with its silver-bottomed fronds, is the official national symbol. A few other distinctive plants make their mark on New Zealand's landscape. The **pohutukawa,** "New Zealand's Christmas tree," has bright crimson blooms during late December and is found in northern regions. The **rata** begins life as a vine and slowly strangles its host tree to death until it casts a peachy-orange glow to the undergrowth with its bright blooms. The world's largest buttercup, the **Mt. Cook lily,** and New Zealand's only native palm trees, the **Nikau palms,** are other examples of the archipelago's biodiversity. Alpine **tussock** grasslands on both North and South Island round out the diverse landscape.

FAUNA

Many animal families that evolved on the supercontinent never developed in New Zealand. Most noticeably, New Zealand has no snakes, and three species of bats are the only native land mammals. Instead, the country has many strange and exotic birds. The four different species of **kiwi** are New Zealand's most recognized celebrity. The small, solitary birds have slender beaks with external nostrils to help scrounge food from the forest floor during their nocturnal scavenging. Like many of their avian cousins, the kiwi is flightless, tail-less, and practically wingless. The **kea,** the world's only alpine parrot, is one of the few birds to reside in the peaks of the Southern Alps. Any visitor to the ski slopes or national parks of New Zealand will quickly realize that the kea is no ordinary bird, but a clever, destructive, and bold menace. Watch your back—and your pack. The **kereru,** the native pigeon, is the only bird able to disperse the large seeds of some native plants. Some of the most recognizable New Zealand bird species include its seven types of **penguins.** Among them, the blue, yellow-eyed, and Fiordland crested are the most common. These fascinating birds are popular with tourists in Otago (p.385). Other fanciful names for New Zealand's astonishing variety of birds abound: the **morepork** (*ruru*, the only native owl), the **muttonbird** (*titi*), the **shag** (*kawau*), and the **wrybill** (*ngutuparore*, with its slender and twisted beak), among others.

Today, many of these rare birds are endangered. Only 160 of the blue-green **takahe,** flightless parrot from the Australian continent, remain. The **black stilt** (*kaki*) are down to under 70. Fewer than 90 nocturnal **kakapo,** the world's heaviest parrot (males can weigh in at 4kg), are still in existence. The sensitive bird is notoriously difficult to breed in captivity. Intensive conservation efforts operated by the Department of Conservation (DOC) and private organizations are underway for all three species, including the creation of predator-free sanctuaries on offshore islands and in remote wilderness areas.

Besides the birds, New Zealand is host to many critters that are both cringe-worthy and fascinating. 1500 species of **land snails** (some carnivorous), 11 species of the **weta**—the world's heaviest insect, teeming crayfish (*koura*), pesky sandflies (*te namu*), and ethereal glowworms (*titiwai*) and their native habitats are all tourist attractions. The extremely rare coastal **katipo spider,** a relative of the black widow, is New Zealand's only poisonous spider. Although people rarely encounter the katipo, the black spiders have a distinctive red stripe on the top of their abdomen and are usually found under logs or other debris. If you do get bitten, you should go to the hospital for an antidote. Although these spiders are poisonous, do not kill them—they are endangered, and will leave you alone if you leave them alone. Another primordial relic found in New Zealand is the **tuatara,** a lizard-like creature old enough to have roamed with the dinosaurs 200 million years ago.

Although land mammals are few and far between, there are plenty of marine mammals flourishing off New Zealand's shores. Orca, seals, and sea lions can be found in the waters off South Island. The islands are also home to almost half of the world's migrating whale, porpoise, and dolphin populations. Marine mammals unique to the area include **Hector's dolphins, beaked whales,** the **New Zealand fur seal,** and the **Hooker sea lion.** At the turn of the century, marine mammal populations reached dramatic lows due to the lucrative whaling and sealing trades. While those early trades are no longer a threat to New Zealand's marine life, climate changes and water pollution continue to threaten these animals' habitats.

INVADERS

Man's arrival to isolated New Zealand brought about the massive destruction of natural habitats and the introduction of invasive, non-indigenous species. The first settlers from Polynesia arrived over 1000 years ago carrying with them breeds of disease-carrying **dogs** *(kuri)* and **rats** *(kiore)*, ushering in the first age of extinction. The Maori, and later the Europeans, cleared forests for agriculture and hunted the giant moa to extinction. Deer, goats, pigs, rabbits, and opossums, brought to make settlers comfortable in unfamiliar surroundings, overwhelmed native species. Stoats and weasels, imported to control the exploding population of introduced rabbits, started feeding on hapless native birds when the rabbit and opossum supply diminished. Millions of years of evolution left New Zealand's birds without any natural predators and no means of defense; even today, many bird species seem uncommonly friendly to tourists. Predation of native species continues to plague New Zealand. The kiwi is now vanishing at an annual rate of almost 6%. **Wasps** hidden in aircrafts entered the ecosystem during WWII and have since reached epidemic proportions, threatening the food of birds and endemic insects. In addition to losing 43% of frog fauna and over 40% of bird fauna since humans first arrived, New Zealand now has more than **600 endangered species.**

Non-native flora has also disrupted the ecosystem by out-competing endemic flora for sunlight, space, and nutrients. These plants, accustomed to harsher weather, thrive in New Zealand's mild climate. Because the introduced plants lack native predators, and because introduced predators often feed on indigenous plant life, the addition of a single foreign plant species can destroy an entire ecosystem. Of the 20,000 non-native species introduced to the country, the DOC reports that over 200 are now weeds.

CONSERVATION EFFORTS

New Zealand is hailed worldwide as a leader in conservation efforts, both on land and at sea. About one-third of the country is set aside as protected land, and a massive international whale sanctuary established in 1994 includes more than 11 million sq. mi. The country is covered with 14 national parks, plus numerous other forest parks, groves, and wildlife reserves. The first national park, **Tongariro National Park,** was created in 1887 as a result of the foresight and efforts of Te Heuheu Tukino IV (Horonuku), the high chief of the Ngati Tuwharetoa Maori tribe. He offered the area as a gift to the New Zealand government on the condition that it be kept *tapu* (sacred). The most recent national park, **Rakiura National Park,** was designated in 2002 to protect the largely untouched wilderness of Stewart Island.

One of the largest governmental organizations, the **Department of Conservation (DOC)** is an environmental behemoth and is the go-to source for all things eco. Nearly one-third of New Zealand is designated as protected wilderness areas and DOC projects range from breeding endangered species to protecting historical mining sites, not to mention keeping a close eye on the 19 separate marine reserves. Alongside other conservation organizations, the DOC also plays a big part in regulating the fishing and energy industries throughout the county. It plays an active role in habitat protection, predator control programs, and relocation of species, and conducts surveys and research on the current status of endangered wildlife. While Auckland is one of the few regions of New Zealand not graced with a national park, the DOC has proposed the creation of a 50,100-hectare Great Barrier marine reserve to protect the 80 species of fish that live beneath Auckland's waters. The DOC has a hotline for conservation emergencies—sick or injured wildlife, vandalism, fishing in marine reserves, etc. If you see a problem, call ☎ 0800 362 468. For more information, visit www.doc.govt.nz/conservation.

TRAMPING

Backpacking, trekking, hillwalking, bushwalking—whatever you call it back home, it's tramping in New Zealand. The country's nine most spectacular and popular tramps (including one that takes place entirely over water) are classified as **Great Walks** and are run by the DOC under a separate administration. The **Rees-Dart Track** (p. 403) a major track, has undergone recent improvements including the construction of a new, modern hut, the addition of several foot bridges and railings, and the widening of the track in certain areas. Many trampers suspect that the Rees-Dart is being groomed for Great Walk status. The DOC is an unparalleled resource for information on the seasonal availability and safety of hikes, the regulations and practicalities for adventuring in New Zealand, weather forecasts, maps, and more. Offices are in every large city, most small towns, and virtually every protected wilderness area. The easiest and cheapest way to book tracks and reserve huts is through the DOC website (www.doc.govt.nz). Still though, the DOC often requires trampers to give detailed information in the DOC intention book before setting out on any DOC monitored track, especially in winter months when traffic is low. Most city DOC offices will also sell hut passes and assist with hut bookings for nearby tracks, though the track may already be booked and the office will charge a small reservations fee. For most tracks, the DOC also produces a brochure with basic but adequate map and track information. Detailed topographic maps are $12-14. The main DOC office is located at 18 Manners St., Wellington (☎ 04 384 7770). For more information on hut passes, Great Walks, and bookings, read further. Check with the local DOC office before venturing forth.

THE GREAT WALKS

The DOC designates New Zealand's grandest tramps as Great Walks, a series of nine tracks that wend through New Zealand's most stunning and unique geography. These offer avid trampers of all experience levels over 400km of glacially carved valleys, tranquil mountain lakes, and forested sea coasts. Ranging from the spectacular Milford Track through mystical Fiordland wilderness to the dazzling Abel Tasman Coast Track along golden beaches and cresting waves of Tasman Bay, the Great Walks deliver unique insights into New Zealand's diverse ecology. All nine walks are well maintained, well graded, and make excellent introductory trips for those with little or no previous experience. However, good maintenance, easy access, and superb facilities make for crowded summer trails. Hardened backpackers seeking a challenging and solitary wilderness trip may wish to explore less-trodden routes. Yet despite crowding, the sheer richness and splendor of Great Walks scenery is irresistible to any nature enthusiast.

Most walks require pre-purchased, time-limited, track-specific **Great Walks Tickets,** except in winter when many revert to the backcountry hut pass system (huts become Standard Huts). The Great Walks Ticket serves as proof of payment for accommodation in a hut or a designated campsite along the track. Since camping is only allowed in certain areas, you must take the ticket with you on the track. Though traffic varies, many of the walks necessitate booking in

THE BIG SPLURGE

ABOVE AND BEYOND

New Zealand is not only a playground for lovers of the great outdoors, it is also a training ground. One way to become acquainted with the landscape beyond the standard tour is to invest in a certification course in a specific activity. Here are our favorites.

1. New Zealand Kayaking School in Murchison: Known for its accessible whitewater, the small town of Murchison also has a world-renowned whitewater school. Intro courses guide novices from putting on a whitewater skirt to shooting the rapids like a pro. 4-day courses start at $695, including accommodation. 22 Grey St. (☎523 9611; www.nzkayakschool.com)

2. Mountaineering Courses in Aoraki/Mt. Cook: Sir Edmund Hillary trained at Aoraki/Mt. Cook. New mountaineers now follow in his footsteps with companies such as Alpine Guides that lead a number of trips including backcountry skiing and ice climbing. 5-day intro ice climbing courses start at $1995. (☎435 1834; www.alpineguides.co.nz).

3. New Zealand Skydiving School at Methven: If tandem skydives aren't enough of a fright, qualify to pull the ripcord yourself at Methven's Skydiving School. 9-stage course costs $7875. Min. age 18. (☎302 9140; www.skydivingnz.com.)

advance for the summer (Nov.-Apr.; bookings for the upcoming season begin on **July 1**), especially the **Abel Tasman, Milford, Heaphy,** and **Routeburn Tracks.** This booking system restricts visitor numbers and guarantees a bunk in a hut, preventing a daily rampage of trampers eager to secure the next night's bed. Cancellations allow date-flexible couples and single trampers the chance to get on the track. Placing your name on the waiting list will often secure you a last-minute spot. For comprehensive information on fees and bookings, visit www.doc.govt.nz or contact the DOC regional office that oversees the track you are attempting to book.

Abel Tasman Coast Track (Abel Tasman National Park): 51km, 3-5 days. Less difficult. The most popular of all the Great Walks, this track offers golden beaches and turquoise ocean views, framed by fern-filled forest. Advance reservations required. See p. 283.

Heaphy Track (Kahurangi National Park): 82km, 4-6 days. More difficult. New Zealand's most ecologically diverse track, passing through lofty beech forests, alpine meadows, lowland podocarp forest, and wild beaches. Advance reservations required. See p. 295.

Kepler Track (Fiordland National Park): 60km, 3-4 days. More difficult. The most accessible of the Great Walks, the Kepler is an awe-inspiring ridge-walk, offering commanding views of Lake Te Anau and Fiordland. See p. 412.

Lake Waikaremoana Track (Te Urewera National Park): 46km, 3-4 days. Moderately difficult. This track climbs bluffs topped with gnarled beech trees. See p. 183.

Milford Track (Fiordland National Park): 54km, 4 days. Moderately difficult. Heralded as "the finest walk in the world," the Milford runs through 2 glacial valleys and over a spectacular mountain pass. Rock faces are watered by countless cascades, including Sutherland Falls—New Zealand's highest. Advance reservations required. See p. 418.

Rakiura Track (Rakiura National Park): 36km, 2-3 days. Moderately difficult. The newest of the Great Walks, this boardwalked track undulates through the primordial forest on Stewart Island. See p. 447.

Routeburn Track (Mt. Aspiring and Fiordland National Parks): 33km, 2-4 days. More difficult. Mostly traveling high above treeline, the Routeburn skirts grand valleys and overlooks rugged mountain ranges. Advance reservations required. See p. 389.

Tongariro Northern Circuit (Tongariro National Park): 51.5km, 3-4 days. More difficult. Winding around 3 great volcanoes, this track passes wild and spectacular lava flows, desolate moonscapes, and technicolor lakes. The **Tongariro Crossing,** "the finest one-day walk in New Zealand," is part of the circuit. See p. 204.

Whanganui River Journey (Whanganui National Park): 145km, 3-5 days by canoe. More difficult. The only Great Walk that requires a paddle; canoeists and kayakers battle the small rapids beneath luxuriant greenery. Two Maori *marae* make the trip a cultural journey as well. See p. 226.

JUST-AS-GREAT WALKS

While many travelers come to New Zealand to hike one of the nine Great Walks, the just-as-great walks tend to be even more awe-inspiring than the great ones. Typically, those tracks not listed with the great nine are longer, cover more difficult terrain and are more difficult to access. Fortunately, New Zealand is well-equipped to handle such difficulties and the rewards for stepping off the great tracks are often exhilarating. The best of the rest are listed below.

Dusky Track (Fiordland National Park): 84km, 8-10 days. Extremely difficult. New Zealand's most rugged track, the Dusky rewards the intrepid with alpine vistas, pristine forests and rivers, lots and lots of mud, and a satisfying challenge. Recommended only for groups of experienced trampers. See p. 430.

Greenstone and Caples Tracks (Wakatipu Recreational Hunting Area): 50km, 4-5 days. More difficult. Cattle graze in paradise, where green mountains overlook the golden meadows of the valley floor. See p. 391.

The Northwest Circuit (Rakiura National Park): 125km, 8-10 days. More difficult. Off the boardwalk and ankle deep in mud, the Northwest Circuit traces Stewart Island's secluded shores and bird sanctuaries before traversing the subalpine meadows of the island's highest point. See p. 449.

Tuatapere Hump Ridge Track (Fiordland National Park): 53km, 3 days. More difficult. New Zealand's newest track, the Hump Ridge is run by a local trust and explores the rugged wilderness of southern Fiordland. Advance bookings required. See p. 430.

Queen Charlotte Track (Marlborough Sounds): 71km, 3-5 days. Moderately difficult. This popular, mellow walk winds along the shimmering inlets of the Sounds. Pampered trampers can stay in trackside hostels and have packs transported by boat. See p. 260.

Rees-Dart Track (Mt. Aspiring National Park): 72km, 4-5 days. More difficult. The Rees and Dart River Valleys are crowned with glaciers galore. A daytrip up to the Cascade Saddle affords one of the most mind-numbing views in New Zealand. See p. 403.

Wangapeka Track (Kahurangi National Park): 52km, 3-5 days. More difficult. Similar in scenery to its brother the Heaphy, the Wangapeka offers a secluded taste of New Zealand's tremendous ecological diversity. See p. 298.

HUTS AND CAMPING

New Zealand's tracks are home to a well-developed backcountry hut system with nearly 1000 huts. The DOC builds huts for three reasons: to increase safety for trampers, to reduce the environmental damage caused by camping and hiking off-trail, and to provide an opportunity to meet fellow trampers. There are **four categories** of huts. **Great Walks huts** ($10-40 depending on the season; Great Walks Hut Ticket required) include mattresses, water, toilets, and heating with fuel available. Cooking facilities are sometimes available. **Basic huts** or **bivvies** (free; no ticket or pass required) are shelters with extremely limited facilities. **Serviced huts** ($10) and **Standard huts** ($5) have intermediate facilities and both require Backcountry Huts or Backcountry passes. Purchase **hut tickets** ($5) online or at any DOC office. Purchasing hut tickets while on the trail from park rangers may mean incurring a heavy penalty. Great Walks Hut Tickets must be purchased online or at the DOC office managing the track. Frequent trampers can buy a **Backcountry Annual Hut Pass** for $90. Children under 11 stay for free and ages 12-17 are half-price.

GREAT OUTDOORS

PENNY SAVED. While DOC offices and i-Sites will often book huts and sell hut tickets to would be trampers, save time and $1-3 by booking online at www.doc.govt.nz.

Those who prefer carrying their own accommodations can backcountry camp for free in designated areas along almost all tracks. There is usually a small charge for camping near huts; camping at a distance from the track is often difficult because of dense foliage. **Camping is not allowed outside designated sites on Great Walks.** As with huts, there are categories of official **DOC campsites:** serviced, standard, and informal. Serviced grounds include flush toilets, tap water, showers, and usually electricity. Standard grounds have toilets, a water supply, and some type of vehicle access, while informal grounds have limited facilities— sometimes only a water supply. Prices depend on the facilities offered and range $3-12. Informal grounds are free of charge. Fees are collected by camp wardens or the local agent. For more information, go to www.nzcamping.co.nz.

CAMPING AND TRAMPING EQUIPMENT

WHAT TO BUY

Good camping equipment is both sturdy and light. North American suppliers tend to offer the most competitive prices. If you bring your own camping equipment with you into New Zealand, make sure it is clean, as customs officials will check and disinfect used equipment, including boots, upon arrival.

Sleeping Bags: Most sleeping bags are rated by season: "summer" means 30-40°F (around 0°C) at night; "four-season" or "winter" often means below 0°F (-17°C). Bags are made of **down** (warm and light, but expensive, and miserable when wet) or of **synthetic** material (heavy, durable, and warm when wet). Prices range US$50-250 for a summer synthetic to US$200-300 for a good down winter bag. **Sleeping bag pads** include foam pads (US$10-30), air mattresses (US$15-50), and self-inflating mats (US$30-120). Bring a **stuff sack** to store your bag and keep it dry.

Tents: A tent is not necessary for tramping in New Zealand; the backcountry huts are excellent and there's little point in lugging the extra pounds on your back. However, if you're keen on self-sufficiency, the best tents are free-standing (with their own frames and suspension systems), set up quickly, and only require staking in high winds. Low-profile dome tents are the best all-around. Worthy 2-person tents start at US$100, 4-person at US$160. Other useful accessories include a **battery-operated lantern**, a plastic **groundcloth**, and a nylon **tarp.**

Backpacks: Internal-frame packs mold well to your back, keep a lower center of gravity, and flex adequately to allow you to hike difficult trails, while **external-frame packs** are more comfortable for long hikes over even terrain, as they carry weight higher and distribute it more evenly. Either way, make sure your pack has a strong, padded hip-belt to transfer weight to your legs. There are models designed specifically for women. Any serious backpacking requires a pack of at least 4000 cubic in. (16,000cc), plus 500 cubic in. for sleeping bags in internal-frame packs. Sturdy backpacks cost US$125-420—your pack is an area where it doesn't pay to economize. On your hunt for the perfect pack, fill up a prospective model with something heavy, strap it on correctly, and walk around the store to get a sense of how the model distributes weight. Either buy a **rain cover** (US$10-20) or store all of your belongings in plastic bags inside your pack.

Boots: The terrain on most New Zealand trails is rough underfoot; be sure to wear hiking boots with good **ankle support.** They should fit snugly and comfortably over 1-2 pairs of **wool socks** and a pair of thin **liner socks.** Break in boots over several weeks before you go to spare yourself blisters and always carry adhesive bandages to help blister riddled feet on trail.

Backcountry Stove and Cookware: Some Great Walks huts contain gas stoves for cooking but lack cookware and matches. For other tramps, pack a camp stove (propane stoves are lighter and more compact, but run through fuel more quickly than liquid fuel stoves) and a spoon and pot for boiling water and preparing backcountry delectables.

Personal Locator Beacon (PLB)/Mountain Radio: For winter-time hiking or climbing in alpine extremes, the DOC recommends carrying a PLB. Most gas stations rent PLBs for about NZ$25 per week. These light transceivers will alert rescuers to your location if disaster strikes. Mountain radios are heavier and more expensive but they allow you to check weather forecasts and transmit information to the DOC or outdoor outfitters.

 AN ITCH TO SCRATCH? Sandflies are notorious in New Zealand. While not pesky as mosquitos, their bites can last for weeks. Fortunately, the buggers don't bite at night. For daytime protection, wear long pants and sleeves and consider using a low-percentage DEET bug spray for infested areas.

Other Necessities: Synthetic layers, like those made of polypropylene or polyester, and a pile jacket will keep you warm even when wet. **Do not bring cotton into the backcountry.** A space blanket (US$5-15) will help you to retain body heat and doubles as a groundcloth. Plastic **water bottles** are vital; look for shatter- and leak-resistant models. While many of the streams at informal campsites are safe to drink from, carrying **water-purification tablets** is advisable for questionable water sources. Ask DOC employees about water quality. Also bring a **first-aid kit, pocketknife, insect repellent,** and **waterproof matches** or a **lighter.**

WHERE TO BUY IT

New Zealand has several renowned outdoor brands, including MacPac, Fairydown, and Kathmandu. The country has also led the charge in the recent resurgence of wool tramping clothing with native brands such as Icebreakers. Renting gear is a cost-cutting option when it's convenient to begin and end a tramp from a town with rental outlets. The mail-order and online companies listed below offer lower prices than many retail stores. A visit to a local camping or outdoors store will give you a good sense of the look and weight of certain items.

Discount Camping, 880 Main North Rd., Pooraka, South Australia 5095, Australia (☎ 08 8262 3399; www.discountcamping.com.au).

Eastern Mountain Sports (EMS), 1 Vose Farm Rd., Peterborough, NH 03458, USA (☎ 888-463-6367; www.ems.com).

Gear-Zone, 8 Burnet Rd., Norwich NR3 2BS, UK (www.gear-zone.co.uk).

L.L. Bean, Freeport, ME 04033, USA (US and Canada ☎ 800-441-5713; UK 0800 891 297; www.llbean.com).

Mountain Designs, 51 Bishop St., Kelvin Grove, Queensland 4059, Australia (☎ 07 3856 2344; www.mountaindesigns.com).

Recreational Equipment, Inc. (REI), Sumner, WA 98352, USA (US and Canada ☎ 800-426-4840, elsewhere 253-891-2500; www.rei.com).

CARAVANS AND THE OUTDOORS

Camping is a popular way to see the wonders of New Zealand without seeing your wallet dwindle. Camping facilities (known as **holiday parks**) vary in size from grassy plots to sprawling compounds. Motor parks and camps usually feature tent sites (from NZ$10 per person) and caravan (campervan) sites (from NZ$20).

Some also feature on-site caravans for rent. Most parks charge for tent and caravan sites per person. Many also offer cabins or flats with singles (from NZ$30), doubles (from NZ$45), and tourist flats (from NZ$75) and bunk rooms (from NZ$20) with varying amenities (e.g., kitchens, linens). The DOC runs campsites scattered in the middle of nature. For more information, see **Camping, 35**. Though frequently illegal, it is also possible to camp for free in New Zealand.

In New Zealand, renting a caravan (campervan) will always be more expensive than camping or hostelling, but the costs compare favorably with the price of renting a car and staying in hotels. Rates vary widely by region, season (summer months are the most expensive), and type of caravan. A no-frills, two-berth caravan can cost as little as NZ$55 per day in low season (NZ$120 in high season), whereas a luxury six-berth camper will run closer to NZ$125 per day (NZ$250 in high season). To arrange a caravan rental, check with your local Automobile Association, contact a major international firm, such as Avis, Budget, or Hertz, or select one of the options listed below. In any case, it always pays to contact several different companies to compare vehicles, amenities, and prices. Those who plan to travel by RV in New Zealand or do a lot of camping may choose to join a network like the **Top 10 Holiday Parks,** 294 Montreal St., P.O. Box 959, Christchurch 8015, to reap consistent 10% discounts at member parks. (☎0800 867 836; www.topparks.co.nz. Membership fee NZ$30.)

Auto Europe (NZ ☎0800 223 5555, US 888-223-5555, UK 0800 169 6414; www.autoeurope.com) rents caravans in New Zealand.

Maui Rentals: New Zealand, 36 Richard Pearse Dr., Mangere, Private Bag 92133, Auckland (New Zealand ☎0800 651 080, elsewhere 09 275 3013; www.maui-rentals.com). Offers diverse RV and camper rentals.

United Campervans (www.campervan.co.nz) is a family-run business that rents 2- to 6-berth caravans.

WILDERNESS SAFETY

Stay warm, stay dry, and stay hydrated. For any hike, prepare yourself for an emergency by packing a first-aid kit, a reflector, a whistle, high-energy food, extra water, rain gear, a hat, mittens, and extra socks. For warmth, wear wool or insulating synthetic materials designed for the outdoors. Cotton is a bad choice since it dries slowly and retains little warmth when wet.

On any hike, however brief, you should pack enough equipment to keep you alive should a disaster occur. For backcountry trips, fill out an **intentions book** at the nearest DOC office (and sign hut books along the way). Always let someone—a friend, your hostel, a park ranger, or a local hiking organization—know when and where you are going. It may be helpful to set up an emergency plan with friends. Know your physical limits and do not attempt a hike beyond your ability. See **Safety and Health,** p. 16, for information on outdoor medical concerns. Weather changes quickly all over New Zealand, especially in mountainous areas— keep your eyes on the skies. The local DOC office will have the latest **weather forecasts.** A good guide to outdoor survival is *How to Stay Alive in the Woods,* by Bradford Angier (Macmillan, US$8).

A major hazard in the New Zealand wilderness is **crossing swollen rivers.** With weather systems constantly skirting across the Tasman Sea, it's always raining somewhere in New Zealand. In the 19th century, British colonials dubbed drowning in a river the "New Zealand death" because it happened so frequently. The safest bet is to wait it out; river levels generally fall as rapidly as they rise.

OUTDOOR AND ADVENTURE ACTIVITIES

▨ BUNGY JUMPING. Bungy is big in New Zealand; the world's first commercial jump has been thrilling Queenstown visitors since 1988. **Queenstown** remains the bungy capital of New Zealand (and the world) and boasts several different jump sites (p. 380). If you can hack it, try AJ Hackett's **Nevis Highwire Bungy** in Queenstown (134m). Bungy jump sites also exist in **Taupo** (p. 199) and **Rotorua** (p. 163).

▧ CLIMBING, CANYONING, AND CAVE RAFTING. New Zealand's turbulent geology has created plenty of crags to scale and its abundant precipitation has sculpted dozens of dramatic canyons to descend. Major rock climbing areas in New Zealand include: the **Port Hills** near Christchurch (p. 334), sport climbing in **Wanaka** (p. 365) limestone near **Golden Bay** (p. 288) and some of the nation's best at **Wharepapa South** (p. 150). Alpine climbing centers on mountainous South Island. Erosive and tectonic forces create marginal rock routes in the **Southern Alps,** but the high elevations and abundant moisture flowing from the Tasman Sea make for excellent ice and snow climbing. **Aoraki/Mt. Cook National Park** (p. 332) offers more mountaineering routes and guiding companies than anywhere else in New Zealand. For more information, visit www.climb.co.nz.

Canyoners descend narrow gorges in wetsuits and helmets to protect themselves from frigid flows and punishing rocks. Canyoning adventures are available in **Auckland** (p. 92), **Queenstown** (p. 381), and **Wanaka** (p. 400).

Tiny **Waitomo** (p. 151) nearly monopolizes the New Zealand caving business. Its multitude of cave complexes hosts a wide variety of subterranean pursuits, from tame glowworm tours to full-day abseiling and rafting adventures. For other opportunities to descend into the bowels of the earth, visit **Westport** (p. 339) and **Greymouth** (p. 345) on South Island's **West Coast.** Both serve as bases for caving adventures in the wild western range.

▨ CYCLING AND MOUNTAIN BIKING. With big distances between cities, New Zealand ensures long days in the saddle. The stunning scenery along the way and the warm hospitality at the day's end make the effort more than worthwhile. South Island contains more mountain passes but generally has flatter terrain than undulating North Island. Some cyclists claim that the wild ride up the **West Coast** is one of the world's best. Bike shops in **Christchurch** and **Auckland** have high-end bike rental packages, but most dedicated cyclists bring their own. For more information on cycling, pick up a copy of the informative *Pedaller's Paradise* (NZ$12) by Nigel Rushton, at any New Zealand bike shop.

New Zealand mountain biking is growing in popularity. If you have the bucks, search the web for one of many companies that offer guided mountain biking tours. The **Southern Alps** region (**Aoraki/Mt. Cook, Queenstown,** and **Wanaka**) boasts excellent single-track riding and several companies offer heli-biking trips. Easy-access riding is available from **Christchurch, Dunedin,** and **Wellington.** The **Central Otago** region has recently become a mountain biking hot spot; the **Central Otago Rail Trail** offers a multi-day mountain bike trip that's well graded and easy enough for beginners.

▣ FISHING. One of the cheapest and best ways to get out of the tourist circuit is to rent a fishing pole and hit the river. Ocean fishing and freshwater fishing are common, though it is the monster freshwater trout in fast running rivers that put New Zealand fishing on the map. Most hostels throughout the country will rent rods and tackle or let guests borrow fishing gear. Just make sure to have the proper fishing licenses, which can be purchased at the local DOC or any tackle shop. Flashy **Taupo** (p. 194) and laid-back **Turangi** (p. 200) both claim the title of

"Trout Fishing Capital of the World," though they are separated more by style than quality of fishing. **Wanaka** (p. 393) makes an attractive base from which to explore South Island's streams. National parks also often allow fishing.

⬦ RIVER SPORTS. A Kiwi original, **jetboats** have whisked tourists up and down New Zealand's waterways since the 1960s. With specialized internal engines, jetboats can travel rapidly over very shallow waters. Professional drivers thrill passengers with 360° spins and dangerously close passes to rocky bluffs. **Queenstown's** narrow gorges and scenic rivers make it a prime spot for jetboating (p. 386) but companies run tours all over New Zealand. The steepest and wildest jetboating river is the **Wairaurahiri** in southern Fiordland (see **Tuatapere,** p. 428).

More than two dozen commercially guided rivers greet rafting enthusiasts in New Zealand. Kiwi rivers offer a variety of difficulty levels (Class I-V) and some chances to drift through remote wilderness. Hot spots include the **Shotover River** in Queenstown (p. 398), the **Buller River** outside Murchison (p. 339), the **Rangataiki River** near Rotorua (p. 162) and the seasonal but spectacular **Wairoa River** (see **Tauranga,** p. 164). For more information, visit www.nz-rafting.co.nz. Whitewater **boogie-boarding** and **sledging** provide a more intimate encounter with raging rapids. Outfitters operate from **Rotorua** (p. 162) and **Wanaka** (p. 399). Experienced **kayakers** can paddle whitewater on many New Zealand rivers, but few opportunities exist for beginners. For those interested in mastering whitewater kayaking, consider taking a multi-day course many of which are operated on the **Buller River** in Murchison (p. 339). With more stable boats and calmer waters, **sea kayaking** is an excellent option for the less-experienced. Sea kayakers have the freedom to explore golden bays and pristine sounds at their own pace, free from the droning hum of a tour boat. Prime sea kayaking destinations include **Doubtful Sound** (p. 423), **Abel Tasman National Park** (p. 280), and the **Marlborough Sounds** (p. 252).

⬧ SCUBA DIVING AND MARINE ENCOUNTERS. New Zealand's coastal waters offer the chance to swim among dolphins. The water can be chilly, but worth it to come face-to-face with the elegant creatures. The waters off **Kaikoura** (p. 266) teem with dusky dolphins, **Akaroa** (p. 318) near Christchurch, abounds with rare Hector's dolphins, and the year-round warmth of **Paihia** (p. 111) assures temperate dolphin swims. **Poor Knights Islands** (p. 110), off the coast near Whangarei, was ranked as one of the 10 best dive sites in the world by Jacques Cousteau. The opaque water on **Milford Sound's** surface creates a unique diving environment (p. 416): fooled by the low light levels, deep sea creatures live close to the surface.

⬧⬧ SKIING AND SNOWBOARDING. With South Island's majestic mountain scenery and North Island's symmetrical volcanic slopes, New Zealand has plenty of fantastic runs for skiers and snowboarders to enjoy. The nation's best snowboarding is at **Treble Cone** outside Wanaka (p. 398) and popular ski fields surround **Queenstown** (p. 383) and **Tongariro National Park** (p. 202). Western **Canterbury** also hosts skiers and boarders at several popular resorts (p. 321). On North Island, the **Mt. Ruapehu Ski Area** (p. 203) is the largest and most developed ski area in the country. Experienced skiers can find excellent backcountry runs at one of the nation's many private ski fields. Most are owned by local clubs and use rope tows instead of lifts. Heli-skiing has become a popular alternative for those willing to spend a little extra money in the **Aoraki/Mt. Cook** region (p. 354).

⬧ SKYDIVING AND PARAGLIDING. Skydiving is cheaper in New Zealand than in the US, the UK, or Australia. As a result, many tourist towns have skydiving operations eager to capture a chunk of the heavy tourist demand. Most companies offer tandem jumps from both 9000 ft. and 12,000 ft. Free-fall on the higher jump generally lasts 45 seconds; the prolonged rush is worth the extra $50. The cheapest skydive is in **Taupo** (p. 198) but its approach can feel a bit impersonal. For a more scenic and personalized fall, try **Wanaka** (p. 382) or **Franz Josef Glacier** (p. 358). Many paragliding outfitters provide both tandem rides and paragliding courses. South Island's mountainous terrain makes leaping and gliding possible. **Queenstown** (p. 399), **Wanaka** (p. 383) and **Christchurch** (p. 313) all have several operators.

☐ ☑ SURFING AND SAILING. Tasman Sea swells crashing into the Kiwi coast inspired the surf-bum flick *The Endless Summer* in 1966. Today, New Zealand remains a popular surfing destination and attracts annual international competitions. Raglan's **Manu Bay** boasts the nation's greatest breaks (p. 146) but the **Taranaki Coast** (p. 215) and **Whangamata** on the Coromandel Peninsula (p. 139) also deliver amazing waves. Those willing to brave colder waters are rewarded for the effort in **Dunedin** (p. 365) and the **Catlins** coast (p. 445). To indulge in surfer culture and learn how to get up on a board yourself, consider visiting **Raglan** (p. 146). The 2002 arrival of the America's Cup sparked a sailing rebirth in **Auckland** (p. 53), and it was redubbed the city of sails. **Paihia's** (p. 111) harbor is home to many tall ships as well as tropical waters.

☑ OTHER OUTRAGEOUS ACTIVITIES. Enjoy a stomach-churning roll downhill in a giant, inflated ball by **zorbing** in Rotorua (p. 163). **Dune surfing** in Northland's Hokianga Region (p. 119) or at Ninety-Mile Beach (p. 122) is a sandier way to look hip atop a fiberglass board. One of New Zealand's wildest new thrills, **Fly By Wire** straps participants to a 60-horsepower aircraft engine and then sends them whipping around on a thick cable (see **Queenstown,** p. 383).

ORGANIZED ADVENTURE TRIPS

Organized adventure tours offer another way of exploring the wild. Activities include hiking, biking, skiing, canoeing, kayaking, rafting, climbing, photo safaris, and archaeological digs. Organizations that specialize in camping and outdoor equipment like REI and EMS (p. 68) also are good sources of info. Alternatively, consult **Specialty Travel Index,** 305 San Anselmo Ave., #313, San Anselmo, CA 94960 (US ☎ 800-442-4922, elsewhere 415-459-4900; www.specialtytravel.com).

USEFUL PUBLICATIONS AND RESOURCES

A variety of publishing companies offer hiking guidebooks. For info about camping, hiking, and biking, write or call the organizations listed below to receive a free catalog. The **Great Outdoor Recreation Pages** (www.gorp.com) provides general info for travelers planning on spending time in the outdoors. *101 Great Tramps in New Zealand* (NZ$27), by Pickering and Smith, and *Adventuring in New Zealand* (NZ$21), by Margaret Jefferies, provide surveys.

New Zealand Department of Conservation, 18 Manners St., Wellington (☎ 04 471 0726; www.doc.govt.nz). A wealth of information concerning national parks, campsites, and conservation efforts within New Zealand.

Sierra Club Books, 85 2nd St., 2nd fl., San Francisco, CA 94105, USA (☎ 415-977-5500; www.sierraclub.org). Publishes general resource books on hiking and camping, as well as specific guides on New Zealand.

AUCKLAND AND AROUND

AUCKLAND ☎09

A visit to Auckland (pop. 1.2 million), New Zealand's largest and most cosmopolitan city, grants travelers a glimpse into an adolescent metropolis grappling with maturity. Multiculturalism continually plants its seeds, as the world's largest Polynesian population interacts with the products of 150 years of European settlement, and the recent arrival of large Asian communities. With the advent of widescale tourism and immigration—not to mention the fleeting 2000 America's Cup growth spurt—urban planners have not quite discovered the most effective way to allow the city to flourish.

Auckland is home to several distinctive neighborhoods. Central Auckland's downtown thrives on the energy of the corporate future. Parnell's Victorian boutiques and vast estates stand as a self-conscious testament to years of British colonization. Mt. Eden plays host to artists and heavenly culinary delights, while hipster Ponsonby, home to Auckland's vibrant gay and lesbian community, jolts visitors to life with late-night caffeine fixes. The islands of the Waitemata Harbour, which dazzle with their unique serenity and beauty, are a short ferry ride away. Most visitors use Auckland as a launching pad to visit the rest of the country, but this city is on the rise as a destination in of itself. With droves of tourists and cash flowing in at an increasingly high level, Auckland is already moving out of adolescence and coming of age.

◪AUCKLAND HIGHLIGHTS

ANYTIME IS A GOOD TIME at Auckland's **Waterfront District** (p. 94), where the party lasts all night.

PICK YOUR POISON in **Ponsonby, Parnell,** or **Mt. Eden,** three character-laden neighborhoods with magnetic charm (p. 91).

ESCAPE IT ALL on **Great Barrier Island** (p. 103), and explore isolated wilderness.

◪ INTERCITY TRANSPORTATION

Flights: Auckland International Airport (AKL), a 40min. drive from Central Auckland, is the point of entry for about 80% of New Zealand's overseas visitors. For international flights, **Air New Zealand** (☎357 3000 or 0800 737 000; www.airnewzealand.co.nz) and **Qantas** (☎357 8900 or 0800 808 767; www.qantas.com.au) both have frequent flights to Australian cities and Pacific islands, including **Brisbane, Fiji, Melbourne, Rarotonga,** and **Sydney.** For domestic flights, Air New Zealand provides service to: **Christchurch** (1¼hr., 1-2 per hr., from $110); **Queenstown** (1½hr., or via Christchurch 3¾hr.; 4-5 per day; from $140); **Rotorua** (45min., 5-11 per day, from $80); **Wellington** (1hr., every hr., from $89). Backpackers and students may receive discounts; see **By Plane,** p. 21. **Super Shuttle** (☎306 3960) runs to Central Auckland ($26, $5 per extra person). From the free phone in the Visitor Information concourse outside the International Terminal, call ☎66 for the Super Shuttle. **Airbus** (☎0508 247 287; www.airbus.co.nz) runs every 20min. from 6am, with the last bus at 10pm, and makes many stops, including the YHA, SkyCity bus station, and Downtown Airline Terminal ($15, children $6; $13 YHA/VIP discount). From the airport, a taxi to downtown Auckland can cost up to $80. **Discount Taxi** (☎529 1000), will send a 3-person car for $30.

Trains: TranzScenic (☎0800 872 467; www.tranzscenic.co.nz) leaves from the **Brito-mart Transport Centre** (☎366 6400) next to QE II Sq. Open M-F 7:30am-6:30pm, Sa-Su 8am-3:30pm. To: **Hamilton** (2½hr., 1 per day, $37); **Palmerston North** (10½hr., 1 per day, $110); **Wellington** (12½hr., 1 per day, $145). Cheaper fares available if booked ahead (see **By Train,** p. 24).

Buses: InterCity (☎913 6100; www.intercitycoach.co.nz) arrives at the travel center of **SkyCity,** 102 Hobson St., at Victoria St. in Central Auckland. Service runs north to **Paihia** in the Bay of Islands (4½hr., 4 per day, $49) via **Whangarei** (2¾hr., 4 per day, $37). Southbound buses run to: **Napier** (7hr., 1 per day, $83); **New Plymouth** (6¼hr., 2 per day, $69); **Palmerston North** (9-10hr., 2 per day, $78); **Rotorua** (3½-5hr., 6 per day, $45-55) via **Hamilton** (2hr., 13 per day, $26); **Tauranga** (4hr., 4 per day, $40); **Wanganui** (8hr., 1 per day, $76); **Wellington** (11hr.; 4 per day; $109, overnight bus $70) via **Taupo** (4½-5hr., 5 per day, $54). Special discounts available by booking ahead and with student ID or YHA card.

Cars: SH1 is the main route in and out of Auckland. To the south, it's called the **Auck-land-Hamilton** or **Southern Motorway,** with on-ramps at the top of Hobson St., Symonds St., and Khyber Pass Rd. To the north, it's the **Northern Motorway,** with an on-ramp at Beaumont St. by Victoria Park. Locals simply refer to either as "the motor-way," using NW or NE to specify direction.

Hitchhiking: While *Let's Go* does not recommend hitchhiking, hitchhikers report that the best rides can be found by taking a bus to the outlying suburbs and asking locals for advice. To head north, hitchers reportedly catch the **Stagecoach** (☎366 6400) #89, the Hibiscus Coast Bus, from the downtown terminal to Orewa ($9.60). To head south, hitchers take the #471 to Papakura and switch to the 475 to Drury ($8.60). It is **illegal** to hitch on the freeway; hitchers recommend thumbing near on-ramps where cars can pull over. (For more info, see **By Thumb,** p. 28.) A safer way to travel is to look for notices in hostels posted by other backpackers wishing to share rides.

■ ORIENTATION

Auckland and its environs stretch across a narrow isthmus that connects North-land to the main landmass of North Island. **Waitemata Harbour** and the Pacific Ocean lie to the east of the city, while **Manukau Harbour** extends southward with the Tasman Sea to the west. **SH1** (the Southern Motorway) shunts traffic up from the south, becoming the Northern Motorway north of the city and converging with **SH16,** which stretches west to the Waitakeres and north to Ninety Mile Beach.

Teeming with modern buildings, banks, and businessmen, **Central Auckland** is the commercial heart of the city. **Queen Street,** the main drag, runs north-south toward the water where it meets **Queen Elizabeth II Square** (known as **QE II Square**). **Victoria Street,** another major thoroughfare, crosses Queen St. and goes east-west from **Victoria Park** (the west side of town) to **Albert Park** (east side).

The **Waterfront** is at the bottom of Queen St. by Waitemata Harbour. The **Ameri-can Express New Zealand Cup Village,** a dense tangle of bars and restaurants built for the 1999-2000 America's Cup, fans out from **Viaduct Basin** near Hobson Wharf along the waterfront. **Quay Street** also runs along the water, while **Customs Street** is parallel to the water and one block inland. The **Ferry Building** is right off Quay St., across from QE II Sq. south of **Aotea Square.** Off of Queen St. lies **Karangahape Road** (known as **K'Road**), the gritty site of bass-heavy clubs. Just west of Central Auckland, K'Rd. leads to the trendy neighborhood of **Ponsonby,** filled with hip cafes and a substantial part of the city's gay and lesbian community. To the east of the city center is the upscale area of **Parnell,** the neighborhood of old money estates and stylish boutiques. Auckland residents go to **Newmarket,** just south of Parnell, to do their shopping. Home to a large number of artists, **Mt. Eden** lies on a

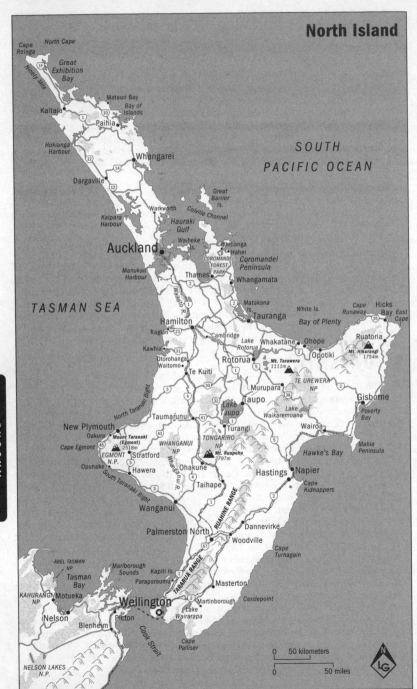

North Island

SOUTH

PACIFIC OCEAN

Cape Reinga
North Cape
Great Exhibition Bay
Ninety Mile
Kaitaia
Matauri Bay
Bay of Islands
Paihia
Hokianga Harbour
Whangarei
Dargaville
Kaipara Harbour
Warkworth
Great Barrier Is.
Colville Channel
Hauraki Gulf
Waiheke Is.
Whitianga
Hahei
Manukau Harbour
Auckland
COROMANDEL FOREST PARK
Thames
Coromandel Peninsula
Whangamata
TASMAN SEA
Matakana Is.
White Is.
Cape Runaway
Hicks Bay
East Cape
Waikato R.
Hamilton
Raglan
Cambridge
Whakatane
Ohope
Ruatoria
Kawhia
Lake Rotorua
Rotorua
Opotiki
Mt. Hikurangi 1754m
Otorohanga
Waitomo
Te Kuiti
Mt. Tarawera 1111m
TE UREWERA NP
North Taranaki Bight
Murupara
Taupo
Gisborne
Taumarunui
Lake Taupo
Lake Waikaremoana
Poverty Bay
New Plymouth
Oakura
Mount Taranaki (Egmont) 2518m
Turangi
Wairoa
Cape Egmont
WHANGANUI NP
TONGARIRO NP
Mt. Ruapehu 2797m
Mahia Peninsula
EGMONT N.P.
Stratford
Ohakune
Hawke's Bay
Opunake
Hawera
Whanganui R.
Hastings
Napier
South Taranaki Bight
Taihape
Cape Kidnappers
Wanganui
RUAHINE RANGE
Palmerston North
Dannevirke
Woodville
Cape Turnagain
ABEL TASMAN NP
Tasman Bay
Marlborough Sounds
Kapiti Is.
TARARUA RANGE
KAHURANGI NP
Motueka
Paraparaumu
Masterton
Nelson
Martinborough
Castlepoint
Blenheim
Picton
Lake Wairarapa
Wellington
Cook Strait
Cape Palliser
NELSON LAKES N.P.

0   50 kilometers
0   50 miles

hill two kilometers south of the city center. Running east of Central Auckland, Quay St. turns into **Tamaki Drive,** which then swoops along the stunning coast. Take a look out at **Orakei Basin,** off **Hobson Bay,** at **Bastion Point** along the ocean, or at **Mission** and **St. Heliers Bays**—top spots for sunbathing. A short ferry ride to the north lies **Devonport** with its many beaches and spectacular vistas of **Mt. Victoria.**

⊏ LOCAL TRANSPORTATION

Public Transportation: In 2003, Auckland introduced the **City Circuit,** a free bus service that carves a path between key inner city points. Runs every 10min. daily 8am-6pm. The **Link bus** runs a complete loop through the central city in 1hr. Stops include: the Auckland Museum, Auckland University, K'Rd., Newmarket, Parnell, Ponsonby, QE II Sq., the Railway Station, SkyCity, Victoria Park (every 10min.; M-F 6am-7pm, Sa 7am-6pm; every 15min. M-F 7-11:30pm, Sa 6-11:30pm, Su 7am-11:30pm; $1.60). The tourist-oriented **Explorer Bus** (☎0800 439 756; www.explorerbus.co.nz) offers hop-on, hop-off service with live commentary on various Auckland sights. An additional **satellite bus** operates Oct.-Apr. Buses leave from the Ferry Bldg. Departs daily Oct.-Apr. every 30min. 9am-4pm; May-Sept. every hr. 10am-4pm. Day pass $30, children $15. Ordinary city buses run by **Stagecoach** (www.stagecoach.co.nz) are a bit more challenging to negotiate but cheaper; full schedules available on the website. Fares are calculated by the number of stages traveled, and range from Stage 1 ($1.60, children $1) to the all-day, unlimited-travel Auckland Pass ($11), also good on Northshore-Downtown Fuller ferries. Explorer and Stagecoach buses are concentrated at the **Downtown Bus Centre**, which may feel unsafe at night, or across from **QE II Square**, both on Customs St. **Rideline** (☎366 6400) provides info on the Auckland public transportation system. Open M-Sa 7am-8pm, Su 8am-6:30pm.

> **EASY RIDER.** Those planning on using public transportation in Auckland may want to consider investing in a **flexi-pass**. The pass can be used on an InterCity/Newmans buses or ferries and can be purchased in 5hr. increments. $55 per 5hr. (☎0800 222 146; www.flexipass.co.nz).

Ferries: Ferries leave from **Prince's Wharf** behind the Ferry Bldg., across from QE II Sq. Contact **Fullers** (☎367 9111) for schedules. To: **Devonport** (round-trip $9, children $4.40); **Rangitoto** ($20/11); **Waiheke** ($28.50/14.30). Summer ferries depart from Mechanic's Bay to **Great Barrier Island** (round-trip $105/50).

Taxis: **Alert Taxis** (☎309 2000), **Auckland Co-op Taxis** (☎300 3000), and **Discount Taxis** (☎529 1000) can be found at Victoria St. East and Queen St., and on K'Rd.

Car Rental: Ace Rentals, 39-43 The Strand (☎303 3112), in Parnell. Economy cars in summer from $55 per day; in winter $34 per day. Discounts for long-term rentals (20 days or more). Unlimited mileage, insurance, AA coverage, and tax. **Omega Rental Cars,** 75 Beach Rd. (☎ 0800 525 210 or 377 5573), or at the airport (☎275 3265). Budget cars from $39 per day (4-day min.). Unlimited mileage, insurance, and AA service. One-way rentals to joint offices in Christchurch, Nelson, Picton, Queenstown, and Wellington available. **Maui Rentals,** 36 Richard Pearse Dr. (☎0800 651 080; www.maui-rentals.com), 2km from the airport. Campers in summer from $124 per day, with toilet and shower $162; reduced prices in winter. Worldwide chains **Avis** (☎526 2847 or 0800 655 111), **Budget** (☎976 2222 or 0800 652 227), and **Hertz** (☎0800 654 321) have offices at the airport. **Spaceships,** 31 Beach Rd. (☎309 8777), offers minivans with cooking areas, refrigerators, A/C, water and pumps, extending double beds, and DVD players. High-season $129 per day, low-season $49.

Car Buying and Selling: If you'll be in New Zealand for a while, you might consider buying a car. The cheapest way is to keep your eyes open for postings by backpackers on bulletin boards. **Car auctions** are another option: **Turners Car Auctions** (☎525 1920; www.turners.co.nz), at the corner of Leonard and Penrose Rd. in Penrose, sells budget cars. Call for auction times. **Hammer Auctions,** 830 Great South Rd. (☎579 2344), also in Penrose, sells cars M-Th at 6pm, F at 1pm, and Sa at 11am. **Car fairs** are another way to buy or sell a car; **Sell it Yourself,** 15-17 Silvia Pk. Rd., Mt. Wellington (☎270 3666; open daily 8am-6pm), and **Manukau City Park and Sell,** at the Manukau City Centre (☎358 5000; open Su 9am-1pm), are possibilities. On Beach Rd., opposite the many car rental agencies, sits **Auckland City Car Fair** (☎021 932 287; carfair@ihug.co.nz), which is put on every Sa (9am-late), is free for buyers, and charges sellers $20. Or you can try **guaranteed buy-back services** such as **New Zealand Guaranteed Buy-Back Vehicle Associates,** 825 Dominion Rd. (☎620 6587), in Mt. Roskill (open M-Sa 8am-6pm). Alternatively, **Budget Cars Sales,** 12 Mt. Eden Rd. (☎262 6530), will take you to the warehouse to view and buy a car. Open daily 8am-7pm. For more information on short-term car purchase, see **Buy-backs,** p. 27.

Car Resources: Automobile Association, 99 Albert St. (☎966 8800, 24hr. breakdown line 0800 500 222), in Central Auckland. Open M and W-F 8:30am-5pm, Tu 9am-5pm; Nov.-Apr. also Sa 9am-1pm. Pick up free road maps and *The Road Code of New Zealand* ($25), a worthwhile investment for motorists new to the country. The

Driver's Guide indicates all of Central Auckland's one-way streets and parking areas. Parking officials ticket regularly, and motorists can expect to pay up to $200 if caught in violation of parking laws.

Bike and Motorcycle Rental: Adventure Cycles, 1 Laurie Av. (☎309 5566 or 0800 335 566; adventurecycles@xtra.co.nz), in Parnell. Mountain bikes from $25 per day, $100 per week, $230 per month; touring and racing bikes $20/90/200. Open M-Tu, Th-F 7am-7pm. **New Zealand Motorcycle Rentals,** 35 Crummer Rd. (☎360 7940; www.nzbike.com), in Ponsonby. Motorcycles and scooters from $95 per day. Unlimited mileage, insurance, and 24hr. service. Open in summer M-Sa 8:30am-5pm.

■ PRACTICAL INFORMATION

TOURIST AND FINANCIAL SERVICES

Visitors Center: Auckland i-Site (☎363 7180; www.aucklandnz.com), in SkyCity near the Victoria St. entrance, in Central Auckland. Open daily 8am-8pm. **Branch** in the Viaduct at the corner of Quay and Hobson St. Complete domestic booking system and a seemingly infinite number of brochures and maps. Open M-F 9am-5pm. There's also a **branch** at the airport. Open 24hr.

Department of Conservation (DOC): (☎379 6476; www.doc.govt.nz), on Quay St. in the Ferry Bldg. Open M-F 9:30am-5pm, Sa 10am-2pm.

Budget Travel: STA Travel, 187 and 267 Queen St. (☎309 0458 or 356 1550; www.statravel.co.nz), in Central Auckland. Open M-F 9am-6pm, Sa 10am-3pm. Also at 229 Queen St., 8th fl., above Auckland Central Backpackers. **Backpacker's World Travel,** 23 Victoria St. East (☎368 1742). Books everything from tours to flights. Open M-F 9am-7pm, Sa 10am-5pm. Internet access. There are also travel centers at most of Auckland's downtown hostels.

Consulates: Australia, 188 Quay St., 7th fl. (☎921 8800). **Canada,** 48 Emily Pl., 9th fl. (☎309 8516). **Ireland,** 18 Shortland St., 6th fl. (☎977 2252). **UK,** NZ House, 151 Queen St., 17th fl. (☎303 2973). **US,** 23 Customs St., 3rd fl. (☎303 2724).

Banks and Currency Exchange: Interforex, 99 Quay St. (☎302 3066), in the Ferry Bldg. Open daily 8am-7:30pm. **The National Bank,** 205 Queen St. (☎359 9813). No commission on traveler's checks or foreign currency when selling. Open M-F 9am-4:30pm. **ATMs** line Queen St.

LOCAL SERVICES

Luggage Storage: National Mini Storage LTD, 68 Cook St. (☎356 7020). $1 per bag per day. Open daily 8am-6pm.

Bookstores: Whitcoull's, 210 Queen St. (☎356 5400). Open M-Th 8am-7pm, F 8am-9pm, Sa 9am-6pm, Su 10am-6pm. **Unity Books,** 19 High St. (☎307 0731). Open M-Th 8:30am-8pm, F 8:30am-9pm, Sa 9:30am-6pm, Su 11am-6pm.

Women's Resources: Auckland Women's Centre, 4 Warnock St. (☎376 3227), in Grey Lynn, offers counseling for women. Open M-F 9am-4pm. **Wanderwomen** (☎360 7330) coordinates trips for groups of women.

GLBT Resources: Gay and Lesbian Line (☎303 3584; www.gayline.org.nz) provides info, counseling, and referrals. Open M-F 10am-10pm, Sa-Su 5-10pm. **Rainbow Youth,** 281 K'Rd. (☎ 376 4155). Info, referrals, and an events calendar. Open M-F 10am-5:30pm. **Where It's At,** the local guide to nightlife, is available at the tourist office.

Ticket Agencies: Ticketek (☎307 5000; www.ticketek.co.nz) sells tickets for music, theater, and sporting events; book at various locations including the **Aotea Centre** (open M-F 9am-5:30pm, Sa-Su 9am-5pm) and the **SkyCity lobby** (open daily 8am-8pm). $2 surcharge for purchase at location, $6 for purchase over the phone, $8 for purchase online.

AUCKLAND AND AROUND

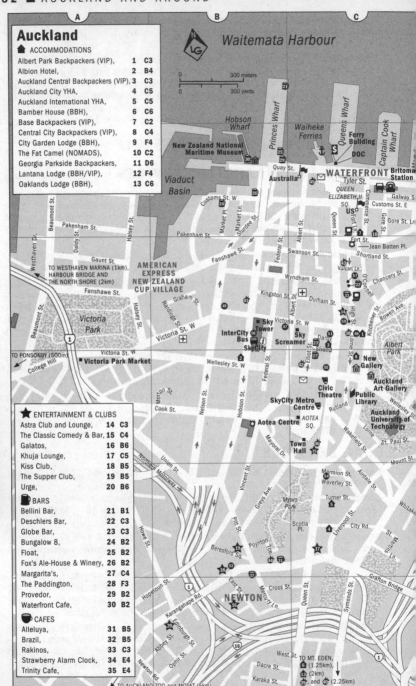

Auckland

🏠 ACCOMMODATIONS

Albert Park Backpackers (VIP),	1	C3
Albion Hotel,	2	B4
Auckland Central Backpackers (VIP),	3	C3
Auckland City YHA,	4	C5
Auckland International YHA,	5	C5
Bamber House (BBH),	6	C6
Base Backpackers (VIP),	7	C2
Central City Backpackers (VIP),	8	C4
City Garden Lodge (BBH),	9	F4
The Fat Camel (NOMADS),	10	C2
Georgia Parkside Backpackers,	11	D6
Lantana Lodge (BBH/VIP),	12	F4
Oaklands Lodge (BBH),	13	C6

⭐ ENTERTAINMENT & CLUBS

Astra Club and Lounge,	14	C3
The Classic Comedy & Bar,	15	C4
Galatos,	16	B6
Khuja Lounge,	17	C5
Kiss Club,	18	B5
The Supper Club,	19	B5
Urge,	20	B6

🍸 BARS

Bellini Bar,	21	B1
Deschlers Bar,	22	C3
Globe Bar,	23	C3
Bungalow 8,	24	B2
Float,	25	B2
Fox's Ale-House & Winery,	26	B2
Margarita's,	27	C4
The Paddington,	28	F3
Provedor,	29	B2
Waterfront Cafe,	30	B2

☕ CAFES

Alleluya,	31	B5
Brazil,	32	B5
Rakinos,	33	C3
Strawberry Alarm Clock,	34	E4
Trinity Cafe,	35	E4

🍎 FOOD

The Bog,	36	F4
Burger Fuel,	37	E4
Cafe 88,	38	C3
Circus Circus,	39	C6
Fraser's,	40	C6
Hackster's	41	B3
The Middle East Cafe,	42	C4
The Occidental,	43	C3
Rasoi Vegetarian Restaurant,	44	B5
St. Pierre's Presents Sushi of Japan,	45	C2
Tanuki Sushi and Sake Bar,	46	C4

● SERVICES

Automobile Association,	47	B3
Backpacker's World Travel,	48	C3
Beat Merchants,	49	B3
Maui Rentals,	50	D6
The National Bank,	51	C3
Omega Rental Cars,	52	D3
Pride Centre,	53	B5
Real Groovy,	54	C5

STA Travel,	55	C4
Ticketek,	56	B3
Unity Books,	57	C3
Newmarket Day and Night Pharmacy,	58	E6
Whitcoull's,	59	C3

Mechanics Bay

Tooley

Jellicoe Wharf

Freyberg Wharf

Quay St.

Tamaki Dr.

Tinley St.
Plumer St.
Tangihua St.
Tajora
Beach Rd.
Mahuhu Cres.
Anzac Ave.
Ten Crescent
Waterloo Quadrant
Parliament St.

Old Railway Station

Te Taou Cres.

The Strand

Ronayne St.

Augustus Terr.
Fox St.
Egron
York St.
Bradford
Earle St.
Bath St.

Churton St.
Farnham
Garfield St.

Kenwyn St.
St. Georges
Faraday St.
Cleveland Rd.
Gladstone Rd.

Constitution Hill

Auckland University
The ClockTower

Alten Reserve

Campus Library

Fraser Park
Parnell Rise

PARNELL

Bay Rd.

Monument Arts Centre

Fred St.

Carlaw Pk.

Stanley St.
Alten Rd.
Grafton Rd.

Bedford
Cracroft
Heather St.

Parnell Rd.
Windsor St.
Falcon

Ruskin St.
Scarborough Terr.

St. Georges Bay Rd.

Cheshire
Gibraltar Cres.

Lower

Domain Dr.

Aerere St.

Edmonds St.

St. Stephens Ave.

AUCKLAND AND AROUND

Auckland Domain

Domain Dr.

Birdwood Cres.

Anglican Cathedral of the Holy Trinity

Cathedral Pl.

Moehau St.
Fern croft
Grafton Rd.

Cenotaph Rd.

The Crescent

Football Rd.

Auckland Museum

Maunsell Rd.

Claybrook Rd.

Laurie Ave.

Auckland City Hospital

Wintergardens

Kings Kid

Domain Dr.

Little George St.

Hordi St.

Ayr St.

Park Rd.

Cowie St.
Parnell Rd.
Sarawia St.

Newmarket Park

View Rd.
Park Rd.
Park Ave.
Boyle
Glasgow

Football Rd.
George St.
Morgan St.

Broadway

Railway St.
Leek St.
Youngs Ln.
Largo Terr.

Carlton Gore Rd.

(27km)
(29km)

TO NEWMARKET, 58 (200m)

Weather Conditions: MetPhone (☎0900 99 909; www.metservice.co.nz).

Publications: The Auckland-based **New Zealand Herald** is the country's most comprehensive daily newspaper. **Metro** magazine takes the pulse of Auckland's pop culture and politics, while **express** is the gay and lesbian paper. **The Fix** and **Infusion** have the goods on Auckland's dance clubs. **Pulp** lists headliner events nation-wide.

EMERGENCY, MEDICAL, AND COMMUNICATIONS

Police: Auckland Central Police Station (☎379 4240), at the corner of Cook and Vincent St. **Downtown Station** (☎379 4500), at the corner of Jean Batten Pl. and Fort St. **Ponsonby Police Station,** 8 Jervois Rd. (☎302 6400). Other stations include **Airport International Terminal** (☎275 9046) and the **Devonport Community Constable,** 19 Anzac St. (☎489 4008), in Devonport.

Crisis Lines: Lifeline (☎522 2999) provides counseling by appointment and phone support. **Auckland Help Foundation** (☎623 1700) aids victims of sexual assault. Call the **AIDS Hotline** (☎0800 802 437) with STD concerns. All hotlines 24hr.

Medical Services: Newmarket Day and Night Pharmacy, 60 Broadway St. (☎520 6634), in Newmarket. Open daily 9am-1am. The **Auckland Hospital** (☎367 0000), on the edge of the Auckland Domain on Park St. in Grafton. **Auckland Metro Doctors,** 125 Queen St. (☎373 4621), Closed Su. You can also go to **CityMed** (☎377 5525), at Albert St. and Mills Ln. On-site **pharmacy** (☎307 1133). Open M-F 8:30am-5:30pm, Sa 9:30am-1pm. **Ponsonby Accident and Medical Clinic,** 202 Ponsonby Rd. (☎376 5555), has its own **pharmacy** (☎378 6075). Clinic open daily 7:30am-10pm; pharmacy 8am-9:30pm. The **Radius Pharmacy** at 104 Queen St. (☎303 4253), in central Auckland has the best hours of the downtown pharmacies. Open M-Th 8am-6pm, F 8am-7pm, Sa 9:30am-5:30pm, Su 11am-5pm.

Internet Access: There are Internet cafes all over the city; the average rate has plummeted to about $3 per hr. Most hostels offer Internet access for a small fee.

Post Office: Wellesley Street Post Shop, 24 Wellesley St., in the Bledisloe Bldg. Poste Restante. Open M-F 7:30am-5:30pm. **Auckland City Post Shop,** 23 Customs St. Open 8:30am-5:30pm, Sa 10am-2pm. For information on all post offices call ☎379 6710.

ACCOMMODATIONS

Accommodations in **Central Auckland** provide easy access to the city's sights at the price of noisy streets and the occasional congestion. Older travelers, campers, families, or those seeking a city location with more relaxed vibes should choose a residential neighborhood instead. The backpackers in **Ponsonby, Parnell,** and **Mt. Eden** are only a short bus ride away from the city center and are generally much homier than the downtown hostels. Most have **Internet** access and **laundry** services, and **key deposit** is usually $10-20.

CENTRAL AUCKLAND

Base Backpackers (VIP), 16-20 Fort St. (☎300 9999; www.basebackpackers.com). Head and shoulders above the rest, base offers amenities including bag storage in every dorm, a rooftop spa, and "sanctuary," a female-only floor with increased security and 5-star linen. The on-site bar, **First Base,** has an inventive selection of mixed drinks ("sex on the bunks," $15), while the travel center offers expert advice on outdoor excursions. Dorms from $25; sanctuary $30; singles $80-90; doubles $70. MC/V. ❷

Albert Park Backpackers (VIP), 27-31 Victoria St. East (☎309 0336; bakpak@albert-park.co.nz). Stocked with twentysomethings and the occasional senior citizen, intimate Albert Park houses a communal kitchen, lounge with a pool table, and satellite TV. With dorms starting at $17, it just might be the best deal in town. Reception 24hr. Dorms $17-20; singles $50; doubles and twins $60. AmEx/MC/V. ❷

Auckland International YHA, 1-35 Turner St. (☎302 8200; www.yha.co.nz), just off Queen St. The long, colorful hallways, huge kitchen, and lounges are spotless. A youthful clientele makes for a convivial atmosphere, and the job search center might help you extend your stay. Dorms $28-29; twins and doubles $78-81. AmEx/MC/V. ❷

The Fat Camel (NOMADS), 38 Fort St. (☎307 0181 or 0800 220 198; www.fatcamel.co.nz). Dorms surround a central living room with kitchenette. Free snacks from 7-8pm are a big draw for hungry travelers. Dorms $19-27; twins and doubles $55, with window $69; triples $85. AmEx/MC/V/D. ❷

Auckland City YHA, 8 Liverpool St. (☎309 2802; yha.aucklandcity@yha.org.nz), at the corner of City Rd. Attracts an older crowd than the YHA down the hill. On-site **Tommy's Bistro** (open daily 7-11am and, when busy, 6pm-late) has cheap eats. Reception 24hr. Dorms $23; singles $67; twins and doubles $77. AmEx/MC/V. ❷

Central City Backpackers (VIP), 26 Lorne St. (☎358 5685; ccbnz@xtra.co.nz). A lively crowd fills this small traveler's haven. Check out the **Embargo Bar** (☎309 1850) in the basement; open M-F 5pm-late, Sa-Su 6pm-late. Female-only dorms available. Dorms $20-23; singles $45; doubles and twins $56. AmEx/MC/V. ❷

Auckland Central Backpackers (VIP), 229 Queen St. (☎358 4877; www.acb.co.nz), at the corner of Darby St. A veritable warehouse for backpackers, ACB is hands-down the busiest and largest of its kind. Services include the popular **Globe Bar,** a travel center, Wi-Fi, TV rooms, kitchens, and a job search center. **STA** has offices on the 8th fl. Single-sex dorms available. Dorms $25-27; singles $68; doubles and twins $88. MC/V. ❷

Albion Hotel, 119 Hobson St. (☎379 4900; www.albionhotel.co.nz), at the corner of Hobson and Wellesley St. Set in a refurbished Victorian building, Albion is a simple reprieve from hostels. Check in by the bar at night. Doubles $100; family rooms $120. AmEx/MC/V. ❹

PONSONBY

🏶**The Brown Kiwi (BBH),** 7 Prostord St. (☎378 0191; www.brownkiwi.co.nz). The Brown Kiwi puts you where you want to be—trendy Ponsonby. This serene 2-story homesports an elegant garden and 2 Japanese-style fish ponds. The owners are friendly both to patrons and to the environment. Free local calls. Reception 8am-noon, 2-7pm. Dorms from $22; doubles and twins $58. MC/V. ❷

Ponsonby Backpackers (BBH), 2 Franklin Rd. (☎360 1311 or 0800 476 676; www.ponsonby-backpackers.co.nz). A large Victorian house just off Ponsonby Rd with a garden and barbeque area. Reception 7am-7pm. Dorms $24; singles $37-42; doubles $58-65. MC/V. ❷

PARNELL

🏶**City Garden Lodge (BBH),** 25 St. George's Bay Rd. (☎302 0880; city.garden@compuweb.co.nz). Once owned by the Queen of Tonga, this lodge gives guests the royal treatment, providing amenities such as a cozy living room and hammock-adorned back porch. Free storage. Reception 8am-1pm, 4-8pm. Dorms $22-24; singles and twins from $48; doubles from $60. Tent sites $10, $12 for 2 people. MC/V. ❷

Lantana Lodge (BBH/VIP), 60 St. George's Bay Rd. (☎373 4546; www.lantanalodge.co.nz). This white-shuttered house charms with a gingerbread porch and flower garden. Small and simple with a homey feel, this hostel grants guests an intimate experience. Free storage, free Internet and Wi-Fi. Reception 8am-10pm. Dorms $22-25; twins and doubles from $60; triples $66. Tent sites $10 per person. MC/V. ❷

MT. EDEN

🏶**Bamber House (BBH),** 22 View Rd. (☎/fax 623 4267; bamber@ihug.co.nz). This colonial home has a spacious living room, two kitchens, and an outdoor pool. Rainwater is

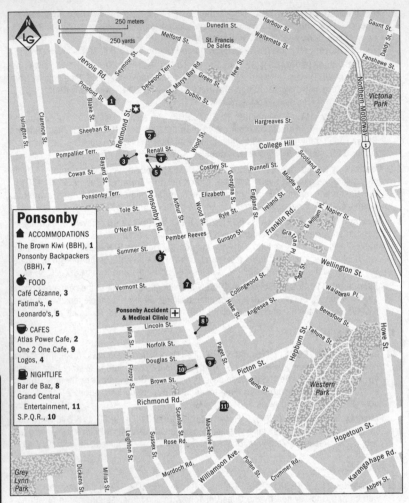

Ponsonby

🏠 ACCOMMODATIONS
The Brown Kiwi (BBH), 1
Ponsonby Backpackers
(BBH), 7

🍴 FOOD
Café Cézanne, 3
Fatima's, 6
Leonardo's, 5

☕ CAFES
Atlas Power Cafe, 2
One 2 One Cafe, 9
Logos, 4

🍸 NIGHTLIFE
Bar de Baz, 8
Grand Central
Entertainment, 11
S.P.Q.R., 10

filtered and piped into the washing machines. Free parking. Reception 8:30am-noon and 4-8pm. Dorms $23; singles $43; twins and doubles $56-60. MC/V. ❷

🔖 **Oaklands Lodge (BBH),** 5a Oaklands Rd. (☎/fax 638 6545; www.oaklands.co.nz), just off Mt. Eden Rd. Green-roofed Oaklands has spacious rooms, a backyard trampoline, and weekend barbeques. Reception 8:30am-1pm and 2-8:30pm. Dorms from $21; singles $45; doubles and twins $60. MC/V. ❷

GRAFTON

Georgia Parkside Backpackers, 189 Park Rd. (☎309 8999; www.georgia.co.nz). A lone hostel in the vicinity of Newmarket and the Auckland Domain, Georgia is a broken-in backpackers with all the necessities and an impressive stained-glass window in the main hall. Reception 8am-9pm. Dorms $22; doubles $48. MC/V. ❷

◘ FOOD

Fusion is the word in Central Auckland. Takeaways and food courts—the cheapest choices for backpackers—dot the city center, but supermarkets are mostly located in Newmarket and Ponsonby. An expansive **Foodtown,** 76 Quay St., is east along the waterfront. (☎275 2567. Open 24hr.) **New World,** 2 College Hill, near Victoria Park, has the most central location; the Link bus stops right outside. (☎307 8400. Open daily 7am-midnight.) Central Auckland options cluster around the middle stretch of Queen St. or along K'Rd. Ponsonby and Mt. Eden feature affordable hipster spots, while Parnell caters to a more upscale set.

CENTRAL AUCKLAND

▓ **The Middle East Cafe,** 23A Wellesley St. (☎379 4843). A funky Middle Eastern falafel house, packed with wooden camels and pictures of deserts. Falafel $7. Entrees, including vegetarian options, $15-17. Open M-F 11am-3pm, Sa 5:15-10pm. Cash only. ❸

▓ **Rasoi Vegetarian Restaurant,** 211 K'Rd. (☎377 7780). An all-veggie refuge. The Deluxe Thali Platter, complete with rice and your choice of curry ($12.50), challenges even the hungriest, as do the freshly made dosa ($6-7). For a snack, stop in for a quick samosa ($1.20, 3 for $3). Open M-Sa 11am-9pm. AmEx/MC/V. ❷

▓ **Cafe 88,** 11 Victoria St. East (☎309 3328). This unassuming eatery is not a cafe, but a family-owned Chinese restaurant with some of the best prices in the city. Steaming plates of traditional stand-bys like Mongolian beef and sweet and sour pork will set you back a mere $6.80. Main dishes $10-15. A great alternative to the food courts and streetside food vendors. Open M-Sa noon-9:30pm. Cash only. ❷

The Occidental, 6-8 Vulcan Ln. (☎300 6226; www.belgian-beer-cafe.co.nz). Rusted french horns and faded photographs line the oak-panelled walls of this European-style bistro. Try one of the mussel pots ($17) while enjoying a selection from the Belgian beer menu ($6.50-14.50). Live music Sa-Su 10pm-midnight. Open daily 7am-3am. AmEx/MC/V. ❸

Jackster's, 66 Hobson St. (☎307 7039). A tasty selection of sweet and spicy chilli spreads make this unassuming sandwich and salad shop worth a stopover for lunch. Design your own sandwich or wrap ($6.50), or go breadless with a homemade salad (small $7, large $9). Open M-F 7am-3:30pm. Cash only. ❷

Tanuki Sushi and Sake Bar, 319 Queen St. (☎379 5353; www.sakebars.co.nz). Delectable Japanese entrees ($5-16.50) and sushi (rolls $8-12). Open daily 5-10:30pm and W-F noon-2pm. In the darker depths of the restaurant, **Tanuki's Cave** (☎379 5151) serves 24 different kinds of sake. Open daily 5:30-11:30pm. MC/V. ❸

St. Pierre's Presents Sushi of Japan (☎377 6695), in the Westfield Downtown Centre food court off QE II Sq. Churns out roll after delicious roll ($6-8). The seafood display makes grab and go easy (shrimp cocktail, $6). Also sells fish by the kg. Locations throughout the city, including 277 Broadway in Newmarket and 167 K'Rd. Open M-Sa 8am-8pm and Su 10am-4pm. AmEx/MC/V. ❷

PONSONBY

▓ **Café Cézanne,** 296 Ponsonby Rd. (☎376 3338). Although the bright, busy mural on the wall is far from a masterpiece, the famous chicken caesar salad ($15) and the remarkable Thai chicken curry ($17) are pure artistry. Also offers homemade baked desserts. Open daily 8am-11pm, kitchen closes at 9pm. AmEx/MC/V. ❸

Fatima's, 240 Ponsonby Rd. (☎376 9303; www.fatimas.co.nz). This healthy kebab stand offers pitas ($9) and shawarmas ($8.40) served by a young, hip staff. Fruit smoothies and frappes $5. Open daily 11:30am-10pm. AmEx/MC/V. ❷

Leonardo's, 263 Ponsonby Rd. (☎361 1556). Well worth the splurge. Leo himself greets diners at this elegant Italian restaurant. Enjoy the wide range of antipasto options (from $15.50) or try the filet of beef with black truffles ($32.50). Open Tu-Su 6pm-late; F-Sa also noon-3pm. AmEx/MC/V. ❹

PARNELL

The Bog, 196 Parnell Rd. (☎377 1510). A Kiwi take on the traditional Irish pub, The Bog dishes up gourmet sandwiches ($13-17.50; until 5pm) and hearty pub fare ($17.50-24.50). Tu trivia night packs the place, with patrons salivating over the $50 bar tab prize. Guinness and Kilkenny await at $8 per pint for the losers. Open daily 10am-3am. AmEx/MC/V. ❸

Burger Fuel, 164 Parnell Rd. (☎377 3345; www.burgerfuel.co.nz). Riffs on the burger. Options like the "Peanut Piston" (peanut sauce, salad, aioli; $8), or the "V8 Vegan" (pumpkin, cashew nut, ginger; $9) dot the menu of this health-conscious fast food chain. Open M-Th and Su noon-10pm, F noon-midnight, Sa noon-11pm. MC/V. ❷

MT. EDEN

Frasers, 434 Mt. Eden Rd. (☎630 6825). This popular neighborhood cafe serves up standard beverages and bites. Chat with a local over the homemade quiche ($8.50) and a cappuccino ($3). Open daily 7am-11pm. AmEx/MC/V. ❶

Circus Circus, 447 Mt. Eden Rd. (☎623 3833). Filled with vintage circus memorabilia, this cafe's select menu ($14-20) makes it a 3-ring steal. Open daily 7am-11pm. AmEx/MC/V. ❸

◧ CAFES

Enjoying Auckland's vibrant cafe scene is a popular way to pass an afternoon or to jump start a long night. In **Central Auckland,** the narrow paths of High and Lorne St., as well as Vulcan Ln. and nearby K'Rd., are brimming with coffee sippers, while the main roads in **Parnell** and **Mt. Eden** feature a wide selection of java joints. Stylish **Ponsonby** wins the caffeine crown for the highest concentration of great cafes. In addition to coffee, most cafes serve light meals and alcohol, and some feature occasional live music.

CENTRAL AUCKLAND

▧ **Rakinos,** 35 High St., 2nd fl. (☎358 3535). Anything but quaint, Rakinos gets grooving with a young crowd and a live DJ from the late afternoon on. The balcony overlooking the nearby park makes for a scenic spot to enjoy the french toast with bananas ($12). Happy hour 3-7pm. Open M-F 8am-late, Sa 11am-late, Su 7pm-late. AmEx/MC/V. ❷

Brazil, 256 K'Rd. (☎302 2677). The fragrance of roasting beans wafts through the air of this hip corridor of caffeine. Breakfast options ($5.50-13) include the vegetarian breakfast ($11). Open M-F 8am-8pm, Sa-Su 9am-8pm. Kitchen closes at 3pm. Cash only. ❷

Alleluya, 183 K'Rd. (☎377 8424), in St. Kevin's Arcade. The youthful staff at this back-corner shop serves huge bowls of coffee ($3.50) in front of an expansive downtown vista. Smoothies $4.50. Brunch $8-14.50. Open M-W 9am-5pm, Th-Sa 9am-midnight, Su 9am-3pm. AmEx/MC/V. ❷

PONSONBY

▧ **One 2 One Cafe,** 121 Ponsonby Rd. (☎376 4954), serves excellent coffee and boasts vegetarian options like the organic brown rice porridge with yogurt and maple syrup ($7), or large breakfasts ($11-15). In nice weather, enjoy your meal in the verdant back garden or out front. Open M-Tu 6am-6pm, W-F 6am-late, Sa, Su 7am-late. MC/V. ❷

Logos, 265 Ponsonby Rd. (☎376 2433; www.cafelogos.com). It would be tough to miss the elaborate, sun-like wooden carving that beckons passersby to this relaxed neighborhood cafe. Serves up healthy gourmet burgers (tofu and satay patty; $13.50). Open M, W, Sa, Su 9:30am-late, Tu 5pm-late, Th-Fr 8am-late. AmEx/MC/V. ❷

Atlas Power Cafe, 285 Ponsonby Rd. (☎360 1295). Good breakfast options (eggs Benedict; $14) are served in the Scandinavian dining room upstairs or out front. Open M-F 6:30am-5:30pm, Sa-Su 7am-5:30pm. Kitchen closes at 3pm. AmEx/MC/V. ❷

PARNELL

Strawberry Alarm Clock, 119 Parnell Rd. (☎377 6959). Named after a popular 1960s band, this technicolor streetside cafe mellows even the squarest of customers. "No Smoking" is inscribed in every imaginable language. Healthy all-day brunch menu ($7.50-14.50). Open M-F 7am-5pm, Sa 8am-4:30pm, Su 9am-4pm. AmEx/MC/V. ❷

Trinity Cafe, 107 Parnell Rd. (☎300 3042). This petite cafe serves fantastic, light fare (chicken salad with crispy noodles, banana, and chutney; $15) as well as the requisite selection of coffee and tea. Open M-F 7am-4pm. AmEx/MC/V. ❷

ⓖ SIGHTS

CENTRAL AUCKLAND

ART GALLERIES. Next to Albert Park sits the ▨**Auckland Art Gallery.** The space includes a beautiful two-story hall with works by lesser-known European masters. Peruse the 19th-century paintings of New Zealand landscape and history, as well as the Maori portraits on the ground floor. Approximately half of the museum has rotating exhibits of mostly contemporary works. *(At the corner of Wellesley and Kitchener St. ☎307 7700; www.aucklandartgallery.govt.nz. Open daily 10am-5pm. Free. Special exhibit prices may vary.)* Its sister gallery, the **New Gallery,** focuses on contemporary art; the steel and glass space holds traveling exhibits. *(Directly across from the Auckland Art Gallery on Kitchener St. Free.)*

AUCKLAND MUSEUM. Auckland's largest museum displays Polynesian, European, and natural history exhibits. Upstairs, **Scars on the Heart** has exhibits on several New Zealand wars; downstairs galleries feature Aotearoa's Maori heritage and house the **Hotunui Whare,** a complete meeting house on loan from the Tainui tribe of the Thames area. The museum is also the venue for **Manaia,** a performance group from Auckland's native tribe, Ngati Whatua O Orakei. *(Take the Link Bus to "Auckland Museum." ☎306 7067 or 0800 256 873; www.aucklandmuseum.com. Open daily 10am-5pm. Shows daily 11am, noon, and 1:30pm, and 2:30pm. Suggested donation $5. Shows $15, students and seniors $11.20, ages 5-12 $7.50.)*

SKY TOWER. Dominating the Auckland skyline, the 328m Sky Tower is 4m taller—and a lot brighter—than the Eiffel Tower. The **observation deck** has a 360° view. The **Sky Deck** is 34m higher and offers almost the same view; step onto the glass in the outer ring or eat at **Orbit,** its rotating restaurant. **Vertigo** (p. 92) lets you climb 44m more. The **Sky Jump** (p. 92) is a testament to New Zealand's adrenaline addiction. *(In the middle of Hobson, Wellesley, Federal, and Victoria St. ☎363 6000; www.skycityauckland.nz. Open M-Th and Su 8:30am-11pm, F-Sa 8:30am-midnight. Last elevator 30min. before closing. $22, ages 5-12 $8, under 5 free. Sky Deck $3 more. 10% discount vouchers available in brochures at the Auckland i-Site.)*

AUCKLAND UNIVERSITY. As you traverse Albert Park, it is impossible to miss the neo-Gothic tower of the **Old Arts Building.** Built in 1926, the Clock Tower is the symbol of Auckland University, the largest of New Zealand's eight public universities. *(22 Princes St. University operator ☎ 373 7599.)* The campus **library** is at the corner of Prince's and Alfred St.

PARKS. Victoria Park, west of Queen St., and the more charming **Albert Park** to the east are a welcome respite from the city's chaos. Across from Victoria Park, the **Victoria Park Market** is abuzz with crafts, clothes, cafes, and weekend flea markets. *(210 Victoria St. West. ☎ 309 6911. Open daily 9am-6pm.)*

AUCKLAND DOMAIN. To the east of Auckland lies the vast expanse of grass and trees that is the Auckland Domain. The band rotunda often hosts free jazz concerts on summer weekends *(www.aucklandcity.govt.nz/akatplay)*. Amid the various attractions in the Domain is the free **Wintergarden,** two botanically oriented glass houses overlooking a lily pond. *(The park is best accessed from the Grafton Bridge, which extends across the motorway 1 block from the intersection of Queen St. and K'Rd. Wintergarden open M-Sa 9am-5:30pm, Su 9am-7:30pm; in winter M-Sa 9am-4:30pm.)*

THE WATERFRONT

It comes as no surprise that the waterfront is one of the busiest and most commercial areas in Auckland, the "City of Sails." Head to the bottom of Albert St. to find **Waitemata Harbour,** site of the renowned America's Cup regatta. Once there, turn left on Quay St. and continue to Viaduct Harbour (just west of QE II Sq.) to reach the **American Express New Zealand Cup Village** for numerous restaurants, bars, hotels, and a summer open-air cinema series.

NEW ZEALAND NATIONAL MARITIME MUSEUM. This waterside museum has meticulously crafted exhibits chronicling New Zealand's historical involvement with the high seas. Highlights include numerous vessels, pre-Polynesian artifacts, and a room that might make you seasick. *(At the base of Hobson Wharf, at Quay and Hobson St. ☎ 373 0800 or 0800 725 897; www.nzmaritime.org. Open daily 9am-6pm; in winter 9am-5pm. $16, students $9. Audio guide included. Cruises leave at noon, Tu, Th, Sa-Su, $15, $7 for students. Museum and cruise package $24/15.)*

FERRY BUILDING. The brick and sandstone 1912 Ferry Building is an important waterfront landmark and home to **Fullers Ferries,** which has service to Great Barrier Island (p. 103), Rangitoto (p. 99), Tiritiri Matangi Island (p. 98), and Waiheke (p. 99), as well as to the North Shore community of Devonport (p. 97). See **Local Transportation,** p. 80, for schedules and prices. The **Harbour Cruise** provides a leisurely tour of Waitemata Harbour with complimentary coffee and cookies. *(99 Quay St. Fullers ☎ 367 9111. 1½hr. 2 per day. $30, children $15.)*

WESTHAVEN MARINA. A parking lot for Auckland's elite, Westhaven is the largest manmade marina in the Southern Hemisphere. Farther down Westhaven Dr. are the upper-crust **yacht clubs,** where crews return from civilized competition to enjoy a civilized drink—or six. Back along Westhaven Dr. toward Central Auckland, the staff at **Sea Tours** on Pier Z can answer questions about charters. *(Take Westhaven Dr. out of Auckland, along Gaunt St. from the American Express New Zealand Cup Village. Sea Tours ☎ 369 1234; www.seatours.co.nz.)*

THE BAYS

Skirting subtropical waters and cream-colored sands, the Bays are a prime venue for in-line skating, kayaking, and parading in the summer months.

KELLY TARLTON'S UNDERWATER WORLD. Deep beneath Tamaki Dr. lurk stingrays, eels, and sharks in possibly the most ingenious use of converted sewage tanks ever. A message board at the entrance serves as a fishy tabloid of who's being fed, who's been born, and who's mating with whom. The moving walkway transports guests into the underwater world, while a Snowcat takes passengers through the Antarctic Encounter, featuring a colony of penguins. *(23 Tamaki Dr., 6km east of Central Auckland. Take either bus #74, 75, or 76 from Tyler St. next to the Britomart, or the Explorer Bus. ☎ 528 0603 or 0800 805 050; www.kellytarltons.co.nz. Open daily 9am-6pm; last entry 5pm. $26, students and seniors $20, children $10, families $40-59.)*

ORAKEI BASIN. The yacht-filled Orakei Basin is the prime sailing territory for the rich residents of **Paritai Drive**, Auckland's wealthiest street, in a gated community of million-dollar mansions. To catch a glimpse of the pleasure yachts, head to Orakei Rd., which abuts Hobson Bay east of Central Auckland.

MISSION AND ST. HELIERS BAY. Mission Bay, a sunbathing outpost with a stretch of lively bars and cafes, is just around Bastion Point from the Orakei Marae of the Ngati Whatua tribe. Nearby is the popular and accessible St. Heliers Bay. Quiet throughout the winter, **Tamaki Drive** and **St. Heliers Bay Road** fill with touristing hordes in the summer. *(To get to Mission Bay from downtown Auckland, take any of the following buses: #745-746, 765, 767, or 769. To get to St. Heliers Bay, take either #767 or 769. All buses depart from platform D-13 at Britomart Station on Tyler St. Rideline, ☎ 366 6400, also has detailed bus information.)*

PONSONBY

No visit to Auckland is complete without a jaunt to Ponsonby. While not a historic district, student and gay populations give the neighborhood a more welcoming feel than Auckland's business district. Both sides of **Ponsonby Road** are lined with bars and trendy cafes. Connecting Ponsonby to the top of the city, the bridge over the K'Rd. motorway hosts an open-air market on Saturdays. *(Open 10am-4pm.)*

PARNELL

On the far side of the Domain is the flashy, upscale neighborhood of Parnell, home to vast estates and expensive shops. The most notable architecture is a group of Victorian homes-turned-boutiques, along Parnell Rd., known as **Parnell Heritage Village**. At the top of the road stands Auckland's 19th-century **Anglican Cathedral of the Holy Trinity**, which was moved completely intact to make room for a larger church. The free and fragrant **Parnell Rose Gardens** at the bottom of the hill bloom from November to March. Parnell Rd. leads straight into nearby **Newmarket**; take Carlton Gore Rd. where Parnell Rd. forks. A shopping mecca for Auckland residents, this tiny suburb bustles along Broadway St.

MT. EDEN AND ONE TREE HILL

The parks of Mt. Eden *(Maungawhau)* provide a bird's-eye (or at least a giraffe's-eye) view of Auckland. Look out for the herd of cows on your way up to the crater summit. One Tree Hill *(Maungakiekie)* is another fine lookout and houses the **Stardome Observatory**, which features a planetarium show. After shows, you can take a peek at the cosmos through the EWB 50cm telescope. *(Mt. Eden: Take bus #274, 275, or 277 from Customs St., near Gore St. Observatory: take bus #312, or 302-305 from the corner of Victoria and Queen St. ☎ 624 1246; www.stardome.org.nz. Shows W-Sa 2 per day. $14, children $7. Telescope $8. Book ahead.)*

WESTERN SPRINGS

A residential suburb, Western Springs is home to two of Auckland's big name attractions: the zoo and MOTAT. To get there, take the #43, 44, or 45 bus from QE II Sq. ($2.60); all stop just opposite MOTAT. Alternatively, take the NW motorway (16) to the zoo/MOTAT off-ramp, turn right over the motorway, left onto Great North Rd. for MOTAT and right onto Motions Rd. for the zoo.

AUCKLAND ZOO. Auckland's zoo features an impressive rainforest section and African "habitats" including Hippo River and the Pridelands, complete with Zulu huts stalked by lions. The kiwi and tuatara exhibits are worth a look, as are the red pandas and Wallaby Walkabout. The aviary showcases some of the country's most famous indigenous animals. Concerts occur throughout the summer on weekend evenings. *(On Motions Rd. ☎360 3800; www.aucklandzoo.co.nz. Open daily 9:30am-5:30pm; last entry 4:15pm. $18, students and seniors $14, children ages 4-15 $9. Concerts $25, children $10; includes zoo admission.)*

MUSEUM OF TECHNOLOGY AND TRANSPORT (MOTAT). A classic streetcar connects the zoo to MOTAT, where visitors find a collection of steam engines and antique cars and conduct physics experiments. The entrance fee includes **MOTAT II,** an exhibit of classic aircraft and seaplanes 500m past the zoo on Motions Rd. *(805 Great North Rd. ☎815 5800 or 0800 668 286; www.motat.org.nz. Open daily 10am-5pm; last entry 4:30pm. $14, students, children and seniors $7, families $30. Streetcar $2.)*

OTARA

For a distinctive shopping experience, head 20km south of Auckland to the **Otara Markets.** This mainly South Pacific extravaganza has a wide range of stalls selling fresh fruit as well as arts and crafts. *(☎274 0830. Take bus #487 or 497 from Customs St. in Auckland or the East Tamaki off-ramp from the Southern Motorway. Open Sa 6-11am.)*

◪ ADVENTURE ACTIVITIES

BUNGY BOBBING. The **Sky Screamer** hurtles two or three passengers 160m in 1½min. and then lets them bob up and down for another 5min. *(At the corner of Victoria and Albert St. ☎0800 932 8649. Open daily M-Th 9am-10pm, F-Sa 9am-2am, Su 10am-10pm. $40, 2 riders min.)* For a higher thrill, the **Sky Jump** is a controlled 192m base jump off the top of the Sky Tower. *(☎0800 759 586; www.skyjump.co.nz. Open daily 10am-5:30pm. $195, students and backpackers $175, children $145.)*

WHEELING. **Auckland Adventures** leads full-day area cycling tours, some of which include several hours of mountain biking. *(☎379 4545 or 025 855 856; www.aucklandadventures.co.nz. $120).* **Adventure Cycles** rents mountain bikes and touring bikes (p. 81). **4 Track Adventures** guides ATV "safaris" through Woodhill Forest and nearby beaches. *(30min. north of the city. ☎420 8104 or 0800 487 225. Motorbike safaris $135 per 1hr., $195 per 2hr., $235 per 3hr., $40 pickup available in Central Auckland.)*

CLIMBING. **Clip and Climb** is the first indoor climb center in New Zealand. *(610 Dominion Rd., in Balmoral. Take any #25 or 26 bus from Queen St. near St. James. ☎630 5522; www.theroxx.co.nz. Open daily 10am-10pm. Climbs start at $20, children $15.)* If the call of the outdoors stirs your blood, however, try **Vertigo.** The 1½hr. climb up the inside of the Sky Tower ends at the highest view of Auckland, a heart-stopping 270m above ground. *(☎368 1917; www.4vertigo.com.)*

SKYDIVING. **Skydive Auckland** offers tandem jumps from 12,000 ft. *(590 Koheroa Rd., in Mercer, 25min. south of the city. Free round-trip shuttle. ☎373 5778 or 0800 865 867; www.skydiveauckland.com. $250, students $240.)*

CANYONING. **AWOL Adventures** leads 7hr. tours that explore the canyons around Piha. Night trips available. *(☎834 0501 or 0800 462 965. $145 per person.)* **Canyonz** runs full-day trips into the Blue Canyons. *(☎0800 422 696 or 025 294 7724; www.canyonz.co.nz. $175-200 per person.)* Both companies include free pickup.

KAYAKING. **Outdoor Discoveries** leads full-day trips to Rangitoto Island (p. 99), as well as an evening excursion to Brown's Island. *(☎813 3399; www.nzkayak.co.nz.*

Rangitoto $95; Brown's Island $95, with barbeque $125.) The **Little Adventure Company** runs guided tours in the Auckland Harbour and Hauraki Gulf. *(☎0508 529 257 or 021 631 376; Half-day $55, full-day $80. Open Jan.-May.)* Fit romantics might want to head to **Ferg's Kayaks** for a moonlight kayak trip to Rangitoto Island. Ferg also rents in-line skates. *(12 Tamaki Dr. ☎529 2230. In-line skates $15 per hr., $30 per day. Kayaks from $10 per hr. Kayak trips $95. Bookings are essential. Open M-F 9am-8pm, Sa-Su 8am-8pm; in winter M-F 9am-6pm, Sa-Su 8am-6pm.)*

SAILING. Designed to sail in the 1995 America's Cup (but not finished in time), the NZL 40, operated by **SailNZ**, now makes several outings daily, as does the NZL 41. *(☎0800 724 569. 2hr. tour $135 per person, 3hr. "match race" between the 2 boats $195.)* **LOGAN Ponsonby Sailing School** conducts dinghy-sailing courses primarily on weekends. *(☎376 0245; www.pcc.org.nz. 23hr. of lessons $185.)*

DOLPHINS. In conjunction with ongoing research projects, **Dolphin and Whale Safari** runs daily day and evening trips from Pier 3 through the Hauraki Gulf Maritime Park. *(☎/fax 357 6032; www.dolphinexplorer.com. 4-5hr. $105, under 10 $65.)*

HIKING. The **Coast to Coast Walk** starts at the Ferry Building (p. 90) and travels through the city from Waitemata Harbour to Onehunga Beach, home to the first European settlements in Auckland. It passes the Auckland Domain, Mt. Eden Domain, and One Tree Hill on the way. The path is marked each kilometer by blue and yellow signs. *(16km, 4-6hr.)*

VITICULTURE. **Aotearoa Van Coach Tours** conducts half-day and full-day trips to three or four of the Auckland-area wineries. *(☎834 5363 or 025 212 3032. $89-155, depending on the type of trip and group size.)* **Auckland Wine Trail Tours** also offers trips to four vineyards as well as full-day tours that visit six. *(☎630 1540 or 027 227 4924; www.winetrailtours.co.nz. Half-day $95, full day $175-225.)*

PARASAILING. **Flying Kiwi Parasail** has just recently brought its popular aerial experience down from Paihia. Float up 800 ft. for a completely unique view of the city; eye-to-eye with the Sky Tower. *(☎402 6078; www.parasail-nz.co.nz. $70-85.)*

🎵 ENTERTAINMENT

Entertainment in Auckland means more than handles at the corner pub. From ballet to underground theater, its local art scene makes Auckland the culture capital of New Zealand. Check out **The New Zealand Herald** for entertainment info or pick up the monthly **Real Groove** ($3.50). Live music energizes many local joints throughout the week (see **Nightlife**, p. 94). When big bands pass through Auckland, they take the stage at the **North Shore Events Centre** (☎443 8199; www.nseventscentre.co.nz). Check at the mother of all record stores, **Real Groovy**, 438 Queen St., for schedule and ticket info. (☎302 3940; www.realgroovy.co.nz. Open M-Sa 9am-9pm, Su 9am-7pm.)

The highbrow highlights of Auckland's entertainment scene cluster around centrally located Aotea Sq. off Queen St.; known as the **Edge** (☎309 2677; www.the-edge.co.nz), the complex includes the Aotea Centre, the Civic, Auckland Town Hall, and the Force Entertainment Centre. In the **Aotea Centre,** the 2256-seat **ASB Theatre** is the regal home of the **New Zealand Royal Ballet,** the **New Zealand Philharmonic,** and world-class productions; the 186-seat **Herald Theatre** and the **Ticketek** box office are also on site. Opposite Aotea Centre, classical music emanates from the **Auckland Town Hall Concert Chamber,** home to the **Auckland Philharmonic.** Other entertainment options are listed below.

Waikaraka Speedway (☎636 5014; www.aucklandspeedway.co.nz), on Neilson St. in One-hunga, next to Manukau Harbour. Join locals in watching the minor stardom of New Zealand's stock car scene, or as Kiwis call it, the "Big Smoke." The grandstand hosts frequent demolition derbies and "Dirt Cups." Races most Sa and some Su throughout summer.

SkyCity Metro Center, 291-297 Queen St. (☎979 2400; www.villageskycity.co.nz). Hollywood films are shown at this complex which houses **Megascreen,** cinemas, restaurants, bars, and arcades. Tickets $15. SkyCity (☎912 6000) has casinos for both seasoned and novice gamblers. Staff obliges gaming ignorance.

The Classic Comedy and Bar, 321 Queen St. (☎373 4321; www.comedy.co.nz), serves up good laughs. Shows range from amateur open mic on M ($5) to the musings of seasoned pros later in the week. Live shows W-Sa start at 8pm and 10:30pm. Cover $5-25. Open Tu-Sa 7pm-late. Student 2-for-1 drink special on W. Backpacker discounts F-Su.

Civic Theatre (☎817 6001), at the corner of Queen and Wellesley St., hosts music and theater functions, including a range of classic films; the opulent interior is worth a peek.

Maidment Arts Centre, 8 Alfred St. (☎373 7599; www.maidment.auckland.ac.nz), opposite the Auckland University Library. Theater, dance, and music performances are often being performed. The **Auckland Theatre Company** makes its primary home here, but also performs at the Herald and the SkyCity Theatre. Tickets $15-49.

Ponsonby Pool Hall, 106 Ponsonby Rd. (☎360 2356). The classiest pool hall in Auckland, with 2 full-size snooker tables, 4 American 9-ball tables, and 10 English pool tables. $12 per hr. Open daily 11am-1am. Reservations necessary at night.

■ FESTIVALS

In mid-July, the **Auckland International Film Festival** captures the attention of movie buffs with two weeks of screenings from all over the world. (☎307 5000. Tickets $12.50-13.50.) Toward the end of summer, the city comes alive with the arts during the annual **Auckland Festival.** Performances throughout the month-long festival include dance groups, concerts, drama, comedy, visual exhibitions, family events, and "fringe" happenings. Many are free, but a few events require expensive tickets. For two weeks in February, the carnivalesque **HERO Gay and Lesbian Festival** celebrates with theatrical performances, film screenings, and outdoor events including a parade and an all-night dance party. Check **express,** www.gaynz.com, or www.hero.org.nz for the schedule.

■ NIGHTLIFE

PUBS

The pub scene in Auckland picks up in the late afternoon when revelers spill out of the cafes and into happy hour (typically 4-7pm) at the nearest watering hole. Wednesday finds the young crowd packing the posh lounges of **Parnell,** while the **Waterfront** bars are popular on weekends. See the **Food** (p. 87) and **Cafes** (p. 88) sections for other places to enjoy a glass of fine wine or an overflowing pint.

CENTRAL AUCKLAND

Deschlers Bar, 17 High St. (☎379 6811). In this classed-up version of a hometown pub, regulars return for the saxophone beer taps, posh dark surroundings, and live jazz on Th. Happy hour 3-7pm: handles $4 (normally $5). Cocktails $15. Open M-W noon-1am, Th-Sa noon-3am. AmEx/MC/V.

Globe Bar, 3 Darby St. (☎357 3980; www.globebar.co.nz). Any night is a good night at Globe Bar, where locals and backpackers alike push their way between bar stools and pool tables to catch a glimpse of the game on the big-screen TVs. Rotating theme nights with drink specials. Open daily 4pm-late. AmEx/MC/V.

Margarita's, 18 Elliot St. (☎302 2764; www.margaritas.co.nz). Backpackers flock here for the popular, long-lasting happy hour specials (3-9pm; handles $3) and weekly events, including a pool tournament. Upstairs, Chili Lounge is a bit less cramped. Mixed drinks $9-16. Cover F-Sa $5. Open daily 4pm-5am. Open M-Th, Su 3pm-3am and F-Sa 4pm-5am. AmEx/MC/V.

Provedor, Hewlett Packard Bldg. (☎377 1114), on Prince's Wharf. The light-footed crowd grooves to 70s and 80s tunes. Daily happy hour (3-7pm) features $4 house spirits and $4 handles. Open daily 3pm-late. AmEx/MC/V.

Float, Shed 19 (☎307 1354), on Prince's Wharf. Built for the America's Cup 2000, this upscale sports bar features 3 bars, stadium seating around a massive projection screen, a lounge, a restaurant, and excellent views of the harbor. Beer $6-8. Mixed drinks $13-15. Happy hour M-Th 4-7pm with half-price specials. Open M-Th 12:30-3pm, 7-9pm and Fr-Sa 7am-5am. AmEx/MC/V.

Bungalow 8, 48 Market Pl. (☎307 1500; www.bungalow8.co.nz), near the corner of Customs St. and Market Pl. This newly opened lounge features aquariums with tropical fish and a bamboo canopy over the bar. Streetside porch looks onto the harbor. Beer $5-8. Open Tu-Th 4pm-2am, F-Sa 4pm-5am. AmEx/MC/V.

Bellini Bar, 147 Quay St. (☎978 2000), in the Hilton at the end of Prince's Wharf. If you're up for the splurge, this hotel bar has the best waterfront location in the city. Up the stairs, the viewing deck is open to the public during the day. Beer $8. Mixed drinks $18-28. Cigar menu $4-77.50. Open M-F 8am-late, Sa, Su 9am-late. AmEx/MC/V.

Fox's Ale-House and Winery, 85 Customs St. West (☎358 2767), in the Viaduct. This concealed corner bar draws the highest concentration of locals of any Viaduct establishment. Catch up on your cricket with a pint of local brew ($7) and some pub grub ($14-24.50; served daily 11:30am-3pm and 5-9pm). Transforms into a nightclub after 10pm on weekends, with a casual dress code for men.

PONSONBY

S.P.Q.R., 150 Ponsonby Rd. (☎360 1710). Lit by candles and glowing orbs, this spacious cafe-bar attracts a large crowd of mostly male twentysomethings. The name refers to the liberal days of the Roman Republic; anything goes here, even outdoor seating. Pizzas (starting at $22.50) seem cheaper after a few brews ($6.50-9.50) or cocktails ($15.50). Open M-F noon-midnight, Sa-Su 10am-late. AmEx/MC/V.

I NEED A HERO

The cornerstone of gay and lesbian life in Auckland has been the often famous, often infamous HERO Festival since 1989. Having occured in a number of guises, the festival has evolved into two weeks of individual events put on throughout the metropolitan area. Recently, however, both financial and community problems have cropped up, putting a damper on the festival's success.

In 1995, HERO added a parade, which quickly became the highest profile event. But the parade had negative financial effects and was thought of by some members of the the gay community as an event put on solely for the straight community. The festival began to lose support from the Auckland city council as it became further mired in money and planning troubles.

The most recent festivals, however, have seen HERO come out of debt and begin to grow, relying wholly on community involvement for its successes. The HERO name branded on independent events has promoted the widely attended Big Gay Out, a picnic with music, food, and craft stalls, which has become one of the most popular events. Plans are now in the works to bring back the flagship parade to the streets of Auckland in 2009.

For more information check out www.gaynz.com/hero.

Bar de Baz, 153-155 Ponsonby Rd. (☎360 1534). The late-20s crowd that frequents Baz might do so for the sleek lounge, plush bar, and down-and-dirty dancefloor, but no one should miss the view of downtown Auckland. Open Th-F 4pm-late, Sa 6pm-3am. AmEx/MC/V.

Grand Central Entertainment, 126 Ponsonby Rd. (☎360 1260). This hip Ponsonby venue has a bar downstairs and popular acts cycling through upstairs. Open M-Th 4pm-3am, F 4pm-5am, Sa 6pm-5am, Su 6pm-2am. MC/V.

PARNELL

The Paddington, 117 St. George's Bay Rd. (☎309 3586), off the Strand. A local pub to beat all, Parnell's Paddy caters to a young executive crowd. A hotspot F after 5pm. Beer is $6-7 and mixed drinks start at $12. Open daily 10am-late. AmEx/MC/V.

CLUBS

While Auckland's surrounding neighborhoods light up with lively bars, **Central Auckland** dances until dawn. Up on K'Rd., style reigns supreme as clubbers don their favorite shade of black and join the line. Adding color to the scene are the drag queens who come out at night and stay until the next day. Gay nightlife is well integrated into the Auckland scene, and most **K'Road** clubs are gay-friendly. For the skinny on events, the free glossy mag **The Fix** can't be beat. **express** newspaper tracks down the hottest gay and lesbian events ($2.50). Pick both up, as well as special events flyers, at **Beat Merchants,** 31 Victoria St. East (☎302 2328), and at **Real Groovy,** 438 Queen St. (☎302 3940).

 URBAN NINJA. While Auckland residents tend to have a fairly laid-back dress code, Auckland clubs do not. Dress sharp and be prepared to pay a cover.

Khuja Lounge, 536 Queen St. (☎377 3711; www.khujalolunge.co.nz), at the intersection with K'Rd. Lebanese for "melting pot," Khuja draws a multicultural crowd. DJs mix everything from soul to drum and bass. W is *Brisa Luca* with samba and bossa nova. Cocktails $14-18. Cover $5 before midnight, $10 after. Open W-Sa 8pm-late.

Galatos, 17 Galatos St. (☎303 1928; www.galatos.co.nz), just behind K'Rd, off East St. Galatos allows aspiring DJs to rent out the huge dance floor for the right to play their favorites (cover $5 and up) while cranking drum and bass in the basement. Big Kiwi names often cycle through. The upstairs lounge is free—if the bouncer thinks you're cool enough to get in. Open F-Sa 10pm-late.

Asta Club and Lounge, 10A Victoria St, E, near the intersection with Queen St. (www.asta.co.nz). Asta's 2 laquered wood bars, cushy leather furniture, and packed dance floor attract the best-looking young crowd in the city. Cocktails $12-15. No cover. Open Th-Sa 10pm-late.

Urge, 490 K'Rd. (☎307 2155). This gay men's club has a "play area" in the back and features frequent theme nights, including dungeon nights and underwear parties on public holidays. A DJ spins F-Sa. Open Th-Sa 9pm-late.

Kiss Club, 309 K'Rd. (☎303 2726; www.kissnightclub.co.nz). This newly renovated club draws cutting-edge DJs to spin for the music-savvy crowd of K'Rd. Upstairs, **Bacio** has house music and R&B (Th), while the downstairs sees mostly UK hard house and trance. Cover $10-20. Open Tu-Sa 10pm-7am.

The Supper Club, 2 Beresford Sq. (☎300 5040), just behind K'Rd. off Pitt St. Once home to Auckland's public toilets, this curiously shaped club now plays host to Auckland's late-night/early-morning/midday crowd. Be patient: the scene matures around 9am. Seriously. Beer $6.50. Open W-F 3pm-late, Sa 10pm-late.

◪ DAYTRIPS FROM AUCKLAND

NORTH SHORE AND DEVONPORT

Devonport accessible by Fullers Ferry ☎367 9111. Departs M-Th 6:15am-11pm, F-Sa 6:15am-1am, Su 7:15am-10pm; returns M-Th 6:10am-11:30pm, F-Sa 6:10am-1:15am, Su 7:30am-10:30pm. $9, children $4.40. Visitors center: 3 Victoria Rd., next to the Esplanade Hotel. ☎446 0677; www.northshorenz.com. Open daily 8:30am-5pm.

Across a narrow stretch of water just northeast of Central Auckland, the North Shore is home to family beaches, suburban shopping centers, and vast commuter highways. The completion of the Harbour Bridge in 1959 led to development of the area, which was soon expanded into an eight-lane megolith to accommodate the growing crowds. Today, Devonport's Victorian charm and Takapuna's stunning natural beauty both deserve a day's visit. North of Devonport, sprawling suburbs mix easily with the natural beauty of the coast. Meanwhile, the coastline beyond Takapuna is characterized by sandy crescent beaches separated into bays by outcroppings of basalt. Some bays are protected environmental havens, and substantial fines (up to $5000) for pocketing shellfish are enforced; heed the posted signs.

 SHORTCUT. While there is no ferry service between Waiheke, Rangitoto, and Devonport, some people visit Rangitoto and Devonport on the same day. Buy a round-trip ticket to Rangitoto ($20), but get off at Devonport on one of the Rangitoto-Devonport-Auckland ferries for a couple of hours before heading back to Auckland on the more regular Devonport-Auckland ferry.

The easy-on-the-eyes town of Devonport feels kilometers away from the minimalist architecture of urban Auckland, yet it's only a 12min. ferry ride. Though Devonport is a budget-friendly daytrip, its accommodation prices are astronomically high; backpackers should catch the last ferry back to Auckland. Most of Devonport's inviting restaurants and cafes are on **Victoria Road,** the main street leading from the ferry wharf. The **Devonport Visitor Information Centre** is just steps from the wharf, across from the harbor park. A jaunt to any of the three extinct volcanoes in town promises an unparalleled view—**Mt. Victoria** offers a comprehensive panorama, including Central Auckland, Rangitoto, and Browns Island.

The northern beaches also offer unspoiled views of Rangitoto and the Hauraki Gulf. Just north of North Head, **Cheltenham Beach** (a protected area) and **Torpedo Bay** (closer to Devonport) are swimmer-friendly two hours before and after high tide. **Devonport Beach,** near the town, or **Narrow Neck Beach,** around the Takapuna Head, are the beaches of choice for all-day swimming. Narrow Neck Beach harbors the recently restored **Fort Takapuna Historic Reserve,** home to a group of old military buildings and parks. Both Narrow Neck Beach and the summit of **North Head Historic Reserve,** once an important lookout and defense site for the Maori and later for the British, provide million-dollar views of the **Hauraki Gulf** and the coastline. The military tunnels on the north and south sides of the hill are open to the public daily 8am-8pm. The broad black sands of **St. Leonard's Beach** and the neighboring **Takapuna Beach** are popular local sunning spots. A coastal walk from Takapuna north along **Thorne Bay** to **Milford Beach** features slick volcanic rock formations and the manmade **Algie's Castle** with battlements from the 1920s. Nearby **Long Bay** is a regional park and marine reserve. Jutting off into the open sea from the top of Long Bay is the lofty **Whangaparaoa Peninsula,** where you can bask in the awe-inspiring views of Gulf Harbour. Town tours in Devonport are popular, particularly the **Devonport Explorer**

AUCKLAND AND AROUND

Bus, which culminates its one-hour tour of Devonport with a stop at the summit of Mt. Victoria. (☎357 6366 or 0800 868 774. Departs from the wharf daily every hr. 10:25am-3:25pm. $20. Purchase tickets at the Ferry Building or onboard.)

THE WAITAKERE RANGES

Buses from Auckland go to Titirangi, 6km down the road, but getting there without a car is nearly impossible. While Let's Go does not recommend it, would-be hitchhikers can first catch a bus to Titirangi. A safer option is the Piha Surf Shuttle, which runs from Auckland to Piha in summer (☎627 2644; www.surfshuttle.co.nz. Departs 8:30am, returns 4pm. $50 roundtrip, $30 one-way). Arataki Visitors Centre, on Scenic Dr./Rte. 24 past Shaw Rd., can help you plan the trip. (☎366 2000 or 0800 806 040; www.arc.govt.nz/arc/auckland-regional-parks/arataki. Open daily Sept.-Apr. 9am-5pm; May-Aug. M-F 10am-4pm, Sa-Su 9am-5pm.)

Unspoiled and undertouristed, the Waitakeres await those exhausted by Auckland's frenzied pace. Lying between **Manukau Harbour** and the **Tasman Sea,** the Waitakeres contain over 250km of walking and tramping tracks through lush, subtropical rainforest.

If you have a car, driving along the coast offers access to some top-notch beaches. **Karekare,** the setting for *The Piano,* is the most scenic—a multi-tiered waterfall is accessible by a short walk from the parking lot. On a hot summer's day, you can burn your feet on the black sands of **Piha,** farther north. Piha's world-class surf attracts expert boarders in summer, when conditions are best. **Piha Surf,** located a stone's throw from the beach at 122 Seaview Rd., is a budget surfer's dream. The friendly owners will rent you a board, give you a lesson, and even put a roof over your head (☎812 8723; www.pihasurf.co.nz. Surf boards $25 per 3hr., $35 per day; surfing lessons $80 per 2hr. lesson; small trailers with refrigerator, stove, and TV, $30 per night, $25 for stays of more than one night). At the southern tip of the Waitakeres, at the ocean entrance to Manukau Harbour, is **Whatipu,** home to rich ocean fishing and secret sea caves. Back along the harbor entrance with the sandbars lie **Cornwallis** and **Huia,** two beaches with excellent picnic potential and calm waters for swimming. **Auckland Adventures** (see **Wheeling,** p. 92) guides treks and mountain bike tours to Muriwai Beach where 700 species of birds, including the rare **gannet** colony, reside. (☎379 4545 or 025 855 856. Full-day tours $120.)

HAURAKI GULF

Natural wonders lie a short jaunt from downtown Auckland in Hauraki Gulf, which consists of 57 islands. Volcanic Rangitoto makes for an educational daytrip through the enchanting forests of Pohutukawa, while Waiheke harbors an artsy vacation community. Great Barrier Island appeals with its lack of traffic, crowds, and electricity, as well as its pristine beaches. Another island worth a look is **Tiritiri Matangi,** an uninhabited bird and plant sanctuary, protected since February 2000. **360 Discovery** runs round-trip boats from Auckland that allow for a day on Tiritiri. (☎0800 888 006. 1½hr.; departs Auckland W-Su 9am, departs Tiritiri 4:50pm; $59, under 15 $28.) Volunteers run guided walks for visitors, proceeds from which go to fund the conservation project. ($5, under 15 $2.50.) The DOC also runs a **bunkhouse** ❷ on the island, which is often booked months in advance. (☎476 0010. $20, under 15 $15.) The Fullers **Harbour Cruise** tours the Auckland harbour, Devonport, and the New Zealand naval base. The full-day **Rangitoto Ferry Cruise** stops at Rangitoto Island and Devonport (☎367 9102 or 0800 385 5377; www.fullers.co.nz. Harbor Cruise 1½hr.; 2 per day; $30, under 15 $15.)

RANGITOTO ISLAND ☎09

Though the given Maori name, *Te Rangi i totongia a Tamatekapua* ("The Day the Blood of Tamatekapua was Shed") proved too much of a tongue-twister for vacationing colonials, Rangitoto stuck. The island was formed by a series of volcanic eruptions that ended about 500 years ago. It wasn't until 1854, however, that the Crown took notice of Rangitoto and shelled out £15 for what then seemed a mere lump of rock. The island has since become a premier hiking and picnicking spot for Auckland daytrippers, with "bach" (traditional New Zealand holiday homes) dating back to the 1920s. Rangitoto's most popular attraction is the **Summit Walk** (2hr. round-trip), which meanders through arboreal glens and lunar fields of volcanic rock. During the summer, walking the track is akin to hiking on charcoal briquettes, so be sure to wear solid shoes and a hat. At the top, you can take a peek into the **crater**. The summit rewards with a 360° view of Auckland, Great Barrier Island, and the Coromandel Peninsula. The **lava caves** are off a well-marked side trail (20min. round-trip); bring a flashlight and wear durable clothes if you plan to explore these jagged passageways. **Fullers** runs a two-hour **Volcanic Explorer Tour** for those who don't want to walk the whole way; the narrated 4WD tram ride drops passengers at the base of the 900m boardwalk that leads to the summit. (Tours run 2-3 per day Nov.-Mar. daily 9:15am-12:15pm; Apr.-Oct. W-Su 9:15am-12:15pm. Departs when the ferries from Auckland arrive. $50, under 15 $26; includes round-trip ferry.) Another worthwhile track leads from the summit to **Islington Bay** and a series of secluded swimming beaches. The Auckland **DOC office** (p. 81) has more info on local hikes. Be sure to check times for the last ferry (usually 5pm) so you're not stuck for the night.

Fit folks can **kayak** to Rangitoto (p. 92), but most take the ferry. Fullers runs to Rangitoto from just behind the Ferry Building. (☎367 9111. 20-30 min.; 3 per day; round-trip $20, under 15 $11.) The only **campsite ❶** is located at Home Bay on adjacent Motutapu Island. Facilities include toilets, running water, and barbeque pits. (Book with DOC. Tent sites $5 per person, children $2.50.)

WAIHEKE ISLAND ☎09

Waiheke's population of 7500 more than quadruples during peak tourism seasons. With a stunning coastline, annual jazz festival, 26 first-rate vineyards, and a vibrant art scene, Waiheke offers travelers a respite from Auckland's high-energy scene.

THE LOCAL STORY

A VOLCANO AWAY FROM HOME

Although it's no longer possible to spend the night on Rangitoto, the barren volcanic island was once a vacation paradise for Kiwis. The 1920s and 30s witnessed the construction of "baches," traditional holiday houses of the rising middle class. These simple private dwellings often consisted of little more than a roof and one or two small rooms, with outdoors cooking pits and longdrop toilets. Built from whatever building materials were cheap and available, many baches were cobbled together from recycled materials such as fibrolite (asbestos) or from the salvaged remains of shipwrecks.

The modesty of the baches on Rangitoto helped foster community. Neighbors often lent each other a hand with the heavy work of building and maintaining their homes away from home. Evenings in the settlements, which consisted a group of baches clustered around communal facilities such as swimming pools, community halls, and tennis courts, were spent playing cards or singing songs under the light of a gas lamp.

Though construction of baches on Rangitoto Island was banned in 1937, several of the distinctive homes are still standing. For more information on how to see the baches contact the island's Historic Conservation Trust (☎634 1348 or 445 1894).

☞ TRANSPORTATION

Ferries: Fullers (☎367 9102) departs Waiheke's Matiatia Bay for Aucklan3d, sometimes via Devonport (35-40min.; 14-20 per day; round-trip $28.50, under 15 $14.30). **Subritzky** (☎300 5900) also offers passenger and car ferries from Half Moon Bay to Kennedy Point (1hr.; 11 per day; round-trip $28.50, students and seniors $24.50, under 15 $15.50. Cars with up to 4 passengers $125 round trip.

Public Transportation: Fullers Waiheke Bus Company (☎372 8823) meets all ferries and loops around the island. $1-4; day pass $8. Fullers also offers a comprehensive **Island Explorer Tour** (10am and noon; $42) which includes round-trip ferry, a 1½hr. island tour, and an all-day bus pass good on any island bus.

Taxis: Waiheke Taxi (☎372 8038) and **Waiheke Island and Taxi Tours** (☎372 9777).

Car and Scooter Rental: Waiheke Rental Cars (☎372 8635; www.waihekerental-cars.co.nz), at the Matiatia Wharf carpark. Cars/SUVs/Vans $50-75 per day, $0.60 per km. Scooters $40 per day. Open daily 8am-5pm. **Waiheke Auto Rentals** (☎372 8998; www.waiheke.co.nz), also at the carpark. Cars/station wagons/mini-buses $50-75 per day, $0.60 per km. Open daily 8am-5pm.

Bike Rental: Waiheke Bike Hire (☎372 7937; www.4waiheke.co.nz/bikehire.htm), at the Matiatia Wharf carpark. Full-day $30, 2 days $45. Open daily dawn-dusk. **Attitude Rentals** (☎372 8767 or 0274 728 767), also at the carpark, rents "motor-assisted" bikes. Half-day $25, full-day $35. Open daily dawn-dusk.

Hitchhiking: Although *Let's Go* does not recommend it, hitchers report success. Waiheke islanders are a charitable bunch, though winding roads can make it hard to find a good spot to stop, and the small population means little traffic.

◪ ⁊ ORIENTATION AND PRACTICAL INFORMATION

The passenger ferry docks at **Matiatia Bay.** A 1km uphill walk (or a 5min. bus ride; see p. 100) takes you to **Oneroa,** the island's main town and the only one with an interesting strip of shops and cafes (along Ocean View Rd.). Other island "centers" include **Surfdale** and **Ostend** (both southeast of Oneroa, roughly 2km and 4km, respectively), **Onetangi** (7km directly east), and **Palm Beach** (4km northeast).

Visitors Center: Waiheke Island i-Site, 2 Korara Rd. (☎372 1234), in the Artworks Centre in Oneroa. Island maps $1. Luggage storage $2 per bag. Internet $5 per hr. Open daily 9am-5pm.

Banks and Currency Exchange: ANZ, 112 Ocean View Rd. (☎372 1280), in Oneroa has an **ATM.** Open M-Tu and Th-F 9am-4:30pm, W 9:30am-4:30pm.

Police: 100 Ocean View Rd. (☎372 1150), in Oneroa.

Medical Services: Centers in **Ostend** (☎372 5005) and **Oneroa** (☎372 8756). The local **pharmacy** is **Waiheke Pharmacy,** 120 Ocean View Rd. (☎372 8312), in Oneroa. Open M-Sa 9am-5:30pm.

Internet Access: The **Waiheke i-Site** offers web access for $5 per hr.

Post Office: 128 Ocean View Rd. (☎372 1026), in Oneroa. Open M-F 8:30am-5pm, Sa 9am-noon.

⌂ ⌂ ACCOMMODATIONS AND CAMPING

All accommodations are a long, hilly walk from the ferry docks. Luckily, island bus service is cheap and extensive; ask drivers or fellow riders when to get off. **Campers** can head out to the **Whakanewha Regional Park ❶** campsite on the southeast side of Oneroa. (☎303 1530. Reservations required. $10 per person, under 18 $5.) Head to **Rock Gas**, 35-37 Tahi Rd., in Ostend for camping supplies. (☎372 3606. Open M-F 8am-5pm, Sa-Su 9am-3pm.)

▨ Hekerua Lodge (BBH), 11 Hekerua Rd. (☎372 8990; www.hekerualodge.co.nz). Take the backpackers track just beyond Little Oneroa Beach, a 1.3km walk from Oneroa along Ocean View Rd. This cabin hideaway is tucked into a plot of native bush, just 5min. from the beach. House music (the owner is an aficionado) can usually be heard around its decks and pool. Jacuzzi. Linen $5. Reception 8am-1pm and 4-8pm. Dorms from $23; women-only dorm $25; singles $45; doubles and twins $75; triples $110; quads $120. Tent sites $15. Ask about discounts on long dorm stays. AmEx/MC/V. ❷

Waiheke Island Hostel (YHA), 419 Sea View Rd. (☎372 8971; www.waihekehostel.co.nz), on the corner of 7th Ave. in Onetangi. Up the long staircase from Onetangi Beach. Brightly colored barracks might not be as glamorous as the Hekerua, but the view of the coast is a worthwhile trade-off. Dorms $24; doubles $54-64. AmEx/MC. ❷

◪ FOOD

Ostend's **Woolworths** can take the sting out of Waiheke's costly restaurant scene. (☎372 2103. Open daily 7am-9pm.) There are also general stores in each town.

▨ The Lazy Lounge Cafe, 139 Ocean View Rd. (☎372 5132; www.thelazylounge.com), in Oneroa. This cool and breezy bungalow lords over the top of Ocean View Rd. Eclectic menu garners rave reviews, including the nachos ($13) and Thai chicken salad ($16). Pizza $16-22. Open M-Th, Su 8am-6pm, F-Sa 8am-late. AmEx/MC/V. ❷

Vino Vino, 153 Ocean View Rd. (☎372 9888; www.vinovino.co.nz), behind Spice in Oneroa. Terrace views and an open fire in winter create a posh atmosphere worth the splurge. Mains $18-30. Open daily noon-3:30pm and 6:30pm-late. AmEx/MC/V. ❸

Oneroa Fish & Chips, 29 Waikare Rd. (☎372 8752), just off Ocean View Rd. in Oneroa. The no frills store front shells out deep-fried fish ($3.50), chips ($3.50), and burgers ($6.50-12). Take it to go—there's only one picnic table out front. Open Tu-Th and Su noon-8pm, F-Sa noon-9pm. MC/V. ❶

Spice, 153 Ocean View Rd. (☎372 7659), in Oneroa. Tiny street-side spot serves coffee ($3.50) and a rotating breakfast menu ($5-18). Open daily 8am-4pm. MC/V. ❷

◉ ⚠ SIGHTS AND OUTDOOR ACTIVITIES

The **Montana Jazz Festival** (☎372 5301; www.waihekejazz.co.nz) shakes things up every Easter weekend, with performances in Auckland and on the island. The festival features the best of Kiwi jazz as well as big names from New Orleans. With five days and 22 venues, it's usually possible to get tickets at the last minute, though true fans may want to book several months ahead for the best shows ($25-35), and more importantly, to get a bed on the island. The relatively young **Waiheke Island Wine Festival** celebrates the island's vineyard tradition with live music, good food, and of course the wine in early February. A few of the vineyards themselves serve as the idyllic venues for the events. (☎372 1324 for information; www.waihekewinefestival.co.nz. $65, includes shuttle bus between venues, a wine glass and glass holder, a complimentary glass of wine, and all-day concerts at each venue.) Less internationally renowned though no less popular, the **Ostend Market** appears every Saturday at the corner of Ostend Rd. and Belgium St. Local vendors hawk goods including pottery, food, books, with some of the proceeds going to the Waiheke Community Childcare Centre. (Open Sa 8:30am-12:30pm.)

TIRITIRI TWEET TWEET

There are many opportunities to volunteer to preserve New Zealand's natural splendor. You need not venture far from Auckland, however, to work for a project of great importance to the Department of Conservation. Tiritiri Matangi Island sits in the Hauraki Gulf. It currently serves as a bird sanctuary, protecting many of New Zealand's endangered aviary population, such as the spotted kiwi, takahe, and kokako.

The spotted kiwi lives only on off-shore islands and is more severely endangered than its brown cousin. The takahe is so rare that it was thought to be extinct for 40 years until it was rediscovered in 1948. Both of these species are currently bred in a small handful of locations.

Travelers of any age and qualification can go to the island for a number of days or weeks to volunteer and, depending on the length of their stay, can receive free accommodation in the department's bunkhouse. The reservation project has been successful in increasing bird populations, but volunteers are still needed for a number of jobs, including filling water troughs, weeding, working in the nursery, and leading tours for day visitors. *For more information on volunteering call ☎307 4853, check out www.123.co.nz/tiri, or email aucklandvolunteer@doc.govt.nz. Visitors can take daytrips to Tiritiri daily from Auckland Harbour ($15).*

BEACHES. Beaches surround Waiheke, but only the island's northern side has white sand. **Oneroa Beach,** just downhill from the town of the same name, is a convenient place to soak up some rays. A bit farther east, **Little Oneroa Beach** is popular with families. Between these two beaches lie two **isolated coves,** which are both beach-accessible at low tide; at high tide, follow the paths over the rocks. **Palm Beach** is another enticing spot, though **Onetangi Beach,** the island's largest stretch of sand, draws the most sunbathers. Flout your tan lines at the western (to the left if you're facing the water), clothing-optional ends of both of these beaches.

THE ARTS. Waiheke's creative nerve centers on the **Artworks Centre** in Oneroa, home to the **Waiheke Community Art Gallery,** which displays varied works of New Zealand artists. *(2 Korora Rd. ☎372 9907. Open daily 10am-4pm.)* The **Artworks Theatre** brings the best of the West End and Broadway to the Hauraki Gulf over the summer. *(☎372 2941.)* **Art on Waiheke,** a free brochure available at the i-Site, includes a map of the island's two dozen other galleries. Aimed at true art buffs, **Ananda Tours** arranges visits to the the homes and studios of local artists *(☎372 7530; www.ananda.co.nz. 4hr. $75; includes a glass of Waiheke wine.)*

KAYAKING. Gulf Adventures has bred at least one kayaking champion (the owners' son is one of New Zealand's top paddlers) and now offers guided trips and rentals in single kayaks only. *(☎372 7262 or 021 667 262. Rentals $45 per day; transport included. 1-3hr. tours $35-55, depending on number of people. $5 backpacker discount.)* **Ross Adventures** runs guided kayaking tours at all hours. *(☎372 5550; www.kayakwaiheke.co.nz. Half-day $70, full-day $135. Moonlight trips $70. Book in advance.)*

WINE TASTINGS AND TOURS. There are 26 vineyards on Waiheke Island; several open regularly to the public for tours and tastings. **Stonyridge Vineyard** is renowned for its Larose. *(☎372 8822. 45min. tours Sa-Su 11:30am. $10.)* **Te Whau Vineyard** offers the widest wine selection in New Zealand. *(☎372 7191. Tastings Nov.-Mar. M and W-Su 11am-5pm; Apr.-Sept. Sa-Su 11am-4:30pm. $3 per variety.)* For a more complete sampling of the local varietals, consider taking a tour. **Fullers' Vineyard Explorer tour** visits three vineyards. *(☎367 9102. 3hr. Nov.-Mar. daily; Apr.-Oct. Sa-Su. $67.50; includes round-trip ferry.)* **Jaguar Tours** swings by your choice of one, two, or three vineyards. *(☎372 7312; www.wiahekejaguartours.co.nz. 1 vineyard $35, 2 $45, 3 $55.)*

WALKS. Two free i-Site pamphlets outline walking routes on Waiheke; *Whakanewha Regional Park Visitors Guide* includes a map of the 270-hectare Regional Park, southeast of Oneroa, while *Waiheke*

Island Walkways describes paths throughout the entire island. History buffs should bike or take a taxi to the **Stony Batter Historic Reserve,** a World War II-era fortress with an extensive underground system of tunnels and chambers located at the northeast end of the island. (*☎027 305 2772 or 027 345 1607; www.geocities.com/stonybatter- waiheke. Admission $5. Guided tours available for an additional $5. Book 24hr. in advance.*)

GREAT BARRIER ISLAND ☎09

As you grab a ferry to the largest and most remote of the Hauraki Gulf islands (pop. 850), check your reliance on modernity at the wharf. Maintaining few connections with the outside world, the island is an isolated haven of deep forests and marshlands, silky white beaches, and blissful silence. Plan to spend at least a night on the island—it's nearly impossible as a daytrip. And take some cash with you since there are **no banks or ATMs,** though most places accept credit cards.

⌐ TRANSPORTATION

Flights: Great Barrier Airlines (☎275 9120 or 0800 900 600; www.greatbarrierai-rlines.co.nz) from Claris Airport to: **Auckland** (35min., 3 per day, round-trip $152-192, depending on how early you book); **Whangarei** (30min., F and Su 2 per day, round-trip $198); **Whitianga** (30min., F and Su 2 per day, round-trip $198). **Great Barrier Xpress,** operated by Mountain Air (☎0800 222 123; www.mountainair.co.nz) flies to **Auckland** (35min., 3-4 per day, round-trip $155-190).

Ferries: Fullers (☎367 9111; www.fullers.co.nz) runs passenger ferries to Tryphena during the height of summer and on holiday weekends. 2½hr. Round-trip $105, children $50. **Sea Link,** 45 Jellicoe St. (☎300 5900; www.sealink.co.nz), makes more frequent trips in a car ferry that departs from Wynyard Wharf, just west of the Viaduct, from late Oct. to Feb. 4hr. Round trip $105, children $72. Cars from $218 (driver included).

> **! ROUGH WATERS.** The strong currents of the Colville Channel can make the ferry crossing to Great Barrier Island quite rough. Come prepared with motion sickness medication or an iron stomach.

Taxis and Shuttles: Hired buses and taxis can be found at the ferry terminals. **Great Barrier Travel** (☎429 0474; www.greatbarriertravel.co.nz) runs shuttles to Port Fitzroy. The shuttle departs Tryphena at 9:30am and drops hikers off at various trail-heads by request. It picks up hikers on its way back from Port Fitzroy. Passes $35, $49 for a weekend, $59 for 5 days. Free pickup.

Car Rental: GBI Rent-a-car (☎429 0062; www.greatbarrierisland.co.nz), at the Claris Airfield. Cars from $50 per day. Mini-moke (4-seat golf cart) $80 per day. Free transfer and pickup. **Better Bargain Rentals** (☎429 0424 or 0800 426 4832), in Tryphena and Port Fitzroy. $55-80 per day. Free transfer and pickup. **Aotea Transport Services** (☎0800 426 832), also in Tryphena and Port Fitzroy, rents more expensive models. $70-99 per day. Free transfer and pickup.

Bike Rental: GBI Rent-a-car (see above) also hires out mountain bikes ($30 per day) and boogie boards ($15 per day) for those inclined to leave the car behind.

Hitchhiking: Although *Let's Go* does not recommend hitching, cars will often stop to pick up hitchers. However, there is little traffic on the island.

✳ ⁊ ORIENTATION AND PRACTICAL INFORMATION

Port Fitzroy in the north is the island's largest settlement, but most backpackers congregate on the southern half of the island, around **Claris** (home to the airfield)

AUCKLAND AND AROUND

and, farther south, **Tryphena** (home to ferry docks). Tryphena encompasses the towns of Mulberry Grove and Pah Beach. Northwest of Claris, **Whangaparapara** is the island's other significant outpost. Buses around the island are scarce and it's easiest to get around with a rented car. Also, there is very little electric light after sunset, so bring a **flashlight** if you're planning on staying overnight.

Visitors Centers: With the indefinite closing of the Great Barrier Island Visitor Center in 2006, there is only one official information center for tourists on the island. The **DOC Field Centre** (☎429 0044), at Akapoua Bay in Port Fitzroy, operates several campsites and provides guidance to hikers. Open M-F 8am-4:30pm. Both **Great Barrier Travel** and **GBI Rent-a-car** (see **Transportation,** p. 79) are happy to provide information to tourists, though they tend to promote their own services.

Laundromat: Sunset Lodge (☎429 0051), in Mulberry Grove. Self-service wash $4, dry $4. Open M-Sa 9am-2:30pm, Su 9am-1pm. **Claris Laundromat** (☎429 0916), in Claris next to the post office. Wash $6, dry $6. Open M-Sa 8am-5:30pm, Su 9am-5pm.

Police: (☎429 0343 or ☎111), on Hector Sanderson Rd. in Claris. Open M-F 8am-4pm.

Medical Services: Community Health Centre (☎429 0356), in Claris by the airfield. Open daily 9am-4pm by appointment.

Great Barrier Pharmacy (☎429 0006), just outside Claris. Open M-Tu, Th-F 8:45am-1:30pm, W 8:45am-12:30pm, Sa during high season. After hours call (☎429 0021).

Internet: Some hostels have Internet access and will let non-guests purchase time. **Claris Texas Cafe** has one computer ($3 per 15min.). Open daily 8am-4pm. You can also try **Barrier Groove** in the Tryphena Stonewall Center. Open daily 10am-4pm.

Post Offices: Pigeon Post (☎429 0242), 129 Hector Sanderson Rd. in Claris. Open M-F 8:30am-4pm, Sa-Su 10am-3pm. **Outpost** (☎429 0610), in the Stonewall Center on Blackwell Dr. just off Pah Beach in Tryphena. Open daily 10am-4pm.

⌂⌂ ACCOMMODATIONS AND CAMPING

December and January draw hostel-filling crowds. The **DOC** ❶ (☎429 0044) runs six **campsites** ($9, under 15 $4.50), and a hut ($10, under 18 $5). **Puriri Bay** ❶, north of Pah Beach, has the only **campsite** with hot showers. (☎429 0184. Adults $9, children $5.) **Mickey's** ❶ (☎4290 140), in Awana, is another non-DOC campsite.

The Stray Possum Lodge (☎429 0109; www.straypossum.co.nz), Cape Barrier Rd., 25min. walk from the ferry dock. Tucked into a grove, this hostel has an excellent restaurant. Dorms $23; doubles $70; 6-person chalets $130; tent sites $12. MC/V. ❷

Pohutukawa Lodge (☎429 0211; www.currachirishpub.com), in Pah Beach. Homey rooms sit beside a sunny garden. Talented musicians are occasionally offered free room in exchange for performances at the adjoining Currach Irish pub. Dorms $25 (linen included); doubles $60; lodge rooms $120. Campsites $15. MC/V. ❷

Medlands Beach Backpackers and Villas (☎429 0320; www.medlandsbeach.com), between Claris and Tryphena, 5min. from Medlands Beach. With free boogie boards and beach views, Medlands is a good location for beach-bound travelers. Dorms from $25; doubles from $70; 4-person cabins $200. Cash only. ❷

⬙ FOOD

There are small **grocery stores** in Mulberry Grove, Pah Beach, Claris, Whangaparapara, and Port Fitzroy, though they are more expensive than in Auckland.

The Stray (☎429 0109; www.straypossum.co.nz), at the Stray Possum Lodge. One of the only sit-down locales on the island, this friendly restaurant/bar serves both locals and guests—of other lodges as well. Enjoy a beer ($4) with your new closest friends in the intimate setting. Music often to follow. Pizzas $11.50. Burgers $9.50. Mussel special $14.50. Open 6pm-late. Kitchen until 9pm. MC/V. ❸

Angsana Thai Restaurant (☎429 0272), 63 Gray Rd., in Claris. Heaping plates of traditional Thai favorites like stir-fry chicken and cashew nuts ($24) give the island some much-needed ethnic flair. Main dishes $24. MC/V. ❸

Claris Texas Cafe (☎429 0811), in Claris. Look for the sign on the main road for the island's most inventive fare. Thick mussel chowder ($9.50), and hearty sandwiches ($9) make the menu. Internet $3 per 15min. Open daily 8am-4pm. MC/V. ❷

The Currach Irish Pub (☎429 0211; www.currachirishpub.com), in Pah Beach. Currach occupies one of the original homesteads in Tryphena, featuring classic jam sessions (Th nights) and a rotating roster of activities throughout the rest of the week. Excellent pub fare with stellar burgers from $12. Death by Chocolate ($8.50) is the best way to go. Veggie options. Mains $16.50-24. Open daily 9am-late. Kitchen from 4pm. MC/V. ❸

◔ 𝕄 SIGHTS AND OUTDOOR ACTIVITIES

The Barrier's main draws are its endless beaches and undisturbed nature—more than half of the island's land belongs to the DOC. East coast beaches facing the South Pacific earn points with surfers. With its graceful dunes, sapphire sea, and blissful breezes, **Medlands Beach** is the island's most popular. Other east coast beaches include: **Kaitoke, Awana, Haratonga,** and **Whangapoua Beaches,** all equally alluring and secluded. The west coast beaches are calmer and popular among yachtsmen, and those in **Tryphena Harbour**—Puriri Bay, Pah Beach, and Mulberry Grove—are good for snorkeling.

For boot-bound travelers, there are dozens of tracks for all abilities. Pick up the indispensable **DOC guide map** ($2) from a visitors center or the DOC office. The easy **Kaitoke Hot Springs Track** (2hr. round-trip) leads to a set of steamy swimming holes. Another non-strenuous, albeit longer, trek is the **Harataonga/ Okiwi Coastal Walkway** (5hr. one-way), which follows the old road. The **Te Ahumata Track** (2hr. round-trip), also known as the "White Cliffs Walk" for the quartz-studded stream beds along the way, climbs gradually to a 398m summit that offers 360° views of the ocean, Mt. Hobson, and the Coromandel. The last part is a fairly challenging, steep hike. Look out for mine shafts. Day hikers often combine the Te Ahumata and Kaitoke tracks and end up at the hot springs (4-5hr.). Significantly more challenging routes are the **Kaiaraara** and **Palmers Tracks** (5hr. round-trip in conjunction), which ascend steeply through subalpine forest to the island's highest point, 621m **Mt. Hobson (Hirakimata).**

For seafaring parties, **Aotea Kayaks,** in Mulberry Grove, runs a variety of guided kayak tours. (☎429 0664. Free pickup. 2hr. trip $30; 4-5hr. trip with snorkeling $55; 6hr. trip with fishing $75; night trip $50; multi-day trip $85 per day. Kayaks $35 per day.) **GBI Adventure Horsetreks,** in Nedlands, rides along the beach and road. (☎429 0274. $40 for 1hr. trek.) Great Barrier's network of rugged roads also makes for superb **mountain biking;** the well-graded **Forest Road,** which runs between Whangaparapara and Kaiaraara and is closed to all non-DOC vehicles, is a favorite ride.

NORTHLAND

Home to the first landings of legendary explorers Kupe and Captain Cook, Northland is rich with the history of New Zealand's Maori and European cultures. The sparkling Bay of Islands on the east coast harbors New Zealand's oldest settlements and is admired by tourists and residents alike for its historical import—most notably as the site of the signing of the Treaty of Waitangi. The quiet west coast shelters the semi-tropical Kaipara and Hokianga Harbours. At the terminus of North Island, the empty stretch of Ninety Mile Beach offers a welcome retreat for travelers willing to forego the trappings of predictability and convenience.

⬛NORTHLAND HIGHLIGHTS

GET WET on the shores of **Poor Knights Islands** (p. 110); the world-class scuba diving here made Jacques Cousteau's top 10 list.

GO WILD and say a prayer as you submit yourself to a parasail in **Paihia** (p. 111).

BUT DON'T GO BROKE in **Kerikeri** (p. 117), where you can pick kiwifruit as a temporary laborer.

▐ TRANSPORTATION IN NORTHLAND

Rent a **car** if you can; it will allow you to explore the **Twin Coast Discovery Highway** (SH1, SH10, and SH12) at your own pace, especially the western and interior regions, which are hard to access. But beware; gas pumps are rare when away from tourist towns. If you travel by bus, strongly consider buying a pass that lets you travel at your discretion. *Let's Go* doesn't recommend hitchhiking, and **hitchers** on the east coast, north of the Bay of Islands report long waits and little success. On the west coast, SH12 is the road less traveled, but the locals are more accommodating.

🗚TIP **SHACK UP.** Campers should note that annual hut passes do not apply in the Northland region. Instead, you must book in advance for all huts and lodges or pray that a blight drives out the fruit pickers.

WHANGAREI ☎ 09

The journey to Whangarei (FAIN-ga-ray; pop. 48,000), a 2½hr. drive north of Auckland, is a quiet and popular escape from frenzy of Auckland. Often neglected by backpackers eager to hit Paihia, Whangarei is the largest city in the area, offering a base for nearby beaches, scuba diving, fishing, kayaking, and the obligatory grocery stock-up before heading into the most remote regions of Northland.

▐ TRANSPORTATION

Buses: The bus stop is across from **Northland Coach and Travel,** 3C Bank St., near Walton St. Open M-F 8am-5pm, Sa-Su 8:30am-2:30pm. **Northliner** (☎438 3206), **Inter-City** (☎623 1503), and **Newmans** (☎438 2653) head to **Auckland** (3hr., 10 per day, $37) and **Kaitaia** (4hr., 1 per day, $45) via **Paihia** (1hr., 3 per day, $24). **Whangarei Bus Services** (☎438 6005) stops on Rose St., just off Bank St., and provides transport to the hospital and airport ($2).

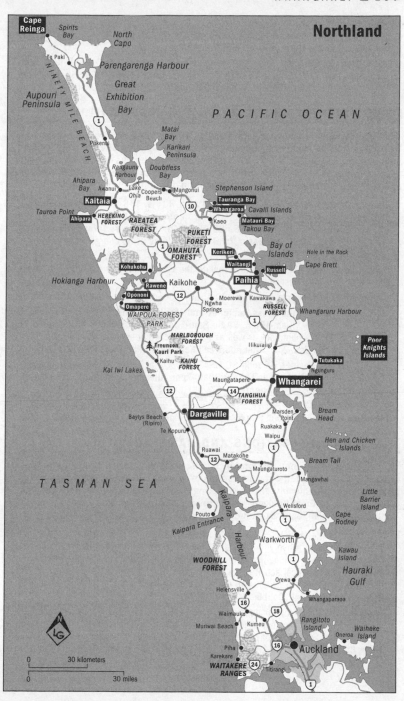

Northland

Taxis: A1 Cabs (☎438 3377) runs 24hr.

Car Rental: Rent-a-Cheepy, 69 Otaika Rd. (☎438 7373). From $35 per day. **Budget** (☎438 7292) and **Hertz** (☎438 9790) have offices on Water St.

Hitchhiking: Though *Let's Go* doesn't recommend it, hitching to Auckland is reputed to be easiest from the Whangarei i-Site in Tarewa Park; those heading to the Bay of Islands often thumb it on SH1 (Western Hills Dr.) before traffic picks up to 70kph.

■■ 🔢 ORIENTATION AND PRACTICAL INFORMATION

Whangarei wraps around **Whangarei Harbour,** 167km north of Auckland up **SH1** on the east coast. The main drag, **Bank Street,** bisects **Cameron Street** at a pedestrian mall that buzzes during the day; the surrounding four blocks contain the majority of restaurants and bars. **Hatea Drive** runs north from the basin. Moneyed tourists and yachtsmen gravitate toward the **Town Basin** development by the harbor.

Visitors Center: Whangarei i-Site, 92 Otaika Rd. (☎438 1079; www.whangare-inz.org.nz), in Tarewa Park, at the southern entrance to the city. Internet $1 per 10min. Open M-F 8:30am-5pm, Sa-Su 10am-4pm. **Quayside Information Centre** (☎438 3993), in the Town Basin, books reservations at no charge. Internet $2 per 10 min. Open daily 9am-5pm.

Banks: Banks with **ATMs** proliferate toward the city center. You can find two at the corner of Bank and Rust St.

Police: 91-97 Lower Cameron St. (☎430 4500). For emergencies, call ☎111.

Medical Services: White Cross Accident and Medical Clinic, 121 Bank St. (☎430 0046). Open M-F 7:30am-10pm, Sa-Su 8am-10pm. **Orrs Unichem,** 48 Cameron St. (☎438 3113), is a pharmacy as well as a fully stocked beauty supply store. Open M-F 8:30am-5pm, Sa 9am-2pm. After hours call **Kensington Pharmacy** (☎437 3722).

Internet Access: Easinet, 46 John St. (☎430 0930), at Robert St., allows laptop connections. $1 per 20min. Open M-Sa 9:30am-7pm. **Klosenet,** next door at 34 John St., has a slightly faster connection. $4 per hr., $3 for laptops. (☎438 8111; www.klosenet.co.nz. Open M-Sa 10am-9pm, Su 11am-6pm.)

Post Office: 16-20 Rathbone St. (☎430 2761). Open M-F 8:30am-5pm, Sa 9am-1pm.

🏠 📷 ACCOMMODATIONS AND CAMPING

Though the best accommodations in Whangarei have always been situated just outside the city center, the recent exodus of several downtown nightclubs has all but eliminated the advantages of shacking up near the bars. Campers can purchase supplies at **Great Outdoors,** at the corner of Robert St. and James St. (☎438 7990. Open M-F 9am-5pm, Sa 9am-4pm.)

🛏 **Bunkdown Lodge (BBH),** 23 Otaika Rd. (☎438 8886; www.bunkdownlodge.co.nz). Take your shoes off when you enter and make yourself at home in this turn-of-the-century villa. You're a houseguest of owners Peter and Noelle, artistic polymaths who delight in booking local activities for their guests. They also organize trips to the Bird Recovery Center, where visitors can touch a real live kiwi ($5). Free pickup. 2 kitchens. Dorms $22; twins $48; doubles $50. MC/V. ❷

Whangarei YHA Hostel, 52 Punga Grove Ave. (☎ 438 8954; yhawhang@yha.org.nz), off Riverside Dr. in a quiet residential area. The arduous 20min. hike up the hill from the bus stop rewards visitors with a view of peaceful but growing Whangarei. Inquire about tours of the Abbey Caves. Internet $2 for 20min. or $10 for 2hr. Off-street parking. Reception 8am-1pm and 5-8pm. Free linen and towels. Dorms $24; twins and doubles $54-58. MC/V. ❷

Whangarei Holiday Park, 24 Mair St. (☎437 6856 or 0800 455 488; www.whangareitop10.co.nz), a 25min. walk up Hatea Dr., to the right. More trailer park than backpacker accommodation, these cabins at the city's outskirts might be the best option for a group. Reception 8am-9pm. Internet and WiFi $2 for 20min. Tent sites $15, under 14 $8. 2-person cabin $55, with bath $80; 8-person unit with kitchen and bath $250. MC/V. ❷

🄴🅂 FOOD AND NIGHTLIFE

The **Pak 'N Save,** 4 Walton St. at Quay St., is cheap and central. (☎438 1488. Open M-F 8am-9pm, Sa-Su 8am-8pm.) For those opting to eat out, most restaurants in the city center are reasonably priced. Those looking for a night out on the town might be better off making the trip back to Auckland, but if you are really hard up for a drink, **Danger Danger** (see below) doubles as a bar for the late dinner crowd.

Bogarts, 84 Cameron St. (☎438 3088; www.bogartscafe.co.nz). Small Uncle Scrooge pizza ($13) is not stingy, and the rock-encrusted bar adds to the ambience. Open M-Th and Sa 5pm-late, F 11:30am-late, Su 6pm-late. AmEx/MC/V. ❷

Killer Prawn, 26-28 Bank St. (☎430 3333; www.killerprawn.co.nz). Catering to a mature crowd, ye olde Prawn is happy to satisfy seafood cravings; watch that the giant prawns ($29.50), prepared 6 different ways, don't eat you first. Killer Pizza, upstairs, offers alternatives to seafood ($22-26). Open M-Sa noon-midnight. AmEX/MC/V. ❹

Danger Danger, 37 Vine St. (☎459 7461). The closest thing to nightlife that Whangarei has to offer, this no-frills bar fills up with a young crowd on W, F, and Sa nights. Mains $6-18. Open Tu-F 10:30am-late, Sa 2pm-late. AmEx/MC/V. ❷

Frings, 104 Lower Dent St. (☎438 4664; www.frings.co.nz), near the Town Basin. This brewery puts quality over presentation. The industrial facade and homebrewed drafts ($5) are accompanied by sky-high burgers ($7.50-16.50) and fish 'n chips ($10). Open M-Sa 10am-10pm, Su 10am-9pm. MC/V. ❷

Caffeine, 4 Water St. (☎438 6925; www.caffeinecafe.co.nz), near the intersection with Bank St. The best cafe in Whangarei displays local art on its walls and offers a menu with just enough inventiveness to satisfy discriminating tastes. Blueberry oak cakes $12.50, Vego Quesadilla $15.50. Open M-F 7am-2pm, Sa-Su 7am-1pm. MC/V. ❷

🄶🄰 SIGHTS AND OUTDOOR ACTIVITIES

In its heyday, Whangarei's tourist center was its waterfront, known to the masses as the **Town Basin,** where eccentric museums and upscale cafes connect via paved walkways. The area still offers the nicest ambience and is a pleasant spot to unwind after playing hard all day. With its 1400 clocks, watches, and music boxes, the **Clapham Clock Museum,** begun in the early 1900s on Dent St., now shares space with the town's newest visitors center. Be sure not to miss the Victoria music box, built around 1880 and still in operation, and the French atmos clock, which runs solely on chemical diethyl chloride. (☎438 3993. Open daily 9am-5pm. $8, students and seniors $6. Guided tour included.) Don't miss the outside square's gargantuan **sundial.** Next door, you can watch expert glass-blowing at **Burning Issues.** (☎438 3108. Open daily 10am-5pm.) A 10min. walk from Bank St. on Rust St. (which turns into Selwyn Ave.) leads to the **Craft Quarry,** a collection of open art studios. (☎438 1215. Quarry open daily 10am-4pm.) **Town Basin Leisure Craft Hire,** Jetty 1, on Riverside Dr., middle of the bridge, rents in-line skates and scooters ($10 per hr.), mountain bikes ($20 per half-day), and kayaks ($10 per hr.) on summer weekends. (☎437 2509. Open in summer Sa-Su 11am-5pm; in winter Su 11am-4pm.) The **Fernery,** at the end of First Ave., populates its premises with the world's oldest plants. (Open daily 10am-4pm. Free.) The landscaped lawn in **Cafler Park** and the **Rose Gardens,** next to the Fernery on Water St., make good spots for picnicking. For Whangarei's more athletic options, numerous 1hr. **walking tracks** wind through the hills that embrace the town; it's best to leave from Mair Park, on Rurumoki St. off Hatea Dr., and follow the map from the Whangarei i-Site. No visitor should miss the 25m **Whangarei Falls,** located 5km from town, off Kiripaka Rd. on the way to Tutukaka. Though *Let's Go* does not recommend initiation rituals, Maori youths have jumped off the dangerous cliff for hundreds of years as a rite of passage. Spelunkers can whet their appetites at the **Abbey Caves** before heading south. As your eyes adjust, thousands of glowworms light up the overhangs like a planetarium. The caves are open to the public, but you might want help navigating them—inquire about free guided tours at the Whangarei YHA hostel; bring a flashlight and clothes and shoes that can get wet. For a heart-pounding afternoon, connect with the friendly folks at **The Bushwacka Experience** for two tours of varying intensity, which include rock climbing and rappelling. Both end at the **farm base,** where you can complete the New Zealand trifecta of activities by milking cows or shearing sheep. (☎434 7839 or 021 578 240. Free pickup with a day's notice. Full tour $85, tour without rappel $55.)

Those who want to venture farther should explore the **Whangarei Heads,** a 30-40min. drive east from Whangarei. **Ocean Beach** offers great surf and a rocky coastline. Just south, the **Bream Head Scenic Reserve** challenges amblers with several walks. A manageable 1½hr. walk to **Peach Cove** departs from near Ocean Beach; **Mount Manaia,** a 1hr. summit hike, provides a 360° view. You can access Mt. Manaia from the **Early Settlers Memorial,** just past McLeod's Bay.

TUTUKAKA AND POOR KNIGHTS ISLANDS ☎09

Eleven million years ago, the Poor Knights Islands emerged from the sea 23km off the coast from Tutukaka. Although the Ngatiwai tribe had long inhabited these islands (calling them the Tawhiti Rahi and Aorangi Islands), a string of invasions and deaths in the 1800s led the tribe's chief, Te Tatua, to declare them *tapu* (forbidden) in 1822. Today, landing on the islands without a permit is also *tapu*, but by decree of the DOC. Thanks to the dearth of human interference, the islands are a haven for rare creatures, including prehistoric tuatara lizards and the world's heaviest insect, the weta, or "demon grasshopper."

Tutukaka (pop. 24), 30km east of Whangarei is on the rise and remains the base from which most ventures to the Poor Knights Islands depart. The biggest draw is world-class ■scuba diving; Jacques Cousteau rated the area one of the 10 best sites in the world. Special mooring buoys off the coast serve as landing points for the scores of scuba, snorkel, kayak, and fishing trips that run out of Tutukaka and Whangarei. Overhanging sea caves encourage the proliferation of marine life, making for awesome kayaking and snorkeling among DOC-protected moray eels, stingrays, and subtropical reef fish. The two dive wrecks are also popular choices for experienced divers.

Dive! Tutukaka runs a professional, friendly operation from the Marina Complex. Competent guides brief divers on the topography of each dive site and where the resident fish like to gather, then have complimentary hot soup and drinks awaiting the divers' return. Free shuttles to and from your accommodation in Whangarei leave at the crack of dawn. They also host kayaking and snorkeling expeditions for non-divers. (☎434 3867 or 0800 288 882; www.diving.co.nz. 2-dive day with full equipment hire $209 for certified divers. Lunch $10. Free kayak use. Supervised single dive with full equipment hire for novices $250. Lunch included.) **Knightdiver** Don Pringle also offers dives, supplying gear and an underwater guide. (☎0800 766 756; www.poorknights.co.nz. Full equipment hire for certified divers $190. Supervised 2-dive day with full equipment hire for novices $220. Free pickup in Whangarei.) You can rent kayaks at **Tutukaka Kayak Hire** at the marina beach. (☎0800 559 559 or 0274 901 111. Single $15 per hr., double $30 per hr.) From the park, you can take a guided kayak tour (2hr.; $30 per person) of the beautiful Matapouri Estuary.

Sugarloaf, next to the Oceans Hotel, is a makeshift visitors center and books dives, fishing expeditions, and accommodations free of charge (☎434 3678. Open daily 8am-6pm in summer, 10am-4pm in winter. Internet $5 per hr.) The lone lodging option for backpackers is **Tutukaka Holiday Park ❷,** on R.D.3, 100m past the turn-off for the marina (☎434 3938; www.tutukak-holiday-park.co.nz. 2-person cabins $50-100, $20 per extra person. Dorms $25. Linen $5. Campsites $14 for adults, $6 for children. Hot showers $0.50. AmEx/MC/V.) Before heading out to sea, stock up on groceries at the **General Store** on R.D.3, which also houses a small **post office** (☎434 4652. Open daily 7am-7pm.) Post-

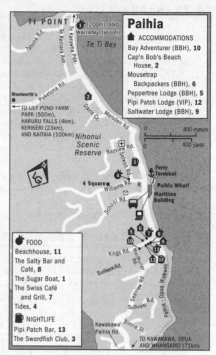

Paihia

▲ ACCOMMODATIONS
Bay Adventurer (BBH), **10**
Cap'n Bob's Beach
  House, **2**
Mousetrap
  Backpackers (BBH), **6**
Peppertree Lodge (BBH), **5**
Pipi Patch Lodge (VIP), **12**
Saltwater Lodge (BBH), **9**

🍎 FOOD
Beachhouse, **11**
The Salty Bar and
  Café, **8**
The Sugar Boat, **1**
The Swiss Café
  and Grill, **7**
Tides, **4**

🍷 NIGHTLIFE
Pipi Patch Bar, **13**
The Swordfish Club, **3**

dive martinis and fine dining can be found at **Oceans ❹,** next to the hotel of the same name. (☎470 2000. Marinated and seared sea scallops $17.50. Other mains $26.50-31.50. Open daily 7am-late. AmEx/MC/V.) More down-to-earth but no less satisfying is the dockside **Moocho's Bistro ❸,** which serves up fresh seafood as well as traditional landlubber pub fare. (Light meals $7.50-14. Mains $19-22. Cash only.)

BAY OF ISLANDS

Temperate climate and a beautiful coastline have long attracted summertime travelers to the Bay of Islands. The most famous visitor, Captain Cook, dropped anchor in 1769, befriended the Maori, and then sent word back to England to set in motion permanent European settlement. Not particularly creative, the captain named the region after the 144 islands that continue to draw tourists and bolster the local economy. To best appreciate the Bay of Islands, follow Cook's lead; board a boat and discover the coast for yourself.

PAIHIA   ☎09

Paihia, the center of commerce in the Bay of Islands, combines an inlet full of green isles with a strip of packed motels. In summer, the low-season population of 3000 explodes to nearly 40,000, overwhelming the bay. Agents on each corner try to convince visitors to cruise, fish, sail, dive, and even fly, while the friendly and relaxed locals patiently watch the annual feeding frenzy. A large backpacker following has drawn the youthful masses north before they head south from Auckland, helping to make Northland a must-see on country-wide itineraries.

⌐ TRANSPORTATION

Buses: Buses depart from the **Maritime Building**. **Paihia Travel** (☎402 7857) arranges travel for **Northliner Coaches, InterCity,** and **Newmans,** which run daily to **Auckland** (4½hr.; $49, backpackers $42, students and seniors $39) via **Whangarei** (1¼hr.; $24, backpackers $20, students and seniors $19) and to **Kaitaia** (2hr.; 1 per day; $34, backpackers $29, students and seniors $27) via **Kerikeri** (30min.; $15, backpackers $13, students and seniors $12).

Ferries: Kings Red Fast Ferry (☎402 8288) zoom to **Russell** in 5min., leaving every 20min. (8:30am-late), while **Fullers Passenger Ferry** (☎402 7421) takes 15min., departing every hr. (7:20am-10:30pm). Both cost $5 one-way ($9 round-trip). The **Fullers Vehicle Ferry** departs from Opua (about 5km south of Paihia) for **Okiato** (5min.; every 10min. 6:50am-10pm; cars $17 round-trip, includes 1 passenger; $1 per extra passenger each way).

Taxis: Haruru Cabs (☎402 6292) or **Paihia Cabs** (☎402 5948).

Hitchhiking: Although *Let's Go* doesn't recommend it, hitchhiking to Kerikeri or points north is reportedly best attempted near the roundabout at the end of Marsden Rd. To head south, hitchers wait on Paihia Rd. at the edge of town.

◪🛈 ORIENTATION AND PRACTICAL INFORMATION

Marsden Road runs along the waterfront and is Paihia's main artery. **Paihia Wharf** is roughly in the middle of town beside the Maritime Building and opposite the town's commercial center along **Williams Road. Kings Road** is backpacker central.

Visitors Center: Bay of Islands i-Site (☎402 7345; visitorinfo@fndc.govt.nz), in the white octagonal pavilion next to Paihia Wharf. Staff books accommodations, adventure activities, and transportation. Internet $4 per hr. 24hr. ATM. Open daily 8am-8pm. In winter 8am-5pm.

Banks: Banks with 24hr. **ATMs** cluster around the commercial block bordered by Williams, Marsden, Selwyn, and Bay View Rd. The **ASB** at the corner of Williams and Selwyn St. is open M-F 9am-4:30pm.

Police: Paihia's **police station** is on Williams Rd. Dial ☎402 7130 for non-emergencies, ☎111 for emergencies.

Medical Services: Bay View Medical Centre, 7 Bay View Rd. (☎402 7132). Open by appointment M-F 9am-5pm. **Paihia Pharmacy,** 2 Williams Rd. (☎402 7034). Open M-F 8:30am-5pm, Sa 8:30am-1pm.

Internet Access: Connections in Paihia follow the same pace as life: slow. The Bay of Islands i-Site offers the best rates, at $4 per hr. Most others are $6 per hr. **Paihia Photos,** on Williams Rd., offers wireless ($6 per hr.) Open daily 8am-6pm.

Post Office: On Williams Rd. (☎402 7800), next to the pharmacy. Open M-F 8am-5:30pm, Sa-Su 9am-3pm. In winter M-F 8am-5:30pm, Sa 8:30am-1pm.

⌐ ACCOMMODATIONS

A steady influx of overnighters has created a backpacker community on **Kings Road,** minutes south of the bus station. Light sleepers beware: the street can get as loud as a frathouse row at night. A fancier option is an overnight cruise, which combines a desire to see the bay by ship with a need to find a bed.

▨ **Cap'n Bob's Beach House (BBH),** 44 Davis Cres. (☎402 8668; www.capnbobs.co.nz), about 800m north of the wharf past the bluffs. Belying its campy name, this smaller, quieter hostel is all class. Removed from swamped Kings Rd., Bob's sits on a hill with porch views of the bay far more valuable than its prices indicate. Contains two lounge spaces—one with a TV, the other without. Female-only dorms available. Dorms $23 (linens $2); singles $45; doubles $56. Book ahead Nov.-Feb. MC/V. ❷

Mousetrap Backpackers (BBH), 11 Kings Rd. (☎402 8182; www.mousetrap.co.nz). If the lounge and kitchen are empty, check the terrace—the ocean view makes it a popular hangout. Cabinets shelved with bric-a-brac of the sea gives the place the feel of a private beach house. Key deposit $20. Dorms $22-24; twins and doubles $58. MC/V. ❷

Peppertree Lodge (BBH), 15 Kings Rd. (☎402 6122; www.peppertree.co.nz). Kind owners Angela and Ken offer massive living areas, solid bunks, and hotel-quality mattresses. Free bike and kayak use, tennis rackets, videos, and storage. Key deposit $20. Dorms $23-25 (linens $1); twins and doubles $65-75. MC/V. ❷

Saltwater Lodge (BBH), 14 Kings Rd. (☎402 7075 or 0800 002 266; www.saltwaterlodge.co.nz). New Zealand's first 5-star backpacker lodge feels like part of a cruise ship. Superbly clean, it offers baths, a large TV, a small gym, a parking lot, tennis rackets, and bikes. Free bag storage. Reception 7:30am-7:30pm. Dorms $24-26; doubles $90-120, $15 per extra person. AmEx/MC/V. ❷

Bay Adventurer (VIP), 28 Kings Rd. (☎402 5162; www.bayadventurer.co.nz). Party-ready backpackers dip in the pool and towel off on the sun terrace before an afternoon of tennis. Free parking, bikes, and kayaks. Reception 8am-9pm. 6-bed dorms $23; doubles $85; 2-person studios $125, $18 per extra person; 4-person single-unit apartments $191, $18 per extra person. ❷

Pipi Patch Lodge (VIP), 18 Kings Rd. (☎402 7111; www.gobeyond.co.nz). The giant green Kiwi Experience bus parks in front of this party hostel, which offers a well-equipped lounge, swimming pool, and spa. Wi-Fi. Key deposit $20. Reception 7am-7pm. Dorms $25; doubles $66, with bath $84. Discounts in winter. MC/V. ❷

🖪🖻 FOOD AND NIGHTLIFE

Central Paihia has dining choices around each corner. For groceries, try **4 Square** (☎402 8002) on Williams Rd. (open daily in summer 7am-9pm; in winter 7am-7pm), or the larger **Woolworths** (☎402 5524), on Puketona Rd., just north of town (open daily 7am-10pm). For evening entertainment, follow the noise and plant yourself at either the **Beachhouse** (see below), the **Salty Bar and Cafe** (see below), or the **Pipi Patch Bar** in the Kings Rd. hostel of the same name. (☎402 7111. Happy hour 7-9pm; $5 shots. Open daily 3pm-1am.)

🖾 **The Sugar Boat** (☎402 7018), next to Waitangi Bridge. Climb aboard this splurge-worthy vessel not simply for the novelty but also for the culinary prowess of the mess staff. The deckhands deliver dishes like snapper fillet or seafood and chorizo paella (both $29) on this sailboat turned restaurant. Open daily 5pm-late. MC/V. ❹

Beachhouse, 16 Kings Rd. (☎402 7479). In the morning, this juice and coffee bar features homemade cakes ($3-5) and hot breakfast ($8-13.50). As the day progresses, the scene changes drastically. Backpackers and locals come for the dinner-drink specials (burger, chips, and a large beer; $14). Open daily 8am-midnight. MC/V. ❷

The Salty Bar and Cafe, 14 Kings Rd. (☎402 6080), in front of the Saltwater Lodge. The youthful backpacker crowd chomps on pizzas in this popular evening hangout. Pizza $15.50-24.50. Happy hour 7-9pm. Open daily 4pm-1am. AmEx/MC/V. ❷

The Swiss Café and Grille, 48 Marsden Rd. (☎402 6701). Just when you thought no one in town spoke German, the Swiss Café appears out of nowhere. Wiener schnitzel $23.50. Fish 'n chips $19.50. Open daily 5:30-10pm. In winter closed Su. MC/V. ❹

🝆 OUTDOOR ACTIVITIES

The **Maritime Building** by the wharf is the meeting point for many trips and the booking agents who hawk them. (Open daily 7am-9pm; in winter 7am-7pm.) Next door, the Bay of Islands i-Site books activities free of charge. In addition, **Adventure**

Headquarters (☎ 402 7127), located behind the visitors center on Charter Pier, books most companies but specializes in fishing trips. In summer, expect hordes of tourists—advance booking is essential, especially on cruises around the bay or to Cape Reinga. In winter, you may encounter the opposite—fewer trips and many activities requiring minimum numbers. Whatever the season, inquire about backpacker discounts. Many of the trips listed will also pick you up in Russell. The following are the best of hundreds of activities offered in the area.

SAILING. Mike and Debbie have sailed over 60,000 miles in 15 years, and now take travelers on their **Gungha II Supercruise.** They will teach you about sailing this 65 ft. yacht, provide snorkel gear, wetsuits, and on-board lunch. (☎ 407 7930 or 0800 478 900; bayofislandssailing@xtra.co.nz. 6½hr. $85. YHA, BBH, and VIP discounts.) **She's A Lady Island Sailing Adventures,** will take you on a day of sailing, snorkeling, and "see-through bottom" kayaking. (☎ 0800 724 584; www.bay-of-islands.com. 6½hr. $85; includes lunch.) **SailNZ** operates the 72 ft. catamaran *On the Edge*, which can go up to 30 knots. This trip offers the only sail to the Hole in the Rock, a barbeque lunch, and an island stopover. (☎ 402 7900 or 0800 724 569; www.explorenz.co.nz. 6½hr. $135, children $79.) The **R. Tucker Thompson,** a majestic halibut schooner, replicates the Captain Cook experience, minus the hardtack and scurvy. (☎ 0800 882 537 or 402 8430; www.tucker.co.nz. 7hr. Oct.-May $110, children $55; includes cream tea and barbeque lunch.) **Stray Cat Sailing** runs sailing trips with swimming and snorkeling stops on two islands, as well as a chance at the helm. (☎ 402 6130 or 0800 101 007; www.straycat.co.nz. $79, children $45; includes lunch.)

ADVENTURE CRUISES. For those adventure travelers always looking to cram 6hr. into one, several high-speed options make short shrift of the bay's sights. **Mack Attack** is an open-air boat capable of speeding up to 50 knots, cementing a tie for fastest in these waters and making seat belts a necessity. (☎ 402 8180 or 0800 622 528; www.mackattack.co.nz. 1½hr. 4 per day. $70, children $35. 10% ISIC, VIP, and YHA discount.) The Fullers-owned **Excitor** also travels to the Hole in the Rock at up to 40 knots, with an optional stopover on Urupukapuka Island and optional 3hr. guided kayak tour. (☎ 402 7020; www.excitor.co.nz. 1½hr. round-trip. $72, children $36. Island stopover $10/5. Kayak tour $125/79.)

OVERNIGHT CRUISES. The **Bay of Islands Overnight Island Cruise** is an all-in-one cruise, sleep, eat, trek, swim, and play, with a 24hr. stay on the Rock. Activities include a target shooting competition, night kayaking, and mussel diving. (☎ 402 7796 or 0800 762 527. $168.) For a longer stay, sign up with **Bay of Islands Ecocruz,** for a three-day, two-night environmentally-conscious sailing adventure that includes snorkeling, kayaking, and hiking options. (☎ 0800 432 627 or 025 592 153; www.ecocruz.co.nz. Dorms $495; doubles $1150.)

SWIMMING WITH DOLPHINS. While popular, dolphins can be unpredictable. Check to see if the company has a refund policy for trips with no sightings. **Dolphin Discoveries** has been spotting dolphins since 1991 and has a high success rate. (In the NZ Post Bldg. at Marsden and Williams Rd. ☎ 0800 365 744 or 402 8234; www.dolphinz.co.nz or www.explorenz.co.nz. 10% VIP, YHA, and BBH discount.) Recently renovated and upgraded, **Carino** is a 40 ft. catamaran and the only yacht licensed to swim with dolphins. Its trip is a steal, offering a full day of sailing, sunning, fishing, bushwalking, and swimming with dolphins. (☎ 402 8040 or 025 933 872; www.sailinganddolphin.co.nz. $90, children $50. Includes barbeque lunch.) **Kings** offers dolphin swimming during **Day in the Bay** and its **Hole in The Rock Scenic Cruise** (see **Other Cruises,** p. 123).

DIVING. Paihia Dive offers dives to the wreck of the *Rainbow Warrior* and the *Canterbury* as well as the Bay of Islands reef. (On Williams Rd. ☎ 402 7551; www.divenz.com. 2-dive day including all equipment $199. 4-day open water dive course $600. Snorkeling gear hire $10 per day.)

KAYAKING. Coastal Kayakers provides independent kayak rentals, guided kayak tours, package tours, and hardcore 2- to 3-day wilderness expeditions. (☎402 8105; www.coastalkayakers.co.nz. *Kayaks $10 per hr., $30 half-day, $40 full-day. Half-day tour $55, full-day $75. Expeditions Nov.-May from $130. Snorkeling mask and goggles $10 per day.*) **New Zealand Sea Kayak Adventures** offers more remote, multi-day kayaking. (☎402 8596; www.nzkayaktours.com. *Full-day $125, multi-day $150 per day. 3-day trips $525, 6-day trips $1050, 10-day trips $1500. Ask about backpacker specials.*)

FISHING. The good folks at **Adventure Headquarters** are familiar with fishing operators, handle bookings, and will match you with a boat and guide. Generally, trips are 4-6hr. and fish for snapper, marlin, shark, king fish, and hapuka. (*Halfway down the wharf on the left.* ☎402 7127. *Around $65 for small boats. $250 for game fishing.*)

FLYING. Salt Air offers a 30min. prop-plane flight around the **Hole in the Rock,** an island at the extreme eastern end of the bay through which boats pass, as well as a longer Bay Discovery tour and a 20min. helicopter flight to the Hole. They also run a high-priced prop-plane tour of Cape Reinga, which catches the cape before the lunchtime arrival of tour buses. (*Located in a kiosk just to the south of the Maritime Bldg.* ☎402 8338; www.saltair.co.nz. *Trips $115, $195, $190, and $365 per person, respectively.*)

ACTIVITIES ASHORE. Sick of the water? Fortunately, there are plenty of terrestrial activities geared towards summer travelers. **Island Kayaks** rents mountain bikes. (☎402 6078; www.islandkayaking.co.nz. *$5 per hr., $20 per day.*) **Bush 'n Bike** has ATV, go-cart, and horseback tours. (☎404 1142; www.bushnbike.co.nz. *ATV $75 for 1½hr., Go Kart $75 for 1hr., $40 per passenger; horseback ride $55 for 1½hr.*) **Skyline Quads** also has ATV tours through 810 hectares of farm, scrub, pine, and native forest. (☎021 487 357. *Tours $60-145. Free pickup.*) For a unique Paihia experience, visit the **Lily Pond Farm Park.** Activities include horse rides, feeding the friendly eels, milking the friendly cow, gawking at the fat—and friendly—pig, swimming, boating, and potentially getting your eyes pecked out by (not-so-friendly) ostriches. (*On Puketona Rd. on the way to Kerikeri.* ☎402 6099. *Open Su-Tu and F-Sa 10am-4pm. Call ahead for winter bookings. $7, children $5.*) At the end of School Rd., 700m west of Paihia, the **Oromahoe Road Traverse** is a 2½hr. walk through regenerating forest to the **Opua Coastal Walk,** which returns to Paihia (*2hr.*). Alternatively, the **Opua Forest Lookout Track** starts at School Rd. and veers off to ocean views. (*30min. one-way.*) The **Bay of Islands Jazz and Blues Festival** (www.jazz-blues.co.nz) in August and the **Bay of Islands Country Rock Festival** (www.country-rock.co.nz) in May feature local and international talent. Contact the Paihia i-Site (see p. 112) for info.

WAITANGI ☎09

On February 6, 1840, more than 500 Maori, settlers, traders, dignitaries, and missionaries came ashore the beach of Waitangi to witness the signing of the most important document in New Zealand history—the **Treaty of Waitangi** (p. 42). Today, the treaty is the focal point of vigorously debated Maori land grievances.

The **Waitangi National Trust Estate** is a serene and verdant reminder of the all-important document. (☎402 7437. *Open daily in summer 9am-6pm. In winter 9am-5pm. $12, children free.*) To reach the reserve from Paihia, follow Marsden Rd. over the Waitangi Bridge, and then head up the rise about 800m. The **Treaty House** is one of the first architectural products of a British presence in New Zealand. From 1832 to 1844, it was home to watchdog "British Resident" **James Busby** (p. 42); today, it is a museum. To the left of the lawn is the **Whare Runanga,** a Maori meeting house, constructed in 1940 to celebrate the treaty's centennial. The world's largest war canoe, *Ngatokimatawhaorua* (35m), has its own place of honor down the hill. Until 2005, the canoe was hauled out by 80 warriors and paddled around the bay every Waitangi Day (Feb. 6). Take a lunch break at the

NORTHLAND

Waikokopu Cafe ❸ on the Treaty Grounds. (☎402 6275. Open daily 9am-5pm. Cash only.) The **Haruru Falls** can be reached via the **Waitangi National Trust Mangrove Walk**, a beautiful 1½hr. stroll from the visitors center.

RUSSELL   ☎09

On a sunny afternoon in Russell (pop. 800), it's hard to believe that the town was once known as the "Hell Hole of the Pacific," notorious for its thriving brothel industry, seedy sailor activity, and Maori-Pakeha clashes. Today, Russell's romantic, small-town charm provides a quiet alternative to its more boisterous neighbor across the bay. If accommodations in Paihia are full, you can try your luck here.

📧 TRANSPORTATION. The ferries from Paihia are the way to go. For both passenger and vehicular ferry info, see **Ferries**, p. 112. Though Russell is accessible by car, the dirt and gravel road around the bay to and from Paihia is so treacherous that some rental companies specifically prohibit travel on it.

📧🔁 ORIENTATION AND PRACTICAL INFORMATION. Matauwhi Rd. dumps cars into town on **York Street**, parallel to **The Strand**, which runs along the water from the **Russell Wharf**. All the shops are situated within two blocks of each other on these two streets, just west of a residential area, and south of **Long Beach Road**, which leads over a hill to **Long Beach**. The **Bay of Islands Visitor Centre**, on The Strand, one block south of the wharf, is also the main **DOC office** for the Bay of Islands. (☎403 9005. Open daily 9am-5pm; in winter 10am-4:30pm.) The privately run **Russell Booking and Information** is a reliable kiosk on the wharf. (☎403 8020. Open daily 7:45am-7pm; in winter 9am-5pm.) Russell's lone policeman lives in the colonial house on The Strand that has served as a **police station** and residence since the early 1900s (☎403 9090). Other services include: **Westpac Trust**, Cass St. near The Strand (open M-Tu and Th-F 9:30am-2pm, W 10am-2pm), with 24hr. **ATM; laundry** and **shower facilities** on Matauwhi Rd. and Florance Ave. (showers $2; wash $3; dry $2; open daily 7am-10pm); **Russell Medical Services**, on Church St. north of the wharf (☎403 7690; open M-F 9am-4:30pm); **Russell Pharmacy**, 21 York St. (☎403 7835; open daily 8:30am-5pm; in winter M-F 8:30am-5pm, Sa 8:30am-noon); **Internet** access at **Internet and Copying, etc.**, in the Traders Mall on York St. (☎403 8843; $6 per hr.; open daily 9am-5pm); a **post shop** in the Russell Bookshop. (☎403 7674. Open M-F 8:30am-5:15pm, Sa 8:30am-2pm, Su 9am-2pm. Closed Su in winter.)

📧📧 ACCOMMODATIONS AND FOOD. 🏠**Pukeko Cottage** ❷, 14 Brind Rd., offers homestay-style rooms (one of which houses the owner), postcard-quality sunset views from the dining room, and a 1950s-era caravan which has been converted into a cozy, nearly self-contained double. (☎403 8498; www.pukekocottageback-packers.co.nz. All rooms $25 per person. Book ahead for Dec.-Feb. Cash only.) **Sheltered Waters Backpackers** ❷, 18 Florance Ave., is a new option, with a spa, barbeques, and Internet, among other amenities. (☎403 8818 or 021 999 092. Dorms $25; doubles $65, with bath $75; $25 per extra person. Book ahead Dec.-Feb. Cash only.) Flowering plants and trees abound at **Russell Holiday Park** ❶, at the corner of James St. and Long Beach Rd. Dorms are available in winter. (☎403 7826; www.russelltop10.co.nz. Office open daily 8am-8pm, 8am-7pm in winter. 2-person cabins $60, $15 per extra person. Dorms $22. Tent and powered sites $16. MC/V.)

   Waterfront Cafe ❷, on The Strand, one block south of the wharf, has a beautiful beachfront view and an outdoor courtyard in back. The handmade burgers ($12) are patrons' favorites. (☎403 7589. Open Tu-Su 7:30am-3:30pm. 8-3:30. Cash only.) **York St. Cafe** ❶, in the Traders Mall, serves hearty breakfasts (pancakes $7.50), healthy lunches (chicken and kumara salad $18), and cheap takeaways (hamburger $5.) (☎403 7360. Open M-Sa 8am-4pm, Su 9am-4pm. AmEx/MC/V.)

◨ ♫ **SIGHTS AND OUTDOOR ACTIVITIES.** The best collection of local historical treasures is housed at the **Russell Museum**, 2 York St. Displays range from a functional one-fifth scale replica of Cook's *Endeavour* to cow hairballs and swordfish eye sockets. (☎403 7701. Open daily 10am-4pm. Jan. 10am-5pm. $5.) The Anglican **Christ Church**, at Baker and Robertson Rd., with a crowded cemetery in front, is the oldest church still standing in New Zealand. Illustrious worshippers have included Charles Darwin, who attended services here while the *HMS Beagle* was anchored in the bay. Not to be outdone by the Protestants, Bishop Pompallier arrived in 1838, and his Catholic missionaries soon followed suit. The 1841 **Pompallier**, on the esplanade at the end of The Strand, was the first Catholic mission in New Zealand and is the only mission building that remains standing. Now a working museum, it continues to tan leather and bind books in the painstaking Marist tradition. (☎403 9015. Open daily 10am-5pm. $7.50, students $3.50, children free.) On the opposite side of the Russell waterfront is **Flagstaff Hill**. A walking track ascends to the site where the famous Maori warrior, **Hone Heke**, felled the symbol of British rule (the flagpole) four times in 1844-45 (p. 43). When the tide is out, the hill may be approached along the beach at the north end of The Strand; otherwise take the signposted route off Flagstaff Rd. **Long Beach** of Oneroa Bay lies over the hill at the end of Wellington St. Rent kayaks and paddle boats in the summer outside the **DOC office** by the waterfront (from $25 per day) or from Paihia.

Trekkers come to Russell to walk the medium-grade **Cape Brett Lighthouse Track** (20km, 16hr. round-trip). The old lighthouse keeper's house has been turned into a **hut** with a gas cooker, running water, and toilets ($12, children $6). Book ahead at the DOC office in Russell, where you also pay the track fee ($30, children $15). The start of the track is a 1hr. drive from Russell and guides are usually available to introduce you to the history of the region (prices negotiable). One popular option is to be dropped off at the lighthouse (**Kiwi Eco Tours**; ☎403 8823) and then hike back, enjoying the coast and saving a day's walk; contact the DOC for more info. They can also tell you about the two **campsites ❶** ($6, children $3) on the island of **Urupukapuka**, one right at the beach and one at Cable Bay. Both have running water and cold showers but no toilets; digging a hole is not allowed, meaning visitors must bring a chemical toilet, available for rent in Whangarei.

KERIKERI   ☎09

Strategically placed at the head of an inlet, quiet Kerikeri (pop. 6000) was home to the marauding Maori chief Hongi Hika and a group of English missionaries under his protection, making the town an economic center for Christians throughout the Bay of Islands. Meaning "dig, dig," Kerikeri is where the first English plow cut into New Zealand soil. Today, well-preserved European missionary buildings and acres of hikeable trails are the main draws for most tourists.

⌐ **TRANSPORTATION. InterCity** (☎913 6100) buses run to Kaitaia (1½hr.; 1 per day; $30, under 13 $20, backpackers, students, and seniors $24) and Paihia (25min.; 3 per day; $15, under 13 $10, backpackers $13, students and seniors $12). Never far from the tourists, **Fullers** tours Kerikeri from Paihia and hits history, horticulture, and shopping all in 3hr. (☎407 7421. Daily 1:15pm. $55, children $28.)

◪ ♂ **ORIENTATION AND PRACTICAL INFORMATION. Kerikeri Road** (called Main Rd.) is the central street, leading 5km east from **SH10** through town to the water and Rewa's Village. Most of the services are clustered within its triangle with **Hobson Avenue** and **Cobham Road.** The **i-Site** in Paihia handles most queries, but brochures may be obtained from the **Visitors Information Centre,** located in the public library on Cobham Rd., just off Kerikeri Rd. (☎ 407 0774. Open M-F 8am-5pm, Sa 9am-2pm, Su 9am-1pm.) The **DOC office** is at 34 Landing Rd. north of Rewa's Village. (☎407 8474. Open M-F 8am-4:30pm.) **Work opportunities** abound given Kerikeri's fruit-picking industry. Hostels post listings. The best times to work in the area are late March, May, early June, and late December.

All major New Zealand banks with 24hr. **ATMS** line Kerikeri Rd. in town. Other services include: the **Kerikeri Medical Centre,** 4 Homestead Rd. (☎407 7777; open M-F 8am-5:30pm, Sa 9am-2pm, Su 9am-1pm); **McFadziens Pharmacy,** at the corner of Homestead and Kerikeri Rd. (☎407 7144; mcfadziens@xtra.co.nz; open M-Th 8:30am-5:30pm, F 8:30am-6pm, Sa 9am-1pm); **Internet** access at the library's visitors center, $2 per 15min.; and the **post office,** 6 Hobson Ave. (☎407 9721; open M-F 8:30am-5:30pm, Sa 8:30am-1:30pm, Su 8:30am-12:30pm). There's a full-service **laundry** at 11 Cobham St., across from the library (☎407 8942. Open M-F 8am-5pm, Sa 8:30-2pm. Wash and dry $12, wash only $6.)

⚡ ◖ ACCOMMODATIONS AND FOOD. Hostels in Kerikeri are geared toward working backpackers and offer good weekly rates. The closest hostel to town is the **Kerikeri YHA ❸,** 144 Kerikeri Rd., just past the edge of town toward the water. A rustic backpackers, its clutch of whitewashed buildings is reminiscent of an international summer camp. (☎407 9391; yha.kerikeri@yha.co.nz. Pool table. Dorms $25; twins and doubles $56; 2-person cottages $120, $10 per extra person. MC/V.) To reach the **Hone Heke Lodge (BBH/VIP) ❷,** 65 Hone Heke Rd., turn off Kerikeri Rd. onto Hone Heke Rd., and look for the wooden backpackers sign. Its motel-style structure features a comfortable new TV lounge and a sprawling outdoor barbeque area. (☎407 8170; www.honeheke.co.nz. Bike rental $10 per day, $5 for 3 or more days. Free pickup from bus stop. Shuttle to orchards $1. Free parking. Linens $5. Reception 8am-8pm. Dorms $21; doubles $46, with bath $56. Weekly dorms $108 for BBH-members, $126 for non-members. Campsites $15. AmEx/MC/V.) The **Fishbone Cafe ❷,** 88 Kerikeri Rd., specializes in sandwiches ($11-13) and wines ($25-30). (☎407 6065. Open M-F 8am-4:30pm, Sa 8:30am-3pm, Su 8:30am-2pm. AmEx/MC/V.) (☎407 1050. W quiz night, Th karaoke. Open M-Sa 10am-late. MC/V.) Staples are at **New World,** at Homestead Rd. and Fairway Dr. (☎407 7440; open daily 8am-9pm), or at **Woolworths,** down Kerikeri Rd. (open daily 7am-9pm).

◖ ⚡ SIGHTS AND OUTDOOR ACTIVITIES. Head to the **Kerikeri Basin,** a 20min. walk down Kerikeri Rd. toward the water, to view a trinity of Anglican missionary power: **St. James Church,** the graceful white **Mission House** (claims are made for it as the oldest standing wooden European building in the country), and **Stone Store,** constructed in 1832-36 to house supplies for the Church Missionary Society. (☎407 9236. Open daily 10am-5pm; in winter 10am-4pm. Stone Store and Mission House $7.50, students and children $3.50.) Cross the footbridge over the **Kerikeri River** to see **Rewa's Village,** 1 Landing Rd., a recreated pre-European Maori fishing village. A 10min. video provides an instructive overview of the town's history. (☎407 6454. Open daily 9:30am-4:30pm; in winter 10am-4pm. $5, children $1.) The area near the SH10 roundabout has kauri shops, ceramics, wineries, and boutiques. Make sure you check out **Makana Confections,** on the way into town on Kerikeri Rd., to try a free sample. (☎407 6800; www.makana.co.nz. Open daily 9am-5:30pm.)

Burn off chocolate calories by taking a swim in the **Fairy Pools,** serene rock holes near the Kerikeri River. (Follow the track behind the Kerikeri YHA; 30min. round-trip.) Another popular swimming hole is **Charlie's Rock,** 800m past the roundabout on Landing Rd. Further up the river are the basalt, 27m-high **Rainbow Falls.** (Accessible only by car while the heritage trail is closed for repairs. Drive along Waipapa

Rd. 2.5km east of SH10. Ask at the DOC for the current status of the trail.) Approximately 20km west of Kerikeri are the **Puketi and Omahuta Forests.** DOC-published pamphlets detail several walks. Access the park from Puketi, off Puketotara Rd., or from Mangamuka off SH1. The DOC administers a **campsite** at Puketi. ($7, children $3.50. Pay at the on-site donation box.)

THE FAR NORTH

MATAURI BAY, TAURANGA BAY, AND WHANGAROA ☎09

Sparse settlement and secluded beaches make this scenic detour from SH10 wholly worth an overnight stop for the independent serenity-seeker. For the Maori, the area marks the historic landing spot of one of seven *waka* (canoes) that originally transported their ancestors from Polynesia. This was the site of the 1814 arrival of the Rev. Samuel Marsden, the first to preach Christianity to the native population. Today, the rising Cavalli Islands and the sunken *Rainbow Warrior* beckon divers, snorkelers, and kayakers through the warm waters.

■♂ ORIENTATION AND PRACTICAL INFORMATION. Enjoying the area sans auto might prove difficult. To reach the bays, head north on SH10 until the turn-off for Matauri Bay and the Tourist Dr. From there, Matauri is another 15km. To reach Tauranga, continue on the scenic road for roughly 15km more. **Whangaroa** is another 8km down the drive, which rejoins SH10 shortly thereafter.

♬♫ ACCOMMODATIONS AND FOOD. Between Kaeo and Mangonui along SH10 is the fabulous **▧Kahoe Farms Hostel (BBH) ❷,** a dazzling, fifth-generation family farm that spreads from the roadside to the coast. (☎405 1804; www.kahoe-farms.co.nz. Kayak rental $55 per day. Cape Reinga bus tours arranged through **Dune Rider 4x4 Tours** (see p. 123) $55. Homemade pizza $17. Book ahead. Dorms $23; twins/doubles $56. 8-person villa $33 per person. MC/V.) Farther southeast lies **Whangaroa Bay,** a narrow inlet with a serpentine coastline. On the eastern shore is the small town of the same name, home to two bars, a general store, a cafe, and the **Sunseeker Lodge (BBH) ❷.** A steep hill leads to this small but homey accommodation on Old Hospital Rd. Call ahead for free pickup from the bus station in Kaeo. (☎405 0496; www.sunseekerlodge.co.nz. Spa. Dorms $21; doubles $60. Cash only.) **Northland Sea Kayaking ❷,** based 10km east of Whangaroa, leads $80 kayak trips from Orua Bay, with accommodations available. (☎405 0381. Private cabins $20 per person. Cash only.) The **Matauri Bay Holiday Park ❶,** accessible from the Tourist Dr., has equipped caravans and tent sites only steps from the beach. (☎405 0525; www.matauribay.co.nz/camp.html. Showers included. Reception 8am-6pm. Tent sites $15; caravans $65 for 2, $16 per extra person. MC/V.) Similarly, the **Tauranga Bay Holiday Park ❶,** has campsites and log cabins which remove the roughing-it feel, but theoretically increase the hygiene. (☎405 0436; www.taurangabay.co.nz. Tent sites $15. 2-person cabins $90, with kitchen $140. MC/V.)

Cooking your own food at one of the hostels or holiday parks stands as a defensible proposition. Otherwise, **Jake's Cafe ❸,** in Whangaroa, is your best bet. (Lunch and dinner $8-26. Open daily 11am-2pm and 5-10pm. MC/V.) Closer to Matauri and Tauranga, the **cafe ❸** and **takeaway ❶** at the top of the hill, will fill you up. Take a right at the Matauri Bay turn-off from the Tourist Dr. (☎405 1041. Cafe open Tu 11am-6pm, W-F 12:30-10pm, Sa-Su 11am-10pm. Takeaway open M-Tu 8am-6:30pm, W 8am-7pm, Th-Su 8am-7:30pm. MC/V, takeaway cash only.)

NORTHLAND

◑☒ SIGHTS AND OUTDOOR ACTIVITIES. The *Rainbow Warrior* commenced its Greenpeace work in 1978. Used in campaigns against ecological terrorism, the ship set off in 1985 to evacuate those in the South Pacific's Rongelap who had been exposed to radioactive contamination. On July 10, 1985, docked in Auckland before setting out to an anti-nuclear protest in Mururoa, the *Warrior* was attacked by French agents with explosives who killed one of its crew members. Though the ship could not be salvaged, the Maori population of Matauri Bay convinced Greenpeace to sink the ship near the Cavalli Islands, close to the resting place of their ancestral *waka*. Today the ex-vessel serves as a marine reserve and international attraction for the diving community. **Paihia Dive** (p. 114; ☎402 7551 or 0800 107 551; www.divenz.com) offers trips to the *Warrior*, as does **Matauri Kat Charters** (☎407 3483 or 0800 492 774). In 1990, the Ngati-Kura tribe commissioned a **memorial sculpture** to be placed on top of Matauri Bay Hill, in commemoration of the ill-fated, sunken eco-behemoth. Visitors can park at the bottom of the hill and climb to its column-crested apex for an excellent panorama of the Cavallis and the *Warrior's* watery grave. The Oceans Village has **kayaks** ($15 per hr.) and **boats** (half-day $85, full-day $160) for the renting. For those with a bit more disposable green, the **Kauri Cliffs Golf Course** has a beautiful layout.

AHIPARA AND KAITAIA ☎09

Ahipara, 15km south of Kaitaia, is so perfectly positioned at the southernmost tip of **Ninety Mile Beach** that it looks to have been placed by the hand of some benevolent God of Surf. Though no buses pass through the town center, which consists of two small groceries and a liquor store, travelers arriving via private transport will find no shortage of diversions, courtesy of the white sand beach, curling waves, and massive sand dunes—the former site of prehistoric kauri forests—overlooking the Tasman Sea. Though Let's Go does not recommend hitchhiking, backpackers report that lifts to Ahipara are easy to come by near the clocktower in Kaiatai.

The first stop for visitors should be the **☒Endless Summer Lodge (BBH) ❷**, 245 Foreshore Rd., 2km south of the town center. The gingerbread porch of this spacious Victorian house is steps from the beach and also looks out onto a front lawn strewn with hammocks and lawnchairs. (☎409 4181; www.endlesssummer.co.nz. Surf boards $30 per day. Free sand boards. Dorms $24; doubles and twins $58-64. MC/V.) Alternatively, there is free **camping ❶** available along Ninety Mile Beach. For essentials, the **Ahipara Superette** (☎409 4828; open daily 7am-7pm) will serve in a pinch. **Bidz Takeaways ❶**, across the street, serves up fish 'n chips ($5) cooked with the catch of the day (☎409 4722; open M-Th, Su 7am-8pm and F-Sa 7am-9pm).

In addition to ever-popular excursions up the Aupouri Peninsula to **Cape Reinga**, pastimes in Ahipara include surfing, sunbathing, and ☒**sand dune riding. Tua Tua Tours** offers guided tours through the dunes on motorized all-terrain quad bikes. Rocky paths through the forested hills overlooking the beach add variety to the terrain. (☎0800 494 288 or 409 4875; www.tuatuatours.co.nz. $100 for 1½hr., $125 for 2hr., $175 for 3hr. BBH discounts. MC/V.) The **Ahipara Adventure Centre,** on Takahe St. next to Bidz Takeaways, rents everything from quad bikes ($60 for 1hr., $40 each additional hr.) to mountain bikes, kayaks, and surfboards ($40 per day), to "blokarts"—windpropelled beach vehicles ($30 for 30min., $20 for each additional 30min.) (☎409 2055; www.ahipara.co.nz/adventurecentre. Open daily 9am-5pm. MC/V.) Mark and Fiona offer **surfing lessons** for the downright reasonable price of $55 for a 2hr. lesson. Advanced lessons also available. (☎409 4009; www.surfcoaching.com. Board and wetsuit provided.)

The **Far North Regional Museum,** on South Rd., displays a artifacts ranging from ancient Maori carvings to the anchor from the vessel piloted by French Captain de Surville on his exploration of the Aupouri Peninsula. (☎408 1403.)

Open M-F 10am-4pm. $4, children $1. Guided tours available upon request.) Just 13km north of Awanui, **Gumdiggers Park** invites visitors to walk through a gumdiggers' shanty town as it might have looked 100 years ago. (☎406 7166; www.gumdiggerspark.co.nz. $10. Open daily 9am-5pm.)

Head to the extensive trails on the **Karikari Peninsula**, 20km northeast of Kaitaia between **Rangaunu** and **Doubtless Bays.** Alternatively, the **Herekino Forest (Orowhana) Track** (8hr.) begins at the Herekino Saddle on the road between Kaitaia and Awaroa, goes 15km, and exits on Diggers Valley Rd. The saddle (Te Arai) is the mythical door where Maori spirits pause before proceeding to Cape Reinga. After two hours of hiking, trampers come across one of the largest standing kauri groves in the north. The **Lake Ohia Gumholes** showcase the fossilized remains of a kauri forest. In Awanui, **Ancient Kauri Kingdom**, 229 SH1 (☎406 7172; www.ancientkauri.co.nz), digs up kauri logs that were felled into the swamp 30,000-50,000 years ago, and carves the naturally preserved wood into high-quality crafts. Farther east along the base of the Karikari peninsula, **Coopers Beach** offers sunbathing good surfcasting in Doubtless Bay. **Tokerau Beach,** on **Matai Bay** at the end of the peninsula, is less crowded. A nearby DOC trail winds along the beach (1¾hr. round-trip). Camping is available at the popular Matai Bay **DOC campsite ❶**. (☎408 6014. Tent sites $8, children $3.)

Visitors without cars normally arrive on **InterCity** or **Northliner** at the visitors center. Buses head south daily to **Auckland** (7hr., $72, backpackers $61, students and seniors $58) via **Kerikeri** (1¾hr., $30, backpackers $26, students and seniors $24) and **Whangarei** (3½hr., $45, backpackers $38, students and seniors $36). For answers to all cape queries and **Internet** access, seek out the **Far North i-Site Visitor Centre,** on South Rd. across from the Mobil station. (☎408 0879. Internet $2 for 20min. Open daily 8:30am-5pm.) The **post office,** 104 Commerce St. (☎408 6411), has full services. Open M-F 9am-5pm.

To spend the night in Kaitaia, try **Main Street Lodge (BBH) ❷**, 235 Commerce St., on the eastern edge of town. This colorfully painted hostel is notable for its huge *Whare Wananga*, where visitors can learn bone carving ($30) from local artisans. (☎408 1275; www.mainstreet.co.nz. Key deposit $10. Reception 7am-10pm. Dorms $25; singles $50, with bath $60; doubles and twins $56, with bath $64. Small tent sites $15. MC/V.) **Rumours ❶**, 42 Commerce St., is the best of the local cafes. Blueberry pancakes ($13) or Cajun chicken salad ($13) add spice to standard fare. (☎408 0058. Open daily 9am-3:30pm. MC/V.) **Mussel Rock ❷**, 75 Commerce St., doubles as a

THE LOCAL STORY

A KAURI PRIMER

If the kauri tree seems a constant presence in Northland, it's with good reason: the entire country was covered in the massive tree before the late 19th-century timber boom nearly drove the forests to extinction. The same time period also witnessed a rush for kauri gum, which was valued as a main ingredient in varnish and lacquer. Traditionally, the Maori used the gum for its antiseptic properties. The amber-colored gum is produced by the tree to shore up structural damage to the trunk or branches.

But it wasn't only mankind that doomed the forest giant. A massive natural disaster of uncertain origin (some scientists suggest that it was a meteor, while others argue for a tsunami) leveled the forests on the eastern side of the Aupouri peninsula more than 45,000 years ago, burying the forests in debris. The late 19th centurey gum digging boom was an effort to unearth small pieces of the gum from the underground prehistoric forests—a sort of poor man's gold rush. Today, visitors can visit the majestic tree at the Kauri Museum on Church St. in Matakohe, which offers an intriguing glance into the life of the tree and its human followers. *(☎09 431 7417; www.kauri-museum.com. Open daily 9am-5pm).*

casual lunch spot in the afternoon and an intimate gathering place in the evening. (☎408 0094. Open M-Th 9am-6pm, F 9am-10:30pm, Sa 10am-8pm. AmEx/MC/V.) For an island feel, hula over to **Big Kahuna Cafe and Bar ❷**, 71 Commerce St., for pizza ($15) and coke floats ($4). It's especially popular on Friday night, when a DJ spins danceable tunes. (☎408 0003. Open M 9:30am-2:30pm, Tu-Th 9am-4:30pm, F 9am-5pm and 8:30pm-1:30am. AmEx/MC/V.) The **Pak 'N Save**, on Commerce St., stocks groceries. (☎408 6222. Open daily 8am-8pm.)

CAPE REINGA AND NINETY MILE BEACH ☎09

The Aupouri Peninsula, a narrow finger of rolling sand, extends up from the northern coast into the subtropical waters of the Tasman Sea and Pacific Ocean. Maori believe that spirits of the dead travel to Cape Reinga and dive into the Pacific to return to the mythical homeland of Hawaiki. For visitors, Ninety Mile Beach is an increasingly popular locale for adventure activity and camera cross-hairs, while Cape Reinga marks the meeting of two oceans.

⬛▼ ORIENTATION AND PRACTICAL INFORMATION. The path to the afterlife is flanked on the west by **Ninety Mile Beach,** a name more poetic than "ninety kilometer beach" or "fifty-six mile beach," both of which would be more accurate. Near the top, the sands are interrupted by the **Te Paki Stream,** which empties into the Indian Ocean. This is part of the **Te Paki Reserves,** administered by the **Te Paki DOC Field Centre** (☎409 7521), off SH1. Don't venture out to the very tip of the beach, which is sacred Maori land known as **Pohutukawa.** On the Pacific side of the peninsula, boarders boogie in the ocean waters of **Tapotupotu** and **Spirits Bay.** Slightly south is **Great Exhibition Bay,** a favorite spot among anglers. The Cape Reinga bluff is capped with a **lighthouse. Cape Maria van Diemen** to the west and the **North Cape** to the east have breathtaking, if less celebrated, scenery.

▼▼ ACCOMMODATIONS AND CAMPING. Travelers with cars should steer toward **Pukenui** (pop. 1000), a tiny and charming coastal town with New Zealand's northernmost hostels. ▨**North Wind Lodge Backpackers (BBH) ❷**, positioned on a remote site a stone's throw from the ocean, offers a convivial cooking space, a sunny deck, and a nearly private beach. Turn off Henderson Bay Rd., 9km north of the Pukenui shops, or call for free pickup from Pukenui. (☎409 8515; www.north-wind.co.nz. Reception 8am-9pm. Dorms $20; twins $44; doubles $56. Cash only.) The **Pukenui Lodge (BBH) ❷**, at the corner of SH1 and Wharf Rd., has a welcoming backpacker cabin adjacent to its motel accommodations; both come with pool access, assuming the nearby ocean doesn't interest you. (☎409 8837; www.pukenuilodge.co.nz. Free parking. Dorms $22.50; twins and doubles $50; motel rooms $99-119. AmEx/MC/V/D.)

For more rustic accommodations, the DOC (☎409 7521) maintains two **campsites** in the area of the Te Paki Reserve, but they are only available in summer. One is **Tapotupotu Bay ❶**, south of the Cape region, which features sheltered golden sands accessible by a posted turn-off 3km before the end of the road to the Cape. The site is about 2hr. on foot from Cape Reinga and 1½hr. by car from Kaitaia. (Tent sites $6, children $3.) The other is at **Kapowairu ❶**, along the east coast of Spirits Bay. (200 tent sites. $6, children $3.) The DOC maintains a third campsite near the center of the Aupouri Peninsula at **Rarawa ❶**. Follow the signs one kilometer north of Ngataki on SH1. (Open Labour Day-Easter. Tent sites $6, children $3.) All three feature DOC minimalism: cold showers, running water, and toilets. Bring your own cooking equipment and remember that open fires are prohibited. Consult the DOC at the Te Paki field center (☎409 7521; www.doc.gov.nz)

or in Kaitaia (☎408 6014) for more info. **Waitiki Landing** (☎409 7508) runs shuttles from the Landing up to Cape Reinga for the steep fee of $50.

🄖 🄜 **SIGHTS AND OUTDOOR ACTIVITIES.** There are several ways to tackle the sands of Cape Reinga. One option for motorists with 4WD vehicles is to drive along the beach, a scenic route with the attendant risk of getting stuck in the sand—or worse, floating out to sea. Those attempting to drive the beach should first seek advice at local hostels and take great care to avoid getting caught at high tide. If you do get stuck, **Bradley's Truck and Tractor** (☎409 8501) runs a towing company that will remove cars. The other option for motorists is SH1, which north of Waitiki Landing turns into loosely-packed gravel that can be treacherous at high speeds. As with the beach, drivers should exercise great caution on this stretch of road. The safest and most informative way to see the Cape is via a **guided day tour** in a specially designed sand- and surf-worthy craft. Tours leave from both Kaitaia and Paihia, but those leaving from Kaitaia, significantly closer to the area, spend more time among the panoramas.

From Kaitaia, land-based tours of Ninety Mile Beach usually include a stop on the beach for swimming, a stop for lunch, and an excursion to the 🄜**Te Paki Sand Dunes** for toboganing. Among the tours departing from Paihia, a good bet is **Northern Exposure Tours,** which provides a day of sport and scenery and a tree-hugging stop at the kauri in Puketi. (☎0800 573 875; www.northernexposure.co.nz. 11hr. $92. YHA, VIP, and BBH discounts. $83.) Companies that offer similar trips include **Far North Outback Adventures** (☎408 0927; www.farnorthtours.co.nz; $120-150) and **Sand Safaris** (☎408 1778; www.sandsafaris.co.nz; $60, children $30). **Dune Rider 4x4 Tours** tours the beach in a rugged, air-conditioned Mercedes Benz bus and offers pickups in Kerikeri, Kaeo, Mangonui, Taipa, and Kaitaia. (☎402 8681; www.dunerider.co.nz. $95, children $50. Backpacker discounts.) Their **Paihia Duck Tour** travels land and sea and stops in Paihia, Waitangi, Russell, and Opua along the way. (www.paihiaduck.co.nz. $50, children $25.) With larger buses, **Kings** (☎402 8288; www.dolphincruises.co.nz; $99, children $50) and **Fullers** (☎402 7421; www.fboi.co.nz; $118, children $69) cater to a tamer clientele. **Marty's Pack or Paddle's** "Bite of the North Tour" ($175) includes guided kayaking, fishing, and dune surfing or snorkeling. (☎409 8445; www.packorpaddle.co.nz. Tours $75-220.)

HOKIANGA REGION ☎09

Though it sits directly opposite Paihia on the west coast of the Aupouri Peninsula, the Hokianga feels worlds removed from that hub of adventures. If nature seems a playground for visitors to the east coast, it demands proper reverence and respect from those passing through the west. The massive, century-old kauri trees of the Waipoua Forest are nothing if not humbling. The constellation of tiny towns surrounding Hokianga Harbour—Rawene, Kohukohu, Omapere, and Opononi—provide excellent opportunities for bushwalking, swimming, and sand dune surfing.

🄵 **TRANSPORTATION IN HOKIANGA**

Bus service among the Hokianga towns is limited to the **Magic Bus** (☎358 5600; www.magicbus.co.nz), which stops at the Opononi i-Site. From Paihia, **Westcoaster** buses run to Kaikohe, 55km northeast of Omapere (30min.; in winter M, W, F, Su 9am; $9), and eventually on to Auckland (8¼hr., $50). Although *Let's Go* does not recommend hitchhiking, many hitchers stand on the straightaways; those heading north or south take the Rawene-Kohukohu ferry and ask drivers on board.

🔢 PRACTICAL INFORMATION

The **Hokianga i-Site Visitor Centre,** in Opononi on SH12, has faded 1950s newsreels about Opo the Dolphin in the museum upstairs. (☎405 8869; hokianga@visitnorthland.co.nz. Internet $10 per hr. Open daily 8:30am-5pm. Museum open daily 9:30am-4:30pm.) There are no banks, ATMs, in the Hokianga Region, so bring EFT-POS or an adequate supply of cash. For medical assistance, **Hokianga Health** (☎405 7709; open M-F 8am-6pm) is on SH12 just outside of Rawene; call ahead.

OMAPERE AND OPONONI   ☎09

Keeping watch over the dangerous waters at the mouth of the Hokianga Harbour, Omapere and Opononi (combined pop. 600)—3km apart on SH12—are breathtaking spots to pause before heading south to Waipoua or east to Kaikohe and the Bay of Islands. The latter was once home to **Opo the Dolphin,** who in 1955 befriended locals and captured the affection of the nation. Since Opo put it on the map, Opononi has changed little. It is still a small resort town with sand, sea, and simple food. **Kupe's monument,** an anchor stone and commemorative plaque, sits at the top of a hill on the harbor side of SH12, between Opononi and Rawene. The **grave** of Opo the Dolphin is located in front of the South Hokianga War Memorial. **Hokianga Express** offers water taxi service across the harbor to the dunes, which lure sand surfers keen on sliding down the dunes and into the water. They will even loan you boards and pick them up at the end of the day. (☎405 8872 or 021 405 872. $20, children $10. Cash only.) A short drive from SH12 along Waiotemarama Gorge Rd. leads to the maize maze at **Labyrinth Woodworks.** (☎405 4581; www.nzanity.co.nz. Open daily 9am-5pm. Maze open in summer. $4, children $2.)

   Globetrekkers (BBH) ❷, off SH12, makes a good home. The cottage has a water view, a telescope, and a deck. (☎405 8183; www.globetrekkerslodge.com. Free pickup from the Opononi i-Site. Dorms $22; singles $45; doubles $55. Cash only.) The other option for backpackers is **House of Harmony (BBH) ❷,** in Omapere. (☎405 8778; www.houseofharmony.co.nz. Dorms $23; twins and doubles $50. Tent sites $14. MC/V.) For a quick bite, stop in at **Opo Takeaways ❶** and try a dolphin-free Opo Burger—fish, cheese, and tartar sauce ($4.80). (☎405 8065. Open daily 10am-7:45pm.) **4 Square** has a **post office** inside. (☎405 8838. Open daily 7:30am-7:30pm. Post shop open M-F 9am-5pm.) **Omapere Food Mart** on SH12 has a **post office** inside and a **pay phone** outside. (☎405 8892. Open M-Sa 7:30am-7pm, Su 8am-7pm.)

RAWENE   ☎09

Rawene's (pop. 300) central location once made it vital to the kauri shipping industry. Without the kauri, however, there's no industry—just a sleepy town and a lone **ferry** to **Kohukohu.** (8min.; nearly every hr. 7:30am-7:30pm; $2, cars $14.)

   The **Far North District Council,** on Upper Parnell St. up from the wharf on the right, is not a visitors center but can answer travel queries. (☎405 8900. Open M-F 8am-4:30pm.) ▧**The Boatshed Cafe ❷,** a short walk up from the ferry landing, makes Italians proud with their foamy cappuccinos ($3.50). The connected craft shop sells Hokianga souvenirs. (☎405 7728. Lunch menu $8-15. Open daily 8:30am-4:30pm. MC/V.) **4 Square,** at the waterfront, has a **post shop.** (☎405 7848. Open M-F 7:30am-5:30pm, Sa-Su 8:30am-4:30pm.) Meander among "fluted" basalt boulders at the **Wairere Boulders Nature Park** near Horeke, just 14km from SH1 and SH12. (☎401 9935; www.wairereboulders.co.nz. $10, students and children $5.)

KOHUKOHU   ☎09

Most commonly known as the other end of the Hokianga ferry, Kohukohu (pop. 165) is renowned among budget travelers for its distinctive hostel. (Ferry departs

for Rawene daily at 7:30, 8:15, 8:45, 9:30am, then every hr. until 8pm; $2, cars $14.)
◙**The Tree House (BBH)** ❷, 2km from the ferry 168 West Coast Rd., is a wooden-planked network of decks and rooms in a 17-acre forest. A shop sells basic food and phone cards. Reservations are essential. (☎405 5855; www.treehouse.co.nz. Call from Rawene for free pickup from the ferry landing or from town. Linen $2. Duvets $3. Dorms $22; singles $45; twins and doubles $60. Tent sites $16. MC/V.)
Away from the forest in the town proper, the ◙**Waterline Cafe** ❷, on Beach Rd., gives its neighbor across the river a run for its money. (☎ 405 5552. Open M-Th, Sa-Su 10am-4pm, F 8am-10pm. Breakfast and lunch $6-15. MC/V.)

WAIPOUA FOREST PARK   ☎09

North of Dargaville on Northland's west coast, Waipoua is New Zealand's only primary kauri forest. Inaccessibility protected the virgin woods of the Waipoua region from 19th-century axe blades. 1940s demand for shipbuilding timber stirred up controversy that resulted in Waipoua being declared a sanctuary in 1952.

Everyone who visits the forest wants to see "the big tree" in northern Waipoua, and most buses (including InterCity) stop at least for a snapshot. A trek from parking off SH12 leads through rainforest to the 2000-year-old, 52m high, 14m wide **Tane Mahuta.** "God of the Forest" is the world's largest living kauri and New Zealand's largest tree. The boardwalk keeps admirers at a distance to protect the Almighty's shallow root system. A parking lot food trailer provides snacks.

Waipoua's other "big trees" are accessible via clearly marked walking tracks from the parking lot, two kilometers south of Tane Mahuta on SH12 ($2 requested donation). A 20min. walk leads to the "diminutive" 30m ◙**Te Matua Ngahere** (Father of the Forest), at 1500-2000 years old the second-largest living kauri, which is also the widest, oldest, and most impressive; the close-knit **Four Sisters,** four inseparable kauris standing side-by-side, are just 10min. away. A 30min. walk goes to the **Yakas Kauri,** the seventh-largest kauri, named after kauri gatherer Nick Yakas. The **Waiotemarama Walk** begins off Waiotemarama Gorge Rd. near Omapere next to Labyrinth Woodworks, reaching a spectacular waterfall within 30min. and ending at the Hauturu Highpoint. From here trekkers can either continue on the track to Mountain Rd. or return the way they came—either way, the walk will take about 6hr. at a leisurely pace. A less taxing walk along mostly flat beach is the two-day **Hokianga Kai Iwi Coastal Tramping Track,** linking Hokianga Harbour to the **Kai Iwi Lakes** (see **Sights and Outdoor Activities,** p. 126). The first part of this track, the **Arai te Uru Heritage Walk,** is only 5min. but grants spectacular views of the harbor. Follow signs south of Omapere to the turn-off from SH12.

DARGAVILLE   ☎09

Dargaville (pop. 4600) has few attractions and is normally used as a place to stock up on provisions—gas, food, and batteries. While proximity to the kauri forests may sound appealing, most visitors use this riverside town as a stopping point rather than a final destination.

🖪 🔊 **TRANSPORTATION AND PRACTICAL INFORMATION.** Buses from Dargaville head in two directions. **Main Coach Line** (☎278 8070; www.main-coachline.co.nz) runs to Auckland (3hr., 1 per day, $42, backpackers, students, and seniors $32), while **Westcoaster** runs to **Whangarei** (1hr., M-F 2 per day. $10). Passengers have to change buses in Whangarei to head north to Paihia and Kaitaia.

Dargaville borders the **Northern Wairoa River,** 187km north of Auckland on the west coast. **Normanby Street** is the road by which **SH12** traffic passes through town. Most points of interest cluster on nearby **Victoria Street.** For information, try the **Kauri Coast i-Site,** 69 Normanby St.,where there is also **Internet** access. (☎439 8360;

www.kauricoast.co.nz. Internet $4 per 30min. Open M-F 8:30am-5pm, Sa-Su 10am-4pm.) If you do nothing else in town, get plenty of money at one of the **banks** or **ATMs** on Victoria St., as there are no banks farther north in the Hokianga Region. Other services include: the **police** (☎439 3400), on Portland St.; the **Dargaville Medical Centre**, in the hospital at 77 Awakino St. (☎439 8079; open M-F 7:30am-5pm, Sa-Su 9am-noon); the **post office**, 80 Victoria St., in the Terartz Stationery Shop. (☎430 6051. Open M-F 8am-5pm, Sa 9am-1pm.)

▞ ◖ ACCOMMODATIONS AND FOOD. The **Greenhouse (BBH) ❷**, 13 Portland St., has a large, mural-decorated sleeping hangar with beds separated by shoulder-high, primary school-style dividers, remnants of the building's past as a primary school. (☎439 6342; greenhousebackpackers@ihug.co.nz. Dorms $21; singles $31; twins and doubles $50. Cash only.) The **Northern Wairoa Hotel ❸**, at the corner of Hokianga Rd. and Victoria St., is a majestic antiquity turned budget lodge. Backpackers may feel out of place among the older locals at the bar. (☎439 8923; northernwairoahotel@win.co.nz. Singles $35, with bath $60; doubles $53, with bath $78. AmEx/MC/V.) **blah, blah, blah... cafe/bar... ❸**, 101 Victoria St., is the best of a small handful of upscale options, featuring a standard cafe menu for slightly less-than-standard prices. (☎439 6300. Lunch $15-24. Dinner $18-28. Happy hour Tu-Sa 4-6pm. Open M 9am-3:30pm, Tu-Sa 9am-1am, Su 9am-3:30pm. AmEx/MC/V.) **Woolworths** is at the end of Victoria St. (☎439 3035. Open daily 7am-9pm.)

◙ ⚠ SIGHTS AND OUTDOOR ACTIVITIES. The **Kai Iwi Lakes**, rimmed with pure white silica sand, are a summertime mecca for water enthusiasts. **Lake Taharoa** is the largest of the three and the best bet for swimming. Waterskiing is available at the Kai Iwi Lakes Water Ski Club at **Lake Waikere**. The smallest and most serene is **Lake Kai Iwi** itself, trafficked solely by sailboats and dinghies and offering excellent fishing at Wi Wi Cove. **Buses** make the turn-off on Omamari Rd., 24km north of Dargaville on SH12, but you'll have to be resourceful to cover the remaining 11km. Thankfully, once there, the Kauri Coast i-Site administers two **campsites ❶** at which to rest your weary bones. (Tent sites $10, children $5.)

Closer waters lap the expanse of **Baylys Beach** (also called Ripiro Beach), which, at 100km, squeaks by as New Zealand's longest. Astonishing in breadth and length, its vanishing point is often obscured by mist. As with many, the beach is officially a public highway, but only 4WD vehicles should even attempt the trip.

The ▓**Kauri Museum**, on SH12 in Matakohe, 45km south of Dargaville, is a must for any traveler interested in the settlement of the area. Visitors can walk through a replica boardinghouse from 1910 and a replica kauri settlers' villa, both complete with costumed mannequins and props. Also includes a collection of photographs by Tudor Collins and a room filled with gum carvings. (☎431 7417; www.kaurimuseum.com. Open daily 8:30am-5:30pm. $15, students and seniors $12, children $3.)

COROMANDEL PENINSULA

Isolated, if not entirely removed from the tourist loop, this idyllic peninsula harbors some of the best of North Island's natural beauty. The towns along the Coromandel first rose out of the dust of 19th-century gold mining and kauri logging. Since the 1960s, when potters and hippies moved here in search of communal bliss, the area has flourished as a refuge for artists, retirees, and surfers. Thames, more than just a transport gateway to the southwest, provides historical anecdotes, necessary conveniences for heading up the northern coast, and its own wonders. Here, the Firth (a narrow inlet of the sea) gently curves up to the artisan town of Coromandel and then to the wild Coromandel Walkway. The west coast showcases some of the most scenic, inviting, and secluded beaches the country has to offer. While the peninsula is packed with Aucklanders and other Kiwis during holidays (avoid it altogether right after Christmas), there are no tour buses, no crowds, and no worries for most of the year.

▨ COROMANDEL PENINSULA HIGHLIGHTS

STEAM in a self-dug spa at Hahei's **Hot Water Beach** (p. 138).

SCOUT out the tranquility of the **Northern Tip's** untouched beauty by bike (p. 134).

SNACK on affordable delicacies in hippy-happy **Coromandel Town** (p. 132).

▛ TRANSPORTATION IN THE COROMANDEL

Flights: Great Barrier Airlines (☎0800 900 600; www.greatbarrierairlines.co.nz) flies from **Whitianga** to **Auckland** (30min.; 1 per day F, Su; $99 one-way) and **Great Barrier Island** (30min.; 1 per day F, Su; $99 one-way).

Buses: Travelers without private transportation should consider buying a **Pacific Coast Highway Pass** from **Intercity**. The pass covers fare to **Auckland,** the **Coromandel Peninsula loop, Tauranga, Rotorua, Whakatane, Gisborne, Napier, Palmerston North,** and **Wellington,** conveniently skipping 8hr. of East Cape coastline. (The Pacific Coast Highway loop runs daily Oct.-Apr.; May-Sept. Su-F. $209, Book each leg the day before.)

Shuttles: Go Kiwi Shuttles (☎07 866 0336 or 0800 446 549; www.go-kiwi.co.nz) services the eastern peninsula to and from downtown **Auckland** and the **airport.** The Auckland service ($46-70) leaves **Whitianga** at 7:30am and **Thames** at 9:20am, arriving downtown at 11:45am. **Go Kiwi Flexi Passes** are valid for 30 days and offer one-way transport through **Auckland, Paihia, Whitianga, Coromandel town, Thames, Tauranga, Rotorua,** and **Hamilton.**

Cars: Most roads are paved and in good repair but have harrowingly narrow shoulders, steep drop-offs, and hairpin turns. Unpaved roads up the Kauaeranga Valley, north to Fletcher Bay, and across the peninsula require caution and patience. A vehicle with 4WD doesn't hurt. Be sure to check your rental agreement carefully for restrictions on driving in the Coromandel. The only gas north of Coromandel town is in Colville.

Bikes: The ride to Coromandel town from Thames is a solid 4-5hr. drive with additional 2-3hr. segments up to Colville and Fletcher Bay. The biking past Colville is difficult and remote. Instead of doubling back, cyclists with appropriate tires can investigate the sin-

Coromandel Peninsula

Cape Colville Fletcher Bay
Port Jackson
Coromandel Walkway
COROMANDEL FOREST PARK
Stony Bay
Fartail Bay
Moehau Range
Port Charles
PACIFIC OCEAN
Waikawau
Colville
Great Mercury Island
Red Mercury Island
Kennedy Bay
Whangapoua
Opito Bay
Long Bay
Kuaotunu
25
Coromandel
Te Rerenga
Coromandel Harbour
Castle Rock
25
Mercury Bay
309
Whitianga
Manaia
Waiau Kauri Grove
Hahei
Cooks Beach
Kereta
Hot Water Beach
25
COROMANDEL RANGE
Whenuakite
Waikawau
Coroglen
Te Mata
Tapu
Alderman Islands
Waiomu
COROMANDEL FOREST PARK
Te Puru
Tairua
Pauanui
25
Pinnacles
Whakatete Bay
Slipper Island
Hikuai
Kauaeranga Valley
DOC Park Headquarters
Thames
Opoutere
Kopu
25A
Firth of Thames
Matatoki
Onemana
25
Puriri
TO AUCKLAND (90km)
Whangamata
2
Ngatea
Mangatarata
Wentworth Valley
26
Kerepehi
COROMANDEL FOREST PARK
2
Whiritoa
25
Patetonga
27
Paeroa
2
TO HAMILTON (60km)
Waikino
Waihi
TO TAURANGA (70km)
Waihi Beach
2

0   6 kilometers
0   .6 miles

COROMANDEL

gle-track to Stony Bay and continuing down the east coast. The entire peninsula loop requires 3-5 days. **Gateway Backpackers**, 209 Mackay St. (☎868 6339), in Thames, rents 21-speed mountain bikes with all necessary gear ($30 per day). **Tidewater Tourist Park**, 270 Tiki Rd. (☎866 8888), in Coromandel town, also rents mountain bikes for $20 per day. Other bike rental outfitters are listed by town.

Hitchhiking: Although *Let's Go* does not recommend it, hitching between the major towns is reportedly easy. Thumbers report long waits from some of the smaller towns (Hahei, Opoutere); arranging a ride back is advisable.

THAMES   ☎07

Thames (pop. 6700) earned its claim to fame through the original get-rich-quick scheme—gold-digging. The 1870s were a prosperous decade, and, with a steady influx of hopeful miners, the city briefly enjoyed status as the largest in all New Zealand— over 100 hotels and bars poured whiskey for its 18,000 inhabitants. Today, Thames is a small, vibrant city offering travelers a glimpse at New Zealand's colonial history, as well as a convenient base for exploring the scenic Coromandel Peninsula. While in town, visitors should dig up some cash of their own; ATMs are scarce hereafter.

⌐ TRANSPORTATION

InterCity departs the Thames i-Site for: Auckland (2hr.; 2-3 per day, $26; backpackers $21); Coromandel Town (1¼hr., daily 9:50am, $16); Tauranga (2hr.; 2-3 per day; $24, backpackers $21, students and seniors $19); Whitianga on a non-loop run (1¾hr.; 3:30pm; $33, backpackers $28, students and seniors $26). For a taxi, ring **Thames Gold Cabs** (☎868 6037). Although *Let's Go* does not recommend **hitchhiking,** hitchers report that it's possible to get to Coromandel town from Pollen or Queen St., and to Whitianga by waiting on either side of the SH25 bridge into town.

✴ 🔁 ORIENTATION AND PRACTICAL INFORMATION

From Auckland, **SH25 (Pacific Coast Highway)** traces the east coast of the **Firth of Thames** before wrapping around the tip. Thames itself lies between the Firth and the sweep of the Coromandel Range. Most of Thames's shops line **Pollen Street.** Parallel is **Queen Street,** the local stretch of SH25.

Visitors Center: Thames i-Site, 206 Pollen St. (☎868 7284). Open M-F 8:30am-5pm, Sa-Su 9am-4pm. **Kauaeranga Valley Visitors Centre (DOC;** ☎867 9080), 13km from town—turn off Pollen St. onto Banks St., turn right onto Parawai Rd., and follow it all the way out. Open daily 8am-4pm.

Banks: BNZ, 501 Pollen St. (☎868 5811). Open M and Th-F 9am-4:30pm, Tu-W 9:30am-4:30pm. Other major banks with 24hr. ATMs line Pollen St.

Police: 402 Queen St. (☎867 9600), across from Goldfields Mall. Dial ☎111 for emergencies. Station open M-F 8am-4pm.

Medical Services: Goldfields Amcal pharmacy (☎867 9232), in the Mall. Open M-Th 9am-5:30pm, F 9am-8pm, Sa 9am-4pm, Su 10am-4pm. **Thames Medical Centre** (☎868 9444), 817 Rolleston St., down from the hospital's side entrance. Open M-F 8:30am-5pm. **Thames Hospital** (☎868 6550), on MacKay St., parallel to Pollen St.

Internet Access: Computer Geeks Limited, on Pollen St. next to the Thames i-Site, charges $6 per hr. and has laptop connections. (☎0800 243 357 or 868 7912. Open daily 9am-8pm). **United Video Thames,** 456 Pollen St. (☎868 8999), charges $7 per hr. Open M-Th, Su 8:30am-8:30pm, F-Sa 8:30am-10pm.

Post Office: 517 Pollen St. (☎868 7850). Open M-F 8:30am-5pm, Sa 9am-noon.

ACCOMMODATIONS AND CAMPING

Several motor camps lie along the coastal road between Thames and Coromandel town, and the DOC runs eight **campsites** ($7) in the Kauaeranga Valley (see **Coromandel Forest Park,** p. 131). Dorms fill up fast on summer weekends; be sure to book ahead. Contact the i-Site to investigate numerous B&B options.

Sunkist Backpackers (BBH/VIP), 506 Brown St. (☎868 8808 or 0800 786 547; www.sunkistbackpackers.com). A former gold-rush hotel and the oldest building in Thames, Sunkist is a slice of historical heaven. The spacious rooms and serene garden are also perks. Free road bike use. Shuttles to the Pinnacles $25. Reception 7:30am-9pm. Dorms $19 (linens $2); twins and doubles $58. Tent sites $14. MC/V. ❷

Gateway Backpackers, 209 Mackay St. (☎868 6339), behind the i-Site. The only other hostel in town, this tucked-away backpackers offers free road bikes, and mountain bikes for $30 per day. Shuttles to the Pinnacles ($25). Free laundry. Dorms $22 (linens $1); singles $40; doubles $50. MC/V. ❷

FOOD

Takeaways and cafes line **Pollen Street.** Fend for yourself at the **Pak 'N Save,** in the Goldfields Mall. (☎868 9565. Open daily 8am-8pm.)

Di Luca's, 640 Pollen St. (☎868 7976). This unassuming local favorite serves fettucine so fresh, the Italian owner's right hand is imprinted with the mark of the machine's crank. Pasta dishes $16, pizzas $13-21. Reservations advisable. Takeaways are a quicker option. Open Tu-Sa 6pm-late. MC/V. ❷

Sola Cafe, 720b Pollen St. (☎868 8781; www.solacafe.co.nz). A hip vegetarian cafe with a relaxed coffee shop atmosphere amid cool artwork. Everything on the menu is homemade. Quiche $9. Open daily 8:30am-4pm. MC/V. ❷

Food for Thought, 574-576 Pollen St. (☎868 6065). Fresh breakfast options ($5.50-$9.50), homemade savory pies ($1.60-3.50) and hot sandwiches ($6.50) excuse the cafeteria ambience. Open M-F 6:30am-3:30pm, Sa 7am-1:30pm. Cash only. ❷

SIGHTS AND OUTDOOR ACTIVITIES

Not only has Thames retained its 19th-century good looks, but most of its activities also throw backpackers a good hundred years into the past. An impressive memorial to the gold industry, the **Gold Mine Experience,** on SH25 at the north end of town, hosts rock-crushing and sifting demonstrations that will take you into a prospecting shaft, and breaks the illusion of gold-digging glamour. (☎868 8514. Open daily 10am-4pm. $10, children $5.) Illuminated at night, the **WWI Peace Memorial,** up Monument Rd. from Waiotahi Rd. at the north end of town, provides a panorama of both the town and the Firth. The **Karaka Bird Hide,** a small nature preserve just past Goldfields Mall, was built with French compensation funds for the bombing of the *Rainbow Warrior* (p. 120). It is also home to several species of heron, gull, and mallard.

One of the best walks not maintained by the DOC is **Rocky's Goldmine Trail** (2½hr. round-trip with optional 1hr. sidetrip to waterfall), which starts and ends at the Dickson Holiday Park (☎868 7308) on Victoria St. at Tararu. The area is riddled with old and dangerous mine shafts—stay on the path. Tararu Creek Rd. leads to the **Tararu Valley Conservation Trust,** a native tree nursery that accepts volunteers. (☎868 8988.) Do not cross the fords if the water is overflowing. Also at the Holiday Park is the **Butterfly and Orchid Garden,** with 400 colorful insects fluttering inside a climate-controlled greenhouse. (☎868 8080. Open daily 10am-4pm; in winter 10am-

3pm. $9.50, students and seniors $9, children $5.) To explore the natural wonders around Thames on horseback, call Vicky for **K Valley Horse Treks**, 607 Kauaeranga Valley Rd., 8km from Thames, which will take you on 2½hr. ($80), half-day ($150), and moonlight ($95) tours. (☎868 6129. Pickups from the Thames i-Site $10.) **Canyonz** runs full-day trips into the Sleeping God Canyon, which includes the second-highest commercial rappel (70m) in New Zealand. (☎0800 422 696 or 027 294 7724; www.canyonz.co.nz. $175-200. Pickup and lunch included. MC/V.)

The winding 55km **scenic drive** to Coromandel town, with rocky inlets and bays shifting from muddy brown to jewel blue, is the most stunning drive on North Island, especially when the road turns inland, revealing **Coromandel Harbour**. Along the way, the **Waiomu Kauri Grove**, one of the finest old-growth stands in New Zealand, contains ancient, stout kauri. Turn right off of SH25 at the sign for Waiomu Bay Holiday Park and walk 1hr. through farmland and bush from the end of Waiomu Creek Rd., 15km from Thames. About 5km farther is the turn-off for the **Tapu-Coroglen Road**, which cuts across the peninsula. Follow it for about seven kilometers to find the **Rapaura Watergardens**, a lovely area of waterfalls, bushwalks, and garden art, with a tea room and accommodations. (☎868 4821; www.rapaurawatergardens.co.nz. $10, children $4. Open daily 9am-5pm.) Another few kilometers finds a sign marking a steep 10min. walk through native bush to the 1200-year-old "square kauri tree."

COROMANDEL FOREST PARK ☎07

The hills of the 72,000-hectare Coromandel Forest Park are tangled with regenerating bush, crawling with creepers, and laced with high waterfalls and small, fern-lined creeks. Deep within the hills that stretch up the peninsula's volcanic backbone, old kauri dams and mine shafts are interspersed with the few remaining patches of original forest. Active efforts to replant native species are underway, as are rigorous pest management techniques (especially in the north, where opossums have not fully infiltrated). Regardless of the terrain, travelers should arm themselves with high-powered bug spray.

Getting to Kauaeranga Valley without your own car, motorcycle, or donkey can be quite difficult. **The Sunkist Lodge** (p. 130) runs a round-trip shuttle service ($25). Though *Let's Go* does not recommend it, **hitchhiking** is common along Parawai and Kauaeranga Rd., especially on the weekends. Most hitchers wait in Thames at the corner of Bank St. Arrange a return ride or run the risk of getting stuck among the evergreens. The **Kauaeranga Visitors Centre (DOC)** is 13km up Kauaeranga Valley Rd., a winding half-paved road that branches off at the BP station at the south end of Thames. Be sure to stop here to pick up a helpful Kauaeranga Kauri Trail brochure ($1) and fill out safety registration forms before hitting the trails. (☎867 9080. Open daily 8am-4pm.)

DOC campsites ❶ are liberally scattered throughout the valley, with eight off the road and three accessible by trails from the road's end; the sites are cheap and basic ($9, children $4.50). The only hut in the area is the relatively upscale **Pinnacles Hut** with views, year-round warden, wood stove, gas cooking (bring your own utensils), 80 mattresses with fitted sheets, solar-powered lighting, and toilets. It's about a 3hr. climb from the gravel's end. (Book in advance at the visitors center; hut passes not applicable. Tent sites $7.50; hut $15, children $7.50.)

The **Kauaeranga Valley** is one of the most popular hiking spots on the peninsula, with a wide variety of walks leading off the main road. A 5min. hop from the visitors center leads to a scale model of the kauri dams that used to exist in the region. A walk to two of the valley's only surviving large **kauri** stands departs from the **Wainora campsite** (2-3hr. round-trip). The **Kauaeranga Kauri Trail** heads up to Pinnacles Hut and the sheer, jagged bluffs of the **Pinnacles** themselves. It's well worth the swing bridges and the thousand-step staircase through fern-laden bush, but the scrambling towards the end is challenging (6hr. round-trip from the road's end.) An alternative to the Pinnacles walk is the **Billy Goat circuit,** which takes hikers part of the way to the Pinnacles and then loops back with great views of the **Atuatumoe Falls** from above (4-5hr. round-trip). Ambitious trampers can combine the Pinnacles walk with the return loop of the Billy Goat for the best of both worlds (8hr. round-trip). The **Kauaeranga River,** which runs along the road up the valley, sports tons of swimming holes. Find your own, or check out **Hoffman's Pool,** 1km past the visitor's center (☎867 9080).

COROMANDEL TOWN ☎07

At the close of the 60s, most Kiwi hippies traded in their bell-bottoms for slacks and their peace signs for business cards. Others, however, headed to Coromandel (pop. 2000), where they continue to groove in harmony with art and nature. Ambitious visitors undertake treks along the coast or into the interior, while the less ambitious toast the sweeping green hills.

📲 TRANSPORTATION AND PRACTICAL INFORMATION. Transport services change rapidly and vary considerably by season—check with the visitors center for schedules. **InterCity** runs to Whitianga (1½hr.; daily 11:10am; in winter M-F and Su; $18, backpackers, students and seniors $15), continuing to Thames (1hr.; daily 7:30am; $30, backpackers $26, students and seniors $24). **Coromandel Discovery** (☎0800 668 175) goes to Fletcher's Bay and the Coromandel Walkway (pickup after walk at Stony Bay) daily in the summer and on the weekends in winter (2-person min.; departs 9am, returns about 5:30pm; $90). **360 Discovery** (☎0800 888 006) runs a ferry from Auckland that lands at Hannaford's Wharf in Te Kouma, 8km south of Coromandel (2hr.; 4 per week; $49, $82 round trip, backpackers, students, and seniors $44/75). Although *Let's Go* does not recommend it, **hitchhiking** to Thames is reportedly easy, and slightly more difficult to Whitianga. The SH25 road that turns off past the fire station on Tiki Rd. sees more traffic than the 309 Rd. Hitching north in winter is difficult.

The **Coromandel Information Centre** is at 355 Kapanga Rd. (☎866 8598; www.coromandeltown.co.nz. Open daily 9am-5pm.) The **DOC field office,** in the same building, will not issue passes or permits. **Internet** access is available at the **Information Centre** for $6 per hr. Other services include: **BNZ,** at Tiki and Kapanga Rd., with a 24hr. **ATM** (open M-F 10am-3pm); the **police,** next to the visitors center (☎866 8777); the **post office,** 190 Kapanga Rd. (☎866 8865. Open M-F 8:30am-5pm.)

🔓 ACCOMMODATIONS. It's a good idea to book ahead for the summer, when each bed in town is filled. Travelers planning to camp in peak months should be prepared to deal with crowds. Alternatively, homestays spring up during the holiday season. **▧The Lion's Den (BBH) ❷,** 126 Te Tiki Rd. (☎866 8157). This laid-back hostel bests the rest with a friendly host and a communal feel. Free vegetables from the organic garden, homestays in the Hippie House, and savory, home-cooked seafood on request ($16). Dorms $25; doubles $50. Cash only. **Anchor Lodge (BBH) ❷,** 448 Wharf Rd. (☎866 7992; www.anchorlodgecoromandel.co.nz). The newest hostel in town sits right across from the water. This relaxed group of bungalows surrounds a heated pool and spa. Free road bike use. Dorms $20 (linen $1); doubles $55-65; motel rooms $110-165. MC/V. **Long Bay Motor Camp ❶** (☎866 8720), 3km from town at 3200 Long Bay Rd. Take your tent to remote Tucks Bay with beautiful views and escape the motoring masses. Kayaks $10 per hr. Metered showers. Reception 7:30am-7:30pm. Tent and powered sites $15. 2-person cabins $65, $15 per extra person; 2-person bunkhouse $45. MC/V. **Tidewater Tourist Park (YHA) ❷,** 270 Tiki Rd. (☎866 8888; tidewatr@world-net.co.nz). Explore on a mountain bike ($20 per day) or kick back and enjoy the bay from the standard YHA hostel. Sauna $5 per 30min. Kayaks $20 per day. Reception 7:30am-9:30pm. Dorms $23; twins $48; doubles $52; 6-person cabin $180. Tent sites $12.50. MC/V.

▮▮ FOOD AND NIGHTLIFE. Coromandel's restaurants are small in number but high-quality, with some verging on gourmet. **4 Square,** on Kapanga Rd., is a good place to stock up on groceries. (Open daily 7:30am-7:30pm.) ◾**The Success Cafe ❸,** 104 Kapanga Rd. (☎866 7100). More restaurant than cafe, this excellent little eatery has outdoor seating and a covered deck for both coffee and meals. Order wine to complement your meal, or bring your own bottle ($3 corking fee). Mussel chowder $9. Local fish $24.50. Open daily 8:30am-late. AmEx/MC/V. **The Pepper Tree Restaurant and Bar ❹,** 31 Kapanga Rd. (☎866 8211; peppertreecrandb@xtra.co.nz), town center. Specializes in fresh seafood like mussel spring rolls ($14). Dinner menu $23.50-32.50. Open daily 10:30am-9pm. AmEx/MC/V. **Umu ❷,** 22 Wharf Rd. (☎866 8618; umucafe@xtra.co.nz). Umu offers several specialty pizzas ($11.50-25), vegetarian dishes, and all-organic produce in a sleek pseudo-Swedish setup. Open daily 9am-9pm. AmEx/MC/V. **Driving Creek Cafe ❷,** 180 Driving Creek Rd. (☎866 7066; www.drivingcreekcafe.com), 3km north of town before the railway. Pancake breakfast ($12), organic veggie garden, and pottery sales that no earth-friendly traveler can resist. Organic tofu burger $13.50. Internet $2 for 15min. Open M-Tu, Th-Su 9:30am-5pm. Closed in winter. MC/V. **Star and Garter Hotel ❷,** 5 Kapanga Rd. (☎866 8503). The hip (and only) night spot for Coromandel dwellers, this old-time saloon serves food from both Umu and Pepper Tree, sports Internet ($8 per hr.), and has a pool table and rear patio seating. Local beer on tap (handles $6). Open daily noon-1am. MC/V.

▮▮ SIGHTS AND OUTDOOR ACTIVITIES. Coromandel town displays pottery, weaving, sculpture, and woodwork of local artisans on nearly every corner. The **Weta Design Studio,** 46 Kapanga Rd., is the best of the local shops, offering reasonably priced curios. (☎866 8823. Open daily 10am-6pm; in winter 10am-5pm.) Besides crafts, Coromandel town's biggest attraction is the **Driving Creek Railway,** 3km north of town. Begun as a pet project in 1975 to extract clay and kiln fuel from the surrounding hills, the railroad has become the passion of owner and potter Barry Brickell. The ever-lengthening track snakes through glowing forests, tunnels, and bridges. (☎866 8703; www.drivingcreekrailway.co.nz. $20, seniors $18, children $11. Train departs 7 times per day in summer 10:15am-4:30pm. In winter 10:15am, 2pm.) North of town, visitors can pan for their own gold ($5) at the **Coromandel Gold Stamper Battery,** 410 Buffalo Rd., while learning about the gold-mining industry that was once the pillar of the peninsula. (☎866 7933. Open M-Tu and Th-Su 10am-4pm. $10, children $5.)

The arts and crafts-oriented community of Coromandel draws much of its inspiration from the area's natural surroundings. The **309 Road,** branching off 4km south of Coromandel and ending in Whitianga, may be a budding artisan's best venue. Although the unpaved road is winding and narrow at times, it's passable by car; just go slowly around the bends and keep to your side of the road. The most eccentric attraction on the peninsula is the **Waiau Waterworks,** 9km from Coromandel town, with engineered, water-powered kinetic sculptures and activities. (☎866 7191; www.waiauwaterworks.co.nz. Open daily 9am-5pm. $10, children $5.) One hundred meters past Waiau Waterworks, the **Castle Rock Trail** (1½hr. round-trip), the best tramp in town, yields 360° views of the peninsula. The trail is of medium difficulty, though the last 100m are steep. The **Waiau Falls,** set in a glade 7.3km from Coromandel, is a good place to cool off after a dusty ride. Be sure to make it up to the **Waiau Kauri Grove,** about 15km from Coromandel. Walk for 10min. to join other astonished visitors in the cathedral of soaring trees that once covered the peninsula. The daring who push just a bit farther make it to **High Zone** (p. 136), several hundred meters after the end of the 309 Rd.

Mussel Barge Snapper Safaris offers group and casual outings on their 11m catamaran. They also run **Coromandel 8 Wheel Argo**, an adventure tour exploring the old mine roads off 309 Rd. (☎866 7667. Fishing trips $40. 3hr. 8-wheel argo $40-150, depending on numbers. Cash only.) **The Mad Fisherman** also indulges aspiring anglers for 5hr. outings. (☎866 8103. $50. Cash only.)

THE NORTHERN TIP   ☎07

Upon heading north of Coromandel, travelers bid farewell to the comforts of hostels and cyber cafes and fend for themselves in mother nature. With jumbled green hills, deserted crescent bays, and twisting trees, the natural wonders of the North unfold around every corner and may even help you to make friends with those blasted sandflies. The Coromandel Walkway, between Fletcher and Stony Bays, is noteworthy as a relatively easy tramp through untouched kauri forests, intermittently broken by panoramic views of the craggy coast.

⌧ TRANSPORTATION. The quality of roads in the region is inversely proportional to the "gasp" factor—the more beautiful the scenery, the more harrowing the drive. The narrow gravel roads do add charm and a pleasant sense of isolation, though they have a tendency to flood. One road winds up the west side to **Fletcher Bay** at the top of the Tip; another branches off just past **Colville** (28km north of Coromandel) and finds its way to Stony Bay. The well-stocked **Colville General Store** is the northernmost opportunity to fill up on **gas** and groceries on the Tip. (☎866 6805. Open daily 8:30am-5pm.) Check your rental agreement about the area before setting off—poor road conditions will be murder on your vehicle. Mountain biking is a great, but strenuous way to circuit the Tip along the track connecting Fletcher and Stony Bay. **Hitchhiking** is all but impossible here in the winter. Some succeed in the summer (once past Colville, thumbers usually only accept rides going all the way); however, *Let's Go* doesn't recommend it, and prospective hitchers should keep in mind that it's easy to get stuck out on the road. Inquire at the visitors center about the rural delivery man who makes the trip up to Fletcher's Bay every Wednesday and often welcomes tag-alongs.

⌂ ACCOMMODATIONS. Colville Farm Backpackers (BBH) ❷, less than 1km south of the general store, offers down and dirty rural fun (horses, glowworms, and cow milking) and tidy accommodations. Many cyclists spend two nights here and then ditch their saddlebags to lighten their load for a daytrip around the Tip. Colville Farm also offers horse treks for $27. (☎ 866 6820; www.colvillefarmholidays.co.nz. Dorms $19; singles $22; doubles $44; self-contained 2-person huts $55-100, $10 per extra person. MC/V.) **Fletcher Bay Backpackers ❶,** next to the Coromandel Walkway trailhead, is a comfy base for tramping, swimming, or fishing. Owned by the DOC, Fletcher has just 12 beds, making advance bookings essential. (☎866 6712; js.lourie@xtra.co.nz. Dorms $14.) The DOC also manages five basic **campsites ❶** in the northern region, the locations of which are mapped out on the pamphlet, **Coromandel Recreation Information** ($1), available at the Coromandel i-Site.

⚑ OUTDOOR ACTIVITIES. The peninsula's 7.5km **Coromandel Walkway** (3-4hr. one-way) explores lonely coves, bushy valleys, and overlooks turquoise waters from high bluffs between Fletcher and Stony Bays. Apart from a few steep climbs, the walkway is not difficult, though it can be a bit hairy in winter before it's cleared (it becomes overgrown and quite muddy). **Coromandel Discovery** runs their own full-day tour (9am-6pm) of the coastal walkway, with hiking from Fletcher to Stony Bay and resting in a van on the return trip. Good historical commentary, free bottled water and tea, and transport to and from your accommodations explain the steep price. Be sure to wear sturdy shoes. (☎866 7405. Book ahead. $90. MC/ V.) **Go Kiwi** meets up with Strongman in Coromandel from Whitianga. (☎0800 446 549. $120.) While a number of tramps were once available—like the trail up **Mt. Moehau** (892m), the peninsula's highest mountain—many have been indefinitely closed after human contact caused the native frogs to disappear. Mt. Moehau remains closed; contact the Coromandel DOC or i-Site for more information.

WHITIANGA ☎07

Extending east across the peninsula, the coastline softens from mud and rocks into sandy beaches, where Whitianga (fit-ee-ANG-guh; pop. 3700) is almost lost among the dunes. Recent development and an influx of travelers and residents have better established the town as a regional hub and destination. With a relaxed vibe interrupted by weekend arrivals from Auckland, Whitianga has become Coromandel's main resort town.

⌷ TRANSPORTATION. InterCity (☎623 1503) buses leave the Whitianga i-Site for Thames (1½hr.; 2 per day; $33, backpackers $28, students and seniors $26) with a connection to Auckland (1½hr.; 2 per day; $57, backpackers $48, students and seniors $45) via Whenuakite, Tairua, and Hikuai. To get to Whangamata, try **Go Kiwi** (☎0800 446 549 or 866 0336; www.go-kiwi.co.nz), which departs daily at 7:30am (1½hr., $33). Otherwise, take the InterCity bus through Waihi, a much more circuitous route. Also runs to Auckland ($48), Rotorua ($70) and Coromandel ($21). **Mercury Bay Taxis** (☎866 5643) will also run to Coromandel town for about $100 per van (11-person max. Cash only.) Book bus transport at the **Whitianga i-Site** (see below) or through **United Travel/Travel Options**, 75 Albert St. (☎866 4397. Open M-F 9am-5pm.) **Whitianga Water Transport** sends shuttles to Ferry Landing. (☎866 5472. 5-10min., daily 7:30am-10:30pm, $4 round-trip.) **The Bike Man**, 16 Coghill St. (☎866 0745), is a pedal purveyor (Full-day $25. Includes helmet and lock. AmEx/MC/V.)

◼⚡ ORIENTATION AND PRACTICAL INFORMATION. Whitianga sits where **Mercury Bay's** beach meets **Whitianga Harbour. SH25** newly bypasses the town, becoming part of **Buffalo Beach Road,** north of town along the beach. Going south into town, Buffalo Beach Rd. merges with **Albert Street,** the main drag. The **Whitianga i-Site,** 66 Albert St., produces a brochure packed with information about the Mercury Bay area. It also offers **Internet** access. (☎866 5555; www.whitianga.co.nz. Internet $3 per 15min. Open Dec.-Jan. daily 8am-6pm. Feb.-Nov. M-F 9am-5pm, Sa-Su 9am-4pm.) So does **Inter-earth,** on Blacksmith Ln. (☎866 5991. $3.60 per 30min. Open M-F 9am-9pm, Sa 10am-7pm, Su 10am-5pm.) **Baywash Laundromat,** 15 Monk St., charges $8 for self-service wash and dry (☎866 2288. Open daily 9am-9pm.) Other services include: **Westpac Trust,** with an **ATM,** on Albert St. (☎866 4532; open M-Tu and Th-F 9am-4:30pm, W 9:30am-4:30pm); the **police,** at 3 Campbell St. (☎866 4000; open M-F 8am-4pm); **Mercury Bay Medical Centre,** at Albert and Owen St. (☎866 5911; open M-F 8:30am-5pm, Sa 9-11am); **Mercury Bay Pharmacy** next door (☎866 4592; open M-F 8:30am-5:30pm); the **post office,** 72 Albert St. (☎866 4006. Open M-F 8:30am-5pm).

⌂⚡ ACCOMMODATIONS AND CAMPING. In a stout converted motel about 1km from downtown, **On the Beach Backpacker's Lodge (BBH/YHA) ❷,** 46 Buffalo Beach Rd., scores points for location. The enthusiastic owners joke with guests and provide a courtesy van, as well as free kayaks, fishing rods, boogie boards, and shovels for Hot Water Beach. (☎866 5380; www.coromandelbackpackers.com. Reception 7am-7pm. $20 key deposit. Bike rental $20 per day. Dorms $24; twins and doubles $58, with bath $86. MC/V.) Near town is **The Cat's Pyjamas Back-**

packers Lodge ❶, 4 Monk St., off Albert St. Ask Buster, the affable owner, about scenic flights in his single-prop plane. A former retirement home, The Cat's Pyjamas makes you feel as if you've been there for years. (☎866 4663; www.cats-pyjamas.co.nz. $20 key deposit. Free boogie board use. Bike rental $20 per day. Reception daily 7am-8pm. Dorms $21; twins and doubles $48. Tent sites $12. MC/V.) **Bay Watch Backpackers (VIP) ❷**, 22 The Esplanade, is along the bay beyond where Buffalo Beach Rd. turns into Albert St. (☎866 5481; www.whitianga.co.nz. Bikes available. Dorms $23; doubles and twins $60; motel units $65-140. MC/V.) **The Mercury Bay Motor Camp ❶**, 121 Albert St., is 500m south of the town center with standard motor park amenities. (☎866 5579. Reception 8am-8:30pm. Camping shower $0.10 per min. Tent and caravan sites $12. Dorms $18. Cash only.)

🛈🍴 **FOOD AND NIGHTLIFE.** Visit **4 Square**, 3 Albert St., for groceries. (☎866 5702. Open daily 7am-8pm.) The **New World**, 1 Joan Gaskell Rd., on the outskirts of town, is a bit better stocked. (☎867 1900. Open daily 8am-8pm.) A block from busy Albert St., 🍴**Cafe Nina ❷**, 20 Victoria St., is a perfect reprieve. The muffins melt in your mouth, and the lunch menu (from $13) always has veggie options. (☎866 5440. Open daily 8am-3pm. MC/V.) **The Fire Place ❸**, 9 The Esplanade, across from the wharf, is the spot to splurge; the older locals seem to. Brick-oven pizzas ($20) are especially good. (☎866 4828. Open daily 11:30am-late, in winter M-F 11:30am-2pm and 5:30-9pm, Sa-Su 11:30am-9pm. AmEx/MC/V.) The Whitianga Marina Hotel, 1 Blacksmith Ln., has two options. For the backpacker set, **The Blacksmith's Kitchen ❷** has plate-sized burgers ($6-12.50). (Open daily noon-late. AmEx/MC/V.) **Smitty's Bar and Grille ❸**, 37 Albert St., is all about the love of the game. Handles $5.30. Bangers and mash $12.50. (☎866 4647. Open daily 11am-late. AmEx/MC/V.) The **Upper Crust Cafe ❶**, 47 Albert St., is a diner based around the age old idea that breakfast is the best meal; sandwiches ($3-6.50) are just a distraction from the real deal, served all day. (☎866 5669. Open daily 6am-4pm. MC/V.)

🎭🎿 **SIGHTS AND OUTDOOR ACTIVITIES.** There's no reason to stay indoors in Whitianga. Cross the river and take the path to the small **Scenic Reserve** on the right. Follow the water up to the 24m bluff of **Whitianga Rock**, an old Maori *pa* (fortified village), from which stone for the old landing wharf was taken. Gorgeous views reward those who walk from **Ferry Landing** up to the **Shakespeare Lookout**, named for a resemblance to the Bard; you can also drive on highway 25 (40min.) The walk follows along **Front Beach** to the crescent of **Flaxmill Bay** and climbs from the sign on the pohutukawa tree at the far end. The view from the top includes a glimpse of **Lonely Bay.** Isolated from unsightly buildings and roads, the cove's golden sands and turquoise surf are accessible by boat or by the steep footpath down from Shakespeare Lookout. The next beach over is **Cooks Beach,** a shallow 3km stretch. **Buffalo Beach,** directly on the shores of Whitianga, is named for the *HMS Buffalo,* which wrecked in 1840 while collecting kauri for England. In order to explore the area on the other side of the harbor, rent a **bike** either in town or at Ferry Landing and ride out to Hahei and Hot Water Beach. Intensely blue water draws most people to the **Mercury Bay** area. With **Cathedral Cove Marine Reserve** nearby and the Mercury Bay Islands off the coast, water activities include windsurfing, kayaking, and cruising. Whitianga also has some of New Zealand's best **big-game fishing** from December to March.

For a thrill, venture just south of the junction between SH25 and the 309 Rd. to **High Zone,** 49 Kaimarama Rd. New owners Penny and Geoff have turned the immaculate colonial house into a B&B, but the main event remains in their front yard: the nine different ropes course activities, 12m above the ground. The 14m free-falling high swing gives your adrenal glands a workout. (☎866 2113; www.highzone.co.nz. High swing $15. 3-activity combo $40. Full course $60.

Cash only.) From Whitianga, hop aboard the **Cave Cruzer,** which jaunts to the bays and stops for a musical experience in giant sea caves. Captain Bob also has fishing trips, snorkeling trips, group picnics, and island tours. (☎866 2275 or 0800 427 893; www.cavecruiser.co.nz. Departs in summer 9, 10:30am, 2, 6pm. $30-50.) The **Glass Bottom Boat** explores the marine reserve and gives visitors an onboard mask into the depths below. (☎867 1962; www.glassbottomboatwhitianga.co.nz. $75, backpackers $65, children $40. MC/V.) Exercise your artistic fingers at **Bay Carving,** on the Esplanade opposite the wharf beside the museum. The metamorphosis from paper to polished pendant in 3hr. is satisfying, particularly for the otherwise talentless. (☎866 4021; www.baycarving.com. Designs and tutelage from $40. Classes 10am-4pm. Call ahead.) Next door, the **Mercury Bay Regional Museum** displays shipwreck artifacts and details Maori history. The nature exhibit showcases a 7 ft. stuffed emu, among other flightless birds. (☎866 0730. Open daily 10am-4pm. $5, under 15 $0.50.) **Twin Oaks,** 9km north of town on the road to Kuaotunu, takes horseback riders of any level. (☎866 5388; www.twinoaksridingranch.co.nz. 2hr. $35. Cash only.) **Kauri Connections** leads 5hr. guided tours up the 309 Rd. to the Kauri Grove, Waiau Waterfall, Castle Rock, and Egan Park. (☎027 682 9294. $45.)

HAHEI ☎07

The name Hahei (HA-hey; pop. 5400) stems from Chief Hei of the Arawa canoe, one of the original seven Maori canoes that docked somewhere off the coast around AD 1350. Today, most visitors to Hahei stop for the waters of Cathedral Cove Marine Reserve and the steaming pools at nearby Hot Water Beach.

⌐ TRANSPORTATION. Go Kiwi (☎866 0336) runs vans from the Ferry Landing to Hot Water Beach, Hahei, Shakespeare Reserve, Purangi Winery, and Cooks Beach. (Departure times vary daily to suit the tide. Book 3hr. prior to departure. $35, min. 3 people.) The **Purgani Winery** (☎866 3724 or 021 262 5742) also runs a shuttle service from the Ferry Landing to Cooks Beach or the winery ($5, min. 5 people), Hahei ($10, min. 2 people), or Hot Water Beach ($15, min. 2 people), as well as a shuttle between the latter two ($5, min. 2 people).

⌐⌐ ACCOMMODATIONS AND FOOD. ◙**Tatahi Lodge (BBH) ❷,** on Grange Rd., has the distinct advantage of being in Hahei instead of Whitianga. Its solid wood bunkbeds, inviting lounge, and affable crowd foster post-beach bliss. (☎866 3992; www.dreamland.co.nz/tatahilodge. Book ahead in summer. Linens $3. Dorms $22; twins and doubles $60; cottages and motel units $120-220, $15 per extra person. AmEx/MC/V.) **Hahei Holiday Resort ❷** and the accompanying **Cathedral Cove Backpackers (VIP) ❷,** at the end of Harsant Ave., are posh for their genre. (☎866 3889; www.cathedralcove.co.nz. Dorms $22; twins and doubles $50. Tent sites $14; powered and caravan sites $15-17. Prices for non-backpacker units jump in high season. MC/V.) The **Hahei Store,** on Beach Rd., sells groceries and doubles as a **post shop.** (☎866 3885. Open daily 8:30am-7:30pm, in winter daily 8:30am-5:30pm.) Around the corner next to the Tatahi Lodge, **Luna Cafe ❷** has a rotating menu with salads, pizza, and other meals for under $15 until 2:30pm, after which time the Cafe turns into a restaurant with considerably steeper prices. (☎866 3016. Open daily 9am-"until we've closed." In winter M and Th-Su. AmEx/MC/V.)

⋔ OUTDOOR ACTIVITIES. Hahei's **beach** is sheltered by offshore islands, providing perfect calm for swimmers. Surfers head to **Hot Water Beach** (p. 138) for the bigger breaks. To the south of Hahei rises the dramatic bluff of **Hereheretaura Point,** an ideal spot for an old Maori *pa;* cross the creek at the beach's end and follow the path (1hr. round-trip) for 360° views. To the north, around a green hill, gaze out at

COROMANDEL

the small islands speckling the ocean and amble down to the **Cathedral Cove Marine Reserve (Te Whanganui-a-Hei).** To reach the majestic rock formations over the cove, you can either walk from the beach or turn left past the Hahei Store to reach the 1hr. track to the cove (45min. from the parking lot atop the hill). The hugely popular path snakes through pastures and descends hundreds of steps.

Gemstone Bay contains a snorkeling path, with buoys arranged informing swimmers what they might see below. The next stop, **Stingray Bay,** has been temporarily closed due to landslides. These two bays, however, are merely preludes to neighboring **Mare's Leg Cove** and the famous ■**Cathedral Cove.** With a pristine, white beach and arching rocks, this idyllic expanse of subtropical water is only accessible through a stone archway carved out by the sea (which might require a short wade at high tide). To enjoy the cove's many splendors, swim out to the warped stone formations, or sample the freshwater falls trickling over the white cliffs. For a closer look at some of the bay's more distinctive ecological features, take a guided kayak trip with **Cathedral Cove Sea Kayaking,** which includes pickup from the Ferry Landing for Whitianga-based folk. Studly Nathan gives a briefing on geology, biology, local history, and percolation. (☎866 3877 or 0800 529 258; www.seakayaktours.co.nz. Half-day trips $75.) Nigel and his **Hahei Explorer** provide motorized scenic trips any time of the year to explore the local islands, hidden caves and archways, and a cavernous 30m blowhole. (☎866 3910; www.haheiexplorer.co.nz. 1hr. $59.) He also rents snorkel gear with wetsuits ($35 per day). The organic **Purangi Winery,** situated on the road between Ferry Landing, Hahei, and the Hot Water Beach area, makes 23 varieties of wines and liqueurs, and will let you taste them for free. (☎866 3724; www.purangi.co.nz. Shuttle service available. Open daily 10am-8pm. Call ahead.)

HOT WATER BEACH ☎07

Proving once again that Mother Nature can outdo the resort industry, the golden crescent of steaming sands at Hot Water Beach is a free spa, bubbling with water as hot as 65°C (149°F). Shovels are available for rent from the beachfront store. (Shovels $4 per 2hr. $20 deposit. Open daily 9am-5pm.) For two hours on either side of low tide, you can soak in your own hollowed series of pools. The pools don't always work; locals say the nature gods cooperate only 60-70% of the year. Chances are better in summer, though you may not have the only set of legs poking out of the sand; the Kiwi Experience Bus stops here, and as many as 1500 people try to dig pools in the limited space. The beach is beautiful, but the rips, reefs, and sandbars that bring good surfing breaks also make for treacherous swimming. **Go Kiwi** and the **Purangi Winery** both run shuttles to the beach (see above).

OPOUTERE ☎07

Linger by the tides for a day or two to experience the sound of silence, punctuated only by the echo of shorebirds and the wash of surf along one of the last undeveloped beaches in Coromandel. Lying on a harbor estuary at the mouth of the Wharekawa River, Opoutere (oh-POH-tury) isn't a town—it's just a home to an idyllic hostel, motor camp, and little else but 5km of perfect, lonesome beach.

The **Wharekawa Harbour Sandspit Wildlife Reserve** is one of New Zealand's few remaining nesting places for the New Zealand dotterel (only 1200 remain). During nesting season (Oct.-Feb.), the DOC fences off and guards the exposed sand where these claustrophobic birds nest (they require an almost 360° view of their surroundings to guard their young). **Ocean Beach,** on the opposite side of the sandspit from the estuary, is a great spot to study the jagged outline of the **Alderman Islands** far offshore. Fantails (small, sparrow-like birds that Maori believe brought death when they entered a home) and numerous other native birds clamor around

Opoutere on their way to the summit of **Maungaruawahine pa**. The summit itself towers over the hostel and is accessible by trail from the hostel (1hr. round-trip). Capitalizing on this refuge from civilization is the appropriately peaceful ⍟**Opoutere YHA Hostel ❷**, 4km from the Opoutere turn-off from SH25. Housed in a group of school buildings, this backpackers is a communal oasis. Relief manager Tony also gives eco-tours of the area. (☎ 0800 278 299 or 865 9072; yhaopout@yha.org.nz. Dorms $22-25; twins and doubles $61; cabins $76, with bath $86; $10 per extra person. Tent sites $18. MC/V.) About 1km down the road at the far end of the estuary is the **Opoutere Motor Camp ❶**, 460 Ohui Rd. Pine plantings afford tent sites privacy, while tourist flats and chalets rest near massive old pohutukawa trees, just 200m from the beach. (☎ 865 9152. Kitchen. Showers $0.50. Reception 8am-10am and 4:30-7pm. Open Dec.-Apr. Tent sites $15, children $10. 2-person tourist flats $85, $20 per extra person. Prices reduced before Dec. 26 and after Jan. 31. MC/V.)

Opoutere is a 15min. drive north of Whangamata. **Go Kiwi** (☎ 866 0336 or 0800 446 549) travels daily 5 days per week to **Whangamata** and **Whitianga** ($33). **Whangamata Tours** runs through town to connect with InterCity. (☎ 863 8627. Runs Nov.-Mar. daily. Apr.-Oct. 3 per week. Book ahead through InterCity.)

WHANGAMATA ☎ 07

With 4km of white sand cradling an island-studded bay, Whangamata (fahn-ga-muh-TAH; pop. 5000) deserves its reputation as one of North Island's top surf spots. Apart from the summer surfers scattered on its shores, Whangamata is delightfully residential and hospitable.

🖭 TRANSPORTATION. No major bus lines run to Whangamata; local shuttles carry passengers out to meet them. Make arrangements at the **Whangamata i-Site**, 616 Port Rd. (☎ 865 8310; www.whangamatainfo.co.nz. Open M-Sa 9am-5pm, Su 9am-5pm. In winter Su 10am-2pm.) **Intercity** runs to Auckland (4½hr.; 1 per day; $59, backpackers $50, students and seniors $47), Rotorua (5hr.; 1 per day; $54/46/44), and Taupo (6½hr.; 1 per day; $90/76/73), among other destinations. **Go Kiwi** (☎ 866 0336 or 0800 446 549) runs to Auckland ($70), Auckland airport ($78), Rotorua ($56), and Whitianga ($33). **Whangamata Tours** offers a shuttle to Waihi for connections to Tauranga. (☎ 863 8627 or 025 727 708. 30min.; 1 per day; $20.) **Whangamata Taxi** (☎ 865 8294) zooms around town if you really can't bear the walk.

🖪🖫 ORIENTATION AND PRACTICAL INFORMATION. Port Road is the main drag. The Whangamata i-Site (see above) can reserve tours. Other services include: **Westpac Trust Bank,** 606 Port Rd. (☎ 865 0600; open M-F 9am-4:30pm); **Whangamata Medical Centre,** 103 Lincoln Rd. (☎ 865 8032; open M-F 8:30am-5:30pm, Sa 9am-12:30pm); **Internet** access at **Bartley Internet and Graphics,** 706 Port Rd. (☎ 865 8832; $3 per 15min., $10 per hr.; open M-F 9am-6pm, Sa 10am-4pm); and a **post office,** 600 Port Rd. (☎ 865 8230; open M-F 8am-4:45pm, Sa 9am-noon).

🖬🖫 ACCOMMODATIONS AND CAMPING. The **Whangamata Backpackers Hostel (BBH) ❷**, 227 Beverly Terr., is a worn surfers' haunt as comfy as home, but with more wetsuits. (☎ 865 8323. Free laundry. 9-bed dorms $18; doubles $46; triples $69. Cash only.) The rooms at the **South Pacific (BBH/VIP) ❷**, 500m south of the town center on Port Rd. at Mayfair Ave., are clean, comfortable, and very green. (☎ 865 9580; www.thesouthpacific.co.nz. Reception 8:30am-8pm. Dorms $26; doubles $63; motel units from $110. MC/V.)

◘ FOOD. The summer influx of surfers causes Whangamata's dining scene to sizzle; things lower to a simmer in the winter. **Vibes Cafe ❷**, 638 Port Rd., brings the beach indoors with sand paintings on its walls. Salads ($10-14) are the highlight of the menu. (☎865 7121. Open daily 8am-5pm. AmEx/MC/V.) **Phil's Take-aways** ❶, set back from Port Rd. side between the post office and the surf shop, serves up burgers, tacos, and burritos ($5-8) for cheap. (☎865 8351. Open M-Tu 11am-8pm, W-Su 11am-late. Cash only.) Get fresh food at **Quarry Orchards,** 612 Port Rd., next to the post office. (☎865 8282. Open daily 7am-6pm.)

⚑ OUTDOOR ACTIVITIES. Most come to Whangamata to marinate in the sun and to take low-tide wades out to **Hauturu Island** (a.k.a. **Clark Island**). Check with the visitors center about accessibility. Surfers say the best waves are near the mouth of the harbor. **Whangamata Surf Shop,** 634 Port Rd., is owned by a longtime surfer who rents boards and wetsuits at fair prices. (☎865 8252. Surfboard $40 per day; wetsuits $15; boogie boards $20. Open daily 9am-5pm.)

Good **hiking** and **biking** trails abound in the 12,890-hectare **Tairua Forest,** north of town. **Wentworth Valley,** down Wentworth Valley Rd., 3km south of town on SH25, is the center for outdoor activities in Whangamata. The river valley's walks are strewn with mine shafts. A 2hr. walk leaves the **campsite** ❶ (tent sites $9) and heads up to Wentworth Falls. At low tide, the cramped sea tunnel at **Pokohino Beach** leads to a rocky cove with isolated white sand. A short, steep walk leads to the beach from a parking lot at the end of Pokohino Rd., a forest road that branches off Onemana Rd. 6km north of Whangamata on SH25. The Tairua Forest is owned by Matariki Forests Company, and while hiking on their land is free, biking requires a $10 monthly permit, available at the i-Site. **Whangamata Mowers and Cycles,** 652 Port Rd., provides mountain bikes. (☎865 8096. $7.50 per hr., $25 for 4hr., $50 per day. Deposit $50.) Classic hot rods, dragsters, and motorcycles parade through the streets of Whangamata each year in late April for the **Beach Hop,** a 5-day festival celebrating the culture, fashion, and music of the 50s and 60s. Attendance in past years has been estimated at 70,000 (www.beachhop.co.nz).

THE WAIKATO AND KING COUNTRY

Today, tranquility reigns in the lush pastureland and lazy streams of the Waikato and King Country, but living in these parts has not always been so easy. In the 1840s and 50s, the Maori tribes of the Waikato united to resist encroaching European settlement, proclaiming Potatau Te Wherowhero the first Maori king in 1858. The king's signature white top hat was passed on to his son, King Tawhiao, who used it during the Waikato War (1863-64) to make a legendary gesture of defiance, casting it onto a map of North Island and proclaiming, "There, I rule!" As a result, his people called the region *Rohe Potae*, "the brim of the hat." To the Europeans, however, it was simply "King Country," in grudging deference to the Maori dominance that lasted until the 1880s. Modern times brought a different kind of power to the region; the Waikato River, the longest river in New Zealand, churns out 50% of North Island's electricity.

WAIKATO HIGHLIGHTS

UNDERGROUND CAVES in **Waitomo** (p. 151) allow curious spelunkers and adventurers to explore New Zealand's mysterious underworld.

UNDERGROUND CULTURE of a different color defines the world-class surfing outpost of **Raglan** (p. 146).

HIGH-ABOVE-GROUND CLIFFS in sleepy **Wharepapa South** (p. 150) make for some of the best rock climbing in New Zealand.

HAMILTON ☎07

The home of Waikato University, Hamilton has a reputation as a lively town; the extraordinary number of bars is a testament to its youthful exuberance. Due in part to all these youngsters, Hamilton is the fourth-largest city (pop. 188,000) in New Zealand. Other than the scenic Waikato River and winter's mystically foggy nights, Hamilton has few noteworthy geographical features. It does, however, have a central location—half of North Island and its wonders are a few hours' drive away. Weekends are when the town really jumps, so if you're hoping for an exciting layover here, shoot for a Friday or Saturday night.

▐ TRANSPORTATION

Trains: Hamilton Railway Station, at the end of Frasier St. From Tainui St., go right on Lake St. and left onto Queens Ave. Frasier St. is on the right. **TranzScenic** (☎0800 872 467) heads daily to **Auckland** (2½hr., 1 per day, $41) and **Wellington** (9hr., 2 per day, $135) via **Palmerston North** (6½hr., $100) and **National Park** (3hr., $54).

Buses: InterCity/Newmans (☎834 3457) head daily to: **Auckland** (2hr., 11 per day, $21-32); **Gisborne** (7hr., noon, $58-70); **Palmerston North** (7hr., 3 per day, $52-66); **Rotorua** (2hr., 5 per day, $30-40); **Wellington** (9hr., 3 per day, $65-85). **Guthreys** (☎0800 759 999) runs to **Auckland** (2hr., 2 per day, $20-22) and **Rotorua** (1½hr., 2

WAIKATO

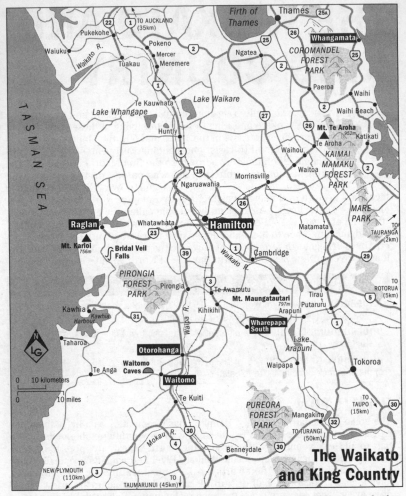

The Waikato and King Country

per day, $22-25). **Dalroy Express** (☎06 755 0009 or 0508 465 622) runs to **Auckland** (2hr.; M-Sa 11am, Su 1pm; $20) and **Hawera** (4½hr.; M-Sa 3:20pm, Su 5:20pm; $44) via **New Plymouth** (3½hr.) and **Stratford** (4hr.).

Public Transportation: From the transportation depot next to the visitors center, **Hamilton City Buses** ($2) stop around the city, including the university (#13) and the gardens (#10). They also go to **Raglan** (#23; 55min.; M-Sa 3 per day, Su 2 per day; $5.50).

Taxis: Taxis gather at Victoria and Hood St. during evening hours and in front of the Hamilton i-Site. Try **Hamilton Taxis** (☎847 7477 or 0800 477 477).

Car Rental: Rent-a-Dent, 838 Anglesea St. (☎839 1049 or 0800 736 822). From $55 per day. Unlimited km.

Hitchhiking: *Let's Go* does not recommend it, but hitching to Raglan is reportedly easiest along SH23/Whatawhata Rd. Follow Norton Rd. away from the city center and go left on Hall St., which turns into Whatawhata Rd. To go north, many try from SH1 past the junction of Te Rapa St. and Avalon Dr., though some say chances are better taking a bus to the outskirts of town. Southbound thumbers try Cambridge or Ohaupo Rd.

◢◤🛈 ORIENTATION AND PRACTICAL INFORMATION

Hamilton lies northeast of **SH1 (Cobham Drive)** and is bisected by the **Waikato River.** Most commercial activity and nightlife is on the river's west bank. **Victoria Street** is the main drag, with the stretch between **Ward** and **Hood Streets** prime for shopping and nighttime carousing. **East Hamilton** houses **Waikato University** and many cafes.

Visitors Center: Hamilton i-Site (☎839 3580; www.visithamilton.co.nz), in the ultra-modern Transport Centre at Bryce and Anglesea St. Internet $3 per 30min., $5 per hr. Open M-Th 7:15am-5:30pm, F 7:15am-6:45, Sa 9am-4:45pm, Su 9:30am-4:45pm.

Banks: Many banks and **ATMs** dot the downtown area. **BNZ** (☎824 8607), across Victoria St. from Garden Pl. Open M and Th-F 9am-4:30pm, Tu-W 9:30am-4:30pm.

Library and Internet Access: The **library,** 9 Garden Place (☎838 6826). Internet $3 1st 30min., $5 1st hr., $4 each additional hr. Open M-F 9am-8:30pm, Sa 9am-4pm, Su noon-3:30pm. Or try **CITYInternet,** 545 Victoria St (☎849 4580). $3 per hr. Open daily 9am-1am.

Police: 6 Bridge St. (☎111 or 858 6200).

Medical Services: Hamilton Pharmacy, 750 Victoria St. (☎834 3444). Open daily 8am-10pm. **Anglesea Clinic** (☎858 0800), at Thackeray and Anglesea St. Open 24hr.

Post Office: 36 Bryce St. (☎838 2233). Open M-F 8:30am-5pm.

🏠 ACCOMMODATIONS

A recent rash of hostel closings have left Hamilton with a serious shortage of budget options. For those craving city living, a few budget options are available, but travelers are better served staying in nearby Raglan. During National Fieldays in June (p. 144) prior bookings are essential.

J's Backpackers (BBH), 8 Grey St. (☎856 8934; www.jsbackpackers.co.nz). Take bus #10 to Hamilton Garden's Gate 2. It's across the street at the intersection of Grey St. and Cobham Dr. From Bridge St., take a right onto Grey St.; it's 2km on the left. A petite house with a kitchen, lounge, and impeccable restrooms. Free pickup. Linen $2. Dorms $22; twins $25; triples $24. $2 BBH discount. MC/V. ❷

The Commercial Hotel Accommodation (VIP), 287 Victoria St. (☎839 4993; www.hotelcommercial.co.nz). This renovated vintage hotel has private rooms along a long, dim corridor, 2 resident bars, and a restaurant. Lounge has Satellite TV. Linen $2 for dorms. Dorms $25; singles $45-75; doubles $60-90. MC/V. ❷

🍴 FOOD

Universities mean students, and students mean cheap food. Droves of ethnic restaurants line **Victoria Street,** mostly between Hood St. and Garden Pl. A staple is the $8 set lunch at **Masala Club ❶,** 237 Victoria St. (☎839 4045. Open M-F 11:30am-2pm, 5pm-midnight, Su 5pm-midnight.)

GelatAmore, at Garden Place. This little hole in the wall serves perfectly textured gelato in classic and Kiwi flavors, like feijoa and, of course, kiwi. Small cups and cones $4, 1L containers $12. Open daily 10am-7pm. MC/V. ❶

Metropolis Cafe, 211 Victoria St. (☎834 2081). "Metro" serves mostly wine and coffee to power-lunchers but offers staples like Thai curry ($14) and a selection of seasonal specialities like pork loin with caramelized apple couscous ($26). High ceilings and metal-framed interior create an urban feel. Open daily 9am-midnight. MC/V. ❷

Gengy's, 191 Victoria St. (☎838 2924). Choose your own meats, seafoods, veggies, and sauces and watch it cooked at this bottomless Mongolian dinner buffet ($24). Savory pancake lunch meals ($15). Open daily 10:30am-2pm, 5pm-late. MC/V. ❷

Gourmet Sushi (☎838 3500), in The Marketplace off Hood St. Fresh fish to go. Vegetarian rolls under $1. Sushi by the piece $1-2. Inventive tofu-wrapped rice pieces or a small selection of fish rolls and sashimi $1.70-2.30. Open M-Sa 10:30am-4:30pm. MC/V. ❶

Rocket Lounge, 109 Victoria St. (☎834 4365), at the intersection of Hood St. Potent espresso ($3), airy scones ($3.50), and delicious panini (with salad $8) will send you into orbit. Open daily 8am-4pm. Cash only. ❶

🜚 ❀ SIGHTS AND FESTIVALS

A walk through the **Hamilton Gardens,** on Cobham Dr. 2km southeast of the city center, is a highlight of the many cerebral diversions in town. The 58-hectare historic gardens are more than simple greenery; the enlivening Japanese tea garden has a serene picnic pavilion, and, in the American Modernist Garden, Marilyn Monroe's visage smiles upon strollers. (☎856 3200; www.hamiltongardens.co.nz. Open 7:30am-sunset.) At the **Waikato Museum of Art and History,** at Victoria and Grantham St., you can admire Maori carvings, an epic totara wood canoe, and rotating exhibits. (☎838 6606; www.waikatomuseum.org.nz. Open daily 10am-4:30pm. Admission by donation.) Next door, the Waikato Society of Arts showcases local artists at **Artspost,** 120 Victoria St. (☎839 3857. Open daily 10am-4:30pm.)

Most of Hamilton's recreation happens along the river, with paths on either side enticing amblers. The paddle-wheel replica, **M.V. Waipa Delta,** launches three times per day, Thursday to Sunday, from the Memorial Park Jetty. The lunch (12:30-2pm; $45) and afternoon coffee (3-4pm; $20) cruises are cheaper, though the dinner trip (7-10pm; $59) features live entertainment. (☎854 7813 or 0800 472 335; www.waipadelta.co.nz. Bookings essential.)

Accommodations in Hamilton fill a year in advance for June's ⬛**National Fieldays;** in 2007 and 2008, roughly 150,000 people will descend on tiny Mystery Creek (15min. away, toward Cambridge) for the Southern Hemisphere's largest A&P (agricultural and pastoral) show. With chainsaw demonstrations, head-to-head tractor pulls, a fashion show of recycled farm material clothing, and a rural bachelor-of-the-year competition, stereotypes of the simple farmer will be uprooted. (☎843 4497; www.fieldays.co.nz. Book hostels at least 1 mo. in advance. Tickets $12, children $6.) **Balloons Over Waikato** (☎839 6677; www.balloonsoverwaikato.co.nz), an awe-inspiring hot-air balloon festival, takes place in early April. For information, contact **Events Hamilton** (www.hamiltonevents.co.nz).

🎵 🎬 ENTERTAINMENT AND NIGHTLIFE

With live music venues, university bars, Irish pubs, two movie theaters, and several live theaters, there's plenty to do at night in Hamilton. For those wanting to see the effects of higher education at its best, stop by the city at the beginning of March for Waikato U.'s O-Week, a non-stop party throughout the city. The most impressive venue is the **Meteor,** 1 Victoria St. (☎834 2472), a versatile space for performances, raves, and other community events. The **Riverlea Theatre** on Riverlea Rd. (☎856 5450 or 0800 800 192; www.riverlea.org.nz) features a more diverse theatrical schedule. When in doubt, tap into the scene with **City Happenings,** a brochure available at the visitors center.

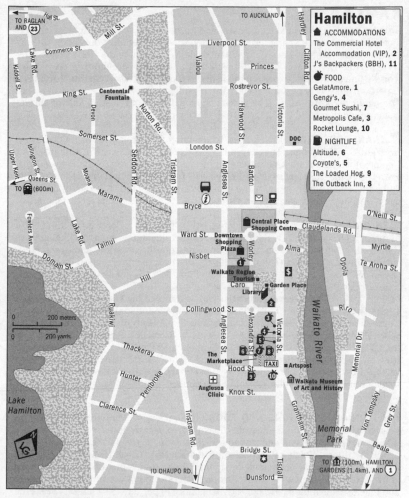

Hamilton

♠ ACCOMMODATIONS
The Commercial Hotel
  Accommodation (VIP), 2
J's Backpackers (BBH), 11

🍴 FOOD
GelatAmore, 1
Gengy's, 4
Gourmet Sushi, 7
Metropolis Cafe, 3
Rocket Lounge, 10

🍸 NIGHTLIFE
Altitude, 6
Coyote's, 5
The Loaded Hog, 9
The Outback Inn, 8

The Outback Inn, 141 Victoria St. (☎839 6354), in the Marketplace off Hood St. Waikato U's students try to memorize all 100 shooters ($6 each), but forget after a few drinks. Outback turns into a veritable meat market on weekends, with more techno than ambience. Happy hour 7-11pm. Open M noon-late, Tu-Su 9am-3am.

Altitude, 30 Alexandra St. (☎838 2221; www.altitude.net.nz). This cavernous nightclub hosts big bands when they come to town, and the weekly cover-free, two-level dance floor is the largest and most popular in town. Wear closed toed shoes. Pint $5. Open W-Sa 10pm-3am.

The Loaded Hog, 27 Hood St. (☎839 2727). Rock, hip hop, and R&B spill out from this hog heaven, rivaled only by rugby on the big screen. Handles $2.50 W-Th. Open M-W 10:30am-late, Th-F 10:30am-3am, Sa 10am-3am, Su 9am-late.

Coyote's, 171 Victoria St. (☎838 2171). Eclectic array of music in a less eclectic atmosphere of stucco walls and wood floors. Monteith's on tap ($5). Open daily 8pm-late.

RAGLAN ☎07

Bronzed skin, wraparound sunglasses, and hordes of surfers cutting through perfectly cresting waves characterize the beach town of Raglan (pop. 3500). In New Zealand's premier surf haven, inhabitants take relaxation and a "no worries" lifestyle seriously. The left-handed break at Manu Bay is considered one of the world's finest. Short of experiencing it first-hand—which is dangerous for all but expert surfers—it is best appreciated in its full splendor in the classic 1966 film *The Endless Summer*. Kick back with the locals or join the stampede of surfers from around the world that migrate here each summer.

☐ TRANSPORTATION. Buses head to **Hamilton** from a variety of Raglan stops (☎0800 4287 5463; 45min., 3 per day M-F, 2 per day Sa-Su; one-way $6). Although *Let's Go* does not recommend it, **hitchhiking** is practiced regularly along SH23, at the edge of town before the traffic picks up to 100kph. The favorite spots are the top end of Bow St. by the water tower (look for the giant surfing mural) and at the Te Uku outpost dairy. Heading to the western beaches, many catch rides at the Stewart St. church.

⚡🔢 ORIENTATION AND PRACTICAL INFORMATION. Forty-eight kilometers of mountain road **(SH23)** winding around extinct volcanoes separate Raglan from Hamilton. The town rests on the harbor, 6km from the coastline and the western surfing points. The **Raglan i-Site,** 4 Wallis St., lies near the intersection with Bow St. (☎825 0556; fax 825 0557. Open M-F 10am-5pm, Sa-Su 10am-4pm.) Exchange currency or use the **ATM** at **Westpac Trust,** at the top of Bow St. (☎825 8579. Open M-F 9:30am-4:30pm.) **Volunteer opportunities** can be found at the **Whaingaroa Environment Centre** (☎825 0480; open Tu-F 10am-4pm), in the Municipal Building on Bow St. Come here to plant trees with organizations like **Friends of Wainui Reserve.** Other services include: the **police,** 3 Nero St. (☎111 or 825 8200); **West Coast Medical Centre,** 12 Wallis St. (☎825 0114; open M-F 8am-5pm, Sa 9am-1pm); **Raglan Pharmacy,** 8 Bow St. (☎825 8164; open M-F 9am-5pm, Sa 9am-7pm); **Internet** access at **Raglan Video,** 9 Bow St. ($5 per hr.; open daily 10am-9pm), or at the **library,** across from the Raglan i-Site ($5 per 45min.; open M-F 9am-5pm, Sa 9am-12:30pm); the **post office,** 39 Bow St. (☎825 8007; open M-F 9am-5pm).

🔟☐ ACCOMMODATIONS AND FOOD. Raglan's wee population increases to nearly 15,000 during the summer. In the winter, expect to find a number of visitors who came for a weekend and stayed for the season, as the surf is good regardless of the weather. ◪**Raglan Backpackers and Waterfront Lodge (BBH) ❷,** 6 Nero St. (☎825 0515; www.raglanbackpackers.co.nz). Posh rooms open onto an airy inner courtyard with a hammock, flowers, and surfers soaking up the sun. Free kayak and bike use. Surfboards $15 per day. Wetsuits $10 per day. Surf lessons $89. Free drop-off to beaches, walking tracks, and other surf destinations. Dorms $20; twins and doubles $42. $2 BBH discount. Cash only. **Solscape (BBH) ❷,** 611 Wainui Rd. (☎825 8268; www.solscape.co.nz), 6km from the town center. With the raging waves of Manu Bay only 2km away, this is a favorite among surfers and those with their own transportation. The brightly painted retired railway cars offer great views. Free pickup in town. Linen $3. Dorms $20; singles $30; doubles $55; triples $66; self-contained cottages $120. Tent sites $12. BBH discount. MC/V. **Sleeping Lady Accommodations (VIP) ❷,** 8km from the town center up Wainui Rd., just past the Whale Bay roundabout (☎825 7873; www.raglansurfingschool.co.nz). This converted youth camp run by Raglan Surfing School offers a range of accommodations. Free pickup in town. Linen $3. Towels $2. Laundry $3. Internet $1 per 10min. Dorms $22-24; doubles $60; private houses $120-210. $2-3 VIP discount. MC/V. **The Raglan Kopua Holiday Park ❶** (☎825 8283; raglanholidaypark@xtra.co.nz), over the

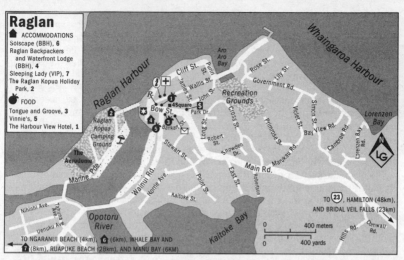

Raglan

♠ ACCOMMODATIONS
Solscape (BBH), **6**
Raglan Backpackers
and Waterfront Lodge
(BBH), **4**
Sleeping Lady (VIP), **7**
The Raglan Kopua Holiday
Park, **2**

🍴 FOOD
Tongue and Groove, **3**
Vinnie's, **5**
The Harbour View Hotel, **1**

WAIKATO

footbridge on Marine Pde., next to the airstrip. This vast area can accommodate 2000 travelers and fills up during the Christmas holidays. Tent and powered sites $10. Dorms $15-18; basic 2-person bunk chalets $65; doubles $50-80. MC/V.

Farmers and surfers chow down at the **Tongue and Groove ❸,** at the corner of Bow St. and Wainui Rd. The veggie-friendly menu includes breakfasts until noon ($6-16) and dinner mains ($16-26) from 6pm. (☎825 0027. Open daily 9am-late.) In 1847, scores of pre-fabricated kauri wood cottages were deposited in Raglan in anticipation of a wave of immigrants. Though it's hard to tell through the heavy vines and the landmark sailboat, one of the only units remaining is now **Vinnie's ❶,** 7 Wainui Rd., formerly a church, school, town hall, pizza joint, and smoothie bar. Now the menu covers all manner of tastes, including fruit smoothies ($3-6) and venison burgers ($7). (☎825 7273. Open Tu-F 10:30am-6:30pm, Sa-Su 9:30am-8:30pm. Cash only.) Raglan's only bar, **The Harbour View Hotel,** adjacent to the eponymous hotel on Bow St., is a popular local hangout with gambling machines and a killer deck. (☎825 8010. Open daily 11am-1am. $10 cover for live performances. Closes earlier on slow nights.) **4 Square,** 16-18 Bow St., is a market, auto supply, and sundry shop all in one. (☎825 8300. Open daily 6:45am-8pm. MC/V.)

🎦🏄 SIGHTS AND OUTDOOR ACTIVITIES. Raglan's black sand beaches alone are worth the trip. If you have a car, make sure to lock it while at the beach; although security has been tightened, theft is still a problem. Of the many choices for beach fun near the town center, **Te Kopua Beach** is the most convenient, accessible via the footbridge at the base of Bow St. Accessibility has its price, though, as the beach is overrun with families and their screaming children in the summer. Te Kopua also occupies a perfect location for wind and kitesurfing. The less crowded **Cox's Bay** and **Puriri Park (Aro Aro Bay)** are ideal for children and picnics; walk along Wallis St. away from the visitors center.

Beginning surfers should start at **Ngaranui Beach** (4km from town), where the surf is less challenging and the sandy bottom is much more forgiving. During the summer months, lifeguards place flags to show where it's safe for swimmers. To access the beach, turn right off of Wainui Rd. onto either Riria Kereopa Memorial Dr. or Wainui Reserve Rd. Only experts head to rocky **Manu Bay** (Waikeri; 6km from town) for world-class breaks. Another 2km farther down the coast is **Whale**

BEACH BLUES. Although many beaches in Raglan are safe for surfing and swimming, be sure to check the current surf report for information on rip currents before hitting the waters as currents often change according to the incoming swell. **Raglan Surf Company** has regular surf updates on their website. (www.raglansurf.co.nz.)

Bay (Whaanga; 8km from town), where green surf and a rocky shore are accessible by a walking path from the cul-de-sac at the end of Calvert Rd. The surf here really heats up in the autumn, when there are often professional surfing competitions. Farther down the coast, **Ruapuke Beach** (36km from town) offers a rugged coastline and the chance to beat the crowds, even in summer. Of course, your car will have to endure winding, unpaved roads to find solitude.

For first-time surfers, instruction on technique and water safety is extraordinarily important and helpful, unless you want to spend your first days of surfing buried by waves and gasping for breath. ◼**Raglan Surfing School** gives 3hr. lessons for $89. They also rent out surfboards, boogie boards, swim fins, and wetsuits by the hour. (☎825 7873. Lessons daily 10am, 3pm. Equipment provided. Kiosk at Ngaranui Beach open daily 10am-6pm.) The **Raglan Surf Company**, 3 Wainui Rd. (☎825 8988; www.raglansurf.co.nz) can set you up with a board and wetsuit. They also run a surf phone with daily beach updates; as does "The Rock" 93 FM. Call the **Raglan Museum,** on Wainui Rd. to see the photographic chronicle of the town's surfing legacy. (☎825 8129. Open Sa-Su 1-3:30pm. Free.)

Although surfers might lead you to believe otherwise, Raglan has more to offer than the ocean. If you can't catch a wave, take a hike to the inactive volcanoes of **Mt. Karioi** in **Pirongia Forest Park.** One glance at Mt. Karioi's feminine silhouette explains why Maori legend refers to it as "the sleeping lady" (look southwest from town in order to see her). With curves in all of the right places, **Whaanga Road** wraps around the mountain's coastal side, making for terrific mountain biking and entertaining driving. Whaanga Rd. begins where Wainui Rd. ends at the Whale Bay roundabout. Refrain from careening around curves—the one-lane gravel road carries a considerable amount of traffic, and vehicles come perilously close to the edge. To find the walk to the top of Mt. Karioi, follow Whaanga Rd. all the way to **Te Toto Gorge.** Park in the first available lot on the beach side, just across from the signs, and begin the walk from that side of the gorge. With some hairy spots of steep, muddy climbing and ladder stretches, the scenic climb to and from the peak (6hr. round-trip; 4hr. round-trip to the "lookout," a false summit on the mountain) requires good footwear.

Freshwater wonders also await. The locals are proud of **Bridal Veil Falls** and the fact that they are higher than their Niagara counterpart. Thirteen kilometers off the main road between Hamilton and Raglan, their thin, delicate spray is best photographed from the lookout, a 10min. walk from the parking lot on Kawhia Rd. The hike to the base is a steep one, but the pool is swimmable. Soak out many of life's aches and pains at the **Waingaro Hot Springs,** 32km north of Raglan on SH22. (☎825 4761. Open daily 9am-9:30pm. $.) With the proper DOC permits, you can also hunt wild pigs or fly fish in the Kaniwhaniwha Stream.

OTOROHANGA ☎07

"The place of outstretched arms," Otorohanga (OAR-to-ra-ha-nga; pop. 2650) has long been a rest stop for travelers. Legend has it that a great Maori chief once paused here to multiply his meager supply of fish, and with a few magical incantations turned the small catch into a proper feast. Today's adventure travelers use

Otorohanga as a gateway to nearby Waitomo Caves, while others stay for the first-rate bird house and Wiki, the town's giant kiwi.

 THE REAL DEAL. Although Otorohanga is proud of its kiwiana, the nearby Waitomo Caves are the real reason to visit this quiet enclave. *-Lauren Holmes*

⌐ TRANSPORTATION. The **train station** is on Wahanui Cres., behind the Otorohanga i-Site. **TranzScenic** goes to Auckland (2½hr., 1 per day, $37-51) via Hamilton (1hr., $18-24) and to Wellington (8hr., 1 per day, $95-120) via Palmerston North (6hr., $64-87). The **bus stop** is at Wahanui Cres. and Maniapoto St., next to the visitors center. **InterCity** heads to Auckland (3hr., 2-3 per day, $22-48) via Hamilton (1hr., $23) and to Wellington (8hr., M-F and Su 12:05pm, $69-90) via Wanganui (5hr., $47). **Dalroy Express** runs service to Auckland (3hr., 1 per day, $33; www.dalroytours.co.nz) and to Hawera (3½hr., 1 per day, $45) via New Plymouth (2½hr.). To get to Waitomo, take Bill and Irene Millar's **Waitomo Shuttle** from the Otorohanga i-Site or any accommodation. An informative history of the area is given during the 15min. ride. (☎0800 808 279. 5 per day, $10.) Bill also operates **Otorohanga Taxis** (☎0800 808 279). Although *Let's Go* does not recommend it, **hitchhiking** is said to be best from the bypass road, Huiputea Dr., north of town.

▊▞ ORIENTATION AND PRACTICAL INFORMATION. Maniapoto Street is the central road in town where most business takes place. While at the **Otorohanga i-Site,** 21 Maniapoto St., keep an eye out for Wiki, the giant kiwi who greets visitors. (☎873 8951; www.otorohanga.co.nz or www.kiwianatown.co.nz. Open M-F 9am-5:30pm, Sa-Su 10am-4pm.) **Westpac Trust,** 64 Maniapoto St. (☎873 6806; open M-Tu and Th-F 9am-4:30pm, W 9:30am-4:30pm), has a 24hr. **ATM.** Fill up at one of the **gas stations** in town, as there is no gas in Waitomo. Other services include: the **police,** 4 Ballance St. (☎873 7399); the 24hr. on-call **doctor** (☎873 8399); a **pharmacy** at the corner of Main and Maniapoto St. (☎873 7294; open M-F 8:30am-5pm, Sa 9:30am-1pm); **Internet** access at the **Otorohanga i-Site** ($2.50 per 15min.) or at the **public library,** on Maniapoto St. across from the ANZ (☎873 7175; $10 per hr.; open M-Th 10am-5pm, F 10am-6pm, Sa 10am-noon); the **post office,** inside **King's Paper Plus,** 39 Maniapoto St. (☎873 8816. Open M-F 8:30am-5pm, Sa 9am-2pm.)

▐▐ ACCOMMODATIONS AND FOOD. A stone's throw from the kiwi house, the **Oto-Kiwi Lodge (BBH) ❷,** 1 Sangro Cres., provides rooms at the end of the suburban cul-de-sac. An excellent option for Waitomo cavers who seek civilization in addition to stalactites. Signs point the way from the north end of Maniapoto St. (☎873 6022; oto-kiwi@xtra.co.nz. 4-bed dorms $20; doubles and twins $44. Tent sites $10. $3-4 BBH discount. MC/V.) On the bypass road east of town lies **Otorohanga Holiday Park ❶,** 12 Huiputea Dr., a well-groomed facility just across from the railroad tracks. With a lawn, a fitness center, and a sauna ($5), this place caters to a wide crowd. (☎873 7253; www.kiwiholidaypark.co.nz. Tent and caravan sites $12. 2-person cabins $50; 2-person self-contained units $85. $12 per extra person. MC/V.)
     Residents are proud of their **Woolworths,** at the southern end of Maniapoto St. (☎873 7378. Open daily 7am-10pm.) The most reliable meal in town is at **The Thirsty Weta ❷,** 57 Maniapoto St. **Free Internet** for patrons makes this a backpacker staple. Fresh mussels ($15) and savory breakfasts ($4-13) satisfy cold, hungry cavers. (☎873 6699. Open daily 10am-1am. Closes earlier during the week. MC/V.)

◙ SIGHTS. The residents of Otorohanga will no doubt remind adventure-hungry travelers to slow down and hang with the birds. The **Otorohanga Kiwi House and Native Bird Park,** on Alex Telfer Dr., where two shifts of birds "perform" daily for

TATTOO FOR YOU

If you have kept your eyes open for the Maori traditions prominent in New Zealand society, you might have noticed the facial tattoos around the mouths of some women. Called *tamoko,* these markings have special significance within many tribes. The gender gaps in Maori society are undeniable, but women privileged to be chosen for *tamoko* have great status within the community. They are granted the ability to speak out for themselves and others.

Modern tattooing procedures have made the *tamoko* much easier to perform and the process easier to endure. While the lines carry the same significance—each mark represents a river flow, a mountain peak, or some other landscape feature central to tribal tradition—the antiquated procedure used to be a greater trial. Traditionally, the tribes would starve a dog for a few days or weeks, ultimately feeding it a black beetle. Upon quick digestion, the dog's droppings would come out thick black in color and consistency. The lines of the *tamoko* would then be carved with a blade into the face and the pungent black "ink" would be applied. This process would be repeated over a number of years until the *tamoko* had become permanent.

4hr., is the best bet to get up close to New Zealand's elusive airborne population. The walk-through aviary also houses tuataras, geckos, and cave wetas, possibly the world's oldest insects. (☎873 7391; www.kiwihouse.org.nz. Open daily 9am-5pm. June-Aug. 9am-4pm. Last entry 30min. before closing. Kiwi feeding daily 1:30, 3:30pm. $15, children $4. $1 BBH/YHA discount.) By prior arrangement, the Kiwi House operates a nightly **Kiwi Watch;** bookings before 4pm are essential. (Groups of 2-6 people. 1½-2hr. $25. Call for times.)

The visitors center hopes to market Otorohanga as the **"Kiwiana capital"** of New Zealand; 24 posted explanations of Kiwi culture are spread throughout every third shop window along Maniapoto St. These informational posters explain such cultural staples as pavlova, "Ches 'n Dale," gumboots, and the multifaceted word "kiwi." Murals of popular Kiwi icons decorate the town; *Pou Pou* (wooden poles) carved to depict Maori legends stand in front of the library.

WHAREPAPA SOUTH   ☎07

As you drive toward the crossroads of Wharepapa South and the four or five buildings that pass for a "place on the map," and pat yourself on the back for venturing so far afield. Wharepapa South and its environs hide some of the most affordable adventure sporting on North Island, from rock climbing and flying fox-ing to extreme mountain biking and tramping. Out of the hills tower incredible ignimbrite (volcanic tuft) crags, home to half of North Island's sport climbing and bouldering. The unique volcanic rock can be tricky even for expert climbers, but bolted routes in the most popular areas allow climbers to get accustomed quickly. Most climbing lies on privately owned farmland; climbers need permission from the owner before ascending. Major climbing areas include **Waipapa, Smith Rocks, Wharepapa Crags,** and **Froggatt Edge;** the latter two are owned by **Castle Rock Adventure Lodge** (see below), whose management charges a $6 access fee. Castle Rock also offers full-day climbing lessons ($100-120) and bike and equipment rental.

 MAP THAT. Before setting out to visit the Wharepapa area, ensure that you are armed with detailed maps from the Otorohanga or Te Awamutu i-Sites. Even road atlases sometimes mislabel the main roads of the remote region.

The ■**Castle Rock Adventure Lodge (YHA) ❷,** 1250 Owairaka Valley Rd., 2km before the crossroads and 45min. from Waitomo Caves, is one of the reasons that New Zealand hostels have a world-wide reputation. The center caters to outdoor enthusiasts, with access to Froggatt Edge, Wharepapa Crags, and four established biking tracks, and draws loyal patrons from all over North Island for regular weekend trips. The luxurious lodge boasts a beautiful pool deck overlooking the rocks. (☎0800 225 462; www.castlerockadventure.co.nz. Spa. Tennis courts. Mattresses in shed $10; dorms $27; doubles $82. Tent sites $8. $4-5 YHA discount. MC/V.) A surefire way to learn more about climbing in the area is to visit **Bryce's Rockclimbing Centre** ❷, 1424 Owairaka Valley Rd. Bryce lets well-maintained rooms to weary climbers as well as providing an infinite source of climbing information. (Dorms $20; private rooms $52 per person. MC/V.) Also at the center is **Bryce's Cafe** ❶, which offers the best coffee ($3) for kilometers and is the only food service in "town." (☎872 2533; www.rockclimb.co.nz. Open daily 9am-4pm. MC/V.)

To reach town and the crags, leave SH3 in Kihikihi and go east on Whitmore Rd. toward Putaruru. After 9km, turn right on Owairaka Valley Rd. heading to Mangakino, which leads 14km to an intersection with Wharepapa South Rd. This intersection serves as the town center, with a store and a cafe. Believe it or not, the **Waitomo Wanderer** (☎0508 926 337; www.waitomotours.co.nz) will make a daily stop for pre-booked reservations on its way between Rotorua and Waitomo (1hr., $20). *Let's Go* does not recommend **hitchhiking**, which can be very difficult here due to thin traffic. There are **no gas, ATM, police,** or **medical services** in this area. The closest proper municipality is **Te Awamutu**, about 18km away.

WAITOMO ☎07

Back in 1887, Maori chief Tane Tinorau and English surveyor Fred Mace chose to ignore Maori warnings and to explore the depths of the local river cave. Although they found no displeased gods, the two spelunkers were treated to an other-worldly display of glowworm bioluminescence and dazzling cave formations. Within a year, Tinorau opened the cave for a few visitors to experience the ethereal wonder. Over 100 years later, the glowworm population remains stable, but the number of tourists has soared to nearly 500,000, putting this miniscule hamlet (pop. 300) squarely on the map. Every morning, about 30 tour buses roll into town and, a few hours (and several million glowworms) later, they cruise on out again. While most visitors come for the "light show," the unique adventure-caving industry attracts its own crowd for trips of varying degrees of difficulty.

🖪 🛛 TRANSPORTATION AND PRACTICAL INFORMATION

Nearly 70% of visitors arrive by bus, and most transportation schedules accommodate same-day arrival and departure. **InterCity** runs daytrips from Auckland (4hr., 12:30pm, $55-65) and Rotorua (4hr., 9am, $44). The **Waitomo Wanderer** offers service between Rotorua (7:45am) and Waitomo (3:45pm), with a pre-arranged stop at Wharepapa South. (☎0508 926 337; www.waitomotours.co.nz. 2hr; $40, round-trip $68.) The **Waitomo Shuttle** is the best option for those making **InterCity, Dalroy Express,** or **TranzScenic** connections in Otorohanga, providing pickup from Waitomo hostels. (☎0800 808 279. 15min.; 5 per day.; $10, by arrangement $23.) Although *Let's Go* does not recommend it, **hitchhiking** is reportedly easiest from the junction of Waitomo Caves Rd. and SH3.

The **Waitomo i-Site** is inside the Museum of Caves. (☎878 7640; waitomoinfo@xtra.co.nz. Internet $1.50 per 15min. Open daily Jan.-Feb. 8am-8pm. Feb.-Easter 8am-5:30pm. Easter-Labour Day 8am-5pm. Labour Day-Jan. 8am-5:30pm.) The **post office** is inside the museum; card **phones** and **public toilets** are

WAIKATO

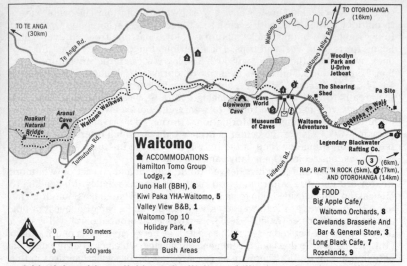

TO OTOROHANGA (16km)

TO TE ANGA (30km)

Te Anga Rd.

Waitomo Stream

Waitomo Valley Rd.

Woodlyn Park and U-Drive Jetboat

The Shearing Shed

Pa Site

Glowworm Cave

Cave World

Ruakuri Natural Bridge

Aranui Cave

Waitomo Walkway

Tumutumu Rd.

Museum of Caves

Waitomo Adventures

Opapaka Pa Walk

Waitomo Caves Rd.

Fullerton Rd.

Legendary Blackwater Rafting Co.

TO ③ (6km), RAP, RAFT, 'N ROCK (5km), ⑥ (7km), AND OTOROHANGA (14km)

Waitomo

🏠 **ACCOMMODATIONS**
Hamilton Tomo Group Lodge, **2**
Juno Hall (BBH), **6**
Kiwi Paka YHA-Waitomo, **5**
Valley View B&B, **1**
Waitomo Top 10 Holiday Park, **4**
- - - - Gravel Road
▒ Bush Areas

🍎 **FOOD**
Big Apple Cafe/ Waitomo Orchards, **8**
Cavelands Brasserie And Bar & General Store, **3**
Long Black Cafe, **7**
Roselands, **9**

0 ___ 500 meters
0 ___ 500 yards

outside. **Internet** is available at the Waitomo i-Site (see above) or at the **Long Black Cafe** ($3 per 30min., $5 per hr.).

🏠🏕 ACCOMMODATIONS AND CAMPING

Despite Waitomo's popularity as a daytrip, overnight accommodations fill rapidly in the summer. Book ahead if you plan on spending the night. For those who want to stay overnight in a converted 1950s Bristol Freighter plane, contact **Billy Black** at Woodlyn Park (p. 154). (☎878 6666. $125 per couple, $12 per extra person.)

Hamilton Tomo Group Lodge (☎878 7442), 2km past the village up Te Anga Rd. A line of beds support the sleep-where-you-fall philosophy at this laid-back, hyper-clean lodge popular with local caving clubs. Free laundry. Dorms $12 for 1st night, $10 thereafter. Tent sites $6 per person. Cash only. ❶

Kiwi Paka YHA-Waitomo (☎878 3395; waitomo@kiwipaka-yha.co.nz), directly behind Waitomo Caves Tavern on School Rd. This encampment of red-and-gray corrugated metal chalets is immense, even without the attached pizzeria and cafe. Dorms $26; twins and doubles $60; triples $78. MC/V. ❷

Waitomo Top 10 Holiday Park, 12 Waitomo Caves Rd. (☎0508 498 666; www.waitomopark.co.nz), across the street from the Museum of Caves. Relax in the pool or hot tub before toweling off and tucking in. Tent and powered sites $116-18. Budget beds depending on number of room occupants $20-45; 2-person cabins $50, $10 per extra person; self-contained units $95-114 for 2, $10 per extra person. MC/V. ❶

Juno Hall (BBH), 600 Waitomo Caves Rd. (☎/fax 878 7649; www.junowaitomo.co.nz). Perched on a hill just outside the village proper, Juno offers amenities like a swimming pool and tennis court. Free pickup. Dorms $22; doubles $50, with TV and bath $60. Tent sites $10 per person. MC/V. ❷

Valley View B&B (☎878 7063), just up the hill and across the road from Hamilton Tomo Group Lodge on Te Anga Rd., 2km out of town. The large, partially self-contained unit holds up to 5 easily on comfy beds and the private lounge (with Sky TV) gives everyone his or her own space. Breakfast included. Singles $60; doubles $80. $10 per extra person. Cash only. ❺

◗ FOOD

There are grocery stores in Waitomo, but the best meals lie outside the village proper. If you're hungry in the village, **Cavelands Brasserie and Bar and General Store** ❷, next to Waitomo Adventures, serves takeaway breakfast, lunch, and dinner items for $5.50-16.50. (Open daily 7am-7pm. Reduced winter hours. MC/V.)

Roselands (☎878 7611). Ironically, the best lunch in town is 3km out of it, up Fullerton Rd., east of the village. The barbeque buffet ($26) is more than enough for you and a few sumo wrestlers. Full salad bar $18. Open daily 11am-2pm. MC/V. ❸

Long Black Cafe (☎878 7361), 1km east of the village inside the Legendary Black Water Rafting Co. Lots of tasty fare from large breakfasts ($3-15) to fresh lunch items ($4.50-7). Specialty "skinnyccinos" ($4). Hurry out of your wetsuit or face the queue. Internet $8 per hr. Open daily 8am-4pm. MC/V. ❷

The Big Apple Cafe and **Waitomo Orchards** (☎873 8753), are next to each other on SH3, 9km from the Waitomo i-Site. Besides free coffee for drivers, cheap produce, and apple pies ($6), the cafe has a strange hollow apple structure that visitors can climb for views of the countryside. Come for the lunch barbeque (includes steak and salad; $23 per person) if you're ravenous. Cafe open M-Th and Sa 8am-5pm, F and Su 8am-late. Fruit stand open daily 8:30am-6pm. MC/V. ❷

◉ SIGHTS

The holes dotting the green pastures around Waitomo are gateways to a mystical world where neither time nor temperature seem to exist. Centuries are measured by centimeters of change, and the caves stay dark and cool regardless of conditions outside—unless, of course, there's a flood.

WAITOMO CAVES. If you are curious to see where all of those tour buses are headed, and eager to empty your wallet, visit the caves that everyone talks about. A stage-like boardwalk traces the dramatically lit formations for a theatrical experience. **"The Cathedral"** has served as a venue for the likes of Kenny Rogers, the Vienna Boys' Choir, and Kiwi opera diva Dame Kiri Te Kanawa (p. 50). The Disneyesque boat ride at the end is so striking that it typically creates the only moments of silence anywhere in the tourist-filled cave. Midday trips bulge with large bus tours. *(On Waitomo Caves Rd., 500m around the bend, west of Waitomo village. ☎0800 456 922; www.waitomocaves.co.nz. Tours daily every 30min. 9am-5pm. $33, children $15.)*

ARANUI CAVE. This cave holds a treasure trove of rock formations, and you don't even have to get your feet wet to see them. *(Tours daily every hr. 10-11am, 1-3pm. $30, children $14. Combination trip with the Waitomo Caves $49, children $25.)*

SPELLBOUND. A family-friendly interpretative tour brings visitors on a boating journey beneath a canopy of glowworms. *(☎0800 773 552; www.waitomospellbound.co.nz. 3½hr. 4 per day. $48, children $25.)*

MUSEUM OF CAVES. Any visit to Waitomo should include a trip to this revamped shrine to all things subterranean. Inside, learn how the caves were formed, contemplate resident wildlife, and take in a multimedia glowworm experience. All of the companies provide a complimentary museum pass as part of their adventure on request. *(☎878 7640; www.waitomo-museum.co.nz. Open Jan.-Feb. 8am-8pm. Feb.-Easter 8am-5:30pm. Easter-Labour Day 8am-5pm. Labour Day-Jan. 8am-5:30pm. $6, children free.)*

THE SHEARING SHED. It's not what you think. Each day visitors are treated to a free, unique experience—a shearing show of Angora rabbits. Native to the Pyrenees, they only survive in captivity. The bunnies are buzzed right before your eyes, but don't feel sorry for them—they would overheat and die without a regular haircut. *(On Waitomo Caves Rd. ☎878 8371. Open daily 9am-4pm. Shearing 12:45pm. Free.)*

WOODLYN PARK. Farmer, historian, and globe-trotting sheep-shearer Billy Black puts on an entertaining **Pioneer Show.** Expect animal antics, audience participation, and general agricultural hijinks. *(1177 Waitomo Valley Rd., 700m off of Waitomo Caves Rd. ☎878 6666; www.woodlynpark.co.nz. Daily 1:30pm. $20, children $12.)* **U-Drive Jetboat** lets first timers and old pros behind the wheel. Not to worry; the sloping walls of its water course are safely lined with tires. *(Open daily 9am-5pm. In summer also open 6:30-8pm. Runs available except during the Pioneer Show. 8 laps $50. Book ahead.)*

◪ ADVENTURE CAVING

Always go caving with a guide; never cave solo, even if you are an experienced spelunker. Virtually all caves are privately owned, and trespassing is illegal. Before you suit up, you may want to consider testing yourself for claustrophobia—head to the Museum of Caves and try the cave "crawl-through." Experienced cavers can to contact **Paddy Vetsch,** president of the local caving club (www.htg.org.nz), or **Kieran McKay** at Absolute Adventure (see below).

OPERATORS

The training of the guides, gear quality, and safety standards are uniform, but each company operates in a different cave system, giving the tours their own character.

Waitomo Adventures (☎878 7788 or 0800 924 866; www.waitomo.co.nz), next door to the Waitomo i-Site, has the greatest variety of adventure caving trips. All trips require cavers to be at least 10 yr. old. $95-225.

Absolute Adventure (☎0800 787 323; www.absoluteadventure.co.nz). The newcomer in the adventure caving business, Absolute Adventure is as close as you'll get to caving with a commercial operation. Photos of trip included in package. Trips depart from in front of the Waitomo i-Site. $125-175.

The Legendary Black Water Rafting Company (☎878 6219 or 0800 228 464; www.blackwaterrafting.co.nz), 3km east of the Waitomo i-Site, on Waitomo Caves Rd. Founded in 1987, LBWR is the oldest operator in town. Black Abyss tour $175.

Rap, Raft 'n Rock (☎873 9149 or 0800 228 372; www.caveraft.com), 7km east of the Waitomo i-Site, Waitomo Caves Rd. Trips daily 11am, 3pm. In winter 9am, 2pm. $99.

Cave World (☎878 6577 or 0800 228 396; www.caveworld.co.nz). Cave World offers 3 tours, departing from the Cave World building next to the Waitomo i-Site. Designed to cater to a wide range of age groups, including children. Each trip emphasizes tubing, adventure caving, or abseiling. $90. 12.5% student and BBH/YHA discount.

TRIPS

Adventure tours in Waitomo cater to all levels of experience and enthusiasm. Standard protocol for caving involves slapping on a wetsuit and coveralls (or just the coveralls if it's a "dry" trip), a hard hat with a head lamp, and gumboots. Check if a snack or meal is included, and if you need to bring swimwear, a towel, or shower supplies. Don't expect many rapids in blackwater rafting. Blackwater rafters float down an underground river in a rubber tube, and any rapids along the way are contingent on heavy rain. Most trips require a minimum number of people to run; advance bookings are essential. Unless otherwise noted, all trip lengths include transport to and from the caves. Time underground and optional adventures (extra abseils, climbs, and jumps) will vary according to the fitness of the group.

FOR THE FAINT OF HEART. The emphasis in these trips is on viewing as much of the underworldly formations as possible. **Black Magic** provides the longest underground glowworm rafting, but a number of artificial structures (including a water slide) mar the beauty of the cave. *(CW. 3hr. About 5 per day. $99.)* **Tumu Tumu TOObing** features optional jumps and small rapids to spice up the float. *(WA. 4hr. 4 per day. $95.)* The progenitor of all underground tubing tours in Waitomo, the **Black Labyrinth** trip involves a gentle float, a waterfall jump, and the obligatory glowworm sighting. *(LBWR. 3hr. 5-10 per day. $90.)*

FOR THE DRY AND HEARTY. St. Benedict's Cavern features spindly stalagmites and -tites with the added bonus of two abseils (20m and 40m), and a flying fox. *(WA. 3½hr., 2 per day. $120.)* **Richie's Canyon,** abseiling 50m into cave known as the "Baby Grand" gives real adventurers a little extra bang for their buck—abseiling twice. This trip is also offered at night, when the lights are turned out for a space walk in a galaxy of glowworms. *(CW. 2hr. 4-7 per day. Night tour, 1 per day on demand. $99.)* The **Lost World Four Hour Abseil** features one of the tallest commercial abseils in the world, a 100m free-hanging abseil into an ethereal world of mist and miniature ferns, self-dubbed a "fairyland without the fairies." The most daunting part of the trip may be stepping out from the 100m high platform or the 27m ladder climb back. Dress for adventure; no denim allowed. *(WA. 4hr. 4 per day. $225.)*

ABSOLUTELY WET AND HEART-STOPPING. The next level of cave tours is a cross between Indiana Jones-style antics and being flushed down the loo on a string. These trips require fitness and comfort with tight spaces. The **Black Abyss** tour includes a 30m abseil, a flying fox, waterfalls, rock climbs, and tubing. *(LBWR. 5hr. 3 per day. $175.)* The **Rap, Raft 'n Rock** trip provides a 27m rappel, blackwater rafting, and a 20m rock climb. *(RRR. 5hr., 2-4 per day, $125.)* Not for the faint of heart, the **Haggas Honking Holes** includes three abseils (5-22m), plenty of climbing (up to 8m), squeezing, and admirable formations, all at a fast pace. Prepare to get wet, dirty, and exhilarated. *(WA. 4hr., about 2hr. underground. 2 per day. $165.)* If you've got the cash, spend it on the **Lost World All Day Epic Adventure.** The 7hr. odyssey begins with the epic abseil (see Lost World Four Hour Abseil above), but skips the ladder for swimming, scrambling, wading, and walking a few kilometers upstream, passing through cathedral-high passages. *(WA. 7hr. 1 per day. $355; includes lunch and dinner.)* **Absolute Adventure's** trips are for the serious adventurer seeking the experience closest to genuine caving with a commercial operator. Unlike many other trips, you can lead your own way through portions of the caves, guide in tow. *(4hr. $125; 6hr. $175.)*

BAY OF PLENTY

At the junction of natural wonders, cultural spectacles, and flowing tourist dollars, the Bay of Plenty is one of North Island's most popular regions. Land of lakes, geysers, and pools, the inland town of Rotorua captivates visitors with its sulfur springs and its wealth of Maori culture. Along the coast, Mt. Maunganui rises from sun-warmed beaches while neighboring Tauranga pulses with nightlife. At the east end of the bay, lively Whakatane, with the smoking White Island volcano in the background, opens onto the uncompromising natural beauty of the East Cape.

🔖 BAY OF PLENTY HIGHLIGHTS

BEAUTIFY in **Rotorua's** thermal wonders (p. 160), where geysers spray, ponds glow, and thermal spas and gurgling mud pools relax, reinvigorate, and exfoliate.

SATISFY your cravings at a Maori **hangi** (p. 163), a tasty cultural experience.

SANCTIFY your soul on **White Island** (p. 172), an eerie and spiritually refreshing escape from the mainland, hidden in a perpetual cloud.

ROTORUA   ☎07

As you slip into the heart of the Bay of Plenty, don't be alarmed by the smell of sulfur in the air and the threads of steam rising from the pavement. The name of the town (*roto*, meaning lake, and *rua*, meaning two) refers to the Maori discovery of the second of 15 lakes in the region. Today, the city is a hotbed of well-structured tourist highlights: geothermal activity and Maori offerings.

▐ TRANSPORTATION

Flights: The **Rotorua Airport** is off SH30, around the east side of Lake Rotorua, 9km from town. **Air New Zealand,** 1103 Hinemoa St. (☎343 1100), has at least 3-4 flights per day to: **Auckland** (45min., $150-290); **Christchurch** (1¼hr., $150-486); **Queenstown** (3-4hr., $200-833); **Wellington** (1hr., $100-337). Bus #10 connects the airport to town, as does **Super Shuttle.** (☎0800 748 885. $15, $3 per extra person.)

Buses: All buses come and go from the **bus depot** (☎348 5179) in front of the Rotorua i-Site. **Newmans** and **InterCity** depart daily for: **Auckland** (4hr., 2-7 per day, $40-51) via **Hamilton** (1½hr., $22-27); **Napier** (4½hr., 2 per day, $59-65); **Wellington** (7¼hr., 2 per day, $65-82) via **Taupo** (1½hr., $20-29). **Waitomo Wanderer** (☎349 2509 or 0508 926 337) goes to **Waitomo** (2¼hr., 7:45am, $58 round-trip), with pickup.

Public Transportation: City Ride (☎0800 422 928) runs M-Sa ($2). The main stop is Pukuatua St. between Tutanekai and Amohia St. Bus #1 goes to Skyline; bus #2 to Whakarewarewa.

Taxis: Fastaxis (☎348 2444 or 0800 221 000) and **Rotorua Taxis** (☎348 1111 or 0800 500 000) operate 24hr.

Car Rental: EZI-Rent, 1234 Fenton St. (☎349 1629 or 0800 652 565; www.ezirentcarhire.co.nz). "Super saver" cars $52 per day, $0.18 per km. Open M-F 8am-5pm, Sa-Su 8am-noon. **Rent-A-Dent,** 14 Ti St. (☎349 3993 or 0800 736 823), off Fenton St., past Countdown Supermarket. $45 per day, $35 in winter; 100km free. Open M-F 8am-5pm, Sa-Su 8am-noon. **Avis, Budget,** and **Hertz** have offices around Rotorua.

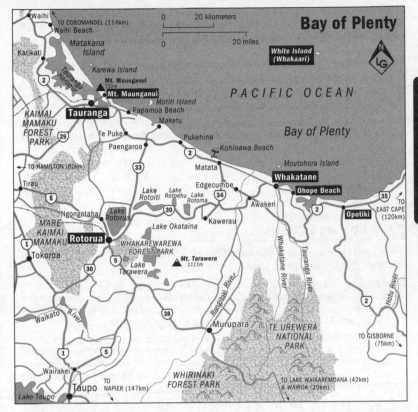

Bike Rental: Planet Bike (☎348 9971; www.planetbike.co.nz), on Waipa Mill Rd. Take the first left off SH5, 2km south of Sala St. Mountain bikes $35 per 2hr., $55 per day. Free bike delivery to accommodations and shuttles to Whakarewarewa Forest. Guided bike tours $65-110; combo bike and kayak or bike and raft $95-150. Open daily 9am-6pm. MC/V. **Lady Jane's Ice Cream Parlour** (☎347 9340), at Tutanekai and Whakaue St., rents antique roadbikes for afternoon cruising. $10 per hr., $25 per day. Open M-F 10am-9:30pm, Sa-Su 10am-8pm. In winter M-F 10am-6pm.

Hitchhiking: Although *Let's Go* doesn't recommend hitchhiking, hitchers report that it's easy to hitchhike from Rotorua. Heading south toward Taupo, many hitchers start past Amohau St. and work toward Whakarewarewa. Amohau St. is also the branching-off point for SH5 north and SH30 east; many hitchhikers head a few blocks away from Pak 'N Save to go east. Catching a ride north is reportedly easier before Rainbow Springs.

■🛈 ORIENTATION AND PRACTICAL INFORMATION

Rotorua lies at the southwestern end of **Lake Rotorua,** but many geothermal and recreational attractions are spread along **SH5** and **SH30,** which wrap around parts of the lake. Downtown is a rectangular grid, defined by **Fenton, Arawa, Ranolf,** and **Amohau Streets.** The crossroads of **Tutanekai** and **Hinemoa Streets** serve as a city center with stores, cafes, and banks. Rotorua is easily walkable.

Visitors Center: Rotorua i-Site, 1167 Fenton St. (☎0800 768 678; www.rotoru-anz.com), between Arawa and Haupapa St. Contains a cafe, showers, toilets, Internet, and currency exchange. Open daily 8am-6pm. In winter 8am-5:30pm.

Department of Conservation (DOC): 14-16 Scott St. (☎348 3610). Open daily 9am-6pm. In winter 9am-5:30pm. Most services also at the booth in the Rotorua i-Site.

Banks and Currency Exchange: Banks with **ATMs** line Hinemoa St. Most open M-F 9:30am-4:30pm. Currency exchange in the Rotorua i-Site (see above).

Police: (☎111 or 348 0099), kitty-corner from the Rotorua i-Site.

Medical Services: Lakes Care Pharmacy (☎348 4385), at the corner of Arawa and Tutanekai St. Open daily 8:30am-9:30pm. Next door, **Lakes PrimeCare** (☎348 1000) has a doctor on call 24hr. Open daily 8am-10pm.

Internet Access: The **library** has the cheapest rates in town, $1 per 15min. Open M-F 8am-5:30pm. Also at the Rotorua i-Site, $3 per 30min., $5 per hr.

Post Office: 1189 Hinemoa St. (☎349 2397), in Kiwi Bank near Tutanekai St. Open M-F 7:30am-5pm, Sa 8:30am-4pm, Su 10am-3pm.

⌐ ACCOMMODATIONS

Some good budget lodgings line **Ranolf Street,** while the strip of motels along **Fenton Street** give Rotorua its nickname, "Roto-Vegas."

▣ **Funky Green Voyager (BBH),** 4 Union St. (☎346 1754). An oasis for laid-back backpackers in a desert of motels. Gregarious owners make guests feel at home. Even the dorm rooms are spacious. Yoga classes. Reception 8am-11pm. Dorms $20-21; twins and doubles $47, with bath $51. Tent sites $12-14. Cash only. ❷

▣ **Treks,** 1287 Haupapa St. (☎0508 487 357; www.treks.co.nz). Opened in the summer of 2004, the facilities at Treks are still sparkling. Cavernous modern kitchen for feeding armies of backpackers. Reception 7:30am-7:30pm. Linen provided, towels with ensuite rooms. Internet $5 per hr. Laundry, safes available. $20 key deposit. Four-share dorms $26; doubles and twins $62, with bath $72; triple $84. MC/V. ❸

Base Backpackers (VIP), 1140 Hinemoa St. (☎350 2040 or 0800 227 369; www.basebackpackers.com). 3 floors of large rooms overlook an indoor climbing wall. A hip crowd lazes in spacious common areas. Game room. Key deposit $10. Dorms $23-25; twins and doubles $55, with bath $68. Female only dorms $28. MC/V. ❷

Kiwi Paka YHA, 60 Tarewa Rd. (☎347 0931; www.kiwipaka-yha.co.nz), 1km from the town center. An upbeat spirit reigns in this quasi-resort, complete with a thermal pool and an in-house cafe. Free shuttle to bus stop. Key deposit $10. Reception 7:30am-9:30pm. Dorms $24; singles $38; twins and doubles $55, with bath $68; triples $75; quads $100. Tent sites $9, powered $10.50. MC/V. ❷

Rotorua Central Backpackers (BBH), 1076 Pukuatua St. (☎349 3285; rotorua.central.bp@clear.net.nz). From the bus station, turn right down Fenton St. and left on Pukuatua St. 6 mattresses fill a bunk-free dorm room in the comfortable old house. Indoor spa. Key deposit $20. Dorms $18-20; doubles $44; triples $60; quads $80. MC/V. ❷

Cosy Cottage International Holiday Park, 67 Whittaker Rd. (☎348 3793; www.cosy-cottage.co.nz), 2km from town off Lake Rd. Thermally heated pools and a private beach make up for the tired communal facilities. Tent sites on geothermally heated ground. Bike rental $16-35. Flats $50-75. MC/V. ❸

Hot Rocks (VIP), 1286 Arawa St. (☎348 8636; www.acb.co.nz/hotrock). Night owls flock to Lava Bar's for all-hours thermal pools and hordes of grooving bodies. Pool. Duvet $2. Key deposit $20. Dorms $23-27; doubles and triples $31 per person. ❷

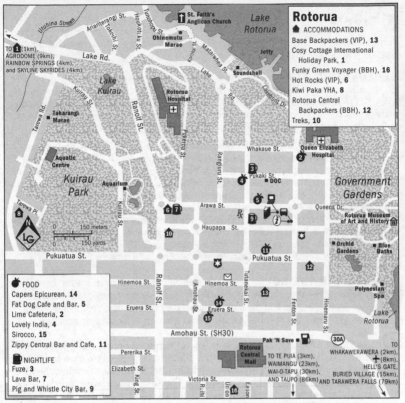

Rotorua

♠ ACCOMMODATIONS
Base Backpackers (VIP), **13**
Cosy Cottage International
    Holiday Park, **1**
Funky Green Voyager (BBH), **16**
Hot Rocks (VIP), **6**
Kiwi Paka YHA, **8**
Rotorua Central
    Backpackers (BBH), **12**
Treks, **10**

🍎 FOOD
Capers Epicurean, **14**
Fat Dog Cafe and Bar, **5**
Lime Cafeteria, **2**
Lovely India, **4**
Sirocco, **15**
Zippy Central Bar and Cafe, **11**

🍸 NIGHTLIFE
Fuze, **3**
Lava Bar, **7**
Pig and Whistle City Bar, **9**

🗂 FOOD

An alternative to the usual fare is the enlightening Maori *hangi* (p. 163). Although the meals exceed the normal backpacker allowance, they shouldn't be missed. A **Pak 'N Save** is at the corner of Fenton and Amohau St. (Open daily 8am-10pm.)

■ **Lime Cafeteria,** (☎ 350 2033), at the corner of Fenton and Whakaue St. This cafe transports customers from the sulfur fumes to what could be the center of any European city. Excellent salads and breakfast menu (from $8). Open daily 8am-4:30pm. MC/V. ❷

■ **Sirocco,** 1280 Eruera St. (☎347 3388). Sophisticated gourmet fare at reasonable prices. Enjoy spooning an ultra-thick feijoa smoothie ($6) on their sunny deck. Open daily 9am-9pm. Entrees from $9, mains from $13. MC/V. ❸

Capers Epicurean, 1181 Eruera St. (☎348 8818). The culinary deli is a popular takeaway joint. Jamaican rum-baked chicken $15. Tantalizing wraps and panini $4.50-9. Open M 7:30am-5pm, Tu-Sa 7:30am-9pm, Su 7:30am-4pm. MC/V. ❷

Fat Dog Cafe and Bar, 1161 Arawa St. (☎347 7586). This low-key cafe is packed with tourists and locals looking for satisfying fried foods. Lunch ($7) and dinner specials ($10.50). Open M-W 8am-9pm, Th-Su 8am-9:30pm. Kitchen closes 9pm. MC/V. ❷

Zippy Central Bar and Cafe, 1153 Pukuatua St. (☎348 8288). Kitschy decor infuses with a dose of funk. With an rotating menu, the tuna melt bagels ($8) are a tasty constant. Veggie and vegan options around $10. Open daily 9am-9 or 10pm. Cash only. ❷

SIGHTS

Some of Rotorua's sights are inaccessible without transport. **Geyser Link Shuttle** runs to Wai-O-Tapu and Waimangu. (☎0800 000 4321. Daily 9am; $20, both $25.)

GEOTHERMAL WONDERS

Rotorua is known for its thermal activity, caused by an active fault line running from White Island to Mt. Ruapehu in Tongariro National Park. Colliding tectonic plates created the spectacular mountains, the bizarre landscape, and the innumerable steaming pools, craters, and vents of the geothermal parks.

■ **WAI-O-TAPU.** This "Thermal Wonderland" is the most colorful—and probably the finest—geothermal spot in the nation. Leased from the DOC by private operators, the reserve is explored via self-guided tour, weaving around boiling mud, an expansive silicate terrace, brilliantly hued pools, and—inevitably—crowds of tourists. While veiled in steam, the stunning ochre and turquoise colors of the bubbling **Champagne Pool** make the celebratory beverage pale in comparison. Erupting up to 21m each day at precisely 10:15am, **Lady Knox Geyser** is another Wai-O-Tapu attraction. Mother Nature isn't that regular—the geyser is soaped every morning to relieve surface tension. (30km south of Rotorua on SH5. ☎366 6333; www.geyserland.co.nz. Open daily 8:30am-5pm. Last admission 3:45pm. $25, children $10.)

> 🔥**TIP** **FIRE IN THE HOLE.** For unexpected and free geothermal activity, head to Kairau Park—affectionately know as KP by locals. Small explosions and geysers go off fairly regularly in the park, although they are nowhere near as regular as at a commercially operated geyser. The park is unsafe for strolling after dark.

■ **POLYNESIAN SPA.** If you're going to spend three days breathing in geothermal fumes, you might as well do it while soaking. The newly expanded adult-only pools and **Priest Spa** ($15), filled with acidic water that reaches 39-42°C (102-108°F), have purported healing powers. The **Lake Spa**, a landscaped terrace of caves and waterfalls, claims to be one of the best in the world. The half-hour spa treatments ($70) are an include entrance to the Lake Spa pools. (At the Government Gardens end of Hinemoa St. ☎348 1328; www.polynesianspa.co.nz. Open daily 6:30am-11pm. Last entry 10:15pm. Pools and spas $12-35.)

WAIMANGU VOLCANIC VALLEY. This enormous box canyon complex created by Tarawera's eruption hosts several hot geothermal phenomena. The **Echo Crater** is home to the world's largest hot springs, while the ice blue and extremely acidic **Inferno Crater Lake** is actually a geyser whose hydraulic activity revolves around a 38-day cycle. The extensive trail system also passes the site of **Waimangu,** once the world's largest geyser, whose blast heights regularly reached 185m—some even exceeded 800m. White crosses mark the site where four tourists were killed in 1903. There is a one-hour guided boat cruise to the former sites of the **Pink and White Terraces**. (23km from Rotorua off the Taupo Hwy. ☎366 6137; www.waimangu.com. Open daily 8:30am-5pm. Valley tour $28, with boat ride $63. Boat ride alone $35.)

TE PUIA. Containing the **Te Whakarewarewa Thermal Reserve** and **Maori Cultural Centre,** this attraction combines nature and culture in one. Boiling mud pools, a kiwi house, and demonstrations of carving, weaving, and crafts are included with admission. Along the walking tour, New Zealand's largest and most famous geyser, **Pohutu,** spurts to lofty heights of nearly 30m daily. (3km south of town, past Sala St., off Fenton St. ☎348 9047; www.tepuia.co.nz. Open daily 8am-6pm. In winter 8am-5pm. Admission includes guided tour. $35, children $17.50.)

Lake Rotorua

HELL'S GATE. While George Bernard Shaw christened the park "Hell's Gate," to some it is a slice of heaven. Not only is Hell's Gate home to 50 acres of seething mud, bubbling pools, and a steaming hot waterfall, but is also home to New Zealand's only mud bath. *(16km northeast of Rotorua on SH30. ☎ 345 3151; www.hells-gate.co.nz. Booking necessary for complimentary shuttle. Open daily 8:30am-8:30pm. Park entry $25, children $10. Mud bath $70.)*

MAORITANGA

OHINEMUTU. A visit to this lakefront Ngati Whakaue tribe village rewards visitors with a patient introduction to Maori culture. Of the compound's buildings, the **Tamatekapua Meeting House,** built in 1939, is the most symbolically important. The interior showcases a smattering of paua shells and rich, red carvings. *(Off Lake Rd., down Mataiwhea St. ☎ 349 3949.)*

ST. FAITH'S ANGLICAN CHURCH. Across from Ohinemutu, this church has an incongruous combination of Tudor exterior and Maori interior. The pulpit is supported by carved figures of Maori ancestors, while an etched window shows Christ clad in the cloak of a Maori chief—from a certain angle, he appears to be walking on Lake Rotorua. To protect the corpses from being steamed underground by geothermal forces, the coffins were all "buried" above ground.

OTHER SIGHTS

ROTORUA MUSEUM OF ART AND HISTORY/TE WHARE TAONGA O TE ARAWA. A former luxury spa, this museum houses permanent exhibitions on the eruption of 1886, the Te Arawa people, the B Company 28 Maori Battalion of World War II, the area's geology, and the former spa itself. *(In the Tudor-style Bath House, to the right of the Government Gardens.* ☎349 4350; www.rotoruamuseum.co.nz. Open daily 9am-8pm. $12, children $6. Museum admission includes admission to the Blue Baths.)*

THE BLUE BATHS. Begun as the first unisex pool in the country, today this site houses a museum devoted to the history of the baths, an elegant outdoor hot pool, and a charming tearoom that serves tiered cakes on antique trolleys. *(Next to the Rotorua Museum.* ☎350 2119. Museum open daily 10am-5pm. Pools open daily 10am-8pm. In winter 10am-6pm. Museum $12. Pools $9.)*

AGRICULTURAL DIVERSIONS. Entertaining busloads of tourists, the **Agrodome's** resident "farmer" shears 19 breeds of sheep, performs a mock auction, leads sheepdog trials, and coaxes the camera-happy crowd to milk cows and pet baby lambs. You can also tour the actual working farm. *(From Rotorua, take SH5 toward Hamilton for about 10km and turn right onto Western Rd.; it's 500m down on the right. Free shuttle from the Rotorua i-Site.* ☎357 1050 or 0800 339 400; www.agrodome.co.nz. Agrodome Show $20, children $10. Farm Tour $28, children $15. Agrodome Show and Farm Tour Combo $40, children $20.)* For a less polished agricultural experience, the **New Zealand Farm Show** gives visitors four chances per day to see its bovine extravaganza. *(On SH5, 5km north of town, opposite Rainbow Springs.* ☎347 9301. $18.50, children $9.50.)*

⚡ OUTDOOR ACTIVITIES

WHITEWATER RAFTING. Adrenaline junkies craving their next fix rush to the short but sweet **Kaituna River,** where the 7m Okere Falls spill into Lake Rotoiti. Trips to other area rivers, including the Rangitaiki and Tongariro, are offered by many companies, but are contingent on good weather and safe water levels. On Sundays, the **Wairoa River** is flooded by the hydroelectric plant, creating the best rapids in the area. The longest running company, **Kaituna Cascades,** receives strong local endorsement. *(☎357 5032; www.kaitunacascades.co.nz. From $78.)*

WHAKAREWAREWA FOREST PARK. It may not be native bush, but this 5667-hectare exotic pine plantation draws visitors with its awesome ⚡**mountain biking** trails and lake-skirting walks. For walking or riding, get maps from **Redwoods Visitor Centre.** *(On Long Mile Rd., 5km from the city center off of SH30.* ☎350 0110. Open M-F 8:30am-5:30pm, Sa-Su 10am-4pm. In winter M-F 8am-5pm, Sa-Su 10am-4pm.)*

KAYAKING. Kaituna Kayaks offers tandem whitewater kayaking over Class V rapids. No experience needed, just a hearty sense of adventure. *(☎0800 465 292; www.kaitunakayaks.com. Half-day lessons $130, full-day $240. 1½hr. tandem trips $130.)*

MT. TARAWERA. The volcanic Mt. Tarawera (1111m), the cause of the 1886 commotion, is now privately owned; you can only access the mountain through guided tour. Inquire at the visitors center before heading out. **Mt. Tarawera NZ** leads half-day 4WD tours, which include a guided walk around the crater and helicopter trips with a landing on Mt. Tarawera. *(☎349 3714; www.mt-tarawera.co.nz. 4WD tours depart 8am, 1pm. $121. 45min. flights $415.)* **Volcanic Air Safaris** also flies over Mt. Tarawera and the Crater Lakes District. *(☎0800 800 848; www.volcanicair.co.nz. Tarawera: float-plane $175; helicopter $295. Crater Lakes: $125/175.)* **HELIPRO** runs similar trips. *(☎357 2512; www.helipro.co.nz. Tarawera $275. Crater Lakes $170.)*

SLEDGING. Sledging is a unique form of insanity for a generation jaded with rafting or kayaking whitewater. **Kaitiaki Adventures** will lead you down chutes and rapids in a buoyant plastic sled. The experienced guides also run rafting trips. (☎0800 338 736 or 357 2236; www.kaitiaki.co.nz. Sledging $125. Rafting $75.)

SKYDIVING. Those who chickened out in Taupo might consider jumping with **Nzone**, a reputable skydiving option in Rotorua. The company offers a drop over the spectacular Lake District. (☎345 7520 or 0800 3767 9663; www.nzone.biz. 9000 ft. $245; 12,000 ft. $295. 15,000 ft. $395. Book ahead.)

SKYLINE SKYRIDES. Rotorua is the semi-official luge capital of the country, thanks to **Skyline**. After ascending in a scenic gondola, the luge hurls you back down on a three-wheeled plastic cart with your choice of three tracks. (4-5km from the city center, next to Rainbow Springs on SH5. ☎347 0027; www.skylineskyrides.co.nz. Open M-Th and Su 9:30am-5pm, F-Sa 9:30am-9pm. Gondola $22. Luge $7.50.)

AGRODOME ADVENTURE CENTRE. With five original attractions, this adrenaline mecca draws the bold. You can **bungy jump** off a 43m tower, zip around a small rubber-banked pond in a tiny 450-horsepower **Agrojet boat,** or roll down a hill in a **Zorb.** Next, the **Swoop** raises one to three people linked in sleeping-bag-like sacks to a height of 40m, and then drops them like a sack of potatoes. **Freefall Xtreme** rockets 120mph winds from under you to simulate a sky-diving free-fall—lift guaranteed. (☎357 4747 or 0800 021 211; www.agrodome.co.nz. Call for free shuttle from the Rotorua i-Site. Open daily 9am-5pm. Zorb open until 6:30pm. In winter 9am-5pm. Bungy $90. Agrojet $40, children $30. Wet or dry Zorb $45. Swoop $30-40. Freefall Xtreme $70 for 4min.)

FISHING. With all its lakes and purportedly more trout per capita than even Lake Taupo, Rotorua is an angler's dream. Popular fishing spots include Lake Rotoiti and Ngongotaha and Hamurana Streams. Lakes Rotorua and Okareka are open year-round; Tarawera, Okataina, and Rotoiti Lakes are open October through June. (Fishing guides begin at $75 per hr. 1-day license $18.50; weekly, monthly, or seasonal licenses $88; available at the Rotorua i-Site or at any fishing store.) **Mana Adventures,** 1271 Fenton St., rents gear and can arrange charter boats and guides. (☎348 4186; www.manaadventures.co.nz. Open M-Th 8am-5:30pm, F 8am-6pm, Sa 9am-2pm, Su 9am-1pm.)

🎵 🎭 ENTERTAINMENT AND NIGHTLIFE

A MAORI EVENING: THE HANGI

The best way to learn about Maori culture is through participation in a Maori *hangi*, or feast. Be aware that many evening commercial packages tread a delicate line between education and exploitation; the package you choose and the attitude of the sponsoring company can significantly alter your experience. Some emphasize learning about Maori history and traditions, while others consist solely of song and dance. Some *hangi* are held on real *marae*, some in specifically built commercial locations, and others in motel restaurants. That said, this may be your best chance to move beyond postcard images of tattooed Maori warriors to get a glimpse of the beauty, power, and richness of the Maori tradition. Full evening tours by several Maori-owned operators usually include an introductory communication protocol, a challenge and welcome ceremony (finalized with the *hongi*, the pressing of noses to forge friendships with visitors), followed by a concert, and a *hangi*—all with transport from any accommodation.

MITAI. Spending a night with the Mitais is one of the least touristy ways to experience Maori culture in Rotorua. Groups are smaller than those of other tours, and the affable Mitai family uses interaction rather than just entertainment as means for teaching Maori history, culture, and language. The evening ends with a walk through the family's sacred grounds. *(192 Fairy Springs Rd. ☎343 9132; www.mitai.co.nz. Book ahead. Daily 6:15-9pm. $85, children 10-15 $42, under 10 $16.)*

TAMAKI TOURS. Although not as intimate as Mitai, Tamaki is another good way to learn about Maori culture through a polished evening of song and dance. *(☎346 2823; www.maoriculture.co.nz. Vegetarian options. Book ahead. $63, children $36.)*

MAI ORA. At a replica of a pre-European village in Te Puia overlooking the Whakarewarewa Thermal Reserve, this *hangi* is prepared using the underground heat of the water. Te Puia also offers daytime concerts. *(☎348 9047 or 0800 494252; www.tepuia.co.nz. Summer only. $85, children $50.)*

PUBS AND CLUBS

Rowdy tourists feed a lively Rotorua nightlife scene. Even after a long day of mud and *marae*, travelers manage to hit the beers and bars with gusto.

■ **Lava Bar,** 1286 Arawa St. (☎348 8618). Obligatory stop for anyone who wishes to see the social options of Rotorua's youth. Greenbus backpackers crowd this wood-paneled mixer nightly, grinding to Clear Channel dance hits and pounding Lava's special shooters ($5) with rafting guides. Happy hour 4:30-6pm. Open daily 4:30pm-late.

Fuze, 1122 Tutanekai St. (☎349 6306). Sleek Fuze is the upscale answer to Lava Bar hosting hip bands for no cover Tu, Th, and Sa. Crowds fill the dance floor on weekends and sip innovative mixed drinks ($9-14). Open Tu-Sa 3pm-late.

Pig and Whistle City Bar, 1152 Tutanekai St. (☎347 3025), at Haupapa St. Grab a bar stool at this former police station and get down to rock'n'roll cover bands. Live bands F-Sa. Handles $4.50. Cover F-Sa $2. Open daily 11:30am-late. Kitchen closes 10pm.

◤ DAYTRIPS FROM ROTORUA

TARAWERA FALLS. Following the Tarawera River's course as it slips underneath and bursts out of a rock, falling 20m, makes for a pleasant day walk through native bush. It's a 10-15min. walk from the parking lot to the falls viewpoint; another 15-20min. uphill leads to a second tier of smaller cascades. Another 5min. rewards you with a swimming hole, while a further 1½hr. will take you to a popular campsite on the shores of Lake Tarawera *(tent sites $5),* which is also accessible by car. From Rotorua, head eastward on SH30A to SH30. At the SH34 intersection (49km), take the road to Kawerau (6km). While the falls are on DOC land, the 24km gravel road to the falls goes through private forestry, and a vehicle permit *($2.50)* is required. The Kawerau Visitor's Center, located in the Tarawera Court shopping center on Islington St., issues permits and provides maps from Kawerau to the falls. *(☎323 7550. Open M-F 8:30am-5pm, Sa-Su 9am-3pm.)*

BURIED VILLAGE. Once renowned as a stagepost for the silica White and Pink Terraces, the 19th-century tourist center **Te Wairoa village** became a little too hot when the 1886 eruption of Mt. Tarawera destroyed the so-called "Eighth Wonder of the World" and its surrounding villages. The tourist draw today is the aftermath of the destruction, where paths meander around the excavated, heavily reconstructed *whares*, settler's houses, and shops. *(On Tarawera Rd., 10km from town. ☎362 8287; www.buriedvillage.co.nz. Open daily Nov.-Mar. 8:30am-5:30pm; Apr.-Oct. 9am-4:30pm. 30min. guided tours, included in admission, at 11am, 1:30, 3pm. Adults $25, children $8.)*

TAURANGA   ☎07

While some travelers still view Tauranga as a quick breath of sea air before sulfurous Rotorua, the city's warm weather and commercial conveniences have made it one of New Zealand's fastest growing areas (pop. 108,000). This sprawling town has many attractions including a lively waterfront, nearby beaches, kiwifruit orchards in nearby Te Puke, and proximity to formidable Mt. Maunganui.

TRANSPORTATION

Buses: Station at the Tauranga i-Site. **InterCity/Newmans** heads daily to: **Auckland** (4hr.; 8am, 1:30pm; $32-40); **Hamilton** (2hr.; 7:50am; $23-29); **Rotorua** (1½hr.; 4 per day; $21-30). Transfers from Rotorua for **Whakatane** and points in the **East Cape**. **Supa Travel Express** (☎571 0583) runs additional service to **Auckland** (M-F 8:30am, Sa 11am; $55) and to the Auckland airport ($80-85).

Ferries: Kiwi Coast Cruises (☎579 1325) run from **Coronation Pier** to **Mt. Maunganui** (in summer daily 10 per day; $6, children $3). Purchase tickets on board.

Public Transportation: Bayline Coaches (☎578 3113) runs **The Bay Hopper** between Tauranga and Mt. Maunganui ($2.50) and to some of the suburbs. Buses depart from Wharf St., around the corner from the Tauranga i-Site.

Tauranga

♠ ACCOMMODATIONS
Bell Lodge (BBH), **11**
Harbourside City Backpackers, **8**
Just the Ducks Nuts (BBH/VIP), **1**
Loft 109 (BBH), **10**
Tauranga YHA, **9**

♥ FOOD
Shiraz Cafe, **6**
Sunrise Cafe, **7**
Zeytin Café and Eaterie, **4**

⬛ NIGHTLIFE
Cornerstone Pub, **3**
The Crown & Badger, **5**
Usual Suspects, **2**

Taxis: Tauranga Taxis (☎578 6086), **CitiCabs** (☎577 0999), and **Coastline Taxis** (☎571 8333) are all available 24hr.

Hitchhiking: Although *Let's Go* does not recommend hitching, hitchhikers heading to Auckland or the Coromandel often try Waihi Rd., past Jonathan St., about 500m beyond the Otumoetai Rd. roundabout. Thumbers to Whakatane or Rotorua often start on Dive Cres. before the bridge and head east via Mt. Maunganui.

◤◢ ORIENTATION AND PRACTICAL INFORMATION

Downtown Tauranga is located on a narrow northern peninsula in **Tauranga Harbour**. With most attractions on **The Strand**, a strip of cafes and clubs along the eastern coast of Waipu Bay, the commercial area spreads west to **Cameron Road** and south to **Elizabeth Street**. Cross-streets south of Elizabeth St. are numbered in a southward ascending order. The continuation of SH2 is **15th Avenue**. The bridge to Mt. Maunganui begins at the northeastern tip of the peninsula, while the bridge to Otumoetai starts at the northwestern tip on Chapel St.

Visitors Center: Tauranga i-Site, 95 Willow St. (☎578 8103; www.bayofplentynz.com). Open M-F 8:30am-5:30pm, Sa-Su 9am-5pm.

Department of Conservation (DOC): 253 Chadwick Rd. West (☎578 7677), in West Greerton, 7km south of the city center. Take Cameron Rd. south to the 2nd roundabout in West Greerton and turn right; the DOC is on the right, just across from the police station. Open M-F 8am-4:30pm.

Banks: BNZ, 124 Willow St. (☎578 8009), and **ANZ** (☎578 2049), at the corner of Spring and Grey St., are both open M-F 9am-4:30pm and have 24hr. **ATMs.**

Work Opportunities: Fruit-picking opportunities abound Apr.-June. Many accommodations have info on available jobs; **Just the Ducks Nuts** (p. 166) and the **Pacific Coast Lodge** in Mt. Maunganui (p. 169) are well connected to the fruit industry.

Library and **Internet Access: Cyberzone,** 75 Grey St. (☎578 6983), has late hours and an all-night weekend special ($25 for 9pm-6am F-Sa) and an all-day rate ($35). $6 per hr. Open daily 10am-10pm. The **library** (☎577 7177), on Willow St. next to the Tauranga i-Site, also has web access for $6 per hr. Open M-Tu and Th-F 9:30am-5:30pm, W 9:30am-7pm, Sa 9:30am-4pm, Su 11:30am-4pm.

Police: (☎577 4300), at the corner of Willow and Monmouth St.

Medical Services: John's Photopharmacy (☎578 3566), at the corner of Cameron Rd. and 2nd Ave. Open daily 8am-9pm. The **hospital** (☎579 8000) is on Cameron Rd.

Post Office and Bookstores: Take Notes, 17 Grey St. (☎577 9911). Open M-F 8:30am-5:30pm, Sa 9am-4pm, Su 10am-3pm. **Browser's Secondhand Bookshop,** 26 Wharf St. (☎577 0990), is the best of many used book purveyors in town. Open M-Sa 9:30am-5:30pm, Su 10am-4pm.

▌ ACCOMMODATIONS

While those without vehicles may prefer to stay downtown, more mobile visitors can find an array of suitable motorparks and motels with parking along Waihi Rd. (coming from Auckland) or along Turret Rd./15th Ave.

Harbourside City Backpackers (BBH), 105 The Strand (☎579 4066; www.backpack-tauranga.co.nz). The newest option in town is a converted hotel with an in-house bar in an unbeatable location—on the downtown waterfront. Free bike rental. Dorms $24-26; doubles and twins $60. MC/V. ❷

Bell Lodge (BBH), 39 Bell St. (☎578 6344; www.bell-lodge.co.nz), southeast of town, near the Otumoetai Rd. roundabout. Mix of accommodations makes for a variable, multi-national crowd, with many long-term residents. Free shuttle into town and to hitching points. Dorms $23; doubles $60; motel rooms $80, $15 per extra person. Tent sites $14. MC/V. ❷

Tauranga YHA, 171 Elizabeth St. (☎578 5064; yha.tauranga@yha.co.nz), a 10min. walk from The Strand. Enjoy the communal atmosphere in the grassy backyard. The staff organizes activities in the area. Dorms $24; doubles $60. Tent sites $16. MC/V. ❷

Just the Ducks Nuts (BBH), 6 Vale St. (☎576 1366; www.justtheducksnuts.co.nz), in Otumoetai. Take Chapel St. from Tauranga and veer left after the bridge, 30min. from downtown. Amenities include a conservatory, fireplace, 2 lounges, and a stellar view. Free bike rental. Free pickup. Dorms $21-23; doubles and twins $50. Ask about reduced weekly rates. ❷

Loft 109 (BBH), 109 Devonport Rd. (☎579 5638; www.loft109.co.nz). This cozy 2nd-floor spot in the middle of Tauranga has a great balcony overlooking the active street below. Reception 8am-8:30pm. Dorms $22 (linens $2), weekly $120; doubles $54-60; triples $70. MC/V. ❷

▐ FOOD

Up-and-coming Tauranga offers backpackers several well-priced and diverse restaurants. Head to the intersection of Wharf St. and The Strand for the best dining options or just a good view of the water.

Shiraz Cafe, 12 Wharf St. (☎577 0059). A sweet Middle Eastern aroma greets you at the door of this tasteful cafe. Mains from $15.50 merit the splurge. Hummus $6.50. Falafel $9. Open M-Sa 11am-2:30pm and 5pm-late. AmEx/D/MC/V. ❸

Sunrise Cafe, 10 Wharf St. (☎578 9302). Salads ($13) and sandwiches ($10-13) offer a respite from deep-fried fare. All-day big breakfast $13. Open M-F 7am-4pm, Sa 8am-2:30pm. MC/V. ❷

Zeytín Café and Eaterie, 83 The Strand (☎579 0099; www.zeytin.co.nz). Enjoy Turkish and Greek mainstays, or pizza ($17) from the wood-fired grill. Doner kebab $10. Open Tu-Su 11am-10pm. MC/V. ❷

◉ SIGHTS

For the odd day of calm between adventure activities, Tauranga is home to a wealth of historical sights. Start the day at **Te Awanui,** an intricately carved replica of a Maori *waka* (canoe) at the northern end of The Strand, crafted in 1973. The greenhouse and rose gardens of **Robbins Park** provide a great picnic site. Up Cliff Rd. and left on Mission St., the beautiful territory of **Te Papa Mission Station** (now called **The Elms**) was established in 1839 as Tauranga's first mission. Farther off is the mission's cemetery, on a mound just to the right of the intersection of Dive Cres. and Marsh St. Ask about concerts during summer weekends. (☎577 9772; www.theelms.org.nz. Grounds open 24hr. Building open W and Sa-Su 2-4pm. $5.) The **Mills Reef Winery,** 143 Moffat Rd., off Waihi Rd. after it merges with SH2 on the way out of town, has free tastings of grape and kiwifruit wine. (☎576 8800 or 0800 645 577; www.millsreef.co.nz. Open daily 10am-5pm.) Those with unquenchable thirst can spend 6hr. with **Tauranga Tasting Tours;** the fast-paced tour visits an antique brewery, two wineries, a distillery, and New Zealand's leading maker of cocktails. (☎544 1383; www.tastingtours.co.nz. Pickup available. $130.) If you're around for Easter, check out the annual **Montana National Jazz Festival,** five days of food, drink, and music ranging from big band to blues. (☎577 7188; www.jazz.org.nz. Tickets for performances range from $15-30.)

◎ NIGHTLIFE

Young crowds hit Tauranga's night spots in full force each weekend. A few establishments on Harington St. cater to a younger, hard-partying crowd, while those on The Strand offer live music and harborside views.

The Crown and Badger, 91 The Strand (☎571 3038), at the corner of Wharf St. More Irish than it realizes, this homage to cricket offers a pub atmosphere, ample space, and live music on weekends. The perfect place for a pint ($5.30) and a bite ($5.50-18.50 until 9:30pm). Tu quiz night. Open daily 9am-late. AmEx/D/MC/V.

Usual Suspects, corner of Hamilton St. and The Strand (☎927 3325). Sleek minimalist decor and a euro-chic upstairs lounge account for this bar's appeal. The great harbor view from the terrace doesn't hurt either. Gourmet pizzas $9-12. Live music Th-Sa nights. Open M-Sa 3pm-late. AmEx/D/MC/V.

◪ OUTDOOR ACTIVITIES

Tauranga's outfitters make the most of the town's natural endowments. **Dolphin Seafaris,** on Coronation Pier, offers takes passengers out for a dip with everyone's favorite aquatic mammals. (☎577 0105; www.nzdolphin.com. Tours depart 7:45am. $120. Breakfast included.) A full-day excursion with **Butler's Tauranga Dolphin Company** also promises a swim with dolphins, as well as a visit to several offshore islands and seal colonies. (☎0508 288 537; www.swimwithdolphins.co.nz. Tours depart 9am. $100.) Newcomer Simon takes his catamaran, the **South Sea Vagabond**—replete with licensed bar—out for snorkeling, kayaking, and dolphin viewing and swimming. (☎579 6376; www.southseasailing.com. Departs 10am, returns approx. 4:30pm. $100, children $75.) Romantic adventurers should ask about full moon kayaking at **Oceanix** (☎0800 335 800; www.oceanix.co.nz), which includes a tour ($95) of a glowworm canyon and a barbeque.

Tauranga is not far from the **Wairoa River** and its gut-wrenching Class V rapids. However, the river is only raftable 26 days a year from September to May, mainly on Sundays, when the dam on its upper reaches is opened. On those rare days, **Wet 'n Wild Rafting** runs 1hr. jaunts down the Wairoa. (☎348 3191 or 0800 462 7238; www.wetnwildrafting.co.nz. Run $80, double run $130.) Based in Rotorua, **Raftabout** (☎343 9500 or 0800 723 822; www.raftabout.co.nz) and **River Rats** (☎0800 333 900; www.riverrats.co.nz) run similar trips. **Waimarino,** 10min. west of Tauranga.is a water-themed park has a climbing wall, floating pontoons, hydro slides, and kayaks. (☎576 4233; www.kayaks.co.nz.) Venture to the depths with **Dive Tauranga,** 50 Cross Rd., and spend the night in one of the bunk rooms. (☎571 5286; www.diveunderwater.com. Trips from $95, equipment $70.) Whether it's deep-sea fishing or reefer-game, most trips are booked at—and leave from—the **Fishing and Boat Charters Office** (☎577 9100), on Coronation Pier. (Daily reef fishing trips from $70.)

If you're averse to water, you can still perfect your swan dive in a 2500m fall with **Tandem Skydiving Ltd.** (☎576 7990; freefall@xtra.co.nz. $190.) Less precipitous for body and budget, the **Tauranga Gliding Club** offers varying altitude levels in ultralight gliders. (☎575 6768. From $90.) **O'Hara Wildlife Estate,** 30min. east of Tauranga, has archery, target shooting, and a variety of wild animal-based activities. (☎533 1484; www.outdoorsnz.com.) Papamoa is home to the only speedway track built specifically for blokarts. The staff at **Blokart Heaven,** 176 Parton Rd., will be delighted to strap you into a motorless go-kart attached to a windsail and wish you the best of luck. (☎572 4256 or 0800 425 652. $10 per 15min.)

The **McLaren Falls Park Track,** which begins a 15min. drive down SH29 toward Hamilton, is a pleasant pastoral hike. The **Kaimai Mamaku Forest Park,** extending west of town, provides 37,140 hectares of forests and rivers laced with trails. With the connecting web of north-south trails, ambitious and experienced trampers can trek the entire spine of the range. The area, with its volcanic origins and andesite plugs, is essentially an extension of the **Coromandel Forest Park** without the crowds. From **Waihi Beach,** 1hr. north of Tauranga, a series of tracks explores the less developed coastlines and harbors to the north. Once you reach the north end of Waihi Beach, the trail leads 2.4km to **Orokawa Bay** (45min. one-way) and 8.2km to **Homunga Bay** (2½hr. one-way). A 25min. drive towards Welcome Bay leads to the trailhead of the **Te Rerekawau (Kaiate Falls)** hike, which terminates at the base of a massive waterfall (1hr. round-trip). If you stick around the city, prepare to duke it out with joggers on the boardwalks around the popular **Waikareao Estuary.**

🦎 ISLANDS

Thirty-five kilometers offshore lies **Mayor Island,** an isolated, undeveloped volcanic protrusion under Maori ownership. Snorkeling and diving areas abound, but the island has no amenities beyond a rugged **campsite** and **huts** with a few backpacker beds (dorms $10; tent sites $5). Good supplies and gear are necessary for any trip here, as bad weather might keep you there longer than you anticipate. **Blue Ocean Charters,** at the pier, makes runs to the island depending on demand, weather, and season. Fishing trips and upscale accommodations are also available. (☎578 9685; www.blueocean.co.nz. Departs Tauranga in summer 7am; returns 5:30pm. Time on island is 9:30am-3pm. Daytrips $95. Fishing trips $95, with equipment $120.) Go down to **Coronation Pier** and ask for other transport options. Even fewer people make it out to the 24km of largely private beaches at nearby **Matakana Island**—you can only get there by swimming across the channel, and even then it's considered trespassing. However, stretching across the entrance to Tauranga Harbour and absorbing the blows of the Pacific, the island makes for good surfing according to locals. *Let's Go* does not recommend trespassing, no matter how good the surf.

MT. MAUNGANUI   ☎07

The extinct volcanic cone of Mt. Maunganui (pop. 30,400) rises from the otherwise flat shoreline of Tauranga Harbour. Formerly a Maori stronghold, the mountain now reigns over the industrial-turned-resort suburb that bears its name. "The Mount" bustles with activity in the summer, attracting cruise ships and tourists with its white beaches.

⌨ TRANSPORTATION. Local and **InterCity** buses run daily to Tauranga (15min.), with stops at the Mt. Maunganui i-Site and the Bayfair Shopping Centre (3km from town). Depending on the bus, service may continue to Auckland ($46), Hamilton ($31), Hastings ($78-86), or Thames ($30). **Go Kiwi** also runs to Auckland ($42) via Tauranga three times per day. In the summer, take the **ferry** to Tauranga from Salisbury Wharf (7 per day; $8). Mt. Maunganui has 24hr. **taxi** companies; try **Taxi Cabs** (☎575 5054) or **Mount Taxis** (☎574 7555).

⚃⚇ ORIENTATION AND PRACTICAL INFORMATION. Mt. Maunganui's main drag is **Maunganui Road,** and the center of town is almost directly below The Mount. **Marine Parade/Ocean Beach Road** traces the ocean toward the fine sands of **Papamoa Beach Reserve. The Mall** runs on the harbor side of downtown. The **Mt. Maunganui i-Site** is on Salisbury Ave. west of Maunganui Rd. (☎575 5099. Open daily 9am-5pm.) Other services include: **banks** on Maunganui Rd.; **Internet** access at **Mount Internet,** which doubles as Mount Backpackers ($2 per 20min, $4 per hr. during "happy hour" 9-11am; open daily 9am-8pm); the **Post Shop and Copy Centre,** 155 Maunganui Rd. (☎574 3505. Open M-F 8:30am-5pm, Sa 9am-12:30pm.)

⚐ ACCOMMODATIONS. Bright blue ▨**Pacific Coast Lodge (BBH) ❸,** 432 Maunganui Rd., 2km from the town center, has plenty to offer, including comfy mattresses, a recycling program, employment opportunities, and free parking. (☎574 9601; www.pacificcoastlodge.co.nz. Key deposit $20. Dorms $25-27; singles $65; doubles $70. MC/V.) A stone's throw from the beach, **Mount Backpackers (BBH) ❷,** 87 Maunganui Rd., attracts long-term residents. Space is tight, but hosts are helpful in scheduling local activities. (☎575 0860; mountinternet@xtra.co.nz. Dorms $23-25; doubles $62. MC/V.) At the base of the mountain is **Beachside Holiday Park ❶,** 1 Adams Ave., with powered tent and caravan sites stretching to the beachfront. (☎575 4471; www.mountbeachside.co.nz. Tent sites, vehicle sites, and 2-person caravans from $30. MC/V.)

⚃▨ FOOD AND NIGHTLIFE. Restaurants are concentrated on Maunganui Rd. The laid-back ▨**Two Small Fish ❹,** 107 Maunganui Rd., serves the freshest catch in town and is well worth the splurge. (☎575 0096. Tua tua and paua fritters $16. Blackboard fish specials $29.50. Open M-Th 6-9pm, F-Su 6pm-late. MC/V.) For the best value, **Kwang Chow ❷,** 241 Maunganui Rd., next to the cinema, offers excellent all-you-can-eat Chinese food (lunch and dinner mains $12-25). (☎575 5063. Large takeaway $9. Open 11:30am-10pm. AmEx/D/MC/V.) Next door, the Indian smorgasbord (Th-Sa lunch; $10) at **Swagath ❷,** 245 Maunganui Rd., serves a similar purpose. (☎574 9909. Mains $10-16. Open daily 5-10pm, also Th-Sa 11:30am-2:30pm. AmEx/D/MC/V.) **Cafe Turkish Delight ❷,** 97 Maunganui Rd., serves up fresh kebabs ($8) smothered in your choice of several tasty sauces. (☎575 9676. Open M-Th 11am-9:30pm, F-Su 10:30am-10:30pm. AmEx/MC/V.) Two doors down from Kwang Chow, **Bin Inn,** 237 Maunganui Rd., has beach snacks and other groceries. (☎575 2050. Open M-F 8am-6pm, Sa 8am-5pm, Su 9am-4pm.)

The young crowd at the **Astrolabe**, 82 Maunganui Rd., won't flinch at your dreds, and the Pacific Rim cuisine makes the pre-dusk hours worthwhile. (☎574 8155; www.astrolabe.co.nz. Beer $5. Mains $12-32. Kitchen open 9am-3pm and 6-10pm. Open daily 9am-late. AmEx/D/MC/V.) The heart of Maunganui's live music scene, **Mount Mellick**, 317 Maunganui Rd., hosts jam night every Tuesday and live bands Friday and Saturday. (☎574 0047. Pints $6. Open daily 11am-1am. AmEx/D/MC/V.)

⚄ ⚀ SIGHTS AND OUTDOOR ACTIVITIES.

It doesn't take a genius to find the must-see attraction in The Mount—it sticks out of the sea like a 232m sore thumb. To reach the **extinct volcano**, follow Adams Ave. or The Mall to where they peter out into a paved lot and a well-maintained track around the base of the volcano. The track is an easy, scenic 35min. walk with crashing surf on one side and sheep on the other. Routes go up the mountain at several spots off the base track, each offering a strenuous 40min. ascent and a knee-knocking 25min. descent. There's also a short jaunt out onto the peninsular **Moturiki Island** and the nearby **Blow Hole**.

The Mount's other major draw (beaches notwithstanding) is the **hot saltwater pools**, located at the base of the mountain. A tepid lap pool, private pools, storage lockers, and multi-trip passes are all available. (☎575 0868. Open M-Sa 6am-10pm, Su 8am-10pm. $5, children $3. Private pools $6 per 30min.) The prime **surfing beach** is next to the mountain, but white sand stretches for miles to the east, and sheltered waters await across the peninsula in **Pilot Bay**. **Mount Surfshop**, 96 Maunganui Rd., rents surfboards, bodyboards, and wetsuits. (☎575 9133. Surfboards $30 per day, bodyboards $20, wetsuits $15, mask and fins $25. 2hr. surfing lessons $50. Open daily 9am-5pm.) Local surf schools, especially **Assault**, 24 Pacific Ave. (☎575 7831), just off Maunganui Rd. near The Mount, offer rentals and lessons of varying rigor ($55, $35 per person for groups). If you haven't yet learned to hang ten, **New Zealand Surf School**, usually stationed at Tay St. on the main beach, will happily take you under its wing. They guarantee successful surfing or a free lesson. (☎021 477 873; www.nzsurfschools.co.nz. Lessons daily 10am, noon, 2pm. 1hr. lesson $50, 2hr. lesson $80. Cash only.) To see The Mount and Tauranga from above the water, mosey over to Pilot Bay and strap into the **Big Sky Parasail**. (☎0800 7244 759; www.bigskyparasail.com. Daily every hr. 10am-5pm. 400 ft. $60, 800 ft. $70, 1200 ft. $80. $10 discount for students and groups of 4 or more.)

WHAKATANE   ☎07

The town of Whakatane (FAH-ka-tah-nee; pop. 18,000) entices travelers with its rich natural attractions—the beaches, the climate, and White Island, the ominously smoking volcano 50km offshore.

▐ TRANSPORTATION.

InterCity departs from the Whakatane i-Site to: Auckland (6½hr.; daily; $45-56), Gisborne (3hr.; daily 3:40pm; $32-40) via Opotiki (45min.; $15-19); Tauranga (5¾hr.; daily 11:05am; $47-59) via Rotorua (1¾hr.; $24-30). For Wellington, catch the bus to Rotorua and connect there. The **Bay Hopper** cheaply traverses the stretches between Whakatane and Ohope, Opotiki, and Tauranga. (Departs M-Sa 9:25am; $6-11. Check the Whakatane i-Site for more info.) For **taxis**, call **Dial-a-Cab** (☎0800 342 522). Rent a **bike** with **Pacific Adventures**. (☎0800 467 529. $45 per day; rates negotiable for longer rental.) Although *Let's Go* doesn't recommend it, **hitchhikers** often head just across the Whakatane River Bridge. The roundabout where Gorge Rd. branches off Commerce St. toward Ohope is considered the best spot for going east.

▐▐ ORIENTATION AND PRACTICAL INFORMATION.

Whakatane is built on drained wetlands between high bluffs and the final bend of the Whakatane River. The commercial center is along **The Strand**, with **Boon** and **Richardson Streets** branching off. **Landing/Domain Road**, the west entrance of SH2, and **Commerce**

Street are the main routes in and out of town. The ■**Whakatane i-Site**, at Kakaharoa and Quay St., is a trove of area knowledge. (☎308 6058; www.whakatane.com. 30min. free Internet. Open M-F 8am-6pm, Sa-Su 10am-4pm.) Other services include: **Westpac Trust,** 167 The Strand, between Boon and Commerce St. and housing a 24hr. **ATM** (☎0800 400 600; open M-Tu and Th-F 9am-4:30pm, W 9:30am-4:30pm); the **police,** 62-70 Boon St. (☎308 5255); the **hospital** (☎306 0999), left (south) on King St. from Domain Rd. and right on Stewart St.; a **post office,** on Commerce St. at The Strand. (☎307 1155. Open M-F 8:30am-5pm, Sa 9am-noon.)

⚏⚏ ACCOMMODATIONS AND FOOD. For beachfront views on the cheap, head 7km over the hill to the campsite or motels at **Ohope Beach** (p. 172). ■**Lloyd's Lodge (BBH)** ❷, 10 Domain Rd., combines the hostel experience with a Maori education, offering an intimate *hangi* and cultural concert once a week ($30). Owner Hare greets all guests with a Maori welcome song. (☎307 8005; www.lloydslodge.com. Internet $2 per 15min. Linens $1. Dorms $24; doubles $56. Cash only.) Under new ownership, **Karibu Backpackers (BBH)** ❷, 13 Landing Rd., near the corner of King St., more than compensates for its farther-from-town location by providing all the comforts of home. (☎307 8276. Free parking. Free bike use. Internet $2 per 20min. Linens $2. Dorms $23; doubles and twins $56. Tent sites $14. Cash only.) The **Whakatane Hotel (VIP)** ❷, 79 The Strand, is centrally located with a kitchen and lounge area, but life focuses on the downstairs Irish pub. (☎307 1670; whakatanehotel@xtra.co.nz. Free Internet. Dorms $20; singles $40, with bath $50; twins and doubles $50, with bath $65. AmEx/MC/V.) The **Whakatane Holiday Park** ❶ offers no surprises. Follow Beach Rd. to the end of McGarvey Rd. to find typical facilities, plus a kitchen. (☎308 8694. Reception 8am-8pm. Tent sites and vehicles $12-14. Cabins from $50-90 for 2, $15 per extra person. MC/V.)

For the best fish 'n chips in town ($5.80), head to **Hare's Whare Kai** ❷, 122 Commerce St. (☎308 7939. Open Tu-Su 11:30am-7pm. Cash only.) More sophisticated tastes can be satisfied at **The Wharf Shed** ❹, on the waterfront in the Main Wharf beyond The Strand. The catch of the day ($27) never fails to please. (☎308 5698. Open daily 10:30am-9:30pm. AmEx/MC/V.) Marginally more affordable, **Barnacles** ❸, 122 The Strand, is virtually indistinguishable from other dining options. However, the fish of the day ($18.50) makes a satisfying splurge, and those with shallow pockets can snack on starters ($10.50). (☎308 7429. Open M-Sa 10am-2pm, also W-Sa 6pm-late. MC/V.)

⚏ OUTDOOR ACTIVITIES. The two biggest attractions in the area are trips to **White Island** (p. 172) and dips with dolphins. **Dolphins Down Under,** on the wharf at the end of The Strand, boasts a 95% success rate for swimming with the comedians of the sea. They provide equipment, instruction, refreshments, and even hot showers after the 3-4hr. trip. (☎0800 354 7737; www.dolphinsdownunder.co.nz. $130, children under 13 $120.) **Whale and Dolphin Watch,** 96 The Strand, runs a similar trip aboard the good ship *Taniwha*, with an underwater camera system filming the experience. (☎308 2001; www.whalesanddolphinwatch.co.nz. $130, children under 13 $120.) For those who long for isolation, **Merry Marine Charters** takes kayaks out from Whale Island; it's only 4hr. on calm seas. (☎307 7260. $90, under 15 $80.) There are three **scenic reserves** in the small area around Whakatane, providing a number of fine bush walks: **Kohi Point,** atop the hill over Whakatane, has panoramic views; **Ohope Scenic Reserve** is home to one of New Zealand's largest remaining pohutukawa forests; **Mokorua Bush Scenic Reserve** is a recovering pasture land. The walk around the hill between Whakatane and nearby Ohope Beach is breathtaking but of only moderate difficulty, so it won't leave you gasping for air. A long walk, the **Nga Tapuwae o Toi** (Footprints of Toi) connects the three reserves. While the 17km trail can be covered in about 5hr., it may be more enjoyable to split it into three shorter segments; the Whakatane-Ohope route is the most popular. The local **Beach Runner** bus (☎0800 442 2928) runs from the Whakatane i-Site to Ohope Beach and back (M-Sa 4-5 per day; $1.50 each way).

WHITE ISLAND   ☎07

Fifty kilometers off the coast, Whakaari ("that which can be made visible, uplifted to view") and its vapor sheath are in fact visible from Whakatane on most sunny days. Captain Cook, in his circuit around New Zealand, coined the name "White Island" because of the steam cloud perpetually hanging above its volcanic peaks. Composed of three distinct cones, two of which are now extinct, White Island is a landscape of lunar quality, with craters and steaming vents, boiling sulfuric acid pools, and sinuous flows of solid rock. The volcano occasionally becomes more active, spewing out ash carried as far as Whakatane by the wind. Even in such an inhospitable environment, ever-resourceful humans attempted to eke out profit with a sulfur mine that operated intermittently throughout the late 1800s and early 1900s. This evidently did not please the gods: a violent explosion and landslide killed 10 men in 1914. Today, mining for tourist dollars has become White Island's most profitable enterprise. For a price, anyone can strap on a gas mask, brave the noxious sulfur fumes, and make his or her own offering to the volcano. The last eruption was in 2000; today a 400m diameter lake of teal-blue acid has been rising ominously at the epicenter of the volcano's most seismically active area.

On clear weather days, the most affordable approach is by boat. **PeeJay Charters** was named "guardian" of White Island. The company's near monopoly on transport means it can charge steep rates, but few travelers who make the splurge come away disappointed. (☎308 9588 or 0800 733 529; www.whiteisland.co.nz. 6hr. $150; includes lunch and morning tea.) Alternatively, call **Dive White** to scope out White Island's underbelly. (☎307 0714 or 0800 348 394; www.divewhite.co.nz. 2 dives $225, children under 13 $80.) **Air Discovery** offers flights. (☎308 9558 or 0800 535 363; www.scottair.co.nz. 55min. $199, 2hr. $349.) For a touchdown on the surface, contact **Vulcan Helicopters.** (☎0800 804 354; www.vulcanheli.co.nz. $395 per person.) Planes and helicopters are at the airport on Aerodrome Rd.

OHOPE BEACH   ☎07

Ohope Beach is 11km of unbroken sand blessed with rolling blue waves and views of the rugged East Cape. Visitors come to marinate in the sun or to tramp around **Mokorua,** the hill between Ohope and Whakatane. A 2hr. journey by sand allows travelers to traverse the length of Ohope's narrow strip of land, from the steep bluffs of Mokorua to the entrance of Ohiwa Harbour, a historically rich shellfishery. Ask at the information center about the 1hr. walk to the **Tauwhare Pa.** The main road, branching off at the end of the highway, is West End Rd., becoming Pohutukawa Rd. as you move east, and then turning into Harbour Rd. Information can be found at the **Port Ohope General Store,** 200m before the Port Ohope Wharf toward the east side of the beach; it doubles as the **Ohope Information Centre.** (☎312 4707. Open daily 7am-7:30pm.) A medical center and pharmacy sit on Pohutukawa Rd. at the center of the beach. **Buses** on the way to Opotiki arrive at the Mobil station on Pohutukawa Rd., 300m down from the West End Rd. turn-off (daily around 4pm; book in Whakatane). Although *Let's Go* doesn't recommend hitching, hitchhikers report that prospects are good. The **Ohope Beach Holiday Park ❶,** 367 Harbour Rd., offers views, a pool, and mini-golf. (☎312 4460; www.ohopebeach.co.nz. Tent and powered sites $19-20. 4-person cabins from $115. Prices reduced in winter. MC/V.) For a quick bite, hit up **Ohiwa Oyster Farm ❶,** just past town on SH2, toward Opotiki. (☎312 4565. Marinated mussels $5.80. Fish 'n oyster burger $7. Open daily 9am-7pm. Cash only.)

OPOTIKI ☎ 07

The last town of any size (pop. 4000) before the remote Maori settlements of the East Coast, Opotiki makes an adequate gateway to the attractions of SH35 and a good pit-stop before the undulations of SH2. About 7km from town is **Hukutaia Domain,** an 11-acre park with a collection of New Zealand's native plant species. You can almost skip a stone across the surf from the porch of the **Opotiki Beach House Backpackers (BBH) ❷,** on Appleton Rd. at Waiotohi Beach, 5km west of town on SH2. (☎315 5117; slowry@paradise.net.nz. Free bike, kayak, and bodyboard use. Dorms $23; doubles $56. Tent sites $17. Cash only.) Beyond out-of-the-way, farther than secluded, and transcending isolated are the phrases that best describe **Bushaven Lodge ❷,** a one-of-a-kind backpackers set on a 160-acre plot of wilderness. From Opotiki, take SH2 toward Gisborne, turning onto Otara Rd., 500m outside of town, and travel for 14km—the pavement dissipates after the first 10km. Follow the sign to the right of the wooden bridge another 4km. (☎027 201 0512; www.bushaven.co.nz. Fire pit. Vehicle security $5 per day. Dorms $23; doubles and twins $56. Tent sites $10. Cash only.) The **Masonic Hotel ❷,** at Elliot and Church St., has small rooms and a popular restaurant and bar. (☎315 6115. Restaurant open daily noon-2:30pm and 6pm-late. Lunch and dinner mains $16-24. Singles $25; doubles with shared bath $45-55. MC/V.) The **Hot Bread Shop and Cafe ❷,** 43 St. John St., has delightfully low prices for breakfast (french toast; $6.50) and hot veggie sandwiches ($9.50). (☎315 6795. Open daily 5am-5pm. MC/V.) If you're in the mood for Indian cuisine, the **Oriental Palace ❷,** 120 Church St., has a $10 takeaway special on Tuesday and Wednesday. Mains $12. (☎315 5879. Open Tu-Su 10:30am-3pm and 5-10:30pm. MC/V.) Stock up on vitals at **New World,** 19 Bridge St. (☎315 6723), south of town centre off SH2, before heading east. (Open M-Sa 8am-8pm, Su 9am-8pm.) The **bus depot** is next to the Hot Bread Shop and Cafe at the corner of St. John and Bridge St., 1km from the Opotiki i-Site. **InterCity** runs to Gisborne (2hr., 1 per day, $26-32) and Rotorua (2hr., 1 per day, $26-32) via Whakatane (45min., $17-21). Book tickets at the **Opotiki i-Site,** at St. John and Elliot St. (☎315 8484; infocentre@odc.govt.nz. Open M-F 8am-5pm.) The **DOC** office is in the same building but closes at 4:30pm. The **Opotiki Superette,** 97 Church St., provides Internet and laptop connections at $4 per hr. (☎315 7632. Open M-Sa 6am-7pm, Su 1-6pm.) The **ANZ,** 108 Church St., has a **24hr. ATM.** (☎0800 180 935.) For the **police,** go to 29 King St. (☎315 1110.) **Kerry Nott,** 116 Church St., is the last **pharmacy** until Gisborne (☎315 5874. Open M-F 8:30am-5pm, Sa 9am-noon.) The **post office** is at 106 Church St. (☎315 6155. Open M-F 8:30am-5pm, Sa 9am-noon.)

EAST COAST AND HAWKE'S BAY

Of all the countries in the world, New Zealand sees the sun first each day, and virtually every town along the East Coast proclaims itself to be the very, very first. Sun-drenched villages give rise to orchards and fields overrun with luscious produce and grapes, ripening the "Fruit Bowl of New Zealand." The area also offers visions of primordial New Zealand, including remote Maori towns on the East Cape, the dense wilds of Te Urewera National Park, and North Island's largest remaining tract of native forest.

◙ EAST COAST AND HAWKE'S BAY HIGHLIGHTS

NATURAL SPLENDOR abounds among the waterfalls and tramps of the virtually tourist-free **East Cape** (p. 179).

NATURAL DIVERSITY flourishes in the isolation of the **Lake Waikaremoana Track** (p. 183), which supports a wide range of New Zealand's flora and fauna.

MANMADE ARCHITECTURE brightens the streets of **Napier** (p. 185) in garish Art Deco fashion.

EAST COAST

GISBORNE   ☎ 06

The site of Captain Cook's first landing in 1769, Gisborne (pop. 30,000) has a long history it won't let you forget. Nearly 50% Maori, the city is New Zealand's largest center for contemporary Maori art. Although the idyllic town lacks the high-quality comforts of many Kiwi destinations, the endless beaches, and surf to rival Raglan make Gisborne a must see for adventurous travelers.

▣ TRANSPORTATION

Flights: The **airport** is barely west of the city, at the end of Chalmers Rd. off Gladstone Rd. **Air New Zealand** (☎0800 737 000) has many daily flights to **Auckland** (1hr., 5-7 per day, $89-329) and **Wellington** (1¼hr., 3-5 per day, $89-369). You can book at the **Air New Zealand Travel Centre,** 37 Bright St. (☎868 2700). Open M-F 9am-5pm, Sa 9am-noon. Taxis downtown run about $10.

Buses: The **bus station** is at the Gisborne i-Site. **InterCity** leaves daily to **Auckland** (9½hr., 7:55am, $60-75) via **Rotorua** (4½hr., $45-56) and **Whakatane** (3hr., $32-40) and to **Wellington** (10hr., 9am, $56-70) via **Napier** (4hr., $32-40).

Taxis: Gisborne Taxis (☎867 2222) and **Sun City Taxis** (☎867 6767) run 24hr.

Car Rental: Scottie's, 265 Grey St. (☎867 7947), just south of the river from the visitors center and part of Ray Scragg Motors, offers the cheapest rates. Standard economy vehicle from $35 per day. Open daily M-F 7:30am-5pm, Sa 7:30am-noon. For weekend service, try **Better Bargain Rentals** (☎868 3407).

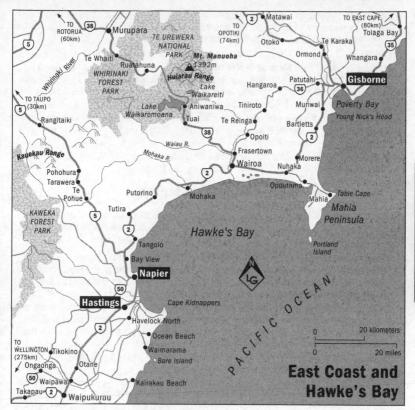

East Coast and Hawke's Bay

Bike/Surf Rental: Maintrax Cycle (☎867 4571), at the corner of Roebuck and Gladstone Rd. Bikes $15 per day, discounts for longer rental. Open M-F 8am-5pm, Sa 8:30am-noon.

Hitchhiking: To head to the surf beaches at Wainui or Makorori, many hitchhikers start out along Wainui Rd. Hitchers going southwest toward Wairoa or north to Opotiki head to the end of SH35/Gladstone Rd. at Makaraka Rd., where the highway branches off to its respective destinations. Let's Go doesn't recommend hitchhiking.

ORIENTATION AND PRACTICAL INFORMATION

Gisborne is located where the **Taruheru** and **Waimata Rivers** join to form the **Turanganui River** (one of the world's shortest, at 1200m). **Gladstone Road (SH35)** is the main drag; it turns into **Wainui Road** over the Turanganui Bridge and then becomes **Moana Road** once it reaches Wainui Beach. Orient yourself relative to the **clock tower** at Gladstone and Grey St., just past the replica of Captain Cook's *Endeavour*. The **Esplanade** runs along the Wainui Rd. side of the river, while **Awapuni** and **Salisbury Roads** run parallel to the main beaches in town.

Visitors Center: Gisborne i-Site, 209 Grey St. (☎868 6139; www.gisbornenz.com). Internet $5 per hr. Open M-F 8:30am-5pm, Sa 9am-5pm, Su 10am-5pm.

Department of Conservation (DOC): 63 Carnarvon St. (☎869 0460). Open M-F 8am-4:35pm.

Banks: Major national banks line Gladstone Rd. **Westpac** (☎867 1359 or 0800 400 600), at the corner of Gladstone Rd. and Peel St., has a 24hr. ATM. Branch open M-Tu and Th-F 9am-4:30pm, W 9:30am-4:30pm.

Police: (☎111 or 869 0200), at the corner of Peel St. and Childers Rd.

Medical Services: Kaiti Medical Centre (☎867 7411), at Turenne St. and De Lautour Rd., off Wainui Rd. Open M-F 8am-8pm, Sa-Su 9am-6pm. For **urgent care** only, look to the **hospital** (☎869 0500), on Ormond Rd. **Bramwells Unichem Pharmacy**, 232 Gladstone Rd. (☎867 1291). Open M-F 8am-6pm, Sa 9am-2pm, Su 10am-2pm. Closed Su in winter.

Internet Access: Treb-Net (☎863 3928), in the Treble Court between Peel and Bright St. $2 per 20min. Open M-F 10am-7pm, Sa 10am-6pm, Su 11am-4pm. Also available at the Gisborne i-Site (see above).

Post Office: The Gisborne Post Shop, 166 Gladstone Rd. (☎867 8220), inside **Paperplus.** Open M-F 8:30am-5:30pm, Sa 9am-4pm, Su 10am-4pm.

🏠 🏕 ACCOMMODATIONS AND CAMPING

While summer finds the occasional worker who stays in Gisborne for an extended period, hostels attract semi-permanent boarders in the low season who rent out rooms for months at a time, creating a more subdued atmosphere.

Gisborne YHA Hostel (☎867 3269; yha.gisborne@clear.net.nz), at the corner of Wainui Rd. and Harris St. A 5min. walk from downtown, this orange compound is an early 20th-century mansion. New owner Clive has been making constant improvements. Dorms $21-23; singles $36; twins and doubles $50; family room with bath $56 for 2, $20 per extra person. MC/V. ❷

Flying Nun Backpackers (BBH), 147 Roebuck Rd. (☎868 0461; yager@xtra.co.nz), off Childers Rd. This convent-turned-hostel has traded piety for a set of rowdy and often shirtless surfers. Key deposit $20. Linens $2. Dorms $19; singles $28; twins and doubles $48. Tent sites $11. Cash only. ❷

Waikanae Beach Holiday Park (☎867 5634; www.gisborneholidaypark.co.nz), at the end of Grey St. Right on the beach, this municipal property has excellent facilities. Tent sites made private by rows of pines. Reception daily 8am-9pm. 2-person tent and powered sites $24. 2-person cabins $70, $15 per extra person. MC/V. ❷

🍴 FOOD

Gisborne's nicer downtown cafes and restaurants, most on **Gladstone Road,** offer a respite from the usual artery-clogging budget cuisine. Of course, there's always **Pak 'N Save,** 274 Gladstone Rd. (☎868 9029. Open daily 8am-8pm.)

The Meetings Irish Ale House (☎863 3733), on the corner of Gladstone Rd. and Reads Quay. This modern, upscale Irish pub offers solid meat-and-potatoes options ($11-22). Many lagers and the imported canon on tap ($5.50-7). Food served 11:30am-2pm and 6-9pm. Open daily 11:30am-late. AmEx/MC/V. ❸

Food For Thought, 124 Gladstone Rd. (☎868 1110). The cheap alternative to more expensive cafes on Gladstone St. Lip-smacking a la carte sandwiches ($5-7) are great with house coffee ($2.20). Open M-F 7:30am-5pm, Sa-Su 8:30am-3pm. MC/V. ❶

Verve Cafe, 121 Gladstone Rd. (☎868 9095). Airy Verve has mosaic mirrors on the walls, couches in the back, and Internet access. The falafel wrap ($12.50) and fish of the day ($18) are highlights of the eclectic menu. Open M-F 7:30am-5:30pm, Sa-Su 8:30am-3:30pm. AmEx/MC/V. ❸

👁 SIGHTS

Titirangi Domain, also known as **Kaiti Hill,** is a good starting place for seeing Gisborne's sights. Once across the river, follow the signs from Hirini Rd. At the base

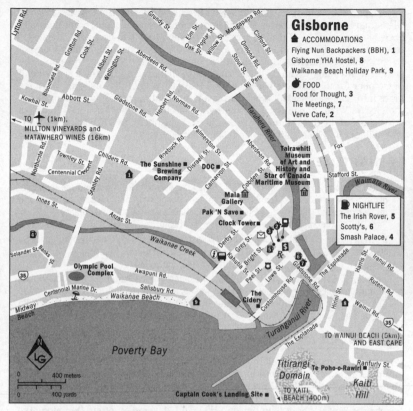

Gisborne

⌂ ACCOMMODATIONS

Flying Nun Backpackers (BBH), **1**
Gisborne YHA Hostel, **8**
Waikanae Beach Holiday Park, **9**

🍎 FOOD

Food for Thought, **3**
The Meetings, **7**
Verve Cafe, **2**

🍸 NIGHTLIFE

The Irish Rover, **5**
Scotty's, **6**
Smash Palace, **4**

EAST COAST AND HAWKE'S BAY

of the hill sits **Te Poho-o-Rawiri,** one of the largest traditional *marae* built from modern materials in New Zealand. The cavernous and expertly crafted structure features painted rafters, woven tukutuku reed panels, and intricately carved wood panels with iridescent paua shell eyes. Ask permission at the office and remove your shoes before entering. The Maori church **Toko Toru Tapu** sits nearby. Continue up the steep hill for a series of phenomenal views of the city and Poverty Bay. You can also see the white cliffs of **Young Nick's Head,** named after Captain Cook's cabin boy—alleged illegitimate son of King George III—Nicholas Young, who first sighted New Zealand. You can also climb Kaiti Hill via a winding path from the base of the Cook Landing Site (a 15-20min. walk from the Esplanade). The **Tairawhiti Museum of Art and History** (☎867 3832; www.tairawhitimuseum.org.nz), on Stout St., features permanent and rotating displays on natural and cultural history. The attached **Star of Canada Maritime Museum** stands in the transplanted bridgehouse of a British steamer that grounded on Kaiti Beach in 1912. (Both museums open M-F 10am-4pm, Sa 11am-4pm, Su 1:30-4pm. Jan. daily 10am-4pm. $1 or $2 donation expected.) For contemporary art-in-progress, head to the **Maia Gallery,** on Cobden St. between Gladstone Rd. and Palmerston St. This airy showroom and workshop is a studio for students in the Maori Visual Arts course at the local Tairawhiti Polytechnic. (☎868 8068. Open M-F 8am-5pm. Free.)

For touring and tasting of a different spirit, enjoy free tastings of Bulmer Harvest's cider as you watch it being made at **The Cidery,** 91 Customhouse St. (☎868

8300. Open M-F 9am-4pm.) The **Sunshine Brewing Company,** 109 Disraeli Rd., off Gladstone St., makes Gisborne Gold, Sundowner, Moonshine, and other naturally brewed sources of local pride. (☎867 7777. Open M-Sa 9am-6pm. Call ahead for free tour.) Visit New Zealand's first certified organic vineyard, **Millton Vineyard** (☎862 8680), in Manutuke on Papatu Rd. off SH2 toward Wairoa, to sample the area's finest vintages. Thirsty travelers flock to Gisborne during the last weekend of October for the **Gisborne Wine and Food Festival;** contact the Gisborne i-Site for more info. The **Eastwoodhill Arboretum** is a popular attraction 35km northwest of the city on Wharekopae Rd. Laid out by a meticulous collector, its 64 hectares grow some of the finest flora in the Southern Hemisphere. (☎863 9003; www.eastwoodhill.org.nz. Open daily 9am-5pm. $8, children free.)

🔊 NIGHTLIFE

Smash Palace, 24 Banks St. (☎867 7769). Take Awapuni Rd. west into the industrial district. Smash Palace is steeped in surreal junk decor, from antique cars suspended in mid-air to an old DC-3 flying around the roof. Handle specials $2.50. Open M-Tu 3pm-3am, W-Th 1pm-3am, F-Sa noon-3am, Su noon-11pm.

The Irish Rover, 69 Peel St. (☎867 1112). Vast open spaces yield plenty of room for Su $5 shots and $4 pints. Weekends often feature free live music. $2 drinks W 6-9pm. Tap beers $4. Open M-F 11am-3am, Sa-Su 3pm-late. AmEx/MC/V.

Scotty's, 35 Gladstone Rd. (☎867 8173). The oldest bar in Gisborne is fairly low-profile, with a big dance floor and house DJs on weekends. Enjoy one of the 13 beers on tap ($4.50) in the back garden. All-day menu $10-20. Open M-Tu 10am-midnight, W-Sa 10am-3am, Su 9am-9pm. AmEx/MC/V.

🔌 OUTDOOR ACTIVITIES

For the area's most convenient waters, try **Waikanae Beach,** stretching from the end of Grey St., crowded with locals at peak summer times. The shore becomes **Midway Beach** farther along Poverty Bay, with soft sand and a surfable break at its western end. Many surfers with more experience head north of the city to the beaches at **Wainui,** about 6km out on SH35, and **Makorori,** another 4km along the highway. These largely uninhabited beaches are swimmable, but have the occasional riptide. With plenty of open land between the road and the beaches, the area is popular with campers. Most camping sites on the east coast require a Freedom Camping Permit, available at the Gisborne i-Site. (Up to 4 people per permit. $10 for 10 nights, $28 for 25 nights.) **Kaiti Beach,** at the base of Kaiti Hill, is rocky and unpatrolled, but the exposed location provides strong gusts for windsurfing. **Surfing with Frank!** (☎867 0823; coach.russell@clear.net.nz), and **Gisborne Surf School** (☎868 3484; www.gisbornesurfschool.co.nz) offer rentals and lessons. Those who prefer their waves small can play it safe one block inland from Waikanae Beach at the **Gisborne Olympic Pool Complex,** on Centennial Marine Dr. Take your pick of the 50m heated indoor pool, the 98m hydroslide, or the spa and therapy pools, all for one low price. (☎867 6220. Open daily 6am-8pm. $3, children $2.)

THE EAST CAPE

The East Cape's stunning craggy coastline, North Island's final frontier, draws travelers in search of the purest New Zealand. From Gisborne to Opotiki, the Pacific Coast Highway (SH35) passes dozens of small towns on its way around the Raukumara Mountains. The majority of residents are Maori, and signs of Maori culture abound in the traditional carvings adorning the churches and *marae.*

▐ TRANSPORTATION

Buses: Bottom Bus (☎03 437 0753) is the only bus that navigates the region, running a weekly 3-night, 4-day circuit ($340), letting passengers on and off as they like. Buses depart **Taupo** M, W, F; go through **Rotorua**; spend 2 nights on the **East Cape** in **Te Kaha** and **Rangitukia**, 1 in **Napier**; then return to Taupo the following day.

Courier Transport: These minivans deliver parcels from **Opotiki** and **Gisborne** to the settlements and farms around the Cape, allowing passengers to see much that would be missed from the main highway. **Polly's Passenger Courier Service** (☎06 864 4728) runs between **Gisborne** and **Hicks Bay** (3hr.; M-F departs Gisborne 6:30am; $40). **Eastland Couriers** (☎315 6350) leaves Whakatane M-F at 8am and returns from Cape Runaway at 2:30pm ($30). **Cooks Passenger Courier Services** (☎06 864 4711 or 021 371 364; cook.teararoa@xtra.co.nz) travels between **Hicks Bay** and **Gisborne** (4½hr.; M-Sa departs Hicks Bay 7:30am, Gisborne 12:30pm; $35).

Hitchhiking: Hitchhikers find friendly rides around the cape in summertime; late afternoon is peak traffic time as people return from Gisborne or Opotiki. In winter, increased rain and reduced traffic make hitching a more dubious prospect, particularly on the less-populated northern coast. *Let's Go* does not recommend hitchhiking.

▐▟ ORIENTATION AND PRACTICAL INFORMATION

Well-maintained and fully paved, **SH35** runs the Cape's 334km perimeter except along the very tip. Most towns along the way have at least one store, takeaway, and postal pickup. Gas pumps are few and far between and charge the equivalent of highway robbery—upwards of $2 per liter.

Visitors Center: The visitors centers in **Opotiki, Gisborne,** and the **Te Puia Springs Service Centre** (☎06 864 6853) are the best bet for answers regarding the southern coast. Open M-F 8am-4:30pm. The comprehensive, free **Opotiki and East Cape,** available at all of the above, lists most travelers' resources and sights of interest, kilometer by craggy kilometer.

Banks: Westpac (☎06 864 8443), in Ruatoria, is the only bank in the East Cape. Open M-Tu and Th-F 9am-4:30pm, W 9:30am-4:30pm. There are **no ATMs.**

Telephone Codes: ☎07 from Opotiki to Hicks Bay; ☎06 from Hicks Bay to Gisborne.

▐ ▐ ACCOMMODATIONS AND FOOD

The coastline between Gisborne and Hicks Bay contains several designated spots for **free camping** (Labour Day-Easter), usually recognizable by a plethora of caravans. Try **Pouawa Beach** (17km north of Gisborne), **Loisel's Beach** at Waihau Bay (50km), **Tokomaru Bay** (90km), **Waipiro Bay** (106km), or **Hicks Bay** (180km); the East Cape's northern shore tends to restrict camping. As for food, the East Cape lacks restaurants and supermarkets—take advantage of the occasional takeaway or StarMart for travel grub. The **Te Kaha Cafe ❶** and **Te Kaha General Store,** next to the Te Kaha Holiday Park and Motel, are also good bets for basic food and supplies (cafe open daily 8am-4pm; store open daily 8am-8pm). Departing from ordinary

Let's Go format, the following accommodations are listed in **geographical order** (following SH35 from Opotiki to Gisborne), rather than in order of quality.

 BRIGHT LIGHTS, TENT CITY. The East Cape is a smorgasbord of free camping unlike any other part of New Zealand. Take advantage of the early sunrises and sandy dunes and bring your own camping gear.

Te Kaha Lodge (☎07 325 2194), in Te Kaha, sits on a majestic plot of bayfront land. Time your stay with or against the Kiwi Experience bus which rolls in M, W, F. You may have to fight for a spot in the sunset-positioned spa. Internet $3 unlimited use. In-house bar. Dorms $25-30; doubles $50. Tent sites $10. Cash only. ❸

Te Kaha Holiday Park and Motel (☎07 325 2894; www.tekahaholidaypark.co.nz), at the eastern end of Te Kaha. A luxury backpackers with reading lamps, TV, and in-room kitchens, but sadly no view. Reception 8am-8pm. Dorms $20. Cabins $78 for 2; $12 per extra person. Tent sites $11.50, powered $12. MC/V. ❷

SunRise Lodge and Beachcamp (☎06 864 4854), in Te Araroa. This windswept patch of land and its homey rooms are as peaceful as it gets. Continental breakfast $10-15. Dorms $25; doubles and twins $60. Tent sites $10. Cash only. ❷

Eastender Farmstay (BBH) (☎06 864 3820; eastendersfarmstay@xtra.co.nz), near Tikitiki, 8km from SH35 on Rangitukia Rd. Play ping pong next to sheep shearing and bone carving. Kiwi Experience stops here Tu, Th, Sa. 2hr. horse treks $60. Possum and pig hunting available. Dorms $23. Tent sites $10. Cash only. ❷

⊙ ꛂ SIGHTS AND OUTDOOR ACTIVITIES

From Opotiki to Hicks Bay, the highway skirts the lush green coast and reveals the Cape's spectacular views, especially in December when the pohutukawa trees explode with red flowers. In **Whanarua Bay,** the road across from the macadamia nut farm leads down to a DOC-protected section of rocky beach full of tidal pools. After Hicks Bay, the road moves inland. The beachfront schoolyard in **Te Araroa** holds the world's largest pohutukawa tree, named Te Waha o Rerekohu. Te Araroa is also the gateway to the lonely **East Cape Lighthouse,** 21km away at the easternmost point in mainland New Zealand.

Tikitiki lies 24km south of Te Araroa. **St. Mary's Memorial Church** perches on a hill in town, overlooking SH35. One of the most impressive Maori buildings in the region, the church's exterior hides an ornately carved inner sanctuary. Another 36km toward Gisborne, **Tolaga Bay** harbors the longest former wharf in the Southern Hemisphere, a deteriorating 600m testament to the days before highways, at the end of Wharf Rd., 1.5km off SH35. The jetty also marks the beginning of the **Cook's Cove Walkway,** an easy trip to the site of one of Captain Cook's first landings in *Aotearoa*. (5.8km; 2½hr. round-trip. Closed Aug.-Oct. for lambing.)

ꙮ MT. HIKURANGI

The highest non-volcanic mountain on North Island, Mt. Hikurangi (1754m) lords over surrounding peaks and enjoys the first offerings of sunlight to the world. Located 137km from Gisborne and 205km from Opotiki, Hikurangi has great spiritual significance for the Ngati Porou people. Adorning the mountain 1000m above sea level are nine carved *whakairo* (sculptures) representing Maui-Tikitiki-a-Taranga, a famed Maori patriarch, and his *whanau* (FAH-noh; family). At the summit, you can see the northernmost alpine vegetation in the country.

To reach the trailhead for the summit track, find the signposted turn-off from SH35, Taupuaeroa Valley Rd., north of Ruatoria, which leads 3km to Pakihiroa Station, 20km from Ruatoria. Yellow markers designate the route from the parking lot to the hut (10km; 4-5hr.) and orange markers denote the rest of the track from the hut to the summit (2.5km; 2-3hr.). All closures will be publicly announced, so inquire about the status of the track with **Te Runanga O Ngati Porou,** 1 Barry Ave. (☎ 06 864 8660 or 06 864 3012), in Ruatoria, custodians of the hut, track, and Pakihiroa Station. Book ahead to stay overnight in the hut ($15), which has a stove, long-drop toilet, communal bunks, and a limited water supply.

The following are prohibited from the mountain: fires, camping, drugs, alcohol, mountain bikes, motor vehicles, dogs, and guns. The Ngati Porou also ask visitors not to reproduce images of the mountain or of the Maui *whakairo* for commercial use without prior written consent of the CEO of Te Runanga O Ngati Porou. Te Runanga O Ngati Porou also offers 4WD tours of the mountain and the *whakairo* which last about 4hr. ($200 for a group of 4.)

TE UREWERA NATIONAL PARK   ☎ 06

Best known for its "Great Walk," which is consistently rated one of the top ten tramps in the country, the Te Urewera National Park is indisputably the largest and arguably the most impressive national park on the North Island. Maori influence remains strong: the region has long been home to the Tuhoe (TOO-hoy) Maori, who resisted European intrusion with greater force and success than most other tribes. One result of this succesful resistance is that the floor of Lake Waikaremoana and several adjoining parcels of land remain under Maori ownership. The Maori have given their hard-earned slice of paradise a most unusual name: "Te Urewera" loosely translates to "burnt penis." According to one legend, a Maori chief who has remained understandably anonymous in the historical record inspired the name after rolling over in his sleep a few inches too far. The anonymous chief would be glad to know that most campers these days in the misty ridges and untamed valleys of the Te Urewera opt for portable gas stoves over large, unguarded bonfires.

AT A GLANCE

AREA: 212,672 hectares.

CLIMATE: Warm weather Oct.-Mar. Cold and boggy Apr.-Sept.

FEATURES: Largest forested wilderness in New Zealand. Hunting, fishing, boating.

HIGHLIGHTS: Lake Waikaremoana, Lake Waikareiti.

GATEWAYS: Whakatane, Taneatua, Murupara, Ruatahuna, Wairoa.

CAMPING: Fully serviced motor camp at Lake Waikaremoana. Unserviced campsites. Backcountry huts.

FEES AND RESERVATIONS: Book ahead in summer. Huts $20, camping $10.

⌐ TRANSPORTATION

Often unpaved, **SH38** cuts through the park on its way from Wairoa to SH5 (which leads north to Rotorua and south to Taupo). The Kiwi Experience **East As** (☎ 09 366 9830) also drives the road's length as part of a multi-day shuttle tour (p. 179). *Let's Go* doesn't recommend **hitchhiking,** which is difficult in the park.

 WHEN TO GO. The park is best enjoyed in the summer (mid-Oct. to Mar.) since the winter weather can be wet and cold; the walks are open year-round with the right equipment. Always be prepared for all weather conditions.

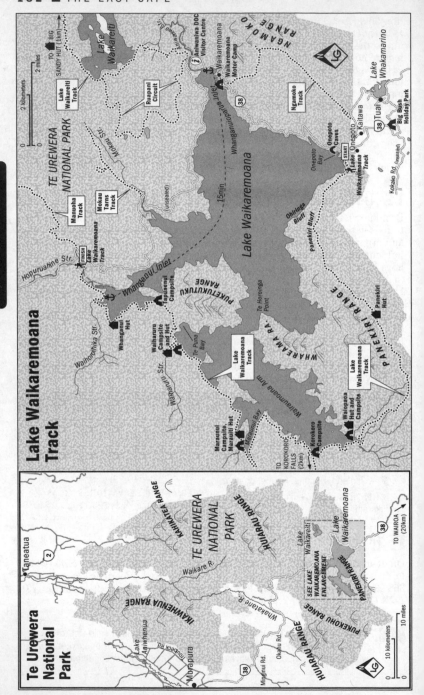

Lake Waikaremoana Track

TE UREWERA NATIONAL PARK

Lake Waikaremoana

Lake Waikareiti Track

Ruapani Circuit

Manuoha Track

Mokau Tarns Track

Whanganui Inlet

Whanganuiopaoa Inlet

Aniwaniwa DOC Visitor Centre

Waikaremoana Motor Camp

Ngamoko Track

Onepoto Caves

Onepoto Bay

Lake Onepoto

START

Lake Waikaremoana Track

Kokako Rd. (unsealed)

Big Bush Holiday Park

Tuai

Kaitawa

Lake Whakamarino

Ohrineg Bluff

Patekiri Bluff

Te Horeinga Point

PUKETUKUTUKU RANGE

Tapuaenui Campsite

FINISH

Lake Waikaremoana Track

Hopuruahine Str.

Whanganui Hut

Waihohonia Str.

Waihararu Campsite and Hut

Te Puna Bay

Waiharuru Arm

Maraunui Bay

Maraunui Campsite
Marauiti Hut

Korokoro Campsite

TO KOROKORO FALLS (2km)

Lake Waikaremoana Track

Waiopaoa Hut and Campsite

Panekiri Hut

PANEKIRI RANGE

WHARAMARA

Te Urewera National Park

Taneatua

TE UREWERA NATIONAL PARK

KAHIKATEA RANGE

HUIARAU RANGE

Waikare R.

Whakatane R.

IKAWHENUA RANGE

Lake Aniwhenua

Murupara

Roubeck Rd.

Minginui Rd.

Okahu Rd.

HUIARAU RANGE

PUKEKOHU RANGE

Lake Waikareiti

Lake Waikaremoana

SEE LAKE WAIKAREMOANA ENLARGEMENT

PANEKIRI RANGE

TO WAIROA (20km)

▄★ 🖪 ORIENTATION AND PRACTICAL INFORMATION

SH38 bisects Te Urewera north of Lake Waikaremoana. Most visitors stay at one of the two holiday parks within the park's limits (see **Accommodations and Camping**, below); both lie east of the **DOC Aniwaniwa Visitor Centre** on Lake Waikaremoana. (☎837 3803 or 0800 492 665. Open daily 8am-4:45pm.) There are small **general stores** in Tuai and Murupara, and at the Waikaremoana Motor Camp, but supermarkets in Wairoa and Rotorua have better prices and **ATMs.** The Waikaremoana Motor Camp's **parking** lot (free even for non-guests) is safer than the trailheads.

🏠 🔀 ACCOMMODATIONS AND CAMPING

The **Waikaremoana Motor Camp ❷** occupies a gem of a location on the lake shore, with a small store and a gas pump. Nearby activities include bushwalks (30min. walk from camp), fishing (equipment available at the camp), hunting, and boating. They also run a $30 shuttle/water taxi service for the Great Walk. (☎837 3826; www.lake.co.nz. Kitchen. Store open daily 8am-6pm, 8am-5pm in winter. Powered tent sites $10 per person. 4- to 5-person fishing cabins $42 for 2, $11 per additional person; 2-person tourist flats and 4- to 5-person chalets $72 for 2, $13 per additional person; 7-person family cabin $84 for 2; 10-person bunkhouse $130. MC/V.) **Big Bush Holiday Park ❷** lies 3km south of the lake and the Onepoto trailhead, and offers shuttle services to the lake track. (☎837 3777 or 0800 525 392; www.lake-waikaremoana.co.nz. Kitchen. Restaurant open evenings. Round-trip Great Walk shuttle $30. Dorms $25; motel rooms $75 for 2 people. Tent sites $12. AmEx/MC/V.) Free **camping** is permitted around the lake, as long as tents are pitched more than 500m from all tracks and not on the clearly marked private land.

🌋 OUTDOOR ACTIVITIES

Ample challenging dayhikes of varying difficulty await you in Te Urewera, including the well-graded **Lake Waikareiti Track** (2hr. round-trip). The walk begins 200m from the DOC and travels through forest to island-dotted █**Lake Waikareiti,** improbably set on a lush green hilltop. From 300m up, you'll get a look at the beech forest below, as well as New Zealand's endangered parrots if you're lucky. The lake itself contains no aquatic plant life, resulting in fairytale clarity. One of the lake's small islands contains its own separate lake. Another option is the **Ruapani Circuit** (6hr. loop), which visits the Waipai Swamp and Lake Ruapani, in addition to Lake Waikareiti. Pick up the dayhikes pamphlet and a map ($2.50) from the DOC. The less-traveled northern reaches of Te Urewera provide even more remote tramping experiences. The **Six Foot Track** (3 days round-trip) cuts through the Tauranga Valley and demands solid navigational skills, while the nearby **Whakatane Loop Track** (4-5 days round-trip) makes a full circuit through the Whakatane Valley.

Since all of the desirable fish and game in the park are introduced species, the DOC allows **fishing** and **hunting.** Fishing licenses are available at **Waikaremoana Motor Camp,** which also rents and sells gear. (Fishing license $18 per day, $88 per year. Rods $30 deposit.) The DOC rents rowboats. ($15 per 4hr.; $45 per day.)

▨ LAKE WAIKAREMOANA TRACK

With its vast tangles of native trees and the sounds of kiwis crying throughout the night, the Lake Waikaremoana (wie-KAH-ray-moe-AH-nah) Track (known locally as the "Great Walk") affords an ideal opportunity to experience New Zealand's serene ecology. The lake itself formed only 2200 years ago, after a massive landslide blocked up a narrow gorge of the Waikaretaheke River; evidence of the landslides dominates the scenery around Onepoto to the east. All bookings for the park are handled by the Aniwaniwa Visitor Centre or through the DOC website.

Length: 46km, 3-5 days.

Trailheads: Trampers can begin at **Onepoto** (which tackles the toughest climb first), a 20min. drive south of the DOC and 500m off SH38, or at **Hopuruahine**, which leaves Panekiri Bluff, 30min. north of the DOC, 1km off SH38.

Transportation: Waikaremoana Guided Tours (☎ 837 3729 or 0800 469 879) shuttles trampers between the Waikaremoana Motor Camp and **Onepoto** ($15), **Hopuruahine Landing** ($25), **Waiopaoa Hut** ($80), **Korokoro Campsite** ($80), **Marauiti Hut** ($70), and **Waiharuru Hut** ($70). **Big Bush Holiday Park** also offers a shuttle service with round-trip pickup in either direction ($25) or water taxi pickup at one of the huts or campsites along the lake ($50-80). In the summer, they also operate a shuttle between the lake and Rotorua ($60). Though *Let's Go* does not recommend it, **hitch-hiking** to and from the trailheads is a cheaper but far more time-consuming endeavor.

Seasonality: While it is possible to complete the track year-round, it gets awfully boggy and cold in winter. The best weather generally lasts from mid-Oct. to Mar. Check weather forecasts at any of the DOC offices before departing.

Huts and Campsites: 5 huts and 5 campsites. Booking system operates year-round. Huts have bunks and mattresses, untreated (rain) water, and long-drop toilets. No stoves. The visitors center (p. 183) handles reservations. Huts $20, under 18 $10; camping $10/5.

Storage: Free at the Waikaremoana Motor Camp store.

Safety: Report any hazardous areas by calling ☎ 0800 999 005.

ONEPOTO TRAILHEAD TO PANEKIRI HUT. *8.8km, 3½-5hr.* The track starts on the small trail beside the DOC sign in the grassy field just off SH38. After passing a small shelter, the trail briefly follows a wide grassy track until it reaches a fork for **Lake Kiriopukae** (20min. round-trip). From the fork the track makes a quad-burning 600m ascent up **Panekiri Bluff**. After about the first hour, panoramic lake vistas grant solace to your troubled mind and exhausted legs, reminding you why it's not called the "Easy Walk" or the "Delightful Walk." The wind-swept moss hanging like spider webs from the grandfatherly trees is another highlight of this leg. After the first hour, the incline mellows somewhat as it winds up the ridge of the Panekiri Range. There is no water along this section of the trail until you reach the **Panekiri Hut** (1180m; 36 bunks), perched on a ridge with a two-way view: the lake lies to the north, while the cleaved hills of the Hawke's Bay region roll into the southern horizon. This leg would make the most worthwhile daytrip.

PANEKIRI HUT TO WAIOPAOA HUT AND CAMPSITE. *7.6km, 2½-4hr.* From Panekiri Hut, the track drops steadily, often steeply, passing plenty of tree ferns, tea trees (kanuka), and mossy rock walls, before eventually reaching the shore of Lake Waikaremoana. This leg has no water, either. New **Waiopaoa Hut** (40 bunks) sits with the lake on its doorstep; adjacent **Waiopaoa Campsite** lies by a frog-filled inlet. As with all of the lakefront sites, sandflies occasionally pester this spot.

WAIOPAOA HUT AND CAMPSITE TO MARAUITI HUT. *12.1km, 3½-4½hr.* An hour-long flat stretch of lakeside track leads to the turn-off for the ▧**Korokoro Falls** (40min.-1hr. round-trip), where rivulets rush down a 30m vertical stone slab. Trampers must grip a steel cable and find their footing over slippery rocks for a short stretch in order to reach the falls. **Korokoro Campsite** lies on a lagoon just past the turn-off for the falls (head right after the bridge). From the campsite, the track winds above the shoreline. Past a private hut and the DOC warden's quarters sits **Maraunui Campsite,** with a choice inlet view and surrounding bluffs. **Marauiti Hut** (22 bunks), 20min. farther, waits on the other side of a hill, and edges a cove perfect for fishing or swimming.

MARAUITI HUT TO WAIHARURU HUT AND CAMPSITE. *6.2km, 1½-2hr.* Beyond Marauiti, the track continues to undulate; this portion has the potential to be incredibly muddy. Immaculate **Waiharuru Hut** (40 bunks) features separate kitchen and bunkroom buildings, a gas furnace perfect for drying wet boots, plenty of wash basins, and porches overlooking the lake. Nearby **Waiharuru Campsite** borders what could almost be called a beach.

WAIHARURU HUT AND CAMPSITE TO HOPURUA-HINE TRAILHEAD. *10.5km, 2½-3½hr.* One kilometer past the Waiharuru complex, the track runs a steep 100m over the **Puketukutuku Peninsula.** Keep your ears open for the sounds of kiwi birds after nightfall. On the other side of the hill, sites at the **Tapuaenui Campsite** are segregated by shrubbery. Mostly level hiking along some of Waikaremoana's most striking inlets leads to **Whanganui Hut** (18 bunks), which rests next to a creek but has minimal lake access and no faucets. The remaining walk to **Hopuruahine Landing** (where most water taxis pick up their passengers) is brisk and undaunting, as are the last kilometers through grassy fields and up a river valley to the swinging bridge leading to the **Hopuruahine Trailhead.**

HAWKE'S BAY

On February 3, 1931, a massive earthquake (7.9 on the Richter scale) rattled much of Hawke's Bay into rubble. Though the history of the region didn't begin with the quake, it certainly seemed to freeze there. Almost immediately following the disaster, teams of architects poured into Napier and Hastings, determined to rebuild in the inexpensive Art Deco and Spanish Mission architectural styles popular at the time. Today, the area's main attractions are its anachronistic buildings and scenic vineyards. Most tourists zip past Hawke's Bay, leaving the region pleasantly uncrowded for those who decide to stay a while. Travelers who do stop will not be disappointed by the viniculture and host of off-beat sights.

NAPIER ☎ 06

You know you've hit Napier (pop. 57,000) when cafes outnumber takeaways, and even the McDonald's is McDeco. The 1931 earthquake killed 162 residents, but also lifted areas of the town previously underwater to new heights above sea level, leaving 3,000 extra hectares on which to rebuild. While the tectonic plates continue to shift underfoot (lifting more than 1cm per year), modern Napier is a living, breathing homage to

LEAVE A MESSAGE

"Billy likes Kate." "Jody is a loser." "Billy *really* likes Kate." "Jody is a *big fat lying* loser."

I was in a backcountry hut, somwhere along the Lake Waikaremoana Track, when the thought occurred to me: should some terrible disaster befall me out here in the Te Urewara National Park—a landslide, flood, massive earthquake—my last written record would be forever preserved in neat handwriting under the words, "Jody is a *big fat lying* loser." Each hut along the trail has a log where hikers can record their names, nationality, destination, main activity pursued on the trip, and comments, and there's some space built in for creativity. A quick glance at top of the page informed me that Billy and Jody were part of a school group that had passed through the previous night; under the "destination" category their teacher had written five words: "home and a hot shower."

Some remarks were basic, many left intensely personal records. Someone who identified himself as "Alexei from Russia" listed "drinking vodka" as his main activity. Several others responded to the main activity question: "thinking" (or, in one case, "working through a midlife crisis.") The primary purpose of the logs aside, they rarely failed to entertain after a long day of solo tramping.
—*Mark Giangreco*

the zigzags, ziggurats, bubbling geometric fountains, neon-lit clock towers and confectionery color schemes that characterize Art Deco.

▛ TRANSPORTATION

Flights: The **Hawke's Bay Airport** (☎835 3427) is north of Napier on SH2. The **Air New Zealand Travel Centre** (☎833 5400), at the corner of Hastings and Station St., books flights to **Auckland** (10 per day, $94-400) and **Wellington** (5 per day, $99-400). Open M-W and F 9am-5pm, Th 9:30am-5pm, Sa 9am-noon. The **Supershuttle** (☎844 7333 or 0800 748 885) offers service to the **airport** ($15). Taxis make the trip for comparable prices.

Buses: Coaches leave from the Napier Travel Centre (☎834 2720), at the train station on Munroe St. **InterCity/Newmans** departs for: **Auckland** (7hr., 3 per day, $66-83) via **Taupo** (2hr., $26-42); **Gisborne** (4hr., 1 per day, $32-40) via **Wairoa** (2hr., $22-28); **Wellington** (6hr., 3 per day, $24-30) via **Palmerston North** (3hr., $15-39). **Nimbus** (☎877 8133) departs from the bus terminal on Dalton St. near Dickens M-F roughly every hr. 7am-5:45pm, Sa 5 per day, to **Hastings** (55min., $5.70). To get to **Hastings** on Su, catch an InterCity/Newmans bus heading south ($11). **Bay Xpress** (☎0800 422 997) goes daily to **Wellington** ($35) in 5hr. **Guthrie's** (☎09 309 0905; www.guthreysespress.co.nz) runs daily to **Auckland** ($64), **Hamilton** ($45), **Rotorua** ($34), and **Taupo** ($23).

Taxis: StarTaxis (☎835 5511) and **Napier Taxis** (☎835 7777 or 0800 627 437).

Car Rental: Metro Rentals (☎835 0590 or 0508 350 590), on Corunna Bay off Hyderabad Rd. Economy cars from $69 per day; insurance $10 per day. **Auto Rental Vehicles,** 3 Dunlop Rd. (☎843 0045 or 027 288 8278), in Onekawa. 25+. Touring cars from $35 per day.

Hitchhiking: Although *Let's Go* doesn't recommend it, hitchhikers heading south recommend getting rides along Marine Pde. A bit past the aquarium, it becomes SH2 and picks up more traffic. Heading north, the best spot is reputed to be across Pandora Rd. Bridge. Most traffic heads to Taupo; those going to Wairoa or Gisborne should ask to be let out where SH5 branches off.

◢▐ ORIENTATION AND PRACTICAL INFORMATION

Napier is compact and easy to navigate. The main boulevards in town, **Marine Parade** and **Hastings Street,** run parallel to each other, stretching southward along the bay. Central Napier's streets abut the bluffs. Be careful when walking through palm-lined **Emerson Street**—despite the brick landscaping, it's a main traffic thoroughfare. **Tennyson** and **Dickens Streets** run parallel to it on either side. The gardens of **Clive Square** mark the edge of the town center.

Visitors Center: Napier i-Site, 100 Marine Pde. (☎834 1911; www.hawkesbaynz.com). Distributes maps and brochures and will book everything from wine tours to domestic flights. When lines are long, play a round of mini-golf out back ($7.50, children $4.50). Internet $8 per hr. Open M-Tu and Th-F 8:30am-5:30pm, W and Sa-Su 9am-5pm. Open later in summer. Mini-golf open daily 9:30am-7pm, 9:30am-4:30pm in winter.

Department of Conservation (DOC): 59 Marine Pde. (☎834 3111). Open M-F 9am-4:15pm.

Banks: ASB (☎834 1286), at the corner of Hastings and Emerson St., houses two 24hr. **ATMs.** Open M-F 9am-4:30pm. Other major banks crowd the center of town.

Police: (☎831 0700), on Station St.

Medical Services: Napier Health Centre, 76 Wellesley Rd. (☎835 4999), has a 24hr. emergency ward.

Internet Access: Cybers, 98 Dickens St. (☎835 0125; www.cybers.co.nz). $6 per hr. Open daily 9am-midnight.

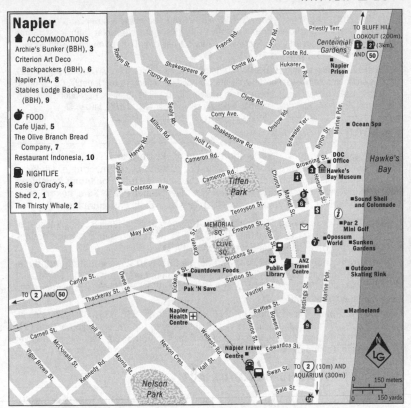

Napier

🔺 **ACCOMMODATIONS**
Archie's Bunker (BBH), **3**
Criterion Art Deco
  Backpackers (BBH), **6**
Napier YHA, **8**
Stables Lodge Backpackers
  (BBH), **9**

🍎 **FOOD**
Cafe Ujazi, **5**
The Olive Branch Bread
  Company, **7**
Restaurant Indonesia, **10**

🍺 **NIGHTLIFE**
Rosie O'Grady's, **4**
Shed 2, **1**
The Thirsty Whale, **2**

Post Office: 57 Dickens St. (☎835 3725), at Dickens and Hastings St. Open M-F 8am-5pm, Sa 9:30am-12:30pm.

Laundry: Taylor's Laundromat (☎835 4863), at the intersection of Browning and Hastings St. Wash $4. Dry $3.50 per 15min. Open daily 7:30am-8pm.

🏠 ACCOMMODATIONS

Be aware that during the fruit-picking season (Nov.-Apr.) some hostels fill up with eager backpackers seeking work.

🏠 **Criterion Art Deco Backpackers (VIP),** 48 Emerson St. (☎835 2059; www.criterionart-deco.co.nz). The building that houses this distinctive backpackers is such a remarkable specimen of Art Deco extravagance, it merits its own stop on the walking tour. Residents enjoy discounts at the Napier-style cafe downstairs. Bike rental $15 per day; scooter rental $50 per day. Wi-Fi $2 per 20min. Key deposit $20. Private parking $4 per day. Reception 8:30am-8:30pm. Dorms $24, weekly $110; singles $32-40/130-150; twins and doubles $55/250, with bath $70; triples and quads $26 per person. MC/V. ❷

Archie's Bunker (BBH), 14 Herschell St. (☎833 7990; www.archiesbunker.co.nz), opposite Hawke's Bay Museum. It's all in the family at Archie's. Spotless facilities and an enormous upstairs lounge. Bike rental $20 per day. Free pickup. Dorms $23; singles $30; twins and doubles $48-56. 4-person shared rooms with bath $100. MC/V. ❷

Napier YHA, 277 Marine Pde. (☎835 7039; yha.napier@yha.co.nz), at Vautier St. Winding hallways and colorful walls give this YHA more character than most. Some rooms have an ocean view. Storage lockers $2 per day. Reception 8am-8pm. Dorms $23; singles $33; doubles $62. MC/V. ❷

Stables Lodge Backpackers (BBH), 370 Hastings St. (☎835 6242; www.stableslodge.co.nz). This environmentally aware hostel is slightly cramped but otherwise very liveable. Comfy bunks plus free tea, blankets, and Internet help make up for the tight quarters. Reception 9am-9pm. Dorms $20; twins and doubles $51. 4-person shared rooms $92-100. MC/V. ❷

◖ FOOD

Upscale cafes cluster around the intersection of Hastings and Tennyson St. while the ethnic restaurants are off Marine Pde. For essentials, the meeting of Dickens, Munroe, Station, and Thackeray St. has three huge options, including **Countdown Foods.** (☎835 2496. Open daily 6am-midnight.) The Napier **Pak 'N Save,** next door, is the second-largest in the country. (☎843 3179. Open daily 6am-midnight.)

Cafe Ujazi, 28 Tennyson St. (☎835 1490), represents the funkiest and freshest of the Napier cafe scene. Breakfast mains $15-17.50. Vegetarian a la carte options $3.50-7.50. Open daily 8am-5pm. AmEx/MC/V. ❸

Restaurant Indonesia, 409 Marine Pde. (☎835 8303; www.restaurantindonesia.co.nz). The signature 13-dish "Rijsttafel" (Dutch-Indonesian banquet; $32-40 per person) makes this restaurant one of a kind. Open W-Su 6pm-late. Reservations recommended. AmEx/MC/V. ❹

The Olive Branch Bread Company, 216 Hastings St. (☎835 8375). Lunchers come for the ready-made sandwiches ($4) and surrender to the freshly baked breads ($1-5). Open M-Tu and Th 8am-3pm, W and Sa 8am-4pm, Su at the Hastings city market 8am-noon. Cash only. ❶

◐ ⚠ SIGHTS AND OUTDOOR ACTIVITIES

Tours in Napier come in two varieties: local architectural tours paying tribute to Art Deco, and winery tours that travel farther afield in pursuit of the perfect vintage. If you choose the latter, plan an extra half-day to sober up. Closer to home, a stroll along Marine Pde. takes you past manicured gardens, burbling fountains, and statues like **Pania of the Reef** (a distinctively toothy mermaid). February's spectacular ▨**Art Deco Weekend** is the yearly event in Napier (a lesser version, called "Deco Decanted" takes place in July). The runner-up, also in February, is the **International Mission Estate Concert** at the Mission Estate Winery, a big regional deal in a gorgeous setting. (www.missionconcert.co.nz.) There are impromptu jazz concerts at the wineries and other entertainment at the Sound Shell.

ART DECO ARCHITECTURE. The town itself is perhaps the main sight in Napier—even the manhole covers can't escape the Art Deco craze. Tennyson St. has a row of classic structures: the Maori Deco of the **Antique Centre,** the Shamrock Deco of the **Munster Chambers,** and the Deco-overload of the **Daily Telegraph Building.** Market St. features Deco glass windows; the peach and green **Countrywide Bank Building** off Dalton and Emerson St. is likewise impressive. Don't forget to check out the Greco Deco of the **Colonnade** and the **Sound Shell.** The **Tom Parker Fountain** in the gardens along Marine Pde. gets technicolor light treatment from dusk until midnight. Perhaps most famous of all, however, is the **National Tobacco Company Building** (formerly known as the Rothmans Building), built in 1933 at the corner of Bridge and Ossian St., outside of town, incorporating elements of Art Deco, Art Nouveau, and the Chicago School headed by Louis Sullivan. The **Art Deco Trust** runs a 1.5km guided walking tour of Napier's Deco. For the cheapest tour, just buy a brochure ($4) at the tourist office. *(163 Tennyson St. ☎835 0022; www.artdeconapier.com. 2 per day. Morning tour departs 10am from the visitors center. 1hr. $10. Afternoon tour departs 2pm from the Art Deco Trust. 2hr. $15. The Trust also runs a 3rd tour in summer that departs from the visitors center at 5:30pm. 1½hr., $12. All walking tours include complimentary tea or coffee and an informative 20min. video. Tour in a vintage automobile, 3 people $99.)*

WINERIES. Napier sits on the edge of the Hawke's Bay plains, one of New Zealand's major wine-producing regions. Pick up a free **Hawke's Bay Winery Guide** at the tourist office or visit these stand-outs. Originally set up by priests to make ceremonial wine, **Mission Estate Winery** is New Zealand's oldest winery, and houses a cellar, craft gallery, and gourmet restaurant. *(198 Church Rd. ☎845 9350; www.missionestate.co.nz. Open M-Sa 9am-5pm, Su 10am-4:30pm. Cellar tours daily 10:30am, 2pm. Free tastings. Restaurant open daily 10am-late.)* **Ngatarawa Wines** is a small winery in a restored stable on lovely grounds. *(☎879 7603; www.ngatarawa.co.nz. Tastings daily 11am-5pm.)* Several tour operators offer guided tours and tastings. Greg of the **Grape Escape** runs a top-notch operation, catering tours to his guests' tastes in wine. *(☎0800 100 489; www.grapeescape.net.nz. Half-day tour $45, full-day $90.)* **Vicky's Wine Tours** *(☎845 2736)*, **Vince's Vineyard Tours** *(☎836 6705; vincestours@hotmail.com)*, and **Toast The Bay Wine Tours** *(☎876 2849)* run 3½-5hr. tours ranging $45-65 per person with free pickup. Those with a high tolerance and a passion for cycling might consider **Bike D'Vine** *(☎833 6697; www.bikedevine.com)*, which drops cyclists off in the Havelock North area near a cheese factory and several wineries ($50 per person, 3-person min.). **Bike About Tours** *(☎844 0601 or 845 9034; www.bikeabouttours.co.nz)*, offers a city tour ($40).

HAWKE'S BAY MUSEUM. In addition to its garishly colored cylinders, this museum has exhibits on the earthquake, the East Coast Ngati Kahungunu Maori, and, of course, Art Deco. A video display on the lower level has some fascinating first-hand accounts from survivors of the quake. The in-house cinema also shows recent releases in the evenings. *(9 Herschell St. ☎835 7781. Open daily Oct.-Apr. 10am-6pm. May-Sept. 10am-5pm. $7.50, under 16 free.)*

NATIONAL AQUARIUM. Suiting up to help out in the daily shark feeding ($60; gear $30; tank $6), certified scuba divers can become celebrities at this modern marine complex. Keep an eye out for "Izzy," an ambassador of the world's most aggressive crocodile species. The aquarium also has a handful of tuatara, direct descendants of dinosaurs. *(☎834 1404; www.nationalaquarium.co.nz. Open daily Dec. 26-Jan.*

FROM THE ROAD

A MAORI PRONOUNCIATION GUIDE

If you're traveling in Northland, you might come across the following on a map: Taumatawhakatangihangakoauauotamatcapokaiwhc nuakitanatahu. It's a hill overlooking Hawke's Bay credited by The Guinness Book of World Records with having the longest place name in the world. But have no fear—just keep the following tips in mind when pronouncing this and other Maori proper nouns:

1. "Fut's" up with those pesky digraphs? The "wh" consonant pair, pronounced as an English "f" sound, is one of two digraphs in Maori—the other is "ng," pronounced as it sounds in the English word "singer."

2. Know your vowels: "a" as in "about," "e" as in "enter," "i" as in "eat," "o" as in "awful," and "u" as in "put." A macron (bar) appearing over the vowel indicates that it is lengthened during pronunciation.

3. Roll those Rs. Remember that old potato chips commercial, the one with the catchy tagline, "Rrruffles have rridges?" Let this be your guide when pronouncing the letter "r" in Maori.

Think you're ready for the advanced course? Go back to the beginning and try to pronounce the name of that record breaking hill in Hawke's Bay.

THE LOCAL STORY

FIX YOUR GREAT DEPRESSION

Let's Go caught up with John Cocking, the man behind the cheeky period character "Bertie," the official Napier Tourist Ambassador since 2000.

LG: You're quite the local celebrity in Napie your image appears on postcards, life-sized cardboard cutouts, and brochures. They even call the straw hats they sell "Bertie-type boaters." How did you come into this role?

JC: I was working as an actor while living here in Napier and was asked to provide a character for a [1920s-era] "tea dance." That's when I had the idea for Bertie. He's in some ways like P.G. Wodehouse's Bertie Wooster, but he's cleverer and much more of a ladies' man.

LG: Bertie is a major presence at Napier's Art Deco Weekend. Describe the event for the uninitiated among our readers.

JC: We close the major streets. Everybody dresses up in period costume There's music, dancing, vintage cars, everything to do with the era of Art Deco and the way of life that the style represents. There's a strange thing that happens when people dress up—they lose their inhibitions, and the costume allows them to feel a special sense of freedom.

LG: I heard about something called the "Depression Dinner." How does that figure in the jolly festivities?

9am-7pm; Feb.-Christmas 9am-5pm. Hand feeding at 10am, 2pm. Behind-the-scenes tours at 9am, 1pm. $14, children $7.50. Tours $27/13.)

MARINELAND. Two of the largest and oldest attractions at this mecca of undersea activities are Shona and Kelly, aging dolphins who like human company. (☎834 4027; www.marineland.co.nz. *Dolphin shows daily 10:30am, 2pm. $11, children $5.50. Dolphin swim $45; gear rental $10. Behind-the-scenes tour daily 9am. $16, children $8. Book at least a week ahead in summer. No open-toe shoes. Penguin workshops daily 1-1:45pm. Arrive 15min. early. Advance booking required. $16.)*

ODDBALL ANIMAL ATTRACTIONS. Opossum World is a shrine to the unique fur of one of New Zealand's most harmful introduced pests, featuring a display on opossum trapping and a boutique tannery that borders on fetish fascination. *(157 Marine Pde. ☎835 7697. Open daily 9am-5pm. Free.)* The **Classic Sheepskins** tour provides insight into what really happens to 80,000 of those cute fluffy herbivores each year. At the retail shop, don't miss the bins of "seconds" skins, available for as little as $21. *(22 Thames St., off Pandora Rd./SH2 North. A courtesy van picks up from the visitors center. ☎835 9662 or 0800 170 171; www.classicsheepskins.co.nz. Shop hours M-F 7:30am-5pm, Sa-Su 9am-4pm. Free tours daily 11am, 2pm.)*

OTHER SIGHTS AND ACTIVITIES. One building able to withstand the Art Deco craze was the **Napier Prison,** 55 Coote Rd., the oldest in New Zealand. Originally a quarantine facility, then an army barracks, then an insane asylum, the building served as a lockup from 1862-1993. It now doubles as a backpackers (p. 188) and a somewhat depressing attraction. (☎835 9933; www.napierprison.com. *Tours daily 9:30am, 3pm. $15, children $7.50.)* To reinvigorate, head to **Ocean Spa,** just north of Tom Parker Fountain on Marine Pde. This aqua complex has outdoor pools and hot tubs and offers a number of other body therapy services. (☎835 8553. *Admission $6. Open M-Sa 6am-10pm, Su 8am-10pm. AmEx/ MC/V.)* The **Centennial Gardens,** just off Marine Pde. on Coote Rd., across from the prison, were initially quarried for limestone by the neighboring inmates and now offer a lovely high waterfall.

Though not known for adventure, Napier has its fair share of fun. For a calm jaunt through the air, **Airplay Paragliding** offers tandem flights and various training programs. (☎027 451 2886. *Intro course $180 per day. Tandem $140.)* **Early Morning Balloons** embarks on one-hour hot-air balloon rides over the bay. (☎879 4229; www.early-am-balloons.co.nz. *8+. Weather dependent. $285, children $240.)* If you prefer to keep your feet on the ground, or at least much closer, try **Mountain Valley** for scenic horse treks. (☎834 9756. *1hr. ride $65 per person; 2hr. $80; 3hr. $100; 4hr. $150.)*

NIGHTLIFE

The bar scene in Napier picks up on weekend nights—the most popular watering holes in town are the Irish pubs on **Hastings Street**. Later in the night, serious partiers head to the nightclubs on West Quay, a 40min. walk through an industrial zone or a $20 taxi ride from the city centre.

TIP

BUNKER DOWN. Walking through industrial Napier from the clubs on West Quay after dark has been known to present hazards. Instead of stumbling home alone, try to walk in packs or, alternatively, catch the free weekend Archie's Bunker shuttle back to town center.

Rosie O'Grady's, 37 Hastings St. (☎834 1235), by Tennyson St., is an authentic tavern that pleases both novice and veteran drinkers. Late hours, theme nights, the occasional live music, and a prime location make this Irish pub a perennial favorite. Pints $5.50. Bangers and mash $12.50. Open daily 10am-3am. AmEx/MC/V.

The Thirsty Whale, 62 West Quay (☎835 8815; www.thethirstywhale.co.nz). With a name worthy of Herman Melville's New Bedford, this bar and club features a massive bar, big screen TV, and a dance floor to complement the inevitable nautical decor. Handles $5-6. Mains $11-35. Open M-Th and Su 10am-midnight, F-Sa 10am-3am. MC/V.

Shed 2 (☎843 4100), next to the Thirsty Whale, offers a wide, selection of inexpensive draught beers (pints $5-6.50) to wash down the munchy-quenching woodfired pizzas ($17). The dance floor picks up around 1am. Open Tu-Su 11:30am-late. AmEx/MC/V.

HASTINGS ☎06

Hastings (pop. 74,000) may be known as Napier's twin city, but the resemblance is strictly nominal. Only 19km away, it fell victim to the same quake of 1931 but was partially rebuilt in Spanish Mission style. The architecture never reached the same gaudy heights as Napier, and little effort has been put into promoting the style as an attraction. Though Hastings may lie in Napier's shadow, the nearby kiwifruit orchards draw hordes of fruit pickers during the annual harvest season.

TRANSPORTATION. Napier and Hastings are about 30min. (19km) apart by bus. **InterCity/Newmans** runs to various destinations including **Auckland** (8hr., 3 per day, $69-86) via **Taupo** (2¼hr., $35-44) and **Wellington** (5hr., 3 per day, $24-30). **Bay Express** also runs to Wellington (5hr., 2 per day, $35). All buses leave from across the street from the Hastings i-Site on Russell St. Book

JC: The busiest night of the weekend is Saturday. Everybody wants to eat out, and there just aren't enough restaurants in town to handle the crowds, so we figured we would have to feed people outside, picnic style. I said to myself, "If it has to be basic, let's make it *really* basic." That's when the idea for the Depression Dinner was born. People dress in tattered clothes and carry a tin cup on a piece of string around their necks. They march through the town and we fill the cups up with soup and give them a piece of bread. The Salvation Army band even marches in front. They lecture the masses on the evils of "the demon rum" and really fit in beautifully.

John and his partner, Penelope Freeman, run tours in their vintage Buick and operate Deco Affair, a deco-devoted costume shop in the Mid City Plaza.

tickets through the Hastings i-Site. **The Nimbus** leaves from Eastbourne St. near the Russell St. corner, with stops in Napier and Havelock. (☎877 8133. Every hr. M-F 7am-5:30pm, Sa reduced service. $5.20.) **Car rental** is available from **Metro Rentals** (p. 186) in Napier. While *Let's Go* does not recommend **hitchhiking,** hikers going south often head out past the 30kph zone beyond the race course; those going to Napier usually hitch from Karamu Rd. North, while those heading to Taupo, Wairoa, or Gisborne take the route that bypasses central Napier by getting rides from Pakowhai Rd.

■**■** **ORIENTATION AND PRACTICAL INFORMATION.** Flat and orderly Hastings is disturbed only by the railway track slicing through the heart of the city center. **Heretaunga Street,** the main road, turns pedestrian-only for a block on either side of the railway; a herd of ceramic sheep assemble at the Market St. end of this stretch. Designations between east and west streets are based around the railway station, while south and north designations split at Heretaunga St. The **Hastings i-Site** is at the corner of Heretaunga and Russell St., and offers free Internet. (☎873 5526; www.hawkesbaynz.com. Open M-F 8:30am-5pm. In summer Sa-Su 9am-4pm. In winter 9am-3pm.) From November to April, there are numerous **work opportunities** for fruit picking around Hastings. Other services include: **ANZ,** on the corner of Heretaunga St. and Karamu Rd., with a 24hr. **ATM** (branch open M-F 9am-4:30pm); the **police** (☎873 0500), on Railway Rd.; a **pharmacy and medical center** at **The Doctors,** 110 Russell St. (☎876 8445; pharmacy open M-F 8am-8pm, Sa-Su 8am-6pm; medical center open daily 8am-9pm); the **post office,** at the corner of Heretaunga and Market St. (Open M-F 8:30am-5pm, Sa 10am-1pm.)

■ ■ **ACCOMMODATIONS AND CAMPING.** Most accommodations will help arrange work for fruit-picking travelers. Barbeques fill the summer at **Travellers Lodge (BBH) ❷,** 606-608 St. Aubyn St. West, which also boasts a sauna. (☎878 7108; www.tlodge.co.nz. Free pickup or parking. Bike rental $25 per day. Key deposit $10. Dorms $21, $110 per week; singles $30/150; doubles $44. $52/250. MC/V.) At the well-hidden **Hastings Backpackers (BBH) ❷,** 505 Lyndon Rd. East, between Hastings St. and Willow Park Rd., you can kick back on the patio after a long day of fruit picking. (☎876 5888; www.medcasa.co.nz. Reception 9am-noon, 2-8pm. Dorms $20, weekly $110; singles $26/140; doubles and twins $48/260. Cash only.) **AJ's Backpackers ❷,** 405 Southland Rd., just off Southhampton St., will do in a pinch. (☎878 2302; ajsbackpackers@xtra.co.nz. Key deposit $10. Dorms $24, weekly $110. Tent sites $15/70. Backpacker discounts. Cash only.) The **Hastings Top 10 Holiday Park ❶,** 610 Windsor Ave., near Splash Planet, 20min. from town on foot, has lots of green space, large trees, and a duck-filled creek. (☎878 6692 or 0508 427 846; www.hastingsholidaypark.co.nz. Reception 8am-7pm. Tent and powered sites $14-15. 4-bed cabins $48 for 2, $11 per extra person; 6-bed cabins $70 for 2, $13 per extra person; 7-bed self-contained unit $95 for 2, $14 per extra person; 8-bed motel $120 for 2, $15 per extra person. MC/V.)

■ ■ **FOOD AND NIGHTLIFE.** While the **Corn Exchange ❹,** 118 Maraekakaho Rd., may sound like an agricultural economist's daydream, it's actually a popular restaurant with a large bar and well-designed fireplace. The menu features steaks, game, and fish ($25-28), as well as wood-fired pizzas ($19). (☎870 8333. Open M-Th 10:30am-11pm, F-Sa 10:30am-1am. AmEx/MC/V.) At **Rush Munroe's Ice Cream Gardens ❶,** 704 Heretaunga St. West, the indulgent lose themselves in an extra-large waffle cone for a mere $3.80. (☎878 9634. Open M-F 11am-8pm, Sa-Su 10am-9pm.) Those in the industry know the express lunch special ($9) at **Bollywood Stars ❷,** 102-106 Heretaunga St. East. (☎876 8196. Open daily 9:30am-late. AmEx/MC/V.) Hippies should feel at home at **Pataka Organics ❷,** 217 Heretaunga St. Mains $9-12. (☎870 9535. Open M-F 8am-3pm, Sa 8am-2pm. Cash only.) A **Pak 'N Save** sits at the corner of Heretaunga and Charles St. (Open 6am-midnight.) **Countdown Foods,** on the royal corner of Queen St. West and King St. North, also stocks groceries. (☎878 5091. Open daily 7am-10pm.) Nightlife usually includes a pint of Steiny ($5) or cider under exposed pine beams at the **Cat and Fiddle Ale House,** 502 Karamu Rd. North. (☎878 4111. Open daily 11am-late.)

◨ 火\ **SIGHTS AND OUTDOOR ACTIVITIES.** Like Napier, Hastings embraced 1930s architectural styles following the 1931 earthquake. Most buildings are in either Art Deco or Spanish Mission. Pick up a **Heritage of Hastings** brochure at the Hastings i-Site to spot them. Otherwise, Hastings shares many of its attractions with Napier (p. 185), such as **wineries, Cape Kidnappers** (p. 193), and killer surfing at **Ocean Beach** on the south side of the Cape and **Waimarama** farther south. In Hastings proper, amusement-seekers enjoy **Splash Planet,** New Zealand's only water theme park, offering year-round (heated indoor pools, jeeps, mini-golf course) and summer attractions (water slides). The six-hectare park is a 25min. walk from downtown Hastings. (☎876 9856 or 0508 775 274; www.splashplanet.co.nz. Open Sept.-Apr. daily 10am-5pm. $25, children $20.) Lose yourself in **The Amazing Maze 'n Maize,** on Longlands Rd., in between SH2 and SH50A south of Hastings, a corn labyrinth which features Friday night "Haunted Mazes" for those over 16. (☎878 8117; www.maze.co.nz. Open daily Dec.-Apr. 10am-6pm, also F last entry 10pm. $9, students $7, CornEvil $13.) Sample over 85 different varieties of pitted fruits (in season) at **Pernel Fruitworld,** 1412 Pakowhai Rd., about a 5min. drive northwest of Hastings. (☎878 3383; www.pernel.nzliving.co.nz. Tours daily every hr. 9am-3pm. $11, children $5.50.) **On Yer Bike Winery Tours** offers tours of local wineries on two wheels from $50. (☎879 8735; www.onyerbikehb.co.nz.) The **Hawke's Bay Exhibition Centre,** 201 Eastbourne St. East, exhibits local and national art. (☎ 876 2077; www.hawkesbaymuseum.co.nz. Open daily 10am-4:30pm. $4.) **Te Mata Peak,** a 20min. drive from the city center, offers walks and a not-to-be-missed view of the Bay. Inquire about directions and pick up a free brochure at the Hastings i-Site.

CAPE KIDNAPPERS   ☎ 06

Locals claim, Captain Cook coined the name "Kidnappers" after local Maori tried to steal a Tahitian boy off Cook's *Endeavor.* From September to March, the area is home to the world's largest mainland nesting grounds of the **Australasian gannet.** Fifteen-thousand large, tawny-headed, white and black birds arrive in early September and set up their nests in orderly rows at the 13-hectare **Cape Kidnappers Gannet Reserve.** Chicks hatch in early November and mature over the summer before flying the coop on their ambitious maiden air voyage 2800km across the Tasman Sea to Australia. The Cape consists of three nesting colonies: the Saddle Colony, visible from the plateau lighthouse, the Black Reef Colony along the beach, and the Plateau Colony, at the apex of the Cape track. The birds make a scene straight from Alfred Hitchcock; male gannets bear down like jet planes toward the teeming colony before dropping nesting material to their mates below.

The area is closed to the public between July and Labour Day weekend (in Oct.), when the birds are in the early nesting stage. At other times, you're free to visit the gannets of the Cape either by tour or on your own. **Gannet Beach Adventures** runs tractor excursions which leave from the motor camp in Clifton. Be prepared for a bumpy, occasionally wet ride along the beach, past an impressive geological display movement caused by faultlines. Once reaching the Cape, you have 1½hr. to observe the birds or take a swim. (☎875 0898; www.gannets.com. Tours run daily Oct.-late Apr. Times depend on the tides. $33, children $19.) **Gannet Safaris** runs a 3hr. bus tour that departs from Clifton and traverses the Cape, ending at the Plateau Colony. (☎875 0893 or 0800 427 232; www.gannetsafaris.com. $50, students and children $25.) Alternatively, you can be your own guide by picking up a **Guide to Cape Kidnappers** ($1) at the Napier DOC. Take SH2 to Clive, turn onto Mill Rd., and continue until you hit Clifton (30min.). From there, you can begin walking up the path that leads to the Plateau Colony (4hr. round-trip). It's a brilliant walk at any time of year, even in winter, when the birds are gone. For further info, check with the Napier DOC (p. 186), which has the latest tour and weather updates.

TAUPO AND TONGARIRO

Lake Taupo, the largest freshwater lake in the Southern Hemisphere, fills a crater formed by a monumental explosion 26,500 years ago. With fire and brimstone beneath its surface and snow-capped peaks towering at its center, the Taupo and Tongariro region uneasily awaits further geological tantrums. In the background tower the mighty trio of Mounts Ruapehu, Ngauruhoe, and Tongariro, home to the famed Tongariro Northern Circuit tramp (in Tongariro National Park) and the popular Whakapapa and Turoa ski fields.

▓ TAUPO AND TONGARIRO HIGHLIGHTS

BASK in the steaming turquoise pools of the splendid **Tongariro Crossing** (p. 204), often called the best dayhike in New Zealand.

TRAWL for trout in **Lake Taupo** (p. 199); averaging 4.5kg each, these famed fish bend the rods of fishermen from around the world.

PLUNGE from the sky with one of the cheapest skydives in the world in **Taupo** (p. 198).

TAUPO ☎ 07

The sunny community of Taupo (pop. 23,000) lies at the headstream of the Waikato River and presides over the largest lake in the Southern Hemisphere, Lake Taupo (616 sq. km). The lake lures anglers with its world-class trout fishing year after year. If trout fishing isn't enough to get your blood racing, Taupo is also home to world-class adventure activities guaranteed to set your teeth on edge. The western terminus of the Pacific Ring of Fire, Taupo rides the same belt of smoking volcanic activity that powers Mt. Ruapehu and White Island.

▐ TRANSPORTATION

Flights: The **airport** (☎378 5428) is 7km south on SH1. **Air New Zealand** (☎0800 737 767) flies daily to: **Auckland** (55min., 2 per day, $150-281); **Christchurch** (2¼hr., 5 per day, $197-486); **Nelson** (2hr., 3 per day, $200-406); **Queenstown** (5hr., 2 per day, $250-753); **Wellington** (1hr., 5 per day, $130-315). Taxis downtown (10min., $11).

Buses: InterCity/Newmans leave from Taupo Travel Centre (☎378 9032), on Gascoigne St. to: **Auckland** (5hr., 4 per day, $25-54); **Hamilton** (3hr., 4 per day, $18-36); **Napier** (3 per day, $18-38); **Rotorua** (1hr., 4 per day, $12-25); **Wellington** (6hr., 4 per day, $34-72). InterCity connects daily with **Turangi's Alpine Scenic Tours** (☎378 7412 or 025 937 281) to reach **Whakapapa** and **National Park Village** (2hr., 2:30pm, $30). During ski season, **Tongariro Expeditions** (☎377 0435; www.thetongarirocrossing.co.nz) runs daily from Pointons Ski Shop to the **Whakapapa ski field** (7:30am, $45 round-trip). In summer, they also head to and from the trailheads for the **Tongariro Crossing** and **Northern Circuit** (departs Taupo 5:40, 6:20am; arrives at Mangatepopo Carpark 7, 8:15am; departs Ketetahi Carpark 3:30, 4:30pm; $35-39 round-trip).

Taxis: TOP Cabs (☎378 9250) and **Taupo Taxis** (☎378 5100) have 24hr. service.

Rentals: Cycle World, 30 Spa Rd. (☎378 6117), rents mountain bikes. From $25 per day. **Pointons Ski Shop,** 13 Tongariro St. (☎377 0087; www.pointonskishop.co.nz). Ski rental package $30 per day. Snowboards $40 per day. Open daily 7am-7pm. If ski fields are closed open 9am-5pm. **Taupo Rod 'n Tackle,** 7 Tongariro St. (☎378 5337; www.tauporodandtackle.co.nz). Fly-fishing outfit $33 per half-day, $40 per day. Spin-fishing outfit $10/20. Open daily 8am-5:30pm. May-Oct. closed Su.

Hitchhiking: To head north on SH1, many thumbers cross the Waikato to the intersection of Norman Smith St. *Let's Go* does not recommend hitchhiking.

▟ ▟ ORIENTATION AND PRACTICAL INFORMATION

Taupo is tucked into the northeastern bulge of the river where the **Waikato River** runs from **Lake Taupo**. SH1 and SH5 are in town as **Tongariro Street**, home to the Tauranga i-Site, and bend south along the lakeshore as **Lake Terrace**. **Spa Road** runs east along the south bank of the Waikato. Following the Waikato River north of the town center, **Wairekai Park** is the site of Huka Falls. Parallel to SH5, **Huka Falls Road** runs 3km north-south. At its northern end, a turnoff leads to **Karetoto Road.**

Visitors Center: Taupo i-Site, 30 Tongariro St. (☎376 0027; www.laketauponz.com). Open daily 8:30am-5pm.

Department of Conservation (DOC): on Tauranga Pl. (☎378 3885). Open M-F 8am-4:30pm.

Banks and Currency Exchange: ATMs line Tongariro and Horomatangi St. **ASB Bank** (☎376 0063), at Tongariro and Horomatangi St. Open M-F 9am-4:30pm.

Police: (☎378 6060), behind the Taupo i-Site on Story Pl.

Medical Services: Main Street Pharmacy (☎378 2636), at Tongariro and Heu Heu St. Open M-F 8:30am-8:30pm, Sa-Su 9am-8:30pm. **Taupo Health Centre,** 117 Heu Heu St. (☎378 7060). Open M-F 8:30am-5pm. The **hospital** (☎378 8100) is on Kotare St., east of town.

Internet Access: Cybershed, 115 Tongariro St. (☎377-4168). Internet $3.50 per hr. for backpackers. Also has **laundry** ($4 wash, $6 dry). Open daily 9am-9pm. **Log On,** 71 Tongariro St. (☎376 5901). From $6 per hr. Backpacker rate $4.50 per hr. Open M-F 10am-8pm, Sa-Su 11am-8pm. In winter 9am-9pm. Alternatively, try **Max Cafe** (see below).

Post Office: At Horomatangi and Ruapehu St. Open M-F 8:30am-5pm, Sa 9am-2pm.

▟ ▟ ACCOMMODATIONS AND CAMPING

Older, cheaper accommodations are clustered along the streets a few blocks east of the town center. Otherwise, the least expensive riverfront bed in town is the free **camping** available at Reid's Farm 2km north of town along Huka Falls Rd.

Rainbow Lodge (BBH), 99 Titiraupenga St. (☎378 5754; www.rainbowlodge.co.nz), just off Spa Rd. The spacious kitchen and outdoor patio are great for socializing. Free coffee and pickup. Mountain bike and fishing rod rental. Free sauna. Key deposit $10. Dorms $19-22; singles $35; twins and doubles $46, with bath $52. MC/V. ❷

Action Down Under (YHA), (☎378 3311; www.laketaupo.com), at the corner of Tamamutu and Kaimanawa St. Enjoy spotless rooms and views of snow-capped peaks from the large deck. Bike rental. Free spa. Dorms $23-25; singles $30; twins and doubles $54, with bath $60; family rooms with bath from $90. Tent sites $12. MC/V. ❷

Orakei Korako Geyserland, 35km from Taupo (☎378 3131; www.orakeikorako.co.nz). Take SH1 or SH5 to Wairaki, turn right onto Tutukau Rd., then 14km later turn right again. Highly recommended for those who have a car and want to avoid the "urban center," this hidden lakeside lodge across the water from Taupo's best geothermal site is scenic, peaceful, and has 3 hot tubs. Bring your own bedding, food, cutlery, and crockery. Rustic communal lodge and bunks $25; 4-person tourist flats from $100, $25 per extra person. MC/V. ❷

Taupo Urban Retreat Backpackers (VIP), 65 Heu Heu St. (☎0800 872 261; www.taupourbanretreat.co.nz). Handsome lodge with large common areas and is working to wean itself off the tourist bus circuit. All rooms with A/C. On-site bar, pool tables, and wide-screen TVs to facilitate socialization. Reception 24hr. Dorms $21-25, twins and doubles $56. MC/V. ❷

Burkes Lodge and Backpackers (VIP), 69 Spa Rd. (☎378 9292; www.burkesbp.co.nz). This renovated motel hidden among car dealerships has private baths, a barbeque area, and a central courtyard. Key deposit $20. Dorms $21; twins and doubles $50, with bath $55; triples $69; family rooms from $52. Tent sites $10. Cash only. ❷

🔲 FOOD

For the true Taupo experience, delight in some trout. Many places around town will prepare your catch for a fee. **Pak 'N Save,** at Ruapehu and Tamamutu St., stocks groceries and has a nightly wine sale. (Open daily 8am-9pm.)

Villino, 45 Horomatangi St. (☎377 4478). This flashy option claims to define neo-Italian, which apparently involves confit of duck ($32) and serious consumption of mixed drinks ($9-20). Open daily 10am-4pm and 6pm-late. MC/V. ❹

Replete Cafe, 45 Heu Heu St. (☎378 0606; www.replete.co.nz). This wonderland is replete with inventive and palate-pleasing dishes. Most items under $7. Lunchtime draws crowds. Open M-F 8:30am-5pm, Sa-Su 8:30am-4pm. Cash only. ❶

Max Cafe, 36-38 Roberts St. (☎378 8444), around the corner from Mulligans and the Holy Cow. Cheap takeaways make this a good spot to grab food for the road. Or hang for a while and use the Internet ($2.50 per 15min.). Burgers $7, other mains less than $15. Coffee $2.80-4.50. Outdoor seating. Open daily 6am-10pm. MC/V. ❶

◎ SIGHTS

The incredible geothermal energy that seethes beneath Taupo's surface has captivated scientists and spectators for decades. Manifesting itself in the form of geysers, springs, and lunar landscapes, this energy powers much of Taupo's tourist activity, drawing in thousands of visitors year after year.

CRATERS OF THE MOON. A 1954 explosion, resulting from the drilling of a geothermal bore, created a steaming pockmarked landscape of craters and boiling mud pools so special that it is now managed by the DOC. *(Turn-off is 6km north of town on SH1; it's an additional 4km from SH1. Open daily until dusk. Parking lot closes at 6pm. Free.)*

ORAKEI KORAKO GEYSERLAND AND CAVE. Though distant and inaccessible to those without their own transport, this dramatic and less developed private geothermal reserve is well worth the trip. A shuttle boat crosses the idyllic lake during the day to reach a range of steamy wonders. Don't miss the spectacular fern-lined amphitheater of **Aladdin's Cave** with its warm mineral pool. *(Follow the signposted road that winds through hills off SH1 about 25min. north of Taupo. ☎378 3131; www.orakeikorako.co.nz. Open daily 8am-4:30pm. In winter 8am-4pm. $25, children $10.)*

TAUPO HOT SPRINGS. After a day of touring, pay a visit to one of Taupo's bubbling pools of tranquility. Public and private indoor or outdoor pools are available. *(On the Taupo/Napier Hwy. or SH5, 3km from town. ☎377 6502; www.taupohotsprings.com. Open daily 7:30am-9:30pm. Last entry 9pm. Public pools $12. Private pools $15.)*

WAIRAKEI PARK. Following the Waikato River north of town, Wairakei Park is a slightly bizarre agglomeration of tourist sights and recreational areas: Huka Falls, Hukajet (p. 200), and the Taupo Volcanic Activity Centre. Maori for "long white water," the **Huka Falls** are a popular place to watch nature fight reason—here, the 100m wide, 4m deep Waikato River forces itself into a 15m wide, 3m deep rock chute. Spurting out of the bottleneck, the water rushes below a footbridge over the channel and finally ejects into a pool below, dumping enough water to fill two Olympic-size pools every second. The cheapest and most aerobic way to capture the falls on your roll of film is via the **Huka Falls Track.** *(Leaves from Spa Thermal Park, off Spa Rd. at the end of County Ave. 1hr. round-trip. For those who would rather watch from their car, Huka Falls is accessible off SH1 on Huka Falls Rd., about 4km north of town. Parking lot open 8am-6pm.)* The public side of the adjacent Institute of Geological and Nuclear Sciences (IGNS), the **Taupo Volcanic Activ-**

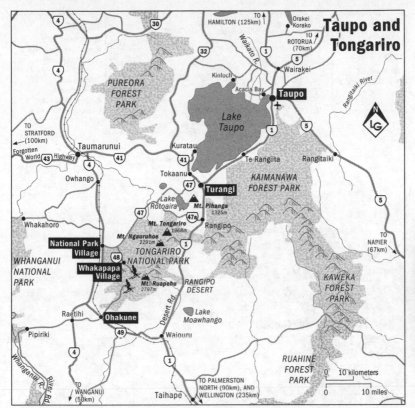

Taupo and Tongariro

ity Centre has a team of researchers who monitor the Taupo volcanic zone. Check out the seismograph readings of Mt. Ruapehu and eruption film footage. *(Take the Huka Falls Rd. turn-off from SH1. 1km north of Huka Falls, on Karetoto Rd. ☎374 8375; www.volca-noes.co.nz. Open M-F 9am-5pm, Sa-Su 10am-4pm. $8, children $4.)* **Wairakei Geothermal Power Development** (built 1959-64) has a jumbled terrain of massive, steaming, stainless-steel tubes that worm along the ground as part of the world's first geothermal power station. *(Across the Waikato Bridge on SH1, less than 8km north of town.)*

🎤 NIGHTLIFE

Taupo nightlife revolves around the influx of backpackers and businessmen that flood the town during the summer months. For late night hunger cravings, **the stand ❶**, across the street from Finn MacCuhal's serves heavenly kumara chips with sour cream and chilli ($4.50). (Open Th-Sa 10pm-4am. Cash only.)

📧 **Mulligans,** 15 Tongariro St. (☎376 9100). The up-and-comer in town, Mulligans is an anything-for-a-laugh potluck of backpackers and locals. Start off your night here with a Murphy's ($6.50) and a game of pool. Open daily 4pm-3am.

Finn MacCuhal's (☎378 6165, ext. 3; www.finnmaccuhals.co.nz), on Tuwharetoa St. at Tongariro St., right below Go Global. It's all about the Guinness at this relaxed alternative to rowdy nightlife. Handles $5.50. Happy hour 5-6pm. Open daily 9:30am-late.

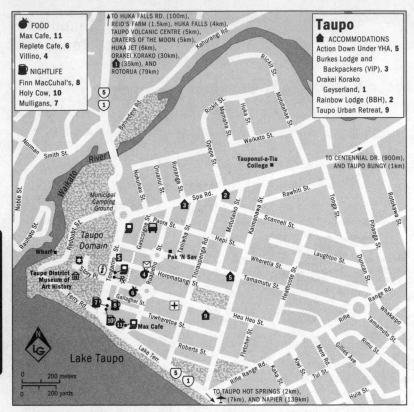

🍎 FOOD
Max Cafe, **11**
Replete Cafe, **6**
Villino, **4**

🍸 NIGHTLIFE
Finn MacCuhal's, **8**
Holy Cow, **10**
Mulligans, **7**

TO HUKA FALLS RD. (100m),
REID'S FARM (1.5km), HUKA FALLS (4km),
TAUPO VOLCANIC CENTRE (5km),
CRATERS OF THE MOON (5km),
HUKA JET (6km),
ORAKEI KORAKO (30km),
🛏 (35km), AND
ROTORUA (79km)

Taupo
♦ ACCOMMODATIONS
Action Down Under YHA, **5**
Burkes Lodge and
  Backpackers (VIP), **3**
Orakei Korako
  Geyserland, **1**
Rainbow Lodge (BBH), **2**
Taupo Urban Retreat, **9**

Holy Cow, 11 Tongariro St. (☎378 0040). Look for the cow-patterned door. Once the alcohol sets in, every backpacker, her uncle, and the hitchhiker they picked up heads to this shameless animal house. Tables are mounted fairly early. DJs mix hits nightly. 2 pool tables. Handles $3.50. Happy hour 7-10pm (jugs $8). Open daily 7pm-3am.

🏔 OUTDOOR ACTIVITIES

IN THE AIR
If you've been resisting peer pressure or sudden impulses, Taupo is the place to throw caution to the wind and your body from a plane at 12,000 ft. Or, you and your fears can plummet toward water attached only to an elastic cord. For a deal on 4hr. of four activities (bungy, skydiving, Huka jetboating, and a helicopter ride), complete the **Fourplay.** (☎374 8572; www.hukajet.co.nz. $500. Book ahead.)

TAUPO FOR CHEAP(ER). Jason's "Encounter New Zealand" Activities Directory brochure gives coupons, most worth a 10% discount for activities in Taupo and Rotorua. They are available at Taupo and Rotorua i-Sites.

🛩 **SKYDIVING.** A tandem jump with **Taupo Tandem Skydive** is cheaper than any-where else in the world, and the views on a clear day will take your breath away.

That is, if you haven't lost it already. This professional organization has been sending people up and "escorting" them back down since 1990. (☎377 0428 or 0800 275 934; www.tts.net.nz. 100kg weight limit. 12,000 ft. $219; 15,000 ft. $314. Call ahead for early-bird specials.) Newcomer **Skydive Taupo** knows that the best way to throw yourself at the ground is with style; from free limo pickup to a complimentary chilled wine or beer, this well-run tandem team gets it right. (☎0800 586 776; www.skydivetaupo.co.nz. 100kg weight limit. 12,000 ft. $220; 15,000 ft. $315. Freefall video $150, DVD $150.)

ROCK 'N' ROPES. This playground for grownups has several ropes and adventure exotica including the Chicken Walk and Heebie Jeebies. (Located at Taupo Adventure Park, off SH5, just 15km north of Taupo. ☎374 8111 or 0800 244 508; www.rocknropes.co.nz. Free transport from Taupo. 15m swing $15. High beam, 12.5m giant trapeze, and swing combo $40. Half-day $65.)

BUNGY JUMPING. Since 1991, more than 180,000 have ventured off the cantilever platform 47m above the hauntingly crystalline Waikato River at **Taupo Bungy.** For $99, you can hook up and ponder the leaden cliffs, the impending water, and the pickup raft below. Or, you can just close your eyes and take the plunge. (202 Spa Rd. Free shuttle. ☎377 1135 or 0800 888 408; www.taupobungy.com. Open daily 9am-5pm.)

ON THE GROUND

KAIMANAWA HELIBIKING. Combining air and land in a remote location, Kaimanawa will take you up in a helicopter 2500 ft. and then down on a mountain bike for 10km of purpose-built track. (☎384 2816; www.kaimanawahelibiking.co.nz. Free pickup from Taupo. Bikes and safety gear provided. 4hr., $345 per person. 2-person min. Bookings essential.)

ACTION QUADS. Ride ATVs through farmland, forest, and native bush, with a hilltop view of Ruapehu and Ngarahoe. Located 12.7km north of Taupo off SH1, down Poihipi Rd. toward Kinloch. (☎0800 342 420; www.actionquads.co.nz. Free pickup from Taupo. 1st hr. $70, each additional hr. $30. Bookings essential.)

ON THE WATER

Lake Taupo's blue waters fill the crater of the volcano responsible for one of the most violent eruptions ever witnessed. The final blast, an estimated 1810 years ago, ejected ash and pumice across the globe creating blood-red skies recorded in ancient Chinese and Roman literature.

KAYAKING. Kayaking Kiwi offers half-day paddles to the Maori carvings ($95) and customized kayaking trips and forest walks. (☎0800 529 255; www.KayakingKiwi.com.) **Kiwi River Safaris** takes adrenaline junkies and first-time adventurers on whitewater rafting and kayaking excursions. (45min. north of Taupo. ☎0800 7238 577; www.krs.co.nz. 1-day rafting $95, 2 days $350. 2hr. kayaking $40.)

LAKE TAUPO BOAT TOURS. On calm days, you can affordably navigate the placid waters with a rented boat or narrated cruises. The western shores of **Acacia Bay** end in dramatically shear rockfaces and narrow inlets. Along part of the northern coastline, a set of impressive (if not ancient) Maori carvings have been chiseled into the rock faces at **Mine Bay**—on private land accessible by boat only. Many cruises include the **carvings,** the **Western Bays, Hot Water Beach,** and much of the lake itself; contact the **Charter Launch Office** at the harbor to book (☎378 3444). The Charter Launch Office also owns the **Barbary,** a 1920s sailing yacht once owned by famous Hollywood swashbuckler Errol Flynn, is now captained by the colorful Bill Dawson, who teaches you to sail it. (☎0800 227 2279 or 378 3444; www.barbary.co.nz. 2½hr. 3 per day. $30, children $10, under 5 free.) The **Earnest Kemp,** a 1920s steamboat replica, is a less arr-gressive, yet informative scenic tour of the lake. (☎378 3444. Book ahead. 2hr. $30, under 15 $10.)

FISHING. The world-famous Taupo trout, both brown and rainbow, were introduced from California and Britain in the late 1800s. Regulations appear on the **fish-**

ing license you must purchase before hitting the river; licenses are only valid for Taupo. The apex of the fish phenomenon is the **Mighty River Power Lake Taupo International Trout Fishing Tournament** (*www.taupotroutfishingtournament.org.nz*); 450 anglers descend on Taupo on ANZAC day (Apr. 25) eager to take the biggest, prettiest, and feistiest trout of the lake. *(Spinning and fly fishing permitted year-round. On rivers except for the Waikato, only fly fishing is allowed. 3 fish per 24hr. license $18.50; one-week license $55. Available from the i-Site, sports shops, or the offices at the harbor. Charters $75-140 per hr.)*

HUKA JET. Take this heart-racing 30min. jetboat blast down the Waikato, performing 360° turns for the photo-snapping crowds at Huka Falls. *(In Wairakei Park, 6km north of Taupo off SH1. ☎374 8572 or 0800 485 2538; www.hukajet.com. Free shuttle. Boats run every 30min. $79, children $49. Bookings essential.)*

TURANGI   ☎07

The self-proclaimed "Trout Fishing Capital of the World," Turangi (pop. 3500) is the smaller, wilder, and fishier cousin of Taupo. Waters teem with anglers, but there is plenty of space, tackle, and catch to go around. Alternatively, fishers and travelers use the abundant hostels in town as bases for the justifiably popular Tongariro Crossing and other hikes in the remote Kaimanawa Forest Park.

⌐ TRANSPORTATION. InterCity/Newmans stops at the **Travel Centre** (☎386 8918), at the corner of Tautahanga Rd. and Ngawaka Pl., and heads daily to: Auckland (5½hr., 5 per day, $56-60) via Taupo (45min., $16-20) and Hamilton (3½hr., $43); Rotorua (2hr., 5 per day, $36); Wellington (5½hr., 4 per day, $59) via Palmerston North (3hr., $40). InterCity's **Starlighter** overnight service heads to Auckland daily at 1:10am and to Wellington daily at 1:45am. The laid-back folks of **Alpine Scenic Tours** (☎0800 872 258; www.alpinescenictours.co.nz), also at the Travel Centre, run daily shuttles to Whakapapa Village by way of the Tongariro Crossing trailheads (45min.; 7, 7:30am; returning from Ketatahi Carpark at 4, 5:15pm; round-trip $30), or on demand to National Park Village (1hr., 1 per day, $25). **Tongariro Expeditions** also runs to the Tongariro trailheads. (☎377 0435 or 0800 828 763; 6:25, 7:15am; arriving at Mangatepopo Carpark at 7, 8:15am; returning from the Ketatahi Carpark at 3:30, 4:30pm; $30-35.) On all of the shuttles, the early-bird service is for those who want to try (in futility) to beat the crowds; it will generally cost $5 more. Although one should consider the risks involved and *Let's Go* does not suggest it, **hitchhiking** to Taupo is reportedly not too difficult; those heading north on SH1 wait at the corner of Pihanga Rd. near the visitors center or the Shell station.

■⎘ ORIENTATION AND PRACTICAL INFORMATION. Turangi is about 6km from Lake Taupo on **SH1**, which continues north around the lake to Taupo and south where it's known as the **Desert Road**. Parallel to SH1 is **Ohuanga Road** (Tautahanga Rd. in its northern stretch), the main road through town. Connecting SH1 to Ohuanga Rd., Pihanga Rd. is the site of the **Town Centre** complex, which holds virtually all essential shops and services. The **Turangi i-Site** is just across from the Town Centre. Check here in winter to make sure the Desert Rd. is open before heading south. (☎386 8999; turangivc@laketauponz.com. Open daily 8:30am-5pm.) For park information and before attempting any Tongariro walks, stop by the Turangi i-Site or the **DOC** at Ohuanga Rd. and Turanga Pl., at the south end of town. (☎386 8607. Open M-F 8am-4:30pm.) Other services, all in the town center unless otherwise noted, include: a **bank** (open M-F 9am-4:30pm) and **ATM;** the **police** (☎386 7709), at Ohuanga and Tautahanga Rd.; **Turangi Pharmacy** (☎386 8565; open M-F 9am-5:30pm, Sa 9:30am-12:30pm); a 24hr. emergency **doctor** (☎378 7060); **Internet** access at the Turangi i-Site ($2 per 20min.); the **post office** is inside Naylor's Bookshop (☎386 7769; open M-F 9am-5pm).

⚑ ⚑ ACCOMMODATIONS AND CAMPING. Turangi's accommodations will set you up with shuttles and discounts for affiliated outfitters and may provide reason enough to use Turangi as a base for Tongariro's trails. With a serene courtyard, state-of-the-art kitchen, and log fire in the Sky TV lounge, **⬛Extreme Backpackers (BBH) ❷**, 26 Ngawaka Pl., around the corner from the bus depot, is better than home—unless home includes a 14m climbing wall. (☎386 8949; www.extremebackpackers.co.nz. Climbing wall $5 for guests. Linen $2. Gear rental for tramping and camping $5. Key deposit $5. 4-bed dorms $21; singles $34; doubles $48, with bath $58. MC/V.) Newcomer **⬛Riverstone Backpackers (BBH) ❷**, 222 Tautahanga Rd., packages itself as a boutique hostel with leather couches, lantern lit deck, outdoor wood-burning pizza oven, and modern kitchen. There is space for anglers to clean their catch out back. (☎386 7004; www.riverstonebackpackers.co.nz. BBH discount. Dorms $25; shares $28; doubles 62, with bath $74. MC/V.) Former bunkhouse of the Tongariro Power Scheme workers, the **Turangi Cabins and Holiday Park ❶**, off of Ohuanga Rd., southwest of the center of town, maintains the small cabins and poor lighting of yore. (☎386 8754; cabinsgalore@xtra.co.nz. Linen $4. Tent sites $11. Cabins and chalets $20 per person; 2-person on-site caravans $44. MC/V.)

◖ FOOD. The **⬛Grand Central Fry ❶**, 8 Ohuanga Rd., has excellent individual meals (under $5) and five-person packs ($15) for the hordes. The four-fillet fish burger is the house special ($5.80). (☎386 5344. Open daily 11am-9pm. In winter, Su-Th 11am-8:30pm, F-Sa 11am-9pm. MC/V.) The imposing **Four Fish Restaurant ❸**, at Pihanga and Ohuanga Rd., lives up to its name, serving large sizes of the fresh catch ($23-30) and specialty pizzas galore ($16-20). (☎386 6340. Open Tu-Su 11am-10pm. MC/V.) The **Turangi Truck Stop ❶**, 1km west of town where Atirau Rd. meets Tukehu St., stays open 24hr. (☎386 8760. Grub $2-8. Cash only.) For groceries, head to **New World,** in the town center. (Open daily 8:30am-7pm. MC/V.)

◷ ⚑ SIGHTS AND OUTDOOR ACTIVITIES. The **Tongariro River** is Turangi's biggest attraction. Knowing, perhaps, that they are the center of attention, husky 1.5-2kg trout are a sure-fire bite. **Fishing guides** start at $80 per hr. That cost does not include **licenses** ($18 for 24hr.; one-week $50), which are available at the Turangi i-Site as well as several tackle shops. **Barry Grieg's Sporting World**, in the Town Centre, rents fishing gear packages from $57 per day and charters boats. (Open M-Sa 8:30am-5:30pm, Su 8:30am-4:30pm. Charter boats $65 per hr. 3hr. min. Waders $15 per day, rods and reel $15 per day.) Those who prefer a hands-off approach should head to the DOC's **Tongariro National Trout Centre**, 4km south of town on SH1, where visitors can learn more than they ever wanted to know about milking (yes, milking) trout. There is also an informative on-site museum. (☎386 8085; www.troutcentre.org.nz. Open daily 10am-4pm; May-Nov. 10am-3pm. Donations requested.) Several operators raft down the Class III upper section of the river, featuring over 60 rapids closed in by walls of bush. **Rock 'n River** will take you rafting, let you jump off a hidden waterfall, and soak you in a hot pool at the end of the day. (☎386 0352 or 0800 865 226; www.raftingnewzealand.com. $99.) The **Tokaanu Thermal Pools** are off the main road of tiny Tokaanu Village down SH41 from Turangi. (☎386 8575. Open daily 10am-9pm. $6 per 20min., cooler public pool $4.)

Turangi's other big attractions are tracks, like the nearby **⬛Tongariro Crossing** (p. 204)—often hailed as the finest one-day trek in the world—and paths in the rugged hills east of Tongariro that constitute part of the **Kaimanawa Forest Park.** Kaimanawa, primarily used for multi-day hunting and tramping trips, is huge (77,348 hectares), hard to access, and not developed for visitors. If you choose to visit, plan your trip carefully and consult with the DOC about huts, hunting season, and private land regulations. An easier option for travelers is the **Lake Rotopounamu**

Walk, which leaves from a signpost 11km up SH47. The short hike makes a quick 5km loop through native fern forest around the small lake hidden at the base of **Pihanga** (the 1325m extinct volcano towering over Turangi). Those itching for a summit but too timid to try the Tongariro trinity tackle **Mt. Tihia** (4hr. round-trip), also near town, which is accessible from Te Pananga Saddle, 7km up SH47.

TONGARIRO NATIONAL PARK

Three larger-than-life volcanic peaks tower over North Island: massive, blocky Ruapehu (rue-uh-PIE-oo; 2797m), conical Ngauruhoe (nair-uh-HO-ee; 2291m), and sprawling Tongariro (1967m). These volcanoes—all still active—were once considered so sacred that all but the highest-born Maori shielded their eyes against their grandeur. An eerie, wind-scoured land, Tongariro National Park encloses New Zealand's only "desert" (the desolate Rangipo), native beech forests, hardy alpine scrublands, and gem-like crater lakes set against colorful volcanic scoria.

AT A GLANCE

AREA: 78,651 hectares.

CLIMATE: Mild climate in summer; extreme conditions in winter.

FEATURES: Craters, active volcanoes, ski fields, tussock, semi-arid desert.

HIGHLIGHTS: Emerald Lakes, Tongariro Crossing, Tongariro Northern Circuit.

GATEWAYS: Turangi, National Park Village, Ohakune. Whakapapa is in the park.

CAMPING: Accommodations and camping in Whakapapa. Backcountry huts along tramping routes.

FEES AND RESERVATIONS: Late Oct.-early June, hut pass $20, tent sites $15. At all other times, huts $10, tent sites $5.

■ TRANSPORTATION

Highways encircle Tongariro National Park. To the east, **SH1,** also called the **Desert Road,** streaks through the Rangipo Desert; ice occasionally closes this road in winter and flash floods temporarily block it during summer. To the south, **SH49** splits from SH1 at **Waiouru** and continues west until it hits **SH4,** which flanks the park's west side. **SH47** traces the park's north edge between SH4 and SH1. **SH48** (also called Bruce Rd.) branches south from SH47 to Whakapapa. **Mt. Ruapehu** runs a daily shuttle bus from Whakapapa Village to the Whakapapa ski area. (☎07 892 3738. Departs 8:45am, returns 4pm; $10 round-trip.) **Hitchhiking** along any of these roads, not recommended by *Let's Go,* can be a slow process, but traffic is particularly sparse along SH48. Those determined to get past Whakapapa Village should start early to catch ski field employees and never wait until dark to try their luck. The same is true for those hitching along Ohakune Mountain Rd., which heads north from SH49 to the base of Ruapehu and Turoa ski fields. Most visitors to the park stay in **Turangi** (p. 200), **National Park Village** (p. 206), **Whakapapa Village** (p. 208), or **Ohakune** (p. 208). Whakapapa Village is the most convenient to the **Tongariro Northern Circuit** and the **Whakapapa ski fields,** while Ohakune provides the easiest access to the **Turoa ski fields.** Operators shuttle walkers to the **Tongariro Crossing** trailheads from Turangi, National Park Village, Whakapapa Village, and Ohakune.

■ ? ORIENTATION AND PRACTICAL INFORMATION

Tongariro National Park lies just southwest of Lake Taupo. Start your exploration at the **DOC's Whakapapa Visitor Centre,** which presents two high-tech audiovisual shows and a treasure trove of ecological, cultural, and geological displays. It also

WHEN TO GO. Though the Tongariro National Park can be visited year-round, extreme weather conditions and avalanches make winter tramping dangerous. Trampers must be experienced and have appropriate gear, including crampons, ice axes, and clothing. Skiers should also dress warmly and are advised to keep an eye on both Mt. Ruapehu and Mt. Ngauruhoe, which have been known to end ski seasons with a bang.

sells gear for the inevitable trip up the volcano. (☎07 892 3729; whakapa-pavc@doc.govt.nz. Open daily 8am-6pm. Shows $3, children $1. Discount for 2-show package.) Its **Tongariro Summer Programme** (late Dec.-early Jan.) features changing ranger-led activities from backcountry heli-hikes ($110) to free evening talks. There are also smaller **DOC offices** in Turangi (☎07 386 8607; open M-F 8am-5pm) and Ohakune (☎06 385 0010; open M-F 9am-3pm). Turangi and Ohakune harbor **supermarkets** and **ATMs.** The DOC advises travelers to park only in the well-watched lot across from the Whakapapa Visitor Centre; vandalism and theft run rampant in many other area lots, particularly those at trailheads. The **phone codes** for this region are ☎06 at Ohakune and ☎07 at all points further north.

▌ OUTDOOR ACTIVITIES

For information on the **Tongariro Northern Circuit** or the **Tongariro Crossing**, see p. 204. Less crowded than the park's namesake walks, the **Round-the-Mountain Track** (4-6 days round-trip; huts $10, camping $5) runs around Mt. Ruapehu, traversing windswept slopes, crossing a deep gorge, and passing along the edge of the forsaken Rangipo Desert. The track intersects the Northern Circuit at both Whakapapa Village and Waihohonu Hut; people often walk the two in conjunction—storing food for the second half of the journey in Whakapapa means a 10min. detour off the trail, but a much lighter pack during the initial days. Contact the DOC before your tramp; they are currently conducting tests on volcanic mudflow.

Many **dayhikes** start right from Whakapapa Village. The relatively easy **Tama Lakes Walk** (14km; 5hr. round-trip), which follows an undulating, tussocked landscape past Taranaki Falls to the incongruous blue of Tama Lakes, is one of the best. The unmarked climb to the active **Ruapehu Crater** is the most difficult official dayhike in the park. Ice, snow, and volcanic activity can make the trip a risky one, and several unprepared trampers have died along the route. Most begin the trek from the top of Bruce Rd. (SH48) near the base of the Whakapapa ski lifts (7hr. round-trip); others ride the lifts to their terminus (open daily 9am-4pm; $20 round-trip) and start from there (5hr. round-trip). Staff members from the **Mt. Ruapehu Ski Area** conduct **guided walks** along this route. (☎07 892 3738. Daily walks depart at 9:30am. Bookings essential. $75, under 16 $45. Price includes lift.)

Alpine-savvy rock climbers will find a challenging 120m route on Pukekaikore called the **Bomb Arete** off the track near Mangatetopo Hut (mere mortals need not apply—seriously). Also nearby, the walls of **Mangatetopo Valley** provide a more reasonable challenge for casual climbers who might be interested in chalking up on the park's unique volcanic rock.

▙▟ SKIING AND SNOWBOARDING

The commercial ski fields that hug Ruapehu's slopes are many people's reason for visiting Tongariro National Park. The **Mt. Ruapehu Ski Area** is the largest and most developed ski area in New Zealand. One pass provides access to lifts on both sides of the mountain (Whakapapa and Turoa). The mountain was a sacred gift from a Maori chief in 1887 and the ski area still respects the sanctity of the crown—no lifts or groomers

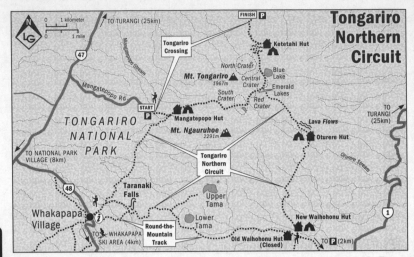

touch the top, which seduces powder-hungry skiers and boarders. Although Mt. Rua-pehu attracts bad weather like a 2797m magnet (gale-force winds and storms often close the fields), the management offers a weather guarantee that allows refunds or credits if lifts have to close or if you're unhappy with the conditions. Even so, volcano skiing is, by nature, unpredictable. Lack of sufficient snow can severely limit the mountain's operations. Recent Mt. Ruapehu eruptions cut both the 1995 and 1996 sea-sons short. (☎ 07 892 3738, snowphone Whakapaka 08 322 22182, Turoa 08 322 22180; www.mtruapehu.com. Open July-Oct. Lifts open daily 9am-4pm. Lift pass $80, under 16 $44; half-day $48/26. Ski, boot, and pole rental $35, under 16 $25. Snowboard and boot rental $43/35. Discounts on multi-day and lift passes.)

WHAKAPAPA. The Whakapapa side of the mountain has daunting views of Mt. Taranaki on clear days. The ski field includes 1360 acres, six chairlifts, eight T-bars, six rope tows, a beginners' area, open terrain, and lots of easily accessible backcountry areas. Snowboarders are welcome, but most seem to prefer Turoa. *(At the top of Bruce Rd. 7km from Whakapapa Village.)*

TUROA. With the country's longest vertical drop (720m) and 500 hectares of snow, Turoa is known for open terrain and long runs (the longest is 4km). Trails slope down from four chairlifts, three T-bars, four platter lifts, and one rope tow. Turoa also offers some off-trail skiing; it's even possible to haul gear up to Crater Lake and ski down (always check with the Ski Patrol first). Snowboarders love Turoa for the natural half-pipes in its gulleys and the lack of flats. Turoa is also home to one of the most exten-sive parks in the country with linked features like boxes, rails, jumps, a beginner park, and a groomed half-pipe. *(At the top of Ohakune Mountain Rd. 17km from Ohakune junction.)*

◪ TONGARIRO NORTHERN CIRCUIT

Winding around the park's trinity of volcanoes, the Tongariro Northern Circuit is one of the country's most jaw-dropping tracks. The otherworldly terrain is riddled with steaming vents, technicolor lakes, and bizarre rock formations, not to men-tion the three volcanoes: Mt. Ngauruhoe, Mt. Tongariro, and Mt. Ruapehu. The ◪**Tongariro Crossing,** a head-spinning highlights-reel day track, is by all accounts the best dayhike in the country. Though the Northern Circuit spans almost the entire length of the Tongariro Crossing, its highlights are not limited to this segment. Beyond where the tracks fork, the Circuit leads to a field of angular, naturally-sculpted lava flows, a few tranquil (if mystifyingly isolated) patches of native forest, the Tama Lakes, the Taranaki Falls, and views of the volcanoes.

Length: Tongariro Northern Circuit: 51.5km, 3-4 days. **Tongariro Crossing:** 17km one-way, 6-8hr.

Trailheads: Start from **Whakapapa Village,** the **Mangatepopo** road end (6km off SH47), the **Ketetahi** road end (1km off SH46), or **SH1,** across from Rangipo Intake Rd. To avoid the crowds, spend the night before at Mangatepopo Hut or hit the trail mid-morning—most Tongariro Crossing trampers arrive 7:30-8:30am. Most trampers walk clockwise to avoid the flow of Tongariro Crossing mobs.

Transportation: Alpine Scenic Tours (☎0800 872 258 or 021 563 109; www.alpinescenictours.co.nz) shuttle between Taupo and the **Mangatepopo** and **Ketatahi trailheads,** via **Turangi, National Park Village,** and **Whakapapa Village** on request. (2 per day, $30 round-trip). **Tongariro Track Transport** (☎07 892 3716 or 021 563 109) runs Oct.-Apr. daily from **National Park** (7:45am) and **Whakapapa Village** (7:15, 8am) to **Mangatepopo** (round-trip $25), and picks up at **Ketetahi** (4, 5:30pm). From Ohakune, **Matai** runs one shuttle to the **National Park Village, Whakapapa Village,** and the **Mangatepopo trailhead** (☎0800 462 824; 7:30am, $30 round-trip). Some area hostels also run on-demand shuttles in the summer. **Hitchhiking** to any of the trailheads is usually difficult, and *Let's Go* does not recommend it. Leaving a car unattended is a bad idea—the Mangatepopo and Ketetahi carparks are among the country's most unsafe.

Seasonality: Harsh conditions and extreme exposure are possible in any season due to high altitudes; even the heat of summer may yield to strong gusts and snow. A winter circuit is a technical tramp requiring equipment and experience. Dec.-Mar. are less challenging; Feb. usually has the most stable weather patterns. As with any outdoor activity, always check weather forecasts before embarking.

Huts and Campsites: From late Oct.-early June, the 4 26-bunk DOC huts have on-site wardens, gas cookers, toilet facilities, rainwater supply (sometimes scarce during droughts), and require a **Great Walks Hut Pass** ($20 per night, children $10). There is no booking system, so a bunk is never guaranteed during the busy season. Each hut has a cluster of tent sites ($15, children $7.50). From late June-early Sept., fees revert to the backcountry ticket system (huts $10, tent sites $5), and huts have fewer amenities.

Storage: Whakapapa Visitor Centre ($3 per bag); most accommodations store for free.

 A SCREE-CHING HALT. For the brave souls heading to the summits of any of the volcanoes, watch for falling rock and scree. It is the number one cause of accidents in exposed terrain. Gloves and pants can also protect hands and legs from the rough scoria rock.

WHAKAPAPA VILLAGE TO MANGATEPOPO HUT. *8.5km, 3-5hr.* The section of track from Whakapapa Village to **Mangatepopo Hut** crosses several streams and affords memorable views of solitary Pukeonake and the jumble of adjacent volcanoes—an enticing teaser of what's to come. The downside: it is extremely rutted and can get very muddy in adverse weather, leading some folks to skip this section by starting at the Tongariro Crossing Trailhead on Mangatepopo Rd. The hut itself, 5min. from the track, faces Mt. Tongariro, Mt. Ngauruhoe, and the saddle between.

MANGATEPOPO HUT TO EMERALD LAKES. *8km, 3½hr.* From the hut, the trail follows Mangatepopo Stream up the valley to its origin, **Soda Springs,** which is a 10min. marked spur from the main trail. Due to high mineral content, the water from the springs and the stream is not drinkable, even when treated. From there, the track up to the saddle, popularly known as the Devil's Staircase, is steep, but short—clocking in at less than 1hr. At the top, strong winds blow across **South Crater,** a Mars-like world almost entirely devoid of plant life. A demanding side-trip leads up the great **Mt. Ngauruhoe** (2291m; 2¾hr. round-trip). Much of the climb is unmarked, but if you stay left along the rocky outcrop on the way up and find the scree chute on the way down, you shouldn't lose your bearings.

The main track continues across South Crater's flat expanse, then climbs another steep slope to the rim of steaming **Red Crater.** From here, a well-marked spur route leads gradually up to the peak of **Mt. Tongariro** (1967m; 1½hr. round-trip). Meanwhile, the main track skirts Red Crater's edge and climbs to the track's highest point (1886m), where first views of the tranquil **Emerald Lakes** reward the effort. It's just a quick, steep scree-run down to their scenic and—we have to say it—smelly shores.

EMERALD LAKES TO KETETAHI HUT OR OTURERE HUT. *4.2km one-way, 1½hr.* At the **Emerald Lakes Junction,** just beyond those amazing green pools, trampers completing the Northern Circuit have a choice; they can head north to **Ketetahi Hut** or veer southeast to **Oturere Hut.** A 1½hr. hike off the main Circuit via a trail that skirts the steep eastern slope of North Crater, ridge-top Ketetahi Hut offers thrilling views of Lakes Rotoaira and Taupo. Unfortunately, the Tongariro Crossing traverses its front porch—literally—so the place turns into a major thoroughfare on pleasant afternoons. The nearby Ketetahi Hot Springs are on private land and off-limits. Past the hut, the track drops steeply, the surrounding vegetation changes from tussock to podocarp forest, and eventually the Ketetahi road end appears (2hr.), marking the end of the Tongariro Crossing.

Heading toward Oturere Hut from the Emerald Lakes Junction, the track descends into a valley strewn with chunks of jagged hardened lava. The Circuit cuts a relatively flat path across the valley floor, at the end of which, on a ledge overlooking a waterfall and stream, sits Oturere Hut. This is the quieter and better hut from which to catch a breathtaking sunrise.

OTURERE HUT TO NEW WAIHOHONU HUT. *7.5km, 3hr.* Beyond Oturere, the track winds down into sandy washes and over a series of gravel hills studded with the occasional wind-whipped treelet. After about 2hr., the path crosses a river to enter the forest, ascends through cool beeches to a scenic ridge, and descends again through forest to **New Waihohonu Hut,** which stares Mt. Ruapehu straight in the face. Those who reach the hut with energy to spare can drop their packs and head a bit farther along the track, straight through a junction, following signposts to the pond-like **Ohinepango Springs** (1hr. round-trip), where exquisitely cold water gushes straight out of the ground.

NEW WAIHOHONU HUT TO WHAKAPAPA VILLAGE. *14.3km, 5½hr.* Just a bit beyond New Waihohonu, a spur trail leads past the century-old **Old Waihohonu Hut** (30min. round-trip), which is unused and filled with decades of tramper graffiti. Stick by the stream here to follow the main track, which rises and falls slightly (but repeatedly) as it continues through stream-furrowed tussocks to the pass between Ngauruhoe and Ruapehu. If you have time, make the side-trip to the Tama Lakes: **Lower Tama** (10min. round-trip), a shining blue pool in an volcanic crater, and crescent-shaped **Upper Tama** (1½hr. round-trip), which lies uphill amid wind-buffeted vistas. The final stretch forks about an 1hr. short of Whakapapa Village; an upper route travels through more rutted tussock terrain, while the equidistant, forested lower route passes the 20m **Taranaki Falls.**

NATIONAL PARK VILLAGE ☎07

National Park Village is little more than a cluster of hostels and a gas station at the junction of SH4 and SH47 established to service the hordes flocking to the nearby Tongariro Crossing, Whakapapa ski fields, and Whanganui River Journey.

TRANSPORTATION. The **train station** is on Railway Rd. at the end of Findlay St. **TranzScenic** (☎0800 872 467) runs daily to: Auckland (5½hr., $70-85); Hamilton (3½hr., $35-50); Palmerston North (3½hr., $30-52); Wellington (5½hr., $55-84). **Buses** depart from the dairy near Carroll and Ward St. at the "Ski Hire" sign. **Inter-City** (☎386 8919) heads daily north to Auckland (5½hr., $39-49) via Hamilton (3½hr., $26-32) and south to Wellington (5½hr., $55) via Ohakune (30min., $18) and Wanganui (2½hr., $30). **Ski Haus** and **Howard's Lodge** (p. 207) handle bookings. **Alpine Scenic Tours** (☎0800 872 258 or 021 563 1093; www.alpinescenictours.co.nz) runs pre-booked trips to Turangi (1¼hr., 4:30pm, $25).

PRACTICAL INFORMATION. National Park Village has **no visitors center or ATM**. For **ski** and **snowboard rental**, head to **Roy Turner Ski and Board Shop** (☎892 2757; www.snowzone.co.nz) or **Ski Biz** (☎892 2717). Both charge $30-60 for ski, boot, and pole rental and $40 for snowboard and boot rental. The small **police station** (☎892 2869) is on Buddo St., parallel to SH4. The nearest **hospital** is in Taumarunui (☎896 0020). **Internet** access and gear rental are available at most accommodations. The **BP station/4 Square** at the highway junction stocks basic groceries and provides postal services. (Open daily 7:30am-7pm.)

ACCOMMODATIONS AND CAMPING. The quality lodges of National Park Village are packed with hordes of winter skiers and summer trampers. Near the corner of Findlay St. and SH4, the eye-catching **National Park Backpackers and Climbing Hall (YHA, BBH)** ❷ has a two-story climbing wall, a spacious kitchen, hot tub, and several concrete kiwis on the grounds. Shuttle services to the Crossing ($20 round-trip) and glowworm (1½hr., $9) and *Lord of the Rings* (3hr., $65) tours. (☎892 2870; www.npbp.co.nz. Climbing wall $9 per day for guests. Internet. 8-bed dorms $18-20; 4-bed dorms $21-23; shared twins and doubles $27; private twins and doubles $42, with bath $61. Tent sites $12. MC/V.) Clean and hospitable, **Howard's Lodge (BBH)** ❷, 11-13 Carroll St., pleases travelers with a variety of shuttle services, a free spa, and rentable ski clothing. (☎892 2827; www.howardslodge.co.nz. Mountain bikes $20 per 2hr., full day $40. Ski, boot and, pole rental package $30 per day. Snowboard $40 per day. Ski jackets from $10. Linen $3. Laundry. Internet. Book 3 weeks ahead in winter. Dorms $22; twins and doubles $60, with bath $80-120. In winter dorms $25; twins and doubles $80, with bath $90-150. MC/V.) **Pukenui Lodge (BBH)** ❷, at SH4 and Millar St., attracts an older crowd with utilitarian rooms, a serene common space, and free Internet. (☎892 2882 or 0800 785 368; www.tongariro.cc. In summer dorms $23; twins and doubles $60, with bath $70. In winter rooms $45-90 per day. MC/V.) For summer visitors who require few amenities, the **DOC Mangahuia Campsite** ❶, 4km from National Park Village on SH47, has a streamside location with pit toilets. (Tent and caravan sites $4.)

FOOD. Due to restricted hours and limited options, the best bet is to stock up on groceries before reaching this isolated outpost. **Eivins Cafe Bar** ❸, on Carroll St. at SH4, serves hefty mains at equally hefty prices ($16-27). The view, however, is choice. (☎892 2844. Open daily 4pm-late. MC/V.) The unassuming spot at **Schnapps Hotel** ❸, at Findlay St. and SH4, rocks the ski season with occasional bands and a bizarre grab-bag of drinking games. Unwind with one of the mains ($12-25) and a tall $9 shot of Jäger. (☎892 2788. Open daily 11am-2am. In summer M-Sa noon-2am, Su noon-10pm. Closes earlier when slow. MC/V.) Otherwise, the **National Park Hotel** ❷, up Carroll St., close to the rails, is a popular choice for affordable pub fare and takeaways. (☎892 2805. Open daily 11am-late. MC/V.)

OUTDOOR ACTIVITIES. The **Tongariro Forest Conservation Area,** just north of town, is home to the **42nd Traverse,** one of the country's most satisfying mountain bike trails. Not for the faint of heart, the organ-jiggling 4-7hr. ride follows 46km of well-maintained old logging trails, with a stream crossing and a 570m descent. It is not pleasant in inclement weather. The eastern trailhead begins 18km north of the National Park on SH47; take a left on Kapoors Rd. Howard's Lodge (see above) runs an on-demand shuttle service to the start and end points ($25 per person, min. 4 people). For a warm-up on bike or foot, follow the 21km **Fisher's Track** (2-3hr. round-trip) from the end of Carroll St. on the other side of the tracks. The wooded path leads to a forested summit 4km from town with views of Taranaki. The descent on the opposite side makes for great coasting, but bikers should keep the return climb in mind. For those too tired to backtrack uphill, Howard's Lodge also provides shuttle services from the end point ($20 per person, min. 4 people.)

WHAKAPAPA VILLAGE   ☎07

This tiny clutch of establishments, owned in entirely by the decidedly non-budget Grand Chateau, is the foundation of ski operations in Tongariro National Park and is the most immediate base for skiing on the north side of Mt. Ruapehu.

The perky **Skotel ❸** has—hands down—the finest view of any budget accommodation on North Island. Follow the road between the Grand Chateau and the visitors center for 200m. Bask in all the ski-lodge amenities—Internet, spa, sauna, games, cushy mattresses, and a small communal kitchen. (☎0800 756 835 or 892 3719; www.skotel.co.nz. Laundry. Reservations recommended. Dorms $30; singles and twins $35-60; 4-person cabins $135-160. From July-Sept. dorms $45; singles and twins $45-85; 4-person cabins $180-205.) Set beside a stream just across from the visitors center, the **Whakapapa Holiday Park ❶**, is a favorite among Kiwis. The basic park offers good kitchen facilities and small sites carved out of the overgrown bushes. Spartan bunks fill the backpackers lodge. An on-site store stocks only basic and tramper-friendly groceries. (☎892 3897; whakapapaholpark@xtra.co.nz. Bring bedding. Reservations recommended. Store open daily 7am-7pm; May-June 8am-6pm. Tent and caravan sites $13. Dorms $23; 2-person cabins $46, $14 per extra person; tourist flats $65. MC/V.)

Refined, historic, and upscale, the **Grand Chateau Hotel** dominates the village both in size and cuisine. Aside from the in-house bar and restaurant at the Skotel, all of the town's dining establishments are run by the Chateau. Lodge-like **Fergusson's Cafe ❶**, serves soup, hot quiches, and sandwiches for $3.50-6. (☎892 3809, ext. 8835. Open M-F 7:30am-3:30pm, Sa-Su 7am-4:30pm.) Across the road, the elegant **Pihanga Cafe ❸**, has surprisingly affordable mains ($16-24) like braised lamb. (☎892 3809, ext. 8126. Open daily 11:30am-late. Kitchen closes 9pm.)

Whakapapa Shuttle (☎892 3716) provides winter service from the village to the ski field ($10, round-trip $15); in summer, it becomes Tongariro Track Transport, which runs a daily shuttle to Mangatepopo and from Ketetahi ($20 round-trip). **Alpine Scenic Tours** (☎0800 872 258; www.alpinescenictours.co.nz) leaves Whakapapa Village for National Park Village (15min., 4:15pm, $15), the Tongariro Crossing endpoints at the Ketetahi and Mangatepopo Carparks (on request), and Turangi ($25). Service can be flexible to accommodate tight schedules, but book in advance. Reportedly, many travelers hitchhike to the ski fields, though *Let's Go* cautions against hitching. The **Whakapapa Visitor Centre** doubles as the **DOC**; see Tongariro National Park, p. 202. There are **no banks** or **ATMs** in the village and **postal services** are provided in Fergusson's Cafe (see above).

OHAKUNE   ☎06

At one end of Ohakune (pop. 1500) stands Mt. Ruapehu, a massive snow-covered time bomb whose fine skiing causes the town's population to triple in winter. At the other end lies Ohakune's alter-ego—a statue of a mighty carrot, symbolizing the importance of post-ski-season farming. When the snow melts and the frozen visitors trickle out of town, Ohakune produces world-class carrots, sprouts, and potatoes from the area's rich volcanic soils, making it a hotbed of volunteer and work opportunities.

TRANSPORTATION

Trains: TranzScenic (☎0800 802 802) runs daily to **Auckland** (6hr., 1 per day, $75-85) via **National Park** (30min., $16) and to **Wellington** (5hr., 1 per day, $75-85) via **Palmerston North** (3hr., $43).

Buses: InterCity runs M-F and Su to **Auckland** (6hr., 1 per day, $68) and **Wellington** (5hr., 1 per day, $60). To get to **Taupo**, take the train to Waiouru and catch a bus just north of the public toilets—check at the visitors center for schedules.

Ski Shuttles: The **Snowliner Shuttles** (☎385 8573) and **Dempsey Buses** (☎385 4022) run on demand to the ski fields of **Turoa** ($10, $15 round-trip). From June-Oct., **Matai Shuttles** (☎0800 462 824) also run to the Turoa ski fields ($15 round-trip). From Nov.-May, Matai also departs from town (7:30am) and goes to the **Tongariro Crossing** ($35 round-trip; departs Ketetahi Hut 5:30, 6pm).

Hitchhiking: Although *Let's Go* does not recommend it, hitchhiking is reportedly not too hard between Ohakune and National Park or Waiouru. Hitching up the mountain is said to be easier in the morning, but success depends on your amount of gear. Catching a ride is significantly more difficult in the summer.

✦⚡ ORIENTATION AND PRACTICAL INFORMATION

The south end of town, where **SH49** merges with the main drag **(Clyde Street)**, has the most services and is active year-round. The north end, known as the **Junction**, lies by the railroad tracks and comes alive during the winter with seasonal chalets and a jumping nightlife. It also marks the start of the **Ohakune Mountain Road**, leading up past the trailheads to several scenic tramps and the ski lifts of **Turoa**. **Goldfinch Street/Mangawhero Terrace** (the road changes names) runs between Clyde St. and Ohakune Mountain Rd. (20-25min. by foot).

Visitors Center: Ohakune i-Site, 54 Clyde St. (☎385 8427; www.ohakune.info), has a relief map of Tongariro National Park. Open M-F 9am-5pm, Sa-Su 9am-3pm.

Department of Conservation (DOC; ☎385 0010), beyond the railroad tracks on Ohakune Mountain Rd. 1 of Tongariro's 3 field centers. Open M-F 9am-12:30pm and 1-3pm. During school and public holidays open daily 9am-4pm.

Work Opportunities: The seasonal gig (Feb.-Apr.) in Ohakune relates to local agricultural pursuits: carrot and potato sorting and packing. If you're looking for your roots, contact **Mountain Carrots** (☎385 9490). Pay is about $10-12 per hr. There are also plenty of work options on Mt. Ruapehu's **ski fields** during winter months (p. 203).

Ski and Snowboard Rental: Powderhorn Ski and Board Shop (☎385 8925), at the bottom of Ohakune Mountain Rd. Ski rental package $30-55. Snowboard rental package $40-55. Open M-Th and Sa-Su 7:30am-7pm, F 7:30am-midnight.

Banks: Several banks line Goldfinch St., including an **ATM** at **Westpac Trust** (☎385 8154), next to New World. Open M-F 9 or 9:30am-4:30pm.

Police: (☎111 or ☎385 0100). Clyde St., opposite Matai Lodge.

Pharmacy: 21 Goldfinch St. (☎385 8304). Open M-F 9am-5pm. July-Oct. also open Sa 8:30am-12:30pm.

Internet Access: Ohakune Video, 27 Ayr St. (☎385-8224), at the corner of Goldfinch St. $3 per 15min., $9 per hr. Open M-W 11am-8:30pm, Th-Su 10:30am-8:30pm; summer hours Su-Th noon-6pm and F-Sa noon-7pm.

Post Office: 5 Goldfinch St. (☎385 8645), in **Takenote Bookshop.** Open M-F 7:30am-5pm, Sa 7:30am-7pm, Su 8am-4pm.

🏠 📷 ACCOMMODATIONS AND CAMPING

Ohakune has an impressive number of accommodations, given its small size. For travelers not requiring amenities, the DOC-run, shower-free **Mangawhero Campsite ❶**, about 1.5km up Ohakune Mountain Rd., is ideal ($6).

Rimu Park Lodge and Chalets, 27 Rimu St. (☎385 9023; www.rimupark.co.nz). Close to the Junction's nightlife, Rimu has an open fire, free pickup, continental breakfast, and an outdoor spa for ski-sore legs in winter. Linen $2. Key deposit $10. Dorms $20-30; twins and doubles $45-75. MC/V. ❷

Matai Lodge (YHA/BBH; ☎0800 462 824; www.matailodge.co.nz), at the corner of Clyde and Rata St. A clean and spacious YHA with central heating, free local phone access, and a game room. Free pickup from Waiouru or the train station. Dorms $22; twins and doubles $30. MC/V. ❷

The Hobbit Motel Lodge (☎385 8248 or 0800 843 462), at the corner of Goldfinch and Wye St., 1km north of town. Once a used bookstore, this Hobbit predates the latest Tolkien craze. All beds come equipped for the winter with electric blankets. A renovated kitchen is expected to open by winter 2007. Free spa. Lodge from June-Oct. $25-35. Motel rooms Nov.-May $70-125. June-Oct. $95-220. MC/V. ❸

Ohakune Top 10 Holiday Park, 5 Moore St. (☎385 8561 or 0800 825 825; www.ohakune.net.nz), off Clyde St. A quiet haven on the banks of the Mangateitei Stream, except when the nearby police-operated air raid signal sounds off. Spa $5. Linen $4. Powered tent sites $14. Basic cabins $24-44, $13 per extra person. July-Oct. 20-40% more. ❶

🍴 🍷 FOOD AND NIGHTLIFE

What Ohakune lacks in nightlife, it more than makes up for with its hipster-happy afternoon cafe scene in winter. **◀Utopia ❷**, 57 Clyde St., makes hearty gourmet breakfasts, like poached eggs on sourdough toast with bacon and tomatoes ($14). (☎385 9120. Open daily 8am-3pm. Cash only.) **Mountain Kebabs Cafe ❷**, 29 Clyde St., has filling meat and vegetarian kebabs (medium; $7.50) served in toasted wraps. (☎385 9047. Open daily 10am-10pm. Frequently closed in summer.) One of the few places open year-round, **The Mountain Rocks Cafe ❷**, at Clyde and Goldfinch St., rocks out to Bob Marley and serves up panini ($9.50), curries ($16), and an infamous Big Breakfast ($14.50). (☎385 8295. Kitchen open daily 8am-2:30pm and 5-9pm. Cash only.) Open daily 6pm-late. Closed in summer.) Stock up for your own virtuoso cooking at **New World ❶**, 12 Goldfinch St. (☎385 8587. Open M-Sa 8am-7pm, Su 8am-6pm.) At the corner of Ohakune Mountain Rd. and Thames St., in the Powderhorn Chateau, the polished wood of the **Powderkeg Bar ❶**, explodes on winter weekends with DJs and drink specials. (☎385 8888. Handles $4.50. Open daily 7am-late. Summer 4pm-late. MC/V.)

🏔 OUTDOOR ACTIVITIES

Most people come to Ohakune to ski the fine slopes of **Turoa** (p. 204), but the area does have summer activities. The paved 17km **Ohakune Mountain Road** makes for exhilarating and scenic **biking** when the ski traffic is gone. Trampers will revel in the **Round-the-Mountain Track** (p. 204), which comes through the Ohakune side of Ruapehu, following Ohakune Mountain Rd. for about 3km before diving back into wilderness on the west side of the mountain. Other good walks depart from the upper reaches of the road, including a short jaunt over to **Waitonga Falls** (1½hr. round-trip) from a trailhead 11km up the road. From October to April, Ohakune is a secondary point of departure for **canoe trips** on the Whanganui River, a tranquil ride running through the heart of the wilderness. Many rental and guide companies either operate in town or offer pickup (p. 208). Before you leave, check out the **giant carrot** on SH49.

TARANAKI AND WANGANUI

The pinnacle of Mt. Taranaki (Mt. Egmont) is the focal point of North Island's westernmost peninsula. Maori legend describes Taranaki as a restless, sorrowful place, a reputation commensurate with its volcanic heart. Yet the green slopes surrounding the peak nourish one of the richest dairylands in the world, defying geological instability with charm. The region's rural setting affords travelers year-round relaxation with its balmy summers and gentle winters. Cows also seem to enjoy the climate, earning Taranaki its reputation as the "Udder of New Zealand."

⚓ TARANAKI AND WANGANUI HIGHLIGHTS

TACKLE the surf and ski challenge by accomplishing both feats in a single day (p. 218).

PADDLE along the **Whanganui River Journey** (p. 225), the only Great Walk where you float to the finish line.

CRUISE the contemporary art galleries and skate-friendly coastal walkway of **New Plymouth** (p. 214).

NEW PLYMOUTH ☎ 06

Residents of New Plymouth (pop. 49,200) love to point out that surfing the Tasman and skiing Mt. Taranaki are both within an hour's drive. While this is indeed an enticing proposition for sports enthusiasts, Taranaki's only urban center manages to make waves of its own. Featuring art galleries, renowned parks, and numerous walks, New Plymouth might capture your attention as more than just a fueling station between snow and surf.

▐ TRANSPORTATION

Buses: Depart from Ariki St., near Egmont St. **InterCity** (☎ 759 9039) runs to **Auckland** (6¼hr., 2 per day, $55-65), via **Hamilton** (4hr., $35-41); **Wellington** (6¾hr., 2-3 per day, $50-59), via **Stratford** (30min., $13-15); **Hawera** (1¼hr., $18-21); **Wanganui** (2½hr., $26-30); and **Palmerston North** (4hr., $34-40). **Dalroy Express** (☎ 759 0197 or 0508 465 622; www.dalroytours.co.nz) runs to **Auckland** (5hr., 1 per day, $57), via **Hamilton** (3½hr., $35); and **Hawera** (1hr., $15). **White Star** (☎ 758 3338) runs to **Wellington** (6¼hr., 1-2 per day, $48), via **Wanganui** (2½hr., $24); and **Palmerston North** (4hr., $32).

Taxis: Energy City Cabs (☎ 757 5580) wait at Brougham and Devon St.

Car Rental: First Choice (☎ 758 0546) and **Rent-a-Dent** (☎ 757 5362) are both located at 585-595 Devon St. East. Daily rates from $45.

Hitchhiking: Although *Let's Go* doesn't recommend it, hitchhiking to Wanganui is easiest near the outskirts of town on SH3, near the racecourse.

▌▐ ORIENTATION AND PRACTICAL INFORMATION

New Plymouth is located at the junction of SH3 and SH45. The main thoroughfare is **Devon Street,** which runs east-west through town. Pukekura Park sits in the center of the city while the Tasman Sea makes waves to the north.

Visitors Center: 🗽 **New Plymouth i-Site** (☎ 759 6060; www.newplymouthnz.com), inside the Puke Ariki museum. Internet $2 per 20min.; $5 per hr. Open M-Tu and Th-F 9am-6pm, W 9am-9pm, Sa-Su 9am-5pm.

Department of Conservation (DOC): 220 Devon St. West (☎ 759 0350). Open M-F 8am-4:30pm.

Banks and Currency Exchange: TSB Foreign Exchange, 120 Devon St. East (☎ 968 3712). Open M-F 9am-4:30pm, Sa 10am-noon.

Library and Internet Access: New Plymouth Library (☎ 758 4544), in Puke Ariki on Brougham St., has Internet for members. Open M-Tu and Th-F 9am-6pm, W 9am-9pm, Sa-Su 9am-5pm.

Police: 89-95 Powderham St. (☎ 757 5449).

Medical Services: Care Chemist, 10 Egmont St. (☎ 757 4614). Open daily 8:30am-9:30pm. **Accident and Medical Clinic** (☎ 759 4295), in Richmond Centre on Egmont St. Open daily 8am-8pm. **Taranaki Base Hospital** (☎ 753 6139), on David St.

Post Office: (☎ 759 8931), on Currie St. Open M-F 7:30am-5:30pm, Sa 9am-1pm.

🏠 🏕 ACCOMMODATIONS AND CAMPING

Hostels in town are reliable, if not outstanding. For a step up in creature comforts and privacy, call the i-Site for information on New Plymouth's B&Bs ($35-150).

🏖 **Belt Road Seaside Holiday Park,** 2 Belt Rd. (☎ 758 0228 or 0800 804 204; www.beltroad.co.nz). The 25min. walk from town yields rewards: a giant jumping pillow and an exquisite view of the sea. Linen $5. Tent spots on grassy knolls and powered sites $14 per person. 2-person cabins $45, with bath $75; self-contained units $8. MC/V. ❶

🏖 **Seaspray House (BBH),** 13 Weymouth St. (☎ 759 8934; seaspray@maxnet.co.nz), a 10min. walk to town. Sisters Sarah and Janine welcome backpackers to spacious, bunk-free rooms styled like a boho chic playground. Internet $6 per hr. Pick-up from bus stop available. Dorms $25, doubles $60. $5 BBH discount. Cash only. ❷

Shoestring Backpackers (BBH), 48 Lemon St. (☎ 758 0404), a 5min. walk from the town center. Placid surroundings make this backpackers tops, and that's not counting the sauna ($8). Call ahead for pickup. Linen $3. Dorms $24; singles $38; doubles $57, with TV $59; motel units $80. $3 BBH discount. MC/V. ❷

Sunflower Lodge (BBH), 25 Ariki St. (☎ 759 0050; www.sunflowerlodge.co.nz), across from the i-Site. A social crowd and key location make for an exciting night—why not spend it on the rooftop patio? On-street parking. All rooms have bath. Surfboard and bike rental $20. Linen $2. Key deposit $10. Dorms $20-22; singles $50; twins and doubles $55. MC/V. ❷

Egmont Eco Lodge (BBH/YHA), 12 Clawton St. (☎ 753 5720; www.taranaki-bakpak.co.nz). Take Frankley Rd. at the Dawson St. fork and follow the signs. Nightly servings of mountain-shaped "Egmont Cake" and the TV-free lounge encourage loafing. Ask the owner about his Hawera farmstay. Key deposit $10. Reception 8-10am, 5-9pm. Dorms $25; doubles $60. Tent sites $12. Cash only. ❷

🍴 🍷 FOOD AND NIGHTLIFE

Devon Street is sprinkled with an assortment of takeaways. For groceries, try **Woolworths,** at the corner of Leach and Cameron St. (open daily 6am-midnight), or **Pak 'N Save,** in the Centre City Shopping Centre on Gill St. (Open daily 8am-midnight.)

Burgers Wisconsin, 144 Devon St. East (☎ 757 8226). Creative burger options from pumpkin and garlic to chicken chilli jam and cheese ($7-11). Open daily 5pm-late, W-Sa also 11:30am-2pm. MC/V. ❷

E.S.Presso, (☎ 759 9399; espcafe@xtra.co.nz), on Brougham St. The food may not heighten your 6th sense, but it will satiate your tastebuds. Veg-heads welcome. Creative breakfast options $9.50-17. Open daily 8am-5pm. MC/V. ❸

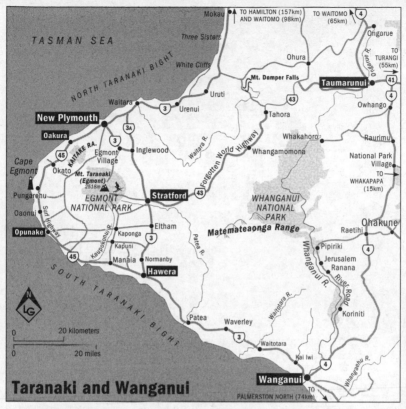

TASMAN SEA

NORTH TARANAKI BIGHT

Three Sisters

White Cliffs

Mokau

TO HAMILTON (157km) AND WAITOMO (98km)

TO WAITOMO (65km)

Ongarue

TO TURANGI (55km)

Ohura

Mt. Damper Falls

Taumarunui

Owhango

Uruti

Urenui

Tahora

Whakahoro

Raurimu

Waitara

New Plymouth

Oakura

3A

Egmont Village

Inglewood

Whangamomona

National Park Village

Cape Egmont

Okato

Mt. Taranaki (Egmont) 2518m

Stratford

WHANGANUI NATIONAL PARK

TO WHAKAPAPA (15km)

Pungarehu

EGMONT NATIONAL PARK

Matemateaonga Range

Raetihi

Ohakune

Oaonui

Opunake

Kaponga

Eltham

Kapuni

Pipiriki

Jerusalem

Ranana

Manaia

Normanby

Hawera

Patea

Waverley

Koriniti

Waitotara

Kai Iwi

Wanganui

PALMERSTON NORTH (74km)

Taranaki and Wanganui

0   20 kilometers

0   20 miles

Sandwich Extreme, 52 Devon St. (☎ 759 6999). This tiny spot lures caffeine addicts and frugal lunchers with sandwiches ($7-9) and veggie mains. Wash them down with an extreme espresso ($2-4). Open M-F 8am-4pm, Sa 8am-3pm. MC/V. ❶

el Condor, 170 Devon St. (☎ 757 5436). Renowned for its Argentinian cuisine, el Condor draws flocks of voracious carnivores. Pasta ($18) and gourmet pizzas ($14-24) redeem the restaurant's tiny size. Open Tu-Sa 5-10pm. MC/V. ❸

India Today, 40 Devon St. (☎ 769 9117), serves the best regarded and authentic North Indian cuisine in town. Mains $14-19. Open M-F 11:30am-2:30pm and daily 5:30pm-late. MC/V. ❷

Snappers (☎ 769 9344), in the shopping plaza at the corner of Leach and Gover St. Locals rave about the fish 'n chips ($4.20)—sometimes waiting up to 40min. for service. Paua fritters $2. Open Su-Th 4-9pm, F-Sa 11am-9pm. Cash only. ❶

Matinee, 69 Devon St. West (☎ 759 2088). A converted movie theater that showcases jazz bands on F evenings. Sa night DJs. Open Tu-Sa 11am-late. MC/V. ❷

Metropol, 32a Egmont St. (☎ 758 9788). This handsome restaurant and bar has plenty of outdoor seating on breezy Egmont St., serving up Mediterranean fare and seafood (gingered scallops $27) in the evenings and mixed drinks at night. Open daily 11am-late. MC/V. ❹

The Mill, 2 Courtenay St. (☎ 758 1935), at the south end of Currie St. Once a functioning flour mill, the grinding at this local club now involves bodies, not wheat. Music pumps in the basement dance area dubbed **Underground.** Handles $4.50. Open daily 11am-late. Some nights $10 cover. Underground open Sa 11pm-3am. MC/V.

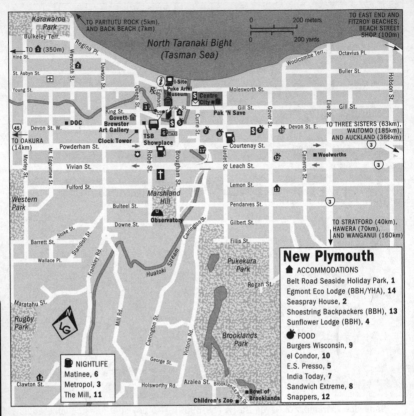

New Plymouth

🏠 ACCOMMODATIONS
Belt Road Seaside Holiday Park, **1**
Egmont Eco Lodge (BBH/YHA), **14**
Seaspray House, **2**
Shoestring Backpackers (BBH), **13**
Sunflower Lodge (BBH), **4**

🍴 FOOD
Burgers Wisconsin, **9**
el Condor, **10**
E.S. Presso, **5**
India Today, **7**
Sandwich Extreme, **8**
Snappers, **12**

🍸 NIGHTLIFE
Matinee, **6**
Metropol, **3**
The Mill, **11**

👁 🏔 SIGHTS AND OUTDOOR ACTIVITIES

On rainy days, head to the town center to see why New Plymouth is the only real roost for Taranaki's cultural connoisseurs. **Devon Street** reveals the city's 19th-century heritage, evinced by artful moldings above storefronts. A few blocks away, at King and Queen St., the sleek ◾**Govett-Brewster Art Gallery** houses contemporary art, including the work of legendary Kiwi artist Len Lye. Those amused by Lye's playful twist on modernity will appreciate his **Wind Wand,** outside the New Plymouth i-Site. Valued at $300,000, the controversial structure demonstrates Lye's affinity for using advanced engineering and technology in his artwork. (☎ 758 5149; www.govettbrewster.org.nz. Open daily 10:30am-5pm. Free.) Adjoining the New Plymouth i-Site is the **Puke Ariki Museum,** housing interactive displays on Taranaki with one section focusing on a Maori perspective. (☎ 758 6060. Open M-Tu and Th-F 9am-6pm, W 9am-9pm, Sa-Su 9am-5pm. Free.)

For a firsthand look at New Plymouth's municipal splendors, head to the contained nature at **Pukekura Park** at the top of Liardet St., reportedly the most breathtaking urban park in New Zealand. If the weather cooperates, visit the calla lilies in **Stainton Dell** or the green grandeur of **King Fern Gully.** Rain or shine, the **Fernery** awaits hushed footfalls on a carpet of cedar chips. (Fernery open daily 8am-4pm. Main gates to Pukekura Park open daily 8:30am-6pm. Other access points 24hr.) Adjacent to Pukekura Park is the **Brooklands,** which has a **children's zoo.** (Open daily 8:30am-5pm. Free.) The annual **Festival of Lights** casts a happy glow over the holiday season from Christmas until early Feb. with rotating musical acts accompanying the lightshow.

Once you've had your fill of manmade parks, head to one of New Plymouth's scenic walkways. The **Te Henui Walkway** (5.9km, 4½hr. round-trip) is one of the best, starting from East End Beach and following the Te Henui Stream through natural splendor down to the sea. Another diversion is the **Coastal Walkway** (7km, 4-5hr. round-trip), which connects Fitzroy Beach in the east to the port area in the west. Watch out for in-line skaters, bikers, and crashing waves. A further 3km west of the port area is **Paritutu Rock.** Paritutu is an old volcanic plug, the remnants of a former volcano, that stands guard over the towns marina. Epic views of the coast and, on a clear day, Mt. Taranaki, reward those souls who brave the very steep 154m vertical scramble.

With its proximity to the Tasman Sea, New Plymouth also offers a variety of aquatic options. Surfers and windsurfers can get their adrenaline fix year-round at **Fitzroy** and **East End** beaches, on the east end of town. The more isolated ▧**Back Beach,** past Paritutu Rock 7km west of town, is popular among surfers. Dave Chadfield of **Happy Chaddy's Charters,** on Ocean View Parade, offers a cruise in a former English lifeboat around the Sugar Loaf Islands, where you can enjoy a visit to the seal colony. (☎758 9133. $50, children $10. Fishing trips 4hr., $60, min. 6 people. Gear provided. MC/V.)

North of New Plymouth, the **Whitecliffs Walkway** (9.6km, 3-5hr. one-way; closed July 1-Sept. 30) offers solitude from the summer crowds at New Plymouth's beaches. Head north on SH3, 37km from New Plymouth, and take a left to the end of Pukearuhe Rd. You can either walk along the beach or along the cliff tops—beware, this area is being developed as lifestyle blocks, so the solitude may not last that long. The walkway ends at Tongaporutu, the site of the **Three Sisters,** three 25m pinnacles cut off from the coastline. By car, drive down Clifton Rd., 63km north of New Plymouth on SH3, just before the Tongaporutu Bridge, and walk another 15-20min. For both the Whitecliffs Beach and Three Sisters, only venture out during low tide.

THE TARANAKI COAST ☎06

Excellent for catching rays on handsome beaches and catching waves on year-round surf, the Taranaki Coast from New Plymouth to Hawera is a surprisingly underappreciated and underdeveloped destination. You can circumnavigate Mt. Taranaki (Egmont) and travel along the coast in two ways. For a scenic journey (1½hr.) with easy access to various bushwalks and the best views of the **Taranaki Bights** and the **Tasman Sea,** take Carrington Rd. from New Plymouth to Okahu Rd. and then circle around. The coastal route (3½hr.) is best done on SH45 (dubbed the **"Surf Highway"**), but unless you stop and walk to the shore, expect only glimpses of the ocean—much of the view on this route is obscured by hedges, great distances, or both. For the best local surf, simply follow the gray signs marked "Surf Beach" between Oakura and Opunake, or the better marked ▧**Stent Beach,** 500m south of Warea on SH45. To explore the area, it's generally best to rent a car or bike. Hitchhikers find sporadic rides at best; in winter frequent rains make the experience even less pleasant. *Let's Go* does not recommend hitching.

OAKURA ☎06

A tiny town (pop. 1300) whose claim to fame stems from its wide, flat, and often family-filled beach, on which was set the world record for the largest number of people surfing the same long board. Oakura is representative of the populated pockets that dot the coast along "The Surf Highway." The town itself provides little diversion for those looking for something other than waves and rays. People pitch tents down by the beach in the summer, but **Oakura Beach Holiday Park ❶,** 2 Jans

WAX ON

The 'Naki has been at the heart of the New Zealand surf scene since the late 1950s when the surf craze first took off in New Zealand. But the sport has a much longer history along the gentle shores of Highway 45. Maori used to ride waves on the *waka* (wooden canoes) until Christian missionaries attempted to ban the water sport in belief that it was indecent to show skin.

Eventually the missionary influence waned, and people made their way back to the beach, forming clubs to protect swimmers. In 1915, Duke Kahanamoku, an Olympic swimming champion, performed two swimming exhibitions in New Zealand. One of these included a surfboard. With this modest beginning, a surf movement took root in the beach clubs of New Zealand.

The modern sport was reintroduced to its shores in the late 1950s by Aussies and Americans. In search of unknown surf spots, these visitors made their way to Taranaki, impressing locals with their skill. The popularity of surfing waxed and waned in New Zealand for the next two decades until the first National Championships hosted by the newly created Taranaki Surfriders Club at Fitzroy Beach.

For a nostalgic visit to New Zealand's wave-rider past visit the Beach Street Surf Shop in Oakura (see p. 215).

Terr., offers oceanside tracts. (☎752 7861; oakura-beachcamp@internet.co.nz. Linen $5. Powered tent sites $14. 2-person cabins $50, with bath $75.) The **Oakura Boardriders Club** provides free toilets, showers, and changing rooms just off the beach, near the corner of Wairau Rd. and Tasman Pde. Three kilometers west of town on SH45 is the **Wavehaven Hostel ❶**. Despite the more than 3km walk to the surf at Ahu Ahu, this chill spot is popular among surfers, who often leave the rooms sand-filled and slightly gritty. Perks include free kayak use, surfing lessons for novices, and Internet. (☎752 7800; www.wavehaven.co.nz. Dorms $18, one week $100; singles $30; doubles $40. 2hr. surfing lessons $60, $50 for 2 people.) Those not staying at the hostel can rent a board in town at **Vertigo Total Surf**, next to the 2-story surf board. (☎752 7363. Surfboards with wetsuit $50 per day.) A few doors down, **Butler's Bar and Cafe ❷**, 1122 SH45, offers pub grub, pizzas ($14-21), and $5 pints. (☎752 7765. Open M-Th noon-late, F-Su 11:30am-late.)

OPUNAKE   ☎06

The closest thing to a metropolis on the coast, Opunake (pop. 2091) is home to the cliffs of Middleton's Bay and the **Opunake Beach**, with its teeming **holiday park ❶**. (☎761 7525; opunakebeach@xtra.co.nz. Powered tent and caravan sites $12, children $6. Min. site charge from Boxing Day-Jan. $21. MC/V.) The town's main attractions are its coastal walkway and easy access to other beaches. For Taranaki views and a good night's sleep, head to the **Opunake Motel and Backpackers ❷**, 36 Heaphy Rd., an often-deserted but comfortable hostel with nary a bunk-bed in sight. (☎761 8330; opunakemotel@xtra.co.nz. Free laundry. Dorms $22; motel units $55, $70 for 2 people, $15 per extra person; 2-person self-contained units $80. MC/V.) Prepare to surf the waves or the net at **Dreamtime Surfshop**, at Tasman Pde. and Havelock St. (☎761 7570. Surfboard rental $45 per day. Internet $5 per hr.) The smoothies are as delicious at ⬛**Sugar Juice ❶**, as the odd pair of legs on their sign is eyecatching. Great for a picnic at the beach. (Smoothies $4.50; snacks $5-14. Cash only.) Buy supplies and snacks at **Beau's Supermarket,** 77-79 Tasman Pde. (☎761 8668. Open M-Sa 7:30am-6pm, Su 7:30am-5pm.)

EGMONT NATIONAL PARK ☎06

The majestic 2518m Mt. Taranaki (Mt. Egmont) dominates the sky, controls the weather, and leaves most visitors stunned by its sheer size. In 1881, everything within a 10km radius of the nearly symmetrical volcano was declared part of New Zealand's second national park, reining in a vigorous logging boom.

With more than 300km of tracks ranging from well-maintained roads to backcountry adventure, Mt. Taranaki remains the country's most accessible national park.

AT A GLANCE

AREA: 33,534 hectares.

CLIMATE: Dictated by the mountain, which attracts foul and unpredictable weather, especially during winter.

FEATURES: Mt. Taranaki (Egmont).

HIGHLIGHTS: Around-the-Mountain Circuit and the Taranaki Summit.

GATEWAYS: New Plymouth and Stratford.

CAMPING: Permitted except at summit. Backcountry huts and lodges managed by the DOC and private alpine clubs.

FEES AND RESERVATIONS: Hut tickets ($5-10) available at the DOC. Tent sites $5.

▐ TRANSPORTATION

No public buses head to Egmont, though **Cruise New Zealand Tours** shuttles trampers daily from New Plymouth (☎ 758 3222; 7:30am, returns 4:30pm; $40 round-trip; booking essential), as does **Taranaki Tours** (☎ 0800 886 877; www.taranakitours.com; $40 round-trip). Guided trips offer transportation as well (see **Outdoor Activities,** p. 218).

 WHEN TO GO. Fall snows bring North Island skiers to Manganui for an early start to the winter season. Tramping is popular from late November to early April, but winter conditions in the alpine zone are extremely dangerous.

▰▰ ORIENTATION AND PRACTICAL INFORMATION

Three paved roads enter the park but do not intersect: **Egmont Road,** from New Plymouth to the North Egmont Visitor Centre; **Pembroke Road,** from Stratford to the Manganui Ski Field; **Manaia Road,** from the Manaia or Stratford to the Dawson Falls Visitor Centre. A fourth road, **Carrington Road,** bisects the northern arm of the park between the Pouakai and Kaitake Ranges. The **North Egmont Visitors Centre,** on Egmont Rd. about 16km south of Egmont Village, is the port of entry for most of the park's visitors. (☎ 756 0990; nevc@doc.govt.nz. Open daily 8am-4:30pm.) About 8km from the park entrance along the southern Manaia Rd., the **Dawson Falls Visitors Centre** has access to a few bushwalks. (☎ 027 443 0248. Open daily 8am-4:30pm. In winter W-Su 8:30am-4:30pm.)

▰▰ ACCOMMODATIONS AND CAMPING

Just 3km from the park boundary is the ▨**Eco Inn (BBH) ❷,** 671 Kent Rd. The delightful owners build their own turbines and offer tasty organic treats in addition to treehouse accommodations. To reach this outpost, leave SH3 just west of Egmont Village and head southwest on Kent Rd. for 7km. (☎ 752 2765; www.ecoinn.co.nz. Singles $25; twins and doubles $48. Tent sites and treehouse $12.) East of Egmont Village on SH3, hop over to **Missing Leg Backpackers (BBH) ❶,** 1082 Junction Rd. The name doesn't derive from a horrific tramping incident, but rather from the three-legged pooch that used to reside at this lodge. (☎ 752 2570; www.missinglegbackpackers.co.nz. Call ahead for pickup. Free bike use. Free Internet. Dorms $18; doubles $44. Tent sites $12.)

Inside the national park, **Camp House ❷** is a sparse but popular accommodation only 50m from the North Egmont Visitors Centre. (☎ 0800 688 272; www.taranaki-bakpak.co.nz. Linen $5. Key deposit $10. $25, children $18.) If you are looking to do some serious mountaineering or climbing in the park, there are several club-owned and operated lodges. The **Tahurangi Lodge** at 1520m is a good place for a summit attempt (accessible from the North Egmont Visitors Center), while the **Manganui Lodge** (20 min. walk from East Egmont parking lot) and **Kapuni Lodge** (1hr. walk from the Dawson Falls Visitor Centre) are nearer trailheads. For all the lodges, prior bookings are essential; contact the North Egmont Visitors Centre (☎756 0990). Most huts charge $15 per person. Near the Dawson Falls Visitors Centre, the DOC runs the **Konini Lodge ❷**. (☎0274 430 248. Bookings essential. $25, children $10.) Camping is not permitted outside the hut areas.

⚠ OUTDOOR ACTIVITIES

TRAMPING IN EGMONT

There are endless trail options in Egmont; visit the DOC visitors centers at Northern Egmont or Dawson Falls to investigate the full range of options. Leaving from any of the main park entrances, **Mt. Taranaki Around-the-Mountain Circuit** (55km, 4-5 days) traverses the upper slopes of the volcano, affording expansive views of the surrounding farmland and coast on clear days. Natural erosion of the track makes for tricky walking and long days. Tall hiking boots are a must. The **Pouakai Circuit** (21km, 2-3 days) is a moderately difficult track with a rare variety of terrain, from rainforest to alpine; start at the North Egmont Visitors Centre and be appropriately prepared for backcountry conditions.

Those wary of tramping alone can call Ross Eden at **Top Guides** (☎0800 448 433 or 021 838 513; www.topguides.co.nz; 1-person summit trips $170, 2-person $225) or Don Paterson at **Adventure Dynamics** (☎751 3589; www.adventuredynamics.co.nz; summit trips from $300 per guide, per day). Or for those wary of heights, the **Around Mt. Taranaki** (☎0800 886 877; www.tarankitours.com.) van tour can offer a lowlanders view of the hulking hill

 ROLLING ON THE RIVER. Egmont National Park is crisscrossed by countless rivers and streams which are prone to overflowing in the spring from mountain run-off and rain. Hikers are advised to wait until water levels subside before attempting to cross; river flows are fast and deceptively deep.

NORTH EGMONT. Well-prepared trampers might make the full-day trek to the **Ahukawakawa Swamp,** home to lichen, mosses, and microbes. For the less hardy, shorter dayhikes abound. One short-but-sweet walk, the **Connet Loop Track** (30min. round-trip), departs from the base of the North Egmont Visitors Centre and winds its way through the "Mountain Forest." For a 1½hr. bush experience, hit the **Veronica Loop Track. Bells Falls,** best reached from **Holly Hut,** is also worth checking out. The safest route to the **summit of Taranaki** begins from North Egmont, following "The Puffer" up to a translator tower. The track then passes Tahurangi Lodge, climbing through a gully and up a long scree-ridden ridge to the rock-scrambling summit block. Laugh heartily at scrawny Mt. Tongariro on the distant horizon. The north side of the volcano offers views of New Plymouth and beyond. The trip (8-10hr. round-trip) should not be attempted or even considered in winter or in otherwise questionable weather.

EAST EGMONT AND DAWSON FALLS. Roughly 20% of park visitors enter from the east by way of Stratford and the **Stratford Mountain House,** with access to the Manganui ski fields in winter and several trails in other seasons. You can attempt direct trips to the summit from this side, but the route is longer (1 day round-trip), and the trail rougher. The northern route up **Taranaki** is accessible from the ski fields by following the Around-the-Mountain Circuit north to the Tahurangi Lodge and connecting there with the summit climb. From the Dawson Falls Visitors Centre, you can hike to the **Wilkies Pools** (1-1½hr. round-trip), a series of pools spilling into one another—be aware that the water is ice cold. The summit of **Fanthams Peak** (1966m) is also accessible from this side (5-6hr. round-trip). **Syme Hut,** on Fanthams Peak, is arguably the best place to watch the sun rise or set; however, the hut's location means it's also exposed to wind and ice.

LITTLE-KNOWN EGMONT. To the north and west of the main peak lie the gentler slopes of the **Kaitake** and **Pouakai Ranges.** These old peaks are the volcanic ancestors of Taranaki, which once spewed lava and ash before being cut off from its magma source. The Pouakais are accessible via Carrington Rd. from New Plymouth and the Kaitakes from Lucy's Gully and other trailheads off SH45.

STRATFORD   ☎06

In this small hamlet (pop. 5300), the moniker is more than half the character. One of 27 towns in the world christened after Shakespeare's birthplace, Stratford has taken this connection to heart by naming most of its streets after the Bard's characters and erecting New Zealand's only glockenspiel, which thrice daily recites lines from *Romeo and Juliet.* Stratford's other claim to fame, and the reason most visitors pass through, is its proximity to Mt. Taranaki's Manganui ski fields.

⧉ TRANSPORTATION. InterCity (☎345 4433) departs from the i-Site and heads to Auckland (7hr., M-F 1 per day, $70) via New Plymouth (35min., $12-15); Wellington (5½hr., 2 per day, $33-55) via Hawera (20min., $12-14), Wanganui (1½hr., $15-25), and Palmerston North (3hr., $25-36). **Dalroy Express** (☎759 0197 or 0508 465 622) heads to Auckland (6hr., 1 per day, $58). **White Star** runs to Wellington (M-F 2 per day, Sa-Su 1 per day, $39) via Hawera (30min., $10). **Stratford Taxis** (☎765 5651) are available for local transportation needs. The **Stratford Leisure Centre,** 420 Broadway, south of town between Romeo and Celia St., rents mountain bikes for $15 per day. (☎765 7580. Open M-F 9am-5pm, Sa 9am-noon.) Although *Let's Go* does not recommend hitching, **hitchhikers** report that getting rides to New Plymouth and Wellington is easier the farther along SH3 one gets from town.

⧉⧉ ORIENTATION AND PRACTICAL INFORMATION. Broadway (SH3) is Stratford's main drag. The Forgotten World Highway (SH43) enters town from the east, where it's known as **Regan Street. Pembroke Road** departs from the north of town and runs to Egmont National Park and the ski area to the west. **Celia Street** (which becomes Opunake St.) departs south of town and runs westward to Egmont National Park's Dawson Falls Visitors Centre. The **Stratford i-Site** is on Prospero Pl., opposite the glockenspiel. (☎765 6708; www.stratfordnz.info. Internet $1.50 per 15min. Open M-F 8:30am-5pm, Sa-Su 10am-3pm.) The **DOC office,** 10km from town on Pembroke Rd., provides only basic info on Egmont National Park. (☎765 5144. Open M-F 8am-4:30pm.) Other services include: **BNZ,** on Broadway (☎765 7134; open M-F 9am-4:30pm); the **police,** on Miranda St. (☎765 8860); a **24hr. doctor** (☎765 5300); the **post office,** 49 Miranda St. (☎765 6009. Open M-F 8:30am-5pm.)

⧉⧉ ACCOMMODATIONS AND FOOD. At ⧉**Pretty Croft B&B ❸,** 193 Regan St., 1km east of town on the road to Taumarunui, hosts David and Edna lovingly spoil guests in their inviting home and gardens. (☎765 6820; davidandedna@xtra.co.nz. Free Internet. Singles $45; twins $100. Cash only.) The **Stratford Top 10 Holiday Park ❶,** 10 Page St., offers a wide variety of accommodations and luxurious touches like the spa and sauna. (☎765 6440 or 0508 478 728; stratfordholpark@hotmail.com. Spa $3. Linen $5. Bikes $10. Reception 8am-10pm. Tent sites $12, powered $14. Dorms from $18; 2-person cabins from $38, $15 per extra person.) The little bistro **Collage ❷**, on Prospero Pl. next to the i-Site, is the exception to Stratford's general apathy toward food. Cheap fusion brunch options ($9-14) are second only to the artistic beauty of the $7 snack bagels. (☎765 7003. Open M 9am-3pm, Tu-F 9am-5pm, Sa-Su 9am-late.) Those camping or graced with kitchens may want to head to **New World,** at the corner of Orlando and Regan St. (☎765 6422. Open daily 8am-8pm.)

◙◿ **SIGHTS AND OUTDOOR ACTIVITIES.** With **Mt. Taranaki** looming in the background, it's little wonder that skiing is a major activity in the area. Unpredictable snowfall means that the season can range from a few weeks to a few months. The **Manganui Ski Field** is the only one on the mountain. (Ski conditions ☎759 1119; www.snow.co.nz/manganui. Lift ticket $30, children $15, over 60 free.) For rentals, call the **Mountain House Motor Lodge,** on Pembroke Rd. north of Stratford. (☎765 6100; www.mountainhouse.co.nz. Skis or snowboard, boots, and poles from $30 per day. MC/V.) Those who want to exercise their eyes as opposed to their knees can head to the **Percy Thomson Gallery** (☎765 0917), next to the i-Site, which showcase various exhibits of contemporary Kiwi art. For an stroll through Stratford's past, head to the **Taranaki Pioneer Village,** south of town on SH3. The 50 fully-restored, turn-of-the-century buildings celebrate Taranaki's history. (☎765 5399; www.stratfordnz.info/pioneervillage. Open daily 10am-4pm. $10, children $4.) Stratford is also the beginning of the Forgotten World Highway (SH43), a 155km scenic drive to Taumarunui (p. 230).

HAWERA   ☎06

Since its 1884 founding, tiny Hawera (pop. 8500), meaning "the scorched place" in Maori, has suffered four devastating fires. It is the heifer, however, not the phoenix, that has risen from the ashes. Today, Hawera's tourism industry relies almost solely upon the dairy industry, offering farmstays and education at Dairyland for travelers eager to experience Taranaki's rural life.

▐ **TRANSPORTATION.** The **bus station** is at the base of the water tower and is the point of departure for **InterCity,** which leaves daily for New Plymouth (1hr., 2-3 per day, $19) and Wanganui (1hr., 2-3 per day, $21), with continuing service to Palmerston North (3hr., $30) or Wellington (5½hr., $48). **Dalroy Express** (☎759 0197 or 0508 465 622) heads to Auckland (6½hr., 1 per day, $65) via New Plymouth (1hr., $13) and Hamilton (5hr., $44). **The White Star** (☎758 3338) goes to New Plymouth ($15) and Wellington ($36). **Hawera Taxis** (24hr. ☎0800 278 7171) has a stand on Victoria St. near High St. While *Let's Go* doesn't recommend **hitchhiking,** hitchers often find a ride on High St. between Argyle and Albion St. or at the junction of SH3 and SH45 (South and Waihi Rd.). Most cars head to New Plymouth or Wanganui via SH3; hitchhiking to the coastal beach communities of western Taranaki along SH45 can be more difficult.

◼▐ **ORIENTATION AND PRACTICAL INFORMATION.** The main drag through town is **High Street.** At the west end of High St., **Waihi Road** (SH3) is the primary northern route to New Plymouth. Parallel to High St., **South Road** becomes the coastal route to New Plymouth (SH45) heading west and to Wanganui (SH3) heading east. The **South Taranaki I-Site,** 55 High St., is located at the base of the water tower and sells **DOC hut passes** for area tracks. (☎278 8599; visitorinfo@stdc.govt.nz. Open M-F 8:30am-5pm, Sa-Su 9am-4pm.) Other services include: **ATMs** and **banks** along High St.; the **police** on Princes St. (☎278 0260); the **hospital** on Hunter St., off

Waihi Rd. (☎278 7109); **Internet** access at **Hawera Library**, 46 High St. ($4 per hr.; open M, W-Th 8:30am-5:30pm, Tu 9:30am-5:30pm, F 8:30am-6pm, Sa 9am-1pm); the **post office**, 162 High St., in **Paperplus** (☎278 7197; open M-F 8am-5:15pm, Sa-Su 9am-4pm).

ACCOMMODATIONS AND CAMPING.
Fifth-generation farm and entrepreneur Gary Ogle gives backpackers hands-on experience at the The Wheatly Downs Farmstay (BBH) ❷, 7km out of town on Ararata Rd. To get there on your own, head to the Tawhiti Museum, and continue 3km on Ararata Rd. Enjoy views of Mt. Taranaki from the front lawn, take a dive in the lake, or ask about flights around the mountain. (☎278 6523; www.taranaki-bakpak.co.nz. Linen $5. Book in advance. Dorms $25; singles $38; doubles $55, with bath $85. Tent sites $12.) For those not quite ready for an encounter with nature, King Edward Park Motor Camp ❶, 70 Waihi Rd., reigns over a kingdom of communal showers, kitchens, and toilets. (☎278 8544. Linen $3. Tent sites $8 per person, powered $9. 2-person cinderblock cabins from $28, 4-person $48, $10 per extra person; 2-person caravans $20, $10 per extra person. Cash only.)

FOOD AND NIGHTLIFE.
If you don't mind eating off the floor, Morrieson's Cafe and Bar ❷, 60 Victoria St., might work for you. The tables here are floorboards from the demolished home of local novelist Ronald Hugh Morrieson (1922-68). The menu features a medley of delectable mains ($13-21) and traditional brews for $3.60. (☎278 5647. Open M-F 11am-1am, Sa-Su 9:30am-10:30pm.) Though the name may conjure images of a smoky dive, Rough Habits Sports Bar and Cafe ❸, 79-81 Regent St., has a well-groomed look. Try one of the light meals ($9.50-15) and wash it down with a $3.50 handle. (☎278 7333. Open daily 11am-late. Kitchen closes around 10pm.) For a "kwik" bite, Kreative Kebabs ❶, 135 High St., offers savory kebabs ($6-10), burgers ($4.50-9), and more. (☎278 5552. Open Tu-Sa 11am-8:30pm, Su 4-8pm.) Buy groceries at Countdown, at the corner of Union and Nelson St. (☎278 0026. Open daily 7am-11pm.)

SIGHTS AND OUTDOOR ACTIVITIES.
The decaying water tower, a response to Hawera's frequent fires, is the most prominent landmark in town. Climb its prison-like structure for views of Mt. Taranaki, the coast, and acres of dairy farmland. (Open daily 10am-2pm. $2.) Nigel Ogle's Tawhiti Museum, near the corner of Ohangi and Tawhiti Rd., displays his subtle sense of humor and surprisingly realistic fiberglass figures encased in dioramas. (☎278 6837; www.tawhiti-museum.co.nz. Open M and F-Su 10am-4pm; Jan. daily; Jun.-Aug. Su only. $10.) For a taste of Maori history, Turuturu Mokai, 2km northeast of town off SH3 on Turuturu Rd., displays the scant remains of a 400-year-old Maori fortress. Use the Hawerea i-Site brochure as the key to the historic kingdom as there are very few signs explaining the otherwise rock-riddled field. Fans of the King will rejoice at Kevin D. Wasley's garage-turned-Elvis Presley Memorial Record Room, 51 Argyle St. Although the King himself is not in the building, you can feast your eyes on a collection of rare recordings, valuable memorabilia, and even Wasley's own Elvisesque haircut. (☎027 498 2942; www.digitalus.co.nz/elvis. Visits by appointment only. Donation recommended.)

The closest Hawera gets to extreme sports is **Dam Dropping**. Plunge over an 8m dam, followed by 3hr. of "whitewater sledding" on the nearby Waigongoro River. (☎0800 338 736; www.damdrop.com. 1½hr. $70, 3hr. $89. Book ahead.)

WANGANUI   ☎06

Home to an art school, an opera house, and a regional museum, Wanganui (pop. 43,000) merges bohemian mentality with historic sensibility to create the most funky and cosmopolitan spirit in the region. Despite its welcoming charm, vestiges

TARANAKI AND WANGANUI

of colonial animosity linger passively in the background. Tensions between Maori and European cultures are apparent in the grassroots movement among locals to restore the "h" to the town's name—Anglicized in the early 20th century. Regardless, Wanganui remains a pleasant stop for a stroll by the Whanganui River.

TRANSPORTATION

Buses: InterCity stops at the **Wanganui Travel Centre**, 156 Ridgway St. (☎345 4433). Open M-F 8:15am-5:15pm. Buses leave for: **Auckland** (8hr., 2-3 per day, $72) via **Hamilton** (6hr., $53); **New Plymouth** (2½hr., 1-2 per day, $30); **Palmerston North** (1½hr.; M-F 3-4 per day, Sa-Su 2-3 per day; $17); **Wellington** (3hr., 2-3 per day, $35). **White Star Buses** operates from the i-Site (☎347 6677) to **New Plymouth** (2½hr., 2 per day, $27) and **Wellington** (4hr., 2 per day, $36).

Public Transportation: Tranzit CityLink (☎345 7100) handles bus transport to **Castle-cliff Beach** and the suburbs. All buses depart from Maria Pl. between Victoria Ave. and Saint Hill St. and run until early evening ($2).

Taxis: River City Cabs (☎0800 345 333) and **Wanganui Taxis** (☎343 555).

Car Rental: Rent-A-Dent, 26 Churton St. (☎345 1505). Economy cars $45 per day plus 100km. Free insurance. Open M-F 7am-5:30pm, Sa 7:30am-5pm, Su 8am-1pm. MC/V.

Hitchhiking: Though *Let's Go* doesn't recommend hitching, hitchers often head to the outskirts of town. People traveling toward Taranaki do so by way of Great North Rd., toward Ruapehu by way of Anzac Pde., and toward Wellington by way of Main South Rd.

ORIENTATION AND PRACTICAL INFORMATION

Wanganui rests at the junction of **SH3** and **SH4**; the latter is called **Anzac Parade** in the city and runs alongside the east bank of the **Whanganui River**. (**Taupo Quay** and **Somme Parade** follow a similar course on the west bank.) They're linked by **Victoria Avenue,** which runs perpendicular to the river and is the town's main street.

Visitors Center: Wanganui i-Site, 101 Guyton St. (☎349 0508; www.wanganuinz.com), near Saint Hill St. next to the District Council. Open M-F 8:30am-5pm, Sa-Su 9am-3pm. Extended hours in summer.

DOC: 74 Ingestre St. (☎348 8475), at the corner of Saint Hill St. Open M-F 8:30am-4:30pm.

Banks: Money ebbs and flows along Victoria Ave. at **BNZ, ANZ, Westpac Trust,** and **National Bank** (all with **ATMs**). Most open M-F 9am-4:30pm.

Police: 10 Bell St. (☎349 0600).

Medical Services: Wanganui Hospital (☎348 1234) on Heads Rd.**Esquilant Unichem Pharmacy,** 145 Victoria Ave. (☎345 7529). Open M-F 8:30am-5pm, Sa 9am-2pm. After-hours service at **Wanganui City Doctors,** 163 Wicksteed St. (☎348 8333).

Post Office: Main Branch, 226 Victoria Ave. (☎345 4103). Open M-F 8:30am-5pm.

Internet Access: Available at the **library,** in Queens Park (☎345 1000; $2 per 1st 15min., $1 per 15min. thereafter; open M-F 9am-8pm, Sa 9am-4:30pm, Su 11am-4:30pm), and at the **i-Site** for $4 per hr.

ACCOMMODATIONS AND CAMPING

Most of Wanganui's backpackers and campsites are rooted on the riverbanks beside English oak trees.

The Tamara Backpackers Hostel (BBH), 24 Somme Pde. (☎347 6300; www.tamaral-odge.com), 5min. from the center of town. Amiable hostel with heated rooms, river views, and lounges. A guitar, piano, and pool table provide amusement. Free pickup and local calls. Linen $1. Key deposit $10. 4-bed dorms $22; singles $38; twins and doubles $48, with bath $58; triples $66; quads $86. Cash only. ❷

Braemar House (YHA), 2 Plymouth St. (☎347 2529; www.braemarhouse.co.nz), 5-10min. from the center of town. The intensity of the pink exterior has faded over the years, but the B&B vibe of this century-old Victorian house still spills over into the backpackers units. Dorms $22; doubles $50; B&B singles $55, doubles $80. Tent sites $12. Cash only. ❷

Wanganui River Top 10 Holiday Park, 460 Somme Pde. (☎343 8402 or 0800 272 664; www.wrivertop10.co.nz), 7km from the center of town. "Aramoho" bus stops at the gate. Sidle up to the river in this tranquil setting shielded from the road by tall pines. Spa $5 per 30min. Kayak trips from $40. Linen $4. 2-person cabins $50, with kitchen $60; 2-person motel units $110. Powered sites $17. MC/V. ❶

Crellow House B&B, 274 Taupo Quay (☎345 0740), 1.5km southwest of the town center. The 3 rooms share a bathroom, but the riverside location and impressive international cheese dish collection make communal rituals a pleasure. Free laundry. Rooms $45; double $65. MC/V. ❸

🌃🍴 FOOD AND NIGHTLIFE

Eateries cluster around **Victoria Avenue** and its sidestreets from the river to **Guyton Street.** Whip up your own dish after a stop at **Countdown Foods,** at Taupo Quay and Saint Hill St. (☎345 8720. Open daily 7am-9pm.)

Red Eye Cafe, 96 Guyton St. (☎345 5646). Secondhand furniture, funky blues, and streamers above create a bohemian atmosphere. Brunch $8-12. Curries $19. Open M-W 8am-3:30pm, Th 8am-10:30pm, F 8am-late, Sa 9:30am-late. MC/V. ❸

Amadeus Riverbank Cafe, 69 Taupo Quay (☎345 1538). Delicious burgers, salads, and sandwiches ($7-16) satisfy salt-receiving tastebuds. Sweets from the Calorie Gallery ($4-6) and river views top it all off. Open daily 8:30am-4pm. Cash only. ❷

Kebabholic, 155 Victoria Ave. (☎348 8332). Popular with the hungry teen set. Expect cheap and filling although not the most savory kebabs ($7.50-8.50.) Lamb kebabs $10-12. Open daily 10:30am-9:30pm. Cash only. ❷

Ceramic/Orange, 51 Victoria Ave. (☎348 4449). The nighttime navy blue interior of the jazzy wine bar complements the daytime bright orange decor of the cafe. Brunch $9-10. Panini $6. Tapas $13. Mains $23-25. No cover. ❸

🔆🏔 SIGHTS AND OUTDOOR ACTIVITIES

Before heading out into the wilderness, get your bearings and survey the land from the top of the **Durie Hill Lookout Tower.** The journey begins from Anzac Pde. at the base of Victoria Ave. where a long tunnel takes you 205m into the hill. An elevator whisks you 66m up through the hill, depositing you at the top. (Elevator runs M-F 7:30am-6pm, Sa 9am-5pm, Su 10am-5pm. One-way $1.) But why stop there? Climb the nearby 34m **Durie Hill Memorial Tower** for the ultimate view. The **P.S. Waimarie** navigates the silty Wahanganui waters from a closer distance. Built in 1899, the restored paddle steamer—the last in New Zealand—chugs from the Whanganui Riverboat Centre 16km up the river. (☎783 2637; www.wanganui.org.nz/riverboats. 2hr. round-trip departs daily Nov.-Apr.; May-Oct. Sa-Su. $30.) Fifteen kilometers north of town off SH4, the narrow and winding 79km **River Road** (p. 229) also heads upriver and makes a good daytrip.

Get your fill of culture in **Queens Park,** a block away from Victoria Ave. Overlooking the green hills is the reflective white-domed exterior of **Sarjeant Gallery,** notable for its collection of 19th-century and contemporary regional and British art. (☎349

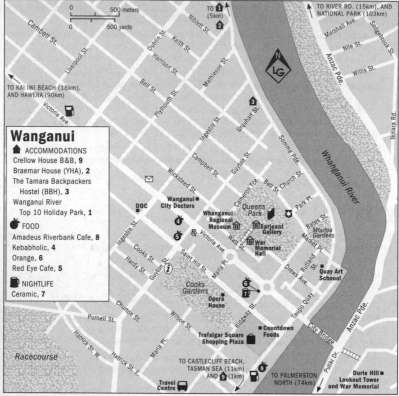

Wanganui

▲ ACCOMMODATIONS
Crellow House B&B, **9**
Braemar House (YHA), **2**
The Tamara Backpackers
 Hostel (BBH), **3**
Wanganui River
 Top 10 Holiday Park, **1**

🍴 FOOD
Amadeus Riverbank Cafe, **8**
Kebabholic, **4**
Orange, **6**
Red Eye Cafe, **5**

🍸 NIGHTLIFE
Ceramic, **7**

0506; www.sarjeant.org.nz. Open daily 10:30am-4pm. Donation appreciated.) Just steps away, modernity gives way to Maori history at the **Whanganui Regional Museum.** Its "Te Ati Haunui a Paparangi" gallery (a place for people to "anchor their canoes") houses the largest surviving *waka taua* (war canoe) in the region. (☎349 1110; www.wanganui-museum.org.nz. Open daily 10am-4:30pm. Free.)

Sports enthusiasts circle **Cooks Gardens,** on Maria Pl., home to a rugby pitch, one of two wooden cycling velodromes in New Zealand, and a running track that was the site of Peter Snell's world-record mile (p. 52). For recreational water action, head to one of the local beaches. **Castlecliff Beach,** where the river meets the sea, is notable for black sand and good surf. To get there, take Taupo Quay West to Heads Rd. and continue another 9km. Alternatively, head for Maria Pl. in town and catch the bus. Farther up the coast, **Kai Iwi Beach** also has good swells and attracts locals who wish to avoid the crowds, but is not accessible by public transport. **Mountain bikers** in the area get their kicks on a host of rugged single-track trails built by the Wanganui Mountain Bike Club up the river at Hylton Park in Aramoho.

The **Blooming Artz Festival,** a celebration of visual arts, occurs in September of odd-numbered years, whereas the **Wanganui Arts Festival** features performing arts and occurs at the end of February in even-numbered years. Every Boxing Day, accommodations fill to the brim, and the town is rattled to its bones by the grave-rumbling **Cemetery Circuit Motorcycle Race.**

WHANGANUI NATIONAL PARK ☎06, 07

According to legend, the great mountains Tongariro and Taranaki fought over an alluring summit named Pihanga. Spurned by Pihanga, Taranaki fled westward and gouged a furrow in the earth, a cleft his triumphant rival filled with water. As a result, lush foliage surrounds the Whanganui (fang-gah-NEW-ee) River—the longest navigable course (234km) in New Zealand—as it flows to the Tasman Sea. Historically, Maori *pa* (fortified village) topped these high ponga-lined bluffs before European missionaries, steamboats, and logging operations altered river life during the 19th century. In recent times, local Maori families have reclaimed parts of the river bank, establishing *marae* (sacred meeting ground) for weary paddlers.

AT A GLANCE

AREA: 74,231 hectares.

CLIMATE: Variable, mild summers.

FEATURES: Hills and valleys through one of North Island's largest tracts of lowland forests and mudstone cliffs.

HIGHLIGHTS: Whanganui River, the longest navigable river in New Zealand.

GATEWAYS: Wanganui, National Park Village, Ohakune, and Taumarunui.

CAMPING: Tents permitted. Backcountry huts available.

FEES AND RESERVATIONS: Huts $5-10. From Oct.-Apr., River Journey Huts Pass $45-60.

◗ TRANSPORTATION

Few roads penetrate the park's boundaries. The **River Road** (p. 229) dips into the southern limits, while a road from Owhango heads to **Whakahoro Hut** (p. 228). Most people planning a Whanganui excursion stay in **National Park Village** (p. 225), **Taumarunui** (p. 230), or **Ohakune** (p. 208) and arrange transport with the operators who rent equipment for the river journey (see **Gear Rental**, p. 226). Trampers who require river transport to return to their point of departure can call **Bridge to Nowhere Lodge** (☎0800 480 308 or 06 348 7122; www.bridgetonowheretours.co.nz); rides can be costly depending on the endpoints. People who have hitched report that patience is necessary. *Let's Go* does not recommend hitchhiking.

 WHEN TO GO. The park is better enjoyed in the summer since its greatest attraction is the Whanganui River, but the river can be run year-round. Be sure to bring warm clothing and waterproof gear for unpredictable weather.

◼◆⟩ ORIENTATION AND PRACTICAL INFORMATION

The Whanganui National Park encompasses various pockets west of SH4. Despite its similar name, the city of **Wanganui** is not the best base for exploring the Whanganui River, though it does contain the park's main **DOC office.** (☎06 348 8475. Open M-F 8am-5pm.) The **DOC field centers** in Taumarunui (☎07 895 8201) and Pipiriki (☎06 385 5022) are open sporadically. In Taumarunui, you'll find a **supermarket** and **ATMs;** in Pipiriki, you won't find much of anything. Most gear outfitters (p. 226) can provide secure **parking;** however, there are no places to stay directly adjacent to the park. The **phone code** for Taumarunui, National Park Village, and points in between is ☎07; Ohakune, while points farther south use ☎06.

⚠ OUTDOOR ACTIVITIES

The **Mangapurua** and **Kaiwhakauka Tracks** combine to form a 40km (3-4 days round-trip) adventure. Mangapurua takes off from **Mangapurua Landing** (p. 229) on the river, then heads over the **Bridge to Nowhere,** through the Mangapurua Valley, and past large open sections of former farmland. The track then climbs to the **Mangapurua Trig,** which offers panoramic views of Mt. Tongariro, Mt. Taranaki, and the junction with the Kaiwhakuaka Track on clear days. From there, it's down through farms and bush to the Kaiwhakauka Valley and the **Whakahoro Hut** (p. 228). This is the only hut along the whole track, though flat campsites are plentiful.

The park's other major trail is the **Matemateaonga Track,** which tempts diehard hikers with 42km (4-5 days round-trip) of serpentine trail following an old Maori route. The path leads from the **Kohi Saddle** on Upper Mangaehu Rd. east of **Stratford** (p. 219) and across to **Tieke Marae** (p. 229) on the Whanganui River. There are three huts ($10 each) on the track, which is flatter than the Mangapurua/Kaiwhakauka route. A significantly shorter option, the **Atene Skyline Track** (6-8hr. round-trip) leads to a lookout with views of Mt. Ruapehu, Mt. Taranaki, and the Tasman Sea, almost forming a complete loop. The Skyline makes a good daytrip from Wanganui, as the trailhead is only 36km north of town on the River Rd.

🛶 WHANGANUI RIVER JOURNEY

Not only is the Whanganui River Journey the only **Great Walk** on water, but it also provides an outdoor experience unique to New Zealand. Those who paddle between the river's steep banks will encounter rapids, wild goats, and hundreds of waterfalls. The journey passes many reminders of its long human history, from the Lombardy poplars planted by missionaries to the iron moorings used by steamers headed upstream. The tramp also has a living legacy in its two *marae*, Tieke and Mangapapapa, both of which welcome overnight guests.

I AM KAYAK. Solo river warrior? No problem. Gear outfitters can set you up with well-matched groups. This may require patience and a good phone card, but it is worth the effort.

Length: 145km, 5 days, by canoe. Time between destinations varies greatly based on water levels, river traffic, and paddler experience. The most popular and scenic section is the 3-day trip from Whakahoro to Pipiriki.

Trailheads: Heads downstream from Cherry Grove, near Taumarunui, to Pipiriki Landing. Other put-ins include Ohinepane and Whakahoro.

Transportation: Landlubber **shuttle service** to the put-in and take-out points is included in the kayak and canoe rental packages (see **Gear Rental,** below).

Seasonality: Dec. to Feb. and weekends are most crowded. The water gets cold and the weather gets rainier June-Sept., making crowds a non-issue and experience a must.

Gear Rental: The *Guide to the Whanganui River* ($10 from the DOC), compiled by the New Zealand Recreational Canoeing Association, describes the river and its rapids. Outfitters include: **Wades Landing Outdoors** in Whakahoro (☎0800 CANOE 1 or 07 895 5995; www.whanganui.co.nz; 5-day kayak or Canadian canoe rental $175, 3-day $140, 2-day $120); **Blazing Paddles** in Taumarunui (☎07 895 5261 or 0800 252 946; www.blazing-paddles.co.nz; 5-day kayak or Canadian canoe rental $230, 3-day $200, 2-day $140, all prices include DOC passes; additional transportation charge for individual travelers); **Canoe Safaris** in Ohakune (☎0800 272 3353; www.canoesafaris.co.nz; 3- to 5-day kayak or canoe rental $145-165; specializes in upmarket guided trips). All outfitters typically assist in procuring the DOC passes necessary for using huts.

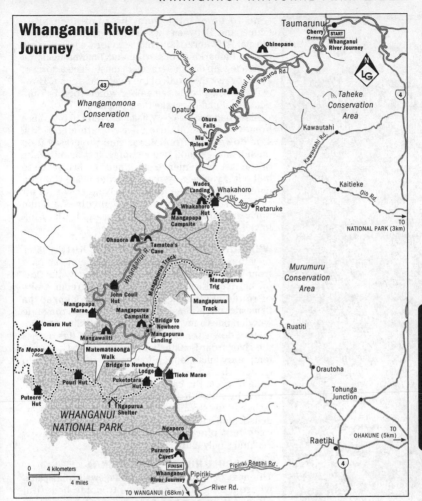

Whanganui River Journey

Storage: Most outfitters will hold onto extra gear.

CHERRY GROVE TO WHAKAHORO HUT. *57km.* This two-day leg covers the vast majority of the journey's largest rapids (but still only Class II). Paddlers begin near Taumarunui at **Cherry Grove,** where the Ongarue and Whanganui Rivers meet. Roads and grazing farm animals surround the introductory stretch of river, and include ⛵**Lauren's Lavender Farm,** where you can moor your ship and take in a morning coffee in a field of fragrant lavender before setting out for the raging waters. (☎07 896 8705; on the River Road in Taumarunui. Open daily 8:30am-4:30pm. Iced coffee $2.50. Cash only.) **Ohinepane Campsite** provides the first opportunity to stop and camp, 22km downriver from Cherry Grove. The next two campsites are the most popular Day 1 layovers; **Poukaria** (14km from Ohinepane) and **Maharanui** (17km from Poukaria) feature flat ground and abundant bush, and

THE FIRE WITHIN

When not masked under a cloak of clouds, Tongariro National Park's mighty triumvirate of volcanoes dominates the surrounding landscape.

To the Tangata Whenua, the original inhabitants of the area, the mountains symbolized the link between the environment and the home of their ancestors. Legend says that when their ancestor the high priest Ngatoroirang arrived in the Bay of Plenty and saw the peaks for the first time, he immediately set out to climb the mountains. As he climbed Tongariro, a sudden, violent blizzard swept through. Near death, he cried out for the gods to create fire for warmth and light. The gods responded by sending fire from beneath him, creating the volcanic fires of White Island, Taupo, and Tongariro.

During the 19th century, the tribe discouraged European settlement. The Ngati Tuwharetoa clan also struggled to keep the lands from other tribes. In 1887, their chief donated the land to the Crown on the condition that it would not be used for settling or grazing. In 1894, Parliament established it as New Zealand's first national park. In 1991, the park was designated the first natural World Heritage Sight to be included as a cultural site, reaffirming what locals have always known: the mountains should be treated with respect for its spiritual and physical power.

tend to be quieter than the road-accessible Ohinepane. Between these rise the imposing carved **niu poles**, where Hau Hau warriors used to pray before embarking for battle, and **Taniwha Rock**, on which legend dictates travelers must place a sprig of green or risk the wrath of the river's guardians. However, as few people remember which rock is Taniwha, most paddlers take their chances.

Also road-accessible, **Whakahoro Hut** (16 beds) is a homey old schoolhouse blessed with electricity, 4km down river from Maharanui; the grassy field outside makes good tent camping. It is also the site of the last convenience store and the last place to bail out if you've gotten in over your head. Unfortunately, reaching this former *pa* is no easy task for those already on the river—it involves a 600m upriver paddle (to a landing past the bridge) followed by a 500m uphill climb.

WHAKAHORO HUT TO JOHN COULL HUT. *37.5km.*
As you paddle into the borders of the national park from Whakahoro on, dramatic cliffs steady the flow of the river. Eleven kilometers downstream, stairs of rounded stone lead up to grassy **Mangapapa Campsite**, but it's easier to land by the less romantic wooden ones a few meters down river. Sixteen kilometers downstream, **Ohauora Campsite** lies across the river from **Tamatea's Cave**, named for a former temporary inhabitant (who was also the first man to explore the whole river). More like a shallow overhang of rock, the cave exhibits a small glowworm show by night. Roomy **John Coull Hut** (30 beds), 10.5km downstream, sports plenty of burners, wardens from October to April, and is known to be an excellent place to spot long-tailed bats, New Zealand's only native mammal.

JOHN COULL HUT TO TIEKE KAINGA. *19.5km.*
The next possible stop is at **Mangawaiiti Campsite**, where a long staircase leads to some beautiful plots, set among ponga trees. Nine kilometers downriver from John Coull Hut, **Mangapurua Campsite** rests on the river's right bank across the water from **Mangapurua Landing**. From the landing, an easy 30-40min. walk (one-way) leads deep into the bush, opening onto an astounding view of the ponga canopy, with a tannin-stained stream far below and, in the middle of it all, a perfectly ordinary concrete bridge. This **Bridge to Nowhere** is the last remnant of an isolated post-WWI rehabilitation settlement, which officially closed in 1942.

Back on the water, the river leads 10.5km to the well-marked **Tieke Kainga** (TEE-eh-kee), a hospitable settlement with a Maori caretaker who urges guests to partake in the *powhiri* (welcoming) ceremony. Whether or not the Maori are in residence, guests are welcome to make themselves at home in the kitchen, on the mattresses in the bunk room, or on the beautiful lawn. Across the river, the privately owned **Bridge to Nowhere Lodge ❶**, (☎0800 480 308) charges $10 per person for camping, $15 for cabins. There are also B&B units available.

 ROCK IT TO THE RIGHT. Between the Tieke Kainga and the Ngaporo Campsites, there is a well-known rock in the middle of the river that has been the site of more than one high-speed canoe collision. It may be tempting to dodge left, but the easier move and better current lies to the right.

TIEKE KAINGA TO PIPIRIKI LANDING. *21.5km.* This final stretch holds several of the journey's largest rapids. Set between two choppy sections of water 12.5km downriver from Tieke Kainga, **Ngaporo Campsite** provides well-positioned tent sites, framed by sheer gray rock faces. The **Puraroto Caves,** filled with spa-quality mud, make a good last stop for exploration and body painting. They are near a small stream on the right after the river turns sharply to the left. By the time **Pipiriki Landing** appears at the journey's end, the native forest has again yielded to cleared sheep fields.

THE RIVER ROAD ☎06

After a 30-year construction project fraught with floods and mudslides, 1934 saw the opening of the aptly named **River Road.** Dancing with the bushy banks of the Whanganui River, the road affords the only automobile access to settlements upstream from Wanganui. Defined by its well-preserved natural beauty and enriched by long-standing Maori enclaves and Pakeha missions, the River Rd. seems to be a time and place apart, allowing visitors who linger to gain new appreciation for fluvial life. From Wanganui, the River Rd. begins 15km north of the city off SH4, and winds its way 64km to **Pipiriki.** From Pipiriki, the road turns east and out of Whanganui National Park to meet up with SH4 at **Raetihi** (27km), less than 15km from the ski town of **Ohakune** (p. 208). If you don't have your own car, riding along with **Take it Easy Tours** (a.k.a. the Rural Mail Coach Tour) is a great way to get into the heart of the river valley and meet locals at the same time. The run returns to Wanganui around 1:30-2:30pm, or you can ask to be dropped off anywhere along the way and be picked up the next day. (☎344 7465 or 027 406 5788. Departs M-F 7:45am from behind the old Post Office on Saint Hill St., opposite the Opera House. $40.) **Whanganui River Road Tours** covers the same route as Take it Easy, but also visits the *marae* at Koriniti. (☎345 8488; www.whanganuiriverroad.com. Departs daily 8:30-9am, returns 3pm. $50.)

Travelers heading up the road from Wanganui soon see the white **Oyster Cliffs,** which take a large bite out of the river—a reminder of a time when oceans enveloped the valley. Farther up, there's riverside camping at the **Otumaire Campsite** with toilets and water. Continuing upstream, the accommodations get plusher. Omaka Farm 1, 35km north of Wanganui, is another option for tenting along this beautiful stretch of river. For non-rustic souls, a proper bed awaits in the welcoming Rivertime Lodge 3, just up the road. (☎342 5595; www.rivertimelodge.co.nz. Doubles $100 first night, $80 each night after. Tent sites $8.) Those who venture farther arrive at one of the most jaw-dropping homestays in New Zealand, ▨**The Flying Fox 4,** 44km north of Wanganui before Koriniti. Truly off the beaten track, it is accessible only by boating down the river or via an aerial zipline—a "flying fox" in Kiwispeak—suspended 20m above the river. Self-proclaimed hippie proprietors Annette and John may feel personally insulted if you don't gulp down a home-brewed beer made entirely from ingredients grown organically on site. Due to access limitations, only booked guests are invited to use the zipline. (☎342 8160;

THE OTHER 2005 ELECTION

Politicians may be like pigs, but rarely are they actual pigs. This is a real possibility, however, in the village of Whangamomona, where past presidents have included a poodle and a goat, the latter of whom tragically died in active service while eating weeds. Whangamomona (pop. 40) is one of the world's smallest countries. As you approach the "republic," signs beg you to stay and increase the population.

Whangamomona residents celebrate Republic Day, held biennially in January. Its beginnings go back to 1988, when the government partitioned half of Whangamomona from Taranaki into the Wanganui/Manawatu district. Outraged, three citizens declared the village's independence. While you don't have to be a citizen to participate in the festivities, border patrols are set up and a $3 passport is issued to foreigners.

The day's festivities include sheep races, opossum-skinning, and gumboot-throwing competitions. Fun and games aside, however, the main purpose of the day is to elect the next president. The 2005 ballot was unusual in that all of the candidates were human. Murt, the local fix-it man, was hoisted onto the highest seat of the land: a toilet bowl.

For more info, visit www.stratfordnz.info.

www.theflyingfox.co.nz. Canoes $35 per day. Free laundry. Tent sites $10. Cottages $90-110. Advance booking required. Cash only.)

A trio of Maori villages stands farther upstream; visitors should only enter the *marae* upon prior invitation. **Koriniti** features the never-captured Opeiriki *pa*, a lovely *marae*, and the first Anglican church on the river (est. 1840). **Ranana** is one of the larger villages on the river and retains traces of its past as a traditional center of agriculture. **Hiruharama,** once home to a French Marist Mission, guards the grave of the poet James K. Baxter. A **convent ❶** built in the 1890s welcomes travelers for some serious quiet. (☎342 8190. No linen. Dorms $20. Book ahead.)

Just before Hiruharama is **Moutoa Island,** from which Maori followers of Hauhauism (a xenophobic religious sect) launched ritualized battles against the tribes of the lower river. Continuing upstream, find the cascading beauty of **Omorehu Waterfall.** A bookend of a town, **Pipiriki** is at the end of the River Rd. and is also the beginning for many jetboat rides and walking tracks.

TAUMARUNUI ☎07

When Chief Pikikotaku fell ill here about two centuries ago and commanded his men to construct a cover over his bed, the town of Taumarunui ("place of shelter") was christened. If only travelers could command the same attention as they wander the underdeveloped town. Despite its shortcomings, Taumaranui (pop. 4500), situated at the confluence of the Ongarue and Whanganui Rivers and the junction of SH4 and SH43, is one of the starting points for the Forgotten World Highway and a Whanganui River Journey that begins just south of the municipality.

⟁ TRANSPORTATION. TranzScenic heads to Auckland (4½hr., 1 per day, $36-80) and Wellington (6½hr., 1 per day, $49-98). **InterCity** also runs to Auckland (4¾hr., M-F and Su, $37-50) and Wellington (6hr., M-F and Su, $72). **Taumarunui Taxis** (☎895 5444) will help you get around town. Though *Let's Go* does not recommend hitchhiking, most hitchers try the area by the Hakiaha St. railyards, past the former Main Trunk Cafe. Toward Te Kuiti, thumbers go from Ongarue River Rd. (SH4).

⧆⛉ ORIENTATION AND PRACTICAL INFORMATION. Taumarunui sits along the **Main Trunk Railway** at the junction of **SH43** and **SH4** (called **Hakiaha Street** within the town limits). The **Taumarunui i-Site** is located in the railway station on Hakiaha St. (☎895 7494; www.ruapehu.tourism.co.nz. Open M-F 9am-4:30pm, Sa-Su 10am-4pm. Internet $5 per hr.) Take a nature walk through Cherry Grove to get to the **DOC**

field centre. (☎895 8201. Open M-F 8am-5pm.) Other services include: **banks** with **ATMs** (open M-F 9am-4:30pm) on Hakiaha St.; a **pharmacy,** 93 Hakiaha St. (☎895 7326; open M-F 8:30am-5pm, Sa 9:30am-12:30pm); the **police** (☎895 8119), on Hakiaha St.; **Taumarunui Hospital** (☎896 0020), on Kururau Rd. (SH43), just west of town toward Stratford; **Internet** access at the **library** in the center of town ($3 per 15min.; open M-F 10am-5pm, Sa 10am-1pm) or at the i-Site ($2 per 20min.); the **post office,** 47-49 Miriama St. (☎895 8149; open M-F 9am-5pm).

⚡☐ ACCOMMODATIONS AND FOOD. While Taumarunui's glaring lack of budget accommodations will have you yearning for anything with four walls and a ceiling, **Taumarunui Holiday Park ❶,** 4km south of town on the Whanganui River, is an option. Activities include fishing, swimming, and kayaking. (☎895 9345 or 0800 473281; www.taumarunuiholidaypark.co.nz. Kayaks $45 per half-day. Linen $3. Tent sites $10, powered $11. 2-person cabins $35; tourist flats $55, $12 per extra person. MC/V.)

Though quality dining establishments are scarce, **Ruddies Cafe ❷,** on Hakiaha St. across from the library, stands out. Contemplate local artists' paintings as you enjoy huge breakfasts, panini, salmon, and kumara fishcakes ($7.50 each). (☎896 7442. Open M-Tu 8:30am-4pm, W-F 8:30am-5pm, Sa-Su 9am-4pm. Cash only.) **Rivers II Cafe ❷,** 43 Hakiaha St., has French toast with bacon ($12) and stellar $6-7 roast beef sandwiches. (☎895 5822. Open M-Th 8am-5pm, F-Su 7am-5pm. Cash only.) Stock up at **New World** supermarket, at the northern end of Hakiaha St., the only major supermarket in the area. (Open daily 8am-7pm.)

◎🏃 SIGHTS AND OUTDOOR ACTIVITIES. Most people who visit Taumarunui use the town as a stopover before their trip down the **Whanganui River** (p. 226). Taumarunui's sights alone are not be worth a prolonged stay. Those lucky enough to have their own wheels can get a taste of the backcountry by traversing the **Forgotten World Highway,** a 155km stretch of SH43 connecting Taumarunui to Stratford. Established in 1990 to introduce travelers to the region's history, the mostly paved road winds through historic towns, farmland, and scenic reserves. After negotiating switchbacks and hairpin turns, drivers are rewarded with saddletop views of Mt. Ruapehu and Mt. Taranaki on clear days. Highlights include the **Tangarakau Gorge,** a 1920s wooden truss tunnel called the Hobbits Hole, and **Whangamomona Village,** whose proud residents declared their independence from New Zealand in 1988 (see **The Other 2005 Election,** p. 230). Seventy-three kilometers from Taumarunui, an 18km gravel road off the highway leads to **Mount Damper Falls.** Plunging 85m into a horseshoe-shaped papa bluff, the falls is one of North Island's highest and is best seen after heavy rains. The lookout is a 20min. walk from the parking lot. Despite its being only 155km, plan 2½-3hr. for the drive, without stops. There is no gas along the route, so it's best to fill up in Taumarunui or Stratford.

WELLINGTON AND AROUND

WELLINGTON ☎04

Although it lies on a major fault line and is one of the windiest cities on earth, the compact capital city of Wellington (pop. 400,000) is a better place to catch your breath than to lose it. Overlooking scenic Wellington Harbour near North Island's southern tip, New Zealand's second-largest city entertains visitors with an impressive series of festivals, renowned museums, and some of the country's best theater and dance. A ten minute drive from the bustling city center brings visitors to wild shorelines and nature preserves.

▨ WELLINGTON AND AROUND HIGHLIGHTS

SNACK on delicious baked goods on **Cuba Street** (p. 239), where the highest density of cafes in the Southern Hemisphere turns up the heat at night.

DRINK the fine wines of nearby **Wairarapa** (p. 247).

AND BE MERRY at the Kiwi cultural epicenter of **Te Papa Museum** (p. 239), Wellington's pride and joy.

✕ INTERCITY TRANSPORTATION

Flights: Wellington International Airport (☎385 5123) spans the Miramar Peninsula in the southeastern suburbs with international flights to **Sydney, Brisbane,** and **Melbourne** on **Qantas** or **Air New Zealand (ANZ;** ☎474 8950 or 0800 737 000). ANZ has an office at the corner of Lambton Quay and Grey St. and covers most domestic destinations; it flies to **Auckland** (1hr., 1-2 per hr., from $100) and **Christchurch** (45min., 1 per hr., from $80). **Soundsair** (☎801 0013 or 0800 505 005; www.soundsair.com) flies to **Picton** (25min., 6-8 per day, $79). The **Stagecoach Flyer** (☎801 7000) runs service every 30min. between the airport, downtown Wellington, and Upper Hutt ($2.50 between the airport and downtown).

Trains: Railway Station, on Bunny St. at Waterloo and Customhouse Quay, is also home to the bus depot. The **Travel Centre** books for TranzScenic and InterCity. Open M-F 7:15am-5:30pm, Sa-Su 7:15am-12:15pm. **TranzScenic** (☎0800 872 467; www.tranzscenic.co.nz) provides daily service to **Auckland** (12hr., 8:40am, $94-157) via **Palmerston North** (2hr., $19-38), **National Park** (5½hr., $50-84), and **Hamilton** (9hr., $66-132). **TranzMetro** (☎801 7000; www.tranzmetro.co.nz), a regional commuter line, leaves from the Railway Station. There are 4 regular lines including routes up **Hutt Valley,** the **Kapiti Coast,** and the **Wairarapa.** The **Wairarapa Line** offers limited service to **Masterton** (1½hr., M-F 5 per day, $13). A taxi to downtown costs $8-15.

 EASY RIDER. Those planning on using public transportation in Wellington may want to consider investing in a **flexi-pass.** The pass can be used on InterCity/Newmans buses or ferries and can be purchased in 5hr. increments. (☎0800 222 146; www.flexipass.co.nz. $55 per 5hr.)

Wellington and Around

Buses: InterCity/Newmans (☎385 0502; www.newmanscoach.co.nz) runs daily from the Railway Station to: **Auckland** (11hr., 4 per day, $45-100) via **Hamilton** (9hr., $67-80); **Napier** (6hr., 2-3 per day, $35-59); **New Plymouth** (6hr., 2 per day, $35-59) via **Wanganui** (4hr., $18-35); **Palmerston North** (2hr., 1-6 per day, $14-28); **Rotorua** (7¼hr., 5 per day, $43-85) via **Taupo** (6hr., $34-72). **InterCity** runs a night bus to Auckland and points between (daily 6:50pm, $10-15). **Freeman's Lotto and Cafe,** 23 Lambton Quay, sells tickets for **White Star Coach Services** (☎478 4734; www.whitestarbus.co.nz), which runs to **New Plymouth** (6¼hr., 1-2 per day, $45) via **Palmerston North** (2¼hr., $20) and **Wanganui** (3½hr., $27).

Ferries: Bluebridge (☎0800 844 844; www.bluebridge.co.nz), opposite the Railway Station on Waterloo Quay. This former freighter runs to **Picton** (3¼hr.; 2-3 per day; $45, cars from $120). **Interlslander** (☎0800 802 802; www.interislander.co.nz) operates the **Lynx,** a high-tech, high-speed catamaran, which departs from Waterloo Quay in downtown Wellington for **Picton** (2¼hr.; 2 per day; $35-68, cars $115-215). The **Interlslander,** inconveniently located

FLICKS FOR FREE

While Peter Jackson's *Lord of the Rings* put New Zealand on the international film map, the country already had a significant film tradition before the hobbits journeyed to Tongariro National Park. Anyone interested in the moving image, social history, or who simply wants to view a free feature film, should head to the **New Zealand Film Archive**, one of the country's hidden cultural treasures.

Built in 1994, the archive is housed in three floors of a converted commercial building. Downstairs, the film library provides free viewings of over 20,000 videos and DVDs. The collection ranges from mainstream New Zealand features like Jane Campion's *The Piano* (1994), to rare treasures like the video art of Philip Dadson and film art of Len Lye, to newsreels, documentaries, and historic personal home movies. Upstairs, the media gallery displays contemporary art using video and computer technology.

The 120-seat media theater has screenings Wednesday through Saturday nights, ranging from international documentaries and rarely seen Kiwi feature films to experimental videos.

The Film Archive, *84 Taranaki St., Wellington (www.filmarchive.org.nz). Open daily noon-6pm. W screenings by donation; other nights $8. Library and gallery free.*

in **Aotea Quay,** north of town on SH1, runs daily to **Picton** (3hr.; 6 per day; $35-65, cars $115-215). There's a free shuttle for the Interislander from Platform 9 of the Railway Station 40min. before each scheduled departure and back to the station upon ferry arrival. Advance bookings are essential; fares drop with significant lead time. Ask about 1-day or 3-night excursion fares.

Hitchhiking: While *Let's Go* does not recommend hitchhiking, travelers report that riding from Wellington can be difficult. The Aotea Quay or the Railway Station are the best bet. The old main road (where SH1 and SH2 branch a few kilometers north of the ferry station on Hutt Rd.) is also known to be a successful spot, although it is a 3-4km walk from downtown. Many say it's best to take the train to Paraparaumu (on SH1) or Masterton (on SH2) and catch a ride from there.

✦ ORIENTATION

Central Wellington is remarkably compact, though its suburbs sprawl around the harbor into nearby valleys and out onto the **Miramar Peninsula.** Easily explored in a day, downtown Wellington sits between the **Railway Station** and **Kent Terrace,** at the base of **Mt. Victoria. Lambton Quay,** home to hordes of well-dressed business types and fancy restaurants, is the main drag. **Courtenay Place** hops with nightlife between Cambridge Terr. and **Taranaki Street,** while **Cuba Street** cultivates a more bohemian air between Abel Smith and Manners St. Locals say that the intersection of Cuba and Vivian St. is the "red-light district." The **Civic Square,** near the waterfront, leads to **Queens Wharf, Te Papa,** and **Oriental Bay.** Near the water to the north is the historic area of **Thorndon,** home to the Railway Station and government buildings such as Parliament's **Beehive.** The quiet residential streets and backpackers of the **Mt. Victoria** area form the southern edge of downtown.

▣ LOCAL TRANSPORTATION

Public Transportation: Ridewell Service Centre (☎801 7000 or 0800 801 700; www.stagecoach.co.nz) can answer questions about public transportation. Open daily 24hr. **Stagecoach** (☎801 7000 or 0800 801 700) services the main city and most surrounding suburbs. Main line buses run daily 6:30am-11pm. Most backpackers use the line between the Railway Station and the Cambridge Terr. end of Courtenay Pl. ($1-2.50). Buses #1 and 2 run between these points every 15min. during the day and every 30-45min. on evenings and weekends. The **City Circular** runs every 15min. from all major city sights ($2). The **Daytripper Pass** ($15) allows unlimited downtown travel M-F 9am-midnight, Sa-

22

Su 6:30am-midnight. **Stagecoach Eastbourne Connector** (☎0800 200 910) runs buses #81 and 83 between Courtenay Pl. and the Railway Station and around the bay to Petone and Eastbourne every hr. during the day and fewer in the evenings.

Taxis: Taxis frequent Lambton Quay and Courtenay Pl. **Wellington Combined Taxis** (☎0800 843 222 or 384 4444) or **Wellington City Cabs** (☎0800 388 8900).

Car Rental: Avis (☎802 1088), **Budget** (☎0800 652 227), and **Hertz** (☎388 7070) are at the airport. Arrange pickup at the ferry terminal. **Omega Rentals,** 96 Hutt Rd. (☎472 8466), has free pickup and 24hr. AA breakdown service. Budget cars $39 per day, with 4 days unlimited mileage. **Ace Car Rentals,** 150 Hutt Rd. (☎471 1176; www.acecarrentals.co.nz) typically has the cheapest rates and offers free pickup from downtown.

Automobile Clubs: Automobile Association, 342-352 Lambton Quay (☎931 9999). Open M and W-F 8:30am-5pm, Tu 9am-5pm, Sa 9am-1pm.

▲ PRACTICAL INFORMATION

TOURIST AND FINANCIAL SERVICES

Visitors Center: The Wellington i-Site, at Wakefield and Victoria St. (☎802 4860; www.wellingtonnz.com). Internet $4 per hr. Open M-F 8:30am-6:30pm, Sa-Su 9am-5:30pm. **Airport Visitor's Centre** (☎385 5123). Open daily 7am-7pm.

Department of Conservation (DOC), 15 Lambton Quay, (☎472 7356; www.doc.govt.nz), in the Old Government building across from the Beehive. Open M-F 9am-4:30pm, Sa 10am-3pm.

Budget Travel: STA Travel, 130 Cuba St. (☎385 0561; www.sta.com). Open M-F 9am-5:30pm, Sa 10am-1:30pm. There is also a profusion of discounted ticket consolidators and agents along Lambton Quay and in the Willis St. vicinity.

Consulates: Australia, 72-78 Hobson St. (☎473 6411), in Thorndon, north of the Railway Station. **Canada,** 61 Molesworth St., 3rd fl. (☎499 9895). **UK,** 44 Hill St. (☎472 6049). **US,** 29 Fitzherbert Terr. (☎472 2086), in Thorndon.

Banks and Currency Exchange: Travelex, 358 Lambton Quay (☎472 8328), near Willis St., has long hours. Open M-F 9am-5:30pm, Sa 9:30am-4pm.

LOCAL SERVICES

Tramping Gear: Mainly Tramping, 16 Willis St. (☎473 5353), in the Grand Arcade. Open M-Th 9am-5:30pm, F 9am-7pm, Sa 10am-4pm, Su 11am-3pm. 10% YHA and student discount.

GLBT Resources: Gay Switchboard (☎473 7878) runs a hotline 7:30-9:30pm and provides support and info on the Wellington scene. It's also a contact point for other area groups like **Icebreakers,** a young GLBT support group. **Out! Bookshop,** 15 Tory St. (☎385 4400), has a wide array of gay-oriented magazines and other items. Open daily 11am-10pm. The **Express** newspaper, available at the Wellington YHA (p. 238), has info on Wellington's gay scene.

Limited Mobility Resources: City Mobility, a Wellington City Council and TSB Bank project, offers free mobility scooter rentals with deposit of security item. 4hr. max. per rental. Rent from **Wellington City Council,** 101 Wakefield St. (☎499 4444), or **Botanic Gardens** (☎499 1400).

EMERGENCY AND COMMUNICATIONS

Emergency Assistance: ☎111.

Police: (☎381 2000 or 111), at the corner of Victoria and Harris St.

Crisis Lines: AIDS Hotline, ☎0800 802 437. **Wellington Rape Crisis,** 84 Willis St. (☎473 5357). Both open 24hr.

WELLINGTON

TO OTARI NATIVE
BOTANICAL GARDEN
(1km)

TO KATHERINE
MANSFIELD
BIRTHPLACE
(400m)

Katherine
Mansfield
Memorial
Park

TO (13 km),
(23km), AND (27km)

Westpac
Stadium

TO
INTER-
ISLANDER
FERRY (900m)

Hawkestone St.

THORNDON

Town Belt

Old St. Paul's

St. Paul's
Cathedral

National
Library

National
Archives

Hill St.

Aitken St.

Parliament
Buildings

Kate Sheppard
Pl.

Early Settlers'
Memorial Park

Bowen St.

The Beehive

White Star

InterCity

Anderson
Park

Bolton St.

Aurora Terr.

Blue Ridge
Ferry

Lady Norwood
Rose Garden

The Terrace

Customhouse Quay

PIPITEA
QUAY

The Lynx Ferry

Botanic Gardens

Lambton Quay

Ballance St.

Waring St.

Taylor St.

Dominion Post
Ferry

Carter
Observatory

KELBURN CABLE CAR

Featherston St.

Events Centre
Wellington

POST
OFFICE SQ.

QUEENS
WHARF

300 meters

300 yards

KELBURN

Kelburn
Park

Hunter St.

Museum of
Wellington
City and Sea

Lambton
Harbour

TO KARORI WILDLIFE
SANCTUARY (1.7km)

Boulcott St.

Jervois Quay

Frank
Kitts
Park

VICTORIA
UNIVERSITY

The Terrace

Willis St.

Harris St.

Mercer St.

Bond St.

City Gallery

CIVIC
SQUARE

Capital E

Chaffer's
Marina

Boyd
Wilson
Field

The Terrace

Dixon St.

Town Hall

Michael Fowler
Centre

Wakefield St.

Museum of
New Zealand Te Papa Tongarewa

Herd St.

TO (500m),
AND (8km)

TE
ARO

Ghuznee St.

Manners St.

Cable St.

Wakefield St.

Oriental Parade

ORIENTAL
BAY

Vivian St.

Cuba St.

Marion St.

Film Archive

Courtenay Pl.

Tory St.

Allen St.

Blair St.

TO MT. VICTORIA
LOOKOUT
(2km)

Majoribanks St.

Aro St.

Abel Smith St.

National
Tattoo
Museum

Tennyson St.

Lorne St.

College St.

Frederick St.

Vivian St.

Tory St.

Elizabeth St.

Haining St.

Webb St.

Arthur St.

Buckle St.

National War
Memorial

MT. COOK

TO NATIONAL CRICKET
MUSEUM (100m), (1.3km),
ZOO (2.7km), AND (10km)

Pirie St.

Brougham St.

Queen St.

Austin St.

TO WIND
TURBINE (4km)

Hania St.

Wellington

Medical Services: James Smith Life Pharmacy (☎499 1466), Cuba and Manners St. Open M-Th 9am-6pm, F 9am-8:30pm, Sa 9:30am-6pm, Su 10am-5:30pm. **Wellington Accident and Urgent Medical Centre,** 17 Adelaide Rd. (☎384 4944), in Newtown. Open daily 8am-11pm. After-hours **pharmacy** (☎385 8810) next door. Open M-F 5pm-11pm, Sa-Su 9am-11pm. The **hospital** (☎385 9999), in Newtown on Riddiford St.

Internet Access: Internet cafes cluster around Courtenay Pl. **iPlay,** 49 Manners St., 2nd fl. (☎494 0088; www.iplaynz.com). $4 per hr. Open 24hr.

Post Offices: Post shop, 43 Manners St. (☎473 5922). Poste Restante. Open M-F 8am-5:30pm, Sa 10am-1:30pm.

🏠🏠 ACCOMMODATIONS

For truly spectacular sleeps, head north to one of the many shorefront hostels along the coast. Book your bed in advance during the summer and on weekends.

🏅 **Wellington City YHA** (☎801 7280; www.yha.co.nz), Cambridge Terr. and Wakefield St. Recently renovated and centrally located, this 6-story behemoth has 320 beds, 2 kitchens, a game room, and big lounges. Laundry $4. Internet $2 per 15min. Reception 7am-10:30pm. 6-bed dorms $26; 4-bed dorms with bath $28; twins $66-90; doubles $70-90. $3-6 YHA discount. ❷

🏅 **Moana Lodge (BBH),** 49 Moana Rd. (☎233 2010; www.moanalodge.co.nz), in Plimmerton. Take SH1 north to Plimmerton; turn left into town and follow the coast. Right on the water, with views of the legendary Mana Island. The owners, John and Helen, have created a home away from home in this carefully crafted lodge with a fully stocked kitchen, dining room, and living room with sea views. Choice freebies including kayaks, coffee, and tea. Call for free pickup. Laundry $5. Internet $2 per 15min. Book ahead. Dorms $26-28; singles $40; twins and doubles $56, with view $70. ❷

Nomads Capital, 11 Wakefield St. (☎978 7800; fax 978 7810; www.nomadscapital.com). Across from the Wellington i-Site. Popular with travelers of all ages, this hostel is fully equipped for impromptu barbeques and rowdy rugby matches. Internet $4 per hr. 24hr. reception. Dorms $22-28; ensuite double $85; "elite rooms" with TV and clock $99. ISIC and VIP discounts. ❷

The Cambridge Hotel & Backpackers (BBH), 28 Cambridge Terr. (☎385 8829; www.cambridgehotel.co.nz). Enter from Alpha St. This converted hotel retains all the glamour with none of the cost. Breakfast $2. Laundry $4. Internet $5 per hr. 24hr. reception. 8-bed dorms $23-25; singles $59; doubles $85-99. AmEx/MC/V. ❷

Base Backpackers (VIP), 21-23 Cambridge Terr. (☎801 5666; www.basebackpackers.com). A converted pub, Base hasn't lost its social atmosphere in the change over. The female-only "sanctuary" floor pampers guests with spa-like amenities. Laundry $4. Internet $4 per hr. Key deposit $10. 6- to 8-bed dorms $25; 6- to 8-bed female dorms $28; 4-bed dorms $26-28; doubles with bath $80-85. $1 VIP discount. ❷

Downtown Backpackers (VIP), 1 Bunny St. (☎473 8482; www.downtownpack-ers.co.nz). Across from the railway station and Blueridge ferry station, the historic hotel is great for travelers in transit. Internet, lockers, and a cafe. Key deposit $20. Dorms $24; single with shared bath $58; twin with shared bath $56; double $68. ❷

World Wide Backpackers, 291 The Terr. (☎802 5590 or 0508 888 555). Take Ghuznee St. up the hill, and turn right. Continental breakfast (7:45-9am), shared boxed wine, local calls, and Internet all included. Linen $1 per item. Laundry $6. Key deposit $20. Reception 7:45am-noon, 3-8:45pm. Dorms $24; twins and doubles $60. Weekly dorms $120. $1 YHA/BBH/ISIC discount. ❷

Wildlife House, 58 Tory St. (☎381 3899 or 0508 005 858; www.wildlifehouse.co.nz). Recognizes your animal desires with free condoms at reception. Linen $3. Laundry $5. Free Internet. Key deposit $20. Reception 7:30am-10:30pm. Dorms $25-29; twins and doubles $68, with bath $73-85. ❷

Rowena's (VIP), 115 Brougham St. (☎385 7872 or 0800 801 1414; www.wellington-backpackers.co.nz). Removed from the city center, this brightly painted hostel has great views of downtown. Free shuttle to 12:30pm ferry. Laundry $6. Internet $0.50 per 15min. Key deposit $10. Reception 7am-10:30pm. Dorms $20; singles $30; twins and doubles $50. Tent sites $12.50. ❷

Stillwater Lodge (BBH), 34 Mana Esplanade (☎233 6628; www.stillwaterlodge.co.nz), in the unsigned village of Mana. Take SH1 north past the junction with SH58; it becomes Mana Esplanade. This beautiful home-turned-hostel is a few steps from Paua-tahanui Inlet. Free pool table. Linen $4. Free wash, $2 dry. Internet $2 per 20min. Book ahead. Dorms $23; twins and doubles $57, with bath $65. ❷

Top 10 Hutt Park Holiday Park, 95 Hutt Park Rd. (☎568 5913 or 0800 488 872; www.huttpark.co.nz), in Lower Hutt. Take SH2 to Petone and follow it to the waterfront. Wellington's closest holiday park, although tent campers may be lost amid the cara-vans. Laundry $4. Internet $2 per 10-20min. 1- to 2-person tent and powered sites $30, $13 per extra person; 2-person cabins $40. ❶

🍴 FOOD

Lambton Quay and Willis Street are full of lunch spots, but become dead at night. The young and chic liven up **Courtenay Place** and its side streets on evenings and weekends, while **Cuba Street** is peppered with smaller ethnic restaurants and cafes. You'll find a surprising mixture of food types at the **Wellington Market Food Court**, at Jarvois Quay and Taranaki St. (Open F-Su 10am-6pm.) Buy groceries at **New World**, 279 Wakefield St. (Open daily 7am-midnight.)

▨ Kai in the City, 21 Marjoribanks St. (☎801 5006; www.kaicity.co.nz). All items on the menu are traditional or Maori-inspired dishes. Sample a bit of everything with *Tangaroa* (seafood platter with smoked tuna and prawns, $40) or *Rongo* (vegetarian platter including *hangi* frittata and *kumara*; $32). Call ahead. Open daily 5:10pm-late. ❹

Mac's Brewery Bar and Restaurant, Shed 22 on the waterfront (☎381 2282; www.the-brewerybar.co.nz), at the corner of Taranaki and Cable St. The most scenic outdoor seating in the city serves gourmet pub fare along side it's famous micro-brews. Local brews from $3.50. Open M-F 11am-late, Sa-Su 10:30am-late. ❸

Aunty Mena's Vegetarian Restaurant & Cafe, 167 Cuba St. (☎382 8288). Vegetar-ian and vegan friendly dishes cooked in a variety of Asian styles. The Malaysian *nasi lemak* is aromatic coconut rice, vegetables and tofu ($10). Open Su-M 5:30-9:30pm, Tu-Sa 11:30am-10pm. ❷

Schoc Chocolaterie and Espresso Bar, 11 Tory St. (☎382 8907; www.chocolateher-apy.com). The place to wake up in Wellington. Schoc whips up rich hot chocolate

($3.50), strong espresso ($3), and unique gourmet chocolates. Lime and chili chocolate, anyone? Open M-F 7:30am-6:30pm, Sa 10:30am-6pm, Su noon-6pm. ❷

Daawat, 88 Manners Mall (☎472 0060) between Victoria and Cuba St. *Hotcha,* the god of curry, grants the trinity of backpacker desires: low prices, high quality, and heaping portions. Enjoy a divine *Dal makhani* (black lentils in spicy tomato puree; $11) or chow on the lunch standby (chicken tikka masala with rice and naan; $11). Open M-F 11:30am-2pm, 5:30pm-late, Sa-Su 5:30pm-late. ❷

Aqaba, 186 Broadway Ave. (☎357 8922). Don't let the Egyptian decor fool you—the menu holds no national allegiance. Business types, students, and families enjoy affordable dishes (most $11-23) in the airy environs. Open M-F 7:30am-late, Sa-Su 9am-late. Cash only. ❸

⌐ CAFES

With the highest number of cafes per capita in the Southern Hemisphere (and thankfully, only three Starbucks), Wellington is certainly doing something right. **Courtenay Place** is lined with standard cafes, while funkier finds dot the bohemian stretch of 🔲**Cuba Street.** Most cafes serve food and many extend the party with liquor licenses and late hours.

🔲 **Fidel's,** 234 Cuba St. (☎801 6868). *¡Que vive la revolucion!*—in coffee, at least. Easily the hippest spot in town, this temple to the great leader will place you firmly in the trenches with its tight inside passages, patio military netting, and revolutionary memorabilia. A delicious menu and caffeine buzz ($3-4) vie for control with the milkshakes ($5). Open M-F 7:30am-midnight, Sa-Su 9am-midnight. ❶

Chocolate Fish Cafe, 497A Karaka Bay Road (☎388 2808), in Scorching Bay. Once the spot to escape the city, this small cafe now quietly attracts celebrities and movie producers to its sunny beachside seats. A chocolate-covered marzipan fish lands in the bottom of every drink. Breakfast served all day. Open daily 8:30am-5pm. ❶

Parade Cafe, 148 Oriental Parade (☎939 3935). A favorite for its heaping breakfasts and relaxed atmosphere along the popular jogging boardwalk. The pancakes with bananas and bacon ($16) can satiate even the hungriest hardbodied traveler. Open daily 7:30am-10:30pm. ❶

Midnight Espresso, 178 Cuba St. (☎384 7014). With funky beats, alternative art, and a stellar vegan-friendly menu, Midnight makes you dread the clock striking three. Couple your coffee ($4) with a hunk of midnight chocolate cake ($4). Open M-F 8am-3am, Sa-Su 9am-late. ❶

Ed's Juice Bar, 95 Victoria St. (☎473 1769). Savor an irresistible smoothie ($3-6) or steaming soup ($5). Great selection of vegetarian and vegan food. Open M-F 7am-6pm, Sa-Su 9am-5pm. ❶

⌾ SIGHTS

MUSEUMS

🔲**MUSEUM OF NEW ZEALAND TE PAPA TONGAREWA.** This museum's enormous collection of ambitious, informative, and entertaining exhibits is Wellington's pride and joy; free admission is just a bonus. Permanent exhibits explore New Zealand's land, history, and culture. Upstairs, *Te Marae* offers a contemporary interpretation of Maori iconography. For a fee, try the interactive exhibits, including a virtual bungy jump, virtual sheep shearing complete with virtual blood if you do a bad job, and a virtual tour of prehistoric New Zealand. (*Cable St. at the end of Taranaki St. on the waterfront.* ☎381 7000; www.tepapa.govt.nz. Open M-W and F-Su 10am-6pm, Th 10am-9pm. Free. Interactive exhibits $2-9.)

THE MUSEUM OF WELLINGTON CITY AND SEA. Built in 1892, this museum explores the unique relationship between Wellington residents and the sea. Watch out if you're heading to South Island—the gallery features a video on the 1968 sinking of the *Wahine* interisland ferry. *(At the corner of Queens Wharf and Jervois Quay. ☎ 472 8904; www.museumofwellington.co.nz. Open daily 10am-5pm. Free.)*

OTHER MUSEUMS. The **Dowse Art Museum** features off-beat, contemporary object art; recent raves include skateboard art and "works that have been chosen for their freak factor." The new Cafe Reka is just as freaky as the exhibits and specializes in tapas (5 for $12.50) and wheatgrass shots. *(45 Laings Rd., in Lower Hutt. Take the #83 Eastbourne bus to Queensgate Shopping Centre from Courtenay Pl. ☎ 570 6500; www.dowse.org.nz. Museum open M-F 10am-4:30pm, Sa-Su 10am-5pm. Free. Cafe open M-Tu 7:30am-5pm, W-F 7:30am-late, Sa 8am-late, Su 9am-5pm.)* If you miss the thwack of the national pastime, the **National Cricket Museum** has more old bats than you can shake a stick at. *(Basin Reserve grandstand. ☎ 385 6602; www.nzcricket.co.nz. Open Nov.-Apr. daily 10:30am-3:30pm. May-Oct. Sa-Su only. $5, children $2.)* The **National Tattoo Museum** displays pictures and designs of Maori *moko* plus a preserved skin sample. *(42 Abel Smith St. ☎ 385 6444; www.mokomuseum.org.nz. Open Tu-Sa noon-5:30pm. $5, students $4.)* The **Katherine Mansfield Birthplace** showcases the early years of the beloved short story writer. *(25 Tinakori Rd., in Thorndon. Go up Murphy St. past the Motorway, or take bus #14 to Park St. ☎ 473 7268; www.katherinemansfield.com. Open Tu-Su 10am-4pm. Call ahead to book a group tour. $5.50, students $4, children $2.)*

CITY SIGHTS

■ **VANTAGE POINTS.** Rising from the city's south end, **Mt. Victoria** towers above downtown Wellington and provides panoramic views of the harbor. Catch a ride if you're not keen on the 30min. hike. *(Take bus #20 M-F.)* Some locals say that the view from the **ECNZ wind turbine** is even better. *(Take bus #7 from the Railway Station or drive west on Willis St. to Brooklyn Rd.; follow the signs. Beware: it's a steep climb.)*

PARLIAMENT. The most prominent visual attractions in Wellington, New Zealand's capital since 1865, have prime national significance. The distinctive **Beehive**, a monstrosity of 1970s architecture, houses the offices of the Prime Minister and other bigwigs. Unfortunately, the interior is closed to the public. Next door, the Edwardian Baroque **Parliament House** has a **tour desk** on the ground floor. The carefully designed Maori Affairs Select Committee Room is set off by a huge art installation. The ornate Victorian Gothic **Parliamentary Library,** meticulously restored after a 1992 fire, is also part of the tour. To see the House in action, get a schedule in advance. *(Molesworth St., a few blocks from the Railway Station. ☎ 471 9503; www.parliament.nz. Tours leave on the hour; groups of 10 or more call ahead. Open M-F 10am-4pm, Sa 10am-3pm, Su noon-3pm.)*

CIVIC SQUARE. The public buildings in Wellington's Civic Square offer ample opportunities for people-watching. At one side sits the elegant **City Gallery,** which hosts contemporary exhibitions by top-caliber New Zealand and international artists, the Gay and Lesbian Festival, and short film showings. *(101 Wakefield St. ☎ 801 3952; www.city-gallery.org.nz. Open daily 10am-5pm. NZ exhibits free; international exhibits up to $12.)* In the far corner of Civic Sq. is the circular **Michael Fowler Centre,** an event and conference center which is home to the New Zealand Symphony Orchestra. Inside are the two towering Maori pillars, *Te Pou O Wi Tako* and *Te Pou O Tawiwi,* dedicated to "the people of the land" and "to visitors," respectively *(☎ 801 4242).* Just under the base of the bridge sits **Capital E,** a children's center with a hands-on toy store, constantly changing exhibitions, and a theater. *(Cross the bridge to the waterfront and the green public space of Frank Kitts Park. ☎ 384 8502; www.capitale.org.nz. Open daily 9:30am-5:30pm. Exhibits free to $8. Theater $10.)*

LIBRARIES AND CATHEDRALS

NATIONAL LIBRARY. Home to over 1.8 million volumes, the library displays off-beat cultural oddities in the **Cartoon Archives** and musty photographic archives from early Pacific settlement in the **Alexander Turnbull Library.** *(58 Molesworth St. ☎474 3000; www.natlib.govt.nz. Open M-F 9am-5pm, Sa 9am-1pm. Reference area open Su 9am-1pm. Gallery open M-F 9am-5pm, Sa 9am-1pm. Archive access by arrangement. Free.)*

NATIONAL ARCHIVES. A dim vault at the back of the building exhibits the country's most important documents, including the original copy of the 1840 Treaty of Waitangi and the Statute of Westminster. *(10 Mulgrave St. ☎499 5595; www.archives.govt.nz. Open M-F 9am-5pm, Sa 9am-1pm. Free.)*

OLD ST. PAUL'S. Erected in 1866 from native timber, the colonial Gothic interior of this Anglican church has superb stained-glass windows. The contrast between this charming cathedral and the salmon-colored **St. Paul's Cathedral** is shocking. *(Old St. Paul's, 34 Mulgrave St., next door to the Archives. ☎473 6722. Open daily 10am-5pm. Donation requested. St. Paul's Cathedral is next to Parliament on Molesworth St.)*

GARDENS AND TOURS

BOTANIC GARDENS. A trip to the gardens may call to mind similarities between Wellington and San Francisco, especially if you ride the **Wellington Cable Car** 610m up to the Kelburn Terminal. *(☎472 2199. Departs every 10min. on Cable Car Ln. M-F 7am-10pm, Sa 8:30am-10pm, Su 9am-10pm. $2, students and children $1.)* Established in 1868, the Botanic Gardens cover over 25 hilly hectares just west of downtown. Follow one of the many paths snaking from the herb garden to the **Carter Observatory,** with canopied views of the city and hills in the distance. The observatory features planetarium shows and telescope viewings, as well as a giant sundial. *(☎472 8167; www.carterobservatory.org. Open Nov.-Feb. M-Tu 10am-5pm and W-Sa 10am-late; Mar.-Oct. M-Th and Su 11am-4pm, F-Sa 11am-late. $6-12.)* One of the most memorable spots in the gardens is the **Lady Norwood Rose Garden,** with hundreds of different kinds of roses blossoming around a central fountain. The walkway leads through the dense foliage and follows Bolton St. to a wide terrace and downtown Wellington. *(☎801 3073. Always open, though best if visited during the day. Roses in bloom Nov.-May. Free.)* Anyone with a botanist's eye should visit the 90-hectare **Otari Wilton's Bush,** which is dedicated to native kiwi plants. *(160 Wilton Rd. Take #14 Wilton bus. ☎475 3245. Free.)* In the summer, the wildly popular **Sound Shell** hosts live music and theater daily. *(Shows begin at dusk. Free.)*

IN RECENT NEWS

FLAGGING ENTHUSIASM

Many people, including plenty of Kiwis and Aussies, have trouble telling the Australian and New Zealand flags apart. This isn't surprising, given that a single star is the difference between the two. In recent years, the confusion has led Kiwis to call for change. A 2005 petition calling for a new flag had nearly 100,000 signatures. Many of those passionate about the change claim that the current flag doesn't represent New Zealand, but rather mimics the Australian flag and overemphasizes the country's British heritage while failing to represent the Maori population.

There are two popular options for a new flag. The first pays homage to a great Kiwi icon and the logo for the revered All Blacks—the white fern. The second combines a variety of elements, including the white fern, to represent the diverse aspects of New Zealand.

However, not everyone is in favor of a new flag. Many veterans and veteran groups oppose changing the flag because the current flag is the one that troops, particularly the venerated ANZAC troops, fought and died for.

While the 2005 petition fell short of the required 400,000 signatures needed to garner a referendum, the debate shows no signs of flagging.

WELLINGTON ZOO. New Zealand's oldest zoo, the Wellington Zoo leads the pack with it's world class breeding programs. Exotic animals such as the Sumatran tiger and the Malayan sun bear sit near New Zealand favorites such as the brown kiwi and the giant weta. *(200 Daniell St. in Newtown. 10min. from downtown. Take the #10 or 23 Stagecoach bus to Newtown Park. ☎381 6750; www.wellingtonzoo.com. Open daily 9:30am-5pm. $10, children $5.)*

KARORI WILDLIFE SANCTUARY. Located on a fault line high above the city surrounded by an impenetrable 2m fence used to repel pests, this sanctuary uses its best defenses to recreate a native habitat for endangered species. The 18km of hiking tracks represent an eden for bush-starved visitors while night tours are offer an opportunity to see the elusive kiwi in its natural habitat. *(Through the Karori Tunnel at the end of Waiapu Rd. Take bus #12, 17, 18, 21, or 22, all marked Karori, from downtown. ☎920 9213; www.sanctuary.org.nz. Open Dec.-Mar. daily 10am-5pm; Apr.-Nov. M-F 10am-4pm, Sa-Su 10am-5pm. Call ahead for guided tours, night tours typically begin 8pm. $10, children $5.)*

ALL THINGS RINGS. Though none of the *Lord of the Rings* sets remain and many of the landscapes were altered by computer graphics, Tolkien fans might want to make a driving tour of the area. The **Otaki Gorge Road** winds by the woods and roads of Hobbiton, though the streets and village of Hobbiton were filmed outside of Matamata, east of Cambridge. Rivendell was filmed at **Kaitoke Regional Park,** outside Upper Hutt. **Queen Elizabeth Park,** near Paekakariki, hosted filming for the battle of Pelennor Fields. For more info, go to the Wellington i-Site.

WELLINGTON GUIDED TOURS. If time is at a premium and access to a car is limited, a guided tour is the perfect way to see Wellington and its suburbs. Rover Explorer Tours offers conversational tours with gregarious local guides in small buses that allow hop-on hop-off service at sites in the city and along the coast. Tours include discounts to venues across the city. The scenic southern coastline is reason enough to board the bus. *(Offered daily from the Visitors Center at 9am, 11:30am, and 2:30pm. ☎021 426 211; www.wellingtonrover.co.nz. $40, children $25.)*

▧ OUTDOOR ACTIVITIES

▧WALKS AND RIDES. The Northern, Southern, and Eastern Walkways, detailed in leaflets from the Wellington i-Site or DOC offices, are tame and accessible walks through the city's greenbelt and coastline *(www.feelinggreat.co.nz)*. Or rent a bike from town and ride along the spectacular coast from Oriental Bay around the Miramar Peninsula to the end of the pavement. From there, the Red Rocks Coastal Walk, a terrific 8km round-trip loop along the jagged southern shore, winds past the pillow lava formation of Red Rocks. The walk continues out to the crashing surf of Sinclair Head, where a colony of fat fur seals typically lazes around in winter. A 4WD ride from Sea Coast Safaris travels to the colony along rugged and otherwise inaccessible tracks. *(☎0800 732 527; www.sealcoast.com. 3hr. $70.)*

ADRENALINE BOOSTERS. Fergs Kayaks rents sea kayaks and in-line skates. *(At Shed 6, Queens Wharf. ☎499 8898; www.fergskayaks.co.nz. Kayaks $12-25 per hr. In-line skates $12 per hr.)* **HangDog** and **Top Adventures** specialize in caving, rafting, canyoning, and rock climbing in Titahi Bay. *(453 Hutt Rd., in Lower Hutt. ☎589 9181; www.topadventures.co.nz. Trips from $70.)* In Karori's suburban expanses, **Mud Cycles** rents bikes for the world-famous mountain biking trails at Makara Peak. *(1 Allington Rd. ☎476 4961; www.mudcycles.co.nz. Open M-Tu, Th-F 9:30am-6pm, W 9:30am-7pm, Sa 10am-5pm, Su 10am-4pm. Bike rental $40 per day.)*

AQUATIC ACTIVITIES. Within walking distance from downtown, **Oriental Bay** boasts beautiful sands and bustling crowds. Locals prefer **Lyall Bay,** which has a patrolled swimming stretch and a relatively consistent break at the airport end. If you have the time, **Plimmerton** and the **Kapiti Coast** have superior swimming and sunning. Wellington's **surfing** is wind dependent: winter southerlies cause bigger waves, but breaks are more consistent east of the Wairarapa towns of Martinborough and Masterton. Windsurfing here is popular among the hardened professionals. The **Dominion Post Ferry** is a cheap way to experience the harbor. Full of Wellingtonians escaping the city, it leaves from Queens Wharf and crosses to the quaint community of **Day's Bay,** home to a small but popular swimming beach. Past Day's Bay is the village of **Eastbourne,** similarly saturated with cafes, blue penguins, and a pebbly beach. *(☎499 1282; www.eastwest.co.nz. M-F 9 sailings per day, Sa-Su 5 per day. Round-trip $17, children $9.)* Some ferries also stop at **Matiu/Somes Island** *(20min.; departs daily 10am, noon, 2:15pm; round-trip $17).*

🎭 ENTERTAINMENT

Wellington presents a wide variety of diversions, from high art to high-energy sport. The Wellington i-Site has schedules and information about shows and theaters, and they sell rush tickets for **Downstage, Circa,** and **BATS** (see below). **Ticketek** (☎384 3840), at Queen's Wharf, sells seats for most events, though rugby tickets are sold through **Red Tickets** (☎0800 000,575) or at any **post shop.** Prices for Wellington's many performances vary drastically and are determined by the theater company using the space. Call ahead for showtimes and prices. Wellington also offers many cinematic options, including **Paramount,** 25 Courtenay Pl. (☎384 4080), which dishes out arthouse cinema fare and **Rialto** (☎385 1864), at Cable St. and Jervois Quay. For information on upcoming events in Wellington, the **Jason's What's On Wellington** is a useful guide (www.jasons.com).

Downstage, 12 Cambridge Terr. (☎801 6946; www.downstage.co.nz), at the corner of Courtenay Pl. and Cambridge Terr. Wellington's oldest professional theater hosts a wide range of productions, from classic drama to cabaret and comedy.

Circa, 1 Taranaki St. (☎801 7992; www.circa.co.nz), next to Te Papa. Mainstage plays and a studio with smaller, more experimental shows.

BATS, 1 Kent Terr. (☎802 4175; www.bats.co.nz). An experimental, on-the-fringe venue, often featuring homegrown productions.

The Westpac St. James Theatre, 77 Courtenay Pl. (☎384 3840; www.stjames.com). Restored Edwardian lyric theater, home to the Royal Ballet, opera, and musicals.

The Opera House, 111-113 Manners St. (☎802 4060), is run by the St. James.

Wellington Convention Centre, (☎801 4231; www.wellingtonconventioncentre.com) stages lectures as well as classical and chamber music concerts (even the New Zealand Symphony Orchestra), mainly at the Michael Fowler Centre and Wellington Town Hall.

Westpac Stadium, on Waterloo Quay (☎384 3840). This new, $128-million stadium is jokingly called "The Cake Tin" for its metallic outer shell. But don't let the moniker fool you—Wellington is mighty proud of this tin can, which hosts events like rugby, cricket, soccer, and big-name concerts. Prices vary, but rugby tickets usually cost $30-50.

Basin Reserve, on Kent Terr. (☎384 3840), a 20min. walk from downtown. This stadium has been home to Wellington cricket for more than 125 years and enjoys National Heritage status. It also houses the National Cricket Museum. Most matches Nov.-Mar., with 1-2 international series every year. Tickets usually $10-30.

Bodega, 101 Ghuznee St. (☎384 8212; www.bodega.co.nz). Wellington's top weekend music stop. Impressive selection of quality local ales and imports. Handles $5. Open Su-Th 4pm-late, F-Sa 3pm-late.

Events Centre Wellington, at Queens Wharf (☎470 0190). The main venue for indoor sporting events (like international basketball and netball), popular music concerts, and various weekend festivals and exhibitions.

❊ FESTIVALS

The **Summer City Festival** (☎494 4444; www.feelinggreat.co.nz) is a brilliant cavalcade of festivals like Sunday night jazz in the Botanic Gardens, mass walks up Mt. Victoria, and a Pacific Island festival. Wellington's young crowd flocks to the **Cuba Street Carnival** (☎499 4444) in mid-February for live bands, street performers, and food. The biennial **New Zealand Festival of the Arts** (☎473 0149; www.nzfestival.telecom.co.nz), the country's biggest celebration, draws artists and performers from across the globe. Between February and March, the **Fringe Festival** (☎495 8015; www.fringe.org.nz) takes Wellington to the cutting edge, showcasing underground and experimental theater, music, dance, and spoken word. May plays the fool with the **New Zealand International Comedy Festival** (☎309 9241; www.laugh.co.nz), featuring big-name comedians from New Zealand and abroad. July rolls out the red carpet for the annual **New Zealand International Film Festival** (☎385 0162; www.nzff.co.nz), a regular stop on the post-Cannes film festival circuit. The **New Zealand Wearable Art Awards** showcases outrageous human spectacles each September. For judges, gawkers, and their own entertainment, contestants design themselves as everything from dragonfly beauties to spiked cyberpunks to jellyfish. (☎548 9299; www.worldofwearableart.com. Tickets sell out as early as 6 mo. ahead.) The **Wellington International Jazz Festival** (☎496 5494; www.jazzfestival.co.nz) takes to the waterfront during the last two weeks of October.

▨ NIGHTLIFE

Wellington nightlife comes in flavors ranging from business chic to skater cool. The **Courtenay Place** stretch is clogged with slick bars frequented by after-work businessmen and black-clad students; most establishments are indistinguishable from one another. The chilled-out pubs on **Cuba Street** tend to be just as crowded but are less fond of amped up rock remixes. For the latest happenings, grab the free weekly **The Package** or **Capital Times** from newsstands, or check cafes for fliers. Scope out **Express** for GLBT nightlife listings.

PUBS

▧ Matterhorn, 106 Cuba Mall (☎384 3359; www.matterhorn.co.nz). Walk down a long, dark hallway to enter the realm of Matterhorn. Underground trendsters pack this intimate lounge bar, dropping $5 on beers and coffee, and snacking on a selection of gourmet munchies from $5. Late-night DJs (Th-Sa) and live bands (Su) get a young crowd grooving in the rear courtyard. Open Su-W 10am-midnight, Th-Sa 10am-late.

▧ Good Luck Bar, 126 Cuba St. (☎801 9950), hidden down a stairway across from Tulsi. Lead friends to this underground tribute to China's opium dens, but make them spring for the delicious mixed drinks ($11-16). DJs W-F night. Open daily 4:30pm-3am.

Our Bar, 201 Cuba St. (☎802 4405). Particularly favored by Wellington's gay community, this bar appeals to all with its airy interior and chilled-out bistro bar overlooking Cuba St. Open M-F 3pm-late, Sa-Su noon-later.

Molly Malone's (☎384 2896), at Courtenay Pl. and Taranaki St. Travelers feel right at home in this Wellington institution. A celebration of youth, independence, and beer ($4.30-7). Live bands nightly. Open daily 11am-late.

CLUBS

Shooters, 69 Courtenay Pl. (☎801 7800). Get decked out and cruise past the bouncers to join the gyrating scene upstairs. Mostly top pop, the music keeps an all-ages crowd hopping until the wee hours. Beer $5-7. Open daily 11am-3am.

The Establishment (☎382 8654; www.theestablishment.co.nz), at Courtenay Pl. and Blair St. Get sweaty to thumping techno in a bare-bones warehouse dedicated to the rave. Exposed flesh and strobe lights rule the night. Pints $5.50. Open M-W 3pm-late, Th-Su 3pm-3am.

KAPITI COAST   ☎ 04

Arching gracefully 32km up the west coast from Paekakariki to Otaki, the Kapiti Coast *(KAH-puh-tee)* is Wellington's scenic getaway. Small wildlife sanctuaries, stunning coastline, and the bird-filled Kapiti Island draw visitors to the region. While nearly every town has a public beach, Waikanae Beach is the region's finest, with a long stretch of often secluded sands. Though Porirua's suburban strips and sheltered inlets are not technically within the boundaries of Kapiti's shore, a few diversions and stellar hostels make the town a comfortable stop.

⎐ KAPITI COAST TRANSPORTATION

TranzMetro (☎ 807 7000) trains leave every 30min. from Wellington and stop at **Paekakariki** (45min., $5-7), **Paraparaumu** (1hr., $6-8), and **Plimmerton** (25min., $3.50-5). An unlimited **Capitol Explorer ticket** will get you anywhere for only $15 (travel must begin after 9am on weekdays and excludes the Capitol Connection and Wairarapa line). Trains run weekdays 6am-midnight, with the last outbound train leaving at 11pm. On Saturdays, the final outbound train leaves at 1am. Prices are 25% lower between 9am and 3pm (M-F only) and 20% off for a 10-trip pass. **InterCity/Newmans** (☎ 472 5111) buses also stop along the **Kapiti Coast** (9 per day, from $11), but advance booking is required. **Mana Coach Services** (☎ 0800 801 700) operates a number of buses within the Kapiti Coast and Porirua ($2-3). The **Discovery Pass** ($10) allows one day of unlimited travel by bus within Wellington and along the Kapiti Coast. There's also a fair amount of regional traffic from Otaki to Paekakariki, north of where the motorway ends. Although *Let's Go* does not recommend it, **hitchhikers** reportedly have a good chance of bumming a ride on the outskirts of each town.

KAPITI ISLAND   ☎ 04

Once the stronghold of the great warrior chief, Te Rauparaha, and an anchorage for whalers, Kapiti Island has been cleansed of introduced mammals as part of a wildly successful experiment in floral and avian regeneration. A bird-lover's paradise, the island is the only accessible wilderness site in New Zealand where you're practically guaranteed to see the rare **takahe** and **kaka,** flocks of melodious **tui,** or one of the few remaining **saddlebacks** or **kokako.** The nature reserve contains toilets, a shelter, and three tracks (2 to the island's summit and 1 along the shore), but no other amenities. The **DOC** limits access to the island to 50 people per day and requires a permit ($9, children $4.50); book ahead with the Wellington office (☎ 472 7356). Spaces fill up far in advance from December to February, especially during the weekend slots, but there's often last-minute availability on weekdays. In winter, there can be too few visitors for the boats to run, and rough seas can bring trips to a halt. **Kapiti Marine Charter** (☎ 297 2585 or 0800 433 779; www.kapitimarinecharter.co.nz) and **Kapiti Tours** (☎ 237 7965 or 0800 527 484; www.kapititours.co.nz) both run daily from Paraparaumu Beach to the island (15-20min.; 9am, occasionally 9:30am; $45, children $20, under 5 free). The former also runs summer cruises, which you can book by calling ahead ($20; 20-person min.).

Kapiti Island lies about 5km offshore from **Paraparaumu Beach.** From Wellington, only the 6:55am **TranzMetro** ($8) reaches Paraparaumu in time to catch the 7:55am **Mana Coach** (☎ 0800 801 700) to Paraparaumu Beach (20min., $2). From the train station, take either bus #71 (20min.; 7:55, 8:15am) and get off at the Beach Shop, or take bus #72 (20min., 7:55am) and get off at Paraparaumu Beach. The boat to Kapiti Island departs at 9am. Visitors are given a nature talk upon arrival and must catch the boats back around 3pm. It's more convenient to spend the previous night on the coast; inquire at the **tourist booth** in the parking lot of the Paraparaumu Coastland Shopping Center, across from the train station.

PARAPARAUMU ☎04

Paraparaumu is the jumping-off point to Kapiti Island. The #4 Mana Coach delivers passengers to the sweet-smelling **Nyco Chocolate Factory and Shop** at the corner of SH1 and Raumati Rd. The mouth-watering aroma is a prelude to the free tastings. (☎299 8098. Open M-Sa 9am-5pm, Su 10am-4:30pm.) Farther north on SH1, the **Lindale Centre** serves scoops of frozen happiness (homemade ice cream) and various Kapiti cheeses. If that doesn't put a cherry on top of your day, then sheep shearing, cow milking, and animal feeding might appeal to your inner farmer. (☎297 0916. Open daily 9am-5pm. Farm walk $8. Shearing and milking demonstrations Sa-Su at 2pm. $13, children $8. Ask for free cheese samples.) Just 1.6km north of Lindale, the **Southward Car Museum** displays 250 vintage autos and motorcycles. You can peek into Marlene Dietrich's custom-made Cadillac or check out the bullet holes in the gangster car. (☎297 1221; www.southward.org.nz. Open daily 9am-4:30pm. $7, children $2.50.) Both Southward and Lindale are on the #75, 76, and 77 **Mana Coach** routes that continue to Waikanae; #71 runs the 3.5km from Paraparaumu Centre to its beach.

The **Coastlands** shopping complex, across from the railroad station, has a **post office, supermarket,** and **pharmacy.** The **Paraparaumu Information Centre** can help you find accommodations. (☎298 8195; alison.lowes@clear.net.nz. Open M-F 9am-5pm, Sa-Su 10am-3pm.) Motels stretch along Kapiti Rd. and down the beachfront. **Barnacles Seaside Inn (BBH/YHA) ❸,** 3 Marine Pde., is seaside. (☎902 5856; www.seasideyha.co.nz. Laundry $2. Internet $2 per 20min. Pickup or drop-off from rail station $5. Dorms $20; singles $35; twins $44; doubles $54. MC/V.)

PAEKAKARIKI ☎04

Maori for "resting place of the green parakeet," Paekakariki is a resting place for the weary. The town's location at the southern point of the Kapiti coastline makes for breathtaking views. If you have your own transport, take **Paekakariki Hill Road** off SH1, up through a blindingly green valley, before turning the corner to a panorama of the Tasman Sea and the entire curve of the Kapiti Coast. Kapiti Island and the Marlborough Sounds can be seen in the distance. ▣**Paekakariki Backpackers (BBH) ❷,** 11 Wellington Rd., on a hilltop, is more a restful retreat than a stop along the highway. A peak off the back porch gives up-to-the-minute reports on the excellent local surfing. (☎902 5967. Free boogie board use. Spa $5. Laundry $4. Internet $2 per 20min. Dorms $23; doubles $52, with bath $58. Tent sites available, BBH discount. MC/V.)

PORIRUA AREA AND MANA ISLAND ☎04

Splitting the distance between the Kapiti Coast and Wellington, Porirua City is little more than a stretch of strip-malls on the edge of Wellington's suburban sprawl. The area is redeemed by its smaller communities, coastal inlets, and coves. **Pauatahanui Inlet** tempers stiff breezes for beginning and intermediate **windsurfers. Wildwinds,** at Wellington's overseas passenger terminal at Chaffers Marina, offers three-hour windsurfing lessons ($120), and $34 for six-hour kitesurfing lessons. (☎384 1010; www.wildwinds.co.nz.) Wellington's adventure operators use the inlet for windsurfing and **Titahi Bay** for rock climbing. Among the worthwhile walks in the area is the climb up **Colonial Knob** (5-6hr. round-trip), accessible from Raiha St., which summits the sizeable hill providing 360° views from South Island to Taranaki. The **Wairaka Walkway** (4-5hr. one-way) leaves from the end of Moana Rd. in Plimmerton and follows an oceanside route all the way to Pukerua Bay, where you can catch a train back to town. The very early Saturday morning **Porirua flea market** offers Polynesian wares at dirt-cheap prices. Take the TranzMetro to Porirua, and you'll see it by the McDonald's. (Open Sa 5-9am.) More information about Porirua can be mined at the **Porirua i-Site,** under the white canvas mountains at the Cobham Court strip mall. (☎237 8088; www.discover-porirua.co.nz. Internet $2 per 15min. Open M-F 9am-5pm, Sa 8am-4pm, Su 11am-3pm.)

Four kilometers offshore from Titahi Bay lies **Mana Island**. It is the site of the first sheep farm in New Zealand and is experiencing ecological rebirth thanks to a massive regeneration program. A number of endangered bird species, including the **takahe**, make the island worthy of a special trip. Of the 100 takahe currently alive, 20 of them make Mana their home. The **Dive Spot** organizes transport to and from the island and diving and fishing trips. (☎233 8238; www.divespot.co.nz. Book in advance. Sa 8:30am. $80 per two-tank dive day-trip; equipment included.) **Friends of Mana Island** (☎292 8582) provides info on the scientific reserve. **Moana Lodge** (p. 237), in Plimmerton, is a stone's throw from Mana Island.

THE WAIRARAPA ☎06

In summer, the Wairarapa buzzes with daytrippers and weekenders from Wellington who brave the highway's twists and turns to seek solace in the pastoral landscape and award-winning wines. The vineyard-studded plains and accompanying yuppies are newcomers to a region of natural austerity. The blocky Tararua Mountains form North Island's tailbone, while Pacific swells rage and retreat along isolated coastal stretches from mighty Castle Rock down to Cape Palliser's prominent lighthouse. Regional transportation is scarce, but after a meal and a glimpse of the hills, travelers realize that there's no reason to head anywhere else.

MASTERTON ☎06

Gateway to the Tararuas, Masterton (pop. 28,000) has outgrown its agricultural roots, but has yet to develop sufficient facilities and accommodations for travelers. One sight that visitors and locals both enjoy is the 32-hectare **Queen Elizabeth Park** on Dixon St. A bit farther afield, 30km north of Masterton on SH2, the **Mt. Bruce National Wildlife Centre** ensures that you will see a kiwi and a tuatara in the same day, a feat not easily accomplished. For $15, a guided walk will help avid birders find the most elusive species. Keep an eye out for eel feedings, which occur after lunch. (☎375 8754; www.mtbruce.doc.govt.nz. Open daily 9am-4:30pm. $8.) Closer to home, the gleaming **Aratoi Museum,** at the corner of Bruce and Dixon St. near the park, hosts rotating local exhibits. (☎370 0001; www.aratoi.org.nz. Open daily 10am-4:30pm. Free.) World-class sheep shearers lay shivering animals bare during the **Golden Shears Competition** (www.goldenshears.co.nz) held annually in late summer.

 THE REAL DEAL. While wine connoisseurs the world over head to the Wairarapa, Masterton is better left alone. Martinborough, the next town over, has better tourist infrastructure and is closer to the vineyards. *-Lauren Holmes*

Queen Street, which runs parallel to **Chapel Street (SH2),** is home to most of Masterton's cafes, stores, and restaurants. The **Empire Lodge ❷,** 94 Queen St., is centrally located with sunny rooms that are cheaper than those of area motels. (☎377 1902; empirelodge.co.nz. Laundry $3. Key deposit $10. Reception 7am-9:30pm. Dorms $20-30; singles $25; doubles $70. MC/V.) **Wairarapa Bakery ❶,** 218 Queen St., fills growling stomachs for under $5. (☎377 0686. Open daily 8am-5pm.) There is a **Woolworth's** near the end of Queen St. (☎377 0050. Open daily 7am-9pm.)

TranzMetro (☎04 498 3000, ext. 44933) is the only ride to Wellington (1½hr., 2-5 per day, $12). **Tranzit Coachlines** (☎377 1227) goes from the Queen St. terminal to Palmerston North (2hr., 1-2 per day, $19) via Mt. Bruce National Wildlife Centre

KIWI POWER

Kiwis are fiercely proud of their commitment to environmental causes. Most famously, New Zealand declared itself a nuclear-free zone in 1985 in response to the dangers of nuclear power and the continued nuclear testing carried out by the US and France in the South Pacific.

This decree forced all US warships to establish themselves as nuclear-free, an action against US Navy protocol. Effectively, this banned all US battleships from New Zealand ports, causing a diplomatic row and ending the prospective ANZUS treaty.

Without nuclear power, New Zealand still produces an impressive 75% of its electricity from renewable sources. Hydropower accounts for about 70%, geothermal 6%, coal 5%, and the remainder from wind, natural gas, and biomass. In Palmerston North, the most prominent symbol of Kiwi interest in renewable energy is NZ Windfarms' Te Rere Hau turbine farm. Opened in May 2005, it is the largest wind farm in the southern hemisphere with 97 turbines.

11km east from Palmerston North. See www.nzwindfarms.co.nz for more information on the wind boom.

(25min., $8-10) and to Featherston (40min., $4). The **Masterson I-Site,** 316 Queen St., is the best source for local information. (☎370 0900; www.wairarapanz.com. Open M-F 8:30am-5pm, Sa-Su 10am-5pm.) The **DOC office** (☎377 0700; open M-F 8:30am-5pm), on South Rd., dispenses a wealth of information. **Banks** with **ATMs** (most open M-F 9:30am-4:30pm) and a **post shop** (in **Paper Plus;** open M-F 8am-5pm, Sa 9am-1pm) are located on the upper end of Queen St.

MARTINBOROUGH   ☎06

Wine connoisseurs and those with pretensions head to Martinborough to revel in its viniculture, reputed for its fine **pinot noirs.** High sunshine and low autumnal rainfall are key elements in cultivating choice vintages from the more than 25 area wineries. The weather also lends itself to long strolls through choice afternoons the diagonals of Martinborough's square, laid out by the town's loyal founder in the shape of a Union Jack. Before embarking on the wine trail, head to the **Martinborough I-Site,** on Kitchener St. (☎306 9043; www.wairarapanz.com; open M-F 9am-5pm, Sa-Su 10am-4pm), and the **Masterson I-Site** (p. 247); they provide maps and comprehensive information for your drinking pleasure. Well-respected year-round wineries include the **Palliser Estate,** on Kitchener St. (☎306 9019; www.palliser.co.nz; open daily 10:30am-4:30pm), **Martinborough Vineyard,** on Princess St. (☎306 9955; www.martinborough-vineyard.co.nz; open daily 11am-5pm), and **Alana Estate,** on Puruatanga Rd. (☎306 9784; www.alana.co.nz; open daily 10:30am-5pm.) The **Martinborough Fair** draws huge Wellington crowds (1st Sa of Feb. and Mar.), while **Toast Martinborough** (☎0800 000 575; www.toastmartinborough.co.nz; 3rd Su of Nov.) provides an opportunity to sample the region's gourmet food alongside paired wines. If you're short on time or transport, the **Martinborough Wine Centre,** 6 Kitchener St. (☎306 9040; www.martinboroughwinecentre.co.nz; open daily 10am-5pm), assembles the best regional vintages in one central location. Thirty-six kilometers south of Martinborough toward Cape Palliser, the ⊠**Putangirua Pinnacles,** a sculpted a badlands of spires and fluted cliffs, stand at attention watching over the desolate coastline. (1½hr. round-trip walk from the parking lot.) Another 20km, on a mostly gravel road, leads to the Cape Palliser lighthouse. The windswept coastline is home to one of North Island's largest **seal colonies.**

Contact the Martinborough i-Site for B&Bs and farmstays in the Martinborough area. In Featherston, 17km from Martinborough, the **Leeway Motel ❶,** 8 Fitzherbert St., offers well-maintained rooms near the train station. (☎308 9811 or 0800 533 929; www.leeway-complex.co.nz. No linen. Laundry $4. Reception 8am-8pm.

2-bed dorms $20 per person; motel units from $75, $85 for 2.) **Wairarapa Coach Lines** (☎308 9352; www.waicoach.co.nz) connects to Masterton four times daily and meets commuter trains in Featherston ($13). They also run a bus to Masterton (M-F 5 per day, $6). Booking is essential. **Tranzit Coachlines** (☎377 1227) also connects with **TranzMetro's** Wellington service on bus #200 and #205 in Masterton (M-F, $5).

TARARUA FOREST PARK   ☎06

There are some great hikes off the tourist radar in Tararua Forest Park. Covering 116,535 hectares and 75% of the Tararua Range, it was the first forest park established in New Zealand. Marked tracks meander through beech forests, alpine grasslands, and even leatherwood shrublands. The popular **Mt. Holdsworth Jumbo Tramp** (24km, 2-3 days round-trip) begins at **Mt. Holdsworth Lodge ❶**, 20min. west of Masterton off SH2, and climbs through bush to an exposed alpine ridge at 1,500m before winding back to the lodge. (Huts $10; tent sites $5.) The Class II **Waiohine River** runs though the Waiohine Gorge in the southeastern part of the Tararuas. A swing bridge crosses the river by the parking lot for the camping and recreation areas nearby, surrounded by rimu, beech, rata, and kahikatea trees. The **Cone Hut Track** (6hr. round-trip) climbs to a terrace of the Tauherenikau River. Though the **Holdsworth Road**, south of Masterton off SH2, and the **Waiohine Gorge Road**, south of Carterton, are the park's main eastern access points, but **Kiriwhakapapa Road,** just south of Mt. Bruce, on the east side, also leads to trailheads. The **Southern Crossing** (6-7 days round-trip) traverses the Tararuas, but arranging transport is difficult. Get hut tickets from the **DOC** in Masterton on South Rd. across from the Aerodrome (☎377 0700; open M-F 8am-5pm), the Holdsworth ranger (☎377 0022), or local visitors centers. For further information about the Tararua Ranges, check out www.tararua.net.

PALMERSTON NORTH   ☎06

About 40% of Palmerston North's 78,000 residents are involved in higher education, giving credence to its nickname, "Student City." Home to the main campus of Massey University, New Zealand's second-largest university, and a host of other schools, "Palmy" is more of a transportation hub than a top destination. However, students of the wind may be interested in checking out the largest turbine wind farm in the southern hemisphere, just a few kilometers from downtown Palmy.

▐ TRANSPORTATION

Trains: TranzMetro (☎04 801 7000) runs to **Wellington** (M-F) via the **Kapiti Coast. TranzScenic** (☎0800 872 467) leaves from the railway station on Matthews Ave. off Tremaine Ave., a 20min. walk from The Square. Trains go to **Auckland** (8½hr.; 11am, 11:10pm; $66-132) via **National Park** ($26-52) and **Hamilton** ($50-100).

Buses: Buses leave from the **Travel Centre** (☎355 5633) at Pitt and Main St. **InterCity/Newmans** goes to: **Auckland** (8-10hr., 78 per day, $36-73); **Masterton** (1¾hr., 1 per day, $18-23); **New Plymouth** (4hr., 3 per day, $27-40) via **Wanganui** (1½hr., $10-17); **Rotorua** (5hr., 4 per day, $21-55) via **Taupo** (4hr., $47); **Wellington** (2hr., 8 per day, $17-28). **White Star** (☎358 8777) leaves from opposite the courthouse on Main St. and runs to **New Plymouth** (4hr., 1-2 per day, $30) via **Wanganui** (1hr., $13) and **Stratford** (3¼hr., $26), and to **Wellington** (2hr., 1-2 per day, $20).

Taxis: Palmerston North Taxis (☎355 5333).

Hitchhiking: Though hitchhiking is not recommended by *Let's Go,* hitchhikers report finding rides along any of the main roads. Rangitikei St. joins SH1 at Bulls, heading toward the volcanic heartland and Auckland. Napier Rd./SH3 (Main St. East) heads to Napier. Farther along, Main St. West and Fitzherbert Ave. both head to Wellington.

WELLINGTON AND AROUND

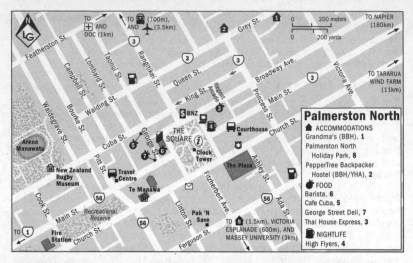

Palmerston North
♠ ACCOMMODATIONS
Grandma's (BBH), 1
Palmerston North
  Holiday Park, 8
PepperTree Backpacker
  Hostel (BBH/YHA), 2
🍴 FOOD
Barista, 6
Cafe Cuba, 5
George Street Deli, 7
Thai House Express, 3
🎵 NIGHTLIFE
High Flyers, 4

◄▶▍ ORIENTATION AND PRACTICAL INFORMATION

Downtown is centered around **The Square,** Palmerston North's well-kept green space. **Rangitikei Street** heads north, while **Fitzherbert Avenue** leads south toward the Manawatu River. **Main** and **Church Streets** head east and west from The Square.

Visitors Center: Palmerston North i-Site, The Square (☎350 1922; www.manawatunz.co.nz) has a huge topographical map of the area. Open daily 9am-5pm.

Department of Conservation (DOC): 717 Tremaine Ave. (☎350 9700), 1km from Rangitikei. Open M-F 8am-4:30pm.

Banks: BNZ (☎358 4149), at the corner of The Square and Rangitikei St. Open M and Th-F 9am-4:30pm, Tu-W 9:30am-4:30pm.

Library and Internet Access: The $13 million ▨**library** (☎351 4100), on The Square, has public showers and Internet ($2 per hr.), as well as the cheapest snacks in the city at their cafe. Open M-Tu and Th 10am-6pm, W and F 10am-8pm, Sa 10am-4pm, Su 1-4pm. **iCafe** (☎357 4578), on The Square between Broadway and Main St., has access for $3 per hr. Open M-Th 9am-11pm, F-Su 24hr.

Police: (☎351 3600), on Church St., off the corner of The Square by McDonald's.

Medical Services: Smart Pharmacy, 120 The Square (☎354 5659). Open daily 8am-8pm. **Palmerston North Hospital,** 50 Ruahine St. (☎356 9169).

Post Office: 338 Church St. (☎353 6900). Poste Restante. Open M-F 8am-6pm, Sa 9:30am-12:30pm.

◄▍◄▍ ACCOMMODATIONS AND CAMPING

Palmerston North's few budget accommodations and plentiful motels along **Fitzherbert Avenue** are not the usual backpackers' fare. For a more collegiate experience, check the availability of dorms at **Massey University.** (☎350 5056; k.l.macey@massey.ac.nz. Singles from $30.)

PepperTree Backpacker Hostel (BBH/YHA), 121 Grey St. (☎355 4054; peppertreehostel@clear.net.nz), at the corner of Princess St. The friendly host, Cherie, keeps the PepperTree spotless, making it the best and busiest hostel in town. Laundry $4. Key deposit $20. Dorms $23; singles $48; twins and doubles $50. BBH/YHA discount. ❷

Palmerston North Holiday Park, 133 Dittmer Dr. (☎358 0349). From Fitzherbert Ave., turn right on Park Rd. toward the Esplanade, then turn left on Ruha St. More trailer than tent friendly, but the facilities are sparkling clean. Tent and powered sites $12. 2-person cabins $24-60. ❶

Grandma's (BBH), 146 Grey St. (☎358 6928). Run by grandma herself. Furniture and bedding straight from the 60s. Laundry $5. Reception 2 doors down across the street. Dorms $20; singles $40; doubles $50. $2 BBH discount. ❷

🕯🍽 FOOD AND NIGHTLIFE

Student City has loads of cheaps eats. The nightlife, however, is sadly lackluster with the exception of Saturday rugby, in which case the locals begin drinking by 3pm. **George Street,** home to funky cafes with long hours, is worth a wander. **The Square** is home to most of the 10 bars in town. Stock up on foodstuffs at **Pak 'N Save,** 335 Ferguson St. (☎356 4043. Open daily 8am-midnight.)

🍴 **Cafe Cuba,** (☎356 5750) at the corner of George and Cuba St. Fresh salads ($3-10), sandwiches ($5-12), and smoothies ($6) consistently bring in the crowds. Open daily 9am-8pm. Cash only. ❶

Thai House Express, 80A Broadway Ave. (☎353 7841). With mains all under $8.50, no one can beat the spice for the price. Open daily 10am-9pm. MC/V. ❶

Barista, 77 George St. (☎357 2614). A real find on George St.'s stretch of cool cafes. Start the day right with Barista's superb coffee ($2-4) and the heart-stopping English breakfast ($17.50), a smorgasbord of all your favorite breakfast goodies. Open daily 8am-midnight. MC/V. ❷

High Flyers (☎357 5155), at the corner of Main St. East and The Square. "Where everybody is somebody." This giant bar is home to the bulk of the local drinkers. A tidy crowd boogies down to DJs Th-Sa. Dress code enforced. Happy hour 5-7pm. Open Su-W 11am-10pm, Th-Sa 11am-3am. MC/V. ❶

👁🏔 SIGHTS AND OUTDOOR ACTIVITIES

Paying homage to the pinnacle of sport, the **New Zealand Rugby Museum,** 87 Cuba St., enshrines The Game one block north and several west of The Square. (☎358 6947; www.rugbymuseum.co.nz. Open M-Sa 10am-noon, 1:30-4pm, Su 1:30-4pm. $4.) On Saturdays in winter, you can watch the real thing at the outdoor **Arena Manawatu** next door.

For more traditional cultural pursuits, disregard the oversized bronze beetles creeping over the roof of the **Manawatu Art Gallery,** 398 Main St. West, and venture inside to view contemporary works by New Zealand artists. (☎358 8188. Free.) The gallery is part of the **Te Manawa** complex, which also includes the **Manawatu Museum and Science Centre,** with rotating exhibits and interactive science displays. (☎355 5000; www.temanawa.co.nz. All open 10am-5pm. Admission to "life" and "art" galleries free; $8, children $5 for "mind" gallery.) **City Rock Adventures,** 217 Featherston St., has indoor **rock climbing** and organizes trips to go caving, canyoning, kayaking, and even bridge-swinging. (☎357 4552. Open M-F 3:30-10pm, Sa-Su 10am-10pm. Climbing $11. Other activities from $15.)

Agricultural enthusiasts disappointed by the overly commercial farm shows in Rotorua should head 15km north of Palmy to **Feilding,** a town with no traffic lights or parking meters, and home to the popular kiwi band Evermore. **The Feilding Info Centre** on Manchester Sq. (☎323 3318; www.feilding.co.nz) provides info on free farm visits in the area. It also books tours of the **Feilding Saleyards,** one of the largest livestock saleyards in the Southern Hemisphere.

MARLBOROUGH AND NELSON

Stretching from the tip of Farewell Spit to the tranquil Marlborough Sounds, the "top of the South" provides visitors with an incredible variety of ecosystems and endless ways to enjoy them. Popular yet pristine, the region presents a choice between taking advantage of the well-developed tourism infrastructure or escaping to the majestic seclusion of the sounds.

▨ MARLBOROUGH AND NELSON HIGHLIGHTS

FROLIC in the shifting sands and turquoise waters of the **Farewell Spit** (p. 290), the northern most point of South Island.

FORGET your troubles in one of **Marlborough's** (p. 265) award-winning wines.

FURROW your brow at the outlandish costumes at the renowned Wearable Art Awards in **Nelson** (p. 274).

MARLBOROUGH

PICTON AND THE MARLBOROUGH SOUNDS
☎ 03

A grand maze of waterways at South Island's northeastern extremity, the Marlborough Sounds, harbor ample sea life and green peaks amid thousands of beautiful coves. While the multi-day Queen Charlotte Track (p. 260) is the best known and most tramped attraction, the area's kayaking, fishing, and marine life draw increasing numbers onto and into the water of the Sounds.

⮐ TRANSPORTATION

Flights: Koromiko airstrip is about 5km south of Picton. **Sounds Air** (☎520 3080 or 0800 505 005; www.soundsair.com), headquartered in the train station with TranzScenic (see below) has daily flights to **Wellington** (25min., up to 8 per day 8:30am-7pm, $59-79). Free shuttle to and from the airstrip. Office open daily 7:30am-5:30pm.

Trains: All trains depart from the **train station,** 3 Auckland St. across from the Picton i-Site. **TranzScenic** (☎0800 872 467) has backpacker carriages available. Trains run to **Christchurch** (5½hr., 1pm, $59-99) via **Kaikoura** (2½hr., $28-55). Bookings can be made at the Picton i-Site or through Sounds Air at the train station.

Buses: InterCity (☎573 7025; www.intercitycoach.co.nz) runs from the ferry terminal to **Christchurch** (5½hr., 2 per day, $38-51) via **Blenheim** (30min., 4 per day, $10-13) and **Kaikoura** (2hr., $24-32), and to **Nelson** (3hr., 3 per day, $24-32). Book early for Super Saver Tickets.

Interisland Ferries: Interislander Ferry (☎0800 802 802; www.interislander.co.nz), in the ferry terminal on Auckland St., goes to **Wellington** (3hr., 5-6 per day 5:45am-10:05pm, $45-75, children $18-43; cars from $99). **Bluebridge** (☎0800 844 844;

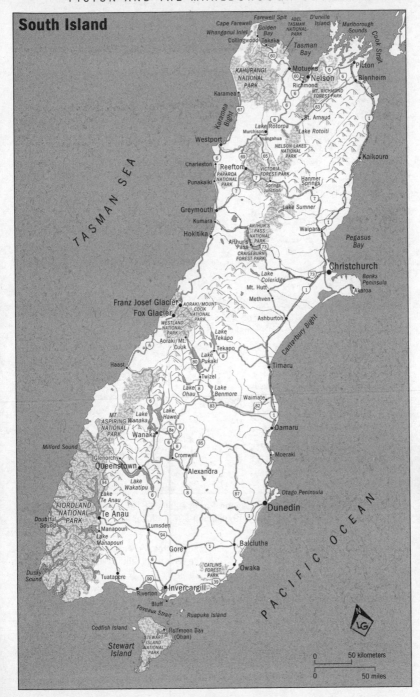

South Island

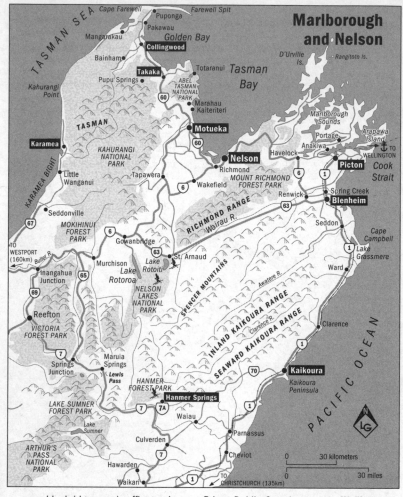

Marlborough and Nelson

www.bluebridge.co.nz), office on Lagoon Rd. at Dublin St., also goes to **Wellington**. Book ahead. (3½hr.; 2-4 per day; $49, children $25, with car $120.)

Taxis: Red Band Taxis (☎577 2072).

Car Rental: Pegasus (☎0800 803 580) across the street on Auckland St., just before the Picton i-Site; **Ace** (☎0800 422 373), in the ferry terminal also has cheap rentals (from $29 per day).

Water Taxis: All transportation departs from the **Foreshore** in Picton, between Wellington St. and the footbridge. **Ferry** services provide the best transport around the sounds. The following 3 companies all offer drop-off and pickup along the Queen Charlotte Track for hikers and day walkers. Prices and services are comparable and most trampers pick a company based on scheduled time. The first 3 companies listed also provide pack transport for the Queen Charlotte Track (p. 260). The first 3 companies also offer a wide range of cruise and hike options; inquire at their offices or the i-Site for further details.

Cougar Line (☎573 7925 or 0800 504 090; www.cougarlinecruises.co.nz) departs for Ship Cove daily in summer at 8, 10am and 1:30pm; in winter 9am and 1:30pm. Queen Charlotte Track: full-day $63, half day $50, twilight cruise $63, round-trip transportation with pack transport $90.

Endeavour Express (☎579 8465; www.boatrides.co.nz) departs daily for Ship Cove 9, 10am and 1:15pm. Queen Charlotte Track: full-day $45-55, depending on section of the track; round-trip transportation with pack transport $80.

Beachcomber Cruises (☎573 6175 or 0800 624 526; www.mailboat.co.nz) departs daily for Ship Cove 9:30am. Queen Charlotte Track: one-day walk $40-55, depending on section of the track hiked; round-trip transportation with pack transport $88, often discounted if booked through your accommodation. The Beachcomber also runs mail cruises and kayak trips.

West Bay Water Transport (☎573 5597; www.westbay.co.nz), office at the ferry terminal, runs 3-5 times daily depending on the season: Anakiwa ($35); Te Mahia Resort ($25), Torea Wharf ($25). They are also available for charter at much higher rates.

◢◪ ORIENTATION AND PRACTICAL INFORMATION

In Picton, the ferry terminal and other crucial transportation links line the harbor area known as the **Foreshore. Auckland Street** is the transport hub in Picton, while **High Street** is home to **Mariner's Mall** and many of the town's shops and cafes. Residential neighborhoods stretch up into the hills. The scenic, paved 35km **Queen Charlotte Drive** connects Picton to Havelock, a small town with some quality budget accommodations and restaurants. Cyclists should avoid Queen Charlotte Drive as there is no shoulder and accidents are frequent. To access the more remote parts of the Sounds, water transport or tramping are the only options, see above for water taxi information. While *Let's Go* does not recommend **hitchhiking**, hitchhikers report that it's not too hard to find rides heading south along the drive.

Visitors Center: Picton i-Site (☎520 3113; www.destinationmarlborough.com), across from the railway station on Auckland St. and the Foreshore. Check here for up-to-date weather forecasts. Open M-F 8:30am-5pm, Sa-Su 9am-4pm.

DOC office: (☎520 3002) inside the Picton i-Site. DOC staffed in summer daily 8:30am-5pm.

Banks and Currency Exchange: BNZ, 56-8 High St., has an 24hr. **ATM.** Open M and Th-F 9am-4:30pm, Tu-W 9:30am-4:30pm. **4 Square,** 49 High St. (☎573 6443), will change money after hours. Open daily 7:30am-9pm.

Police: 36 Broadway St. (☎520 3120).

Medical Services: Picton Medical Centre, 71 High St. (☎573 6092). After hours this number connects straight to the Blenheim Hospital. Open M-F 8:30am-5:30pm, Sa 9am-noon. **Picton Healthcare,** 6 High St. (☎573 6420). Open M-F 8am-6pm; extended summer hours.

Library: 67 High St. (☎578 2784). Open M-Th 8am-5pm, F 8am-5:30pm, Sa 10am-1pm.

Internet Access: Connex i-C@fe, 100 High St. (☎573 6613; www.connexicafe.co.nz), in the Mariner's Mall. Internet $2.50 per 30min., laptops $6 per hr. Open daily 10am-10pm, from 6-10pm enter through the rear parking lot.

Post Office: (☎573 6900), in Mariner's Mall. Open Oct.-Apr. M-F 8:30am-5pm, Sa 9:30am-12:30pm. May-Sept. M-F 8:30am-5pm, Sa 10am-noon.

◤ ACCOMMODATIONS

While the towns of Picton and Havelock can be accessed by road, travelers looking to get away from it all should consider a water taxi to the isolated accommoda-

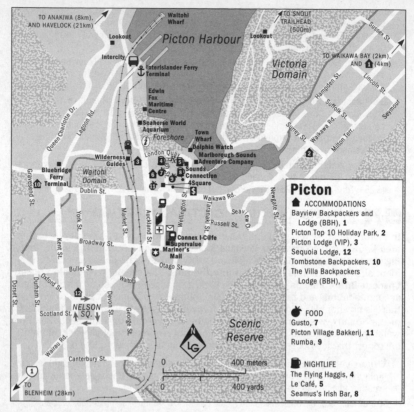

Picton

Picton Harbour

TO ANAKIWA (8km), AND HAVELOCK (21km)

Waitohi Wharf

TO SNOUT TRAILHEAD (500m)

Lookout

Lookout

Intercity

Interislander Ferry Terminal

Victoria Domain

TO WAIKAWA BAY (2km), AND (4km)

Edwin Fox Maritime Centre

Seahorse World Aquarium

Foreshore

Town Wharf

Dolphin Watch

Marlborough Sounds Adventure Company

Wilderness Guides

London Quay

Sounds Connection

4Square

Bluebridge Ferry Terminal

Waitohi Domain

Dublin St.

Waikawa Rd.

Queen Charlotte Dr.

Lagoon Rd.

Gravesend St.

York St.

Kent St.

Market St.

Broadway St.

Buller St.

Auckland St.

Wellington St.

Taranaki St.

Russell St.

Otago St.

Connex I-C@fe

Supervalue

Mariner's Mall

Seav...

Newgate St.

Surrey St.

Waikawa Rd.

Hampden St.

Suffolk St.

Lincoln St.

Seymour

Milton Terr.

Sussex St.

Dorset St.

Oxford St.

Durham St.

Scotland St.

NELSON SQ.

Devon St.

George St.

Waitohi

Wairau Rd.

Canterbury St.

Scenic Reserve

TO BLENHEIM (28km)

0   400 meters
0   400 yards

Picton

♠ ACCOMMODATIONS
Bayview Backpackers and Lodge (BBH), 1
Picton Top 10 Holiday Park, 2
Picton Lodge (VIP), 3
Sequoia Lodge, 12
Tombstone Backpackers, 10
The Villa Backpackers Lodge (BBH), 6

🍴 FOOD
Gusto, 7
Picton Village Bakkerij, 11
Rumba, 9

🍸 NIGHTLIFE
The Flying Haggis, 4
Le Café, 5
Seamus's Irish Bar, 8

tions on the Queen Charlotte Track (p. 260). For campers, the DOC maintains about 40 **campsites ❶,** ($6 per person, under 14 $1.50) throughout the Sounds. All have toilets and untreated water. The Marlborough Sounds: A Guide to Conservation Areas pamphlet ($1), available at DOC offices, contains a complete listing.

🛏 Hopewell Backpackers Lodge (BBH), (☎573 4341; www.hopewell.co.nz), in Kenepuru Sounds, is a full-service eco-retreat far removed from the tourist bustle. Amenities include kayaks and rowboats, a hot tub overlooking the sound ($5), fishing supplies ($5), and a private beach. If you're driving from Picton, take Queen Charlotte Dr. west, turn right onto Kenepuru Rd. at Linkwater, and continue on for 75km (2½-3hr.). Alternatively, book a ferry-car-ferry combo ($80 round-trip) through **West Bay.** Water taxi from Te Mahia round-trip $40. 4-bed dorms $26; twins $54-64; ensuite $84; doubles $64/84. Self-contained cottage $130 for up to 4 people, extra person $25. MC/V. ❸

🛏 The Villa Backpackers Lodge (BBH), 34 Auckland St. (☎573 6598; www.thevilla.co.nz), in Picton. Uncommon amenities raise this restored villa from standard to stellar: pickup, breakfast, apple crumble and ice cream in winter, bicycles, fishing gear, and spa included. Reception 8:15am-2pm and 4:30-9:30pm. Book ahead. Dorms $23-28; doubles and twins $61, with bath $70. $3 BBH discount. MC/V. ❷

Tombstone Backpackers (BBH), 16 Gravesend Pl. (☎573 7116 or 0800 573 7116; www.tombstonebp.co.nz), just off Dublin St. west of Picton. Across from a cemetery,

MARLBOROUGH AND NELSON

this backpackers carries the theme with haunting touches such as a tombstone door and skulls on the keychains. Piano and guitar, pool table, state-of-the-art barbeque, free continental breakfast. Free pickup and drop-off. Single-sex dorms $25; twins and doubles $62, ensuite $68. $2-3 BBH discount. MC/V. ❷

Blue Moon, 48 Main Rd. (☎574 2212; asha@bluemoon-havelock.co.nz), in Havelock. Run by laidback locals, Blue Moon is a great way to get a taste of life in the Sounds. The hosts, Shane and Asha, often grill fresh fish. WWOOFing by prior arrangement. Dorms $23; twins and doubles $52. $3 BBH discount per person. Cash only. ❷

Bayview Backpackers and Lodge (BBH), 318 Waikawa Rd. (☎573 7668; www.truenz.co.nz/bayviewbackpackers), 4km east of Picton. Two-story Bayview has the best views in town and comfy dorms and lambs out back. Free pickup. Free use of kayaks and bikes. Dorms $23; singles $50; twins and doubles $56. New lodge next door has ensuite doubles ($70) and triples ($78). $3 BBH discount. MC/V. ❷

Sequoia Lodge, 3 Nelson Sq. (☎573 8399 or 0800 222 257; www.sequoialodge.co.nz), in Picton. The clean, quiet rooms and staff that can book most of your travel needs compensates for this hostel's inconvenient location on the outskirts of town. Free pickup. Reception 8am-1:30pm and 3:30-9pm. Dorms $23-24; twins and doubles $58, ensuite from $70. Cash only. ❷

Picton Lodge (VIP), 9 Auckland St. (☎573 7788 or 0800 223 367; www.pictonlodge.co.nz). The closest hostel to the ferry, Picton Lodge is a convenient place to crash before heading north or south. Free pickup. Free bike use. Reception 8am-10:30pm. Dorms $22-24; twins and doubles $55. $1 VIP discount. ❷

Atlantis Backpackers (☎573 7390 or 0800 423 676; www.atlantishostel.co.nz), London Quay and Auckland St. in Picton. Live and party like a college student at this large hostel that draws a younger, wilder crowd than other hostels. Free pickup and continental breakfast. Heated pool and pool table. Good bikes for hire half-day $25, full-day $40. Reception 8am-10pm. Dorms $17-21; twins $46; doubles $50. Cash only. ❷

Rutherford (YHA), 46 Main Rd. (☎574 2104 or 027 230 9931; yhahave@yha.org.nz). This hostel offers basic amenities and rooms on the main strip in Havelock. Reception 8am-10pm. Beds from $22; rooms from $50. ❷

The Wedgewood House (YHA), 10 Dublin St. (☎573 7797; wedgewoodhouse@xtra.co.nz), in Picton. This sterile lodge has a large wooden porch and a miniscule kitchen. Pickup and in-room lockers. Reception 8-10am, 1-2pm, 5-6:30pm, 8-10pm. Dorms from $21; doubles and twins from $52. MC/V. ❷

FLEX YOUR MUSSELS

Mussel farming is big business in the Marlborough Sounds. While restaurants in the area charge top dollar for steamed mussels, the savvy traveler can make their own mussels on the cheap.

1. Rent a kayak and paddle into the Sounds.

2. Pick mussels from areas without heavy boat traffic. The less polluted the water, the better the mussels.

3. Choose mussels that are in the water even at low tide and make sure shells are at least 8cm in length.

4. Yank mussels off the rocks. Be aware that you may have a crab or two mixed in. Calmly brush the crabs back into the water (or shriek hysterically and flick them away).

5. Take only what you can eat, typically 15-20 per person.

6. Back in the kitchen, use a table knife to scrape off barnacles and sea debris. Rinse the mussels.

7. Throw a dry white wine (preferably a local vintage), cream, peeled garlic, and chopped onions into a big pot and heat to a simmer.

8. Steam those mussels. Shells should open easily.

9. Bon appetit!

10. After your meal, return the mussel shells to the sea.

Picton Top 10 Holiday Park, 70-78 Waikawa Rd. (☎573 7212 or 0800 277 299; www.pictontop10.co.nz). In a line-up of indistinguishable holiday parks, Picton is a standout with clean, modern cabins and a great hillside location. Spa for 2 people $10. Reception 8am-9:30pm. Tent sites $15, children $8; powered sites $34; 2-person cabins from $50, with kitchen from $70, ensuite from $80. ❶

⛏ FOOD

Picton supports plenty of restaurants with local character to spare. Waterfront **London Quay** has upscale dining, while **High Street** has budget eats. **Supervalue,** in the Mariner's Mall, supplies groceries. (☎573 0463. Open daily 7:30am-7:30pm.)

▨ **Picton Village Bakkerij,** 46 Auckland St. (☎573 7082), at Dublin St. This Dutch bakery has baked goods. Grab a sandwich or baguette before a long hike or treat yourself to one of their sweets afterward. Quality sandwiches $3-6. Meat pies, veggie options, and sweets, as well. Open daily 6am-3:30pm. Cash only. ❶

▨ **Mussel Pot,** 73 Main Rd. (☎574 2824; musselpot@xtra.co.nz), in Havelock. Sample Marlborough's signature green-lipped mussels in creative sauces. Mussels steamed on whole shell or grilled on half-shell for $17. Open daily 10:30am-9pm. Cash only. ❸

Rumba, 32 High St. (☎573 7040), is a raucous cafe with hot meals for backpackers for $10 daily 5-7pm. Thirsty Th handles 4:30pm-close. Toss the Boss F 7-8pm. Open daily 8am-as early as 10pm and as late as 2am; in winter 9am-late. ❷

Gusto, 33 High St. (☎573 7171). Enjoy a savory or sweet snack ($3-5.50) and a cup of Picton's finest tea or coffee ($3-5). Alternatively, splurge on a menu meal, such as squid marinated in coriander chili ($15). Emphasis on local seafood and meat. Open daily 8am-late, kitchen closes 9:30pm; in winter Su-F 8am-3pm. ❸

The Dog and Frog Cafe, 22 High St. (☎573 5650). A smattering of amphibious statues and pudgy stuffed animals complement the filling, all-day brekkie ($12.50) and sweet treats ($6.50). Open daily 7:30am-as late as 1am. ❷

ⓖ 🎿 SIGHTS AND OUTDOOR ACTIVITIES

Rainy day activities are hard to come by, although Picton's new **Seahorse World Aquarium,** at Dunbar Wharf, brings the outside inside for the unlucky. The same building also houses a small movie theater. (☎573 6030; www.seahorseworld.co.nz. Open daily 8:30am-8pm. $16, children $9. Movies $14/11.)

KAYAKING, MOUNTAIN BIKING, AND COMBO TOURS. Marlborough Sounds Adventure Company, on the Town Wharf in Picton, has excellent guides and the most comprehensive lineup of tours, rentals and services, from half-day kayaks to five-day guided trips on the Queen Charlotte Track. Their ▨**3-day hike/kayak/ mountain bike trip** is the best way to sample the Sounds on a tight budget and schedule. (☎573 6078 or 0800 283 283; www.marlboroughsounds.co.nz. Mountain bike rentals $50 per day. Kayak $50 per day, $40 per day for multi-day rental. Half-day and twilight kayak $65, full-day $95. 3-4 day guided kayak trips from $495, including meals and accommodations. 3-in-1 hike/kayak/mountain bike $495, includes accommodation and packed lunches.) **Wilderness Guides,** 3 Auckland St., has a similar lineup of tours. (☎520 3095 or 0800 266 266; www.wildernessguidesnz.com. Kayak rental $40 per day, $30 per day after 2nd day. Half-day kayak $60, full-day $90. One-day kayak and mountain bike combo $130. One-day kayak and hike combo $115. All day trips include lunch.) The most ambitious one-day trip is operated by **Adventure Tours Down Under,** 1 Auckland St. ($210, includes lunch.) It includes jet skiing, mountain biking, and walking or sea kayaking. (☎573 8565 or 021 340 011; www.toursdownunder.com.) **Pacific Coast Kayaks** is based at Anakiwa at the end of the Queen Charlotte Track and is a good option for those wanting to kayak more remote areas of the Sounds, as they provide flexible pickup and dropoff options. (☎574 2765; www.NZSeaKayaking.co.nz. Kayak $25 per 2½hr. $35 per half-day, $60 per full-day. Discounts on day rate for multi-day rentals. Guided tours from $39.)

In addition to water taxi services and mail runs (see below), **Beachcomber** runs a popular sunset sea kayak and barbeque beach party kayak trip. (☎573 6175 or 0800 624 526; www.mailboat.co.nz. Guided one-day kayak trip with taxi transport into the Sounds $80. Sunset sea kayak and barbeque beach party 4:30-9pm $80, includes food and "a few" free drinks. Book early for the barbeque.)

MAIL BOAT TOURS. The unique water delivery of the Marlborough Sounds post offers travelers the chance to come aboard and live the postal dream. Mail boats, **Beachcomber**, in Picton, and **Pelorus**, in Havelock, make the watery rounds. (Beachcomber: ☎573 6175 or 0800 624 526; www.mailboat.co.nz. Wide variety of mail runs from $75. Pelorus: ☎574 1088; www.mail-boat.co.nz. Tu, Th, F 9:30am. $105.)

WILDLIFE TOURS. ◙**Dolphin Watch Ecotours,** on the wharf next to the water taxi companies in Picton, runs a swim with dusky dolphins as well as eco-tours to bird life sanctuary Motuara Island and historic Ship Cove that encounter penguins and dolphins along the way. The guides are all knowledgeable marine biologists. (☎573 5456 or 0800 9453 5433; www.naturetours.co.nz. Warm jacket and sturdy footwear recommended. Weather dependent. Wildlife tours from $75, children from $45. Dolphin swimming $125, spectators $80.) For a balanced mix of myth and reality, consider a **Myths and Legends Eco-Tour** with Pete, Takutai, and Tane. The fun guides have a fabulous 73-year-old Tutanekai boat that perfectly complements a day of learning about Maori traditions and seeing dolphins, seals, and rare birds. (☎573 6901; www.eco-tours.co.nz. Tours on demand. Half-day tours $130; full-day themed cruises like "Captain Cook's Cruise" and "Whale of a Tale" $200.)

Learn about mussels as well as the local wines that best complement them on the **Greenshell Mussel Cruise.** (☎577 9997 or 0800 990 800; www.mtrav.co.nz. Departs from Havelock, Picton, or Portage Bay Resort. $95 from Havelock or Portage, $125 from Picton.) **Sea Safaris** cruises to the outer Marlborough Sounds and d'Urville Island from French Pass to spot birds, seals, dolphins, and more. (To reach French Pass, take State Highway 6, it is about 2½hr. ☎576 5204; www.SeaSafaris.co.nz. Dolphin and seal swim $110, children $90; spectators $75/50. Outer Island Bird Tour $75, children $45.)

FISHING AND SAILING. Sounds Connection, 10 London Quay, runs scheduled and chartered tours. (☎573 8843 or 0800 742 866; www.soundsconnection.co.nz. Half-day from $79.) **Toa Tai Charters** guides half-day fishing and hunting trips and even throws in a barbeque meal. (☎573 7883; www.soundsfishing.co.nz. Half-day, usually 11am-5pm, from $70.) **Huntfish** has heli-fishing tours. (☎575 7604 or 027 541 3801; www.huntfish.co.nz. Heli-fishing tours from $190.) Contact **Go Sailing Picton.** (☎027 473 4886; www.gosailingpicton.co.nz. Min. 2 people. Personalized 2hr. trips from $55 per person. Longer trip options available.)

DIVING. Dive Marlborough, at Waikawa Marina on Beach Rd. off Waikawa Rd., organizes dives to local reefs and the **Mikhail Lermontov shipwreck,** one of the largest wrecks open to divers in the world. (☎0800 463 483; www.godive.co.nz. Max. 6 people. Half-day diving $165; full-day, including Lermontov Wreck $250. PADI certification courses available.) After plunging into the water, take to the air with **Skydive the Sounds** at Koromiko airstrip. (☎573 9101 or 0800 373 1648; www.skydivethesounds.com. Pickup from Picton available. 9000 ft. $245; 12000 ft. $295; additional $155 for DVD and pictures.)

MARLBOROUGH AND NELSON

WINE TOURS. Wine connoisseurs explore the Marlborough region's famous **wineries** on a flexible itinerary with the knowledgeable guides of ▨**Sounds Connection.** (☎573 8843 or 0800 742 866; www.soundsconnection.co.nz. Half-day tour departs 1:30pm $55, full-day departs 10:30am $69. Gourmet tours Nov.-Apr. $149, includes 4-course lunch.) **Waka Whenua** has less structured tours based on demand. (☎573 7877 or 021 133 5946; www.marlboroughtours.co.nz. Half-day $45-50; full-day $60.)

DAY HIKES. Many visitors to Picton come to tramp the 71km **Queen Charlotte Track** (p. 260), but there are a number of short hikes around Picton. The most popular is the **Snout Track** (2hr. one-way from the Picton foreshore, 1½hr. from the trailhead carpark on Sussex St. off Waikawa Rd.). The trail passes **Victoria Domain,** then the **Queen Charlotte Lookout** on its way to **The Snout,** a rocky promontory which overlooks Queen Chorlotte Sound and Waikawa Bay.

▨ NIGHTLIFE

Picton and the Marlborough Sounds are a far cry from the nightlife of urban Christchurch, or even Nelson. However, travelers in search of a cheap pint and some local character will not be disappointed.

▨ **Seamus's Irish Bar,** 25 Wellington St. (☎573 8994 or 027 252 6935). This "traditional Irish nook" is a far cry from the pseudo-Irish bars that are a staple of backpacker life. The Irish staff, traditional Irish music, cheap pints (Guinness $7), and singing drunks. M jam session 8:30-11pm. Pub meals $15. Open daily noon-1am.

The Flying Haggis, 27 High St. (☎573 6969). A Scottish bar with a wide range of malt whiskys and live celtic music most weekends. Cheap pub grub $4.50-10. Foosball table. Pints $4.60-7. Open daily noon-11pm.

Le Cafe, London Quay (☎573 5588; www.lecafepicton.co.nz). While the food at this cafe doesn't warrant accolades, the live music does. All major acts plays here, check out front for a list of upcoming shows. Dinner $18.50-29.50. Open daily 7:30am-10pm, earlier in winter.

▨ QUEEN CHARLOTTE TRACK

Acclaimed for its green and blue beauty, the **Queen Charlotte Track** is the crown jewel of the Marlborough Sounds. Though it is an easier tramp than rugged wilderness adventure, the full 71km track can at times be a challenging outdoor experience. The full track requires a minimum of three days, but (though sometimes pricey) those pressed for time do only part of the track. Thanks in part to its proximity to civilization, Queen Charlotte is the only track in New Zealand where most trampers have their gear transported for them. Moreover, a wide variety of accommodation options from basic camp sites to five-star resorts dot the trail. While diehard survivalists may be disappointed, outdoor enthusiasts will welcome the baggage transport as an opportunity to **run** or **mountain bike** along the trail.

Length: 71km, 3-5 days.

Altitude: 0 to 407m above sea level.

Trailheads: The track runs between **Ship Cove** in the east and **Anakiwa** in the west. Water taxis and luggage transport run from east to west, so most hikers chose to hike the track in that direction.

Transportation: The easiest transportation is by ferry. **Beachcomber, Endeavour,** and **Cougar** (see **Transportation,** p. 252) ferry companies deliver hikers to Ship Cove, transport packs to overnight stops, pick them up in Anakiwa, and take them back to Picton. From Anakiwa at the west end of the track, it is possible to return by land with **Coleman Post Ltd.,** which will run trampers to Picton or Havelock. (☎027 255 8882. Pre-booking essential. From $10 per person.) Though *Let's Go* never recommends it, hitchhikers report that rides are abundant from the parking lot at the Anakiwa end of the track.

Seasonality: Year-round for hiking. The track is also open to mountain bikes, though the section between Ship Cove and Kenepuru Saddle is closed to bikers Dec.-Feb. Droughts present the largest obstacle to traveling the trail, as many of the water sources on the trail are dependent on rainwater.

Campsites and Accommodations: 6 **DOC campsites** vary in amenities and seclusion (DOC $6 per night, children $1.50). All campsites have bathroom and untreated water. Only those noted have cooking shelters. It is recommended that water be filtered, treated, or boiled before drinking. No huts. For tent-averse hikers, numerous **private establishments** provide a variety of dorms and double rooms.

Gear Rental: If you need to rent gear or a mountain bike, contact **Marlborough Sounds Adventure Company** (see **Outdoor Activities,** p. 252). 2-person tent $15 per night, bed roll $1 per night; stove with fuel $5 per day; daypacks $5 per day; sleeping bags $5 per night. 2-person camp set (tent, bed rolls, stove, cutlery) $20 per night.

Storage: Most accommodations in Picton store for free; the visitors center charges $4 per bag per night. Parking is free on the street or $2 per day in the Council parking lot.

Guided Walks: Marlborough Sounds Adventure Company and **Wilderness Guides** lead guided tours of the track, which include accommodation, meals, and water transport. Prices start at $225. **Natural Encounters** specializes in guided walks. (☎021 268 8879; www.natural-encounters.com. Min. 2 people, max. 8 people. Runs on demand. Free pickup and dropoff. Guided one-day $155, includes lunch. Guided 4-day from $1150, includes accommodation, transport, and all meals.)

Mountain Biking: From Mar.-Nov. the whole track is open to mountain bikers. Dec.-Feb. the section from Ship Cove to Kenepuru Saddle. Estimated mountain biking times are: Ship Cove to Punga 4½-5hr., Punga Cove to Portage 3½-4hr., Portage-Anakiwa 3¼-4hr.

 WALK SOFTLY. The slower time is the DOC recommended time for those traveling at a leisurely pace. The faster time is for those who are not winded by inclines and rarely stop for photos. Also note that many accommodations are off the main track, sometimes by more than an hour.

SHIP COVE TO RESOLUTION BAY CABINS. *4.5km, 1½-2hr.* Ship Cove's **Captain Cook Monument** commemorates the many weeks the great navigator spent anchored here on five separate visits, harvesting scurvy-fighting grass for his crew and flogging those who refused it. As the trail climbs steeply to almost 200m over a small saddle, it passes through the track's finest primary forest. Five minutes off the track, **School House Bay Campsite** (DOC) has extra sites on Resolution Bay. The campsite is basic but pleasantly located next to a secluded cove. The sites are mostly used by west-to-east trampers. Farther downhill, at the rustic bungalows of **Resolution Bay Cabins and Bush Cafe ❶,** the shop is always open but is better stocked in the summer. Though few east-to-west hikers stay at Resolution Bay, the freshly baked muffins (Oct.-Apr. 9am-5pm; $3.50) are worth a pit stop. (☎579 9411. No electricity. Free kayak use. Linen $10. Tent sites $15, children $7; basic bunks $35-40; 2-person cottages with bath $140-160. Cash only.)

RESOLUTION BAY CABINS TO ENDEAVOUR INLET. *10.5km, 2¼-3hr.* Past Resolution Bay, the track climbs Tawa Saddle (200m) and then descends to a scattering of accommodations around the northern coast of Endeavour Inlet, traditionally the first stop for those hiking the track in four days. The new **Blue Water Lodge ❸** (☎579 8400 or 021 0222 6220; www.thebluewaterlodge.co.nz.) is a good option. (Bunk bed $35. Double $110, ensuite $130. Cash only). Tiny **Cnoc na Lear ❷,** greets

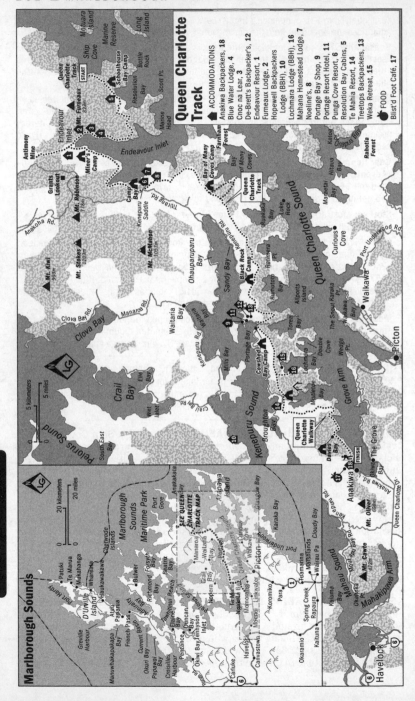

Marlborough Sounds

Queen Charlotte Track

▲ ACCOMMODATIONS

Anakiwa Backpackers, **18**
Blue Water Lodge, **4**
Cnoc na Lear, **3**
De-Brett's Backpacker's, **12**
Endeavour Resort, **1**
Furneaux Lodge, **2**
Hopewell Backpackers
   Lodge (BBH), **10**
Lochmara Lodge (BBH), **16**
Mahana Homestead Lodge, **7**
Noeline's, **8**
Portage Bay Shop, **9**
Portage Resort Hotel, **11**
Punga Cove Resort, **6**
Resolution Bay Cabins, **5**
Te Mahia Resort, **14**
Treetops Backpackers, **13**
Weka Retreat, **15**

▲ FOOD

Blist'd Foot Café, **17**

you with a warm muffin on arrival. The small backpackers only sleeps five, but there's free use of a double kayak and a fishing rod. (☎579 8444; www.cnocnalear.net.nz. Breakfast or packed lunch $10. Linen $5. $30 per person.) The area's other noteworthy accommodation is **Endeavour Resort and Fishing Lodge ❷**, where stunning gardens liven up the basic cabins. (☎579 8381; www.endeavourresort.co.nz. Free canoe and kayak use. Kitchen. Linen $5. Stocked shop. Dorms $30; 2-person cabins $75, self-contained units $125. Cash only.) At the head of Endeavour Inlet, a steep spur trail climbs into the bush to great views from the long-unused **antimony mines** (3½hr. round-trip).

ENDEAVOUR INLET TO CAMP BAY CAMPSITE. *13km, 3-4hr.* As the main track rounds **Big Bay**, its surroundings alternate between towering tree ferns and developed grazing land. This section of the track stays relatively close to sea level, making it the least strenuous section on the track. Not far after Endeavour Resort is the basic farmstay hut known as **The Woolshed ❷** (☎579 8398; adrienne.cathie@clear.net.nz. Meals available by arrangement. Breakfast and lunch $10, dinner $20. Bunk $30. Linen $5. Cash only.) Nearby is the privately run **Miners camp ❶** ($10, children $5; book through the Picton i-Site). After arriving in **Camp Bay** (DOC), a side-trail leads to three excellent accommodations; all are a short hike downhill, and a not-so-short uphill hike back, from an unpaved road. This area, known as Punga Cove, is the first stop for those hiking the trail in three days and the second for those hiking it in four. ▨**Mahana Homestead Lodge (BBH) ❷** isn't just a place to sleep. Owners John and Anne have created a recreational mecca with all the perks of a summer camp. Free use of a kayak, a dinghy, fishing gear, and a swimmable beach. The two-course evening meal is worth the $18, especially the chocolate cake. Breakfast ($10) and a packed lunch ($12) are also available. (☎579 8373; www.mahanahomestead.com. Linen $5. Dorms $33; doubles and twins $75. $5 BBH discount.) **Punga Cove Resort ❸** offers family-style luxury with a pool, spa, and beach-side trampoline. (☎579 8561; www.pungacove.co.nz. Restaurant. Kayaks $10 per hr. Spa and sauna free for guests, visitors $5. Dorms $35, with linen $47. Lodges and chalets from $115.) Up a hill, **Noeline's ❷** has five beds (four in the winter) and panoramic views. During low tide Noeline's is accessible via the beach past Mahana. Alternatively, take the path through Mahana and follow the pink triangles. (☎579 8375. Linen $5. 2-bed dorms $25. Cash only.)

CAMP BAY CAMPSITE TO COWSHED BAY CAMPSITE. *20.5km, 6-8hr.* The Camp Bay to Cowshed section is the longest and most isolated piece of the track. Bring plenty of water or plan to treat water from the campsites. Trampers can reach **Kenepuru Saddle** by a 15min. scramble from Camp Bay Campsite or a slightly longer track up an unpaved road from Mahana. This section of the track is generally considered the most arduous, as the trail rises and falls until arriving at it's high point of 400m. From the saddle, the track travels through scrubby vegetation before reaching the steep spur trail to ▨**Eatwells Lookout** (15min. straight uphill off the track), a 360° panorama that rewards the tough with a worthy lunch spot.

Thirty minutes of rolling track later, the **Bay of Many Coves Campsite** (DOC) has lofty sea views, a cooking shelter, and bumpy, kanuka-sheltered plots. The campsite is on the track, just shy of the ridge. Boat companies will not be able to deliver packs here until Kiwi ingenuity perfects a high-precision baggage cannon. From here, the track encounters tropical primary forests and trademark views, which encompass both Queen Charlotte and Kenepuru Sounds. **Black Rock Campsite** (DOC), also inaccessible by boat, has small, grassy sites, plus a handsome cooking gazebo that overlooks Kumutoto Bay and Picton. From here, the trail slowly descends to **Torea Saddle**, where the track passes a paved road. To get to the next patch of accommodations, make a right on the paved road and walk 10min. downhill to the **Portage Resort Hotel** ❸, with its two restaurants, swimming pool, spa, and 10-bed rooms. The informal **Snapper Cafe** ❷, has affordable meals for around $15 as well as an extensive mixed drink list from $12. (☎573 4309 or 0800 762 442; www.portage.co.nz. Dorms $36, with linen $46. Ensuite rooms from $175. MC/V.) Nearby, **Cowshed Bay Campsite** (DOC) is a caravan-heavy complex with major road access. Trampers can pick up their bags at the Portage Hotel. Two minutes from the Portage Hotel is lovely **De-Brett's Backpackers** ❸, a small family-run lodge. It offers immaculately clean and modern facilities for six and amazing views of the sounds from its wraparound decks. (☎573 4522. Baggage pickup included. Dorms $30, with linen $35. Cash only.) A little farther up the hill from DeBrett's is **Treetops Backpackers** ❸. (Baggage pickup included. Dorms $30, with linen $40. Cash only.) **Portage Bay Shop** (☎573 4445), on the far side of the Resort Hotel, has the most basic rooms, but has the advantage of being in the same complex as a takeaway and water-activity gear rental shop. (☎573 4445; www.portagecharters.co.nz. Mountain bikes $20 per hr., $35 per half-day, $50 per day. Canoes half-day $30, full day $40. Kayaks half-day $30, full-day $50. Fishing rods $15. Linen $10. Baggage pickup $5. Dorms $30; doubles $80, self-contained $120.)

COWSHED BAY CAMPSITE TO MISTLETOE BAY RESERVE. *7.5km, 2½-4hr.* Prepare yourself for a big climb as you ascend the 407m to get back onto the saddle. Once you've reached the ridgeline, the track crosses many switchbacks and passes the steep turn-offs Weka Retreat and Lochmara Lodge (40min. one-way). **Weka Retreat** ❷, down a very steep hill (40min. one-way, more on the uphill return; follow the trail down to the water, then facing the water turn right and take the trail up the stairs to the greenhouse) is a small, six-bed hostel in a local home. (☎573 4747 or 027 201 5113; www.wekaretreat.co.nz. Free dial-up Internet in the evenings. Shop with essentials. Dorm beds $25. One ensuite double room for $110. Cash only.) **Lochmara Lodge** ❸, is one of New Zealand's most renowned eco retreats. With an innumerable list of amenities and perks and plenty of budget-friendly options, Lochmara is worth the arduous detour. (☎573 4554; www.lochmaralodge.co.nz. Reception 8:30am-1:30pm and 5-7pm. Small store. Home-cooked meals available: breakfast and lunch $10-15, dinner $20-25. Lodge water taxi $25 each way. Double ensuite from $85. MC/V.) Past the turnoff for Lochmara is another spur trail to **Hilltop Lookout** (40min. round-trip), with great views over Kenepuru Sound, begins 30min. down the main trail.

MISTLETOE BAY RESERVE TO ANAKIWA. *12.5km, 3-4hr.* Beyond the trail junction for Mistletoe Bay, the track follows the road. Down a side road (20min. off the trail), the tropical **Te Mahia Resort** ❸ has private beach access, motel units, and a backpacker room with a piano. (☎/fax 573 4089. Laundry $4. Doubles from $115; extra person $35.) On the Queen Charlotte side of the saddle, the unpaved road leads to the **Mistletoe Bay Recreation Reserve,** with picnic facilities, secluded campsites and privately-run lodges. (☎573 4048; www.mistletoebay.co.nz. Camping $10, children $5. Water needs treating. Private cabin $120, off-season $80. Backpacker bunk $20. Cabin and backpackers includes linen.) Meanwhile, the main track leaves the road and follows Mistletoe Bay's length before descending to **Davies Bay Campsite** (DOC), situated on an estuary slightly off the path. About 45min. of level walking later, teeny **Anakiwa** marks the finish line; the small but bright and breezy **Anakiwa Backpackers (BBH)** ❶ sits right by the end of the track. Comfortable rooms reward weary trampers. (☎574 1388; www.anakiwabackpackers.co.nz. Dorms and twin shared rooms $25; doubles $54, self-contained $75. $3 BBH discount.) Many hikers enjoy a coffee and a snack at the **Blist'd Foot Cafe** ❶, 257 Anakiwa Rd., 300m past the Tirimoana jetty. (☎574 2627. Open daily 11am-4pm.)

BLENHEIM ☎ 03

While the town of Blenheim (pop. 28,400) itself is hardly worth a second glance, the wineries near to the town are some of New Zealand's finest. More frugal travelers in need of work see these same wineries as a gold mine, seeking vines in need of pruning and grapes in need of plucking.

▛ **TRANSPORTATION.** The **railway station,** which also serves as a **bus station,** is located on Grove Rd. **TranzScenic** (☎0800 872 467) goes to Christchurch (5hr., 1:33pm, $43-86) and Picton (30min., 12:45pm, $18). **InterCity** (☎577 8080) heads daily to: Christchurch (5hr., 2 per day, $25-55) via Kaikoura (1¾hr., $15-30); Nelson (1¾hr., 2 per day, $20-27); Picton (30min., 6 per day, $10-13). **Atomic Shuttles** (☎322-8883) travels to: Christchurch (5hr., 3 per day, $30); Greymouth (4½hr., 1-2 per day, $60); Nelson (1¾hr., 8am, $20); Picton (30min., 3 per day, $10). **Southern Link** (☎525 9434) also runs to: Nelson (1¾hr., 4 per day, $20-27); Picton (20min., 4 per day, $9); Takaka (4hr., 1 per day, $50) via Abel Tasman National Park (3½hr., $38). **Red Band Taxis** (☎577 2072) can give you a ride any time.

◨▟ **ORIENTATION AND PRACTICAL INFORMATION.** From the south SH1 enters Blenheim. To stay on the highway, turn right at the first roundabout. To enter the main strip of town, continue straight at the roundabout onto **Main Street. Scott Street,** the town's commercial center, is a left off Main St. Wineries are scattered throughout the greater Blenheim area. The **Blenheim i-Site,** inside the railway station on Grove Rd., has a $2 map of the Marlborough region. (☎577 8080. Internet $2 per 20min. Open M-F 8:30am-5pm, Sa-Su 9am-3pm; longer hours in summer on demand.) Blenheim offers many **work opportunities** through the area's busy fruit industry. To find employment, talk to hostel owners (see below) or look in local newspapers. The picking season lasts from early March to mid-April. Other services include: the **police,** 8 Main St. (☎578 5279); the **hospital** (☎520 9999); **Internet** access at **PC Media,** 15 High St. (☎578 1100; open M-F 8am-6pm); and the **post shop,** at Main and Scott St. (☎578 3904; open M-F 8:30am-5:15pm, Sa 9:30am-12:30pm).

▙▐ **ACCOMMODATIONS AND FOOD.** Fresh paint, comfy beds, plentiful videos, and a friendly bunch of fruit pickers make **Koanui Lodge and Backpackers (BBH) ❷,** 33 Main St., one of Blenheim's few quality accommodations. (☎578 7487; www.koanui.co.nz. Bike rental $10. Pool table. Reception 8am-9:30pm. Dorms $22-25; singles $43; twins and doubles $52, with bath $68. Weekly dorm $115 with BBH. $3 BBH discount.) To get to Blenheim's other noteworthy hostel, **Grapevine Backpackers (BBH) ❷,** 29 Park Terr., follow Main St. south out of town and take a left on any side street to reach Park Terr., which runs parallel to Main St. Paddle canoes in the adjacent river (free), or rent a bicycle ($10). A house across the street offers less cramped accommodations for long-term fruit pickers. (☎578 6062; stay@thegrapevine.co.nz. Free pickup. Free laundry. Free local calls. Free lockers. Dorms $21; twins and doubles $46-50; triples $69. Tent sites $17. $3 BBH discount.) On your left as you pull into town from Picton, the **Blenheim Bridge Top 10 Holiday Park ❶,** 78 Grove Rd., has options for all budgets. (☎578 3667; blenheim.bridge@xtra.co.nz. Spa $5. Reception 8am-10pm. Tent sites $14 per person; 2-person powered sites $28. 2-person cabins $50-65, with bath $80-100.)

Blenheim offers generic fish 'n chips and Asian takeaways, but no real standout establishments. The **Marlborough Farmers' Market** (☎579 3599) every Sunday 9am-noon in summer at the A&P Showgrounds on Maxwell Rd. is known throughout the area as the spot for fresh produce and street food. **New World,** on Main St., fulfills grocery needs. (☎520 9080. Open daily 8am-9pm.) If you do find yourself stuck in Blenheim for a night, **Copper Bock ❶**, 36 Scott St., has live music, $10 liters of beer, and decent food. (☎577 5050. In summer gourmet barbeque F 4-7pm. Wraps and panini $8.50. Live music Th-Sa, mostly local acts. Open M-Sa 10am-as early as 10pm and as late as 3am.)

▨ WINERIES. The Wairau valley is the largest wine-producing region in New Zealand. So, when life puts you in Blenheim with a bunch of grapes, visit a vineyard, learn about winemaking, and, more importantly, savor Marlborough's signature Sauvignon Blancs. The region celebrates all things alcoholic with two large weekend summer festivals **Wine Malborough Festival** at Brancott Estate (tickets ☎0800 224 224; www.wine-marlborough-festival.co.nz; early to mid-Feb.) and **Blues Brews & BBQs** at A&P Showgrounds. (Early Feb. Tickets $25. Min. age 18, unless accompanied by a guardian.) There are a number of wine tours that run out of both Blenheim and Picton. Overall, the tours from Picton are the better option, providing better service and tour guides as well as pickup options in Blenheim. For a listing of wine tours from Picton, see p. 252. The one notable exception is **Wine Tours by Bike,** 191 Bells Rd. Take SH1 through town and turn left on Middle Renwick Rd., then left on Bells Rd. The friendly owners provide a map of the region as well as extensive knowledge of the various wineries and customized itineraries. (☎577 6954; www.winetoursbybike.co.nz. Safety vehicle on call for break downs. Wine bottle carriers and water provided. 4hr. $40, 4-8hr. $55.)

Marlborough is white wine country, though a few reds are on offer at the larger vineyards. Wineries offer a variety of tour and tasting options, but most close by 4:30 or 5pm. Only Forrest Estate, Montana, and Allan Scott charge for tastings; consult the wine map for a complete list of hours and prices. The following are the region's best and most unique wineries. **Montana** (also called **Brancott Winery** on export labels to the United States) is the most famous and largest of the region's wineries. They offer scheduled tours that give an inside look at how the wines are processed and produced, as well as lessons on the characteristics of the different wines, followed by a lesson in tasting. (On SH1 just outside Blenheim towards Kaikoura. ☎577 5775; www.montanawines.co.nz. Tours 10, 11am, 1 and 3pm. $12, includes structured wine tasting. Cellar door open daily 10am-4:30pm. 3 wines available for complimentary tasting or $5 for tray selection.) **Johanneshof,** SH1 north of Blenheim, is a German-style winery that stores some of its wines in an underground cellar cave. Their pinot gris is award-winning. (☎573 7035; johanneshof.cellars@xtra.co.nz. Tours through cellar by arrangement. Open in summer Tu-Su 10am-4pm, in winter by arrangement.) **Clifford Bay,** 26 Rapaura Rd., has terrific wines and one of the best and most reasonably priced cafes (menu $5-18). Don't leave without trying the shrimp and parsley bread ($7). (☎572 7132; www.cliffordbay.co.nz. Open daily in summer 10am-5pm; in winter 10am-4:30pm. Restaurant open M-F 11am-3pm, weekend hours vary with business.) **Forrest Estate,** on SH6/Blicks Rd. at Foxes Island Rd., is a must-see winery that combines high-grade wines with immaculate grounds. (☎572 9084; www.forrest.co.nz. Open daily 10am-4:30pm. First 2 tastings free; 6 tastings and crackers $5.) **Traditional Country Preserves,** at the corner of Rapaura and Selmes Rd., has concoctions such as pineapple and cauliflower chutney. (☎570 5665; www.traditionalcountrypreserves.co.nz. Open in summer M-F 9am-5pm, Sa-Su 9:30am-5pm; in winter M-F 9:30am-4:30pm, Sa-Su 10am-5pm.)

KAIKOURA ☎03

Kaikoura (pop. 4000) means "to eat crayfish" in Maori. While these crunchy crustaceans can be found scuttling beneath the waves, the offshore waters are also replete with fur seals, albatross, dusky dolphins, and whales. An avid marine enthusiast could spend a lifetime beneath Kaikoura's brilliant blue bay. The local

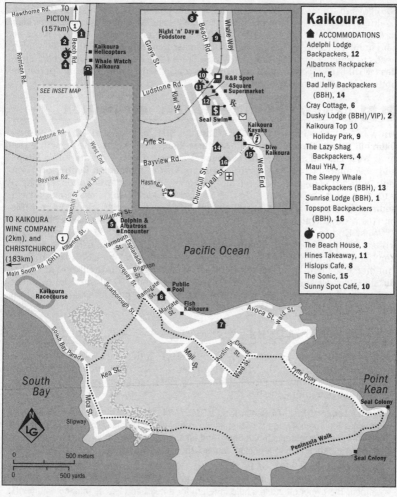

Kaikoura

🏠 **ACCOMMODATIONS**
Adelphi Lodge
Backpackers, **12**
Albatross Backpacker
Inn, **5**
Bad Jelly Backpackers
(BBH), **14**
Cray Cottage, **6**
Dusky Lodge (BBH)/VIP), **2**
Kaikoura Top 10
Holiday Park, **9**
The Lazy Shag
Backpackers, **4**
Maui YHA, **7**
The Sleepy Whale
Backpackers (BBH), **13**
Sunrise Lodge (BBH), **1**
Topspot Backpackers
(BBH), **16**

🍎 **FOOD**
The Beach House, **3**
Hines Takeaway, **11**
Hislops Cafe, **8**
The Sonic, **15**
Sunny Spot Café, **10**

tourism industry has worked out every possible way, short of being swallowed by a whale, to experience this unique environment.

▣ TRANSPORTATION

Sounds Air (☎0800 505 005 or 520 3080; www.soundsair.com) flies to Wellington (45min; daily 9am and 5:30pm; from $100, with good deals for backpackers and students). **TranzCoastal** (☎0800 872 467) has train service to Christchurch (3hr., 3:28pm, from $29) and Picton (2½hr., 9:54am, from $28). **InterCity** (☎365 1113) runs to: Christchurch (2½hr., 2 per day, from $21); Nelson via Blenheim (5hr., 10:10am, from $46); Picton (2hr., 2 per day, from $26). **Atomic Shuttles** (☎349 0697) heads to Christchurch (2½hr., 2 per day, $25) and Picton (2½hr., 2 per day, $25), and can connect with dolphin swims and whale watches. **Southern Link K Bus** (☎0508 458

835) goes to Christchurch (2½hr., 10:30am and 8pm, from $24) and via Blenheim (2¼hr., 2 times daily) to Picton (2½hr., from $39) and Nelson (4½hr.) **Kaikoura Door to Door** (☎319 5922 or 021 319 511) has convenient door-to-door service to Christchurch (M-F 7:45am, from $35). **Hanmer Connection** (☎0800 242 663) also heads to Hanmer Springs (2hr.; Tu, Th, Sa 2pm; $30). For taxis, call **Kaikoura Shuttles** (☎319 6166). The visitors center keeps an up-to-date list of all transportation options out of Kaikoura posted outside its office.

◼️ 🔏 ORIENTATION AND PRACTICAL INFORMATION

Midway between Picton and Christchurch, **SH1** becomes, at various points, **Churchill Street, Beach Road,** and **Athelney Road.** Bear right before Beach Rd. onto **West End** (also called the **Esplanade**), home to most of Kaikoura's shops and accommodations. The terrific **Kaikoura Visitor Information Centre,** on West End, will store luggage ($2 per day), change money on weekends, and help with transport and bookings. (☎319 5641; www.kaikoura.co.nz. Open daily in summer 8:30am-6pm; in winter 9am-4pm.) Other services include: **24hr.** ATMs on West End; the **police** (☎319 5038); a **hospital** (☎319 5040); **Kaikoura Pharmacy,** 37 West End (☎319 7067, after-hours emergencies 021 269 4174; open M-F 8:30am-5:30pm, Sa 9am-12:30pm); **library,** 96 West End (☎319 6280; Internet $2 per 15min., $3 per 30min, $6 per hr.; open M-F 9:30am-5:30pm, Sa 10am-1pm; in summer F 9:30am-7pm); **Internet** access, including laptop facilities, at **Global Gossip,** 19 West End (☎319 7970; $5 for 1st hr., then $0.50 per 10min.; open daily in summer 9am-9pm; in winter 10am-8pm); the **post office,** 41 West End (open M-F 8:30am-5:30pm, Sa 9am-noon).

🏠 ACCOMMODATIONS

Kaikoura has an outrageous number of hostels to lodge the tourists and tourist buses that roll through the city all summer. Most accommodations lie along **West End, Beach Road,** and the **Esplanade** by the beach, while a few others are on the hill overlooking the bay.

▩ Sunrise Lodge (BBH), 74 Beach Rd. (☎319 7444; fax 319 7445). This sunny hostel provides innumerable free services: fishing rods and daily fishing trips, quad bike trips up Mt. Fyffe, sunset tours to the point, and bike rental. Owner-organized pub trip F 5pm. Reception 8am-9:30pm. 4-person dorms $25; twins $56. $3 BBH discount. MC/V. ❷

Dusky Lodge (BBH/VIP), 67 Beach Rd. (☎319 5959; duskyjack@hotmail.com). With hot pools, spa, Thai restaurant (from $10), free breakfast in the winter and a tropical garden, The owner often hires help in return for a free bed (1-week min. commitment). Free pickup. Bike rental $5. Dorms $22; twins and doubles $50, with bath $65. ❷

Cray Cottage, 190 Esplanade (☎319 5152), a 10-15min. walk from the visitors center, opposite the public pools. This tiny hostel is located on the quiet southern side of town and is a favorite of those looking for a peaceful, intimate experience. Impromptu barbeque every couple weeks. Free bike rental. Drop-off and pickup from bus and train station. Lockers $2. Reception 9am-6pm. Dorms $23-25; twins $56. $3 BBH discount. ❷

The Lazy Shag Backpackers (BBH), 37 Beach Rd. (☎319 6662; lazy-shag@xtra.co.nz). Set beside a large, green garden with a creek, this backpackers has rooms that sit off a shady deck and have private baths. Free use of the house kayak on the lazy creek. Free Internet. Dorms $22; twins and doubles $60. $2-3 BBH discount. ❷

Kaikoura Top 10 Holiday Park, 34 Beach Rd. (☎319 5362 or 0800 363 638; www.kaikouratop10.co.nz). Award-winning camping facilities and cabins. Heated pool and spa. Wi-Fi $2 per 15min. Powered sites $35. Cabins $55, with bath $95; self-contained units $100-150. $20 per extra person. Rates lower off-season. ❶

The Sleepy Whale Backpackers (BBH), 86 West End (☎/fax 319 7014 or 0800 319 7014; sleepywhale@xtra.co.nz). This refurbished 48-bed hostel has real mattresses. The view from the upstairs lounge compensates for basic rooms. Towels $2. Key deposit $10. Laundry wash $2, dry $2. Internet $2 per 15min. Reception 8am-8pm. Dorms $23-25; twins and doubles $55-62, with bath $65-67. $2-3 BBH discount. ❷

Albatross Backpackers (BBH), 1 Torquay St. (☎319 6090 or 0800 222 247; www.albatross-kaikoura.co.nz). Set back off the Kaikoura strip, this quiet hostel in a Turkish-style building has all the standard amenities. Barbeque, car park. Reception 8am-late. Dorms $25. Singles $48. Doubles and twins $60, self-contained $75. $3 BBH discount. ❷

Adelphi Lodge Backpackers (BBH), 26 West End (☎0800 423 574 or 319 5141; www.adelphilodge.co.nz). This prominent, historic building houses a large backpackers as well as numerous hotel rooms. The big screen TV is less historical, but a major perk. Reception 8am-9pm; in winter 8am-8pm. Free bike hire, spa, and soup every evening. Dorms $22-25. Twins and doubles $51-54, ensuite $64. ❷

Topspot Backpackers (BBH), 22 Deal St. (☎319 5540; topspot@xtra.co.nz). Walk up the steep path across the street from the visitors center; it's on the right. The loft brings TV-watching to new heights and the garden beckons with barbeques. Free dial-up Internet. Dorms $22; singles $40; twins and doubles $55. $3-5 BBH discount. ❷

Dolphin Lodge (BBH), 15 Deal St. (☎319 5842; dolphinlodge@xtra.co.nz). From the visitors center, walk up the steep path across the street to Deal St. Lounge in the outdoor spa surrounded by roses or in the hammock under the fruit trees (apricot, plum, and nectarine) while gazing at sea and mountain views. Free bike rental. Reception 8am-9pm. Dorms $22; doubles $54, with bath $58. $2 BBH discount. ❷

Maui YHA, 270 Esplanade (☎319 5931; yhakaikoura@yha.co.nz). At Maui, guests eat beside a peaceful ocean view. The hostel is a good 20min. hike from town and well off the main strip. As a result, the crowd here tends to be quieter. Laundry wash $3, dry $3. Internet $2 per 20min. Reception 8:30-10am, noon-1pm and 3:30-7:30pm. 4-bed dorms $28; twins and doubles $62. $3 YHA discount. ❸

❏ FOOD

Kaikoura's delicacy is its namesake—the crayfish served at high-end seafood restaurants: crayfish run $70-90 apiece. However, it's cheaper and more fun to charter a morning fishing trip and catch it yourself (see **Fishing,** p. 271). **4 Square,** 31 West End, has all your grocery needs. (☎319 5333. Open daily 8am-8pm.)

▧ **Hines Takeaway**, 18 West End (☎319 5637), near Beach Rd. Fish 'n chips done right. The blue cod (battered $5.50, grilled $7.50) is without equal. Half-cray and chips ($23, whole cray $40) is one of the cheapest ways to sample the local delicacy. Fish 'n half chips 'n coke special $5. Open daily noon-8:30pm. ❷

▧ **Hislops Cafe**, 33 Beach Rd. (☎319 6971). Even the long, curving bar looks organic at this vegan and vegetarian friendly cafe. Popular breakfast menu ($5-15) available until noon. Daytime meals include such one-of-a-kind dishes such as roast cashew and curried lentil burger ($16.50). Open daily 9:30am-9pm. ❸

The Sonic, 93 West End (☎319 6414). Frequent live music, a pool table, and plenty of outdoor seating make this a popular nightspot. Gourmet pizzas are well-prepared and well-priced (sm. $16.50). Open daily noon-as late as 1am. ❸

Sunny Spot Cafe, 8 West End (☎319 7070). Brews up ridiculously strong coffee ($3.50-4.50) for a thorough caffeine fix. Bagels with cream cheese $6. Open daily 7:30am-4pm. Cash only. ❶

The Beach House, 39 Beach Rd. (☎319 6030), does simple cafe-style food that is popular with local fishermen. Green eggs and ham (bagel, eggs, ham, pesto, hollandaise, and spinach) $12. Open daily 9am-4pm, later on weekends. ❷

The Pier Hotel, 1 Avoca St. (☎319 5037; pierhotel@xtra.co.nz), right on the waterfront. With a prime location overlooking the water, the Pier Hotel is the best place to splurge in Kaikoura. Smoked salmon salad lunch $14.50. Dinner mains around $25.50. Reservations recommended. Open daily noon-9pm. ❹

Black Rabbit Pizza Company, 17 Beach Rd. (☎319 6360). Kaikoura's newest pizza joint has reasonably priced gourmet pizzas with an emphasis on local ingredients. Small pizzas $8.50-12. Open daily 5-around 11pm. MC/V. ❷

⬛🎿 WILDLIFE AND OUTDOOR ACTIVITIES

DOLPHINS. Kaikoura is world-famous for its dusky dolphins. On a typical day, pods average 200-500 dolphins, peaking at over 1000 in winter months. ⬛**Dolphin Encounters** drops humans in the midst of them, for 30min.-1hr. worth of swimming and circling. DOC regulations limit the number of swimmers; only 13 swimmers per each of the three boats are allowed. *(96 Esplanade for booking and base for tours; 58 West End for retail store. ☎319 6777 or 0800 733 365; www.dolphin.co.nz. Book well in advance; waits can be 2-4 weeks or more. If they are fully booked, spectating is a cheaper option that allows a close view of the out-of-water acrobatics. Dec.-Mar. $150, children $140; spectators $80/70. Apr.-Nov. swimmers $130, children $120; spectators $70/60.)*

SEALS. A highlight of Kaikoura is the **Point Kean seal colony,** where visitors can walk among the seals. The reef off the coast is a major breeding site for fur seals and is busiest during the breeding season (Nov.-Feb.), but the furry critters are present year-round. There is no better way to view the entire colony and the beauty of the bay than the **Peninsula Walkway** (2½hr. loop), which starts at Point Kean and has signs explaining the history of the peninsula along the way. *(The trailhead and Point Kean seal colony are a 1hr. walk down the Esplanade from the visitors center.)* If you just can't get enough of the sleepy creatures, **Ohau Point** is the main breeding site on the Kaikoura coast. The DOC has set up a viewing platform overlooking the scores of sunning fur seals. *(24km north of Kaikoura off SH1.)*

By far the best way to experience the these furry sea mammals is to ⬛**swim with the seals.** The seals are consistently responsive to swimmers and unabashedly perform stunts and games of tag. The two main operators of seal swims are **Seal Swim Kaikoura** and **Topspot Backpackers.** Topspot operates a land-based snorkeling tour of Point Kean colony from their hostel (p. 269); it usually gathers a fun, young crowd and has excellent tour leaders. Seal Swim Kaikoura has a boating license, so depending on conditions they do either land-based or boat-based snorkeling tours. Both operate from November to April. *(Seal Swim: 58 West End. ☎0800 732 579 or 319 6182; www.sealswimkaikoura.co.nz. 2½hr. $60-80, children $50, spectators only if with a swimmer $35. Topspot: 22 Deal St. ☎319 5540; topspot@xtra.co.nz. $60, BBH members $55; children $50.)* **Kaikoura Kayaks** runs a half-day seal kayak trip. Dolphins and seals are common in summer, while seals and humpback whales appear more often in winter. *(Departs from Information Centre. ☎319 5641, 0800 452 456, or 021 462 889; www.kaikourakayaks.co.nz. Seal tours daily in summer 8:30am, 12:30, 4:30pm; in winter 9am and 1pm. $70, children $55. Max. 8 people. Freedom kayak hire half-day $55, full-day $70. Kayak school $150. Min. 2 people.)*

WHALES. Whale Watch Kaikoura conducts tours of waters filled with whales and seals, and surrounded by royal albatross and gulls. They offer a refund of up to 80% if no whales are seen during the trip. *(At the old whaleway station. ☎319 6767 or 0800 655 121; www.whalewatch.co.nz. Book 1 week ahead in summer, 3-4 days in winter. Res-*

ervations taken 6am-8pm. Tours daily 7:15 and 10am, 12:45pm; additional tours, up to 16 per day, on demand. 3½hr. $130, ages 3-15 $60. Max. 48 people.) Aerial modes of whale watching are becoming increasingly popular. While the trips are shorter, they are just as successful at finding whales, and allow you to see the whole animal under the water. **Wings Over Whales** operates aerial whale watching tours with a short lesson on the magnificent sperm whales before take-off. *(Located at Peketa Airfield, south of Kaikoura on SH1. ☎319 6580 or 0800 226 629; www.whales.co.nz. 30min. flights daily 9 and 11am, 1 and 3pm; extra flights on demand. $145, children $75. Transport to airfield $5.)* If you'd rather hover over the whales, **Kaikoura Helicopters** will help you do just that. *(Office behind Whale Watch Kaikoura at the old whaleway station. ☎319 6609 or 0274 372 300; www.kaikourahelicopters.co.nz. 30-50min. tours run on demand. From $195.)*

SEABIRDS. Ocean Wings Albatross Encounters runs a boat trip to view Kaikoura's ocean-going birdlife and admire 10 ft. wingspans of the wandering albatross that makes the 1900km flight from their breeding colonies to Kaikoura in a single day. *(96 Esplanade, in the Encounter Kaikoura building. ☎319 6777 or 0800 733 365; www.oceanwings.co.nz. Book at Dolphin Encounters; p. 270. 2-person min. 2½hr. $80, children $40.)*

SURFING. North of Kaikoura 10km, off SH1, Munga Muna is the local surf spot. Get your board and gear at **R & R Sport,** 14 Westend. Beginners can also book lessons with **Board Silly** at R & R. *(R & R: ☎319 5028; rrkai@xtra.co.nz; www.rrsport.co.nz. Surf board half-day rental $30, full-day $45. Wetsuit $15/20. Open daily in summer 9am-7:30pm; in winter 9am-5:30pm. Board Silly: ☎0800 787 352, 027 418 8900, or 319 6464; boardsilly@clear.net.nz. 3½hr. lesson $75. Max. 6 people.)*

FISHING. ▧**Fish Kaikoura** takes out their boat the *Molly D.* The early trip (7am) is recommended, since that's when they pull up last night's crayfish pots. **Top Catch Charters** has a crayfish barbeque on board. *(Fish Kaikoura: 236 Esplanade. ☎319 2012, 0800 768 020 or 027 4426 242; www.fishkaikoura.co.nz. 2½hr. crayfish and fishing tours $60; 1hr. "catch your dinner" $45. Min. 2 people, max. 7 people. Top Catch: 40 Torquay St. ☎319 6306 or 027 498 7613; crayzeesmith@yahoo.com. 3hr. charters from $80, children $45; 4hr. $100/45. Max. 12 people.)*

DIVING. Dive Kaikoura takes divers out into the bay, trains novices, and provides trial dives for first-timers. Diving has the added benefit of enabling one to catch pricey crayfish with their hands. *(☎319 6622; www.divekaikoura.co.nz. First dive $105, each additional dive $75. Intro dives and training $150. PADI certification around $475.)*

WALKS. The circular **Hinau Track** is a flat, easy loop, while the **Fyffe-Palmer Track** is steep but manageable. Keep your eyes open for a black-eyed gecko or the world's heaviest insect, the giant weta—also known as the "demon grasshopper." *(Hinau trailhead 15km from town. To reach the trailhead, take Westend out of town and turn left onto Ludstone; follow Ludstone until it becomes Red Swamp Rd., then turn left on Postmans Rd. and right on Chapmans, then take the first left. 45min. round-trip. Fyffe-Palmer trailhead 8km from town. To reach the trailhead take Westend out of town and turn left on Ludstone, then right on Mt. Fyffe Rd. 1¾hr. round-trip.)* The **Peninsula Walkway** (p. 270) will take you to the fur seal colony. For more ambitious trampers or mountain bikers, the privately owned 40km **Kaikoura Coast Track** takes three days by foot or two days by bike. *(Trailhead 50km south of town. ☎319 2715; www.kaikouratrack.co.nz. Open Oct.-Apr. By bike $75, by foot $150; includes accommodations in homestays.)*

SKIING. Winter time travelers can enjoy **Mt. Lyford,** a mere 60km from Kaikoura. The family-friendly mountain hosts trips from Kaikoura that include ski rental, lift pass, and transport; inquire at the visitors center. Accommodation is available at Mt. Lyford Lodge, call ☎315 6446 for prices and information. *(☎315 6178 or 027 629 8083; www.mtlyford.co.nz. Open June-Sept. Day pass $50, students $45. Ski rental $15-35; snowboard and boots rental $40. For transportation contact Kaikoura Ski Shuttle, ☎319 7354.)*

MARLBOROUGH AND NELSON

HANMER SPRINGS ☎ 03

The rare combination of converging fault lines and connected underground fractures brings Hanmer Springs (pop. 900) to geothermal life. On weekends and school holidays, hordes of Kiwis join in the fun in the steaming waters of the thermal springs at the center of this isolated resort town.

▐ TRANSPORTATION. Check with your bus company in advance to ensure they drop you off in the village proper, rather than at **Hanmer Turn-off,** 10km outside of town. **Hanmer Connection** (☎0800 242 663) runs from the visitors center, and is the best option for heading to Christchurch (2hr.; 11:30am, 2, 5pm; $25, round-trip $45) or Kaikoura (2hr.; Tu, Th, Sa 11am; $30 one-way). **Southern Link** (☎358 8355 or 0508 458 835; www.southernlinkcoaches.co.nz) runs to Christchurch (2hr., 1:55pm, $30 one-way) and Nelson (5hr., 10:30am, $20 one-way) from the turn-off; call ahead to request pickup from the visitors center. **Hanmer Shuttle** (☎0800 800 575) runs to Christchurch (daily 4pm, $25, return $45). To tool around town in style, pick up a two- or four-person bicycle **rickshaw** from **Village Cruisers** at Alpine Crazy Putt Mini-Golf on Conical Hill Rd. (☎315 5177. $17 per hr.)

▐▌ ORIENTATION AND PRACTICAL INFORMATION. Hanmer Springs is about 10km off SH7, on SH7a, and 136km north of Christchurch. Visitors approach the town on SH7a, which becomes the main drag in town. The main drag changes names: first to Hanmer Springs Rd., then to **Amuri Avenue,** then finally **Conical Hill Road** as the road passes the pools on the left. The **Hanmer Springs i-Site,** 42 Amuri Ave., is next to the entrance to the pools. (☎315 7128 or 0800 442 663; www.alpinepacifictourism.co.nz. Open daily Jan. 9:30am-5:30pm, Feb.-Dec. 10am-5pm.) Other services include: an **ATM** at the 4 Square supermarket (☎315 7190; open M-F 8:30am-7pm, Sa 9am-7pm, Su 10am-5:30pm); the **police,** 39 Amuri Ave. (☎315 7117); the **Hanmer Springs Medical Centre,** 20 Amuri Ave. (☎315 7503; open 24hr.) There is a small **post office** behind the 4 Square supermarket. (☎315 7710. Open M-F 9am-5pm, Sa 10am-5pm, Su 10am-3pm.)

▐▐ ACCOMMODATIONS AND FOOD. Only a few budget accommodations are within walking distance of the pools. The lodge-like **Hanmer Backpackers (BBH) ❷,** 41 Conical Hill Rd., a 5min. walk past the thermal reserve on the right, houses travelers in a cozy loft with private rooms in an insulated aluminum house out back. (☎315 7196; hanmerbackpackers@xtra.co.nz. Free hot drinks. Mountain bikes half-day $15, full-day $25. Dorms $23; doubles $52. Tent sites $13. $3 BBH discount.) **Le Gite Backpackers (BBH) ❷,** 3 Devon St., is away from the tourist strip, but its distance from town makes it a better option for those with cars. (As you enter town, travel up Amuri Ave. and make a left on Jacks Pass Rd., just past the pools, then make a left on Devon St. ☎315 5111; www.leg-ite.co.nz. Reception 8:30am-8pm. Reserve 3-4 days ahead in summer, especially for garden chalets. Dorms $22; doubles $50, with bath $60. $2-5 BBH discount.) **Kakapo Lodge Backpackers (YHA) ❷,** 14 Amuri Ave., offers plenty of beds in a somewhat sterile hostel. (☎315 7472 and 027 269 1476; stay-kakapo@xtra.co.nz. Reception 8:30am-8:30pm. Dorms $26; twins and doubles $56, with bath $76; motel rooms $86. $10 per extra person. $3 YHA discount.) **Mountain View Top 10 Holiday Park ❶,** at Bath St. and Hanmer Springs Rd., on the right, crams caravaners into a motor camp, an 8min. walk out of town. (☎315 7113 or 0800 904 545; www.mountainviewtop10.co.nz. Tent sites $22-26; powered sites $28-30. 2-person cabins $45-55, with kitchen $60-70; cabins with bath $60-70, with kitchen and bath $80-95. $10 per extra person on tent sites, $15 in rooms.)

Hanmer Springs doesn't always offer the best bang for your buck in the food department. **Amuri Avenue** is home to takeaway joints and cafes, but the town's most popular restaurants cluster around the small shopping center in town. Share tapas with at **the Rustic Cafe ❷**, in the Conical Hill Rd. shopping center. (Tapas $10. Platter of 4 $35. Open Tu-Su 9am-9pm.) **Jollie Jack's Cafe and Bar ❸**, 12a Conical Hill Rd., is the culinary standout, offering succulent rack of lamb, venison, and fresh blue cod ($28.50), along with a lighter lunch menu. (☎315 7388. Lunch mains $15-16.50. Open daily 11am-9:30pm.) In a town not known for the nightlife, **Saints ❷**, 6 Jacks Pass Rd., behind Rustic cafe, is where Hanmer goes to party. The restaurant becomes the town nightclub at after dinner. (☎315 5262. Takeaway pizza from $21. Half-pints $4. Open M-F 4pm-late, Sa 10am-late, Su, 9am-late.)

🎇 OUTDOOR ACTIVITIES. Hanmer's main attraction is easy to find; if the smell of sulfur isn't enough, follow the plumes of steam to the **Hanmer Springs Thermal Pools and Spa,** on Amuri Ave. The dozen different pools offer something for everyone: swim in the tepid lap pool, soak in the lukewarm hex pools, play on the two waterslides, or prove your superhuman endurance in the 42°C spring-water baths. (☎315 0000; www.hanmersprings.co.nz. Open daily 10am-9pm; spa daily 10am-7pm. Swimsuit rental $5. Towel $4. Locker $2 per 2hr. $12, children $6; same-day return pass $15/7.50. Waterslide $5.) The **Spa at Hanmer Springs** is in the midst of major expansion, and specializes in water massages. (☎315 7567 or 0800 873 529. From $40 for 30min. massage. Open 11am-7pm.)

Hanmer's other claim to fame is the **mountain biking** in the region. The visitors centre sells a detailed, ability graded Hanmer Springs Mountain Bike Track Guide ($2) and the Hanmer Springs Adventure Centre (see below) has rentals as well as a knowledgeable staff. For expert riders, the **Jacks-Jollies Loop** (2-4hr., 25km) covers some of the best terrain. **Hanmer Springs Adventure Centre** (☎315 7233 or 025 221 1568; www.hanmeradventure.co.nz), 20 Conical Hill Rd., just up the road from the visitors center, covers bookings and information for many activities in town. Their **Twin Pass** ($85) gets you a mountain bike with suspension, a ride 19km out of town to the trail on top of Jacks Pass, and, for your return, a pass to the hot springs. The two-hour 🎇**quad bike tour** (tours daily 10am, 1:30 and 4pm; $129) rides over 25km of hills and streams. (☎315 7233. Mountain bikes $19 per hr., 25 per 2hr., $35 per 4hr., full-day $45. Scooters $28 per hr., each additional hr. $12. Fishing rods $25 per day. Archery $20 per 30min. Open daily 9am-5pm.) **Thrillseekers Adventure Centre,** in Thrillseekers Canyon at the Historic Ferry Bridge 18km out of town, has its own little corner of the Waiau River all to itself. It offers 35m baby bungy jump ($135, with pictures $150), jetboat rides (40min.; $99, children $50) and river rafting ($135/75) through the steep-walled gorge, as well as quad bike tours ($119). (☎315 7046; www.thrillseeker.co.nz. Transport available. Office on Conical Hill Rd. Open daily 9am-5:30pm.) To explore the forests and river valleys by horse, contact **Hanmer Horses,** 187 Rogerson Rd. To reach them, turn left after the thermal pools onto Jacks Pass Rd., then left onto Rogerson Rd., the stables are about 1.5km down. (☎315 7444 or 0800 873 546; www.hanmerhorses.co.nz. 1hr. $45, children $35; 2½hr. $90/70.) **Hanmer Air** runs scenic flights over the Southern Alps as well as the stations north of Hanmer Springs. (☎0800 235 942 or 027 435 9810; www.hanmerair.co.nz. 20min. flight $95, children $80; 1hr. flight $185/155.) **Hot Tracks** is a one-of-a-kind tour that puts small groups in a Swedish military vehicle and explores off-road territory. (☎021 718 551; www.hottracks.co.nz. Trips depart every 30min. from the Heritage Hotel on Conical Hill Rd. 30min. ride $35, children $25. Half day trips available. Snowmobile rides available in winter.)

Popular walks include the very easy **Woodland Walk** (45min.), the **Forest Walk** (1hr.) through the "experimental" forests planted in the early 20th century, the moderate **Conical Hill Walk** (1hr.) to a nearby scenic overlook, and the steady climbing **Waterfall Track** (3hr. from trailhead; 6hr. from village center) to the 41m high Dog Stream waterfall. Hikers should check with the visitors center for conditions and maps ($2). During ski season, usually July through September, hit the slopes of **Hanmer Springs Ski Area**, a 45min. drive from town. The skiing is for intermediate and advanced skiers and is mostly off-piste. To reach the slopes, take Clarence Valley Rd., go left at the river, follow signs to Saint James Station, go left through the station, and follow Farm Rd. to the ski area. (☎315 7233 or 0800 888 308; snowphone 366 7766, ext. 5. Tow fees $45, students $35, under 18 $25. Ski rental $25-35; snowboard rental $50. Lift pass $45.) Call Hanmer Springs Adventure Centre (see above) for a shuttle. (Departs 9am. Round-trip $28, children $20.)

NELSON ☎03

Home to the country's first game of rugby, the world's first eight-hour work day, and the New Zealand's oldest railway, "Sunny Nelson" (pop. 45,000) is an oasis of modernity in a region dedicated to ecological conservation. The geographic center of New Zealand, Nelson has a wide range of art galleries, dining, shopping, and nightlife options guaranteed to keep tourists in town for a few extra days.

▛ TRANSPORTATION

Flights: The **airport** is located past the Tahunanui Beach area. **Air New Zealand Link** (☎0800 737 000; www.airnz.co.nz) flies daily to: **Auckland** (1½hr., 9 per day, from $99); **Christchurch** (50min., 9 per weekday, from $94); **Wellington** (35min., 14 per day, from $79). **Vincent Aviation** (☎0800 846 236; www.vincentaviation.co.nz) flies daily to Wellington ($55-75).

Buses: Local buses to Tahunanui, Stoke, and Richmond ($2-5) leave from the Nelson i-Site. **InterCity** (☎548 1539; www.intercitycoach.co.nz) leaves from the 27 Bridge St. depot and heads daily to **Fox Glacier** (10½hr., 1 per day, $73-107) via **Westport** (4½hr., $38), and **Picton** (2hr., 2 per day, $10-29) via **Blenheim** (1½hr., $10-27). You can also take the bus to Blenheim and transfer to a **Christchurch** bus (4½hr., $52-69). **Lazerline** (☎0800 220 001) and **Southern Link** (☎0508 458 835) also go daily to **Christchurch** (7½hr., 1-2 per day, $40) via **Springs Junction** (3½hr., $20-26). **Cains Road Services** runs to **St. Arnauld/Nelson Lakes National Park** (M, W, F, 1 per day, $14). **Atomic Shuttles** (☎322 8883) also goes to **Westport** (5hr., $40). To get to **Abel Tasman National Park** or the **Kahurangi National Park,** call **Abel Tasman Coachlines** (☎548 0285) or **K Bus** (☎0508 458 835; www.kbus.co.nz). Prices and times vary (1½-4hr., 3 per day, from $14).

Taxis: Nelson City Taxis (☎548 8225 or 0800 108 855) and **Sun City Taxis** (☎0800 422 666) run 24hr.

Car Rental: Ascot Cars Limited, 35 Bolt Rd., Tahunanui (☎546 5440 or 0800 500 544). From $29 per day. **Pegasus Rental Cars,** 83 Haven Rd. (☎548 0884 or 0800 354 501; www.rentalcars.co.nz). From $35 per day.

Bike Rental: Stewarts Cycle City, 114 Hardy St. (☎548 1666). Half-day $20, full-day $40. Open M-F 9am-6pm, Sa 9am-1pm.

✳▟ ORIENTATION AND PRACTICAL INFORMATION

Christ Church Cathedral, on Trafalgar St., dominates central Nelson, towering above its surrounding gardens. **Trafalgar, Bridge,** and **Hardy Streets** comprise the main

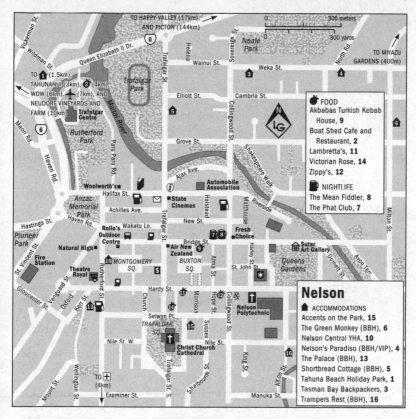

TO HAPPY VALLEY (17km),
AND PICTON (144km)

Neale Park

TO MIYAZU
GARDENS (400m)

🍴 FOOD
Akbabas Turkish Kebab
House, 9
Boat Shed Cafe and
Restaurant, 2
Lambretta's, 11
Victorian Rose, 14
Zippy's, 12

🍷 NIGHTLIFE
The Mean Fiddler, 8
The Phat Club, 7

Nelson

🏠 ACCOMMODATIONS
Accents on the Park, 15
The Green Monkey (BBH), 6
Nelson Central YHA, 10
Nelson's Paradiso (BBH/VIP), 4
The Palace (BBH), 13
Shortbread Cottage (BBH), 5
Tahuna Beach Holiday Park, 1
Tasman Bay Backpackers, 3
Trampers Rest (BBH), 16

shopping district and enclose a plethora of shops, accommodations, and restaurants. From the bus depot, take a left onto Bridge St. to hit Trafalgar St.

Visitors Center: The high-tech **Nelson i-Site** (☎548 2304; www.nelsonnz.com or www.i-sitenelsonnz.com), at Trafalgar and Halifax St. Open M-F 8:30am-5pm, Sa-Su 9am-4pm.

Department of Conservation (DOC): (☎546 9335). The DOC provides information at the desk in the Nelson i-Site. Open M-F 8:30am-5pm, Sa-Su 9am-4pm.

Banks: Major banks with **ATMs** line Trafalgar St. Most open M-F 9am-4:30pm.

Tramping Gear: Rollo's Outdoor Centre, 12 Bridge St. (☎548 1975). Tents $10 per night. Deposits necessary. Open M-F 9am-5:30pm, Sa 9am-3pm.

Police: (☎546 3840), on St. John St. in central Nelson.

Medical Services: Prices Pharmacy, 296 Hardy St. (☎548 3897), at Collingwood St. Open M-F 8:30am-8pm, Sa 9am-8pm, Su 10am-6pm. **Nelson Hospital** (☎546 1800), on Waimea St. **City Care,** 202 Rutherford St. (☎546 8881), has a doctor at night.

Internet Access: Boots Off, 53 Bridge St. (☎546 8789). 60+ terminals. $5 per hr. Specials from $2.50 per hr. Open daily 9am-10pm. Reduced hours in winter.

Post Office: 108 Trafalgar St., kittycorner from the Nelson i-Site. Open M-F 7:45am-5pm, Sa 9:30am-12:30pm.

⌐ ACCOMMODATIONS

As a general rule, the smaller hostels are homier, while larger backpackers compensate for their lack of intimacy with freebies and facilities. Some of Nelson's hostels close for the winter season but are filled during the summer.

🏠 **Trampers Rest Backpackers and Wheelpacker (BBH)**, 31 Alton St. (☎/fax 545 7477), on one of Nelson's historic streets. The owner of this 7-bed oasis specially engineers an atmosphere that fosters relaxed socialization—hence the hammock in the vegetable garden and the TV-free common room.Reserve beds far in advance. Laundry $5. Dorms $23; doubles $56. Cash only. ❷

🏠 **Accents on the Park (BBH/VIP)**, 335 Trafalgar Sq. (☎548 4335; www.accentsonthepark.com), across the street from the church gardens. It's rare that a large hostel feels like a home, but owners Royce and Linda ensure that every guest is looked after in their perfectly located, lovingly restored mansion. Royce bartends and cooks cheap meals in the basement pub. Laundry $5. Internet $6 per hr. Dorms $23-25; singles $39; doubles $50; deluxe queen ensuite rooms $80. ISIC discount. MC/V. ❷

The Green Monkey (BBH), 129 Milton St. (☎545 7421; www.thegreenmonkey.co.nz). 2 gardens beg for barbeques. Dorms $23; doubles $59. $3 BBH discount. Cash only. ❷

Shortbread Cottage (BBH), 33 Trafalgar St. (☎546 6681). Whether you're a sleep-deprived backpacker or a ruthless cookie monster, you'll find a bit of happiness in Shortbread. The brightly colored cottage is one of the most inviting nooks in Nelson. Fresh shortbread baked almost daily. Laundry $6.50. Internet $2 per 20min. Dorms $25; doubles with TV $56. $3 BBH discount. Cash only. ❷

Nelson's Paradiso (BBH/VIP), 42 Weka St. (☎546 6703; www.backpacknelson.co.nz). A social backpacker's paradiso, this hostel is well equipped for summer parties with a sauna, spa, pool, and volleyball court. Surfers line up for the daily breakfast and evening soup. Linen $1. Laundry $6. Internet $2 per 30min. Key deposit $20. Reception 7:45am-9pm. Dorms $22; twins and doubles $52-56. Cash only. ❷

Tasman Bay Backpackers (BBH), 10 Weka St. (☎548 7950; www.tasmanbaybackpackers.co.nz). Although this well-shaded hostel is not on the bay, the bright colors and social atmosphere still attract a host of hard-charging surfers. In winter, continental breakfast included. Laundry $3.50. Internet $2 per 30min. Key deposit $10. Reception 8am-9pm. Dorms $23; twins and doubles $52. Tent sites $12. MC/V. ❷

The Palace (BBH), 114 Rutherford St. (☎548 4691; www.thepalace.co.nz). Turn off Rutherford St. into the Shell gas station, and look for the driveway behind the gas pumps. The Palace occupies a magnificent hilltop historic home and waylays travelers with its laid-back vibe, city views, and 24hr. spa. Free local calls. Continental breakfast included. Laundry $3. Internet $1 per 15min. Key deposit $10. Reception 8am-9pm. Dorms $23; doubles and twins $55; triples $66. Cash only. ❷

Nelson Central YHA, 59 Rutherford St. (☎545 9988; yha-nelson@yha.org.nz). Spotless rooms, an eco-friendly staff, and a location ideal for hitting Nelson's nightlife. Free videos and communal guitars barely compensate for the steeper price. Laundry $5. Internet $2 per 15min. Reception 8-10am, 3-9:30pm. Dorms $27; singles $41; twins and doubles $64, with bath $78. Summer rates increase by $2. MC/V. ❸

Tahuna Beach Holiday Park, 70 Beach Rd. (☎548 5159 or 0800 500 501; www.tahunabeachholidaypark.co.nz), in Tahunanui, 5km from Nelson. With its own store, mini-golf course, and road system, all this 54-acre facility lacks is its own government. Linen $2. Laundry $4. Internet $2 per 20min. Reception 8am-9pm. Tent sites $14 per adult. Cabins $30-40; tourist flats $60-70; studio units $56-75. MC/V. ❶

◪ FOOD

Most of Nelson's attractive restaurants, cafes, and takeaways are located on **Trafalgar, Bridge,** and **Hardy Streets.** Seafood restaurants on **Wakefield Quay (SH6),** along the oceanfront, can be reached by bus or taxi ($3-5). For groceries, head to the centrally located **Fresh Choice,** 69 Collingwood St. (open daily 7am-9pm; MC/V) or **Woolworths,** at Paru Rd. and Halifax St. (☎546 6466; open daily 7am-10pm; MC/V).

Victorian Rose, 281 Trafalgar St. (☎548 7631; www.victorianrose.co.nz). Inside this old British pub is one of the best backpacker eateries in Nelson, with daily meals for $11. The Su roast (from 5:30pm; $13) is an all-you-can-eat affair including soup and dessert. Live music Tu-Sa from 9pm. Beer $4. Kitchen open daily 11am-9:30pm. 10% discount with a coupon available at most hostels. MC/V. ❷

Lambretta's, 204 Hardy St. (☎545 8555; www.lambrettascafe.co.nz). The menu is a mix of lighter meals and mains including innovative pizzas like smoked salmon and apricot ($13-22). Open daily 8:30am-late. MC/V. ❷

Boat Shed Cafe and Restaurant, 350 Wakefield Quay (☎546 9783; www.boatshed-cafe.co.nz), on the oceanfront. Boat shed turned upscale eatery offers blue ocean views and a dose of romance. Known for its seafood—especially crayfish and mussels. Lunch mains from $19. Dinner mains from $28. Wine from $9. Open daily 9am-late. MC/V. ❹

Zippy's, 276 Hardy St. (☎546 6348). Graffiti-painted vegetarian joint with bar-style on-street seating. The muffins are huge ($3-4) and the fresh smoothies are a meal unto themselves ($5). Open M-Sa 10am-7pm. MC/V. ❷

Akbabas Turkish Kebab House, 130 Bridge St. (☎548 8825). A small restaurant and takeaway with low tables and floor pillows. Spicy chicken and doner kebab in flatbread $7-9. Falafels $6-8. Filling lamb kebab $10-12. Open daily 11am-9pm. MC/V. ❶

Yaza (☎528 2849), Montgomery Sq. This hippy-happy cafe hosts open mic acoustic sessions, as well as occasional live music. Focaccia sandwiches $8-9. The savory cheese scones ($3) are a must. Cover around $5. Open M-F 8am-5pm, Sa 7am-4pm, Su 8am-3pm. MC/V. ❶

Spices, 227-229 Hardy St. (☎0508 539 4916; www.spices.co.nz). Savor the spices of Malaysia. The portions of prawn laksa soup ($20) are enormous. Lunch mains $9-10. Dinner mains $14-19. Open M-Sa 11:30am-2:30pm, 5:30pm-late. MC/V. ❷

◉ SIGHTS

If you've got two sturdy legs, pick up a copy of *Walk Nelson* ($5), the best guide to Nelson's natural history. The brochure outlines 30 local walks and is available at the Nelson i-Site. A great way to encounter the many faces of Nelson is to wander through Nelson's weekly **flea market.** Held each weekend in the Montgomery Sq. Saturday is the best day to go. (Open Sa-Su 7am-1pm.) If you have a hankering for a picnic, head to **ANZAC Memorial Park,** off Rutherford St., or to the **Miyazu Japanese Garden,** on Atawhai Dr., north of town. Otherwise, the Victorian **Queens Gardens** has plenty of bold birds guarding the entrances on Hardy and Bridge St. **Suter Art Gallery,** 208 Bridge St., holds a collection of New Zealand and local art, as well as a craft shop, theater, and cafe. (☎548 4699; www.thesuter.org.nz. Open daily 10:30am-4:30pm. $3, students $1. Free on Sa.) A mixture of industrial and Gothic architecture, **Christ Church Cathedral** (☎548 1008) sits atop Church Hill on Trafalgar St. The fine sands of **Tahunanui Beach** ("shifting sands") make it a popular destination accessible by a short bike down SH6, four kilometers west of town. Accessible by car, **Rabbit Island's** expansive beaches (20km west of Nelson off SH60) are often less crowded. To find out how metal shards, seagrass, and insect screen can be incorporated into fashion design, head three kilometers west from Tahunanui along SH6 to the **World of WearableArt (WOW)** and **Collectible Cars Museum.** It showcases the best designs from the WOW Awards Show (now held in Wellington; p. 232). (☎547 4573; www.wowcars.co.nz. Open daily 10am-5pm. $18, children $7.)

Nelson's craftsmen and grape-stompers offer travelers up close and personal insight to local industry just out of town by car or tour bus. **Bay Tours** covers a range of local highlights, including several wineries and craft centers. (☎0800 229 868; www.baytoursnelson.co.nz. Half-day wine and gourmet tour $85. Half-day art tour $69.) Stop by **Mac's Brewery,** 660 Main Rd., in Stoke, about 10min. west of Nelson, for an intoxicating look at the beer-making process. (☎547 0526; www.macsbeer.co.nz. Open Tu-Sa 10am-5pm. Tastings $5, tours $10.) Continuing west on SH6, look for the signposts just before Richmond that mark the way to the **Craft Habitat,** where artisans weave thick wool or perfect their jewelry. (☎544 7481; www.crafthabitat.co.nz. Open daily 9am-5pm. Free.) From SH6, turn right on Queen St. in Richmond, then left on Lansdowne Rd. to reach the **Höglund Art International Glass Centre.** It's free to wander the gallery and store, but you'll have to pay for a 45min. tour of the facilities, where two galleries display glass creations. (☎546 9850; www.nelsonhoglund.co.nz. Open daily 9am-5pm. Tours $15, students $12.) For a hands-on experience, **Creative Workshops** offers informal courses such as Maori bone carving (☎0800 408 020; www.creativetourism.co.nz. 6hr., $65.)

🔺 OUTDOOR ACTIVITIES

Most backpackers in Nelson keep their eyes on the prize: Abel Tasman National Park (p. 288). It's easy to use the city as a base for a variety of trips within the park including kayaking, tramping, and ziplining. If you came to kayak, **Abel Tasman Kayaks** (☎0800 732 529; www.abeltasmankayaks.co.nz) provides pickup in Nelson for guided trips. Additionally, transport from Nelson to various trailheads along the Coastal Track can be arranged. **Happy Valley Adventures** offers the exhilarating Skywire, a zipline that sends you and three others hurtling down the longest 1.6km of your life for $85. They also run 4x4 "Adventure Excursions," such as the Farm Forest and the Bay View Circuits, which visits ancient matai trees that are 40m tall and over 2000 years old. (☎545 0304; www.happyvalleyadventures.co.nz. Farm Forest 1hr., $70. Bay View 2½hr., $95.) **Stonehurst Farm Horse Treks** (☎542 4121 or 0800 487 357; www.stonehurstfarm.co.nz) offers a variety of 1-3½hr. adventures, including the Scenic Farm Trail (1hr., $55) and half-day River Ride ($105).

Self-titled "adrenaline dealers," **Natural High,** 52 Rutherford St., rents mountain bikes and tramping gear, and offers bike tours and kayak trips. (☎546 6936; www.cyclenewzealand.com and www.seakayaknewzealand.com. Bikes from $35 per day. Guided multi-day kayaking from $270.) **Kitescool,** a mix of surf and air, offers windsurfing and kiteboarding lessons. The half-day intro course runs for $170. (☎021 354 837; www.kitescool.co.nz.) See the scenery from the sky with either **Nelson Paragliding** (☎544 1182; www.nelsonparagliding.co.nz; tandem flight $110) or **Nelson Hang Gliding Adventures.** (☎548 9151 or 025 751 436; www.flynelson.co.nz. 15min. tandem flight $160.) For a more daring option, **Skydive Abel Tasman** offers a plunge over the Abel Tasman. (☎528 4091 or 0800 422 899; www.skydive.co.nz. 3000m $210; 4000m $260.)

🎵 🎭 ENTERTAINMENT AND NIGHTLIFE

For good, clean fun, Nelson offers a six-screen cinematic experience at the **State Cinemas,** at Trafalgar and Halifax St., across from the Nelson i-Site. (☎548 8123. Films $11, before 5pm $8. Student discounts.) For a night out, head to **Bridge Street,** where bars and pubs stay open well into the night. Crowds frequently gather at **Victorian**

Rose, 281 Trafalgar St., to celebrate (or mourn) the outcome of the most recent rugby match. (☎548 7631. Live music Tu-Sa from 9pm. Kitchen open until 9:30pm. Open daily 11am-late.) Nelson's main venue for dance parties, DJs, and touring bands is **The Phat Club,** 137 Bridge St. (☎548 3311. Cover usually $5. Open Th-Sa 10pm-3am; in winter F-Sa.) Locals laud **The Mean Fiddler,** 145 Bridge St., for its lack of gimmicks and abundance of excellent local beer. (Handles $4.50. Open daily 4pm-3am.)

NELSON LAKES NATIONAL PARK ☎03

Pristine byways pass through evergreen beech forests, craggy mountains, and tussock grasslands on the banks of Lake Rotoiti and Lake Rotoroa. The forests shelter abundant birdlife and recent efforts by the DOC to control predator populations promise the reintroduction of even more native species. The gateway to the park is the lakeshore village of **St. Arnaud,** which sits on the moraine of the glacier that originally formed Lake Rotoiti.

🚍 TRANSPORTATION. Cain Road Services (☎522 4044) runs to Nelson (M, W, F; 1 per day; $14). **Nelson Lakes Shuttles** (☎521 1900; www.nelsonlakesshuttles.co.nz) runs on demand to trailheads, as well as to Nelson ($30) and Picton ($30) with a four-person minimum. For the cheapest fares, book ahead via email.

 WHEN TO GO. The park can get very cold in winter—be sure to bring adequate clothing and equipment. Huts often become overcrowded in summer.

PRACTICAL INFORMATION. The **DOC office** in **St. Arnaud,** on View Rd. off SH63, also serves as the **Nelson Lakes National Park Visitors Centre.** (☎521 1806, for after-hours emergencies 0800 036 2468; fax 521 1896; starnaudao@doc.govt.nz. Open daily 8am-4:30pm. In summer 8am-6pm.) The **gas station, post office,** and **general store** are all in the **Nelson Lakes Village Centre.** (☎521 1854. Open M-Sa 7:30am-7pm, Su 8:30am-6pm.) There are **no banks or ATMs** in St. Arnaud.

🛏🏕 ACCOMMODATIONS AND CAMPING. Sleeping options are slim in St. Arnaud. The bright **Yellow House (YHA) ❷,** 150m from the gas station, is a good bet with a park-savvy staff. Warm, clean rooms provide the perfect respite from a long day's hike. (☎521 1887; www.nelsonlakes.co.nz. Camping and hiking gear available. Spa $5. Laundry $6. Internet $2 per 15min. Key deposit $10. Reception 8am-6pm, 7:30-9pm. Dorms $24; doubles $56; 2-person cabins $79-119, $16 per extra person. Tent sites $13. Cash only.) Lake Rotoiti has two **DOC campsites ❶,** one at **Kerr Bay** and another at **West Bay.** Both have tent sites, though West Bay is closed in winter. (☎521 1806. Tent sites $8, children $4; powered $10/5. Cash only.) For extended stays in St. Arnaud, it's best to bring your own food to avoid sky high prices. The roadside **Elaine's Alpine Cafe ❷,** on SH6 in front of Alpine Chalet, is the only restaurant in town. Standard all-day breakfast ($15), toasted sandwiches ($8-10), and burgers with chips ($10) will kill your hunger. Dinners ($19-23) will kill your wallet. The **Nelson Lakes Village Centre** (p. 279) has takeaways. (Fish'n chips $5. Open Th-Su 4-6:30pm.)

🥾 OUTDOOR ACTIVITIES. The best-known trail is the strenuous **Travers-Sabine Circuit** (80km, 4-7 days round-trip), which climbs over 1000m to the 1787m **Travers Saddle** and on a clear day can provide a glimpse of the craggy 2338m **Mt. Travers.** An abbreviated and more popular loop (28km, round-trip 2 days) climbs to **Angelus Hut** before returning down the blustery **Robert Ridge** or **Speargrass Creek.** Huts often fill in summer; tickets can be purchased at the DOC ($10 per night). Dayhikes begin in the Kerr Bay Carpark and range in duration from 30min. to 9hr., depending on your ambition; pamphlets ($0.50-2) are available at the visitors center, or just follow the signs. Those crunched for time can do the **Honeydew Walk** (round-trip 45min.), a bushwalk on which you're likely to hear the clatter of tui and bellbirds. If you don't have your own gear, the **Rotoiti Outdoor Education Centre**, on Lodge Rd. on the outskirts of town, rents tramping clothing, packs, sleeping bags, and equipment year-round. (☎521 1820. $2-5 per item. Call ahead.)

The glaciers that carved out the Travers Valley were also responsible for creating Lake Rotoiti—8km long, 80m at its deepest point, and jumping with brown trout. You can fish, canoe, jetboat, or waterski on the lake where Maori once fished for eels and mussels. **Rotoiti Water Taxis** charters boats for trampers and picnickers from Kerr and West Bays. They also rent kayaks and canoes. (☎521 1894 or 021 702 278. Kerr Bay $60 for up to 6, $10 per extra person. West Bay $75 for up to 5, $15 per extra person. Kayaks, canoes and rowboats $30-40 per half day.) Lake Rotoiti's big sister, **Lake Rotoroa**, off SH6, was cut by two glaciers that formed the Sabine and D'Urville Valleys. Jetboating is prohibited on Rotoroa, but trampers, fishermen, and birdwatchers can contact **Rotoroa Water Taxi** (☎523 9199) for a ride.

Wintertime revelers use the **St. Arnaud** ranges as a skiing base. The 350-hectare **Rainbow Ski Area** offers slopes for all skill levels. They also run a shuttle between the ski field and the parking lot. (round-trip $12, children $9). (☎521 1861, snowphone 08 322 2605; www.skirainbow.co.nz. Lift pass $48; half-day $35. Skis, boots, and poles $35 per day. Snowboard and boots $47 per day.)

ABEL TASMAN NATIONAL PARK ☎03

In 1941, conservationist Pérrine Moncrieff was struggling to convince the New Zealand government that a gorgeous swath of coastal forest was worth protecting from the timber industry. On the advent of the 300-year anniversary of Dutchman Abel Tasman's 1642 visit to these shores, Moncrieff found the perfect means to convince the authorities: inviting the Queen of Netherlands to be the patroness of the park. The plan worked, and Abel Tasman National Park was born. With subtropical weather, turquoise waters, golden sands, and bizarre rock formations, New Zealand's smallest national park draws 150,000 visitors each year.

AT A GLANCE	
AREA: 22,530 hectares.	**GATEWAYS:** Marahau and Wainui.
CLIMATE: Mild and sunny.	**ACCOMMODATIONS:** Coast Track has 4 huts and 20 campsites. Inland Track has 3 huts.
FEATURES: Coast and inland tracks; world-class kayaking.	
HIGHLIGHTS: Golden beaches bordering turquoise water.	**FEES AND RESERVATIONS:** Great Walks Ticket required. Coast huts $25, campsites 10. Reserve year-round.

⊏ TRANSPORTATION. Transportation in the park consists of buses and water taxis and centers around the Abel Tasman Coast Track; see p. 283.

▤ 🏖 ORIENTATION AND PRACTICAL INFORMATION. Abel Tasman National Park is east of SH60, on the peninsula that separates the Golden and Tasman Bays. **Sandy Bay Road** breaks off from SH60 between Motueka and Takaka Hill and passes through **Kaiteriteri** before ending in **Marahau** (18km north of Motueka), the tiny tourist village at the southern end of the park. Both Kaiteriteri and Marahau function as bases for exploring the park and many tour operators base out of one or the other or both. **Abel Tasman Drive** heads east from Takaka to **Wainui Carpark** (21km east of Takaka), **Totaranui campground** (32km east of Takaka), and **Awaroa Inlet** (31km east of Takaka), all near the park's northern end. The **Nelson i-Site** (see p. 275) is the main contact center for the park, though the DOC offices in Motueka and Takaka as well as the Motueka i-Site are armed with information. Book huts for the Abel Tasman Coast Track online through the DOC website (www.doc.govt.nz). The nearest **supermarkets** and **ATMs** are in Motueka and Takaka. The best bet for secure **parking** is in hostels' parking lots.

WHEN TO GO. Abel Tasman is fully accessible year-round, although rough seas during the winter season often make water taxi service to the northern reaches of the park difficult.

ⒻⒼ ACCOMMODATIONS AND FOOD. A stone's throw from the Coast Track's Marahau trailhead, **The Barn (BBH) ❷** offers a range of tranquil and cheerful accommodations—some with sea views, many in the fabulously refurbished barn. (☎527 8043; www.barn.co.nz. Small shop. Gas cooker $5 per day, utensils $5 per day. Wash $2, dry $2. Internet $2 per 20min. Free luggage and car storage $3 per day. Dorms $20-24, all female $26; doubles in a teepee $52; seaview doubles and twins $60. Tent sites $12 per person. $2 BBH discount.) Just up the road, surrounded by the same lush hillside, the 100-acre **Old MacDonald's Farm ❶** has a bustling caravan park, some tired indoor rooms, and a clothing-optional swimming hole. It also houses the **Gum Drop Cafe ❷**, which serves fish 'n chips ($7.50), hamburgers ($7), and other "heart attacks" on a plate. (☎527 8288; www.oldmacs.co.nz. Camping gear for rent: stoves $4 per day; sleeping bags $10 per day; 2-person tents $10 per day; equipment deposits $60-100. Small shop with alcohol. Reception 8am-8pm. Internet $2 per 10min. Dorms from $22; cabins $70; doubles $140. Tent sites $12 per adult; 2-person powered sites $40, $12 per extra person. Cafe daily 5-9pm.)

Kaiteriteri has an excellent backpackers and beachside restaurant. **Kaiteri Lodge ❸**, on Inlet Rd. off Kaiteri Rd., has new facilities, including a 2 person swiss infra-red spa ($10 per hr.) and spacious dorm rooms a skip and a hop from the beach. (☎527 8281; www.kaiterilodge.co.nz. Intenet $1 per 10min. Wash $3, dry $3. Mountain bike hire $35 per day. Scooters $20 for 1st hr., $10 each additional hour. Dorms $35-40. Double and twin ensuite $140; triple ensuite $160; quad ensuite $180. 50% discount available off-season.) Next to the lodge, **The Beached Whale** is the beginning and end of nightlife in the area. Live entertainment every night. (☎527 8114. Thirsty Thursday discounts. Pints $6; jugs $8.50. Takeaway fish 'n chips $6. Open Oct.-May daily 4-11pm; in winter open according to business.)

Ⓜ OUTDOOR ACTIVITIES. For information on the **Abel Tasman Coast Track,** see p. 283. The less frequently traversed **Inland Track** (3-4 days round-trip) connects Marahau and Wainui but is considerably more challenging than the Coast Track. Added to the park in the 1970s, it was orginally created for hunters. Trampers who use the track today usually do so only to create a loop with the Coast Track. The Inland Track has three huts ($5, under 18 $2.50). It is also possible to access the track at its midpoint via the 11km unpaved **Canaan Road,** which branches off SH60 halfway between Takaka and Motueka. The end of Canaan Rd. is also the starting point for the walk to the 183m vertical-drop stone splendor of **Harwood's Hole** (1½hr. round-trip), though there isn't much of a view from the edge. Numerous other dayhikes begin from Totaranui campground and Wainui Carpark.

The clear waters, trackless beaches, and fine weather of the park have inspired a sea kayaking explosion in recent years. A dependable tail wind out of the north

MARLBOROUGH AND NELSON

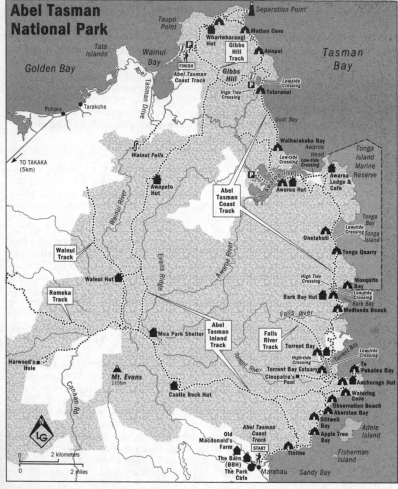

Abel Tasman National Park

means that kayakers are often transported via water taxi to a beach along the Coast Track and then make their way down south, aided by the wind. Kayakers can visit beaches like **Mosquito Bay** and **Observation** that the Coast Track doesn't reach, as well as numerous offshore islands. The profusion of companies can be overwhelming at first, but most offer similar guided excursions, independent rentals (2-person min.), kayak or tramp options, and kayak pickup ($30-40) for paddlers who don't want to double back; all provide extensive instruction before sending anyone out, and most also offer a meal. The following trips and rentals give an idea of each company's prices but do not cover all the offerings. ▨**Kaiteriteri Kayak** has daytrips and several half-day family-oriented trips out of Kaiteriteri Beach with some of the most personable guides in the Abel Tasman area. Most trips pass by the photogenic Split Apple Rock. The "Royale with Cheese" ($165 with water taxi transport, $145 for hikers meeting the tour at Bark Bay), a one-day, one-way trip with the wind at your back, is an especially popular trip. (☎527 8383 or 0800 252 925; www.seakayak.co.nz. Kayak rental half-day $45-55, 2- day $99, 3-day $140, 4-day $170. Half-day guided tours from $80; full-day from $99; overnight from $335, kayak and walk from $175.) **Kiwi Kayaks**, in Riwata, specializes in smaller groups. (☎528 7705 or 0800 695 494; www.kiwikayaks.co.nz. Kayaks $50 for first day, $40 each additional day. Day tours $89-210. Overnight guided tours from $269.) **Golden Bay Kayaks** is the only company based north of the park in Pohara. Its location means their tours often encounter less traffic on the water. (☎525 9095; www.goldenbaykayaks.co.nz. Kayak hire from $40 per day. Snorkel and wetsuits available. Guided tours from $60 for half-day.)

While tramping and kayaking within the national park are the biggest draws, aquatic activities outside park boundaries add history and diversity to the limited park menu. Established in 1993, the **Tonga Island Marine Reserve** stretches one nautical mile into the sea between Awaroa and Bark Bays, and confers full protection to all the creatures that dwell there. **Kaiteriteri Kayaks** runs **Maori Uncut**, the only tour in the Abel Tasman to detail local Maori history. (☎0800 252 925; www.maori-uncut.co.nz. Daily 12:45pm. $110. Lunch $12 extra.) **Abel Tasman Sailing** has laid-back catamaran sailing that lets you choose to participate or just relax and work on your tan. (☎0800 467 245 or 527 8375; www.sailingadventures.co.nz. Departs daily 10am from Kaiteriteri. Lunch included. Transport from Nelson for $32 return. $135, children $68.) **Kitescool** teaches a variety of kitesurfing courses at Marahau and Nelson beaches. (☎021 354 837; www.kitescool.co.nz. Half-day intro course $170. One-on-one instruction $90 per hour.) For a bird's-eye view of the landscape, **Flight Corporation** offers scenic flights over Abel Tasman National Park (1hr., $199), Farewell Spit (1½hr., $269), and Marlborough Sounds (1hr., $199), as well as transport to the Heaphy Track ($199) and Araroa ($175) in the national park. (☎547 8175 or 0800 359 464; www.flightcorp.co.nz. Flights on demand. 2-person min.)

🔣 ABEL TASMAN COAST TRACK

One of New Zealand's best-loved and most-walked tramps, the easygoing Abel Tasman Coast Track promises a colorful outdoor scene. Although the track's lingering pockets of private enterprise and occasionally maddening crowds may not please wilderness-hungry trampers, the scenery remains accessible.

Length: 51km, 3-5 days round-trip.

Trailheads: Marahau in the south and **Wainui Carpark** in the north. An intermediate point at **Totaranui** is car-accessible. Water taxis make any point between Marahau and Totaranul a start or finish, though they only run north of Totaranui by request.

Transportation:

Water Taxis: Inside the park, many **water taxis** service points along the track and most offer pack transport for $10 per bag per transfer. Though times and prices vary slightly, water taxis typically go north from **Marahau** to: **Torrent Bay/Anchorage Bay** (35min., $20-25); **Bark Bay** (45min., $20-29); **Onetahuti Beach/Tonga Bay** (1hr., $25-30); **Awaroa Bay** (1¼hr., $30-34); **Totaranul** (1½hr., $35-36). The following water taxis run daily from Marahau: **Abel Tasman Aqua Taxi** (☎527 8083 or 0800 278 282; www.aquataxis.co.nz); **Abel Tasman Wilsons Experiences** (☎528 2027 or 0800 223 582; www.abeltasman.co.nz.); **Marahau Water Taxis** (☎527 8176 or 0800 808 018; www.abeltasmanmarahaucamp.co.nz); **Kiwi Watertaxis** (☎0800 695 494 or 528 7705; www.adventureabeltasman.com); and **Abel Tasman Sea Shuttle** (☎0800 732 748; www.abeltasmanseashuttles.co.nz).

Buses: Outside the park borders, at the southern end of the Coast Track, **Marahau** is the primary water transport base for the park and the main point of land access from the south. Buses that take travelers out of the park from Wainui Carpark generally run through Takaka, Marahau (by prior request), Motueka, and on to Nelson. **Abel Tasman Coachlines** (☎528 8850; www.abeltasman-travel.co.nz) runs from Nelson via Motueka to Marahau (1¾hr.; 4 times per day; one-way $17, from

Motueka $9), Totaranui (3½hr., daily 6:45am, $34) and Wainui. (3hr., daily 6:45am, $32). and between Takaka and Wainui Carpark (30min., daily 9:15am, $12) and Totaranui (1hr., $16). **Southern Link K-Bus** also runs between Motueka and Marahau (30min.; up to 6 times per day in summer, $9), and for those who walk the entire track south to north, it also runs buses from Wainui Carpark to Marahau (daily 3:30pm, $39) and Motueka (daily 11:10am and 3:30pm, $26) in the summer; call ahead for winter service. **Golden Bay Coachlines** (☎525 8352; mike@goldenbaycoachlines.co.nz) runs between Takaka and Totaranui via Wainui Carpark on demand. **Trek Express** (☎0800 128 735 or 540 2289; rory-moore@xtra.co.nz), **Nelson Bay Shuttles** (☎540 3851; info@nnbays.co.nz), and **Nelson Lakes Shuttles** (☎521 1900 or 021 490 095) run shuttle service to Marahau (1-4 people $100-120) and Totaranui (1-4 people $180-250).

Hitchhiking: Although *Let's Go* does not recommend hitchhiking, hitchers report plenty of traffic in summer and that it is easier to hitchhike to or from Marahau than from the Wainui Carpark.

Tides: The tides can affect one's timing on the track, since **Awaroa Inlet** can only be crossed on foot within 1½hr. before and 2hr. after low tide (Awaroa Lodge runs a launch M-F 1hr. before high tide; $10). **Onetahuti Beach** has a river best crossed within 3hr. of low tide. Anchorage, Bark Bay, Awaroa, and Totaranui all have alternate high- and low-tide routes; low-tide routes are generally 20min.-1hr. faster. **Tide tables** are posted on the DOC website as well as at area visitors centers and in each hut. A general guideline is that early morning low tides are conducive to a south-to-north walk, while late morning and early afternoon tides call for a north-to-south walk. This is not a hard and fast rule, but it is helpful to keep in mind when planning your route.

Seasonality: Year-round. Kiwis crowd the tracks during Christmas and Easter; other visitors flood them just after New Year.

Huts and Campsites: 4 **DOC huts** on a booking system. Huts (Oct.-Apr. $25 per night; May-Sept. $10) must be booked in advance year-round. The DOC accepts bookings starting July 1 for the following season. The track's 21 **campsites** require permits year-round ($10 per night; May-Sept. $7 per night). Max stay at all huts and campsites is 2 nights, except for the DOC-run section of Totaranui which has a max. stay of 1 night.

Water: Anchorage, Bark Bay, Awaroa, Totaranui, and Whariwharangi; water at campsites should be filtered, treated, or boiled for at least 3min.

Gear: Hiking boots are not necessary for the Abel Tasman, and many trampers prefer sturdy sandals.

Storage: Most accommodations store for free. **Kahurangi Bus Services** charges $5 per bag for transport between Motueka and Takaka.

MARAHAU TRAILHEAD TO ANCHORAGE HUT AND CAMPSITE. *11.5km, 4hr.*

Beginning at the southern end of the park, the track proceeds past the unremarkable trailside grass that marks **Tinline Creek Campsite** (15 sites) down to the lovely beach at **Apple Tree Bay Campsite** (15 sites). **Stilwell Bay Campsite** (3 sites) is on a nice beach with views of Adele Island, but access requires a scramble down rocks, which can be difficult at high tide. Shortly thereafter, a switchback descends to **Akersten Bay Campsite** (5 sites), which offers terraced sites among trees next to a small beach. From here, the track rises to a ridge, affording stunning sea views of **Anchorage Bay.** Those planning to stay at Anchorage Campsite will need to detour off the Coast Track here. The side trail forks with a steep track leading down the other side of the ridge to the beachfront **Watering Cove Campsite** (10 sites). The right fork descends gradually to a wide (and often crowded) arc of sand, with the modest **Anchorage Hut** (24 bunks) nearby. Bunks are stacked in two rooms of twelve beds each. The wide field next door is **Anchorage Campsite** (50 sites), a veritable tent town. About a 10min. walk from Anchorage Campsite, the more secluded **Te Pukatea Bay Campsite** (10 sites) is a perfect golden crescent hemmed in by lush headlands popular with kayakers. There's no filtered water on-site, so you'll want to make sure to fill up at Anchorage before moving on.

ANCHORAGE HUT TO BARK BAY HUT. *9.5km, 3-4hr.* To continue to Bark Bay from Anchorage Hut without doubling back up the ridge, go to the western edge of the beach to where a sign points to the high-tide route (1½hr.) and low-tide route (40min.) to Torrent Bay Estuary. A side trip off the high-tide route, **Cleopatra's Pool** (20min. round-trip) sees water spill down a rocky chute into a pleasant pebbled swimming hole. Neither **Torrent Bay Estuary Campsite** (6 sites) nor nearby **Torrent Bay Campsite** (10 sites) is ideal—the former overlooks a mudflat half the time, while the latter is in a grove of pines (though there is convenient beach access). In between the two, a path leads to the densely forested upstream portion of the **Falls River** (3hr. round-trip). Tiny **Torrent Bay Township,** just past the campsites, is a collection of holiday homes most notable for its public phone with free local calls to Motueka. Back in the wilderness, **Medlands Beach Campsite** (6 sites) offers sandy plots framed by a gorgeous combination of estuary and surf. Its white sands offer all the beauty of Bark Bay without the crowds. **Bark Bay Campsite** (40 sites) is usually crowded but the bay is big and beautiful. Just before the spacious rooms and open-air freshwater shower of the inland **Bark Bay Hut** (34 bunks), the small **Bark Bay Hut Campsite** (5 sites) is hidden only paces off the track.

BARK BAY HUT TO AWAROA HUT. *11.5km, 4hr.* The track crosses Bark Bay Estuary (a high-tide route goes around the inlet) and then winds steadily up and over a small peninsula before hitting **Tonga Quarry Campsite** (20 sites). The campsite features a stream, a white stretch of sand, and blocks of stone from the old quarry days that make convenient benches. Another brief up-and-over opens onto the huge arc of **Onetahuti Beach,** host to the **Onetahuti Campsite** (20 sites) and, all too often, scores of buzzing water taxis. The track runs the length of the beach until, after about 20min., it crosses a river at the northern end that can rise chest-high at high tide. It is only safe to cross within 3hr. of low tide. Heading back inland, the track climbs gently toward the **Awaroa Lodge ❺,** a swank resort and restaurant with a cafe and Internet facilities for non-guest use. (☎528 8758; www.awaroalodge.co.nz. Restaurant open daily 7:30am-9pm. Pints $6.50. Public phones. Free toilets and drinking water.) Budget travelers can pass through this posh slice of civilization en route to **Awaroa Inlet;** the route takes 30min. less than the main track, though it cannot be crossed within 1½hr. of high tide. Hikers getting pack transfer to Awaroa should pick their bags up at the beach near the lodge, even if they are staying in the hut. Simple **Awaroa Hut** (22 bunks) and the hard-packed dirt of neighboring **Awaroa Campsite** (18 sites) sit beside the inlet, which becomes a crossable mudflat within 1½hr. before and 2hr. after low tide.

AWAROA HUT TO TOTARANUI CAMPSITE. *5.5km, 1½hr.* After the inlet, the track turns inland through dense forest before arriving at the grassy plots and nearby beach of **Waiharakeke Campsite** (10 sites). The track then passes a couple of huge beech trees, and the long stretch of **Goat Beach** before emerging onto **Totaranui Campsite** (p. 281). Accessible by road, **Totaranui** is a far cry from the natural splendor of the track and is overrun with tourists in peak season. For hikers, DOC runs a small part (40 campers) of the 850-camper capacity campsite. Those booking the DOC campsite must book at least one other campsite on the track. The rest is privately run and only on a booking system Dec. to mid-Feb. Be sure to check road accessibility on arrival. (☎528 8083. Camp office with basic supplies open daily 9am-3:30pm. Trash disposal facilities.)

TOTARANUI CAMPSITE TO WHARIWHARANGI HUT. *13km, 4½hr.* North of Totaranui, the water taxis and kayaks thin out and there are noticeably fewer hikers. Comprised of hillier terrain than other parts of the track, lined with majestic beaches, and featuring superior overnight options, this section is arguably the track's most beautiful. ■**Anapai Bay Campsite** (4 sites) lies next to a beach fringed by fluted rock faces, shrouded by a dense canopy of windswept kanuka. **Mutton Cove Campsite** (20 sites) also sits alongside an elegant beach, though unsightly felled pines mar its plots. A side-trip departs from the campsite around **Separation Point** (1hr. round-trip). This walk over kanuka-clad hillsides leads to a lighthouse with misty views of Farewell Spit, North Island, and the occasional fur seal. The main track descends toward **Whariwharangi Hut** (20 bunks), an old two-story farmhouse with freshwater showers and the **Whariwharangi Campsite** (20 sites) outside. From Whariwharangi Hut, it is possible to loop back to Totaranui to catch a water taxi out of the park via **Gibbs Hill Track.**

WHARIWHARANGI HUT TO WAINUI CARPARK. *5.5km, 1½hr.* The last leg of the track is comprised of one very large (but scenic and gradually graded) hill between Whariwharangi Hut and the Wainui Carpark. The descent offers eye-catching views of Wainui Bay.

MOTUEKA   ☎03

Though its sober appearance is misleading, Motueka (pop. 11,000) was once New Zealand's number one producer of beer and tobacco. The town has since turned its attention toward more wholesome pursuits: namely, fruit picking. Fueled by the area's unusually fertile land, grapes and citrus fruits blossom throughout the summer. Legions of starving backpackers still head to Motueka to line their thinning wallets with some much-needed cash before heading out into the nearby Abel Tasman National Park and Golden Bay.

> **:TIP:** **KEY TO THE KIWI KINGDOM.** To get the real lowdown on picking opportunities in Motueka, chat up local hostel owners and check their work boards before signing on the dotted line.

⌐ TRANSPORTATION. Abel Tasman Coachlines (☎548 0285; www.abeltasman-travel.co.nz) runs to: Marahau (30min., 2-3 per day, $8) via Kaiteriteri Beach (15min., $7); Nelson (50min., 1-3 per day, $9); Takaka (1hr., 1-2 per day, $15). **K Bus** (☎0508 458 835; www.kbus.co.nz) runs to: Marahau (30min., Nov.-Apr. 3 per day, $8) via Kaiteriteri Beach (15min., $10); Nelson (1hr., 3-4 per day, $11); Picton (4hr., 2-3 per day, $30); Takaka (1½hr., 1-2 per day, $17). Two buses leave Motueka for the remote Heaphy Track (2hr., 8am, $35).

◼⁊ ORIENTATION AND PRACTICAL INFORMATION. SH60 becomes **High Street** as it cuts through town. All shops and most hostels lie on or just off High St.; building numbers increase as one heads south (toward Nelson). Buses drop off at the **Motueka i-Site,** 20 Wallace St., which books accommodations and DOC huts. The Motueka i-Site also serves as the main info center for Abel Tasman National Park. (☎528 6543; www.abeltasmangreenrush.co.nz. Open Nov.-Feb. M-F 8:30am-5:30pm, Sa-Su 9am-5pm; Mar.-Oct. M-F 8am-5pm, Sa-Su 8am-4pm.) The **DOC office,** at High and King Edward St., is 2km toward Nelson from the Motueka i-Site. (☎528 1810. Open M-F 8am-5:30pm) Motueka has many **work opportunities** for fruit pickers from Dec.-Jan. and mid-Feb. to June. Ask at the Motueka i-Site for more info.

Coppins Great Outdoor Centre, 225 High St., stocks and rents tramping gear. (☎528 7296. Open Oct.-Mar. M-F 8:30am-5:30pm, Sa 9am-4pm, Su 9:30am-2:30pm; Apr.-Sept. M-F 8:30am-5:30pm, Sa 9am-2pm.) Other services include: three **banks** with ATMs along High St. (all open M-F 9am-4:30pm); the **police,** 68 High St. (☎528 1220); **Unichem Pharmacy** (☎528 9980; open M, W-F 8:30am-5:30pm, Tu 9am-5:30pm, Sa 9am-1pm); after hours **pharmacy** (☎021 528 908); **Internet** access at **Cyberworld Internet Cafe,** 178 High St. (☎528 8090; $5.50 per hr.; open M-F 9am-9pm, Sa-Su 10am-

9pm; extended summer hours); the **post office,** 207 High St., in **Take Note** (☎528 6600; open M-F 8am-5:30pm, Sa-Su 9am-5pm).

⌂ ⌇ ACCOMMODATIONS AND CAMPING. Home to two upbeat Kiwis, **Laughing Kiwi Backpackers (BBH)** ❷, 310 High St., has two houses just a few minutes walk from town. (☎528 9229; www.laughingkiwi.co.nz. Free spa. Laundry $4. Internet $2 per 20min. Reception 7:30am-8pm. 6-bed dorms $21; 4-bed dorms $23; twins and doubles $26, with bath $30. Cash only.) The **White Elephant (BBH)** ❷, 55 Whakarewa St., is a Victorian house offering cushy common spaces, a big garden and a modern kitchen. From the Motueka i-Site, take a left onto High St., turn right after KFC, and continue down Whakarewa St.; the hostel is on the left. (☎528 6208; www.whiteelephant.co.nz. Linen $2. Laundry $2-4. Internet $1 per 10min. Reception 8am-9pm. Dorms $20-21; twins and doubles $50, with bath $60. Tent sites $14. Cash only.) The facilities at the large **Bakers Lodge (BBH/YHA)** ❷, 4 Poole St., are so shiny and sterile that the place still feels new. From the Motueka i-Site, turn right onto High St.; the hostel is two long blocks down on the left. (☎528 0102; www.bakerslodge.co.nz. Laundry $4. Internet $1 per 10min. Reception 7:45-10am, 2-8pm. Dorms $21-25; twins and doubles $52, with bath $62. Two kilometers south of the town center, **Happy Apple Backpackers (BBH)** ❷, 500 High St., has a large backyard and comfortable common room ideal for campers and backpackers alike. The charming hosts can give you the lowdown on the area. (☎528 8652; www.happyapplebackpackers.co.nz. Free pickup. Linen $3. Laundry $4. Internet $3 per 30min. Reception 7:30am-9:30pm. 4-bed dorms $20; singles $24; twins $44; doubles with linen $48. Cash only.)

Motueka Top 10 Holiday Park ❶, 10 Fearon St., just off High St., allows tenters to pitch anywhere in its shady fields. Book ahead December through January. (☎528 7189 or 0800 668 835; www.motuekatop10.co.nz. Linen $5. Laundry $6. Internet $2 per 15min. Reception 8am-9pm. Tent sites $14, $13 per extra person, $7 per extra child. 2-person cabins from $38, with kitchen $65; self-contained units from $69. MC/V.)

◻ FOOD. Bright, muralled walls support the astronomical ceiling at ▨**Hot Mama's Cafe** ❸, 105 High St. Lunch in the garden or sup indoors at the Pollock-inspired tables. (☎528 7039. Mains $10-21. Live music usually F-Sa from 9:30pm. Open daily 8:30am-late.) The **Swinging Sultan** ❷, 172 High St., serves up tangy beef, chicken, vegetarian, and vegan kebabs ($8-10) to eat there or take away. (☎528 8909. Open daily 8am-10pm.) Sweet croissants ($1.40) and sugary cookies ($0.80) are the specialities of the French-inspired **Patisserie Royale** ❶, 152 High Street. (☎528 7200. Open daily 8am-5pm.) Go to **Freshchoice,** 108 High St., for groceries. (☎528 7180. Open daily 7am-9pm.)

◧ ⚠ SIGHTS AND OUTDOOR ACTIVITIES. Kaiteriteri Beach is just a 15min. drive (13km) north from town; buses stop en route to **Marahau** (p. 280). **Takaka Hill** (791m), 20km northwest of town via SH6, serves as a starting point for a multitude of short walks, including the **Takaka Hill Walk** (15min. round-trip) at the very top. Also at the top of Takaka Hill, the **Ngarua Caves** showcase moa bones and illuminated stalactites. (☎528 8093; mte@xtra.co.nz. Open Oct.-May daily 10am-4pm. Call ahead May-Sept. $14, under 8 $5.) Back in town, the **Motueka District Museum,** 140 High St., has an assortment of Maori artifacts and an exhibit on the history of the area. (☎528 7660. Open M-F 10am-4pm, Sa 10am-2pm. In winter open Tu-Th 10am-3pm. $2, children $0.50.) For a night of quiet lounging, **The Gecko Theatre,** 78 High St., at High and Poole St., shows indy and feature films in a tiny playground of a cinema. Grab a bean bag and pretend you're five years old again. (☎528 4272. 3

MARLBOROUGH AND NELSON

shows per day. $8-11, children $5-6.50.) If you're feeling antsy, **Skydive Able Tasman** operates out of the airport (see **Outdoor Activities,** p. 281).

GOLDEN BAY

Golden Bay is where Abel Tasman first spotted *Aotearoa* in 1642. After a brief encounter with local Maori, he quickly turned tail and dubbed the area "Murderer's Bay." Having shed that unfortunate moniker, Golden Bay is now synonymous with earth-centered lifestyles and draws Auckland urbanites, international hippies, and retired ex-pats with its beaches and sprawling wilderness.

TAKAKA   ☎ 03

A convenient access point for the Golden Bay as well as the Kahurangi and Abel Tasman National Parks, Takaka (pop. 1500) is known for its earth-friendly community and offbeat attractions.

☷ TRANSPORTATION. Takaka is 58km north of Motueka, 8km west of Pohara, and 27km east of Collingwood. The Golden Bay i-Site can arrange all bus bookings. **Golden Bay Coachlines,** 98 Commercial St. (☎525 8352; www.goldenbaycoachlines.co.nz), runs to Nelson (2¼hr., daily 6:45am and noon, $28) via Motueka (1¼hr., $19). Transfer in Motueka for Abel Tasman coachlines. They also run to the Heaphy Track mid-December to April (1¼hr., 1 per day, $20) via Collingwood (30min., $15). **Southern Link K-Bus** (☎0508 458 835; www.southernlinkcoaches.co.nz) runs to: Nelson (2hr.; in summer 3 per day, in winter 4 per week; $22) via Motueka (1hr., $15); Totaranui (1hr., 1 per day, $11) via the Wainui Carpark (30min., $10); the Heaphy Track (1¼hr., 1 per day, $20) via Collingwood (30min., $12). For **bike rental,** head to the **Quiet Revolution Cycle Shop,** 11 Commercial St. (☎/fax 525 9555. Mountain and road bikes $15-30 per day. Open M-F 9am-5pm, Sa 9:30am-12:30pm. In winter M-F 10am-5pm, Sa 9:30am-12:30pm.)

◼◪ ORIENTATION AND PRACTICAL INFORMATION. Takaka's main—and some might say only—drag is **Commercial Street,** which becomes **Willow Street** at its southern (Motueka-bound) extremity. **Motupipi Street** branches northeast. Buses arrive and depart from the **Golden Bay i-Site,** on Willow St., just south of Motupipi St. (☎525 9136. Open daily 9am-5pm.) Trampers can get additional insight, including trail updates and hut bookings, at the **Golden Bay Area DOC Office,** 62 Commercial St. (☎525 8026. Open M-F 9am-5pm.)

Takaka and Golden Bay offer many **work opportunities** for WWOOFers. Check the bulletin boards at hostels and cafes for job listings. Other services on Commercial St. include: **Westpac Trust Bank,** 64 Commercial St., with a 24hr. **ATM** (☎525 8094; open M-Tu and Th-F 9am-4:30pm, W 9:30am-4:30pm); the **police,** 155 Commercial St. (☎525 9211); **Golden Bay Pharmacy,** 17 Commercial St. (☎525 9490; open M-Th 8:30am-5:30pm, F 8:30am-6pm, Sa 9:30am-noon), is also good for after-hours emergencies; **Golden Bay Medical Centre** (☎525 9911), north of the city at the corner with Edinburgh Rd.; **Internet** access at the **library,** 63 Commercial St. (☎525 0059; Internet $7 per hr. Open M-Th 9:30am-5pm, F 9:30am-6pm, Sa 9:30am-12:30pm), at **gbnet,** 4 Commercial St. ($6 per hr.; open M-F 9am-5pm, Sa 10am-1pm), and inside **Wholemeal Cafe** ($4 per 30min; see below); the **post office,** 29 Commercial St, inside **Take Note Bookstore.** (☎525 9702. Poste Restante. Open M-F 8:30am-5:30pm, Sa 9:30am-12:30pm.)

▛ ACCOMMODATIONS. Takaka is filled with several cozy backpackers, all of which feature the same relaxed, comfortable vibe. **Kiwiana (BBH) ❷,** 73 Motupipi St., is one of the standout hostels in Takaka. From Commercial St., head down

Motupipi St. 600m; it's on the left. Its "game garage" holds foosball, pool, ping-pong tables, and a guitar, while the garden holds a barbeque, a spa and giant chess and Jenga sets. (☎0800 805 494 or 525 7676. No Internet. Free bike use. Dorms $22; doubles and twins $54. Tent sites $15. $2 BBH discount.) The other standout hostel is nearby **Annie's Nirvana Lodge (YHA/BBH) ❷**, 25 Motupipi St., which lives up to its moniker with soft, fully made beds, a common room, free fruit, Fluffy the cat, and an old-hippie atmosphere epitomized by the backyard lounge area. (☎525 8766; www.nirvanalodge.co.nz. Free bike use. Reception 8:30am-8pm. Dorms $22; doubles and twins $56; triples $78. Tent sites $15. $3 BBH/YHA discount.) A short drive from Takaka, **The Nook Guesthouse (BBH) ❷**, 678 Abel Tasman Dr., just outside Pohara, is the quietest of all hostels with gardens, a swimming beach, and a lot of local art. (☎525 8501 or 0800 806 665; www.thenookguesthouse.co.nz. No laundry or Internet. Reception 8:30am-9:30pm. Dorms $25; twins and doubles $60. Self-contained strawbale cottage with private veranda $160, off-season $140.) Across the way from Annie's, **Get-away (BBH) ❷**, 28 Motupipi St., has a homey feel sure to please couples, though the dorm rooms are plain. There is a great secluded double with TV and fridge. (☎525 6261; marilynn@e3.net.nz. Free pickup from Golden Bay i-Site. Dorms $23; single $40; doubles $54. $2-3 BBH discount.) Past the town center on Commercial St., **Barefoot Backpackers (BBH) ❷**, 114 Commercial St., beds its guests in clean, pastel rooms. (☎525 7005 or 0508 525 7005; www.bare-foot.co.nz. Reception 7am-7pm. Dorms $22-23; single $35; twins and doubles $50. Tent sites $12. $2 BBH discount.)

🄲 **FOOD.** The **Wholemeal Cafe ❸**, 60 Commercial St., embodies the earth-loving free-spirited Takaka with art exhibits and music acts. Fresh ingredients add color to vegetarian curries and pastas ($16-20). Their notice board is a good place to find job opportunities. (☎525 9426. Open daily 7:30am-8:30pm, earlier in winter.) Just down the street, **Dangerous Kitchen ❷**, 46/48 Commercial St., serves strong caffeinated drinks and gourmet pizzas. At night, the beer garden grooves to a DJ. (☎525 8681, takeaways ☎525 8686. Latin night 1st Sa of every month. Spanakopita $6.50-7.50. Pints $5.50. Open in summer Tu-Su 11am-10pm; in winter Tu-Sa 11am-10pm.) Though the meals are pricey, **Brigand Cafe ❸**, 90 Commercial St., has the best jam sessions in town, making it the place to grab a pint ($4.50) and catch a set. (☎525 9636. Live music starts around 9pm. Tu jazzy jam session; Th open mic. Open daily 11am-late, never closes before midnight.) **Golden Fries ❶**, at Commercial and Motupipi St., is the best fish 'n chips shop in Golden Bay. (☎525 9699. Fish of the day $2.40, chips $2.20. Nothing over $7. Open daily 5pm-late.) **Aubergine ❷**, 30 Commercial St., through the Take Notes store, has cheap Asian meals ($6.50-20) as well as Internet ($2.50 per 15min.) and laundry facilities. (☎525 8820. Open daily 6am-8pm; in winter M-Sa 6am-8pm.) **Golden Bay Organics**, 47 Commercial St., peddles organic produce. (☎525 8677. Open M-Th 9am-5:30pm, F 9am-6pm, Sa 9am-1:30pm. Cash only.) **Fresh Choice**, 13 Willow St., across from the Golden Bay i-Site, has groceries. (Open daily 7am-9pm.)Across the way from Annie's, **Get-away (BBH) ❷**, 28 Motupipi St., has a homey feel sure to please couples, though the dorm rooms are plain. There is a great secluded double with TV and fridge. (☎525 6261; marilynn@e3.net.nz. Free pickup from Golden Bay i-Site. Dorms $23; single $40; doubles $54. $2-3 BBH discount.) Past the town center on Commercial St., **Barefoot Backpackers (BBH) ❷**, 114 Commercial St., beds its guests in clean, pastel rooms. (☎525 7005 or 0508 525 7005; www.bare-foot.co.nz. Reception 7am-7pm. Dorms $22-23; single $35; twins and doubles $50. Tent sites $12. $2 BBH discount.) Z

🄲🄰 **SIGHTS AND OUTDOOR ACTIVITIES.** The bubbling 🄽Te Waikoropupu Springs ("Pupu Springs" for short), 7km northwest of Takaka, is said to be the world's clearest freshwater springs system. These crystalline depths afford over 90m of underwater visibility. The Maori consider the springs a sacred source of life; ceremonial blessings at times of birth and death were performed at the site. In the past, the springs were open to the public for swimming, but the presence of didymo (see **Uh oh Didymo, It's Snot Funny,** p. 427) has caused the DOC to discontinue swimming. To reach Pupu Springs, follow Commercial St. north 7km, then turn left on Pupu Valley Rd., then 3km down turn left again on Pupu Springs Rd. The **Rawhiti Caves** are a stunning one-million-year-old hole (with a 60m wide entrance) filled with thousands of colorful stalactites. The caves are best visited with John Croxford of **Kahurangi Guided Walks** (☎525 7177; www.kahurangiwalks.co.nz), who runs informative 3hr. trips ($25). Kahurangi Guided Walks also coordinates guided tours of Abel Tasman and Kahurangi Parks. The **Grove** is a surreal spot where trails lead through the foliage to a view of the entire bay. To reach the Grove, take Motupipi out of Takaka, turn right at the roundabout onto Abel Tasman Dr., then turn right at Clifton. Follow the road to the end and turn right; then at the end of that road, turn right again. **Tasman Tandems** gets visitors involved (and aloft) in one of Golden Bay's favorite pastimes—paragliding off Takaka Hill. (☎528 9283 or 021 544 800. 10-15min. flight $180. Discounts for groups of 3 or more.) Some of the best climbing in New Zealand can be found at **Payne's Ford Scenic Reserve,** a 5min. drive south of Takaka on the main road. Climbers should touch base with **Hang Dog Camp** (☎525 9093; hangdog.camp@paradise.net.nz) to pick up a **Hangdog Camp Guide** and get the scoop on climbing the region's limestone faces.

The highlight of a trip to the **Bencarri Farm and Cafe,** on McCallum's Rd., 5km south of Takaka, is feeding the hungry but harmless native Anatoki eels. Cool your hand in the river before touching their heat-sensitive skin. (☎525 8261. Open Sept.-Apr. daily 10am-5pm. $12, children $6; families $35.) Next to Bencarri, **Anatoki Salmon** guarantees everyone will have the catch of the day. After fishing, Anatoki has sizzling grills ready to go. (☎525 7251; www.anatokisalmon.co.nz. Entry and fishing is free; pay for what you catch.) With antiques, tools, and geological specimens, the **Golden Bay Museum,** in the old post office at the far end of Commercial St., represents the best of the many collections that explain the history of Takaka. The gallery next door has local art as well as souvenirs. (☎525 9990 or 525 6268. Open in summer daily 10am-4pm; in winter M-F 10am-4pm. Suggested donation.) **Labyrinth Rocks Park** is a limestone maze located on two hectares just outside of Takaka. This is a good place to take the kids, but adults might find the paths repetitive. Take Motupipi St. out of the hostel area, turn right on Abel Tasman Dr., then left on Scott Rd. (☎525 8434. Open daily noon-late. $7.)

COLLINGWOOD AND FAREWELL SPIT ☎03

In 1856, New Zealand's first big gold rush made a boom town of Collingwood, where 4000 residents clamored to name it the capital city. Three fires and one depleted gold supply later, Collingwood (pop. 300) may only be a shadow of its former self, but that doesn't detract from its prime location near Farewell Spit.

▐ TRANSPORTATION. Bickley Motors (☎525 8352; www.goldenbay-coachlines.co.nz) runs to Takaka from October to April (30min., 1 per day, $15). **K Bus** (☎578 4075; www.kbus.co.nz) does the same at different times ($12). There is no bus to Collingwood from May to September. While *Let's Go* does not recommend it, **hitchhiking** in Golden Bay is common.

▐▐ ORIENTATION AND PRACTICAL INFORMATION. Collingwood lies at the terminus of **SH60,** 27km north of Takaka and 23km south of **Puponga,** the settlement at the base of Farewell Spit. As SH60 enters Collingwood from the west, the first street on the left is **Tasman Street,** the town's one-block main thoroughfare. One block farther east, **Beach Road** runs parallel to Tasman St. alongside the ocean. ◪**Farewell Spit Visitor Centre** in Puponga is the only info outlet in the area. (☎525 8026. Open Sept.-May daily 10am-4pm.) For information on the Golden Bay area, check out www.heartoftheparks.co.nz. The area has **no ATMs. Internet** access can be found at **Farewell Spit Eco Tours** on Tasman St. ($8 per hr.). The **post office** is on Tasman St. (☎524 8916. Open M-F 8:30am-5:30pm, Sa 9am-noon.)

◪◪ **ACCOMMODATIONS AND CAMPING.** The best places to stay in the area are outside town but easily accessible by car. ◪**The Innlet (BBH) ❷**, 10km from Collingwood toward Farewell Spit, is an eco-friendly spot with several kilometers of marked bushwalks. Luxuries include private forest cottages and two creekside cast-iron hot tubs. (☎524 8040; www.goldenbayindex.co.nz/theinnlet.html. Bike rental. Tandem kayak rental $80. Laundry $3. Internet $6 per hr. Closed June-Aug. Dorms $23; twins and doubles $55; 2-person cottages $70; 2-person Ruru cottage $120, $15 per extra person. Tent sites $15. Cash only.) The serene, environmentally conscious ◪**Shambhala Guesthouse (BBH) ❷**, 12km out of Collingwood toward Takaka, is a solar-powered paradise overlooking the sea. Guests enjoy private beach access, rooms with water views, and a yoga meditation hall. Call for pickup from the Mussel Inn. (☎525 8463; www.shambhala.co.nz. Bike rental. Dorms from $24; twins and doubles $53. Cash only.) **Collingwood Motor Camp ❶**, 6 William St., at the far end of Tasman St., has tent sites overlooking the water. (☎524 8149; langmuir.clan@xtra.co.nz. Laundry $5. Reception 8am-8pm. Tent sites $12.50; huts $20 per person. Self-contained units $75, $15 per extra person. MC/V.)

◻ **FOOD.** Great grub awaits at the ◪**Mussel Inn ❸**, on SH60, 200m toward Collingwood from the turn-off to Shambhala Guesthouse. Bohemian offerings include cryptically named local brews ($4.50) and a mean veggie lasagna ($17.50). Live music (F-Su 9pm) and roaring bonfire bring out the Golden Bay community in full force. (☎525 9241; www.musselinn.co.nz. Open daily 11am-late. Closed for about 6 weeks around Aug. MC/V.) The **Courthouse Inn and Cafe ❸**, where SH60 turns into Tasman St., serves tempting gourmet lunch and dinner. (☎524 8572. Lunch mains $6-10. Dinner mains $23-28. Open daily 9am-late. Reduced winter hours. Cash only.) Stock up at the eco-conscious **Col and Trott's Foodcentre.** (☎524 8221. Open M-Th 8am-5:30pm, F 8am-6pm, Sa-Su 9am-4pm. MC/V.)

◪◪ **SIGHTS AND OUTDOOR ACTIVITIES.** While most of the 30km spit is a nature reserve and is inaccessible to the public, visitors can walk 4km out onto the sand peninsula, stopping first at the visitors center for directions, or they can take a tour with one of two companies licensed to drive to the tip of the spit. Tour structure and departure times change with the tides but run daily most of the year; it is essential to call ahead for bookings. **Farewell Spit Eco Tours** has been running 4WD trips since the mid-1940s. (☎524 8257 or 0800 808 257; www.farewellspit.com. Departs from Collingwood. 5½hr. $80. 6½hr. trip to a gannet colony $110.) **Kahurangi Nature Experience** offers tours to the spit and the cliffs. (☎525 6044 or 0800 250 500; www.farewell-spit.co.nz. Departs from the Farewell Spit Visitors Centre. Cliff tours $40. Spit tours $70. Combo tours $90.)

Puponga Farm Park serves as an environmental buffer for the Spit's unique sand habitat. Thirty kilometers of walking trails allow visitors to roam through a patchwork of native plants and bleating livestock. The park's ◪**Wharariki Beach** is definitely worth a visit: low tide reveals caves that beg exploration. The nearest parking lot to the visitors center lies at the end of Wharariki Rd., 6km west of Puponga town; from there, it's a 20min. walk to the beach. Signs on the beach lead the way to Cape Farewell, the northernmost point of South Island.

MARLBOROUGH AND NELSON

KARAMEA   ☎03

Quite literally at the end of the road, Karamea (pop. 700) is a small town in the shadow of a vast wilderness, and serves as a gateway to the Kahurangi National Park. Best known as the endpoint of the **Heaphy Track** (p. 295) and **Wangapeka Track** (p. 298), Karamea sits at the northern end of SH67. The village is also near the **Oparara Basin**, famous for its huge limestone arches and delicate Honeycomb Hill Cave system. From the parking lot on Oparara Rd. (a well-marked 1hr. drive north of town), the **Oparara (Big) Arch Trail** (45min. round-trip) leads to the 43m high, 219m long arch, while the **Moria Gate Trail** (1hr. round-trip) heads to Little Arch. The Moria Gate trail can also be done as a loop with the **Mirrortarn Lake Trail** (1½hr.). The Honeycomb Hill Caves are only accessible on a guided trip, and only the full-day tour includes transport. (Contact the Information Centre for bookings. ☎782 6652. 2hr. kayak tour $70. 3hr. cave tour $70. 5hr. cave and arch eco tour $195, includes lunch.) The walk to **Scotts Beach** (1½hr. round-trip) through nikau palm forest is a popular day hike on the Heaphy Track (see p. 295). The **Fenian Track** (5hr. round-trip) gives trampers a taste of the rainforest, and ends at Adam's Flat, an old gold-mining site from the 1860s. (Trailhead is 1km from the granite quarry on Oparara Loop Rd.) There are numerous other short hikes near town, though most are only accessible by car.

Mountain bikers can head to **K-Road**, a 27km return track with medium to easy riding that requires some fitness and little experience. To reach K-Road, take Kohaihai Hwy. north for 10km, turn right on McCallums Mill Rd., the trailhead is another 10km down. For bike and kayak rentals as well as kite surfing and fishing, call **Karamea Adventures,** on Market Cross. (☎782 6181. Mountain bikes from $20 for 1hr.; K-Road ride $35, $55 with transport. Kayak rentals from $20 for 2hr. Bike and kayak 3hr. combo on Karamea River $50. Fishing from $15 for 2hr. Kitesurfing lessons: $20 per hr. for "learn to launch;" $30 per hr. for on the water lessons. Kite-surf rentals: $25 for 1hr., $40 for 2hr. Open Sa-Su 9am-4pm; book ahead.)

Though *Let's Go* doesn't recommend **hitchhiking**, Karamea locals reportedly almost always pick up hitchers. However, there's little traffic. **Cunningham's Motors** (☎782 6652 or 789 7177) runs to Westport (1½hr., M-F 5:45pm, $18), as does **Karamea Express** (☎782 6757; info@karamea-express.co.nz. M-F, Nov.-Apr. M-Sa; 7:50am; 1¾hr., $27). The **Karamea Information and Resource Centre,** on Bridge St., has a friendly staff with plenty of local knowledge. They also run the town's only **gas station**. (☎782 6652; www.karameainfo.co.nz. Open in summer daily 9am-5pm; less off-season.) Other local services include: **4 Square** (☎782 6701; open M-Th 8:30am-6pm, F 8:30am-7pm, Sa 9am-7pm, Su 9am-5pm); the **police** (☎782 6801), on Wharf St.; **Karamea Medical Centre** (☎782 6710); a **doctor** (☎782 6737); **Internet** access at the visitors center ($2.50 per 15min.); **postal services** at the **Karamea Hardware Store.** (☎782 6700. Open M-F 8am-6pm, Sa-Su 9am-noon.) There are **no banks or ATMs** in Karamea.

Weary trampers can find BBH comforts at 🏠**Rongo (BBH)** ❷, on Waverly St., a 15min. walk west from the center of town. The gallery, community radio station, and cactus and organic veggie garden send off deep hippie vibes, and the free-spirited hostel makes up what it lacks in cleanliness with character. (☎782 6667; www.livinginpeace.com. Wireless Internet and laundry on donation system. Dorms $25; doubles and twins $60. Tents $20. $2-3 BBH discount. MC/V.) Rongo also runs **Karamea Motels** ❸. (☎782 6838. Doubles $70, extra person $15.) The **Last Resort** ❷, 71 Waverly St., a 7min. walk west from the center of town, is a well-kept, scenic complex that has a spa ($5 per 30min.) and airy rooms, as well as two restaurants. (☎782 6617 or 0800 505 042; www.lastresort.co.nz. Dorms $24; twins and doubles $69, with bath $80; studio ensuite $99; self-contained units from $140. Tent sites $10. MC/V.) The **Hermitage** ❺ monopolizes the rest of the accommoda-

MARLBOROUGH AND NELSON

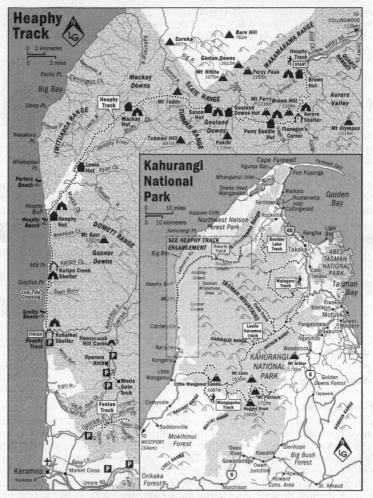

tions in the park; rooms run the gamut from plush to posh, while prices range from very overpriced to "you must be joking." (☎ 435 1809; www.mount-cook.com. Doubles with TV and kitchen from $235; hotel suites from $590. MC/V.)

The pride and joy of the **Karamea Village Hotel ❸**, at Waverly St. and Wharf Rd., is its award-winning whitebait, available to visitors for $18.50. They also have clean and spacious budget rooms that are the best bet in town for couples. An inexpensive takeaway and day menu is also available at this local watering hole. (☎782 6800. Doubles ensuite $95, off-season $85. Open daily 8am-as late as 3am. MC/V.) The no frills community-run bunkhouse in **Karamea Domain ❶**, behind the high-school athletic fields off of SH76, makes DOC huts look flashy and overpriced by comparison. Reception is at the van marked "Caretaker." (No advance bookings. Primitive kitchen. Dorms $9. Powered tent sites $9, $12 for 2, $3 per additional person. Cash only. **Saracens Cafe ❷**, 99 Bridge St., next to the 4 Square in town, serves half-pound hamburgers ($9.50) as well as meat pies ($2.50-3.50), while the adjoining **Bush Lounge Restaurant ❸** grills hearty steak ($24) and provides occasional evening entertainment. (☎782 6600; www.kahurangipark.co.nz. Cafe open in summer daily 8:30am-4pm, restaurant open daily 6pm-midnight; less hours in winter.) **LR Cafe ❷,** at the Last Resort, refuels hungry hikers with pizzas ($15) and bar meals. (Burgers $12-14. Meals $12-22. Open daily 10am-late, licensed until 3am.)

KAHURANGI NATIONAL PARK   ☎03

The vast wilderness that dominates the northwest corner of South Island forms the 452,002-hectare Kahurangi National Park. The country's second-youngest and second-largest national park, Kahurangi accommodates snow-capped peaks, verdant valleys, and palm-lined coasts. This ecosystem supports an astounding array of natural fauna; over half of New Zealand's native plant species grow here (67 of them live nowhere else in the world). Experienced kayakers and thrill seeking white water rafters brave the Class V Karamea River, while trampers looking to escape the crowded Abel Tasman explore Kahurangi's network of challenging tramping tracks.

AT A GLANCE	
AREA: 452,002 hectares.	**FEES AND RESERVATIONS:** The Heaphy Track requires bookings year-round; see p. 295 for prices. Other tracks do not require bookings but do require hut tickets; a single ticket is $5 and huts require 1-3 tickets depending on the quality of the hut. Alternatively, a hut pass ($90) is valid for all huts on the Wangapeka, but not those on the Heaphy.
CLIMATE: Temperate forest.	
FEATURES: Rivers, high plateaus, coastal forest, alpine herb fields.	
HIGHLIGHTS: White water rafting on the Class V Karamea River, trout fishing and over 570km of walking track.	
GATEWAYS: Motueka, Takaka, Collingwood, Karamea, Murchison.	
CAMPING: Backcountry huts.	**TRAMPS:** Heaphy, Wangapeka, Leslie-Karamea.

▐ TRANSPORTATION. Transportation in Kahurangi National Park can be expensive as there are no loop tracks and very few access roads. Coordinating with other hikers makes shuttle transport more available. **Aorere Valley Road** and **Karamea-Kohaihai Road** head southwest from Collingwood and north from Karamea, respectively, to the Heaphy Track's two trailheads; there is no road that connects Collingwood and Karamea on the West Coast. See **Transportation,** p. 295, for information on bus transport to these points. Additionally, **Cobb Valley Road** heads 27km from Upper Takaka to the Cobb Reservoir.

 WHEN TO GO. Kahurangi is beautiful year-round. Most visitors come from December to February; March and April are drier and colder.

▐▐ ORIENTATION AND PRACTICAL INFORMATION. Kahurangi stretches east from the west coast to SH60 and from the base of Farewell Spit south to SH6. The park's sprawl means that both the West Coast and Tasman/Nelson DOC offices are responsible for trail maintenance. This leads to highly decentralized information and access. The **DOC offices** and **visitors centers** in Karamea (p. 292), Motueka (p. 286), Takaka (p. 288), and Westport (p. 336) all sell hut tickets and passes and have information on the park. The Heaphy Track can also be booked on the DOC website (www.doc.govt.nz). There are **supermarkets** and **ATMs** in

Takaka and Westport; Collingwood and Karamea have small food shops. Though most of the trailhead parking lots don't have troubled histories, those who want secure parking can try a hostel lot in a nearby town.

 DEET OR DIE. Sandflies are inevitable when hiking in the Kahurangi. The best way to wage a winning war against the ever advancing swarm of flesheating mercenaries is to use bug repellent with DEET rather than the less powerful citronella-enhanced repellents.

 OUTDOOR ACTIVITIES. There are many subalpine dayhikes around **Mt. Arthur** and the **Cobb Valley.** A steep and narrow track to the incredible viewpoint of **Parapara Peak** (1249m, 9hr. round-trip) begins just 2km off SH60 between Takaka and Collingwood at the end of Ward-Holmes Rd. An intensive tramping option is the **Leslie-Karamea Track** (6-9 days), which connects with the **Wangapeka Track** (p. 298). **Ultimate Descents** (p. 340) and **Eco-Rafting** (p. 348) run **rafting** trips on the **Karamea River** and can organize **kayak** rentals.

HEAPHY TRACK

The longest of the overland Great Walks, the Heaphy Track is also the most diverse, traversing no fewer than four different ecosystems. From east to west, trampers pass through mountain beech forests, flat and tussock-tufted expanses, primary podocarp forests, and palm-fringed west coast beaches at journey's end—there's a new plant or animal waiting around every corner. For the past century, environmentalists have managed to keep the proposed road that would connect Collingwood and Karamea in the planning stages and thus the park is in one of the most remote corners of New Zealand, hard to access, but well worth the effort.

Length: 82km, 4-5 days.

Trailheads: Brown Hut, 28km southeast of Collingwood (p. 290) and **Kohaihai Carpark,** 16km north of Karamea (p. 292). Though the trail can be hiked in either direction, most start at Brown Hut and head west; this finishes the major uphill climb on the first day and rewards trampers with a coastal walk on the last day or two.

Transportation: Arranging transportation between trailheads can be confusing and expensive, especially if you need to get back to the city where you started. Bus schedules to the trailheads change with demand. Transport can usually be arranged most easily by the Nelson or Takaka i-Sites.

Flights: Those looking for convenient one-way transport may be well-served by a scenic flight over the trail to review or scout the Heaphy aerially. **Remote Adventures Scenic Flights** flies between Karamea and Takaka at convenient afternoon times for those finishing the trail. (☎025 384 225; info@remoteadventures.co.nz. 2-person min. Booking essential. $150.) **Abel Tasman Air** flies between Karamea and Nelson and Karamea and Motueka. (☎0800 304 560 or 528 8290. Karamea-Nelson $225 per person; Karamea-Motueka $155. Min. 2 people.)

Buses: Southern Link K-Bus (☎0800 881 188 or 525 9434) runs to Brown Hut from: Collingwood ($20); Motueka ($39); Nelson ($45); Takaka ($23). The same fares apply if going to Brown Hut from those destinations. **Abel Tasman Coachlines** (☎548 0285) heads daily Dec.-Apr. to Brown Hut from: Motueka ($39); Nelson ($46). **Drive Me Wild** (☎546 8876 or 0800 945 369; www.drivemewild.co.nz) runs daily to Brown Hut from: Collingwood (10am, $10); Motueka (8am, $40); Nelson ($50); Takaka (9:30am, $25). They also offer service from Kohaihai to Nelson ($80, return $125) via Westport ($30). **Farewell Spit Tours** (☎524 8257 or 0800 808 257; inquiries@farewellspit.co.nz) runs on demand from Brown Hut to Collingwood ($75 for 1-4 people, after 4 people $20 per person) and Takaka ($100 for 1-4 people, after 4 people $25 per person). **Kahurangi Trampers Services** (☎526 8620) runs between Brown Hut and Motueka ($200 min.) and Nelson ($220 min.). They also run between Karamea and Nelson ($320 minimum). Additionally, they securely store cars for hikers and provide transport in hikers' own cars at discounted rates. From Kohaihai Carpark, most hikers call **Karamea Express** (☎ 782 6757; www.karamea-express.co.nz) from the end of the Heaphy for a lift to Karamea (30min.; Nov.-Apr. 2pm, Dec.-Mar. also 1pm; $12, min. charge $30). Rongos Backpackers in Karamea also picks up guests from the end of the Heaphy ($10). **Trek Express** (☎ 0800 128 735; rory-moore@xtra.co.nz) and **Nelson Lakes Shuttles** (☎ 521 1900) also serve both trailheads on demand. All of the above services also run routes in the opposite direction for the same fare.

Cars: If you have a **car**, it will require a lot of backtracking to pick up your vehicle; your best bet is to leave it in Nelson or Motueka and book a return ticket. If you are driving up the Aorere Valley Rd. to leave your car at Brown Hut (if you are hiking a loop finishing there), beware that the drive entails fording 3 streams, which can be impassable after heavy rain. Otherwise, **Somerset Trampers Transport** (☎ 524 8624) will drive your car back to Collingwood ($45) or Takaka ($70). Perhaps, the simplest option, Derry Kingston of **Heaphy Track Help** (☎ 525 9576; helenk@paradise.net.nz) provides trampers with a van to take to one trailhead while he drives their car to the other. He then hikes the trail and swaps keys halfway. ($250 per vehicle; discounts off-season). **Hitchhiking** to either trailhead can be difficult, as there is no through traffic, and *Let's Go* never recommends it. Kohaihai reportedly sees more cars from daytrippers heading to Scotts Beach from Karamea.

Seasonality: Oct.-Apr. is the peak season for the track; it's most crowded in the middle of summer. Winter hiking (May-Sept.) is more difficult because transportation runs less frequently and fewer DOC rangers are on the trail. Rain is never far off, and in heavy rains the trail can be impassable at some river crossings.

Huts and Campsites: Of 7 **huts**, 5 (Perry Saddle, Saxon, James Mackay, Lewis, and Heaphy) have gas cookers, but bring matches or lighters. Oct.-Apr. requires a hut reservation ($20 per night). May-Sept. hut prices are reduced ($10 per night). Trampers need to bring a printout of their hut reservation with them on the track, or they will face a penalty. The DOC officially permits tenting at 2 **campsites** along the track's coastal section ($10 per night). The following huts and shelters also offer campsites: Brown, Aorere Shelter, Perry Saddle, Gouland Downs, James Mackay, Heaphy, Katipo Creek Shelter, and Kohaihai. Campers are not allowed to use hut cooking facilities.

Storage and Baggage Transport: Most area accommodations store gear. Baggage transport between trailheads can be arranged through bus companies.

BROWN HUT TO PERRY SADDLE HUT. *17km, 5hr.* **Brown Hut** (16 bunks; 10 sites), just 5min. from the parking lot at the track's east end, sports a large fireplace and a phone with free local phone calls for those hiking the trail west-to-east, but lacks cooking facilities. From here, the track follows a broad path, climbing gently but steadily up the **Aorere Valley.** Most of the climbing is finished after 3½hr. when you arrive at **Aorere Shelter** (4 sites), a three-walled affair with a grand view, water, and a toilet. About 1hr. beyond the shelter, a spur trail leads to **Flanagan's Corner** (910m; 10min. round-trip), the highest point on the track, with a panorama of the upper Aorere Valley and surrounding mountains. A gradual descent leads to **Perry Saddle Hut** (880m; 24 bunks; 5 sites), perched on the edge of the valley, which offers more superb views. A rock cairn a 5min. walk down the trail toward Gouland Downs marks a side-trail up Mt. Perry for even more spectacular views, but the trail is not maintained and is recommended only for experienced hikers. Allow at least 2hr. to summit Mt. Perry—even for the ultra fit tramper. For those looking to cool off, take the slightly overgrown trail behind the Perry Saddle toilets down to **Gorge Creek** (15min. one-way). The Creek water is cold, but refreshing after a long hike.

PERRY SADDLE HUT TO GOULAND DOWNS HUT. *8km, 2hr.* About 1hr. after Perry Saddle Hut, the trail leaves behind the patches of beech and opens onto the golden expanse of the **Gouland Downs,** the beginning of the track's most exposed section. Wind-swept grass stretches to the horizon. The track also passes numerous streams. If you can brave the chilly water, feel free to take a dip. **Gouland Downs Hut** (8 bunks; 5 sites) is the smallest and oldest on the track, with a stone hearth but no gas cookers. Its rustic atmosphere makes it an enjoyable place to stay. On clear nights, the area around Gouland Downs as well as Saxon Hut are rumored to be the best spots on the trail to hear or (for the very lucky) see the spotted kiwi. Also coming out at night are the large carniverous *Powelliphanta*, 10cm land snails often found on limestone outcroppings.

GOULAND DOWNS HUT TO SAXON HUT. *5km, 1½hr.* A few hundred meters farther along the track is a brief Tolkien-esque forest, full of moss-shrouded rock formations, caves, and arches. Several beautiful streams wind through and around the limestone. Though many trampers go off the track to explore caves, be warned that it is dangerous to leave the trail; trampers have disappeared in hidden sinkholes and caves in the downs. Perhaps the safest and easiest cave to access is immediately after the Gouland Downs Hut. About one minute down the trail toward Saxon Hut, a small rock cairn marks the short trail (5min.) to the cave. Immediately inside the cave and up to the right, an old meat locker attests to the cave's use by early pioneers. Those with a flashlight can hike into the cave and to the right about 5m to where the cave opens up. Numerous tunnels branch off from here, but it is not safe to explore further as it is easy to become lost or disoriented in the network of tunnels. The track traverses the west end of Gouland Downs—a 500-million-year-old expanse that has been flattened by erosion—before gradually reentering beech forest. This section is home to the first of the terrifying Heaphy Track swing bridges, which should be used for creek crossings when rivers run high. **Saxon Hut** (16 bunks; 5 sites), the newest hut on the trail, sits amid decent scenery, featuring one cozy room with gas cookers and a fireplace.

SAXON HUT TO JAMES MACKAY HUT. *14km, 3hr.* The track climbs gradually uphill, in and out of forest and the **Mackay Downs.** This area sees serious flooding during heavy rain, and the inconsistent boardwalk means wet feet potentially even in dry weather. In heavy rain, trampers should wait for the water to recede before continuing. En route to James Mackay Hut, trampers pass a sign marking the border of the Buller and Tasman region. While the sign itself is not impressive, trampers will undoubtedly be impressed by the flush toilets found in the Buller (western) side of the Heaphy Track. Past many-colored mosses and tannin-tinged creeks flowing through dense forest, **James Mackay Hut** (26 bunks; 4 sites) features views down to the Tasman. Those hiking the trail in four days typically spend their second night here. Energetic trampers can head up the steep, muddy trail behind the DOC warden cabin to ■**Otepo Trig** (20-30 min. round-trip) to watch the sunset and glimpse the west coast in the distance.

JAMES MACKAY HUT TO LEWIS HUT. *13.5km, 3½hr.* From James Mackay, it's all downhill to the sea. As the elevation decreases, the forest changes from beech to rimu and tree fern, entwined with supplejack vines. By the time **Lewis Hut** (20 bunks; no sites) comes into view, the bush has thickened and diversified, the beautiful nikau palm has appeared, and rata lace the hillsides with red (in summer). Lewis Hut sits at the junction of the dark brown Heaphy and sparkling red Lewis Rivers. Be warned: **sandflies** begin to appear here in force.

LEWIS HUT TO HEAPHY HUT. *8km, 2½hr.* After Lewis, the vegetation grows more subtropical. Epiphytes drip from giant rata, and tree ferns grow taller and taller. After traversing four long swing bridges, the track finally reaches the sea. When the river water is low, it is possible to ford the rivers rather than cross on the swingbridges. ■**Heaphy Hut** (28 bunks; 20 sites) overlooks the mouth of the Heaphy River, where the river meets the wild Tasman Sea. The calm river mouth is the best spot on the entire track for taking a dip, though sandflies make soaking up sun on the driftwood-littered beach nerve wracking. One of the highlights of the track is watching the sun slip into the crashing Tasman Sea from the abandoned expanse of sand outside the hut.

HEAPHY HUT TO KOHAIHAI CARPARK. *16.5km, 5hr.* This palm-filled stretch of track runs along the narrow strip of land between limestone bluffs and the coast, and is considered by many to be the finest stretch of the track. Many hikers opt to hike this section as a daytrip or hike in and spend a night at Heaphy rather than hike the entire track and spend money for transport. The Tasman surf is ferocious; riptides make the water too dangerous for swimming. Look for a pair of the very rare blue ducks living in Wekakura Creek; blue ducks have pale beaks with a bluish tinge and are usually found in the fastest rapids in the river, which is where they hunt for food. The dreary **Katipo Creek Shelter** has five tent sites, an aging shelter, and a toilet; visitors can find water at a nearby creek. A few minutes later, the path splits at **Crayfish Point.** The beachside path is safe to use within 2hr. of low tide (check the tide tables posted at Kohaihai and Heaphy Hut); otherwise, the high-water path along the bluff won't tack on more than 5min. Many hikers still walk the low-water route at high tide if the waves are breaking well short of the rocks. The longest stretch of sand before Kohaihai is **Scotts Beach,** popular with dayhikers from Kohaihai. Flax and nikau palms ring **Scotts Beach Campsite** (10 sites), which lies within earshot of the waves. From here, the track does its only real coastal climbing as it skirts **Kohaihai Bluff** before reaching the parking lot. At Kohaihai, there awaits a phone that many hikers use to call for transport, a shelter, and a **DOC campsite** ($6, children $1.50) that is not part of the Great Walk system with water, toilets, and a great view of the bluff. Numerous short hiking tracks branch off from the Kohaihai campsite. The last scheduled shuttle to Karamea departs at 2pm, though a variety of transport options run on demand; just call from the campsite phone—phone numbers are posted near the phone.

◪ WANGAPEKA TRACK

Situated in the southern portion of Kahurangi National Park, the rugged, untouched Wangapeka Track winds up deep river-cut gorges and through moss-covered beech forest. Because the track climbs out of the forest only at the Little Wanganui Saddle, many trampers opt to take a side-track to one of the nearby peaks for better views. As transportation to and from the trailheads can be prohibitively expensive and logistically difficult, some hikers opt to hike in, hike a side trail, and then hike back out the next day.

Length: 52km, 3-6 days round-trip; allow more time if hiking side trails.

Trailheads: The eastern end of the track is **Rolling Junction Shelter,** 31km from Tapawera, best accessed from Motueka or Nelson. **Little Wanganui,** 25km south of Karamea, is the trailhead on the western end of the track. If you plan to hike the Wangapeka as a loop in conjunction with the Heaphy Track (p. 295), it is best to hike the Wangapeka east to west and arrange transport from Little Wanganui north to Karamea, stay one night there, then continue on to the Heaphy trailhead. Most hikers find it easier to hike east to west because Rolling Junction is the more difficult transport to arrange and there is a phone at Little Wanganui to call for pickup.

Transportation: The cheapest option for reaching the Rolling Junction trail head is to take the mail bus with **Cain Road Services** (☎522 4044 or 025 417 511) from Nelson to Tapawera. (1½hr., Bus runs M, W, F 10am and 6pm, $10 per person.) From Tapawera there are 2 options for reaching Rolling Junction, **Tapawera Settle Motels and Campground** (☎522 4334) provides free transport to anyone staying overnight at the motel or campground. Those in a rush can fork out the extra cash and take the **Wadsworth Motors** shuttle. (☎522 4248. Operates on demand. Min. cost $65.) Several small charter bus companies head to the Rolling Junction Shelter on demand from Nelson; all have minimum costs that make them expensive for hikers not with a group. The shuttles and prices are as follows: **Trek Express** (☎0800 128 735; rorymoore@xtra.co.nz. $40 per person. Min. cost $160); **Nelson Lakes Shuttles** (☎521 1900 or 021 490 095; info@nelsonlakesshuttles.co.nz. $35 per person. $140 min.); **Nelson Bays Shuttles** (☎540 3851; info@nnbays.co.nz. 1-8 people $200); **Kahurangi Trampers Service** (☎526 8620. Min. cost $155). **Tasman Taxis** (☎528 1031) goes from Motueka to Rolling Junction (up to 8 people $195). To connect from the Little Wanganui Carpark to Karamea or the Heaphy trailhead, call **Karamea Motors** (☎782 6757 or 782 6718; info@karamea-express.co.nz. $35 min.) or **Little Wanganui Tavern** (☎782 6752. $10 per person. Free transport for overnight guests). For groups with a car, there are 2 convenient options. Derry Kingston of **Heaphy Track Help** provides car relocation services for the Wangapeka for $270. **Helicopter Charter Karamea** runs on demand from Karamea to Rolling Junction. (☎782 6111. From $600 for 3 people.)

Seasonality: The track can be hiked year-round, though the weather is most conducive to hiking in summer. Huts are never crowded. In heavy rain streams may be impassable.

Huts and Campsites: The Wangapeka Track has a variety of hut accommodations, all first-come, first-served. 6 huts on the track (Kings Creek, Stone, Trevor Carter, Helicopter Flat, Taipo, and Belltown Manunui) and 2 on side trails (John Reid and Kiwi Saddle) are fully serviced huts that require 2 hut tickets ($10). Rolling Junction Shelter is a standard hut requiring 1 hut ticket ($5). Cecil Kings Hut, Stag Flat and Little Wanganui Emergency Shelter are free. The huts have pot-bellied stoves or fireplaces, but no gas cookers. Camping is allowed; good campsites are available at Cecil Kings Hut, Stone Hut, and Taipo Hut. Annual hut passes ($90) are valid for all huts on the Wangapeka. Hut tickets work on an honesty system and can be purchased from any DOC office.

Storage: Most area accommodations will store bags for free.

Maps: Though the main track is well marked, anyone considering side-trips should invest in the Wangapeka M28 topographical map ($12.50-13), on hand at most DOC offices.

ROLLING JUNCTION SHELTER TO KINGS CREEK HUT. *9.5km, 3½-4½hr.* After crossing a swing bridge over the Rolling River, the path wanders down through grassy floodplains alongside the Wangapeka River. The view up the gorge is spectacular, particularly when the clouds are rolling up from the west coast. Entering the woods, the track rolls gently but never veers from its course alongside the river. After 2½hr., trampers reach one of the first major turn-offs, the 3hr. track up to **Kiwi Saddle Hut** (6 bunks). The hut serves as a base for those who want to make daytrips along the rough routes to the summit of rocky **Mt. Patriach** (1701m) or **Mt. Luna** (1630m), both of which run 3hr. one-way from the hut. Meanwhile, the main track passes spacious and modern **Kings Creek Hut** (20 bunks), but your first choice should be the historic **Cecil Kings Hut** (4 bunks), another 5min. down the trail. Originally built in 1935, this handmade, wood-slab hut was occupied by prospector Cecil King for many summers until his death in 1982. It is now preserved by the DOC.

KINGS CREEK HUT TO STONE HUT. *6.5km, 2½-3½hr.* Leaving Kings Creek Hut, the track comes to the meeting of the north and south branches of the Wangapeka River and follows the North Branch while climbing through mossy beech forest. Swing bridges span Luna Stream and the North Branch en route to **Stone Hut** (10 bunks), on a grassy field. From here, a second route leads to **Mt. Luna** (3hr.).

STONE HUT TO HELICOPTER FLAT HUT. *8km, 3-4½hr.* Departing the hut, the track emerges onto a rash of boulders tossed about by the 1929 Murchison earthquake. Traversing a long gravel stretch peppered with barren tree trunks and reentering the forest, the track begins to climb in earnest, grinding up switchbacks to the heavily forested **Wangapeka Saddle** (1009m). An actual view of the valley below requires dropping your pack for the 1hr. climb to **Nugget Knob** (1562m) along a well-marked track. After the saddle, the track levels and begins its descent, crossing the Karamea River several times before reaching the modern **Helicopter Flat Hut** (10 bunks). Both Chime Creek and the creek immediately before Helicopter Flat Hut are crossed by the mildly terrifying three-wire bridges, for use if the fords are flooded (or for those with a love of wobbling at great heights).

A popular alternative track leads along a spectacular marked route to **Biggs Tops** and the Leslie-Karamea Track, before descending to the **Trevor Carter Hut** (10 bunks), a few kilometers up the Leslie-Karamea Track. The views on this track are particularly good when the weather is clear. From Trevor Carter Hut, hikers can take the **Lost Valley Track** to Helicopter Flat; the **Saxon Falls Track**, which rejoins the Wangapeka past Helicopter Flat; or follow the Leslie-Karamea Track until it joins the Wangapeka.

HELICOPTER FLAT HUT TO TAIPO HUT. *8km, 3½-4½hr.* The **Lost Valley Track** heads north to Trevor Carter Hut (3hr.), while the main trail continues in a quiet mossy forest with scattered fern stands, and eventually leaves Karamea Gorge. Atop **Brough's Tabernacle Lookout,** there's a gorgeous view of the valley below. In 1898, while surveying the original track, Jonathan Brough set up an A-frame here. Today, only a few tools, a commemorative plaque, and the enduring vista remain. Those finishing the Leslie-Karamea Track to the east join the Wangapeka Track here. From here, it's a 2½hr. gradual climb to **Taipo Hut** (16 bunks).

TAIPO HUT TO BELLTOWN MANUNUI HUT. *10.5km, 6½-7hr.* After crossing the Pannikin Creek, the track pushes upward to **Stag Flat Shelter,** situated in a boggy mess. This shelter serves as a contingency for poor weather on the Little Wanganui Saddle. An intense climb summits the saddle at 1110m, the tramp's highest point. Skirting Saddle Lakes, the trail begins an abrupt drop down to the Little Wanganui River. The tiny **Little Wanganui Emergency Shelter** lies roughly halfway between the two huts. Passing over Tangent Creek and through McHarrie Creek, the climbing begins anew, following the Little Wanganui Gorge and returning to the river atop the bridge to the new **Belltown Manunui Hut** (10 bunks). Highlights include running water and weka footprints in the cement out front.

BELLTOWN MANUNUI HUT TO THE PARKING LOT. *9km, 3-4hr.* A few meters from the hut the path crosses Drain Creek, then continues through Gilmore Clearing, a grassy clearing, reaching the high- and low-water track division after 2hr. The flat, low-water track is faster, but because it crosses the wide, fast-flowing Little Wanganui River twice, it is only safe for use when water levels are truly low. When the river is flooded (or if you'd rather not take your boots off), the only choice is the high-water alternative, which climbs steeply over the river banks before ending about 500m past the trail's end (and past the public phones on Wangapeka Rd.).

CANTERBURY

From the dramatic, untamed Southern Alps to the playful dolphins of Kaikoura, Canterbury is a region of many personalities. Serious skiers shred powder on the slopes, while summer visitors brown on the shores of the Banks Peninsula. In Christchurch, Canterbury gets a dose of urbanity in a city known for its borrowed British sensibility.

◪ CANTERBURY HIGHLIGHTS

DIVE into the scene in vibrant **Christchurch,** with Gothic architecture, botanic gardens, and eclectic street performers (p. 305).

CHUG past breathtaking scenery on the train ride through **Arthur's Pass** (p. 326).

SCALE the heights of formidable **Aoraki/Mt. Cook National Park,** which challenges thrill-seekers with its dramatic peaks, demanding walks, and majestic glaciers (p. 332).

CHRISTCHURCH   ☎ 03

This garden city (pop. 350,000) remains closely bound to its English heritage, most evident in its stone Gothic Revival churches and meeting houses. Named after Oxford's Christ Church College, the city has grown from a settlement on the willowed banks of the Avon River to a bohemian and distinctly Kiwi community of artists and free spirits. The city faithfully preserves its recent past through a network of free museums, galleries, and gardens.

✈ INTERCITY TRANSPORTATION

Flights: Christchurch Airport (☎374 7100), 9km from the city on Memorial Ave., is served by **Air New Zealand, Qantas,** and many Asian and South Pacific carriers. **Air New Zealand** (☎0800 737 000) flies daily to **Auckland** (1½hr., 1-2 per hr., $99-653) and **Wellington** (45min., 1 per hr., $93-409). The Airport "A" bus ($7) departs from the airport (M-F every 30min. 6:35am-7:35pm, every hr. 7:35pm-12:55am; every 30min. Sa-Su 11:40am-5:10pm, every hr. 8:10-11:40am and 5:10-12:55pm.) and Cathedral Sq. (M-F 6am-7pm every 30min., 7-11pm every hr.; every 30min. Sa-Su 10:35am-5:35pm, every hr. 7:35-10:35am and 5:35-10:35pm.) A number of different shuttle operators run passengers from the airport to the city. A shuttle comes at least every 10min. **Super Shuttles** (☎0800 748 8853 and 347 4504; www.supershuttle.co.nz) is one of the best. A shuttle to downtown costs $14-20, $4-5 per additional passenger. A taxi to downtown is around $30.

Trains: Station (☎0800 250 000), 3km from Cathedral Sq. To reach the station, head away from town on Riccarton Ave., turn left on Deans Ave., right onto Blenheim Rd., then left onto Foster St., and left again onto Clarence St. Information office open M-F 6:30am-3:30pm, Sa-Su 6:30am-3pm. Book ahead to utilize student discounts. Lockers at station $1. **TranzScenic** (☎0800 872 467; www.tranzscenic.co.nz) runs both major South Island train lines. **TranzAlpine** goes to **Greymouth** (4½hr., 8:15am, $70-130) via **Arthur's Pass** (2½hr., $70). **TranzCoastal** runs daily to **Picton** (5½hr., 7am, $50-99) via **Kaikoura** (3hr., $29-57). Ticket prices are often lower in the off-season. Taxis to town cost about $12, though **Canterbury Shuttles** (☎0800 021 682) runs a complimentary

Canterbury

shuttle from some Christchurch accommodations. No public buses run directly from the station to the city, although bus #5 from the bus exchange can drop you off at Riccarton Mall. Push the button at Clarence St.—the train station is a 5min. walk away.

Buses: InterCity/Newmans, 123 Worcester St. (☎377 0951; www.intercitycoach.co.nz; www.newmanscoach.co.nz). Open daily 7am-5pm, accepts calls until 9pm. Reserving in advance can often get you lower prices. To: **Dunedin** (6hr.; 8am and 2pm, F 5:15pm, Su 5:30pm; $46, with YHA or VIP card $39); **Kaikoura** (2¾hr.; 7am, 4pm; $28/24); **Nelson** (6½hr., 7am, $69/59); **Queenstown** (express 7½hr., 7:45am and 8:20am, $66/46; via Mt. Cook 9hr., 7:15 and 8:10am, $155/132). The **Flexipass** (from $55 for 5hr.) allows maximum flexibility by coach as you buy amounts of travel time rather than tickets for actual route. Alternatively, the **Coach Passes** are hop-on, hop-off passes that are valid for 1yr. and allow for flexible travel on a variety of routes on both islands. **Atomic Shuttles** (☎322 8883; www.atomictravel.co.nz) often has the best bargain rates for South Island service. **Coast to Coast** (☎0800 800 847; www.coast2coast.co.nz) traverses South Island to **Greymouth** (4½hr., 8am, $35) via **Arthur's Pass** (2½hr., $25). **Great Sights** (☎0800 744 487 or 306 7633; www.greatsights.co.nz), **Southern Link KBus** (☎358 8355 or 0508 458 835; www.southernlinkkbus.co.nz), **South Island Connections** (☎379 9260; www.southernconnections.co.nz), and **East Coast Express** (☎0508 830 900) also run shuttles around South Island. To get to **Akaroa**, take the daily **French Connection** or **Akaroa Shuttle** (see p. 318)

> **GO NAKED.** Southern Link K-Bus sets aside a number of discounted tickets on their backpacker website www.nakedbus.com. When booked far enough in advance, tickets can be purchased for as little as $1.70.

Hitchhiking: Though *Let's Go* never recommends hitchhiking, thumbers report finding rides from the city outskirts, where urban traffic is steady. Those heading north toward Kaikoura often take the **Belfast** bus #16 and ask the driver to drop them off on SH1, while those heading south toward Dunedin take the **Templeton** #5 bus. Hitching west toward Arthur's Pass is possible by taking the **Hornby** #84 bus to the Yaldhurst Roundabout. The best bet for hitching to Akaroa is the **Halswell** #7 bus to Halswell Rd.

◢ ORIENTATION

Christchurch's flat grid of streets extends in every direction from **Cathedral Square,** the city's center, where food stalls and artisans congregate beneath the bell tower of **Christchurch Cathedral.** Cobblestoned **Worcester Street** continues east through **Latimer Square** and west (as Worcester Blvd.) over the **Avon River,** to the gothic **Arts Centre,** the **Canterbury Museum,** and the **Botanic Gardens.** The city's central thoroughfare, **Colombo Street,** is lined with souvenir shops and runs north-south through the square. Arcades and plazas fan out from the **City Mall,** the pedestrian walkway one block south of the cathedral on **Cashel Street.** North of the cathedral, **Victoria Square** fronts the Town Hall. The Avon River runs through the square and is followed on either side by **Oxford** and **Cambridge Terrace. Manchester Street,** Cashel St., and Oxford Terrace form a U-shaped nightlife district. Central Christchurch is bordered to the west by gigantic **Hagley Park,** to the north and east by suburbs, and to the south by **Moorhouse Avenue,** the boundary of the industrial area. In 2008, Christchurch City Council plans to revamp the city mall on Cashel and High St., so tourists should be prepared for construction.

◰ LOCAL TRANSPORTATION

Public Transportation: Bus Crossing at the Exchange (☎366 8855; www.metroinfo.org.nz), at Colombo and Lichfield St., serves as the bus depot and information center. Open M-Sa 6:30am-10:30pm, Su 9am-9pm. Buses depart 6am-11:30pm; frequency depends on the route. Bus schedules at the bus exchange. Christchurch recently expanded its bus service to include a metro card system. Fares are calculated by three zones, and tickets cost $2.50-5, or $1.90-3.75 with a metro card. Metrocards can be purchased at the Bus Exchange. **The Shuttle** is a free service that sends yellow buses up and down Colombo St. every 10-15min. M-F 7:30am-10:30pm, Sa 8am-10:30pm, Su 10am-8pm. Get a route map at the visitors center.

Taxis: First Direct (☎0800 505 550), **Gold Band** (☎379 5795), and **Blue Star** (☎379 9799) provide 24hr. service. Large groups should opt for Blue Star, which provides vans upon request. Corporate taxi companies tend to have higher rates.

Car Rental: The major car rental companies are all in town but for cheaper deals, try one of the following. Most require renters to be 20+, hold a major credit card, and have daily rates around $35-45, though some go as low as $28. **Pegasus,** 127 Peterborough St. (☎0800 354 506, 365 1100, airport branch 358 5890; christchurchcity@rentalcars.co.nz); **Rent-a-Dent,** 132 Kilmore St. (☎365 2509 or 0800 736 822). **Ace Rentals,** 237 Lichfield St. (☎366 3222 or 0800 202 029; fax 377 4610) arranges drop-off and pickup.

Automobile Clubs: AA Centre, 210 Hereford St. (☎964 3650 or 0800 500 444; www.aa.co.nz), sells excellent road maps and dispenses sage traveling advice. Breakdown service available to members. Annual membership standard $77, with vehicle recovery $122. Open M and W-F 8:30am-5pm, Tu 9am-5pm.

Used Cars: Backpackers Car Market, 33 Battersea St. (☎377 3177; www.backpackerscarmarket.co.nz), between Durham and Colombo St. Open M-F 9:30am-5pm.

Bike Rental: Wheels 'n Deals, 159 Gloucester St. (☎377 6655 or 02 7578 9163) rents quality road bikes and mountain bikes. All rentals include lock and helmet. Mountain bike rentals from $19; $24 per day. Road bikes half-day $30, full-day $39. Open M-F 8:30am-5:30pm, Sa 10am-4pm, Su 11am-4pm. **City Cycle Hire** (☎0800 343 848; www.cyclehire-tours.co.nz). Picks up and delivers bikes to you. For city use, half-day $25, full-day $35; mountain bikes $30/45. Open daily 8am-6pm.

🔢 PRACTICAL INFORMATION

TOURIST AND FINANCIAL SERVICES

Visitors Center: Christchurch i-Site Visitor Centre (☎379 9629; www.christchurchinformation.co.nz), in the Old Chief Post Office Bldg. in Cathedral Sq. Open daily in summer 8:30am-7pm, in winter 8:30am-5pm. Other i-Site offices (☎353 0004) are located in the domestic and international terminals of the airport. Open daily 7:30am-8pm and staffed during outside hours for flight arrivals.

Department of Conservation (DOC): 133 Victoria St. (☎379 3706; www.doc.govt.co.nz). Large supply of informational pamphlets about tramps on South Island. They can also book huts on South Island walking tracks. Open M-F 8:30am-5pm.

Budget Travel: STA Travel, 90 Cashel St. (☎379 9098), on the City Mall. Open M-F 9am-5:30pm, Sa 11am-2pm.

Banks: BNZ (☎353 2532), in Cathedral Sq. Provides MC/V cash advances and exchanges money. Open M-W 9:30am-4:30pm, Th-F 9am-4:30pm. 24hr. **ATMs** are available throughout the city.

Work Opportunities: Kelly Services (☎0800 453 559; www.kellyservices.co.nz) and **Adecco** (☎379 9060) are good temp agencies. Temping requires a work visa and min. of 2-3mo. availability. The job board at **Vagabond Backpackers** (p. 305) has a wide selection of short-term opportunities; see also **Beyond Tourism,** p. 54.

LOCAL SERVICES

Maps: Mapworld, 173 Gloucester St. (☎0800 627 967; www.mapworld.co.nz), Manchester and Gloucester St. They sell maps as well as GPS devices. Open M-Th 8am-6pm, F 8am-8pm, Sa-Su 9am-5pm.

Library: 91 Gloucester St. (☎9417923; www.library.christchurch.o-rg.nz). Provides free Internet access to New Zealand pages. Open M-F 9am-9pm, Sa-Su 10am-4pm.

GLBT Resources: 24hr. Gay Information Line (☎379 4796).

EMERGENCY AND COMMUNICATIONS

Police: Main branch (☎363 7400) at Hereford St. and Cambridge Terr. Open 24hr. for emergencies. Regular office hours M-F 7am-8pm, Sa-Su 7am-6pm.

Crisis Lines: Lifeline (☎366 6743 and 0800 543 354); **Victim Support** (☎0800 842 846); **AIDS Hotline** (☎0800 802 437); **Safecare** (☎364 8791). All 24hr.

Medical Services: After Hours Surgery (☎365 7777), at Bealey Ave. and Colombo St. Open 24hr. Next door is **Urgent Pharmacy** (☎366 4439). Open M-Th 6-11pm, F-Su 9-11pm. **Christchurch Public Hospital** (☎364 0640), at Oxford Terr. and Riccarton Ave.

Internet Access: Internet cafes are scattered throughout the city. The cheapest rates and most convenient hours are at the gaming rooms in the High St. mall. **Cybernutz,** 266 High St. (☎379 6688; www.cybernutz.co.nz) has Internet connections for laptops. Internet $3 per hr., $2 per hr. with a membership. Open M-W 10am-late, Th-Sa 24hr., Su midnight-late. **email,** 77 Cathedral Sq., offers fast-access on flatscreen monitors, across from the cathedral. They sell a wide range of phone cards and rent mobile phones. $4 per hr. Open daily 8am-10pm.

Post Office: The main post office is at 736 Colombo St. (☎0800 501 501). Open M-F 8am-6pm, Sa 10am-4pm. Post Restante.

ACCOMMODATIONS

Try to **book ahead** for all Christchurch accommodations particularly if looking for single rooms, though last-minute deals at high-end hotels are occasionally available; ask at the visitors center.

WORCESTER STREET AND SOUTH

Frauenreisehaus: The Homestead (BBH), 272 Barbadoes St. (☎366 2585). From the cathedral, head east on Worcester Blvd. and right on Barbadoes St. Women are fortunate to have this female-only hostel to themselves. Free use of bikes, CD burner, fresh herbs and fruit trees, a hammock, free laundry, and a resident rabbit. Reception 8am-9:30pm. Dorms $23; twins $28; singles $35. Neighboring **French House** has longer stay options doubles $120 per week, singles $180. $3 BBH discount. MC/V. ❷

Vagabond Backpackers (BBH), 232 Worcester St. (☎379 9677; vagabondbackpackers@hotmail.com), 5 blocks east of the cathedral. A Victorian house with a clean, well-maintained interior, lovely garden, friendly hosts, fresh bread for breakfast, and great mattresses. Check the job board for work opportunities. Reception 8am-10pm. Dorms $21-23; singles $35; twins and doubles $48-52. $3 BBH discount. MC/V. ❷

Rolleston House YHA, 5 Worcester Blvd. (☎366 6564; yha.rollestonhouse@yha.co.nz), at Rolleston Ave. The Arts Centre, cafes, and museums are all right outside the door. Small rooms are airy and bright, and the large TV lounge and kitchen promote socialization. Lockers $2. Reception 8am-10pm. Dorms $26-28; twins $68; doubles $70, with bath $92. $3 YHA discount. MC/V. ❷

New Excelsior Backpackers (BBH), 120 Manchester St. (☎366 7570 and 0800 666 237; www.newexcelsior.co.nz), at High St. Fun neighborhood with lots of cafes and shops, with a rooftop deck and pub. Towels $2. Key deposit $20. Reception 7am-8pm. Dorms $23-28; singles $35-45; doubles $60. $3 BBH Discount. AmEx/MC/V. ❷

base backpackers, on the north side of Cathedral Sq. (☎982 2225 or 0800 227 369; www.basebackpackers.com). With one of Christchurch's hottest bars downstairs, base is where backpackers who live on booze and adrenaline occasionally sleep. The 3-story building feels like a dorm room with a big screen TV. Towels $3. Safe $2. Reception 24hr. Dorm $27, ensuite $29. Private room $65, ensuite $85. Book well in advance, especially for private rooms. VIP/YHA $1 discount. AmEx/MC/V. ❷

Thomas's Hotel, 36 Hereford St. (☎379 9536; www.thomashotel.co.nz), across from the Arts Centre. This central hotel has simple, functional rooms to suit any price range.

CANTERBURY

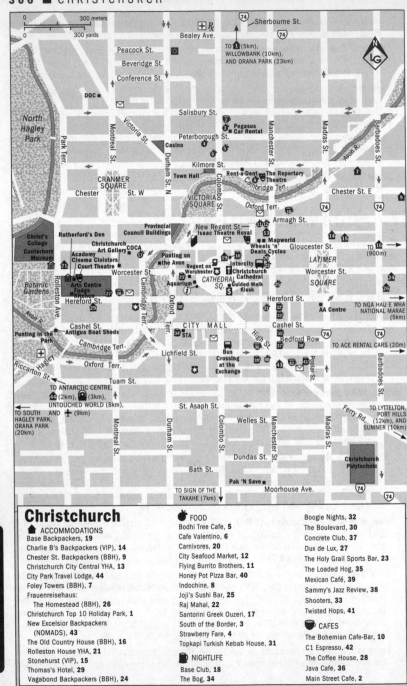

Christchurch

ACCOMMODATIONS
Base Backpackers, **19**
Charlie B's Backpackers (VIP), **14**
Chester St. Backpackers (BBH), **9**
Christchurch City Central YHA, **13**
City Park Travel Lodge, **44**
Foley Towers (BBH), **7**
Frauenreisehaus:
    The Homestead (BBH), **26**
Christchurch Top 10 Holiday Park, **1**
New Excelsior Backpackers
    (NOMADS), **43**
The Old Country House (BBH), **16**
Rolleston House YHA, **21**
Stonehurst (VIP), **15**
Thomas's Hotel, **29**
Vagabond Backpackers (BBH), **24**

FOOD
Bodhi Tree Cafe, **5**
Cafe Valentino, **6**
Carnivores, **20**
City Seafood Market, **12**
Flying Burrito Brothers, **11**
Honey Pot Pizza Bar, **40**
Indochine, **8**
Joji's Sushi Bar, **25**
Raj Mahal, **22**
Santorini Greek Ouzeri, **17**
South of the Border, **3**
Strawberry Fare, **4**
Topkapi Turkish Kebab House, **31**

NIGHTLIFE
Base Club, **18**
The Bog, **34**

Boogie Nights, **32**
The Boulevard, **30**
Concrete Club, **37**
Dux de Lux, **27**
The Holy Grail Sports Bar, **23**
The Loaded Hog, **35**
Mexican Café, **39**
Sammy's Jazz Review, **38**
Shooters, **33**
Twisted Hops, **41**

CAFES
The Bohemian Cafe-Bar, **10**
C1 Espresso, **42**
The Coffee House, **28**
Java Cafe, **36**
Main Street Cafe, **2**

Barbeque, lounge, and kitchen. Reception 6:30am-9pm. Budget dorms $24, with linen $30; singles $65, with shower $95, with bath $109; doubles $69/95/109; triples $80. Rates are negotiable, especially off-season. MC/V. ❷

Christchurch City Central YHA, 273 Manchester St. (☎379 9535; yha.christchurch-city@yha.co.nz), near Armagh St. A typical YHA: central, modern, and ultra-clean. Free shuttle service to the train station, but not the airport. Massage chairs and pool table in the welcoming lounge. Lockers $1 per 6hr. Reception 7am-10pm. Dorms $28-30; singles $63-68; twins and doubles $71, ensuite $91. $3 YHA discount. MC/V. ❷

Foley Towers (BBH), 208 Kilmore St. (☎366 9720; foley.towers@backpack.co.nz). Take Worcester St. east to Madras St., turn left, and then right on Kilmore St. Newly renovated rooms in the a sprawling Victorian house close to a poplar grove lining the Avon River. The mess-hall style kitchen and adopt-a-sock wall in the laundry room give the place a summer camp feel. TV lounge in winter and BBQ. Linen $2. Key deposit $10. Reception 9am-9:30pm. Dorms $21-23; twins and doubles $54, with bath $60. $4 BBH discount. MC/V. ❷

NORTH OF WORCESTER STREET

▨ **The Old Country House (BBH),** 437 Gloucester St. (☎381 5504; www.oldcountry-housenz.com), Stanmore Rd. 20min. walk or short bus ride (#43 or 21). Tucked away in a quiet residential area with herb garden and fresh-baked bread in the morning. Towels $2, linen $2. Reception 8-10:30am and 4-8pm. Dorms $23-33; twins and doubles $55-58, with bath $70; triples $84/99. $3 BBH discount. ❷

▨ **Chester St. Backpackers (BBH),** 148 Chester St. E. (☎377 1897; chesterst@xtra.co.nz). From the city center, follow Worcester St. east to Barbadoes St., turn left, and then right on Chester St. There are only 14 beds at this lovely little hostel, so reserve ahead. Colorful and communal atmosphere with a car-b-q (a barbeque in the trunk of an old car). Reception 9am-9:30pm. Long-term stays available. Dorms $23; doubles and twins $50; triple $73. $3 BBH discount. ❷

Charlie B's Backpackers (VIP/BBH), 268 Madras St. (☎379 8429 or 0800 224 222; www.charliebs.co.nz). A bustling place with a wide range of options. Their super-economy 38-bed dorm room is one of the cheapest sleeps in town, while the ensuite doubles with kitchen and TV are one of the best bargains. Nice lounge area with big-screen TV. Key deposit $20. 38-bed dorm $19; 7- to 12-bed dorm $24; singles $50; doubles $60, with TV and kitchen $65; quads $27 per person; female-only dorm $28. Reservations recommended in summer. $3 BBH, $1 VIP discount. MC/V. ❷

Stonehurst (VIP), 241 Gloucester St. (☎379 4620 or 0508 786 633; www.stonehurst.co. nz). Rooms range from new, hotel-like suites to economy 10-person dorms. Heated swimming pool, barbeque and downstairs bar. Reception 24hr. Dorms $25; singles $55, ensuite $72; doubles and twins $67/105. One- and two-bedroom motel rooms from $120. Powered campervan sites from $30 per night. $1 VIP discount. ❷

Christchurch Top 10 Holiday Park, 529 Cranford St. (☎352 9176 or 0800 396 323; www.christchurchtop10.co.nz). Drive north 10min. from the city center on Sherborne St., which becomes Cranford St. Swimming pool and spa. Tent and unpowered sites $18-35, powered $33-40. 2-person cabins $50-74, $10 per extra person; funky 2-person hexagonal cottages with kitchen $75-80, $15 per extra person. MC/V. ❶

City Park Travel Lodge, 22 Riccarton Ave. (☎0800 33 11 99; www.cityparknz.com), follow Riccarton Ave. west through the park, the lodge is on the right about 500m after the park. This lodge is an excellent options for groups in a car. Cheap but clean and functional motel rooms a 20min. walk from the city center. Reception M-F 8am-9pm, Sa-Su 8:30am-9pm. Rooms sleep up to 3 with bath, fridge, and TV from $89 for 2 people; $15 per extra person. AmEx/MC/V. ❹

CANTERBURY

⬕ FOOD

Many restaurants are concentrated on **Colombo Street,** north of Kilmore St., and on **Manchester Street,** south of Gloucester St. Vendors in **Cathedral Square** sell a range of kebabs and stir-frys around lunchtime; on weekends they take over a corner of the Arts Centre. The **Pak 'N Save,** at Moorehouse Ave. and Manchester St., is the only source for cheap groceries in central Christchurch. (Open daily 8am-10pm.) Fresh produce can be found at the **farmers' market** at Riccarton Raceway. (Orange line on the metro from central Christchurch. Open Su 10am-5pm.)

WORCESTER STREET AND SOUTH

Honey Pot Pizza Bar, corner of Manchester and Lichfield St. (☎366 5853). This fully licensed pizza bar has a menu that puts a twist on traditional dishes. The apricot lamb burger ($15.50) and chicken, cranberry and brie pizza on a naan bread crust ($20) are two stellar options. Breakfast is available all day. Gourmet lunch sandwiches $11-11.50. Open daily 7am-late, usually around 11:30pm. MC/V. ❷

Topkapi Turkish Kebab House, 185a Manchester St. (☎379 4447; www.top-kapi.co.nz). The kebabs at this family-run restaurant are a step above typical kebab fare, with well-prepared meat and falafel on toasted pitas loaded with salad and couscous. Lunchtime kebabs are a deal ($5.50-6.50). Medium kebabs ($6.50-8) are only for takeaway. Large kebabs $11-13. Open M-Tu 11:30am-10pm, W-Th 11:30am-10:30pm, F 11:30am-late, Sa 3pm-late. AmEx/MC/V. ❶

Raj Mahal (☎366 0521), at Manchester and Worcester St. Choose from several traditional tandoori ($12.50-20) and vegetarian ($13-18) dishes, along with lots of spicy curry dishes ($14-19). Takeaways $9-13. Open Tu-Su 4:30-10pm. AmEx/MC/V. ❷

Joji's Sushi Bar, 186 Manchester St. (☎365 0500), look for the bright pink "Joji's" sign. This tasteful sushi restaurant has bargain lunch specials ($9-12) as well as $5 lunch boxes (M-F noon-2:30pm). The service is thoughtful and the portions generous. Sushi rolls mostly $5-9, though the specialty rolls are more expensive. Open daily 11:30am-11pm. AmEx/MC/V. ❶

Carnivores, 207 Manchester St. (☎650 371). Enjoy honey or spicy chicken chopped, garnished, and stuck between bread while you wait. This tiny lunch counter serves chicken in all imaginable combinations. Basic yet filling sandwiches $6.50-7.50. Open M-Th 10:30am-2:30pm, F 10:30am-3:30pm. Cash only. ❶

NORTH OF WORCESTER STREET

▨ Santorini Greek Ouzeri (☎379 6975; www.santorini.co.nz), Cambridge Terr. at Gloucester St. A fun-loving family restaurant with platters of Greek specialties like souvlaki, moussaka, and *paidikan* (barbeque lamb chops; $26). Patrons often drink enough ouzo cocktails ($7) to dance on the wine barrels, and Conga lines have been known to invade the kitchen. Live music F-Sa. Open Tu-Sa 6pm-late. MC/V. ❸

▨ Indochine, Cambridge Terrace (☎365 7323; www.indochine.co.nz), north bank of the Avon River. Christchurch's hottest new restaurant, the locals talk about the food and turn up in droves to eat it. Regular patrons opt for dim sum ($14-16) or mains ($25-30). Th-Sa 2-for-1 dim sum after 10pm. Open M-Sa 5pm-midnight. AmEx/MC/V. ❸

The Bodhi Tree, 808 Colombo St. (☎377-6808). The subtly flavored Burmese cuisine of the Bodhi Tree draws crowds of locals. The meals are designed to be shared, so groups or couples can order dishes to split and sample. Meat dishes $10.50-14; seafood dishes $12-15; vegetarian dishes around $10. Open Tu-Sa 6am-late. MC/V. ❷

Flying Burrito Brothers, Armagh and New Regent St. (☎377 7626; fbbchristchurch@xtra.co.nz). With an incredible tequila list ($6-85) and the perfect dose of spice, the Flying Burrito Bros. is the most authentic of Christchurch's many Mexican joints. Quesadillas $12; heaping burritos $19. Open daily 4pm-late. ❷

City Seafood Market and City Fish 'n Chips, 277 and 265 Manchester St. (Market ☎377 3377; Fish 'n Chips ☎377 4483). For the freshest fish 'n chips in town, you have to make two stops. The first is City Seafood Market to pick out a fresh piece of fish, and the second is City Fish 'n Chips to cook your "catch" for $1. Market Open M-F 9am-6pm, Sa 9am-2pm. Fish 'n Chips open M-Th 11am-6pm, F 11am-7pm. Cash only. ❶

Strawberry Fare, 114 Peterborough St. (☎365 4665; www.strawberryfare.com). A restaurant committed to cooking with fresh, natural ingredients available. Sophisticated entrees (duck confit; $24.50) are a prelude to the Devil's Dream, a light and dark chocolate mousse cake with raspberry coulis ($14.50). Open M-F 7am-late, Sa-Su 9am-late, usually around 10pm weekdays and 11pm weekends; earlier in winter. MC/V. ❸

Cafe Valentino, 813 Colombo St. (☎377 1886). Dean Martin croons in the background at this cosmopolitan Italian restaurant north of the square. The lunch menu features salads and pasta dishes ($14.50-16.50), while dinner adds in a variety of seafood, lamb, and beef mains ($27-30). The 2 bars feature a well-rounded selection of wines ($5-8) and half pints ($5-6). Open M-F noon-10:30pm, Sa-Su 5-10:30pm. MC/V. ❸

◪ CAFES

Christchurch's cafes are some of the city's hippest lounge spots and also some of its best restaurants.

▨ **Java Cafe** (☎366 0195), at High and Lichfield St. The second story of Java looks out over the bustle of Manchester and High St. Multi-layered hot chocolate ($3) served in jam jars and the best breakfast in town ($10.50-14.50). Early Bird special bagel and coffee $5.50. Open M-F 7:30am-6pm, Sa-Su 8am-6pm. ❶

▨ **C1 Espresso,** 150 High St. (☎379 1917; www.c1espresso.co.nz). The best coffee in Christchurch. C1 serves a hipster set in an edgy industrial space. For a non-caffeinated option, try one of their smoothies ($5). Otherwise, choose a coffee ($2.50-5) or tea ($4) from their comprehensive menu. Open M-F 7:30am-10pm, Sa 9am-10pm, Su 9am-8pm. ❶

Main Street Cafe, 840 Colombo St. (☎365 0421). The pumpkin and kumara balls ($13) will have even carnivores contemplating the meaning of tofu as they drink an organic beer ($9). Happy hour F-Sa 5:30-9pm. Th-Sa live band from 9pm. Open M 8:30am-3pm, Tu-F 8am-10pm, Sa-Su 9am-10pm. ❶

The Coffee House, 290 Montreal St. (☎365 6066), near the Arts Centre. Situated near the Arts Centre and museums, The Coffee House is a great place to sip a cappuccino between cultural stops. Mains $15-21. Open M-F 7:30am-late, Sa-Su 8am-8pm. ❷

The Bohemian Cafe-Bar, 256 Oxford Terr. (☎366 2563). Drop in for a cup of coffee ($3) or a pint ($5-7) on the patio and enjoy the riverview. The extensive wine selection is reasonably priced (from $7). Open M-F 7:30am-midnight, Sa-Su 9am-midnight. ❷

◎ ⚠ SIGHTS AND OUTDOOR ACTIVITIES

CATHEDRAL SQUARE

CHRISTCHURCH CATHEDRAL. The centerpiece of Christchurch, this looming 1865 Gothic Revival cathedral combines stones quarried and hewn in Canterbury with wooden beams from native matai and totara. Inside, ornate stained-glass windows imported from England abut Maori *kai kai* (flax) weavings. Climb the 134 steps of the cathedral's tower for a view of the city. (☎366 0046. *Open Oct.-Apr. M-F 8:30am-7pm, Sa 9am-5pm, Su 7:30am-8:30pm. May-Sept. M-Sa 9am-5pm, Su 7:30am-8pm. Su* *morning the cathedral is open for service, closed to tours. 30min. tours M-F 11am, 2pm; Sa 11am; Su 11:30am. Free admission. Tower $4, students and children $1.50. Camera $2.50.)*

ARCHITECTURAL TOURS. In the 1860s and 1870s Benjamin Mountfort designed many of the Gothic Revival stone and brick structures that lend the city its architectural character. At the visitors center, pick up a copy of the *Christchurch City Centre Walks* pamphlet, which details three walks past churches, government houses, and statues along the banks of the Avon River.

The arched wooden ceilings, magnificent stained-glass windows, and imposing, neo-Gothic hallways of the old Provincial Council Buildings, which run the length of Durham St. between Armagh and Gloucester St., have yet to be discovered by most tourists. *(www.ccc.govt.nz/provincialbuildings. Open M-Sa 10:30am-3:30pm.)* Alternatively, **Christchurch Personal Guiding Service** runs 2hr. walking tours from Cathedral Sq., look for the black and red "Guided Walks" kiosk in front of the BNZ. *(Tickets available at the visitors center or the kiosk. Daily tours May-Sept. at 1pm; Oct.-Apr. 10am and 1pm. $10, children free with accompanying adult.)* For a more active tour, pedal around town with **Christchurch by Bike.** *(Tours depart from the bike in front of the Visitors Centre, weather permitting, daily at 2pm. ☎366 0337; www.chchbiketours.co.nz. 2hr. tour $25.)*

SOUTHERN ENCOUNTER AQUARIUM. The small aquarium's cave-like interior is filled with stingrays, sharks, seahorses, and their fishy brethren. Highlights include the hands-on touching tank and the nocturnal kiwi house. The kiwi house is the only opportunity in Christchurch to see endangered kiwi without going to a wildlife reserve outside the city, but those with poor night vision will have trouble seeing anything in the darkened room. The eels are fed at 11am, the salmon and trout at 1pm, and the marine fish at 3pm with a "special feed" at 4pm. *(In Cathedral Sq.; enter via the visitors center or Pathway Shop. ☎359 0581. Open daily 9am-5pm; last admission 4:30pm. $14, students $12, children $5.)*

NEAR HAGLEY PARK

ARTS CENTRE. Formerly the University of Canterbury, the complex now houses cafes, galleries, shops, two cinemas, and the Court Theatre. On weekends, craftsmen and clothiers sell goods in the outdoor market, while ethnic food stalls crowd the back courtyard. *(Bordering the Botanic Gardens on the east and stretching over an entire block toward the city. ☎363 2836; www.artscentre.org.nz. Open daily 9:30am-5pm. Tours by request from 10am. Tours depart from the Arts Centre information center, near the end of Worcester Blvd. Free. Market Sa-Su 10am-4pm.)* **Ernest Rutherford's Den** recreates the university as it was in Edwardian times, chronicling the life of New Zealand's only Nobel Prize winner. *(www.rutherfordsden.org.nz. Open daily 10am-5pm. Suggested donation $1.)* Those with a sweet tooth will love the 1hr. guided tour at the **Fudge Cottage Kitchen,** which features complimentary samples. *(☎363 2836. Tours M-F 2pm. $15, children $7.50. Reservations, which must be made in person, recommended.)*

BOTANIC GARDENS. These free public gardens feature one of the country's best arrays of indigenous tree and plant life, with 10,000 different species sharing 30 hectares of land. The fiery blossoms of the endangered pohutukawa trees excite even the most skeptical naturalists. The 450-acre **Hagley Park,** with jogging tracks and rugby fields, borders the gardens on three sides. *(Gardens open daily from 7am until 1hr. before sunset. Information Centre open M-F 9am-4pm, Sa-Su 10:15am-4pm. 1½hr. guided walks mid-Sept.-May daily 1:30pm. $5. Feb.-Mar. additional 10am walk. Walks depart from Canterbury Museum entrance.)*

CHRISTCHURCH ART GALLERY. This ultra-modern steel and glass building is home to both Kiwi and European art. There are a few sculptures by Rodin, but the real highlights include the many landscapes painted by longtime New Zealand residents Petrus van der Velden and John Gibbs, the eerie birdmen of Bill Hammond, and the primordial landscapes of the Port Hills by Euan MacLeod. *(At Montreal St. and Worcester Blvd. ☎ 941 7300; www.christchurchartgallery.org.nz. Open M-Tu and Th-Su 10am-5pm, W 10am-9pm. Introduction to collection guided tour 11am, tour of feature exhibit daily 2pm and W 7:15pm. Free, suggested donation $5. Audio tour $5.)*

CANTERBURY MUSEUM. Exhibits catalogue the natural history of Canterbury at this excellent regional museum. The coverage of New Zealand's first settlers is stellar—both the moa-hunting Maori in the 15th century and the English in the 19th century. *(Beyond the Arts Centre on Rolleston Ave. ☎ 366 5000; www.canterburymuseum.com. Open daily 9am-5:30pm, in winter 9am-5pm. Suggested donation $5.)*

CENTRE OF CONTEMPORARY ART (COCA). This tribute to Kiwi modernity is an independently supported gallery of innovative modern works with both rotating and permanent exhibitions. They host over 60 exhibitions a year, and exhibits usually change every 3 weeks. Most works in this small but worthwhile gallery are for sale. *(66 Gloucester St., near the Christchurch Art Gallery. ☎ 366 7261; www.coca.org.nz. Open Tu-F 11am-5pm, Sa-Su noon-4pm. Entry by donation.)*

AVON RIVER. The Avon River meanders through the city under willows and arched bridges. Stroll the landscaped banks, or let a boatman do the work for you: **Punting on the Avon** and **Punting in the Park** run regular tours. Punting in the Park, in the Antigua Boat Sheds, also has **canoe rental.** *(Avon: on the river at the intersection with Worcester Blvd. ☎ 354 5994. $12 per 20min., $18 per 30min. Open in summer 9am-7pm; in winter 9am-dusk. Park: where the river meets Rolleston Ave. ☎ 366 0337; www.punting.co.nz. 30min. $16.50 per person, children $8. Min. 2 people. Open in daily summer 19am-6pm; in winter 10am-4pm. 10am-dusk. Both operations sell tickets at the visitors center at their respective boat landings. Antigua Boat Sheds canoe rental: ☎ 366 5885; www.boatsheds.co.nz. Single $8 per hr.; double $16 per hr. Open in summer daily 9am-4:30pm, in winter 9am-4pm.)*

OUTLYING SIGHTS

Some of the area's most worthwhile attractions lie just outside the downtown area; most are accessible by a short bus ride from the city center. Without a car, your best bet is the **Sunshine Shuttle,** which operates on demand. (☎ 379 1699. Departs Cathedral Sq. 10am and 1pm. $15 round-trip to Willowbank, International Antarctic Centre, and Mt. Cavendish Gondola. $20 round-trip to Orana Wildlife Park.) The black **Christchurch's Best Attractions Bus** also runs to major sights. (☎ 0800 484 485; www.chchattractions.co.nz. Call or book at the visitors center. Picks up from Cathedral Sq. daily at 9:30, 11am, 12:30, 2:30, 4 and 5:30pm. $6 round-trip to 1 attraction, $12 for 2 attractions, $17 for all attractions; children $3/7/10. Attractions include Willowbank, International Antarctic Centre, and Mt. Cavendish Gondola.)

NGA HAU E WHA NATIONAL MARAE. The "Marae of the Four Winds"—the world's largest *marae*—provides a window into Maori culture and history. The two meeting houses represent the body of Maui, the fisherman responsible for the creation of New Zealand according to Maori myth (p. 41). An outstanding guided tour plus an evening concert is available, but be warned: you may be "volunteered" to learn a wild-eyed *haka* war dance or *poi* twirling on stage. A complete *hangi* (p. 49), with stone-cooked mutton, pumpkin, and more follows. *(250 Pages Rd., east of Christchurch. Take bus #5 Southside from the depot. If driving, take Hereford St. east out of the city. When Hereford ends, turn right onto Linwood St., then take your first left onto Buckley St., which becomes Pages Rd.; Nga Hau E Wha National Marae is on the right about 2km down. ☎ 0800 456 898; www.nationalmarae.co.nz. Performances at 6:45pm. 15-person min. Call ahead. Guided tour and concert $30, children $19. Hangi, tour, and concert $65/36.)*

CANTERBURY

INTERNATIONAL ANTARCTIC CENTRE. This is as close as most will ever dare to get to the coldest, driest, windiest continent on earth. To make the Antarctic experience even more authentic, the center added a blue penguin area. *(Take the "Airport" bus or catch the free "Penguin Express" shuttle from the Antarctic shop in Cathedral Sq. The "Best Attractions" bus also stops at the Antarctic Centre. To reach the Antarctic Centre by car, drive to the airport and follow the signs; the center is the right just before the airport. Parking $1. ☎ 353 7798 or 0508 736 4846; www.iceberg.co.nz. Open daily Oct.-Mar. 9am-7pm; Apr.-Sept. 9am-5:30pm. $30, student $28, children $20; with Hagglund ride $48/46/36. Audio tour $6.)*

WILDLIFE RESERVES. Willowbank maintains extensive walk-through aviaries and a nocturnal kiwi house. The curious and mischievous kea will attack any unattended baggage and the gibbons keep up an almost constant cacophony. At the same location, the **Ko Tane** Maori cultural performance takes place nightly, showcasing Maori song and dance. *(60 Hussey Rd. Take Sherborne St. north; it will become Cranford St. and eventually T at Main North Rd.; turn right and go over the bridge, turn left on Styx Mill Rd. and go 3km to end, turn right onto Gardiner Rd., then turn right onto Hussey Rd. The only transport option from the city is the "Best Attractions" bus. ☎ 359 6226; www.willowbank.co.nz. Willowbank open daily 9:30am-8:30pm, close earlier off-season; admission after 5pm is only by guided tour. Tours daily 11:30am and 2:30pm and every hr. after 5pm, more often during school holidays. $20, students $17.50, children $10. Ko Tane admission $36/33/20. Ko Tane and park entry $45/39/22.50. Kotane, park entry, and a traditional hangi buffet dinner $85, students $79, age 10-15 $51, age 5-10 $36.50.)* **Orana Park** is a complete African plains park with lions, zebras, rhinos, a nocturnal kiwi house, a variety of savannah animals, native birds, and New Zealand's ageless tuatara. *(To reach the park take Sherborne St. north out of the city; it will become Cranford St. join with Main North Rd.; turn right and follow Main North Rd. to Johns Rd., then turn right on McLeans Island Rd., the park is 6km down on the left. Alternatively, the Sunshine Shuttle runs from Cathedral Sq. to the park. ☎ 359 7109; www.oranawildlifepark.co.nz. Open daily 10am-5pm. $19, students $17, children $7. Lion Encounter daily at 2:30pm. $15. Max. 20 people.)*

ADVENTURE ACTIVITIES

HIKING AND BIKING. In good weather, catch bus #28 from the depot out to **Port Hills** and the **Christchurch Gondola.** Take the gondola or walk up the steep bridle path (about 1hr.) to the top for a view encompassing Christchurch, the distant Southern Alps, and Lyttelton Harbour. *(☎ 384 0700; www.gondola.co.nz. Open daily 10am-8pm, in winter daily until 5pm. Round-trip $22, children $10.)* Once at the summit, you can choose from numerous **walking tracks,** including the ■**Crater Rim Walkway** (see **Lyttelton,** p. 316) and excellent sport-climbing crags. The **Mountain Bike Adventure Company** will bring you a bike at the top of the gondola. *(☎ 0800 424 534; www.cyclehire-tours.co.nz. $50, includes gondola ride to top and mountain bike rental and instruction for the way down. Book online, over the phone, or at the visitors center.)*

SCENIC DRIVE. If you've got a car or bike, head south out of Christchurch on Colombo St., which becomes Dyers Pass Rd. **Sign of the Takahe** stands as one of three Gothic mansions built as a stopping point for travelers decades ago. The Takahe offers a magnificent view of Christchurch and the Canterbury Plains. *(Take the #2 Cashmere bus into the hills. ☎ 332 4052.)* From Sign of the Takahe, continue along Dyer's Pass Rd. until it becomes Summit Rd. Be aware that Summit Rd. is narrow with no shoulder between the road and steep drop-offs on the path to **Godley Head,** a rugged promontory of grassy paths and sheer cliffs overlooking the austere Pacific and **Taylors Mistake.** From Taylors Mistake, visitors can backtrack to Christchurch via Summit Rd. or follow Summit as it turns back to the city.

HOT AIR BALLOONING. Balloon enthusiasts flock to the vast flatness of the Canterbury Plains. Join **Up Up and Away** or **Aoraki Balloon Safaris** for a float.

Aoraki often leads higher-flying trips from Methven that afford better mountain views. *(Up Up and Away: ☎381 4600; www.ballooning.co.nz. $260, children $220, adult price includes champagne. Aoraki: ☎0800 256 837; www.nzballooning.com. $295, with buffet champagne breakfast. Call a week ahead for discount standby rate of $245.)*

OTHER AIRBORNE PURSUITS. Skydiving NZ has a **Christchurch Parachute School,** at Wigram Acrodome, and offers tandem skydiving. Or try paragliding from the gondola down to Sumner with **Nimbus Paragliding.** *(Skydiving NZ: ☎343 5542 or 0800 697 593; www.skydivingnz.com. 9000 ft. tandem jump $245, 12000 ft. $295; pictures and DVD $195, just pictures or DVD $155. Nimbus: ☎326 7373 or 0800 111 611; www.nimbusparagliding.co.nz. Tandem paraglide $140; 3hr. intro course $100.)*

HORSE TREKS. Equestrians have many options for exploring the Canterbury countryside; **Orton Bradley** offers rides through hill country with beautiful views of Lyttelton Harbour. **Waimak Horse Treks** trots through the higher hills with views of the Southern Alps and Canterbury plains. They also have combination packages with Waimak Jet Boating and Jet Thrills. *(Orton: ☎329 4900; www.obhorsetreks.co.nz. 1hr. ride $40; 2½hr. ride $75. Bookings essential. Pickup available. Waimak: ☎323 9064 or 0800 873 577; www.gohorsetrekking.co.nz. 1hr. ride $35, children $30; 2hr. $60/55; half-day $85/80; full-day $150/140.)*

ON THE WATER. ▨**Rangitata Rafts** runs full-day trips over 11km of rapids, including two Class V rapids (the highest class of commercially rafted rapids), on the Rangitata River in the Peel Forest region from September through May. "The Pinch" is an almost 400m long adrenaline rush through Class V rapids. For those with their own car, Rangitata has a lodge in the Peel Forest, so self-drivers can stay there at night and whitewater raft in the morning. **Jet Thrills** leads fast-paced river jetboating adventures, while **Waimak Alpine Jet** runs longer trips into the Waimakariri Canyon. **Canterbury Leisure Tours** runs dozens of different tours in Canterbury and South Island, including an angling trip on local rivers. *(Rangitata: ☎0800 251 251; www.rafts.co.nz. $185 with pickup from Christchurch, $175 for self-drive; pictures on CD $36. Trip prices include lunch and a barbeque dinner. Min. age 13; under 18 requires guardian signature. Jet Thrills: ☎0800 277 729 or 385 1478; www.jetthrills.com. 1½hr. $65, children $35; 2hr. $95/65; heli-jet $210/195. Free pickup. Waimak: ☎318 4881 or 0800 263 626; www.waimakalpinejet.co.nz. $65-90. Canterbury: ☎0800 484 485. Half-day angling $399, full-day $499; per person rates decrease for groups.)*

🎭 ENTERTAINMENT

Christchurch has a professional theater company and several excellent art cinemas; check the back page of *The Press* for current listings. The **Court Theatre** at the Arts Centre has two theaters running some of New Zealand's best professional repertory productions. (☎963 0870; www.courttheatre.org.nz. Box office open M-F 9am-8:15pm, Sa 10am-8:15pm. Late night improv F 10pm $15, students $12. Tickets $12-43.) The **Isaac Theatre Royal,** 145 Gloucester St. (☎366 6326; www.isaactheatreroyal.co.nz; tickets at www.ticketek.com), is the forum for highbrow touring musicals and ballet companies. The **Academy Cinema Cloisters,** 25 Hereford St. in the Arts Centre, shows art and foreign flicks. (☎366 0167; www.artfilms.co.nz. Open 11am-11pm. Films $12.50, students $10.) For your Hollywood fix, hit up **Regent On Worcester,** 33 Cathedral Sq., just west of the square. (☎366 3127; www.regentcinemas.co.nz. Tickets $12-13; Tu $9.50; M and W before 5pm $10.) Gamblers can try their luck at the **Christchurch Casino,** 30 Victoria St., at Victoria and Durham St. While it may resemble a parking garage from the outside, the gaming room and cafe feature tasteful balconies and chandeliers. (☎365 9999; www.christchurchcasino.co.nz. Free shuttle runs from

BUSKING ON A SUMMER AFTERNOON

Perhaps only in Christchurch can an afternoon summer stroll take visitors past a man juggling swords, a pair of clowns on unicycles, and two acrobats performing stunts in spandex. That is the Busker Festival in a nutshell. Over 40 national and international acts draw 250,000 tourists for ten days in late January and early February. Each day presents a full lineup of street performances at locations in Cathedral Sq. and the pedestrian malls on High and Cashel St.

Audience members quickly learn that when it comes to busking, there is not always a clear distinction between performer and audience member. Performers often draw passersby into their acts and the twittering crowds wonder who will be the next "volunteer."

One of the most famous buskers is a Christchurch resident known as the Wizard. Clad in black, the Wizard is loved and loathed in equal measure for his taunting and confounding act. While old age has limited his performances to a few times a year, the busking legend regularly appears in his magic cap for the festival.

A full lineup of performances can be found in The Press in early January or online at www.worldbuskersfestival.com.

hotels and motels in the city 6pm-2am. For shuttle info, call ☎0800 227 466. No jeans, flip flops, or sneakers. 20+. Open 24hr.)

❋ FESTIVALS

Christchurch hosts an amazing number of festivals for a city its size. The **International Buskers Festival** (www.worldbuskersfestival.com) attracts the world's most talented to the streets of Christchurch in late January. The **Festival of Flowers** (☎366 2767; www.festivalofflowers.co.nz) blooms every February. Since 1983, **Summertimes** (www.summertimes.org.nz) has brought a series of concerts and theater performances to the city throughout the summer (events are scattered Dec.-Mar.). The **Christchurch Arts Festival** (www.artsfestival.co.nz) runs in winter of odd years and its multimedia performing arts and exhibitions next come to Christchurch in early August 2009. Also in August, the **Montana Christchurch Winter Carnival** celebrates the ski season with imported snow. In November, **New Zealand Cup and Show Week** (☎379 9629; www.nzcupandshow.co.nz) hits the city with high stakes horse racing, food, and fashion. To find out what's going on in Christchurch during your stay, check out **www.bethere.org.nz.**

▣ NIGHTLIFE

For a small city, Christchurch has a lot of life. Nightlife, that is. On **The Strip,** the row of bars on Oxford Terr., late dinners often become pub sessions. After a few drinks on the Strip, partygoers head to the clubs of **Manchester Street.** Wherever your night takes you, the **After Midnight Express** runs throughout the city on five different routes and can get you home safely. (☎0800 733 287; 379 4260. Runs early Sa-Su morning every hr. on the hr. 1-4am. $4.)

PUBS

▨ **Sammy's Jazz Review,** 14 Bedford Row (☎377 8618). Far removed from the techno clubs of Manchester St., the timeless sounds of cool jazz fill the classy interior and brick courtyard of this bar. On weekends, sets from 5-piece and 2-piece bands in an intimate setting keep Sammy's packed until 2am. Mains from $20. Pints $6. Live jazz from 7:30pm. Open Tu-Th 4-11pm, F-Sa 4pm-2am.

Shooters, 179 Cashel St. (☎365 1046), on the corner of Cashel and Manchester St. A large bar, Shooters manages to have everything twentysomethings look for in a night out on the town: 12 pool tables, a big screen television, a makeshift dancefloor and a bar with cheap drink deals. Pizzas $19. Shooters $7. Th $3 basic spirits and house beer. DJ Th-Sa after 10pm. Pints $5.20. Open daily 11am-late.

The Holy Grail Sports Bar, 99 Worcester St. (☎365 9816). Depending on how the All Blacks are faring, the Holy Grail is the best or worst place to be. Giant screens make the mighty All Blacks larger than life. When the rugby's not on, the bar is an ordinary pub with live vidoes and a dancing crowd. DJ Th-Sa. Pints $5-6; shooters $7. Happy hour daily 6-7pm two-for-one. Su-Th noon-midnight $10 pizza and a beer. Open daily noon-late, the bar is almost 24hr. when a major sporting event is on.

The Bog, 82 Cashel St. (☎379 7141; www.thebog.co.nz), on the City Mall. Live music (Th-Su from 9:30pm) and DJs get a young crowd going on the dance floor until the wee morn at Christchurch's best Irish pub. Burgers $15-18. Tu (The Bog is *the* bar on Tu) and Su night music from 8pm, F-Sa from 10pm. Pints $6.80. Open daily 9am-late.

The Boulevard (☎374 6676), at Oxford Terr. and Hereford St. A cafe and deli by day, the Boulevard transforms in the late evening hours to a riverside pub. Mains from $17.50. Half-pint $6. Happy hour Th-Sa 10:30pm-midnight; buy 1 drink get 1 free. DJ spins in the background Th-Sa. Open Su-W 10:30am-11pm, Th-Sa 10:30am-2am.

CLUBS

▨ **Base,** next to the backpackers on Cathedral Sq. (☎365 9724). For backpackers and locals alike, Base is Christchurch's party mecca. The club has a dance floor and a lofted lounge area with couches and pool tables in back. Base is one of the few places in Christchurch that goes off on week nights. Happy hour 5-9pm has cheap drinks and backpacker promos, often with a local busker as a host. Pints from $6. Open daily 5pm-midnight or as late as 3 days later.

Concrete Club, 132 Manchester St. (☎366 0438). Christchurch's IT club. Arrive before 11:30pm to beat the cue, which on can reach the corner on a busy night. Sign up for the privilege card and get preferential entrance and cheaper drinks W-Th. Th-Sa beats and bubbles. Mostly D&B music with an occasional live sax. The bumb 'n grind really starts around midnight. Smart dress required. Bubbles $3. Pints $7. Open daily 8pm-late, usually around 5:30am.

Mexican Cafe, 110 Lichfield St. (☎377 5515; www.mexicancafe.co.nz). Masquerading as a restaurant in daylight, this cafe becomes a swinging salsa club come night. The first F night of every month is the ▨ Salsa Spectacular. With 140 tequila types even the rhythmically challenged get on the dance floor eventually. Live Latin 6-piece band W from 7:30pm. Margaritas $9.50-12.50. Happy hour daily 5-7pm $7 margaritas, $15 margarita jugs (more margarita for your money). Lunch burrito $11-15. Dinner mains $17-23. Open daily 11:30am-late.

Boogie Nights, 146 Manchester St. (☎377 6375). True to its name, this Dirk Digglersized club grooves to 70s and 80s hits on a light-up dance floor. W ladies night, women get their 1st drink free and $4 cocktails after. Beer $5.50-7.50; cocktails $18. Smart dress required. Crowds usually arrive after 10:30pm. Open W-Th 9pm-late, usually 2 or 2:30am; F-Sa 8pm-late, usually 3 or 4am.

MICROBREWERIES

▨ **Twisted Hops,** 6 Poplar St., off High St. The hops may be twisted, but the beers at Christchurch's best microbrewery all have a simple, crisp flavor that attests to the skill of the brewers. Beers are available both on tap and cask. The creative food menu (plum and brie pizza $18.50) and patio seating are the perfect complements to the brews. Pints $7-8. Live music W-Th. Open daily noon-late, usually 11pm.

The Loaded Hog, 178 Cashel St. (☎366 6674), at Manchester St. The lines are long at this homebrew chain, where bartenders pour an excellent lager. Swing music W, Latin Th from 9:30pm. DJs F from 9:30pm, Sa from 10pm. Pints $6.20. Happy hour Th-Sa 4-7pm $3 "hog" pints. Open M-F 11am-late, Sa-Su 10am-late. Late can be as early as 10pm on dead week nights or as late as 3am on weekends.

Dux de Lux, 41 Hereford St. (☎366 6919), at the Arts Centre. Droves of students pack this enormous old house for its 3 separate bars and 7 freshly brewed beers. The stage here hosts a wide range of musical stylings including local, national, and international acts. Live music Th-Sa, plus a few weeknights. Open daily 11am-11:30pm.

⚡ DAYTRIPS FROM CHRISTCHURCH

LYTTELTON

Just 12km from Christchurch, Lyttelton is a 20min. bus ride (bus #28 or 35, every 15-30min., $2-3) from the city center via the Tunnel Rd.

The small port of Lyttelton (pop. 4000) provides a welcome relief from Christchurch's tour busesComing from Christchurch through the Tunnel, turn left onto Norwich Quay. Turn left on any cross street and one block up from Norwich Quay is London St., one of Canterbury's most famous streets. Going out of town, London St. becomes Sumner Rd. To explore beyond London St., grab a map ($2) from the visitors center (p. 317) and head north to the Major Hornbrook Track. The steep climb (one-way 1-2hr. walking from the Visitors Centre, quicker coming down) provides wonderful views of the old volcanic caldera in which the harbor is situated, and links up with the main attraction, the ⬛Crater Rim Walkway, marked by orange posts with a white "W" on them. To hike the entire walkway allow three days. (Section 1: one-way 5.5km, 3½hr.; section 2: 7.5km, 2½hr; section 3: 8km, 3½hr.) The first section runs above Lyttleton at Godley Head and crosses the Bridle Trail (see below). Those wishing to avoid the climb can either drive up Summit Rd., which parallels Crater Rim, or hop on the Christchurch Gondola (p. 312). Determined hikers can recreate the journey taken by settlers in the 1850s as they moved to their inland homesteads, by taking the 2.4km **Bridle Trail** (1-2hr. up; 30-45min. down), which runs up the Port Hills on the Lyttelton side and down the hills roughly parallel to the gondola lines on the Christchurch side.

The **Lyttelton Time Ball,** 2 Reserve Terr., provides a castle-like lookout tower and fabulous harbor views, as well as insight into maritime history. Lyttelton's time ball guided ships from 1876 to 1934, and although it is no longer a navigational tool, it is still one of the few extant time balls you can set your watch to. (To reach the time ball either follow the walking path from town 10-15min. or drive Sumner Rd. out of town and look for the turn off on the left about 1.5km outside of town. ☎328 7311. Usually open daily 10am-5:30pm; May-Sept. W-Su 10am-5pm, but at press time was closed for renovations, so call. Ball drops 1pm. $7, students $2.)

Quail Island is a good day out for families, as the boats will drop you off on the small island and give you a chance to walk around. **Black Cat Cruises,** 17 Norwich Quay, runs a 2hr. wildlife cruise of the harbor, often encountering Hector's dolphins and other marine life, as well as a Quail Island cruise. (☎328 9078 or 0800 436 574; www.blackcat.co.nz. Wildlife: Departs daily 1:30pm. $52, children $20. Quail Island: Departs daily Dec.-Mar. 12:30pm and Oct.-Apr. 3:30pm. Adults $15, children $7.50.) **Sea Cruises Limited** runs a similar service at a comparable price. (☎328 7720 and 327 3134. Dolphin Watching tour $40, children $20. Quail Trail departs daily from "A" jetty 10am, 2 and 5pm. $14/8.) If you want to see the dolphins while learning to sail a traditional boat, sail **Jack Tar Sailing Companies,** 1903 Gaff Yawl. The boat is available for rental by appointment and the set rates make it a reasonable options for groups. (☎389 9259, 02 7435 5239, or 0800 253 2663; www.jacktarsailing.co.nz. Cost to rent entire boat for 4hr. $250, full-day $500; romantic evening cruise $250. Max. 6 people.) **Salty Dog Charters** takes a more hands-on approach to cruising. (☎328 7021; www.saltydogcharters.co.nz. Cruise by appointment. Min. 8 people. 3hr. $45 per person.)

The **Visitors Centre,** 34 London St., in the Anchor Fine Arts building, has self-guided walking tours, though they provide very little information on attractions beyond Lyttleton. (☎328 9093. Open daily 9am-5pm.) **Tunnel Vision Backpackers (BBH) ❷,** 44 London St., is the town's best and only hostel. Some of the bright, spacious rooms come with a sea-side view. The wooden deck has a barbeque that is put to good use during the peak summer season. (☎328 7576; www.tunnelvision.co.nz. Key deposit $10. Closed June-Aug. In summer reserve a week in advance. Dorms $21-23; doubles $62. $2 BBH discount. Cash only.) **Dockside Accommodation ❹,** 22 Sumner Rd., just out of town on the righthand side, is a small, boutique accommodation. Immaculate suites overlook the harbor and a pleasant garden. (☎328 7344 or 027 4488 133; kathyg@nhf.org.nz. Book well in advance. Twin $80; 2-bedroom queen and twin rooms $100.)

London St. provides a range of culinary options from cheap fish 'nchips to upscale cafes. For groceries, try **Supervalue,** on London St. (☎328 7038. Open daily 8am-9pm.) For those looking for something more than greasy fish 'n chips, The **Volcano ❸,** next door to Tunnel Vision Backpackers, is a highly recommended local dinner joint that serves an eclectic menu. (☎328 7077. Enchiladas $23.50; fish $28; risotto $30. Bar opens daily from 5pm, restaurant 6pm-late.) For a cheap daytime option, **No. 6 Cafe ❶,** 6 London St., has healthy, but still tasty organic food. Their smoothies ($5-6) are made with real fruit, honey, yogurt and milk. (☎328 9566. Lunch panini around $8. Breakfast $9-16. Open daily 8am-4pm.) Bright signs lead the way to the ◪**Wunderbar,** a London St. landmark and one of Canterbury's best bars. Head down the stairs, through the parking lot, and up the ramp—it's worth the walk. Illuminated mannequins in lingerie and neckties shed light on the velvet seats along the bar, as music from scratchy LPs drifts overhead.

SUMNER

Sumner lies to the east of Christchurch, accessible by bus #3 (20min., bus departs every 15min., $2). Drivers take Ferry Rd. out of the city and then hug the coastline. Ferry Rd. becomes Sumner Rd., which turns into Marriner St. in town.

Sumner is Canterbury's beach town. **Taylor's Mistake,** southeast of town, is the town's best break, though beginners should try the waves closer to town center at **Cave Rock,** a natural grotto accessible at low tide. Beware of sudden surges if you choose to venture inside. In summer, the surf breaks can get quite crowded, and those seeking more seclusion should take advantage of some of the area's coastal hikes. Follow sign posts from the beach to **Boulder Bay** (3hr.) via Taylor's Mistake. **Liquefy,** 9 Wakefield St., at Marriner Rd., equips surfers with a board and wetsuit. (☎326 7444; www.liquefy.co.nz. Surfboards 2hr. $20, half-day $30, full-day $40. Wetsuits 2hr. $5, half-day $10, full-day $15. Open daily 10am-6pm, longer in summer.) **Urban Surf,** 25d Marriner St., has beginner foam boards for the less experienced. (☎326 6023. Half-day surfboard rental $40, full-day $50. Wetsuit half-day $10, full-day $25. Open M-F 10am-6pm, Sa-Su 10am-5pm.) The two most highly recommended surf instructors are: **Learn to Surf** and **live 2 surf.** (Learn to Surf: Meets at Stoke St. and the Esplanade. ☎0800 80 7873; www.surfcoach.co.nz. live 2 surf: Meets at Marriner St. and the Esplanade. ☎0508 548 327 873. Lessons from $40.)

Beach bums who don't want to commute from Christchurch can stay at **The Marine Backpackers (BBH) ❷**, 26 Nayland St., Sumner's only hostel. Ample four-bed dorms, a piano, barbeque area, and garden make it a popular surfers' retreat. (☎326 6609; www.themarine.co.nz. Towel $2. Key deposit $20. Reserve ahead a couple weeks in summer. Dorms $21; singles $30, with bath $40; doubles and twins $50/$60. $3 BBH discount. MC/V.) After a beachside stroll, choose a cuppa ($3-4.50) from the 30 different teas of **t is Tea ❷**, 25 Marriner St., at Burgess St. For a healthy option, try one of their fresh fruit and vegetable smoothies. (☎326 7111;www.tistea.co.nz. Meals $9.50-16.50. Open daily M-Tu and F-Sa 9am-10pm, W-Th and Su 9am-6pm.) On **Marriner Road** and **Wakefield Street**, plenty of cheap restaurants dish up fish 'n chips for under $4, or Chinese and Indian food for a bit more. For pizza with a side of surf, ◪**Club Bazaar ❷**, 15 Wakefield Ave., has pizza made from homemade dough in a retro surf setting. (☎326 6155; www.surfbar.co.nz. Open M-Sa 3pm-late, Su noon-late.) Sumner has no shortage of fish 'n chip shops, but for the best, head to **Red Snapper Seafood ❶**, on Wakefield Ave. at Nayland St. (☎326 5726. Fish $2 per piece. Half chips $1.20, full $2. Open daily 11:50am-8 or 8:30pm. Cash only.) The **Ruptured Duck Bar ❷**, 4 Wakefield Ave., has happy hour deals and is a top spot to drink a night away. (☎326 5488. Happy hour W-Su 5-7pm $3 half pints. Upstairs restaurant open M-F 5pm-late, Sa-Su noon-late. Downstairs bar open W-Su 5pm-late.) Pick up groceries at **Supervalue,** 41 Nayland St., in the mall at Wakefield Ave. (☎326 5688. Open M-Sa 7am-8pm, Su 7am-7pm.)

AKAROA AND THE BANKS PENINSULA ☎03

The French settlers who landed in Akaroa (pop. 550) in 1840 didn't succeed in loosening the British stronghold on New Zealand, but they did leave some indelible cultural imprints, from authentic French cafe fare on Rue Lavaud, to shameless knock-offs, like Le Mini-Golf Course. The historic maisons, craft shops, and fishing harbor of the Banks Peninsula seem worlds away from Christchurch.

⊏ TRANSPORTATION. Two shuttle services travel daily between Christchurch and Akaroa, stopping at Barry's Bay Cheese Factory and offering commentary along the way. **Akaroa Shuttle** (☎0800 500 929; info@akaroashuttle.co.nz) departs Christchurch (daily 8:30am, Nov.-Apr. also daily 2pm, F 4:30pm) and returns (daily 10:30am, 3:35, 4:30pm; return ticket $20), while **French Connection** (☎0800 800 575) departs Christchurch (daily 8:45am, day tour departs 9:30am) and returns (daily 2:30 and 4:30pm; Nov.-Apr. additional service at 6:45am; one-way $15, return $25). Both services run about 1½hr. and offer longer scenic tour options. To see the most remote stretches of the peninsula, hop on one of two **mail runs**—part tour, part postal route—for a day. Inquire at least one day in advance at the visitors center. (☎325 1334 or 027 487 6791; www.akaroamailrun.com. Departs M-Sa 9am, returns 2pm. Eastern Bays Mail Run $50; Akaroa Harbour Scenic Mail Run $45; morning tea included.) Although *Let's Go* does not recommend it, **hitchhiking** is possible to and from Christchurch, as most traffic goes all the way to Akaroa; thumbers take the #7 Halswell bus from Cathedral Sq. Those heading back to Christchurch have luck just outside the township, at the bottom of Old Coach Rd.

◪◪ ORIENTATION AND PRACTICAL INFORMATION. Running past **Lake Ellesmere** and through several tiny towns, **SH75** winds 96km southeast from Christchurch, up over the lip of the extinct Akaroa volcano, and back down to the harbor of Akaroa. Drivers enter Akaroa on **Rue Lavaud**, which runs close to the water and becomes **Rue Jolie**. **Beach Road** runs parallel to Rue Jolie along the water and is home to most tour operators and restaurants. The main wharf juts off the coast along the Beach Rd. side of town. The **Akaroa Information Centre**, 80 Rue Lavaud, has information on Akaroa, and can help arrange forays into the greater peninsula. (☎304 8600; www.akaroa.com. Luggage storage $4. Open daily 9am-5pm.) Other local services include: **BNZ**, 73 Rue Lavaud, opposite the visitors center, which changes money and has a 24hr. **ATM** (☎304 1024; open M and Th-F 9am-4:30pm, Tu-W 9:30am-4:30pm); the **police** (☎304 1030); the **hospital** (☎304 7023); a **pharmacy**, 58 Rue Lavaud, across from Bon Accord Backpackers (☎304 7002, after-hours 304 7080; open M-Th and Sa 9am-6pm, F 9am-7pm, Su 11am-5pm); **Internet** access at **Bon-E-Mail**, 63 Rue Lavaud (open daily 9am-8pm; $2 per 20min.) and **Turienne Coffee Shop**, on Rue Lavaud, next to the 4 Square (Internet $2 per 20min. Laptop connections; open daily 7am-6pm); the **post office**, in the same building as the visitors center (☎304 8600; open daily 9am-5pm).

⌂ ACCOMMODATIONS. In Akaroa and the Banks Peninsula, it is hard to go wrong with hostel accommodations. The area has many of New Zealand's best hostels. Built by a Spaniard in 1860, **Chez La Mer Backpackers (BBH) ❷**, 50 Rue Lavaud, still exudes Old World charm with its herb garden, replete with fish pond and gazebo. Play a tune or two on the piano. (☎304 7024; www.chezlamer.co.nz. Free tea and drip coffee in the morning. Reception 9am-9pm. Dorms $23; twins and doubles $58, ensuite $66-76. $3 BBH discount. Cash only.) Cathy and Boots the dog, the welcoming hosts at **Bon Accord Backpackers (BBH) ❷**, 57 Rue Lavaud, welcome all to stay and use the fully equipped kitchens, den, and small porch. The 12-bed hostel sits beside a pleasant stream and its own productive apricot tree. (☎304 7782; www.bon-accord.co.nz. Free lockers, slippers, and hot water bottles. Dorms $23; doubles $56. $3 BBH discount. MC/V.) **Akaroa Top 10 Holiday Park ❶**, 96 Morgans Rd., is 2km before Akaroa. Coming from Christchurch, turn left on Old Coach Rd., then left on Morgans Rd. The cabins offer beautiful views. (☎304 7471; www.akaroa-holidaypark.co.nz. Internet $2 per 17min. 2-person powered tent sites $30. Standard units with kitchen from $60, with bath from $95. MC/V.)

Outside of Akaroa are a wealth of small hostels, each with a distinct personality, amid South Island's trademark scenery. Many backpackers come to the 17-bed **⊠Le Bons Backpackers (BBH) ❷**, Le Bons Bay, just for the charming owner Gary's home-cooked dinners ($12), which use ingredients straight from the garden. The hostel has a prime location overlooking the bay with a network of hiking trails that start in the backyard. Gary also runs marine nature tours from Sandy Beach ($30). Free breakfast and freshly baked bread. (To reach the hostel, take the main road out of Akaroa, turn right on Long Bay Rd. and follow sign to Le Bons Bay, making a right turn onto Le Bons Bay Rd. The hostel is 3km down Le Bons Bay Rd. ☎304 8582; www.lebonsbay.co.nz. Work exchange possible. Lofted dorms $22. Doubles $54. $2 BBH discount. Cash only.) **Half Moon Cottage (BBH) ❷**, on SH75, about 2km before Duvauchele if driving from Christchurch, is more B&B than backpacker. Fortunately, the owner's enjoy free-spirited company and keep the prices on their luxury site low. Muesli in the morning and plums off the tree in season. (The Akaroa Shuttle goes right by the hostel and can drop off and pick up guests with prior arrangement. ☎304 5050; www.halfmoon.co.nz. Bookings essential. Reception 8am-10:30pm. Kayaks $20 for half-day. Dorm $23. Twins and doubles $64. $3-4 BBH discount. MC/V.) While city slickers should avoid the rustic **Onuku Farm Hostel (BBH) ❷**, 89 Hamiltons Rd., those with an affinity for rural living will love the sociable atmosphere. Rumored to have originally been built on whale vertebrae, the historic farm is now the center of 1000 acres of coastal farmland owned and run in conjunction with the hostel. (To reach the hostel follow Rue Jolie out of Akaroa; it will become Onuku Rd. Turn right off Onuku Rd. onto Hamilton Rd. and prepare for a windy drive up the mountain to the hostel. ☎304 7066; www.onukufarm.co.nz. Free pick-up daily 12:30pm from Akaroa Information Centre. Reception 9am-1pm, 2:30-6pm and 8-9pm. Reserve ahead Dec.-Feb. Work exchange available. Dorms $23, stargazer $25. Twins/doubles $54-56. Camping options also available, but not part of BBH. $3 BBH discount.) At Okains Bay, **Double Dutch Backpackers ❷**, 32 Charlton Rd., is the area's newest hostel. (Take Summit Rd. through town and turn left on Charlton Rd. ☎304 7229; www.doubledutch.co.nz. Dorms $23. Twins $56, doubles $66. MC/V.)

❐ FOOD. **By the Green ❷**, 37 Rue Lavaud, offers fresh seasonal dishes ($14-18) and local wines. (☎304 7717. Wines $7-9. Gourmet deli sandwiches $6-7. Open daily 8:30am-5pm.) A few doors down, **The Pepper Tree ❸**, 43 Rue Lavaud, beckons with all-day breakfast (eggs Benedict; $17) served fireside, on the porch, or in the garden near the bocce balls. (☎304 7447. Open daily 9am-8pm.) Head with a group to **Cafe Dooberry's ❷**, 69 Beach Rd., where stonebaked pizzas are big enough to share. (☎304 8060. Pizza for 2 $19-21. Open daily 9am-9pm.) **4 Square**, on Rue Lavaud, across from the museum, has groceries. (Open daily 9am-6pm.)

▨ OUTDOOR ACTIVITIES. Outdoor enthusiasts can encounter area wildlife either by land or by sea. Most companies listed cluster around the main wharf. **Akaroa Adventure Centre**, 64 Rue Lavaud, is a one-stop booking and rental center for activities on the peninsula. (☎304 8709; www.akaroa.com. Bikes $7 per hr., children $5; tandems $10. Volcano rim ride including hire and transport $38. Surfing rental $28 per day, wetsuit $10. Surfing with the seals $60, includes transport to beach. Sea kayaking $12 per hr., half-day $30, full-day $50.) **Dolphin Experience** takes you swimming with rare Hector's dolphins, the smallest marine mammals in the world. The crew does an excellent job of getting swimmers more time with the dolphins than elsewhere on South Island. (☎304 7726 or 0508 365 744; www.dolphinsakarao.co.nz. Max. 10 swimmers. 3hr. tours in summer 6, 8:30, 11:30am, 1:30pm; in winter 11:30am and 1:30pm. Extra tours run on demand. $98, children $80; watching $48/25.) **Akaroa Harbour Cruises,** on the main wharf, tour much of the harbor, including the seal and cormorant colonies. (☎304 7641 or 0800 436 574; www.blackcat.co.nz; www.swimmingwithdolphins.co.nz. 2hr. wildlife tours in summer 11am and 1pm; in winter 1pm. $52, children $20. 3hr. Dolphin swims summer 6, 8:30, 11:30am and 1:30pm; on demand in winter. $105/85, watching $55/30.)

Fox II Wildlife Cruises are tours with an interactive twist. The tours are done on an old sailboat and passengers can help to sail. Tours set sail daily from Daly's Wharf and are run by the people at Chez la Mer. (☎0800 369 7245; www.akaroafoxsail.co.nz. 3hr. tours departs Dec.-May daily 10:30am and 1:30pm. $50 per person, children $25. 30% BBH discount.) **Akaroa Seal Colony Safari** trucks you over the crater and down the outer slopes to the Pacific Ocean, where fur seals await. There are great views of both the harbor and the open ocean from the crater rim. (☎304 7255 or 0274 942 070; www.sealtours.co.nz. 2½hr. $70, children $50. 6-person max. Reserve ahead.) The calm waters of Long Harbour are an ideal spot for novices to take out a sea kayak; the Akaroa Adventure Centre and **Akaroa Boat Hire,** on the waterfront across from Dolphin Experience, can set you up. (☎304 8758 or 304 7136. Small kayak $7 per 30min., $30 per half-day; $40 per full-day.)

Several historical short walks explore the town and waterfront (most are 1hr. round-trip). Longer hikes, like the trek up the volcano to **Heritage Park,** north of town (2-3hr. round-trip), provide views of the hills and water below.

Those spending more time in the region can inquire about the coastal **Banks Peninsula Track** (35km, 2 or 4 days) at the visitors center. The track crosses private property, so reservations are required. (☎304 7612; www.bankstrack.co.nz. Hikers must meet at 5:45pm the day before they leave for orientation. 2-day hike $125; 4-day $225 per person; prices include accommodation, mostly homestays.) Amateur geologists with a car should head to **Kaitorete Spit,** off SH75, between Motukarara and Little River, south of Lake Ellesmere. The narrow formation is rich in agates and other semi-precious stones, which are washed out to this deposit by mainland rivers.

The **Akaroa Museum,** at Rue Lavaud and Rue Balguerie, has informative exhibits detailing the 12-million-year history of the region. Copies of the Treaty of Waitangi are also on display. (☎304 1013. Open daily 10:30am-4:30pm, in winter 10:30am-4pm. $4, students $3.50, children $1.) **Barry's Bay Cheese Factory,** off SH75 on the way to Akaroa, shows visitors the wheys of cheesemaking and is a popular stop between Christchurch and Akaroa. Cheesemaking occurs every other day; call ahead for schedule. (☎304 5809. Open daily 9am-5pm.)

CANTERBURY SKIING ☎03

The ski fields in the Southern Alps explode in the winter, with skiers coming from all over New Zealand to challenge Mt. Hutt. Canterbury's slopes offer great runs, less glitz, and in some cases, lower rates than the tourist-heavy Southern Lakes; they attract more of a Kiwi than an international following.

⌐ TRANSPORTATION

Several companies, including some inevitable mid-season newcomers, shuttle the 1½hr. drive from Christchurch; the best advice is to check at the Christchurch visitors center (☎379 9629; www.christchurchinformation.co.nz) for current departures. As a jumping-off point, **Snowork Mountain Tours** runs to all the club fields listed below from Christchurch. (☎0800 766 967 or 388 7669; www.snowork.com. Daily at 7:30am, return at 4pm. Return fare $45, student $35.) **The Ski Shuttle** runs regularly from Christchurch to **Mt. Hutt** and **Porter Heights** on demand. (☎324 3641. Round-trip $45, students $35.) **Ride Snow Shuttles** brings skiers to the slopes from Methven. (☎021 743 394 or 0800 121 414; www.ridesnowshuttles.co.nz.) Bring snow chains if you're driving, and expect a long walk from the parking lot.

⛷ SKI FIELDS

While none of these smaller mountains and their clubs are as popular as nearby Mt. Hutt (p. 323), each has its own character and loyal following. Most club fields feature overnight accommodations with close proximity to the runs, and all but Mt. Hutt are only 30min. from the comfortable accommodations in Arthur's Pass (p. 326). Each of these clubs offers lessons and packages, but they do not rent equipment unless noted. Student rates mostly apply only to those with a New Zealand student ID. If you plan on skiing for a number of days or in a number of locations, you may want to consider the **NZ Superpass** or the **Chill Pass.** The NZ Superpass allows you to purchase a number of coupons, which can be used for lift passes on Queenstown, Mt. Hutt, and Canterbury ski fields or for other activities. The pass can be purchased through travel agents or at Mt. Hutt, Coronet Peak or the Remarkables. (☎443 4640; www.nzsuperpass.com. 2-day $148, children $75; 3-day $220/111; 4-day $287/147; 10-day $653/333.) The Chill Pass, valid at Porter Heights, Craigieburn Val-

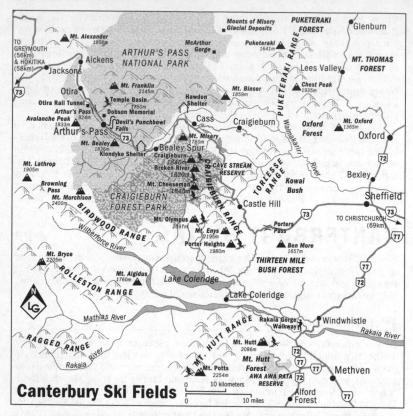

Canterbury Ski Fields

ley, Mt. Cheeseman, Mt. Olympus, Broken River, and Hanmer Springs in North Canterbury (p. 322), is perfect for longer stays. (☎318 4830; www.chillout.co.nz. 3-day anytime pass $160, student $135, children $85; 5-day pass $235/185/120.) For detailed information on ski fields, check out www.nzski.com or www.snow.co.nz, or pick up the free annual **Brown Bear** guide (www.brownbear.co.nz) at the beginning of July.

Porter Heights (☎318 4002; snow phone 366 7766, ext. 06; www.porterheights.co.nz). 1hr. from Christchurch, 12km off SH73. The longest vertical drop in the area as well as excellent terrain for learners. Lift pass $70, students $55; half-day $45/35. Ski, boot, and pole rental $40/30. Snowboard and boot rental $50/40. Toboggan rental $10. Beginner package includes lift pass, ski rental, and 2hr. lesson $75.

Temple Basin (☎377 7798; snow phone 366 7766, ext. 01; www.templebasin.co.nz) has a 40min.-1hr. walk from the parking lot to the field. Some of the best snowboard terrain and night skiing in New Zealand. Lift pass $45, students $35. Ski, boot, and pole rental weekday $30, weekend $40. Snowboard and boot rental $40/70. Accommodations from $40, students $35. 2-day, 1-night pass including meals, 1 night's accommodation, and 2-day lift pass $160, student $125.

Craigieburn Valley (☎318 8711; snow phone 383 8888, ext. 07; www.craigieburn.co.nz). Experts flock to the open powder bowls, steep narrow shoots, and the 600m vertical descent in the middle basin—it's like heli-skiing without the hefty fees. Largest off-piste in New Zealand. Tow fees $60, student $45. Group lessons $20 per hr. Room and board $80/65.

Broken River (☎318 8713; snow phone 383 8888, ext. 03; www.brokenriver.co.nz) requires a 25min. walk. A great bet for intermediate skiers. "Back to basics skiing" means a 70-hectare open basin with a 420m vertical drop. Lift pass $60, students $5; half-day $45/35. Group instruction $22 per hr. Self-catered lodging from $30.

Mt. Olympus (☎0800 686 596, bookings 318 5840; snow phone 383 8888, ext. 04; www.mtolympus.co.nz). 4WD strongly suggested for those providing their own transport. This club ski field is known for light powder, shady mornings, and night skiing under the lights. Lift pass $60, students $30. Self-catered lodging from $25.

Mt. Cheeseman (☎344 3247; snow phone 366 7766, ext. 2; www.mtcheeseman.com), 1½hr. from Christchurch down a well-maintained access road, has a reputation for being family-friendly. Ski or snowboard group lessons from $25 per hr. Lift pass $52, students $40; half-day $39/32. Ski, boot, and pole rental $32/28. Snowboard and boot rental $40/35. Lift pass, room, and board $157/120.

Mt. Potts (☎0800 766 9228 or 303 9060; www.mtpotts.co.nz), 1hr. from Methven near Mt. Somers. Though only accessible via a Snowcat heli-tour, Mt. Potts has become increasingly popular with adventurous skiers searching for the freedom of untracked backcountry. While not for beginners, there are plenty of options for both intermediate and advanced. $399 per day, includes meals, transport, and 10-12 runs.

Alpine Recreation, based in Tekapo, runs shorter, cheaper courses aimed at teaching mountaineering basics. *(☎680 6736 or 0800 006 096; www.alpinerecreation.co.nz. 4-day intro courses from $1000, group discounts available.)* Travelers with mountaineering skills seeking a non-guided option can traverse the Ball Pass Crossing, a popular, challenging route. Alpine Recreation runs guided trips over the pass as well as an easier guided Tekapo Trek. *(Ball Pass: 3 days. $725, all inclusive. Tekapo Trek: 3 days, $650.)*

METHVEN AND MT. HUTT ☎03

The modest farming town of Methven (pop. 1400) swells each winter with skiers and snowboarders enjoying the longest ski season in New Zealand (up to 4 months, starting in June) on the slopes of the nearby Mt. Hutt range.

▐ TRANSPORTATION

Most transport in Methven originates in Christchurch. The **InterCity/Newmans** team (☎365 1113) runs from Christchurch and connects to a shuttle that deposits you in front of the Methven visitors center (1½hr., 7:45am, $33); they also go to Queenstown (6½hr., 8:50am, $53). Book at least a day in advance in winter. Similar options include **Methven Travel,** 93 Main St. (☎0800 684 888 or 302 8106; www.methventravel.co.nz), which drops by the Christchurch airport on the way to the city (1½hr.; M, W, Su once daily, F twice; $48 return, one-way $32; student $48/28).

Transportation directly to Mt. Hutt can come from Christchurch as well as from nearby Methven. Most shuttles to the slope depart Christchurch around 7am and the slopes at 5pm. The **Mt. Hutt Express** (☎0800 808 070 or 388 2042; www.skimthutt.com; $49 return, students $45); **Snowbus** (☎0800 766 928; www.snowbus.com; $45 return, student $40) and **Mountain Mule** (☎383 8995; $49 return, students 45) are good options from Christchurch. Coming from Methven, the **Leopard SkiBus** runs to Mt. Hutt. (☎302 8707 or 027 433 9763. 7:45 and 9:45am, return 3 and 4:15pm. Hostel pickup can be arranged. Round-trip $22, students $17.) **Methven/Mt. Hutt Taxi** (☎302 1728 or 027 431 8604) will shuttle to the ski field anytime at a slightly higher price ($30 return). **Ride Snow Shuttles** runs a six-to eight-passenger 4WD car trips up to Mt. Hutt from Methven. (☎0800 121 515 or 021 743 394; www.ridesnowshuttles.co.nz. 8:15am, with additional service at noon by request. $25 return, students $20.)

✳❓ ORIENTATION AND PRACTICAL INFORMATION

SH77 becomes **Main Street** in town and intersects **Forest Drive/Methven Chertsey Road.** Most services and accommodations lie within a 5min. walk of the **Methven i-Site Visitors Centre,** south of the crossroads on Main St. (☎302 8955; www.methveninfo.co.nz. Internet $2 per 10min. Open daily 8am-6pm. In summer M-F 9am-5pm, Sa-Su 11am-4pm.) **Big Al's,** at the crossroads, is the one-stop adventure shop, renting a variety of clothing and accessories. (☎302 8003; www.bigals.co.nz. Ski rental from $30, students $26. Snowboards from $39/34. Mountain bikes $30 per day. Fishing gear $8 per day. Open in winter daily 7:30am-7:30pm.) **Jace's Ski Hut,** on Forest Dr., stocks a good range of rental equipment. (302 9553; www.balancesports.com. Ski rental from $27, students $21. Snowboard from $40/30. Multi-day discount. Open in winter daily 7:30am-7pm.) Other services include: the **BNZ,** at Banks and Main St., with a 24hr. **ATM** (open M and Th-F 9am-4:30pm, Tu-W 9:30am-4:30pm); the **police** (☎302 8200); the **Methven Medical Centre,** opposite the visitors center (☎302 8105; open M-F 9am-5:30pm; weekends June-Oct.); the **Methven Pharmacy,** next to the visitors center (☎302 8103; after hours 302 8378; open M-F 8:30am-6pm, Sa-Su 4-6pm; in summer M-F 8:30am-5:30pm); **Internet** access at the **Email Shop** (☎302 8982; $5.50 per hr.; open daily in winter 9am-11pm, in summer 9am-8pm); the **post office,** in **Gifts Galore** on Main St. (☎302 8463; open M-F 8am-6pm, Sa-Su 10am-noon, 4-6pm. In summer M-F 8am-5pm.) For **snow reports,** call ☎3085074 or go on line to www.nzski.com.

⛰ ACCOMMODATIONS

Lodges line the streets of Methven, though many accommodations partially close and reduce their rates in the summer. Almost all have the bare essentials: waxing racks and somewhere to put your skis.

▨ **Alpenhorn Chalet,** 44 Allen St. (☎302 8779; timbuma@hotmail.com), the 3rd left past the pubs on Main St. from Forest Dr. Glowing kitchen, resident cat, central heating, thick mattresses and a solarium with spa and view. No Internet. Dorms $25; doubles $60-70, with bath $80. Discounts in summer. ❷

Redwood Lodge, 5 Wayne Pl. (☎302 8964; www.snowboardnz.com). With your back to the Methven i-Site, turn right down Main St., then right onto South Belt, and left onto Wayne Pl. All ensuite dorms and a personable owner make for a pleasant stay. Dorms $25; doubles $55-60; triples $105. Reduced rates in summer. ❷

Snow Denn Lodge (YHA) (☎302 8999; snowdenn@xtra.co.nz), at McMillan and Bank St., features full linen service, free continental breakfast, a wintertime spa ($4 per 30min.), and spacious lounges with mounted deer heads. Free use of bikes, tennis rackets, fishing rods, and cricket set. Internet free, but only 1 computer. Shuttle to Rakaia Gorge $5. Dorms $27-30; singles $45; twins and doubles from $72, with bath $84. $4 YHA discount. No seasonal discount. ❸

Mt. Hutt Accommodation Limited: Bedpost Lodge, 177 Main St. (☎302 8508; www.mthuttbeds.com) A complex of houses near the center of town that are excellent for groups seeking the privacy of self-contained units without a hefty pricetag. Full kitchen and laundry in units. No waxing racks. Twins and doubles from $120, in summer from $85; $18 per extra person. ❸

Skiwi House (BBH), 30 Chapman St. (☎302 8772; www.skiwihouse.com), half a block up Chapman St., which begins behind the Methven i-Site and runs parallel to Forest Dr. at the roundabout. A brightly painted camp of bungalows and lounges. Trampoline in the backyard. Dorms $22; doubles $50. Discounts in summer. $2 BBH discount. ❷

Abisko Lodge, 74 Main St. (☎302 8875; www.abisko.co.nz). A range of private and budget lodgings with a hotel-style lounge. Spa and sauna $3 per 30min. Singles $75-95; doubles $90-105, $15 per extra person; tourist flats with full amenities and 3 bedrooms $240 for up to 8 people. Lower rates in summer. Tent sites $20, powered $25 for 2 people. ❹

◖▣ FOOD AND NIGHTLIFE

In summer, many places shut down or operate on reduced hours. **4 Square,** on McMillan St. (☎302 8114; open daily 7am-9pm, earlier in winter), and **Supervalue,** across the roundabout (☎302 8050; open daily 7am-9pm; in summer 7am-7pm), are the two supermarkets in town.

Arabica, 36 McMillan St. (☎302 8455), on the roundabout between the 2 grocery stores. This classy cafe serves a simple and tasty all-day menu. Cabinet food filos $6. Cajun chicken sandwich $12. All day breakfast Eggs Benedict $12-13. Open in summer Tu-Th and Sa-Su 9am-4pm; F 9am-late, last orders 8pm. In winter Tu-Th and Sa-Su 9am-6pm; F 9am-late, last order at 8pm. ❷

Aqua (☎302 9010), on Main St. next to Paradiso Cinema. What could possibly better after a day on the slopes than sake? Cheap, quality sushi complements the sake menu, not the other way around. Sake $6.80 per bottle. Sushi plate $13.80, 5pc. sushi $5.80. Open in winter daily 11:30am-2pm and 6pm-late, kitchen closes 9 or 10pm; in summer Th-Sa 6pm-late. ❷

Cafe 131, 131 Main St. (☎302 9131). Servers keep the snowbound crowd content with budget eats (steak $15 and sandwiches from $5.50) in a faux-urban setting. All-day breakfast $7.50-14.50. Open daily in winter 7:30am-6pm, sometimes later; in summer 7:30am-5pm. ❷

Lisah's (☎302 8070), on Main St., next to Paradiso Cinema. An upscale venue with fine wines and gourmet cuisine (mains $18-26; rosemary and cashew crusted lamb rump $26). At night, Lisah's is a classy bar. Open in winter Tu-Su 5pm-late; in summer W-Sa 6pm-late. Reservations recommended. ❹

Blue Pub (☎302 8046) announces its azure self—color-coded for easy recall—at the crossroads. Mains runs from burgers ($16) to lamb shanks ($24). Live music weekly in winter. Open daily noon-3am; closes earlier when not busy. ❸

Canterbury Hotel/Brown Pub (☎302 8045), across the road from Blue Pub. The nightly $12.50 roast at this country pub is as good a value as you'll find. Cheap drinks and eats (pub fare $9-17) mean no one worries too much about quality. Open daily 11am-3am; earlier in summer. ❷

🎿 SKIING

With the longest ski season in Australasia and the best snow cover in New Zealand, **Mt. Hutt,** 26km west of Methven, is the main reason that crowds flock to Methven. The 2075m summit looks down upon 365 hectares of beautiful powder, 42 hectares of manufactured snow, and views reaching into the heart of the Southern Alps. The varied terrain includes a 683m vertical drop and provides challenges for all skill levels. Two sweet half-pipes beckon boarders and terrain parks attract tricksters. (☎308 5074, lessons ☎302 8811. Lift pass $84, student $61; half-day $55/41. Group lessons $49 per hr. Ski rental from $41 per day.

Snowboard $48 per day. Discounts for multi-day rental. Slope open June-Oct. daily 9am-4pm.) If your plan includes several days of skiing, you should consider the **NZ Superpass** (p. 321). **Methven Heliski,** office in town next to Paradiso Cinema, specializes in backcountry trips in the area. (☎302 8108; www.heliskiing.co.nz. 5 runs from $825.) **Mt. Hutt Heli-skiing,** 880 Forks Rd., Alford Forest, runs professional heli-skiing trips throughout the Southern Alps. (☎302 8401 or 0800 443 547; www.mthutthelicopters.co.nz. Heli-skiing from $155. Scenic flights from $78. Pickup from Christchurch available.)

🏔 OUTDOOR ACTIVITIES

Those seeking time in nature will find no shortage of **scenic walks** in the Methven area. All of the following require transportation to trailheads 10-20km outside of town. Inquire at the information office to arrange transport ($10-15 per person). If you are up for a longer haul, head for the 1687m **Mt. Somers Sub-Alpine Walk** (7hr. round-trip), frequently hiked over two days. The **Rakaia Gorge Walkway** (3-4hr. round-trip) traces the Rakaia River through forest and shrub past an abandoned coal mine. In order to cross the river, Maori warriors stood side-by-side to break the current (a practice called *Rakaia*), so the rest of their clan could safely pass downstream. Today the river is popular with salmon fishermen. The steep **Scotts Saddle Track** (5hr. round-trip) leaves from the parking lot in the Awa Awa Reserve, at the end of McLennan's Bush Rd., and climbs 1000m to views of Mt. Hutt.

The jetboats of **Rakaia Gorge Alpine Jet** cruise the gorge. (☎318 6574; www.rivertours.co.nz. 35min. tour from $68.) A hot-air balloon ride with **Aoraki Balloon Safaris** is another way to experience the beauty of the southern Canterbury plains and mountains. (☎0800 256 837 or 302 8172; www.nzballooning.com. $295.) **Hassle-free Tours** runs guided tours into the countryside, visiting the site where the fortress of Edoras was filmed for *Lord of the Rings*. (☎0800 141 142; www.hasslefree.co.nz. Depart daily from Christchurch at 9am, return 6pm. $175, with Christchurch transport $199.) Alternatively, the Methven i-Site stocks brochures which will lead you through a self-guided tour of the LOTR region. For extreme rapids, try **Rangitata Rafts** (see p. 313). Though not technically outdoors, **Cinema Paradiso,** 112 Main St., still holds appeals for those looking to unwind after a day on the slopes with an arthouse flick. (☎302 1957; www.cinemaparadiso.co.nz. Tickets $13.)

ARTHUR'S PASS   ☎03

The town of Arthur's Pass (pop. 60) is surrounded by vast mountains of majestic natural beauty. The pass itself snakes through the towering Southern Alps, hiding ski fields and tramping trails. Several major club ski fields compete within 30min. of each other along SH73. Tramping in the 230,000 alpine and subalpine hectares of Arthur's Pass National Park and nearby Craigieburn Forest Park is beautiful, challenging, and uncrowded. In winter, the road through the pass (SH73) is occasionally closed, but the **TranzAlpine Rail Trip** is reliable. Amenities are scarce; it is best to bring groceries if you plan on staying more than a few hours.

🚍 TRANSPORTATION. The aptly named **TranzAlpine** line is run by **TranzScenic** (☎0800 872 461) to Christchurch (2hr., 3:57pm, $79) and Greymouth (1½hr., 10:40am, $49). From the Arthur's Pass Tearooms, **Coast-to-Coast** (☎0800 800 847) runs daily bus service to: Christchurch (2hr., 3pm, $25); Greymouth (1½hr., 11am, $25); Hokitika (1½hr., 1 per day, $25). **Atomic Shuttles** (☎0508 108 359) runs to: Christchurch (3:30pm, $20) and Greymouth (10:05am, $20). Tickets for Coast-to-Coast and Atomic can be purchased at the Arthur's Pass Store. **West Coast Shuttles** (☎ 768 0028 or 027 492 7488) stops at Mountain House before heading to Greymouth (1½hr., 5:10pm, $15) and Christchurch (2hr., 9:20am, $25). For transport to trailheads in the park, ring **Arthur's Pass Taxis** (☎ 027 419 2354).

⬛🔋 ORIENTATION AND PRACTICAL INFORMATION. SH73 runs through Arthur's Pass Village parallel to the railroad tracks, and everything of interest is located right on the highway. Be sure to check in at the **Arthur's Pass DOC Visitor Information Centre** if you're planning a multi-day tramp. (☎ 318 9211; arthurspassvc@doc.govt.nz. Open daily 8am-5pm; in winter 8:30am-4:30pm.) The **police** (☎ 318 9212) are on the main road, across Rough Creek, south of town. For local **breakdown service**, call ☎ 318 9236 or **AA** at ☎ 0800 500 222. **Internet** access is available at the **Arthur's Pass Store** (see **Food**; $2 per 15min.) A tiny **post office** sits just north of the Wobbly Kea. (Open only M-F 9-9:30am.)

🕎🔆 ACCOMMODATIONS AND CAMPING. Mountain House Backpackers (BBH/ YHA) ❸, on the main drag near the visitors center, has a great view of the pass from the comfortable lounge. A true trampers' rest, this lodge has ice-axes and crampons for rentals, as well as a taxi service (max. 6 people) to the trailheads for $10-55. (☎ 318 9258; www.trampers.co.nz. Reception 9am-7pm; sign-in reception all other times. Dorms $27; twins and doubles $66. $3 BBH discount.) For those with their own transport, **Rata Lodge ❸**, on SH73 in Otira, 14km west of Arthur's Pass, has a secluded wood setting, cozy ensuite rooms, free national calls and glowworms. (☎ 738 2822; rata.lodge@xtra.co.nz. No Internet. Dorms $27; doubles $60. $3 BBH discount.) There are **DOC tent sites ❶** and a day shelter opposite the visitors center. (Toilets year-round; running water in summer. Tent sites $5. Cash only.) Seven free roadside **camping** facilities are in the area, all with pit toilets and stream water. On SH73 toward Christchurch, **Greyney's Shelter** is 6km from town; **Klondyke Corner** is 8km from town; **Lake Pearson** is 35km; and **Craigieburn Picnic Area** is 43km. On SH73 toward Greymouth, **Kelly Shelter** is 17km from town. On Mt. White Rd., **Hawdon Shelter** and **Andrew's Shelter** are 27km and 28km from town.

🗐 FOOD. The **Wobbly Kea Cafe and Bar ❷**, in the center of town, serves up large portions of delicious mains (from $16.50; rump steak $28), lunch sandwiches ($10) and light meals. (☎ 318 9101; thewobblykea@hotmail.com. Open Su-Th 8:30am-10:30pm, F-Sa 8:30am-11:30pm.) Across the street, behind the gas pumps, **Arthur's Pass Store ❶** houses a cafe that serves full breakfasts ($7.50-14.50) as well as a deli with a selection of 🖼sandwiches ($4-7). Gas, liquor, and a limited selection of groceries are for sale. (☎ 318 9235. Open daily 7:30am-7pm; in winter 8am-6pm.)

🏔 OUTDOOR ACTIVITIES. Arthur's Pass National Park and the adjacent Craigieburn Forest Park have a diverse terrain of alpine meadows and riverbeds, allowing for both easy and demanding tramps. Overnight trampers in either area should be aware that local weather is volatile. Since there are no bridges in the parks, and overnight huts cannot be reserved, trampers should check with the Arthur's Pass DOC for hut ticket purchase, weather reports, and track conditions before leaving. In addition, DOC sells a brochure ($2) that covers area hikes. Locator beacons are also available for rent from the DOC ($25 for up to 7 days).

Reaching the summit of the aptly named 🖼**Avalanche Peak** (1833m) on a clear day is one of the best day hikes rewards in New Zealand. Though it is an arduous climb over rocky terrain, the reward is a sprawling view to all sides of the peaks of the Southern Alps. Two tracks—**Scotts Track** and **Avalanche Peak Track**—lead to the summit; both are well-marked, but challenging, and should

CANTERBURY

only be undertaken by those with good fitness and moderate tramping experience. Additionally, both tracks are weather dependent—hikers have been killed attempting the hike in inclement weather. Check with DOC to ensure that the weather is clear and dry before hiking. Those wishing to hike a loop should ascend on Avalanche Peak and descend on Scotts Track, as Avalanche Peak is the steeper of the two. Those looking to make the hike a shade easier can hike up and back down on Scotts Track. Both trailheads are in Arthur's Pass Village off SH73. Allow 5-8hr. for the full loop.

When the weather is unfavorable for Avalanche Peak, **Bealey Spur** (trailhead 14km towards Christchurch on SH73), is a popular alternative that often has better weather, and always has comparable views. The **Devil's Punchbowl Waterfall Trail** (1hr. round-trip) begins just past the Chalet Restaurant and leads to an arresting view of the falls. A beautiful spot near the start of the trail rewards early birds with a view of the sunrise over the mountains. The self-guided **historic walk** of the peaceful village (1½hr.) includes directions to original tunnelers' huts on the main road. The **Cass-Lagoon Saddle** (2-3 days round-trip) is a popular summertime tramp (beware of avalanches in winter) and one of the easier overnight hikes. Farther east, dayhikers can explore the limestone formations of **Kura Tawhiti,** formerly known as the **Castle Hill** basin, though local Maori request that climbers stay off the rocks to respect their *tapu* (sacred) status. The **Cave Stream Scenic Reserve,** off SH73, a 45min. drive east of Arthur's Pass and 7km past the turn-off to Craigieburn Forest Park, is a 596m long limestone cave rough even for well-equipped amateur spelunkers. The stream that runs through the pitch dark cave can be waist-high; the DOC recommends wading against the mild current, wearing sturdy shoes or boots and polypropylene or wool socks, and taking at least two flashlights per person. The tramp is not recommended in winter because the water is almost freezing. Do not tramp when it is raining, as the cave floods easily. Though Temple Basin (p. 322), 5km from town towards Greymouth on SH73, is known for its winter skiing, hiking it in summer provides views of alpine flowers.

SOUTH CANTERBURY   ☎03

Travelers choosing to head through the plains of south Canterbury are welcomed by the locals, most of whom stand on four legs. The abundance of flat farmland in this region, however, affords an impressive and uninterrupted view from the central mountain ranges to the coast. The mighty Aoraki/Mt. Cook lies in majestic repose at the northern end of Lake Pukaki, and, in the heart of the Southern Alps, mountains everywhere are reflected in Tekapo, the basin's most famous lake. Covered with tussock grassland and punctuated by brilliant lakes, south Canterbury is the perfect mix of mountainous and pastoral landscapes.

TIMARU   ☎03

Timaru (ti-mah-ROO; pop. 27,200) started out as Te Maru, Maori for "place of shelter." It continues to live up to its name, albeit now as a serviceable, if unexciting, haven for travelers moving up and down the east coast. While most will want to speed right off to the adventure du jour elsewhere, those looking for a place to relax will do well to dip their toes into Caroline Bay, stroll through the town's main streets, and stay for a night or two.

▣ TRANSPORTATION. Atomic Shuttles (☎349 0697) leave daily from the visitors center for Christchurch (2½hr.; 11:10am, 5:10pm; $25) and Oamaru (1¼hr.; 9:50am, 6pm; $20). Operating out of the nearby train station, **InterCity** (☎508 424 368) buses head to Christchurch (2½hr.; 2 per day; 11am, 5:45pm; $27) and Dunedin (3hr., 2 per day, $32) via Oamaru (1¼hr., $21). For taxi service, try **Timaru Taxis** (☎0800 846 829 or 688 8899). **Hitchhikers** report that the base of SH8 is the best way up to Tekapo and Aoraki/Mt. Cook. Otherwise, SH1 is considered the easiest place to grab a ride. *Let's Go* urges readers to consider the risks before hitching.

🔧📱 ORIENTATION AND PRACTICAL INFORMATION. Midway between Christchurch and Dunedin, Timaru slopes down from the foothills of the Central Alps to the sea. **SH1** snakes through the town's rolling hills and changes names several times from Craigie Ave. to Theodosia St. to Evans St. and meets **SH8** to Tekapo and Aoraki/Mt. Cook just north of town. The scenic **Caroline Bay** is a 15min. walk from the visitors center along **Stafford Street**, Timaru's main commercial avenue. Just off Stafford St., across from the train station, the **Timaru i-Site**, 2 George St., is in the old lava-built Landing Service Building; the free map of town is worth the trip. (☎688 6163; fax 684 0202. Open M-F 8:30am-5pm, Sa-Su 10am-3pm.) Other services include: **24hr. ATMs** along Stafford St.; the **police** station (☎687 9808), 20 North St. at Barnard St.; many standard **pharmacies** along Stafford St., with extended service from **Ashbury Amcal** in Northtown Mall next to the Pak 'n Save (☎688 9736, fax 684 5016; open Mo-Su 9am-7pm); the **Timaru hospital** (☎684 4000), on High and Queen St.; **Internet** access at **Computer Shop Timaru 2000**, 329-331 Stafford St., ($3 per hr.; open M-Tu, Th-F 9am-5:30pm, W 9:30-5:30pm, Sa 10am-12:30pm), or **Off The Rail Cafe**, in the train station ($6 per hr.; open M-Th 7:30am-5pm and 7:30-8:30pm, F 7:30am-5pm and 7:30pm-8:30pm, Sa 9am-5pm, Su 9am-5pm and 7:30-8:30pm); the **post office**, 21 Strathallan St., inside "Take Note" between the train station and Stafford St. (☎686 6040; open M-Th 8am-5:30pm, F 8am-6pm, Sa 9am-1pm).

🍴📷 ACCOMMODATIONS AND FOOD. Though rooms can always be found at the motels lining SH1 just north of Timaru's center, their higher prices make booking ahead at the city's few hostels tempting. Life is sweet at **1873 Wanderer Backpackers (BBH) ❷**, 24 Evan St., where fresh apricots from the backyard tree add a touch of sweetness to barbeques thrown by friendly owners Sonya and Greg Sunny rooms offer views of the bay, but you can also pitch a tent in the backyard. (☎0800 1873 92 or 688 8795; 1873wandererbackpackers@xtra.co.nz. Dorms $21; singles $23; doubles $23.50; tent sites $16. Linens $1. $20 key deposit. $2 off with BBH. Cash only.) **334 On Stafford ❷**, 334 Stafford St. at the top of the hill, seems like an echo of its more boisterous past, as evidenced by the graffiti on the walls. Kick back in the lounge with free billiards. (☎684 4729; www.dominion.lodge.xtra.co.nz. 4-6 bed dorms $22-26; singles $25-35; twins and doubles $50-75. Linens $2. MC/V.) At **📷Timaru Selwyn Top 10 Holiday Park ❷**, an extensive camp facility 2km outside of the city center on Selwyn St. at the end of Hobbs St., 100 powered sites sit along a shady creekbed. The video games, TV lounge, well-maintained kitchen and showers, colorful moonbounce, just enhance the convenient location. (☎0800 242 121 or 684 7690; www.timaruholidaypark.co.nz. 2-person powered tent sites $28; standard 2-person cabins $47, with kitchen $57; motel rooms with bath $90-100. $13-17 per extra person.)

For stellar coffee and food at heavenly prices, zip off to **Red Rocket ❷**, 4a Elizabeth St., at the corner of Sophia St. next to the church. If the "Meat-eorite Shower" gets you down, head for "Planet Plantlover"—pizza, that is. (☎688 8313. Pizzas $16-19. Open M-Sa 10am-midnight, Su 11:30am-midnight. Open M-F 8:30am for breakfast, $8-14. BYOB for $5 corking fee. AmEx/MC/V.) **The Coq and Pullet ❶**, 209 Stafford St., sees breakfasters chomp berry muffins ($2.50) at this gourmet deli and juice bar. (☎688 6616. Open M-F 8am-4pm, Sa 10am-4pm.) The **Pak 'N Save Supermarket** is on Evans St. at Ranui Ave. (Open M-F 8am-9pm, Sa-Su 8am-7pm.)

🎿🏕 SIGHTS AND OUTDOOR ACTIVITIES. The highlight of Timaru is **Caroline Bay**, and its shallow sweep of sand, which bustle in summer months. Accessible via the Marine Pde., there are several short walks around the bay, including to the rocky **Benvenue Cliffs.** The neighboring park off Virtue Ave. contains many moderately fun attractions (ferris wheel; $3). (Open daily dawn-dusk.) From December 26 until mid-January, the bay area hosts a **Christmas/New Year Carnival.** For a great view of the bay, climb the tower of the Gothic-revival **St. Mary's Church,** 24 Church St. (☎688 8377. Open Tu-F 9am-1pm. Free.) Next door to the church on Perth St., the **South Canterbury Museum** contains a mix of stuffed birds, historical appliances, and Maori culture. (☎687 7212. Tu-F 10am-4:30pm, Sa-Su 1:30pm-4:30pm. Free.) **Aigantighe Art Gallery,** 49 Wai-iti Rd., features a collection of paintings, with a strong Kiwi focus. Check out the sculpture collection in the backyard. (☎688 4424. Open Tu-F 10am-4pm, Sa-Su noon-4pm. Free.)

LAKE TEKAPO ☎03

The village of Lake Tekapo (pop. 315) is a major rest stop for buses on their way between Christchurch and Queenstown. Consequently, it offers little more than a chance for lunch and a view of the Church of the Good Shepherd, with the impossibly blue Lake Tekapo and snow-capped peaks in the background. Those who choose to spend a day or two will find decent hiking at nearby Mt. John, as well as some of the darkest night skies in New Zealand.

⌷ TRANSPORTATION. InterCity (☎0800 777 707), **Southern Link Shuttles** (☎358 8355), **Wanaka Connexions** (☎443 9122; www.wanakashuttles.co.nz) and **Atomic Shuttles** (☎322 8883) run daily to Christchurch (4hr., $30-50) and Queenstown (3½-5hr., $30-78). **Wanaka Connexions** also travels to Dunedin (7½hr., 11:40am, $50). **InterCity** also runs to Aoraki/Mt. Cook (1½hr., 11:25am, $29), as does **The Cook Connection** (☎0800 266 526 or 435 3116; 8am; $28). Book transport at the information office at **Kiwi Treasures** (☎680 6686). Buses also depart from the **Godley Inn** (☎680 6848), next to the dam.

⬛❼ ORIENTATION AND PRACTICAL INFORMATION. All services, souvenir shops, and food options in Tekapo lie along **SH8. Kiwi Treasures** functions as the official **visitors center** and can book accommodations, activities, and transport, as well as hire fishing rods and sell licenses. (☎680 6686. Open daily 8am-7pm; in winter 8am-6pm. Fishing rods $15 per day, license $18.50 per day.) There are **no banks or ATMs** in Tekapo, although the Shell Station/4 Square changes money and offers cash out on a credit card. In emergencies, call the **police** (☎680 6855). **Internet** access is available at the **Global Gossip** in Tekapo Helicopters on the SH8 strip ($10 per 2½hr; open daily 8am-8pm). The **post office** is inside the same building as the visitors center. (☎680 6861. Open daily 8am-7pm; in winter 8am-6pm.)

⌂ ACCOMMODATIONS. Though Tekapo has about 20 motels and B&Bs to choose from, they are frequently full, and the going rate is $90-100 for a double, and more for lake views. The new **Lakefront Lodge ❸,** 2 Lakeside Dr., sits away from the commercialism of the strip amid a pine grove close to the head of the Mt. John trail. The rooms are simple, but the lounge and its lake vistas are awe-inspiring. (☎680 6227 or 0800 840 740. From SH8, turn toward the lake onto Simpson Lane, then immediately left onto Lakeside Dr.; it's on the left past the motor park. Reception 8am-8pm. 4- and 6-bed dorms $26; doubles and twins $65.) The **Tekapo YHA ❷,** on Simpson Ln., past the pub on the west side of town, has small dorms and lakefront views. (☎680 6857; yhatekapo@yha.org.nz. Reception 8am-1pm, 3:30-7:30pm. Dorms $25-26; twins and doubles $66. Tent sites $16. $4 YHA discount.) The **Lake Tekapo Scenic Resort ❷,** on the strip behind Doughboys, offers sterile dorms typical of a hostel and a convenient location right in town. (☎0800 118 666 or 680 6808; www.laketekapo.biz. Wireless Internet $5 for 30min. Dorms $22-25; budget motel rooms sleeping up to 6 people $60-120.) Formerly a residence for dam-workers, **Tailor-made Tekapo Backpackers (BBH) ❷,** 9-11 Aorangi Cres., is a collection of three buildings with access to the community tennis courts and two stone barbeques. Turn away from the lake onto Aorangi from SH8. (☎680 6700; www.tailor-made-backpackers.co.nz. Linen $2. Dorms $23-27; single $45; twins and doubles $58, with bath $70. $3 BBH discount.) **Lake Tekapo Motels and Motor Park ❶**, next to Lakefront Lodge, is extremely popular with campers and caravans and has cabins for all budgets in a prime lakefront location. (☎680 6825 or 0800 853 853; www.laketekapo-accommodation.co.nz. Showers $2. Powered tent sites $15. Basic cabins $50-55, $12 per extra person; ensuite cabins $80-90/$15; tourist flats with kitchen $90-105/15; motel doubles $120-140/15. MC/V.)

🞐 **FOOD.** Restaurants and takeaways cluster around the Shell gas station on SH8. East of the station on Main St., **Pepe's Pizza and Pasta Company ❷** serves pizzas (venison, sweet potato, and pumpkin with plum sauce; sm. $19.50) to a nightly crowd of locals and tourists. The bar doubles as one of Tekapo's few nightlife spots. (☎680 6677. Open daily 6pm-late.) Behind Pepe's, **Kohan Japanese Restaurant ❸** rolls sushi from $8 and cooks teriyaki dishes for $16. (☎680 6688. Kohan Bento Box $20. Open M-Sa 11am-2pm and 6-9pm, Su 6-9pm.) **Doughboy's Bakery ❶**, on SH8, has all-day breakfast ($7.50-12), as well as surprisingly good pies, baked goods, and toasted sandwiches ($3.50-6.50). (☎680 6655. Open daily 8am-4pm.) **Jade Palace ❶**, on the east side of the village, has decent Chinese food, though you might have to battle loads of bus tourists to get to it. The sit-down menu is a bit pricey (most dishes; $14-25) but the takeaway lunch-boxes ($6-7.50) are a good deal. (☎680 6828. Open daily 11am-10pm.) The **4 Square**, on SH8 near the visitors center, has groceries. (☎680 6809. Open daily 7am-9pm; in winter 7am-7pm.)

🞐 🜨 **SIGHTS AND OUTDOOR ACTIVITIES.** Those just passing through Tekapo invariably stop at the **Church of the Good Shepherd**, a tiny interdenominational church of wood and stone built in 1935. The simple construction sets it off perfectly against the stunning natural backdrop. (Open daily 9am-5pm; in winter 11am-3pm.) Longer walks in the area include the circuit up **Mt. John**, to the observatory through pine forest. The trail begins past the motor park, near the ice-skating rink along the lake's western shore. There are two options for the track, the shorter of the two goes just to the summit (1½-2hr.) while the longer goes to the summit and then along the lakeshore (3-3½hr.). Another track to **Cowan's Lookout** (1½-2hr. one-way) leaves from the eastern side of the lake, park at Cowans Hill Carpark, just off SH8. Follow the green and yellow stakes through the fields to connect the trail to the **Pines Beach Track** (30-60min. one-way) and loop over to the church. Those who prefer two wheels to two legs should explore the mountain biking tracks on the eastern side of the lake. The trails can be accessed off Lilybank Rd., just take SH8 out of town towards Christchurch. Kayak and bike rental is available at the **Lakefront Lodge**, see p. 330. (Kayaks $25 per hr., guided $40. Bike rental $10 per hr., $25 per half-day.)

If you become truly fascinated with Mt. John, it may be worthwhile to return at night for an entirely different look at Tekapo. **Mt. John Earth & Sky Observatory** makes the night skies accessible to both neophytes and practiced astronomers. The Southern Cross, the Jewel Box Cluster, and the double star Alpha Centauri, none of which are visible in the Northern Hemisphere, can all be seen here through a large telescope. (☎680 6960; www.earthandsky.co.nz. Nightly 2hr. tours in English and Japanese, weather permitting. $58, children $25. 1hr. day tours $20/5.) The **MacKenzie Alpine Horse Trekking Company** leads 1hr. rides through the forest, ($45) as well as longer trips up Mt. John. (☎680 6760 or 0800 628 269. 2hr. $75; 3hr. $95; overnight $300, includes all meals and accommodations.) Many **scenic flight** companies serving the Aoraki/Mt. Cook area depart from the Tekapo airport (p. 335). **Tekapo Helicopters** operates scenic flights of the Tekapo lake area. (☎680 6229 or 0800 359 835; www.tekapohelicopters.co.nz. 25min. flight $180. Office on the strip in Tekapo, open daily 8am-8pm.)

CANTERBURY

Small, family-operated **Mt. Dobson** in Fairlie, 30km toward Christchurch off SH8, devotes one-third of its mountain to novice **skiers,** while the rest of the mountain is streaked with intermediate and black diamond runs. (☎685 8039; www.dobson.co.nz. Lift tickets $60, students $45. Ski rental with poles and boots $30/28. Full snowboard rental $47/47. 1½hr. group ski/snowboard lessons $24/24.) **Roundhill Ski Area** provides gently undulating slopes that are perfect for beginners. (☎680 6977; www.roundhill.co.nz. Lift tickets $60, youth $40, children $30; half-day $45/30/20. 1½hr. group lesson $32/27/25. Ski rental with boots and poles full-day $35/25/20. Snowboard rental full-day $45/35/30. Tobogganing $12 per day.)

AORAKI/MT. COOK NATIONAL PARK ☎03

With one-third of its area permanently covered with snow, Aoraki/Mt. Cook National Park and its jagged peaks have an austere and spectacular profile. To many Maori, the mountain represents the most sacred of ancestors, and a recent agreement with the national government has placed restrictions on the use of Aoraki/Mt. Cook. Climbers must not stand on the exact summit, and all references to the mountain must place the Maori name before the English one. Notoriously capricious weather and frequent avalanches make this one of the most dangerous regions in New Zealand. The highest mountain in New Zealand, the longest glacier in Australasia, plus 25 peaks over 3000m make Aoraki/Mt. Cook National Park one of the high points of Down Under.

AT A GLANCE

AREA: 70,696 hectares.

CLIMATE: Severe weather patterns; especially dangerous in winter.

FEATURES: New Zealand's highest mountains and largest glacier coverage (one-third). No forest, but a large variety of alpine plants and wildlife.

HIGHLIGHTS: Aoraki/Mt. Cook, the tallest mountain in New Zealand (3754m).

GATEWAYS: Aoraki/Mt. Cook Village is located within the park; Twizel and Tekapo are outside.

CAMPING: Indoor accommodations only in the village; campsites at Glentanner and White Horse Hill Campground.

FEES AND RESERVATIONS: Inform the DOC of plans and check for necessary hut passes ($5-35).

AORAKI/MT. COOK VILLAGE ☎03

At the end of SH80, a 45min. drive from Twizel along the shores of Lake Pukaki, the buildings of tiny Aoraki/Mt. Cook Village (pop. 120) are nestled in the heart of Aoraki/Mt. Cook National Park and are specially designed to blend into the background. In order to live there, residents must be employed by the DOC or one of the local businesses. The village itself, which is dominated by the overpriced Hermitage, doesn't offer much to budget travelers outside of scenery.

⌨ TRANSPORTATION

InterCity (☎379 9020) buses depart daily from the Hermitage and the YHA for Christchurch (5½hr., 1:50pm, $84) and Queenstown (4¾hr., 2:20pm, $71) via Twizel. **Great Sights** (☎0800 744 487) also runs through Aoraki/Mt. Cook on its way between Christchurch (2:30pm, $105) and Queenstown (2:30pm, $125). Special fare bookings within 48hr. are available for both routes; Christchurch $40, Queenstown $30. **Atomic Shuttles** (☎322 8883) doesn't bus to the village but does serve Twizel. From Twizel, buses connect with Cook Connection (see below). Atomic service from Twizel runs to: Christchurch (3¾hr.; 5:50pm, additional 10:30am service in peak season; $40) via Tekapo (1¼hr., $20); Queenstown (3¼hr.; daily 11:15am, additional service 6:30pm in peak season; $35). **The Cook Connection** (☎0800 266 526) shuttles passengers to: Oamaru (3hr.; 8am, Nov.-May only M, W, F-Sa; $40); Tekapo (1½hr., 3pm, $28); Twizel (45-50min., 2-4 times per day, $20). Though *Let's Go* urges you to consider the risks of hitchhiking, hitchers report success in catching rides to Christchurch, Queenstown, Wanaka or Tekapo from SH80 on the outskirts of the village, though it is reportedly difficult to hitch.

⁊ PRACTICAL INFORMATION

The **Aoraki/Mt. Cook Visitor Centre,** near the Hermitage, is the place to book activities, check track conditions, buy hut tickets, and register for all major trips in the park. (☎435 1186. Open daily 8:30am-5pm; less in winter.) The nearest **doctor** (☎435 0777), **police** (☎435 0719) and **pharmacy** are located in Twizel. For weather conditions, call ☎435 1171. Head to the **Hermitage** (☎435 1645) for overpriced **groceries** (open daily in summer 7am-7:30pm; in winter 9am-5:30pm), **currency exchange** (open daily 6:30am-11pm), **Internet** access (available 24hr., $2 per 8min.), and **post office** (open daily in summer 7am-10pm; in winter 9am-5pm). There is a self-serve **gas** pump that accepts New Zealand EFTPOS; to pay with cash or a credit card ($5 surcharge), pick up the phone to speak with Hermitage staff.

 THE REAL DEAL. While Mt. Cook is New Zealand scenery at its best, the village is commercialism at its worst. Most of the town is owned by one company, and travelers should expect big mark-ups and snooty service. *-Megan Smith*

▐ ⌂ ACCOMMODATIONS AND FOOD

With plush couches, pine-planked walls, a sauna, and a great video collection, the **Mt. Cook YHA ❸** blends comfortably into its alpine surroundings. What's more, despite being pricey compared to hostels elsewhere on South Island, it's the only "budget" place to stay in the village proper. Book at least two weeks in advance. (☎435 1820; yhamtcook@yha.co.nz. Lockers $2-4. Reception in summer 8am-9pm; in winter 8am-8:30pm. Dorms $29; doubles $76. $3 YHA discount. MC/V.) While not exactly budget, **Alpine Lodge ❹** nevertheless has the most reasonably priced rooms and the best lounge in town. Groups should consider paying a bit extra and staying in one of their ensuite rooms. (☎435 1860 or 0800 680 680; www.aorakialpinelodge.co.nz. Ensuite doubles and twins $144-200, for up to 4 people. Book ahead at least 2 weeks in summer. Lower rates available off-season. MC/V.) The popular **White Horse Hill Camping Area ❶** operates on an honor system and has tent sites, untreated water, and flush toilets. The campground is 2km from town on Hooker Valley Rd. (Shower $1 per 5min. at Day Shelter in Mt. Cook Village. Tent sites $6, children $3. Cash only.) Twenty-three kilometers from Aoraki/Mt. Cook Village, the **Glentanner Park Centre ❶** may not have the views of Mt. Cook Village, but it does have better prices, a range of accommodations, and service without a side of pretention. (☎435 1855 or 0800 453 682; www.glentanner.co.nz. Transport to Aoraki/Mt. Cook Village 4 times daily in summer with Cook Connection 30min.; 7:30am-3:20pm; $10, round-trip $15. Transport runs by demand in winter. Restaurant open daily in summer 8am-6:30pm; in winter 8am-5pm. Fish 'n chips $11.50. Linen $7-10. Tent sites $12, powered sites $15. Dorms $25; 2-person cabins $60-95.)

Food options in town are extremely limited. Sir Edmund Hillary attended the opening of **The Old Mountaineer's Cafe ❹,** near the DOC, the only food option not run by the Hermitage. True to their name, they embrace the mountaineer heritage of the area with old photographs and memorabilia. While mains run $20-35, they have takeaway sandwiches from $6.50. (☎435 1890; www.mtcook.com. Open daily 11am-late, kitchen closes at 9pm.)**Bully Hayes ❸**, 57 Beach Rd., serves up breakfast (from $10.50), seafood lunches, and dinners right on the waterfront. (☎304 7533; www.bullyhayes.co.nz. Grilled mussels $18. Seagull attacks free. Open daily 8:30am-late.) The **Chamois Bar ❸**, near the YHA in the Glencoe wing of the Hermitage, has mediocre bar meals ($12.50-18.50), pizzas (from $14), and drinks. (Same phone as the Hermitage. Open Su-W 6pm-midnight, Th 6pm-2am, F-Sa 6pm-1am; close earlier when not busy. Kitchen open 6-9:30pm.)

⚠ OUTDOOR ACTIVITIES

ADVENTURE ACTIVITIES. The Hermitage, Glentanner, Alpine Lodge and the YHA book adventure tours. In the summer, **Glacier Explorers** boats the glacial lake at the mouth of Tasman Glacier, gliding pass icebergs and glacially carved cliffs in an informative tour. (☎435 1077; www.glacierexplorers.com. 3hr. tours Oct.-Apr. $120, YHA/ BBH $95, children $60.) **Glacier Sea-Kayaking** runs one-of-a-kind sea kayaking trips to the Mueller Glacier that include glacier hiking, iceberg views and generally stunning scenery. (☎435 1890; www.mtcook.com. 3½hr. trips 10am and 2pm $98.) To explore the headlands of Lake Pukaki via equine legs rather than your own, call **Glentanner Horse Trekking.** (☎435 1855 or 0800 453 682. Nov.-Apr. only. 30min. rides from $35; 1hr. $50; 2hr. $70; 3hr. $90. 2-person min.) **Discovery Tours** runs **LOTR Tours**—up to five times daily to a location outside of Twizel. (☎0800 213 868. 2½hr. Departs 11am and 1:30pm; additional tours on demand. $75-80, chldren $35-40. Min. 2 people.) At the Twizel airstrip, just off SH8 towards Mt. Cook, **NZ Skydive** has a scenic freefall, if you can keep your eyes open. (☎0800 264 5344 or 435 0813; www.nzskydive.com. 9000ft. $245, 12000ft. $295; digital photos $145, DVD $165, both $195.)

WALKS. The peaks, glaciers, and ice cliffs of Aoraki/Mt. Cook National Park draw visitors from all over the world. The most popular—and thus crowded—walk is the **Hooker Valley Walk,** which runs to Hooker Glacier's terminal lake, providing fantastic views of Mt. Sefton and Aoraki/Mt. Cook at the head of the valley. (4hr. round-trip from the village to the lake, 3hr. round-trip from the parking lot at the end of Hooker Valley Rd.) The uphill climb to **Red Tarns** (1½-2hr. round-trip) rewards exertion with exhilarating views down into the Hooker Valley and up to the cloud-piercing Alps. Much milder, the **Kea Point Walk** (2hr. round-trip from the village; 1hr. from the end of Hooker Valley Rd./White Horse Hill carpark.) leads through clumps of scraggly matagouri and alpine scrubland to a lookout over the Mueller Glacier, with Mt. Sefton's azure ice falls in the background. The only feasible overnight tramping options are the popular and strenuous 3-4hr. route to **Mueller Hut ❷** (1800m, 28 bunks plus toilet, water, and gas stoves; $35) and the scramble along Tasman Glacier moraine to the **Ball Shelter Hut ❶** (3-4hr. from the trailhead at the Blue Lakes Carpark 8km out of town; toilet, but no gas stoves; $5). The walk to the Mueller Hut traverses higher terrain and offers more scenery, while the Ball Shelter walk provides closer views of the glacier.

MOUNTAINEERING. The crags and crevasses surrounding the Cook Range's peaks have trained some of the world's great mountaineers, including Sir Edmund Hillary of Mt. Everest fame; they've also killed or severely injured many climbers, both novices and experts. Aoraki/Mt. Cook and Mt. Tasman average two fatalities a year. If you need a sobering reminder, visit the **Alpine Memorial** just outside the campground in the Hooker Valley or the newly constructed **Sir Edmund Hillary Centre** at the Hermitage. In the spirit of safety, several reputable companies offer guided ascents and multi-day, wallet-slimming courses in mountaineering. **Alpine Guides** and **Southern Alps Guiding** run identical guided ascents and technical courses, with prices beginning around $1750. They also rent equipment, including ice axes, crampons, and avalanche transceivers. If nothing less than the summit will satisfy you, seven-day ascents ($4950) of either

Aoraki/Mt. Cook or Mt. Tasman run Nov.-Jan. based on conditions (Alpine: ☎ 435 1834; www.alpineguides.co.nz. Southern Alps: ☎ 435 1890. 1:1 guide to climber ratio; all equipment provided. Equipment rentals $8-16 per day.) They also run rock climbing trips on the Sebastopol Bluffs. (1:2 guide to climber ratio. 3hr. Nov.-Mar. $150 per person, $240 for 2 people.)

AIR ADVENTURES. Many of the flight operators over Mt. Cook also fly over Fox and Franz Josef glaciers, see p. 358. Heli-biking and guided wilderness hiking adventures are available through **Discovery Tours.** (☎ 0800 213 868; www.discoverytours.co.nz. Flights on demand, 3-person min. Heli-biking from $230. Hiking from $130.) The **Helicopter Line** runs a 20min. flight with a snow landing, as well as several longer and more expensive options. (☎ 0800 650 651 or 435 1801; www.helicopter.co.nz. $195, YHA discount $15.) **Air Safaris** flies a scenic tour called the "Grand Traverse," including Aoraki/Mt. Cook and the Franz Josef and Tasman Glaciers, guaranteeing a window seat and good commentary en route. (☎ 680 6880 or 0800 806 880; www.airsafaris.co.nz. 50min. From Franz Josef and Tekapo airfields from $260, children $180.) **Aoraki/Mt. Cook Ski Planes** runs the popular "Flight Spa 1," with gorgeous views of Murchison and Tasman Glaciers and a glacier landing in-between. Cheaper, non-landing options are also available. (☎ 0800 800 702; www.mountcookskiplanes.com. 40min. $325, children $250.)

SKIING. The small family ski field of **Ohau,** between Twizel and Omarama, is not far from the village and is open mid-July to Sept. The field has slopes for beginner (20%), intermediate (50%), and advanced (30%) skiers. Budget accommodations including a bed, dinner, and breakfast start at $120. (☎ 438 9885; www.ohau.co.nz. Lift passes $62, students $44. 1hr. lessons $40. Ski rental $30, snowboard $45.) All the mountaineering companies listed above run **heli-skiing** and **ski touring** trips in the area, including on trips to **Tasman Glacier.** (Tasman Glacier trips $725-825 per day. Alpine Recreation runs 3-day ski trip on Ball Pass for expert skiers $750, all inclusive.) **Harris Mountain Heli-Skiing** (p. 398), based in Wanaka and Queenstown, also does heli-skiing in Mt. Cook. (5 runs $825, 7 runs $975.)

When UNESCO declared the West Coast a World Heritage site in 1990, the region graciously assumed its place in a hall of fame that included the likes of the Grand Canyon, the Great Barrier Reef, and Mount Everest. Of course, the Kiwis already knew they had a treasure—the towering Southern Alps border the region to the east and form a geological wall a mere 40km from the Tasman Sea. With snow-capped peaks, temperate rainforests, pounding waves, and not a single traffic light in the entire region, it's no wonder that almost 90% of the West Coast is set aside by the government as national parks, forests, and scenic reserves.

▨ WEST COAST HIGHLIGHTS

GET BUZZED on the Monteith's Brewing Company tour in **Greymouth** (p. 345).

GET BUSY with ice axe in hand on **Fox** or **Franz Josef Glacier** (p. 355).

GET BURIED by the roaring rapids of the Buller Gorge in **Murchison** (p. 339).

▄ TRANSPORTATION ON THE WEST COAST

West Coast travelers should keep in mind that there are no banks or supermarkets on the long stretch between Hokitika and Wanaka, and gas stations are few and far between—and often closed by 6pm. Daily **buses** provide a dependable way to travel. While *Let's Go* doesn't recommend **hitchhiking**, those with patience—and good rain gear—report success.

WESTPORT ☎ 03

A 19th-century gold-rush town, the original Westport washed away in a flood in 1872. Gold fever subsided, but the town soon made a comeback of sorts thanks to the coal mining, shipping, and fishing industries. Today, Westport (pop. 6000) attracts those who wish to challenge—either by kayak or by raft—the rough, tempestuous Buller River as well as nature buffs looking to explore the impressive network of caves in the area.

▄ TRANSPORTATION

InterCity (☎379 9020; www.intercity.co.nz) heads daily from Craddock's Energy Center/Caltex Garage, 197 Palmerston St., to Fox Glacier (7hr., 11am, $52) via Punakaiki (1hr., $17), Greymouth (2¼hr., $22), and Franz Josef Glacier (6hr., $49), as well as to Nelson (3¾hr., 3:55pm, $39) via Murchison (1½hr., $30). **Atomic Shuttles** (☎349 0697 or 0508 108 359) departs daily to Fox Glacier (6hr., 2pm, $52) and Franz Josef Glacier (5½hr., $49) via Greymouth (2½hr., $20) and Hokitika (3¼hr., $25) as well as to Picton (6hr., 1:30pm, $55) via Murchison (1½hr., $25) and Nelson (3¾hr., $40). **Southern Link K-Bus** (☎0508 458 835) buses south to Punakaiki (50min., daily 6:50pm, $18) and Greymouth (1¾hr., $26) and northeast to Murchison (1¾hr., 10:30am, $26), Nelson (4hr., $41) and Picton (6½hr., $56). **East West** (☎789 6251 or 0800 142 622) runs daily from Craddock's to Christchurch (4½hr., 8am, $56). **Karamea Express** (☎782 6757) departs from the visitors center and runs to Karamea (1½hr.; Oct.-Apr. M-Sa 11:30am; May-Sept. M-F; $27). **Cunningham's**

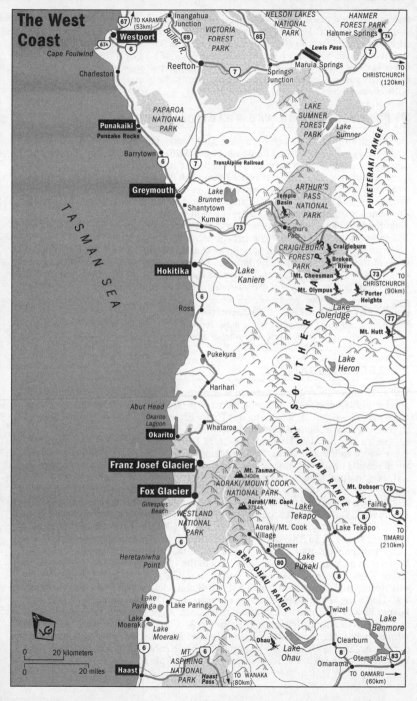

The West Coast

TO KARAMEA (53km)

Inangahua Junction

Nelson Lakes National Park

HANMER FOREST PARK

Hanmer Springs

Westport

Cape Foulwind

Buller R.

VICTORIA FOREST PARK

Lewis Pass

TO CHRISTCHURCH (120km)

Reefton

Maruia Springs

Charleston

Springs Junction

Punakaiki
Pancake Rocks

PAPAROA NATIONAL PARK

LAKE SUMNER FOREST PARK

Lake Sumner

PUKETERAKI RANGE

Barrytown

TranzAlpine Railroad

Greymouth

Lake Brunner

Shantytown

ARTHUR'S PASS NATIONAL PARK

Temple Basin

Kumara

Arthur's Pass

CRAIGIEBURN FOREST PARK

Craigieburn

Broken River

Mt. Cheesman

Hokitika

Lake Kaniere

Mt. Olympus

Porter Heights

TO CHRISTCHURCH (90km)

Ross

Lake Coleridge

Pukekura

Mt. Hutt

Lake Heron

Harihari

TWO THUMB RANGE

Abut Head

Okarito Lagoon

Okarito

Whataroa

SOUTHERN ALPS

Franz Josef Glacier

Mt. Tasman
3498m

Fox Glacier

AORAKI/MOUNT COOK NATIONAL PARK

Aoraki/Mt. Cook
3754m

Mt. Dobson

Fairlie

Gillespies Beach

WESTLAND NATIONAL PARK

Aoraki/Mt. Cook Village

Lake Tekapo

Lake Tekapo

Glentanner

TO TIMARU (210km)

Heretaniwha Point

BEN OHAU RANGE

Lake Pukaki

Lake Paringa

Lake Paringa

Lake Moeraki

Lake Moeraki

Twizel

Lake Benmore

Ohau

Lake Ohau

Clearburn

0 20 kilometers

0 20 miles

Haast

MT. ASPIRING NATIONAL PARK

Haast Pass

TO WANAKA (80km)

Omarama

Otematata

TO OAMARU (60km)

TASMAN SEA

THE WEST COAST

Motors, 179 Palmerston St. (☎789 7177), heads to Karamea (2½hr., M-F 3pm, $18), stopping to drop off mail at various points along the way. **Westport Shuttles** makes trips on demand to area attractions. (☎789 2162 or 027 589 8962. Seal colony $25; Denniston $55; both and Karamea's Nikau Walk $85.) For a lift into town, call **Buller Taxis** (☎789 6900). Though *Let's Go* urges you to consider the risks, **hitchhikers** report success catching rides to Christchurch, Nelson, and Punakaiki outside of town, just over the bridge on the Buller River.

⊀ ② ORIENTATION AND PRACTICAL INFORMATION

The **Buller River** marks Westport's western border. The main drag is **Palmerston Street (SH6),** which intersects **Brougham Street (SH67)** near the center of town. SH6 runs south down the west coast and northeast to Murchison, while SH67 goes north to Karamea. The **Westport Visitor Information Centre,** 1 Brougham St., provides free maps. (☎789 6658; www.westport.org.nz. Internet $2 per 20min. Open daily 9am-5pm; in winter 9am-4pm.) Other services include: **BNZ,** Palmerston near Brougham St., with a 24hr. **ATM** (open M-F 9am-4:30pm); the **police** (☎788 8310), on Wakefield St. close to the intersection with Palmerston St.; **Buller Pharmacy,** 160-162 Palmerston St. (☎789 7629, urgent ☎789 6032; open M-F 8:30am-5pm, Sa 9:30am-12:30pm, Su noon-12:15pm); **Buller Medical Centre,** 45 Derby St. (☎788 8230; open M-F 8:30am-5pm, Sa-Su 10-11am and 5-6pm); **Internet** access at **Dirty Mary's** (see below; $5 per hr.); the **post office,** at Palmerston and Brougham St. (☎788 8193. Poste Restante. Open M-F 8:30am-5pm, Sa 10am-12:30pm.)

> **THE REAL DEAL.** If the backpacker bus scene of the West Coast is wearing you down, consider staying in Hector. The quiet seaside town has a decidely mellow pace of life compared to other West Coast tourist spots. *-Megan Smith*

▛ ACCOMMODATIONS

The most interesting places to stay in Westport are actually outside of town. Solar-powered ▓**Beaconstone ❷,** a carefully crafted eco-lodge set on 52 hectares of bush, has a private swimming hole in the Big Totara River. (☎027 431 0491; www.beaconstone.co.nz. 11km south of the turn-off to Westport off SH6 on a gravel road. Towels $1. Dorms $25; twins and doubles $56-61. $3 BBH discount. Closed June-Sept. MC/V.) A steep walk uphill, ▓**The Old Slaughterhouse ❷,** 34km north of Westport in the small seaside town of Hector, is well worth the hike. The owner built the lodge himself using natural timber, and the deck overlooks some of the best sunsets in New Zealand. (☎782 8333; www.oldslaughterhouse.co.nz. No Internet or TV, but excellent music and book selection. Dorms $25-28. Doubles $64. $3 BBH discount. MC/V.) **Tripinn ❷,** 72 Queen St., off Brougham St., is a lovely Victorian house with good facilities. (☎789 7367; tripinn@clear.net.nz. Reception 8:30am-9pm. Dorms $23-24. Twins $54. Tent sites $14. $3 BBH discount. MC/V.)A favorite with party-crazed Kiwi Experience backpackers, **Bazil's Hostel (YHA) ❷,** 54-56 Russell St., is a large but personable hostel with a toasty lounge. With your back to the visitors center, veer left, then turn left on Russell St. (☎789 6410; www.bazils.com. Bike rental $5 per day. Key deposit $10. Reception 7:30am-9pm. Dorms $24; twins and doubles $60. Self-contained units $80. Tent sites $10; campervan $10 per person. $2-3 YHA discount. MC/V.) **Westport Holiday Park ❷,** 37 Domett St., 1km up Brougham St., offers well-maintained cabins and family-friendly activities such as mini golf. Cook dinner on the covered barbeque deck after a go on the swing set. (☎789 7043; www.westportholidaypark.co.nz. Mini golf $6, kids $4. Dorms $23; basic cabins $55, with bath $65, with bath and kitchen from $90. Tent and powered sites from $24. MC/V.)

◖ FOOD

Honeyman's ❸, on Palmerston St., is a large chillout space with friendly waitstaff and backpacker specials on pizza and beer. (☎789 7928; Pizzas sm. from $14. Open in summer Tu-Sa 8am-4pm and 6pm-late, Su-M 8am-4pm; in winter Su-Th 8am-4pm, F-Sa 8am-4pm and 6pm-late.) Grab a meal or a pint ($5) at the **Denniston Dog ❷**, 18 Wakefield St. (☎789 5030. Daily pasta and fish specials $18 and $26. Quiz night W $2 per person. Internet $2.50 per 20min. Open daily 11am-late.) (☎782 8867. Open daily 9am-6pm, later in summer; hours can be erratic.) Alternatively, hit up **New World**, 244 Palmerston St., for groceries. (Open daily 8am-8:30pm.)

◖ 🆚 SIGHTS AND OUTDOOR ACTIVITIES

The famed West Coast limestone **cave formations** are a regional highlight. ▧**Norwest Adventures** offers an inimitable "Underworld Rafting" adventure that enters the **Metro Cave** system by foot and floats out in total darkness beneath a canopy of one of the world's largest glowworm colonies. Those who want to stay dry can opt for the cave tour. (☎788 8168 or 0800 116 686; www.caverafting.com. Rafting $135, cave walk $80. Extreme tour with 50m abseil from $270 for 5hr.) **Buller Adventure Tours** (☎789 7286 or 0800 697 286; www.adventuretours.co.nz) works out of Westport and runs every imaginable tour, including white water rafting in Murchison, horse trekking (2hr.; $65), quad biking (1½hr.; $105) and jetboating (1¼hr.; $75). **Xtreme Adventures Limited** caters to speed freaks with jetskiing tours along the rocky coast and up rapids. (☎0800 526 405; www.xtremeadventures.co.nz. 1-3hr. From $110.)

The Westport area also harbors several beaches with pounding surf that often have more dolphins than visitors; **Carters Beach,** 6km from town, extends from Cape Foulwind to the mouth of the Buller River, while **North Beach,** 4km from town, stretches along Craddock Dr. to the north end of the Buller. Just 16km out of town, ▧**Tauranga Bay** is famous for some of the best **surfing** in New Zealand. If you need gear, call Mark "the Piranha" Perana at **West Coast Surfing.** They also offer instruction for all levels. (☎0800 927 873; www.wcsurf.co.nz. Board and wetsuit $30 for 2hr., $70 per day. Lessons from $65.) Also in Tauranga Bay is a large **fur seal colony,** a 5-10min. walk from a well-marked parking lot in the northern part of Tauranga Bay. Alternatively, visitors can continue on the path and view the colony from above as well as the lighthouse via the **Cape Foulwind Walk** (3hr. round-trip).

Large industrial machinery, dimly lit mine shafts, and figurines carved from anthracite fill **Coaltown,** Westport's regional museum, south on Queen St. across the railway tracks. (☎789 8204; coaltown@xtra.co.nz. Open daily 9am-4:30pm; longer hours in summer. $8, students $6, children $4.) For those who can't get enough of history and coal, **Denniston,** an abandoned coal-mining town that hit its heyday in the early 1900s, is a popular destination. A great way to see the town is via the 1hr. **Coalbrookdale Walk** (20min. drive from Westport). After exploring the coal history, drink like a miner at the **Miner's Brewery,** 10 Lyndhurst St., which has free tastings of five different beers, including one certified organic brew. (☎789 6201; absalom@xtra.co.nz. Open M-F 10am-5:30pm, Sa 11am-5:30pm.)

MURCHISON ☎03

With just a short block of shops and buildings, the town of Murchison is over almost as soon as it begins. But as the only outpost near the scenic white water of Buller Gorge, Murchison is worth a second look. Whether you are a beginner or an experienced paddler, ▧**NZ Kayak School,** 22 Grey St., has a course for you. World-renowned for its white water kayaking instruction, the school runs multi-day courses complete

1080 KILLS

On the main road south from Karamea, a hand-painted sign proclaims "1080 kills." The sign sums up the arguments both for and against the use of 1080 (sodium fluoroacetate). The Department of Conservation (DOC) and other conservation groups began using 1080 traps to control opossums and stoats. These animals are introduced pests that threaten native birds, including the kiwi. The DOC argues that 1080 should be used because it kills these pests, while others argue that 1080 should not be used because pests aren't the only thing 1080 kills.

. DOC spreads 1080 in pest-ridden areas with nearly one trap every 50 sq. m. According to the DOC, 1080 is a relatively safe substance because all the poison breaks down into harmless substances in water and digestion, and is biodegradable. Hence, the chemical will not accumulate in drinking water or the soil and poses little threat to humans. Moreover, the statistics show that 1080 has a high success rate. As possums and stoats are controlled, native wildlife rebounds.

Critics' main argument against the use of 1080 is its risk to dogs. While most 1080 baited areas are dog-free, many Kiwis still object to the use of the chemical for their favorite four-legged friend. While there is no debate as to 1080's ability to kill, there seems to be plenty about the merits of who it might kill.

with lodge accommodations with communal facilities. (☎ 523 9611; www.nzkayakschool.com. Oct.-Apr. 4-day courses from $695, includes accmmodation. Gear $15 per day for beginner courses, $25 per day for advanced courses. Freedom rentals $45 per day.) Those looking to raft the white water, **Ultimate Descents,** Fairfax St., next to Rivers Cafe, is happy to oblige. They run trips on Class II-IV rapids, including the heart-stopping Ariki Falls. (☎ 0800 748 377; www.rivers.co.nz. Half-day Buller Gorge rafting $105, river kayaking $115. Heli-rafting from $350.) **White Water Action Rafting Tours** also runs rafting trips as well as jet boating. (☎ 0800 100 582 or 523 9581; whitewateraction.com. Half-day rafting from $105, includes barbeque lunch. Jetboating trips 1¼hr. from $75.) Murchison kicks into a white water frenzy for the **Teva Buller Festival** (www.bullerfestival.co.nz) the first weekend in March. The festival features head-to-head racing for kayaks and team rafts and a "Big Air" ramp for some kayak freestyling.

There's more to Buller Gorge than white water. **Skyline Walk** (1½-2hr. round-trip; trailead 1km east of Murchison at SH6 and West Matakitaki Rd.) is a relatively easy hike through native forest to the ridge above Murchison. Another popular hike, **Six Mile Walk** (1-1½hr. round-trip; trailhead 10km south of Murchison at Six Mile hydro power station), passes natural rapids and waterfalls and the hydro power station. Mountain bikers should stop by the Information Centre (see below) for info on trails in the area. **Buller Gorge Swingbridge** allows the tourist masses to walk across New Zeland's longest swingbridge. On the far side of the bridge are hiking trails for those who can brave the sandfly storms. (14km west of Murchison on the road to Westport. ☎ 548 2193; www.bullergorge.co.nz. Bridge $5, children $2. Cometline zipline $25/12.50. Open daily in summer 9am-7pm, in winter open during daylight.)

Murchison lies right on SH6, which becomes Waller St. in town. Most places of interest lie on the main strip or just off it on a side street. **Intercity** (☎ 379 9020) buses to Franz Josef (8¼hr., daily 9:30am, $84) via Westport (1½hr., $30), Punakaiki (3hr., $43), and Greymouth (4hr., $48) and to Nelson (2hr., daily 5:50pm, $36). **Atomic Shuttles** (☎ 0508 108 359) goes down the West Coast to Westport (1½hr., daily 12:30pm, $25), Greymouth (4hr., $35), Franz Josef (7¾hr., $70), and Fox Glacier (8¼hr., $75) and north to Nelson (2hr., 3:30pm, $20) and Picton (4¼hr., $45). **Southern Link** (☎ 0800 881 188 or 0508 458 835) departs from Midwest Cafe to Nelson (2hr., 2 per day, $26) via St. Arnaud (on demand); Christchurch (5hr., daily 10:30am, $41) via Hanmer Springs (3hr., $41); and Greymouth (4hr., daily 9:30am, $31) via Westport

(1½hr., $26) and Punakaiki (3hr., $28). Though *Let's Go* does not recommend **hitch-hiking**, hitchers report that rides are easy to come by on the Waller St. in town. The **Murchison Information Centre**, 47 Waller St., has local information, **Internet**, and gold panning equipment for rent. (☎523 9350; murchinfo@xtra.co.nz. Internet $2.50 per 20min. Gold panning equipment $10 per day. Open daily 10am-6pm; in winter M-F 10am-4pm.) There are **no ATMs** in Murchison, though the **Nelson Building Society** changes money. (☎523 1000. Open M-F 10am-4pm; in winter M-F 10am-3pm.) Services in town include: a **gas station** (☎523 9033. Open daily 6am-9pm; 24hr. pump available); **police**, 15 Fairfax St. (☎523 1170); a small **24hr. hospital**, 58 Hotham St. (☎523 1120); and a **post office** in **Hodgson's General Store**, 48 Fairfax St. (☎523 9006. Open M-F 8:30am-5pm, Sa 8:30am-1pm).

Murchison has limited options for accommodations and food. The town's only hostel, **The Lazy Cow (BBH)** ❷, 37 Waller St., is a home-run hostel with a lot of charm and somewhat cramped facilities. (☎523 9451. Dorms $23, with linen $25. Doubles $55; extra person $15. $3 BBH discount.) **Hampden Hotel** ❸, on the corner of Waller and Fairfax St., has newly renovated rooms that are the best deal in town. (☎523 9008; hampden.hotel@xtra.co.nz. Single $30-45; twins and doubles $50-70, ensuite $90. MC/V.) **Riverview Holiday Park** ❶ has a superb location on the water and a wide range of accommodations. To reach the park take SH6 out of town toward Nelson and follow signs. (☎523 9591; riverviewhp@xtra.co.nz. Reception 7:30am-11pm. Mountain bikes $15 for 3hr.; $25 for 6hr. Showers $2. Tent sites $8, children $5; powered sites $18. Basic cabins from $18 per person, children $5. Ensuite doubles $70-80. MC/V.) Next to Ultimate Descents, **Rivers Cafe** ❷, 51 Fairfax St., is a strange and inimitable blend of country pub and artsy cafe popular with the local white water crowd. (☎523 9009; jude_rivers@xtra.co.nz. Sandwiches $7. Hearty beef, chicken, venison or veggie burgers $14. Open in summer daily 9am-late, kitchen closes 8:30pm; in winter Th-F and Su-M 9am-4pm, later if the rugby is on.) The friendly servers at **Commercial Hotel** ❶, 37 Fairfax St., dish out wraps ($7), pizza slices ($6), and homemade baked goods during the day and more upmarket mains ($19-25) in the evening. (☎523 9696; the commercialhotel@xtra.co.nz. Internet $2 per 15min. Open daily 8am-9pm; close earlier when not busy.) For groceries, the best and only option is the **4 Square Supermarket**, on the corner of Waller and Fairfax St. (☎523 9007. Open M-F 8am-8pm, Sa-Su 9am-7pm.)

PUNAKAIKI ☎03

Punakaiki (pop. 38) is synonymous with pancake rocks and blowholes. Every day, hundreds of tourists put on their raincoats, dash to the cliffs to take pictures of the layered limestone bluffs and geyser-like plumes of water, and then hit the road again. Those who linger find a variety of hikes in the palm forests and sea-carved landscape of Paparoa National Park.

▐ TRANSPORTATION. Almost all bus service through Punakaiki stops long enough (30min.-1hr.) to allow passengers to see the rocks and take pictures. **Inter-City** (☎768 7080; www.intercity.co.nz) passes through Punakaiki daily en route to Greymouth (45min., 12:35pm, $17) and Nelson (4¾hr., 3pm, $68) via Westport (1hr., $24). **Atomic Shuttles** (☎768 5101) provides service south to Greymouth (2:55pm, $15) and Fox Glacier (4hr., $50) and north to Nelson (5hr., noon, $45) and Picton (9hr., $55). **Southern Link K Bus** (☎0508 458 835) runs to Greymouth (40min., 7:45pm, $13) and Nelson (5hr., 9:25am, $46) via Westport (1hr., $18). **Greymouth Taxis** also run from Greymouth. (☎768 7078. Round-trip $25, 3-person min.)

▐ PRACTICAL INFORMATION. The **Paparoa National Park Visitor Centre**, on SH6 across from the blowholes, has park and tramping info. (☎731 1895; fax 731 1896.

Open daily 9am-6pm. In winter 9am-4:30pm.) The nearest **gas** stations are 35-60km away, but the **Wild Coast Cafe** (see below) keeps a small emergency supply of gas. They also offer **Internet** access for $3 per hr. The **police** (☎ 768 1600) are in Greymouth, along with the nearest doctor and **hospital**.

▟ ▢ ACCOMMODATIONS AND FOOD. Punakaiki's accommodations are scattered along SH6. If you're coming by bus, ask the driver to drop you off at your destination. Though many backpackers stay in Punakaiki just long enough for a photo, the area's hostels are reason enough to stay. The ▩**Te Nikau Retreat (BBH/ YHA) ❷**, on Hartmount Pl., is 3km and a 30min. walk north of the visitors center; call for free pickup. This rainforest retreat has the sort of facilities and large common spaces that backpackers dream about. The tiny tent-like "Stargazer" unit has a transparent roof. (☎ 731 1111. Small store. Dorms $20-25; doubles and 2-person cabins $56, with bath $71; self-contained cabins $81-86. Tent sites $15. MC/V.) The **Punakaiki Beach Hostel (BBH) ❷**, at Webb St. and Dickenson Pde., is a 15min. walk north from the visitors center; call for free pickup. Airy rooms open onto a magnificent beach where dolphins are sometimes sighted frolicking in the surf. (☎ 731 1852; www.punakaikibeachhostel.co.nz. Free outdoor spa 6-10pm. Reception 8am-9pm. Dorms $23-24; singles $40; twins and doubles $58. Tent sites $14. $3 BBH discount. MC/V.) **Punakaiki Tavern ❸**, on SH6, 1km north of the village, has economical, modern doubles overlooking a parking lot. (☎ 731 1188. Doubles $110. $15 per extra person. MC/V.) Next door, **Punakaiki Beach Camp ❶** has recently renovated facilities, though cabins remain utilitarian. (☎ 731 1894. Powered sites $13. 2-person cabins $36-50.)

For limited groceries, stop by **Wild Coast Cafe ❶**, near the visitors center. They also serve great coffee and stacks of pancakes ($12) buried in fruit. (☎ 731 1873. Open when they feel like it, but on good days 8am-6pm.) **Punakaiki Tavern and Bistro ❸**, on SH6 at the turn-off for the Beach Hostel, is packed in summer with pubgoers flipping through their day's photos over a pint. (☎ 731 1188. Occasional bands in winter. Pastas from $18.50. Steak $28.50-30.50. Open daily 8am-late.)

◪ ⚠ SIGHTS AND OUTDOOR ACTIVITIES. The 35 million-year-old **pancake rocks** are the product of waves pounding the soft limestone and mudstone cliffs into strange, twisted formations. Subterranean channels have been carved out in three places. When water surges in, it shoots high into the air, creating the **Punakaiki blowholes**. Both are at the end of the **Dolomite Point Walk** (20min. round-trip; wheelchair accessible) across from the visitors center. Check the tide schedule before planning your visit, as the blowholes are practically nonexistent at low tide. The best conditions for viewing the blowholes are at high tide with a westerly or southwesterly swell. A superb alternative is the **Truman Track** (15min.), off SH6, north of the visitors center, which leads through nikau palms to a dramatic lookout point on the ocean's edge. At low tide, explore the rocks and beach below, including the small, 10m long caverns. For a bigger cave, grab a flashlight and head to the 130m long **Punakaiki Cavern,** 500m north of Punakaiki, to the right off SH6. The **Punakaiki Pororari Loop** (3½hr. round-trip) winds through the stretch of rainforest from the Punakaiki River to the Pororari River. Check in advance to see if the rivers can be crossed. More rugged trekkers can explore the **Inland Pack Track** (27km, 2-3 days), which follows the Punakaiki and Pororari Rivers through steep limestone gorges. Fill in the intentions book and get full trail information at the DOC before you go and stay on the track, as there are numerous sinkholes. In addition, the track is very weather dependent and when the rivers are in flood the track is impassable. There is a designated **campsite** at Ballroom Overhang, but no huts along the track. **Green Kiwi** (☎ 731 1843; www.greenkiwitours.co.nz) provides taxi service to trailheads by arrangement and also runs eco-sensitive guided walks (from $60) and caving ($30-200). **Punakaiki Canoe Hire**, 1km north of the visitors center, near the tavern, has guides and rents canoes. (☎731 1870; www.riverkayaking.co.nz. Canoes $30 for 2hr., $50 per day. Guided tours from $70.) Call **Punakaiki Horse Treks** to view the pancake rocks from horseback. (☎731 1839. 2½hr. from $110. Daily rides 9:30am, 3pm. Open Oct.-May.)

GREYMOUTH ☎03

After the gold rush of the late 1800s, Greymouth's timber, coal, and fishing resources facilitated its growth into the largest town on the West Coast. Today Greymouth (pop. 14,000) remains at the heart of extraordinary tramping, caving, and rafting terrain, and marks the western terminus of the TranzAlpine railroad, one of the most breathtaking routes in the world. Those voyaging through Westland should pause here to sample Monteith's brews and stock up on groceries, cash, and gear.

Trains: TranzAlpine (☎0800 872 467; office open M-F 9am-5pm, Sa-Su 10am-3pm) runs from the railroad station, 164 Mackay St. (☎768 7080; www.westcoasttravel.co.nz. Open M-F 9am-5pm, Sa-Su 10am-3pm; Internet $7 per hr.), daily to **Christchurch** (4hr.; 1:45pm; $139) via **Arthur's Pass** (2hr.; $62). Backpackers 20% discount.

Buses: InterCity (☎379 9020) leaves daily from the railroad station to **Fox Glacier** (4hr., 1:30pm, $57) via **Hokitika** (30min., $18) and **Franz Josef Glacier** (3½hr., $53) and to **Nelson** (6hr., 1:30pm, $75) via **Punakaiki** (40min., $17) and **Westport** (2hr., $32). **Atomic Shuttles** (☎0508 108 359) runs south daily to **Queenstown** (10½hr., 7:30am, $90) via **Hokitika** (30min., $15), **Franz Josef Glacier** (3hr., $35), and **Fox Glacier** (3½hr., $40). Atomic also runs north to **Picton** (10hr., 11:15am, $60) via **Punakaiki** (1hr., $15) and **Nelson** (6hr., $50), and east to **Christchurch** (3.75hr., 1:45pm, $30) via **Arthur's Pass** ($25). **Southern Link K Bus** (☎0800 881 188 or 0508 458 835) runs to **Picton** (8½hr., 9am, $66) via **Nelson** (5½hr., $51). **West Coast Shuttle** (☎768 0028; www.westcoastshuttle.co.nz) cruises to **Arthur's Pass** (1½hr., 8am, $13.50) and on to **Christchurch** (3½hr., $35). **Coast-to-Coast** (☎0800 800 847) runs to **Christchurch** (4hr., 12:45pm, $29) via **Arthur's Pass** (2hr., $20). **Coastal Explorer** (☎0800 662 482 or 768 4862) departs to **Punakaiki** (45min., 2pm, $49 round-trip). **Kea West Coast Tours** runs trips to **Punakaiki** (4hr.; 9am, 2:15pm; roundtrip $85).

Taxis: Greymouth Taxis (☎768 7078) runs to **Shantytown** (3 per day; round-trip $30, children $15; admission included; 2-person min.) and **Punakaiki** (2 per day; round-trip $30; 3-person min.).

Car Rental: Greymouth has 15 different car rental companies. Most cluster near or in the train station.

✳🛈 ORIENTATION AND PRACTICAL INFORMATION

From the steps of the **Greymouth Railway Station**, the main drag, **Mackay Street**, runs left to the town center and right to the Grey River, behind the massive "Great Wall" down **Mawhera Quay**. **Mackay** and **Guinness Streets** bustle with activity. **SH6** runs south to Hokitika (40km) and north to Westport (97km); in town SH6 is known as Main South Rd., High St., and Tainui St.

Visitors Center: Greymouth i-Site (☎768 5101), at Herbert and Mackay St. Books accommodations, transportation, and activities. Internet $1 for 10min. Open M-F 8:30am-7pm, Sa 9am-6pm, Su 10am-5pm; in winter M-F 8:30am-5pm, Sa 9am-5pm, Su 10am-4pm.

Banks: Banks cluster around the intersection of Tainui and Mackay St. Most open M-F 9am-4:30pm. All have 24hr. **ATMs.**

Police: 47 Guinness St. (☎768 1600), at the corner of Tarapuhi St.

Medical Services: Mason's Pharmacy, 34 Tainui St. (☎768 7470). Open M-Th 8:30am-5pm, F 8:30am-6pm. **Grey Base Hospital** (☎768 0499), on High St., 1km south of the town center.

Internet Access: Persia and **Tuk Tuk** restaurants, see below, have free wireless. The visitors center and the **library**, 18 Albert Mall., both have access. (☎768 5597. Internet $2 per 15min. Open M-Tu and Th-F 9:30am-5pm, W 9:30am-8pm, Sa 9:30am-12:30pm.

Post Office: (☎768 0123), on Tainui St. Open M-F 8:30am-5pm, Sa 10am-12:30pm.

ACCOMMODATIONS

■ **Global Village Backpackers (BBH),** 42-54 Cowper St. (☎768 7272; www.globalvillage-backpackers.co.nz). Walk down Tainui St. away from town, bear right on High St., go right on Franklin St., then left on Cowper St. This cosmopolitan-themed hostel has ample common space, free hot drinks, kayaks, bikes, and fishing rods, plus spa and gym access ($5 each). Reception 9-11:30am, 1:30-2pm, 5-8:30pm. Dorms $22-24; singles $54; twins and doubles $54/$50; Tent sites $15, $26 for 2. $2 BBH discount. MC/V. ❷

The Duke Backpacker (BBH), 27 Guinness St. (☎768 9470; dukenz@clear.net.nz). From Mackay St., cross to Guinness St. on Albert Mall. Experienced world travelers Dory and Shoshy cater to a young crowd with loudly painted rooms in this historic building. Free pool in the downstairs bar. Reception 8am-8pm. 4-bed dorms $23; singles $35; twins and doubles $52, with bath $61. $3 BBH discount. MC/V. ❷

Kainga-ra YHA Hostel, 15 Alexander St. (☎768 4951; yhagreymouth@yha.org.nz). Turn left off Mackay St. onto Tainui St., left on Chapel St., and right on Alexander St. Simple rooms in this hillside manor, formerly a residence for men of the cloth, command an impressive view of the coast. Female-only dorms and a "chapel" dorm available. Piano, guitar, well-stocked library and a games collection allow guests to make their own fun. Lockers $1-2. Reception 8am-noon, 1-4pm, 5-8pm. Dorms from $25; twins and doubles $62. Rooms discounted off-season. $3 YHA discount. MC/V. ❷

Noah's Ark Backpackers (BBH/VIP), 16 Chapel St. (☎768 4868 or 0800 662 472; www.noahsarkbackpackers.co.nz). From Mackay St., head south on Tainui St. left on Chapel St. The friendly owners, pets, and resident tour bus crowd conspire to keep things lively. Comfortable and spacious TV lounge. Dorms $23; twins and doubles $54. Tent sites $17. $3 BBH or VIP discount. MC/V. ❷

Neptunes Backpackers (BBH), 43 Gresson St. (☎768 4425 or 0800 003 768; www.neptunesbackpackers.co.nz), along the Greymouth Great Wall by the old rail tracks. This former fishermen's pub and motel (one dorm houses the old bar) has been remade into deep-sea digs. Free pickup, pool table, hot drinks, spa, and bubble baths. Dorms $21-23; singles $39; twins and doubles $54. $3 BBH discount. MC/V. ❷

FOOD

While gourmet food options are limited in Greymouth, budget eats are not. **Fresh Choice Supermarket,** on Mackay St., behind the train station, is large and inexpensive. (Open daily 7am-9pm.)

Bonzai Pizzeria, 31-33 Mackay St. (☎768 4170). Crunchy pizzas (sm. from $13.50) run the gamut from standard to wild, with ingredients like mussels, eggs, lemon, and garlic. Read one of the 1980s international newspapers wallpapering the joint while you wait. Open M-Sa 8am-late, Su 3pm-late; kitchen closes at 8:30pm, earlier in winter. ❷

dp: one cafe (☎768 4005), on Mawhera Quay, a few doors down from Railway Hotel. Sip on the best coffee ($3-5) in Greymouth in this laid-back cafe amid local artwork. Gourmet bagels ($5.50-8) during the day and burgers ($10-12) in the evening. Internet $2 for 15min. 5min. free Internet. Open Tu-W 8am-5pm, Th-M 8am-9pm. ❷

Persia, 35 Albert Mall (☎768 5026). Groups looking for a classy night out that won't break the bank head to Persia for tapas platters (for 2 $28, for 4 $50; single tapas $7 each). Free WiFi. Open M-Sa noon-2pm and 6pm-late. Reservations recommended. ❸

Tuk Tuk, Albert Mall (☎768 9747). Run by the same people as Persia, Tuk Tuk curries ($17) favor with budget travelers with its large portions of traditional thai food. Free wireless Internet. Open M-Sa noon-2pm and 5:30-10pm. ❶

Railway Hotel, 120 Mawhera Quay (☎668 7023), on the waterfront near the train station. $5 buys you all the grilled sausages, salad, bread, and pasta salad you can eat in this bar. Throw in another $10 to get a T-bone steak on top of it. Deservedly popular with shoestring travelers and chain-smoking locals who often bond over a game of pool after a few pints. Barbeque daily from 6pm. ❶

SIGHTS

Founded to quench the thirsts of gold rushers, **Monteith's Brewing Company,** at Herbert and Murray St., produces the best beer on South Island. With only 10 full-time employees, the small brewery produces two to four 12,000-20,000L batches of of beer per week. Their informative 1½hr. tour concludes with tastings of their six regular beers plus a seventh seasonal beer. After you've decided which one you like best, there's a 30min. window for visitors to pour their own pints before heading to the Railway Hotel and completing the authentic Greymouth experience. (☎768 4149; www.monteiths.co.nz. Tours daily 11:30am, 2pm, 4pm and 6pm. Book ahead. $12.50, with Railway buffet dinner $20) **Barrytown Knifemaking,** 2662 SH6 in Barrytown, is a tour that captures the spirit of the central West Coast. You spend the day forging your own knife. Then, with newly sharpened objects and goofy grins, everyone sits around and drinks homemade "White Lightning." (☎731 1053; www.barrytownknifemaking.com. $95, includes lunch and "White Lightning." Tu-W and F-Su 9:30am-5:30pm.) **Shantytown,** 11km south of Greymouth on SH6, is a replica 1880s gold-rush town has its own post office, sawmill, working steam engine, horse and cart rides, and gold mine. The main difference between today's Shantytown and that of the 1880s is the number of tourists strolling about. (☎762 6634; www.shantytown.co.nz. Open daily 8:30am-5pm. $12, with gold panning $18; children $8.50.) **Greymouth Taxis** (p. 343) shuttles to Shantytown, as does **Kea West Coast Tours,** which provides chatty commentary. (☎768 9292 or 0800 532 868. 3hr. Departs daily 10am. $60; includes admission.) In town, the **Jade Country,** 1 Guinness St., signals tourists' entry into greenstone territory. The expansive complex holds a shop with expensive wares, cafe, carving studio, and the Jade Trail, which gives a brief historical overview of the significance of jade to Maori, Aztec, Asian, and modern cultures though greener jade pastures await in Hokitika. (☎768 0700. Open in summer daily 8:30am-7pm; in winter 8:30am-5pm.) In the northwest corner of downtown, the **History House Museum,** on Gresson St., is an intriguing jumble of old rugby photos, diving suits, and shipping memorabilia. (☎768 4028; www.history-house.co.nz. Open M-F 10am-4pm and on weekends during the Christmas holidays. $3, children $1.)

OUTDOOR ACTIVITIES

Wild West Adventures, 8 Whall St., operates several adventure activities. Their **Dragon's Cave Rafting** explores the **Taniwha Caves,** including a 30min. rainforest walk, climbing, tubing, and glowworm sightings, followed by a dip in the spa. They can also match you with a **whitewater rafting** trip on one of eight rivers, ranging from a mild cruise to a heli-raft trip over Class V rapids. For a tamer cruise or paddle down the Arnold River in an outrigger canoe, try Wild West's

Jungle Boat Rafting. (☎768 6649 or 0508 286 877; www.fun-nz.com. Cave rafting $145, with optional abseil entry $210. Full-day rafting trips around $185. Helirafting from $95 for a half-day to $575. Jungle cruise $115. Check for last minute discounts at their office on partially full tours.)

For landlubbers, **On Yer Bike!,** 5min north of Greymouth on SH6, runs 4WD farm bike/ATV tours through the mud and bush on demand. (☎762 7438 or 0800 669 373; www.onyerbike.co.nz. From $75 for 1hr.) **Lake Brunner,** 37km inland from Greymouth, is a popular daytrip for those with their own transport. A series of walking trails from easy 20min. strolls to moderate 3hr. hikes explore the terrain around the lake. For those who prefer being on the water to walking around it, the fishing at Lake Brunner is excellent. **Lake Brunner Fish 'n Trips,** 34 Ahau St. (☎738 0144; LBCMotel@xtra.co.nz) rents fishing gear and runs tours.

Nikau palms and the occasional dolphins and seals can be seen along the **Point Elizabeth Walkway** (3hr. round-trip, tide dependent). Head inland past the rail station and across the bridge, turn left down Bright St., and right along the coast on Domett Esplanade toward the trailhead (2hr. round-trip). The self-guided 1hr. tour of the **Brunner Mine Site,** just north of town on SH11, past Taylorville, passes through the site of New Zealand's worst mining disaster. The **Woods Creek Track** (45min.) has infoboards along with tunnels inhabited by glowworms (bring a flashlight), south of town near Shantytown. The moderately challenging **Croesus Track** (8hr., 18km one-way) runs from the Smoke-Ho Creek in Blackball to the tavern in Barrytown and can be done as a dayhike, though most people do it in two, stopping at the **Ces Clark Hut** ($10). While there is bus service from Barrytown, reaching Blackball can be tricky for those without their own transport. Though *Let's Go* does not recommend it, hitchhikers report that locals are quick to provide lifts.

HOKITIKA   ☎03

Virtually all of New Zealand's jade (greenstone) is quarried within a 20km radius of Hokitika (ho-kuh-TEEK-uh; pop. 4000), and as a result jade stores as well as gold, glass and wood craft stores fill the city's quiet streets. Tourist buses passing through Hokitika usually stop only as long as it takes to ring up the orders. Those who stay longer in Hokitika have the opportunity to watch artisans at work, carve their own bone or greenstone piece, or simply meander along the beach to enjoy a magnificent sunset over the Tasman Sea. Hokitika's busiest day of the year features the extremely popular **Wildfoods Festival,** held the second weekend in March.

▐ TRANSPORTATION. InterCity drops off at **Hokitika Travel Centre,** 60 Tancred St. (☎755 8557), and runs daily to Fox Glacier (3hr., 2:55pm, $38) via Franz Josef Glacier (2¼hr., $35) and to Nelson (7hr., 12:30pm, $62) via Greymouth (45min., $15) and Westport (3¼hr., $38). **Coast-to-Coast** (☎0800 800 847) goes to Christchurch (4½hr., 12:45pm, $35) via Arthur's Pass (2hr., $20). **Atomic** (☎0508 108 359) comes to Hokitikia only on demand and runs to Greymouth (45min.; 10:15am, 12:45pm; $10) and on to Christchurch (4½hr., $350) as well as to Queenstown (10hr., 8am, $80) via Franz Josef Glacier (2½hr., $35) and Fox Glacier (3hr., $40).

▐ PRACTICAL INFORMATION. The **Westland i-Site** is in the Carnegie Building, Tancred and Hamilton St. (☎755 6166. Open M-F 8:30am-6pm, Sa-Su 10am-6pm. In winter M-F 8:30am-5pm, Sa-Su 10am-4pm.) The local **DOC** is on Sewell St. near the river. (☎756 8282. Open M-F 8am-4:30pm.) Other services include: **banks** with **ATMs** near the corner of Weld and Revell St.; the **police,** 50 Sewell St. (☎756 8310); **Westland Medical Centre,** 54 Sewell St. (☎755 8180); **Westland Pharmacy,** 10 Weld St. (☎755 8150; open M-F 8:30am-5:15pm, Sa 9:30am-12:30pm, Su 10:30-11:30am); **Internet** access at **Aim West Sports,** 20 Weld St. (☎755 8947. $3 per

30min., $5 per hr.; open M-F 9am-5pm, Sa 9am-1pm) and **Global Gossip**, 15 Weld St. (☎755 7768. Internet $2 per 15min., $5 per hr.; laptops $3 per 30min.; open in summer M-F 8am-6pm, Sa 8:30am-3pm; in winter M-F 8:30am-5:30pm, Sa 9am-1pm); and the **post office**, at Revell and Weld St. (☎756 8034; open M-F 9am-5pm).

⌂ **ACCOMMODATIONS.** If you decide to stay in Hokitika overnight, try the **Blue Spur Lodge (BBH) ❷**, 5km out of the city on Hampden Rd., which becomes Hau Hau Rd. and then Blue Spur Rd.; turn left on unsealed Cement Lead Rd. and follow signs. The wood lodge is as private as hostels get with 100 acres, a 1hr. bushwalk and an open gold mine tunnel where guests can pan for gold using the lodge's free equipment. (☎755 8445; bluespur@xtra.co.nz. Bike rental $15 per day. Dorms $23; ensuite doubles $75. 4-person self-contained cottage $150. MC/V.) **Birdsong ❸**, 124 SH6, 2km north of town, houses backpackers in bird-themed rooms with ocean views. Watch the sunset in the hot outdoor "Bushman Baths" ($4) or from the balcony. (☎755 7179. Dorms $25; singles $40; twins and doubles $60, ensuite $70. $3 BBH discount. MC/V.) **Shining Star ❹**, 11 Richards Dr., 1km north of the town center, provides seaside accommodation for campers and caravaners. The wood cabins are sparkling clean, if lacking in personality. (☎755 8921 or 0800 744 646; www.accommodationwestcoast.co.nz. Doubles from $60, with bath and kitchen $75-149. Tent sites $12 per person; powered sites $14-15. MC/V.) In and old nurse's accommodation, **Seaview Lodge and Kotuku Hostel (BBH) ❸**, Seaview Hill Rd., 1km north of town fork right off SH6, is a sprawling property of accommodations overlooking a view better than other places in town. (☎755 5230; www.seaviewlodge.co.nz. Dorms $30; doubles $50, ensuite $100. $3 BBH discount.) The rooms and facilities at **Mountain Jade (BBH) ❷**, 41 Weld St., are as sterile as, if less flashy than, the jade showroom overlooking the lounge. (☎755 8007; www.jadefactory.com. Reception at Jade Factory in same building. Dorms $18; twins and doubles $45-60; self-contained unit for 2 5 people $80. $3 BBH discount.) **Stumpers ❸**, 2 Weld St., in an old hotel has an upbeat, if impersonal atmosphere. (☎755 6154; www.stumpers.co.nz. Dorms $25; twins $60; doubles $50, with bath $60.)

◻ **FOOD.** ▨**Café de Paris ❹**, on the corner of Tancred and Hamilton St., exudes class. Simple, flavorful dishes like warm lamb or sweet chilli chicken salads are $15.50; mains run $26.50-27.50. Try a wine from Maison Esquilat, an award-winning winery also owned by the proprietor. (☎755 8933. Lunch $12.50-16.50; panini $9. Open daily 7:30am-9pm, closes earlier in winter.) Savor tea and hot meals at **Adz on Tancred ❷**, 39 Tancred St., home to the largest collection of tea cups and some of the finest tea ($3, $4.50 for 2) in New Zealand. (☎755 8379 or 0800 832 768. All day breakfast $8.50-15. Open daily 8am-3:30pm.) The beginning and end of Hokitita's nightlife, **the Tin Shed**, 89 Revell St., lives up to its name with a stripped down decorating scheme, cheap drinks and filling meals. (☎755 8444. All day breakfast $14; large pizzas $20; burgers $12. Beer $3.50-6.50. Open daily 10am-3pm and 6:30-as late as 1am.) Stock up on groceries at **New World**, 116 Revell St. This is the last large supermarket north of Wanaka and has the best prices before then. (☎755 8390. Open M-F 8am-8pm, Sa 8am-7pm, Su 9am-7pm.)

SAVE SOME GREEN. Intricately carved greenstone pieces often fetch hundreds of dollars in the shops, but those looking to take home a piece of the West Coast need not shell out next week's grocery money. Unpolished and uncarved pieces of the stone often turn up on Hokitika's shores fresh from the ocean for free.

◻ **CRAFTS.** In spite of the touristy kitsch that accompanies the sale of crafts, well-made and reasonably priced pieces can be found in Hokitika, often along

A BEACON OF ECOLOGY

Beaconstone (p. 346), an eco-lodge 17km south of Westport, uses solar energy, all-natural bedding, and compost toilets, to name a few of its earth-friendly attributes. Grae and Nancy Stevens have been running Beaconstone since 2000. *Let's Go* caught up with Grae to discuss his eco-lodge and the environment.

LG: Why did you feel so strongly about opening an environment-friendly retreat for backpackers?
A: I bought this land for a backpackers. I live on this piece of land; I'm responsible for it, so I want to be kind to it.
LG: How did you get involved in the environmental movement?
A: It came probably from seeing the use of treated timber and its effects. When it came to building Beaconstone, I thought, "I really don't want to use treated timber." Then from there, each step was, "How can I use something that's friendly to the environment?"
LG: Hypothetical question: You wake up in the middle of the night, and a big, ugly spider, who you know is an integral part of the ecosystem, is about to bite your arm. Do you kill it?
A: Yeah. I'd try and actually pick it up and put it outside, but if he's right there and the pincers are right there, then bam! [hits his arm] Sorry pal, but you're outta there.

with the opportunity to watch artisans at work. At ▨**Bonz 'n Stonz,** 83 Revell St., aspiring jewellers work alongside master craftsman Steve Gwaliasi to create jade, bone, paua shell, or mother of pearl pieces. Would-be carvers have complete creative control, from the initial drawing to the final polish. (☎0800 214 949 or 755 6504; www.bonz-n-stonz.co.nz. Jade pieces start at $90, bone at $60, mother of pearl and paua shells at $45. Open M-Sa 8am-5pm. Carving workshops Tu, Th, Sa. Book ahead to carve your own. $5 BBH discount.) The other create-your-own option in town, **Just Jade Experience Backpackers,** 197 Revell St., might not be as fun as it allows less creative control; numerous travelers have reported a less respectful atmosphere. (☎755 7612; www.madkiwi.co.nz. Simple pieces start at $20.) Though Hokitika is known for greenstone, **Ruby Rock,** 21 Tancred St., sells an equally valuable jewel, known as goodletite. The stone only exists in New Zealand and is a natural fusion of ruby, sapphire and tourmaline. While the stones may be beyond most backpacker's budgets, browsing is free. (☎755 7448 or 0800 388 703; www.nzrubyrock.com. Open in summer daily 8:30am-5pm; in winter daily 10am-3pm.) **Westland Greenstone,** 34 Tancred St., has jade pendants, pins, and paperweights for sale from as little as $8. (☎755 8713. Open daily 8am-5pm.) Across the street at **House of Wood,** 29 Tancred St., carver Quade recycles rimu and kauri salvaged from old buildings into ornamental and practical articles. (☎755 6061. Open daily 9am-5pm; less in winter.) The **Hokitika Glass Studio,** 28 Tancred St., exhibits glass artistry ranging from a whimsical penguin chess set to dainty flowers. (☎755 7775 or 0800 178 445; www.hokitikaglass.co.nz. Open daily 9am-5pm.)

◙▨ **SIGHTS AND OUTDOOR ACTIVITIES.** ▨**Eco-Rafting Adventures** specializes in heli-rafting trips for kayaks or rafts on 22 different rivers, including the Class V Karamea. Knowledgeable guides steer novice paddlers through some of New Zealand's best rapids. (☎768 4005 or 0508 669 675; www.ecorafting.co.nz. Full day from $135, heli-rafting from $220, DVD and photos included. Group discounts available.) The **Glowworm Dell,** a 30min. round-trip walk on the Seaview Lodge property (see above), displays phosphorescent larvae behind a chain-link fence.

The **West Coast Historical Museum,** in the Westland i-Site, walks visitors through the history of New Zealand's gold rushes and "wild west." (☎755 6898. Open daily 9:30am-5pm. $5, children $1.) **National Kiwi Centre,** 64 Tancred St., is part aquarium, part zoo, and home to a tuatara, four kiwis, and giant 60 lb., 120-year-old eels. Exhibits are subject to change. (☎755

5251. Open daily 9am-5pm. $13, children $7.) If it crawls, it's dinner at the phenomenally popular **Wildfoods Festival** (☎756 9010; www.wildfoods.co.nz), during the second weekend in March. Opossum, kangaroo, and grasshopper are among the tamer entrees. Book accommodations at least six months ahead. Tickets $25.

OKARITO   ☎03

On the edge of the 3200-hectare Okarito Lagoon, this tiny seaside community offers serenity unparalleled along the coast. Certainly not known for its size (pop. 35), Okarito is famous instead as a habitat for a vast array of bird species, including the white heron and endangered brown kiwi. Some travelers use the town—just 28km north of Franz Josef Glacier and 13km off SH6—as a retreat from the over-touristed glaciers and their rainy weather. The town is certainly worth a visit for those who have their own transportation.

Okarito's primary attraction is its lagoon and the wildlife that goes with it, and the best way to experience both is by getting out on the water. ☒**Okarito Nature Tours** can supply kayaks, a map, and even a bird guide to help you explore their well-marked routes in the beautiful lagoon. (☎753 4014; www.okarito.co.nz. Kayaks $35 for 2hr., half-day $45, full-day $55. Guided trips from $65, overnight trips from $80. The best time to go is early in the morning when the water is calm and the most birds are out. Min. 2 people. Book ahead.) Using a team approach to locate kiwis, **Okarito Kiwi Tours** has a high success rate for finding the elusive brown kiwi in the wild. (☎753 4330; www.okaritokiwitours.co.nz. 2-3hr. tours depart 30min. before sunset. From $45. Max. 8 people.) **Okarito Experience** runs informative bird-watching tours into the lagoon. Aside from white herons, spoonbills, kingfishers, and paradise ducks all take shelter here. (☎753 4223. 2 trips per day. From $70; group discounts available.) **White Heron Sanctuary Tours** (p. 355) jetboats from the town of Whataroa to see the white herons.

Okarito also has several beautiful hikes. Trailheads are at the far end of the village. The **Okarito Trig Walk** (1¼hr. round-trip) climbs through kahikatea and rimu rainforest to a lookout point with views of Aoraki/Mt. Cook and Mt. Tasman on one side and the ocean and lagoon on the other. The **Okarito Coastal Walk** (a.k.a. the Three Mile Pack Track; 2¾hr. round-trip) follows an old pack track through coastal forest. If the tide is low, take the beach route to the sheltered Three Mile Lagoon. This route is only safe within 2hr. of low tide; a tide table is posted at the trailhead, or check with the DOC.

Kotuku Lodge and Cottage (BBH) ❸, is a chill hostel with welcoming bedrooms and a resident whitebait fisherman who sometimes sells cheap fresh fish to backpackers. (☎753 4330. Laundry wash $2. Doubles and twins $30 per person.) **The Royal Okarito (BBH) ❷** has a new eco-friendly building with bamboo floors and a large kitchen, but the older portions of the hostel are rather plain with cramped common facilities. (☎753 4080; www.okaritohostel.com. Laundry wash $2, dry $2. Dorms $23. Ensuite doubles and twins $60-70. Self-contained cottage $80. $3 BBH discount.) Community-run **Okarito Historic Hostel (YHA) ❷**, runs on a self-check-in system and sleeps guests in bunks stacked three high in a small and very rustic 1870s schoolhouse. (☎753 4151. Showers at the campsite $1 per 6min. Dorms $18.) The **Okarito Campground ❶** only has unpowered sites, plus shelter, water, toilets, a shower, and the village's only public **phone**. (☎753 4151. Tent sites $7.50 per person, children free.) Though back in the gold rush days there were as many as 33 stores in town, there are currently **no shops** or gas stations; bring food, insect repellent, gas, and other necessities with you.

Buses stop (by request) at "The Forks," the turn-off to Okarito on SH6; it's a common place to **hitch** (not recommended by *Let's Go*) and hitchers report a high success rate. Otherwise, it is a 13km walk into town. **Glacier Valley Eco Tours** in Franz Josef runs daytrips to Okarito. (☎752 0699; $45.)

THE GLACIERS

The landscape of southwest New Zealand has been carved out by glaciers. The twin glaciers of Franz Josef and Fox are the most famous of New Zealand's glaciers not only because of their size and speed (they advance up to a foot per day), but also because they descend into temperate rainforest, terminating only 12km from the Tasman Sea. Sandwiched between the sea and the Southern Alps, Fox and Franz are more accessible than most glaciers in the area. Every year, thousands of travelers find themselves face-to-face with several billion cubic meters of rapidly moving (by glacial standards) solid blue ice.

Fox and Franz Josef Glaciers are part of the 117,547-hectare **Westland National Park,** which contains a multitude of hikes and bushwalks highlighting native flora and fauna. There are many ways to explore the glaciers: a guided hike or a bird's eye helicopter tour are the most popular. Franz Josef Glacier, though smaller, has a reputation for more adventurous guided hikes. However, Fox Glacier is less crowded with slightly better weather, and the town of Fox Glacier is noticeably less commercial than its twin.

 YOU CAN'T SAY WE DIDN'T WARN YOU. Signs and barriers exist for your own protection. Tourists have been crushed by falling ice after ducking under the safety ropes to get "just a little closer." It's only safe to venture onto the glacier with a professional guide, and no, this book does not count.

FRANZ JOSEF VILLAGE ☎ 03

Lying 140km south of Hokitika and 27km north of Fox Glacier, Franz Josef Village (pop. 360) owes its existence to its massive glacier. With large Lake Mapourika nearby and more tourist outfitters than Fox, Franz is the destination of most tour groups and backpacker buses. To escape the crowds, nip down to the glacier riverbed for a picnic or a moonlight walk in the glacier's eerie glow.

⬛ TRANSPORTATION

The YHA on Cron St. (☎ 752 0754) serves as the local agent for **InterCity** (☎ 379 9020). Buses head north to: Greymouth (4¾hr., $51), Hokitika (3½hr., 8:30am, $44), and Nelson (11hr., $103) and south to: Fox Glacier (1¾hr., daily 8am, $10), the Copland Track (1hr., $11), Queenstown (9¼hr., $99), and Wanaka (7½hr., $73). **Atomic Shuttles** (☎ 0508 108 359), which books from Scott Base or Chateau Franz, provides northbound service to: Greymouth (3hr., $35), Hokitika (2hr., daily 8am and 3pm, $35), Nelson (9¼hr., only 8am bus service, $75), Picton (11hr., only 8am bus, $85), Punakaiki (5hr., $45), and Westport (5¾hr., $55) and and southbound service to: Fox Glacier (30min., daily 10:15am, $15), Queenstown (7¼hr., $60), and Wanaka (4hr., $50). The pickup area for both shuttle companies is at the bus stop on Main Rd., near the Cheeky Kea Cafe. **Glacier Valley Eco Tours** (☎ 752 0699 or 0800 999 739; www.glaciervalley.co.nz) runs local transportation to the Glacier Carpark and other trailheads in the area (7 per day, 8:45am-6:45pm, $10 round-trip). They also run daytrips to Franz Josef Glacier ($55), Fox Glacier ($60) and Lake Matheson ($60-90) and Okarito ($45). For **bike rentals,** visit **Glowworm Cottages,** see p. 351.

⬛ ⬛ ORIENTATION AND PRACTICAL INFORMATION

Running through the center of town, **SH6,** known as **Main Road,** is the location of most of the town's services—backpackers are located on parallel **Cron Street.** The glacier access road is just north of town, across the bridge. The **Franz Josef i-Site** and **DOC office,** on the southern edge of town on SH6, has displays on glacial dynamics and information on hikes. (☎752 0796; www.glaciercountry.co.nz. Open daily 8:30am-6pm. In winter 8:30am-noon and 1-5pm.) **Scott Base Tourist Info** books activities and can assist with finding accommodations outside Franz Josef. (☎752 0288. Internet $4 per hr. Open daily 9am-9pm, in winter 10am-6pm.) The sole 24hr. **ATM** in town is outside Mt. Cook Ski Planes on SH6; it's the only ATM between Hokitika and Wanaka, so get cash before leaving town. The fastest **Internet** access is available at ■**Red Bus Internet** in—wait for it—the big red bus on Cron St. (☎752 0230. $4 per hr. Open daily 9am-9pm, less in winter.) The **Mobil station** doubles as a **post office.** (☎752 0725. Open daily 8am-8pm. In winter 8am-6pm.)

■ ACCOMMODATIONS

Franz Josef has some stellar hostels, though in peak season all of them fill up, so book ahead and be prepared for cramped living areas. Given the area's rainy weather, it is no surpise that the top hostels provide comfy TV lounges, big screens, and a good selection of movies. In addition, many hostels have free spas or saunas. Rates in most accommodations drop in winter. Look for the roof-scaling mountaineers atop **Chateau Franz (BBH/VIP) ❷,** 8 Cron St., where you can grab a round of pool, eat a bowl of soup, or relax in a great spa, all for free. The ■**love shack** (double $45) is as interesting a place to stay as a B52s music video. (☎752 0738 or 0800 728 372; www.chateaufranz.co.nz. Reception 8am-8pm. Dorms $20-25; twins and doubles $48-55. Self-contained motel units $90-110. Astroturf tent sites $10. $2-3 BBH discount, $1 VIP discount. MC/V.) At **Glowworm Cottages (BBH) ❷,** 27 Cron St., you'll find a spa, rooms filled with backpacker-friendly amenities, a log fire and free homemade soup every night. (☎752 0172 or 0800 151 027; www.glowwormcottages.co.nz. Dorms $21, 4-share ensuite $24; doubles and twins $50-52; motel units $95. $2 BBH discount. MC/V.) **Montrose (BBH) ❷,** 9 Cron St., has spacious dorm rooms, a free sauna and pristine bathrooms, though the disorderly kitchen leaves something to be desired. (☎752 0188. Reception 7:30am-9pm. Dorms $21-23; twins and doubles $58, with bath $88. $3-5 BBH discount. MC/V.) At the **Franz Josef YHA ❸,** 2-4 Cron St., the pool table ($2) and free sauna make for a pleasant end to a gla-cier-filled day. (☎752 0754; yha.franzjosef@yha.co.nz. Reception 7:30am-9pm, in winter 7:30am-8pm. Lockers $2. Dorms $27-30; twins and doubles $67, ensuite $85. $3 YHA discount. MC/V.) **Rain Forest Retreat ❷,** at the end of Cron St., offers a variety of accommodations that are not nearly as impressive as its rainforest setting. The backpackers lodge is plainly furnished and lacking in personality. (☎752 0220; www.rainforestretreat.co.nz. Lounge. Spa and sauna $3 per 30min. Reception 7am-9pm, in winter 7am-8pm. Dorms $20-25; back-packer doubles $55; doubles and twins with bath $69. Gravel tent sites $11, powered $15. Motel rooms and separate treehouses available from $139. MC/V.) ■**Franz Josef Mountain View Top 10 Holiday Park ❷,** 1.5km north of town on SH6, is like camping, but without the mud. Tent sites are on lush grass amid manicured gardens. Immaculate kitchens, bathrooms, and rooms meet any budget. (☎752 0735 or 0800 467 897; www.mountainview.co.nz. Linen $6. Kitchen basket $10. Reception 7:30am-9pm. Spa $10 for 2 people. Tent sites $18 per person. 2-person cabins $62-89, with kitchen and bath from $110; motel rooms from $135. $15-20 per extra person. MC/V.)

◘ FOOD

Dining out in Franz Josef is expensive, especially in the evening. Most ice trek-kers opt to dine in the hostel and crack open a bottle of wine or a couple of

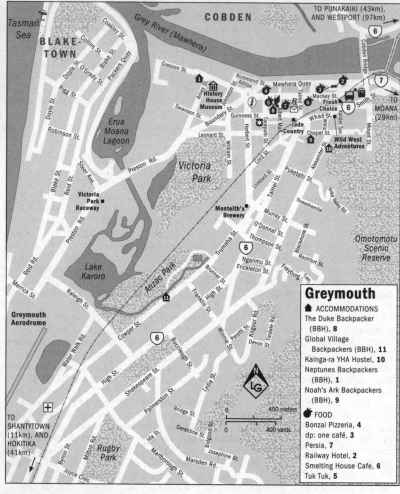

TO PUNAKAIKI (43km),
AND WESTPORT (97km)

COBDEN

Grey River (Mawhera)

Tasman
Sea

BLAKE-
TOWN

Cobden Bridge

TO
MOANA
(29km)

History
House
Museum

Fresh
Choice

Jade
Country

Wild West
Adventures

Erua
Moana
Lagoon

Victoria
Park

Victoria
Park ■
Raceway

Monteith's
Brewery

Omotomotu
Scenic
Reserve

Lake
Karoro

Anzac Park

Greymouth
Aerodrome

TO
SHANTYTOWN
(11km), AND
HOKITIKA
(41km)

Rugby
Park

400 meters

400 yards

Greymouth

🏠 ACCOMMODATIONS
The Duke Backpacker
   (BBH), **8**
Global Village
   Backpackers (BBH), **11**
Kainga-ra YHA Hostel, **10**
Neptunes Backpackers
   (BBH), **1**
Noah's Ark Backpackers
   (BBH), **9**

🍴 FOOD
Bonzai Pizzeria, **4**
dp: one café, **3**
Persia, **7**
Railway Hotel, **2**
Smelting House Cafe, **6**
Tuk Tuk, **5**

beers from the grocery store. For those who do want to get out, Franz Josef
has a few licensed cafes. In a swinging location just up from the gas station,
The Blue Ice Cafe ❸ attracts crowds of young backpackers with a "buy a pizza,
get a pint" meal deal (sm. $16.50; daily 9-10pm). The pub is also the only true
late-night option in town. (☎752 0707. Open daily 4pm-as late as 3am.) A popular early evening destination, **the Landing Cafe and Bar** ❸, on Main Rd., has a
warm fire, hearty servings and rotating drink specials. (☎752 0229. Lunch $10-
15; heaping burgers $16.50-18.50. Open daily 7am-2am, in winter 11am-2am.)
Beeches ❸, in the center of town, serves up a comparable lunch menu ($15.50-
18.50) and takeaway food (lasagna $6.50; wraps $6.50) during the day, but
come dinnertime, pasta and mains start at $26.50. (☎752 0721. Open daily 8am-
10pm, in winter 9am-9pm.) In an electric blue building, **Priya** ❸, 70 Cron St.,
stands apart from the standard pub fare with curries (vegetarian $14, meat

$15.50) at reasonable prices. (☎752 0060. Open daily 11:30am-2:30pm and 5-10pm.) **Fern Grove 4 Square Supermarket**, on Main Rd., is the only option for self-caterers. (☎752 0177. Open daily 7:45am-10pm, less in winter.)

🝙 OUTDOOR ACTIVITIES

GLACIER HIKES

The best way to appreciate the size and majesty of the glacier is up close and personal. Hiking on the glacier solo is dangerous even for experienced mountaineers; veteran trampers should sign on for a tour rather than risk being lost at the bottom of a crevasse. Rain may limit ice time, and the topology of the glaciers is constantly changing—you may or may not find tunnels or caves, depending on recent weather and glacier movement. Those without the money for a guided tour can take advantage of the numerous trails near and around the glacier that provide views. For a guided walk that isn't on the glacier, try **Glacier Valley Eco Tours** (see p. 350). Weather changes rapidly on the West Coast, so plan on rain, even if it's a clear day. Check with the DOC office for track conditions and special warnings.

■**FRANZ JOSEF GLACIER GUIDES.** The oldest and largest company in Franz Joseph, Glacier Guides recently took over the competition to become the only glacier guiding company in town. They have four different tours. The cheapest option is the half-day, which spends most, if not all, of its time on dirty ice. Those with a few extra dollars should upgrade to a full-day tour and a chance to experience the otherworldly landscape of blue ice. The full-day is the best value of all the hiking options. Heli-hiking has become increasingly popular (and expensive) in recent years. Though it only allows three hours on the ice, all of the time is spent on blue ice. The most adventurous tour option, ice climbing gets you up close and personal with the ice. For all trips, Glacier Guides provides necessary weather gear and equipment. *(☎752 0763 or 0800 484 337; www.franzjosefglacier.com. Book ahead. Half-day trips $90, full-day $140; heli-hikes $340; full-day ice-climbing adventures $210. $5-10 BBH/VIP/YHA discount.)*

GLACIER VALLEY WALK. This stroll leads to a view of the terminal face of the glacier. The walk from the parking lot crosses over riverbed gravel, streams, and ice-smoothed rock. Though you may see tourists ducking the ropes and walking the last 200m to the face of the glacier, this is by no means safe; the terminal face often collapses and has severely injured numerous tourists. *(1¼hr. round-trip from Glacier Carpark. From the visitors center, turn right, cross the bridge, and follow the signs. Allow 1hr. to walk to the end of the access road, or drive the 4km. Glacier Shuttle also runs from downtown to the parking lot for $10 round-trip; call ☎752 0699.)*

SENTINEL ROCK WALK. This walk is the fastest, easiest way to get good views of the glacier. The walk begins at the same point as the Glacier Valley Walk, but branches up into a steady, climbing switchback trail to a viewing point of the glacier, the Main Divide, and the glacier valley. The forest lines along the glacier valley indicate the highest levels of advance in the last 100 years. *(20min. round-trip.)*

ALEX KNOB WALK. On a clear day, this tramp steadily climbs through a variety of vegetation to panoramic views of the glacier and the Main Divide. Start early in the morning to be on the mountaintop before clouds cover the view, usually in early afternoon. Boots are essential; take plenty of water with you. Before hiking stop at the DOC office to check weather conditions. *(Trailhead near Glacier Valley and Sentinel Rock Wall, off the Glacier Access Rd. 8hr. round-trip.)*

CANAVAN'S KNOB. The high points along Canavan's Knob, a forested granite outcrop, rise above the rainforest to deliver views of both the glacier and the coast. *(Off SH6, 2km south of town. 40min. round-trip.)*

TARTARE TUNNELS WALK. This track follows the Tartare River and then climbs to old water tunnels. The first tunnel can be explored up to the wooden flume and escape race by flashlight. They're often partially filled with icy water; dress appropriately and watch your head. *(Off the dead-end of Cowan St. 80min. round-trip.)*

ST. JAMES ANGLICAN CHURCH. The glacier view from the altar window of this church is so beautiful that it was featured on a 1946 peace stamp issued to celebrate the end of WWII. *(A 5min. jaunt down SH6; turn onto the path at the right before the bridge. The church is through the brush at the end of the path.)*

SCENIC FLIGHTS

HELICOPTER. Four different helicopter companies operate from Franz Josef and Fox. It pays to book ahead, especially in peak season (Jan.-Mar.). All operators offer similar prices and essentially the same routes, except for **Mountain Helicopters**, which provides a cheaper option as it is only licensed to land on Mt. Cook. *(☎ 0800 369 423; www.mountainhelicopters.co.nz. 10-40min. flights: Fox Glacier from $90; Franz Josef $100.)* **Fox and Franz Josef Heliservices** *(☎ 752 0793 or 0800 800 793; www.scenic-flights.co.nz; located inside the Alpine Adventure Center with The Guiding Company),* **Glacier Helicopters** *(☎ 752 0755 or 0800 800 732; www.glacierhelicopters.co.nz),* and the **Helicopter Line** *(☎ 752 0767 or 0800 807 767; www.helicopter.co.nz; inside the Franz Josef Glacier Guides building; $15 YHA discount.)* have offices on Main Rd. and run identical flights at comparable prices. Helicopter Line also flies a summer "sunset special" ($280) that includes a glacier landing and champagne. *(All tours of the Franz Josef Glacier, Fox Glacier, Tasman Glacier, and/or Aoraki/Mt. Cook with glacier landings $175-355.)*

PLANE. Air Safaris offers a 45min. "Grand Traverse" airplane tour of Fox and Franz Josef, Aoraki/Mt. Cook, and the Tasman Glacier. It does not include a snow landing, but it covers a greater area (approx. 200km total) than the helicopter flights. Air Safaris operates only out of Franz Josef. *(☎ 0800 723 274; www.airsafaris.co.nz. $260, children $180.)* **Aoraki/Mt. Cook Ski Planes** is the only company permitted to do fixed wing glacier landings, although it also runs flights without landings. Pickup is available at Fox Airfield. *(☎ 752 0714 or 0800 368 000; www.mtcookskiplanes.com. From $220 for 20min, with landing from $300.)*

OTHER ACTIVITIES

HUKAWAI. The newest attraction in town, Hukawai is a rainy day alternative to a movie at the hostel with a 10-meter high ice climbing wall. Six different routes ranging from easy to difficult lead to the top. Non-climbers can sip a latte and spectate in the cafe (all cabinet food under $12) after strolling through the museum exhibits on the history of ice climbing and the glacier. *(Cowan and Cron St. ☎ 752 0600; www.hukawai.co.nz. 1½hr. instructed climb $90. Museum admission $28. Open daily 8am-9pm, less in winter.)*

QUAD BIKES. Rev your motor and streak across terrain that the glacier covered 10,000 years ago. **Across Country** runs popular 1-1½hr. quad bike tours of the area just beyond the national park boundary. *(☎ 0800 234 288 or 752 0123; www.acrosscountryquadbikes.co.nz. 4 tours daily in summer; 2-3 in winter. $115, passengers $65.)*

LAKE MAPOURIKA. Glacier Country Tours and Kayaks, at Red Bus Internet on Cron St., runs kayaking trips on Lake Mapourika and includes a CD of digital pictures from the trip that feature a spectacular mountain backdrop. *(☎ 752 0230 or 0800 423 262. 3½hr. 9am, 1:30, 5pm. Additional tours on demand. Tour $75. 3hr. freedom hire*

$60.) The lake is also popular with hunters and anglers. The waters are stocked with brown trout and Quinnai salmon, while the nearby bush is rife with chamois and possums. Hunting licenses are free at the DOC office, and fishing licenses can be purchased at the Mobil Station for $18.50 per day.

HORSEBACK RIDING. South Westland Horse Treks offers rides through bush, rainforest, and rivers with views of the Southern Alps and the glacier. *(☎ 0800 187 357 or 752 0223; www.horsetreknz.com. 1hr. $50, 2hr. $85, 3hr. $110, 6hr. $175.)*

WHITE HERON SANCTUARY TOUR. This eco-tour starts with a jetboat ride and brings a limited number of visitors to observe breeding pairs of white herons in Okarito Lagoon. Held sacred by the Maori, these birds breed only in New Zealand. *(Operates from Whataroa, a 30min. drive north of Franz Josef. ☎ 753 4120 or 0800 523 456; www.whiteherontours.co.nz. Heron-nesting season is Oct. to mid-Feb., but rainforest tours and scenic jetboat rides are year-round. Book ahead. 2½hr. $95.)*

ALPINE ADVENTURE CENTRE. Flowing West, a 25min. movie shown daily, traces the cycle of water in South Westland. *(☎ 752 0793 or 0800 800 793. Up to 7 per day and on demand for groups of 4 or more; guaranteed to show daily at 5pm. $10, children $5.)*

FOX GLACIER ☎ 03

Twenty-seven kilometers south of Franz Josef on SH6, Fox Glacier (summer pop. 200; winter pop. 90) is a little village near a mammoth glacier. Fox offers a more refreshing atmosphere and a bit more elbow room than Franz Josef as well as the mercurial reflections of Lake Matheson—allegedly New Zealand's most photographed lake.

▐ TRANSPORTATION

InterCity (☎ 379 9020) leaves from **Fox Glacier Guiding** and heads north to: Nelson (11hr., 8:30am, $107) via Franz Josef Glacier (45min., $14); Hokitika (3½hr., $49); Greymouth (4¾hr., $57) and south to: Queenstown (8hr., $95) via the Copland Track (20min., $18) and Wanaka (6hr., $70). From Ivory Towers, **Atomic Shuttles** (☎ 0508 108 359) runs north to: Greymouth (3½hr.; 7:20am, 2:15pm; $40) via Franz Josef Glacier (30min., $15) and Hokitika (3hr., $40); the morning northbound bus heads to Picton (11¾hr., $90), Nelson (9¾hr., $80), Punakaiki (4½hr., $50) and Westport (6¼hr., $60) as well. Southbound services goes to: Queenstown (7hr., 11am, $55) via Haast (3hr., $35) and Wanaka (5hr., $45). **Fox Bus** (☎ 0800 369 287) runs shuttles on demand to Fox Glacier, Gillespie's Beach, Lake Matheson, and other local sites ($12 round-trip). The **BP station** on SH6 is the last **gas** station for the next 120km to the south. (☎ 751 0823. Open daily 8am-7:30pm, in winter 8am-6pm.) **Ivory Towers** (p. 356) rents bikes for $4 per hr. and $24 per full-day.

✦ ▐ ORIENTATION AND PRACTICAL INFORMATION

Running through the center of town, **SH6** is known as **Main Road.** It heads north over three arduous hills to Fox's comrade Franz Josef, south to the **Copland Track** trailhead, and then to **Haast** (137km). **Cook Flat Road** leads south from the center of town to wonderful views of the mountains and to the turn-offs for the famously reflective **Lake Matheson** (6km) and seal-colonized **Gillespie's Beach** (20km). The **Fox Glacier Visitor Information Centre,** 37 Sullivan Rd., at the Fox Glacier Inn, is small and has area info and 24hr. Internet. (☎ 751 0022 or 0508 369 466. Open daily 8am-8pm. Internet $1 per 10min.) For information on area trails and to make hut bookings, the **DOC office** is located on SH6 north of the main village. (☎ 751 0807. Open

M-F 9am-noon and 1-4:30pm.) In the center of everything, **Fox Glacier Guiding**, on Main Rd., is the headquarters for the glacier guides and serves as a **currency exchange** and **post office**. (☎751 0825. Open daily 7:30am-9pm, in winter 7:30am-7:30pm.) There are **no banks or ATMs; police** can be reached at ☎756 1070; the local **nurse's clinic** is on SH6 north of town (☎751 0836). While most hostels provide some sort of **Internet, Global Gossip**, run by Helicopter Line next door on SH6, provides high-speed access for $5 per hr. (☎751 0078. Open daily 8am-10:30pm.)

ri rŏ ACCOMMODATIONS AND FOOD

Budget accommodations in town are limited; book early. The only quality budget accommodation in town, **Ivory Towers (BBH) ❷**, on Sullivans Rd., has a large dining room and TV lounge, garden, porch, and sauna ($15 per 45min. for 2 people) that promote mingling. Compared to the other facilities in town, Ivory is noticeably better kept. (☎751 0838; www.ivorytowerslodge.co.nz. Reception 8am-8:30pm. Dorms $25; singles $45; twins and doubles $60, with bath $80. $2.50-3 BBH discount. MC/V.) The **Fox Glacier Hotel ❸**, Cook Flat Rd., just off Main Rd., has a nice but overpriced motel-room wing and separate, less-attractive budget accommodations. (☎751 0839; www.resorts.co.nz. Restaurant and bar. Reception 7am-11pm. Budget doubles from $65, with bath $95. Motel rooms $145-165. MC/V.) The basic facilities at **Fox Glacier Inn ❷**, 39 Sullivan Rd., are the best bet for a budget sleep if Ivory Tower is full. (☎751 0022 or 0508 369 466; www.foxglacierinn.co.nz. Local bar downstairs open daily 10am-3am; earlier if not busy. Breakfast included. Dorms $25. Doubles and twins $65, with bath $95. In winter $55/70. MC/V.) Campers have limited options. **Fox Glacier Holiday Park ❷**, Kerrs Rd. off Cook Flat Rd., has cheap, spartan cabins with facilities that are not worth the pricetag. (☎751 0821 or 0800 154 366; www.foxglacierholidaypark.co.nz. Reception 8am-8pm. Tent sites $14 per person; 2-person powered sites $30. 2-person cabins $56, with bath $89; self-contained motel rooms $120-145. MC/V.)

At **The Hobnail Cafe ❶**, on Main Rd., in the same building as Alpine Guides, pack lunch before your trip on the glacier with homemade pies ($4.50) and sandwiches ($7) or warm up with a bowl of soup ($6) after you get back. (☎751 0005. Open daily 7am-5pm, in winter 8am-5pm.) **Plateau Cafe and Bar ❸**, at SH6 and Sullivans St., brings style to its simple cafe menu with meals like "Monteith's fish 'n chips" ($14). At night, the mains go more upmarket. (☎751 0058. Happy hour daily 4-5pm. Chicken, bacon and brie burger $18.50. $4 Monteith's handles. Open daily 11am-late; kitchen closes around 10pm.) The **Cook Saddle Cafe and Saloon ❸**, on Main Rd., cooks American favorites like barbeque ribs ($23) to match its Western decor. Takeaway fish 'n chips start at $5.50; lunch from $13.50. (☎751 0700. Happy hour daily 6-7pm handles $4, 10pm-midnight shooters $4. Restaurant open daily 11am-9pm; bar is open much later when busy.) Just a few doors down, the swank **Cafe Neve ❺** serves delicious mains to those who can afford them (rack of lamb; $36.50) and tasty pizzas (sm. $14) to those who can't. (☎751 0110. Generous takeaway sandwiches $6 during the day. Open daily 8am-10pm, less in winter.) The only grocery is the **Fox Glacier General Store**. (☎751 0829. Open daily 8am-8:30pm. In winter 8am-6:30pm.)

⚠ OUTDOOR ACTIVITIES

ON THE GROUND

GLACIER HIKES. Fox Glacier Guiding is the only company that leads **guided walks** up Fox Glacier. Their reputation is for an emphasis on safety and providing a kinder, gentler tour; those looking for high adventure might do better to hike at

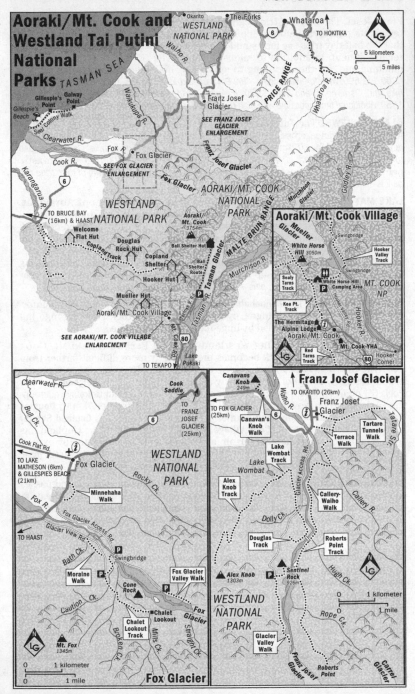

Aoraki/Mt. Cook and Westland Tai Putini National Parks

TASMAN SEA

WESTLAND NATIONAL PARK

Okarito
The Forks
Whataroa
6
TO HOKITIKA

0   5 kilometers
0   5 miles

Waiho R.

PRICE RANGE

Gillespie's Point
Galway Point
Gillespie's Beach
Seal Colony Walk

Waikukupa R.

Franz Josef Glacier

SEE FRANZ JOSEF GLACIER ENLARGEMENT

Whataroa R.

Clearwater R.

Fox R.
Fox Glacier

SEE FOX GLACIER ENLARGEMENT

Cook R.

Franz Josef Glacier

Fox Glacier

AORAKI/MT. COOK NATIONAL PARK

Godley R.

Murchison Glacier

Karangarua R.

6

TO BRUCE BAY (16km) & HAAST

WESTLAND NATIONAL PARK

Welcome Flat Hut

Copland Track

Douglas Rock Hut

Copland Shelter

Hooker Hut

Mueller Hut

Aoraki/Mt. Cook (3754m)

Ball Shelter Hut

Ball Shelter Route

Tasman R. Tasman Glacier

MALTE BRUN RANGE

Murchison R.

P

Aoraki/Mt. Cook Village

Mueller Glacier

White Horse Hill 3050m

Swingbridge

Hooker Valley Track

Sealy Tarns Track

White Horse Hill Camping Area

Swingbridge

MT. COOK NP

Kea Pt. Track

P

Hooker R.

Aoraki/Mt. Cook Village

SEE AORAKI/MT. COOK VILLAGE ENLARGEMENT

Hooker Valley Rd.

The Hermitage Alpine Lodge
Aoraki/Mt. Cook
i

Red Tarns Track

Mt. Cook-YHA
80
Hooker Corner

Mt. Cook Rd.

80

Lake Pukaki

TO TEKAPO

Clearwater R.

Bull Ck.

Cook Flat Rd.

Cook Saddle

TO FRANZ JOSEF GLACIER (25km)

6

i

Fox Glacier

TO LAKE MATHESON (6km) & GILLESPIES BEACH (21km)

WESTLAND NATIONAL PARK

Rocky Ck.

Fox R.

Minnehaha Walk

Fox Glacier Access Rd.

Glacier View Rd.

TO HAAST

Bath Ck.

Swingbridge

P

Moraine Walk

Cone Rock

P

Chalet Lookout

Chalet Lookout Track

Fox Glacier Valley Walk

P

Fox Glacier

Caution Ck.

Browns Ck.

Mills Ck.

Straight Ck.

N
LG

Mt. Fox 1345m

0   1 kilometer
0   1 mile

Fox Glacier

Franz Josef Glacier

Canavans Knob 249m

TO OKARITO (26km)

TO FOX GLACIER (25km)

Waiho R.

Canavan's Knob Walk

Franz Josef Glacier
i

Tatare St.

Terrace Walk

Tartare Tunnels Walk

Lake Wombat Track

Lake Wombat

Glacier Access Rd.

Callery-Waiho Walk

Callery R.

Alex Knob Track

Dolly Ck.

Douglas Track

Roberts Point Track

Alex Knob 1303m

P

Sentinel Rock 926m

Hugh Ck.

N
LG

WESTLAND NATIONAL PARK

Glacier Valley Walk

Franz Josef Glacier

Rope Ck.

Roberts Point

Carrel Glacier

0   1 kilometer
0   1 mile

Franz Josef. The half-day trip begins with a 1½hr. steady, uphill climb through temperate rainforest before stepping onto the top of the glacier. Visitors report that the half-day trips see more mud and rocks than ice; the full-day trip is a better investment. In addition to hikes on the glacier, Fox Glacier provides ice-climbing and, for those looking to spend big, heli-ice-climbing. *(☎751 0825 or 0800 111 600; www.foxguides.co.nz. 4hr.; 9:15am and 1:45pm; $85. 6hr.; 9:30am; $125. Heli-hike 4hr.; 9am, noon, and 3pm; $330. Ice-climbing trips 8am; $215. 8-9hr. heli-ice-climbing $559. Additional times possible with high demand. Book ahead.)*

GLACIER VIEWS. The **Fox Glacier Valley Walk** winds through the gorge carved by the glacier's advance, crossing streams of glacial run-off, and ending within 40m of the glacier's terminal face. *(2km south of town before the Fox River Bridge, take a left on the road to the glacier, the carpark is 4km down.)* The **Chalet Lookout Walk** yields a fantastic peek at the town's namesake. *(Turn off onto Glacier View Rd. 2km south of town.; the carpark is 3km down. 1½hr. return from trailhead.)*

LAKE MATHESON WALK. This walk offers unparalleled views of Aoraki/Mt. Cook and Mt. Tasman reflected upon one of New Zealand's most photographed lakes. Views are best at dusk and dawn, when the water is undisturbed by wind; arrive 15-20min. before sunrise and walk to the nearest lookout point for some unadulterated serenity. Near the trailhead, **Matheson Cafe** *(☎751 0878; Meals from $9; open in summer daily 7:30am-5pm, in winter 8am-3pm)* pours stong cups of coffee for a pick-me-up before or after your walk. *(6km out of town on Cook Flat Rd. 1½hr. loop from trailhead, plus a 20min. walk between the carpark and trailhead.)*

MINNEHAHA WALK. The **Minnehaha Walk** gives a sampling of Westland's rainforest as it wanders across bridges, over small trickling creeks, and through tall moss-covered trees surrounded by huge ferns. *(20min. round-trip.)*

COPLAND TRACK. Connecting Westland National Park to Aoraki/Mt. Cook National Park, Copland Track becomes progressively more difficult farther from Fox. The first leg (17km; 6-8hr.) of the tramp is suitable for moderately experienced trampers. Hot-pool lovers may want to overnight at the **Welcome Flat Hot Pools** (31 bunks; hut $15; annual hut passes not valid, though hut tickets are; camping $5; hut warden Nov.-Apr.). From Welcome Flat it is another 7km to **Douglas Rock Hut** (8 bunks; hut and camping $5). The track continues to **Copland Shelter** before descending into **Mt. Cook Village.** Beyond Douglas Hut, the Copland has huge climbs and unpredictable terrain and should only be attempted by experienced alpine hikers. *(Trailhead 26km south of Fox Glacier. InterCity and Atomic Shuttles make stops daily 9:50 and 11:20am. See DOC office for details and conditions.)*

GILLESPIES BEACH. The **Seal Colony Walk** begins at Gillespies Beach and passes old miners pack tracks as it traces the Tasman Sea for 1½-2hr. out to the seals at Galway Point. Hikers should return the same way they came and not walk on the beach in order to avoid disturbing the seals. *(20km from Fox Glacier, half of it on gravel roads. For transport, see Fox Bus, p. 355. 3½hr. round-trip from trailhead.)*

IN THE AIR

SCENIC FLIGHTS. Fox Glacier offers aerial pursuits similar to those at Franz Josef. All flight companies cluster on Main Rd. in town. While all helicopter companies have branches in Fox, the airplane companies run solely out of Franz Josef.

SKYDIVING. Professional and friendly, **Skydive New Zealand—Fox and Franz Josef Glaciers** is a small operation that provides a pre-jump scenic flight with views of Mt. Cook, Mt. Tasman, and the Tasman Sea. Bring a camera for some unbeatable shots as you fly, and if you dare, dive. *(☎0800 751 0080; www.skydivingnz.com. 9000 ft. $245; 12,000 ft. $285. DVD and photos $170, just photos $30.)*

OTAGO

With rocky coastlines and rolling hills in the east giving way to the snow-capped peaks of the Southern Alps in the west, Otago's geography is an assortment of some of the best South Island has to offer. The friendly citizens of caffeinated college town Dunedin and adrenaline-fueled Queenstown seem to have some idea how lucky they are; the parties there rarely slow down, let alone stop.

■ OTAGO HIGHLIGHTS

TACKLE Queenstown's thrills—bungy jumping, skydiving, and skiing—by day (p. 366), and **Dunedin's** marathon bar-hopping by night (p. 366).

TREAT yourself to some relaxation and enjoy the **Otago Peninsula's** abundant wildlife (p. 367) or hang-out lakeside in laid-back **Wanaka** (p. 393).

TAKE IN the majesty of **Mt. Aspiring National Park** (p. 401) for some of the world's most glorious tramping.

DUNEDIN ☎ 03

The Scottish settlers who arrived in Dunedin (du-NEE-din; pop. 120,000) in 1848 would be proud to see that the city has continued to think big. With one of the largest student populations in New Zealand, Dunedin also plays host to those looking for an education in practical physics. With the steepest streets in the world, one thing is clear: it's easy to roll into town, but it's much harder to roll out.

▐ TRANSPORTATION

Flights: The **airport** is 30min. south on SH1. **Air New Zealand,** 18 Princes St. at the Octagon (☎ 479 6594), flies to **Auckland** (2¾hr., $124-554) and **Wellington** (2hr., $118-408), often via **Christchurch.** Taxi companies run airport shuttles (around $30).

Buses: InterCity, 205 St. Andrew St. (☎ 474 8860), runs to: **Balclutha** (1½hr., 1-2 per day, $22-27); **Christchurch** (6hr., 2-3 per day, $37-46) via **Oamaru** (1½hr., $20-25) and **Timaru** (3hr., $29-36); **Invercargill** (3-4hr., 1-2 per day, $33-41); **Queenstown** (4¼hr., 1 per day, $33-41). **Atomic Shuttles** (☎ 322 8883) is cheap and reliable, traveling once daily from the visitors center to **Christchurch** ($35), **Invercargill** ($30-35) and **Queenstown** ($40).

Public Transportation: 4 **bus** companies travel a variety of routes throughout the city ($1-4, depending on the number of zones traveled). Many depart from the Octagon. **Citibus** offers a $7 day pass. Pick up a Dunedin bus timetable from the visitors center.

Taxis: Stands at the Octagon, on High St. off Princes St., and on St. Andrew and Hanover St., off George St. Try **Dunedin Taxis** (☎ 477 7777) or **City Taxis** (☎ 477 1771).

Car Rental: Jackie's, 23 Cumberland St. (☎ 477 7848). Cars from $55 per day, $0.20 per km over 200km. Unlimited km for rentals over 3 days. Lower rates Apr.-Oct.

Bike Rental: Cycle Surgery, 67 Stuart St. (☎ 477 7473; www.cyclesurgery.co.nz), at the corner of Cumberland St. Half-day $20, full-day $35. Discounts for 5- or more-day rentals. Open M-Th 8:30am-6pm, F 8:30am-9pm, Sa 10:30am-4pm, Su 10:30am-4:30pm.

Hitchhiking: Although *Let's Go* does not recommend hitchhiking, hitchhikers often take a bus from the Octagon out of the city. Those heading north usually take the Pine Hill bus ($2), while those heading south take the Mosgiel bus to Saddle Hill ($4), which leaves from Countdown Supermarket on Cumberland St. A safer and widely used option is to check common room message boards in area hostels for ride availabilities.

◢ ORIENTATION

Dunedin is organized around the Octagon, where a statue of Robert Burns sits in front of the Gothic Revival spires of St. Paul's. **George Street,** Dunedin's main commercial thoroughfare, extends roughly north toward the University of Otago; it becomes **Princes Street** south of the Octagon. Pubs are mostly scattered on and southeast of George St. between the Octagon and the university. **Stuart Street** runs down the hill directly toward the train station and Otago Harbour. The Otago Peninsula extends from the southeastern part of the city along **Portsmouth Drive.**

◪ PRACTICAL INFORMATION

Visitors Center: Dunedin i-Site, 48 the Octagon (☎474 3300; www.cityofdunedin.com). Open daily 8:30am-6pm; winter M-F 8:30am-5pm, Sa-Su 9am-5pm.

Department of Conservation (DOC): 77 Lower Stuart St. (☎477 0677), in the Conservation House. Open M-F 8:30am-5pm.

Tours: Citibus Newton (☎477 5577 or 0800 244 844; www.time2.co.nz) operates city tours starting at $18. Buses generally run 9am-3:30pm. Buses depart from the visitors center. Also provides transportation to **Larnach Castle,** leaving the visitors center for 1½hr. tours ($42) at 10am.

Budget Travel: STA Travel, 207a George St. (☎474 0146; fax 477 2741). Open M-F 9am-5:30pm, Sa 11am-2pm.

Banks and Currency Exchange: Banks dot George and Princes St., most with 24hr. **ATMs. Thomas Cook/TravelEx,** 346 George St. (☎477 1532), inside Broker Travel. Open M-F 8am-5pm. The visitors center exchanges money at other times.

Work Opportunities: The **NZ Immigration Service,** 43 Princes St. (☎0508 55 88 5), near the Octagon, helps travelers to obtain a work permit. Open M-F 9am-3pm. **Adecco Personnel Limited,** 110 Moray Pl., in the Carnegie Ctr. on the ground fl. (☎477 4036; www.adecco.co.nz), can provide short- or long-term placement in the commercial or industrial sectors. For information on fruit-picking jobs (available Jan.-May; mainly peaches, apricots, apples, and cherries), visit www.seasonalwork.co.nz.

Police: 25 Great King St. (☎471 4800). In emergencies, dial ☎111.

Medical Services: The **urgent pharmacy** is at 95 Hanover St. (☎477 6344). Open M-F 6pm-10pm, Sa-Su 10am-10pm. **Urgent Doctors** (☎479 2900) is part of the same building. Open 8am-11:30pm. **Dunedin Public Hospital,** 201 Great King St. (☎474 0999), has emergency facilities.

Outdoor Equipment: Kathmandu, 144 Great King St. (☎474 517; www.kathmandu.co.nz), carries just about everything you need for the next big adventure. M-Th 9am-5:30pm, F 9am-7pm, Sa 10am-5pm, Su 10am-4pm.

Books: University Book Shop, 378 Great King St., (☎477 6976; www.unibooks.co.nz), has a selection of academic books, plus a discount section upstairs. Open M-F 8:30am-5:30pm, Sa 9:30am-3pm, Su 11am-3pm.

Internet Access: The Common Room, 18 George St. (☎470 1730). $4 per hr. Wireless available. Open M-F 8am-9pm, Sa-Su 10am-9pm. **Arc** (p. 364) has 25min. of free, albeit extremely slow, access.

Post Office: 233 Moray Pl. (☎474 0932), just north of George St. Poste Restante. Open M-F 8:30am-5:30pm, Sa 10am-12:30pm.

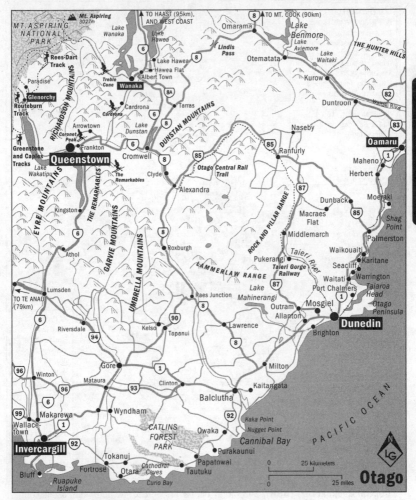

Otago

ACCOMMODATIONS

Most budget choices are within a 10min. walk of the Octagon. Those within a couple blocks thrive on bus traffic and tend to offer less in way of street parking and charm than their outer area counterparts. The farther you move from the Octagon, the more you get in terms of personality, parking, and amenities. Reception generally runs until 8pm. Book in advance during peak season and during rugby games.

CENTRAL OCTAGON

On Top Backpackers (VIP), 12 Filleul St. (☎477 6121; www.ontopbackpackers.co.nz). Perched on an extensive pool hall behind the Municipal Chambers, the close feel of the rooms is balanced out by a large common area and balcony overlooking the city. Key deposit $10. Dorms $23; singles $48; doubles $56. $1 VIP discount. MC/V. ❷

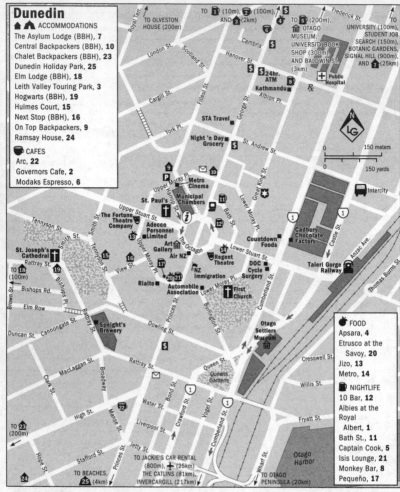

Dunedin

▲ ♠ ⌂ ACCOMMODATIONS

The Asylum Lodge (BBH), **7**
Central Backpackers (BBH), **10**
Chalet Backpackers (BBH), **23**
Dunedin Holiday Park, **25**
Elm Lodge (BBH), **18**
Leith Valley Touring Park, **3**
Hogwarts (BBH), **19**
Hulmes Court, **15**
Next Stop (BBH), **16**
On Top Backpackers, **9**
Ramsay House, **24**

☕ CAFES

Arc, **22**
Governors Cafe, **2**
Modaks Espresso, **6**

🍴 FOOD

Apsara, **4**
Etrusco at the Savoy, **20**
Jizo, **13**
Metro, **14**

🍸 NIGHTLIFE

10 Bar, **12**
Albies at the Royal Albert, **1**
Bath St., **11**
Captain Cook, **5**
Isis Lounge, **21**
Monkey Bar, **8**
Pequeño, **17**

Central Backpackers (BBH), 243 Moray Pl., (☎477 9985; www.dunedinhostels.com). Located in the middle of it all, this hostel is hip on the inside, with a modern TV lounge and sleek kitchen. Dorms $24; singles $38; doubles $62. BBH discount. MC/V. ❷

Next Stop, 2 View St. (☎477 0447; www.nextstop.co.nz), near the Octagon. From Princes St., turn right on Moray Pl. and then left on View St. The slightly small rooms have skylights but no windows. Excellent views from balcony. Dorms $22; doubles, triples, quads, or quints $25 per person. ❷

Stafford Gables (YHA), 71 Stafford St. (☎474 1919). Take Princes St. up several blocks to Stafford St. In this converted hospital, finding your room is like navigating a maze, but the panoramic views from the rooftop balcony are worth the hunt. The TV lounge is in the old morgue. Dorms $26; singles $48; twins and doubles $63. $3 YHA discount. MC/V. ❷

Manor House Backpackers (BBH/VIP), 28 Manor Pl. (☎477 0484; www.manor-housebackpackers.co.nz), 6 blocks down Princes St. Occupying 2 adjacent 1920s houses, Manor House offers ample privacy. Free pickup. Reception 9am-9pm. Dorms $22; doubles $55; triples $69. MC/V. ❷

BEYOND THE OCTAGON

☒ Chalet Backpackers (BBH), 296 High St. (☎479 2075). Take Princes St. to High St. and head uphill. Giant windows in each room wipe away trampers' memory of basement bunks. Dorms $22; singles $37; doubles $50. $2 BBH discount. Cash only. ❷

Ramsay House, 60 Stafford St. (☎477 6313). Across the street from Stafford Gables. This historic home has a spacious kitchen and new, nicer rooms in an annex across the street. Call ahead about closings May-Nov. Dorms $23; singles $40; doubles and twins $50. $3 BBH discount. MC/V. ❷

Hogwarts (BBH), 277 Rattray St. Follow the white spray-painted "277" across the street from St. Joseph's. This addition to the backpackers scene isn't central, but the funky and well-appointed facilities up top encourage socializing in peaceful seclusion. Dorms $22; doubles $51, with bath $66. $3 BBH discount. MC/V. ❷

Elm Lodge (BBH), 74 Elm Row (☎474 1872 or 0800 356 563; www.elmwildlife-tours.co.nz/elm_lodge1.htm). Head up Rattray St. to Brown St., then uphill to Elm Row. Perched high above Dunedin, the Elm offers a homey atmosphere with the added perks of a jacuzzi and wireless Internet. Free pickup and drop-off. Dorms $22; singles $34-40; twins and doubles $54. $4 BBH discount. MC/V. ❷

Hulmes Court, 52 Tennyson St. (☎477 5319 or 0800 448 5637; www.hulmes.co.nz). Offering 1 luxurious single with phone, TV, and VCR, Hulmes makes for a great Dunedin splurge. Free breakfast, laundry, bike rentals, and Internet. Bookings essential. Single $70; doubles $105, with bath $135. MC/V. ❹

WAY BEYOND THE OCTAGON

The Asylum Lodge (BBH), 36 Russell Rd. (☎465 8123), in Seacliff, 33km north of Dunedin. Follow SH1 north from Dunedin and head east on Coast Rd. at the signs for Seacliff. Colorful group of semi-permanents make this perhaps the best-named hostel in New Zealand. Free activities include kayaking, surfing, biking, horseback riding, fishing, and the chance to cruise in a '64 Chevy. Free Internet. Closed May-Nov. Dorms $23; singles $35; doubles $44. $3 BBH discount. MC/V. ❷

Leith Valley Touring Park, 103 Malvern St. (☎467 9936; lvtpdun@southnet.co.nz), 2km from the city. Take the Normanby Bus (M-F, $2) or walk down George St., turn left on Duke St. and continue up to Malvern St. A small, secluded park on Leith Stream with access to trails. Reception 7:30am-10:30pm. Caravan and tent sites $12 per person; on-site caravans $35; 2-person flats $64, extra person $12. Cash only. ❶

Dunedin Holiday Park, 41 Victoria Road in St. Kilda (☎455 4690 or 0800 945 455; www.dunedinholidaypark.co.nz). Take Princes St. south until it becomes King Edward St. and then Prince Albert Rd. Turn left on Victoria Rd. The camp is on your right. Whimsically painted cabins. Token-operated BBQ. Shop. Tent sites $14 per person, powered $18; standard cabins $36; ensuite $76. Cash only. ❶

🔾 FOOD

Catering to students, Dunedin overflows with cheap eats. **George Street** swarms with inexpensive Thai, Japanese, Korean, and Indian eateries. For outdoor dining, choose from any number of nearby takeaways, and get a seat in the lively Octagon. Markets include **Countdown Foods** (☎477 7283), 309 Cumberland St., and **Night 'n Day** (☎477 0313), at the corner of George and St. Andrew St., both open 24hr. On Saturday mornings, the area around the Dunedin train station becomes a lively **farmer's market** from 8am-1pm.

Etrusco at the Savoy, 8a Moray Pl., (☎477 3737; www.etrusco.co.nz), off Princes St. Locals have even gotten married here. Delicious mains (pastas $14-22) served in a warm atmosphere that can be a festive prelude to a night in the Octagon. Most dishes come in medium or large sizes. Open daily 5:30pm-late. MC/V. ❸

Metro, 153 Lower Stuart St. (☎477 7084). An ode to the London Tube. Relax on the torn purple couches as you munch on comforting mains ($10-15). Waffles with bacon and bananas ($10.50) make for a sweet and savory late-night snack. Open M-Th and Su 8am-midnight, F-Sa 8am-2am. Kitchen open 8am-10pm daily. ❷

Jizo, 56 Princes St. (☎479 2692). Dark, stylized interior and slow jazz exude chic as business types and families enjoy high-quality Japanese food. The sushi main ($15.50) defines fresh. Open M-Th 11:30am-9pm, F 11:30am-9:30pm, Sa 5-9:30pm. ❷

Apsara, 380 George St. (☎477 1628), opposite Albert Arms. The big Cambodian noodle soups ($7) warm you from the inside out, and the curry veggies with coconut milk served over rice ($6) are delicious and filling. Open M-Sa 11am-9pm, Su 3pm-9pm. ❶

Barakah, 12 the Octagon, (☎477 3776), on the corner of Lower Stuart St. Enjoy classic tapas dishes ($5-8) in an indoor/outdoor setting on the Octagon. Open daily 10am-late. Kitchen closes 9pm. Brunch 10am-2pm. ❹

Percolater, 142 Lower Stuart St. (☎477 5462), just below the Octagon. Crystal chandeliers add glamor to the otherwise bland decor at Percolater, which makes its mark with excellent fair-trade coffee ($3) and sandwiches ($9-10). Open M-Th and Su 9am-10pm, F-Sa 9am-midnight. ❶

Tangenté, 111 Moray Pl. (☎477 0232), left off Upper Stuart St., 1 block past the Octagon. Settle into this aromatic, family-friendly restaurant. Brunch specials $9-17. Dinner mains from $17. Open daily 8am-3pm; F-Sa nights also open for dinner. MC/V. ❷

Tuatara Pizza, 72 Ardmore St. (☎443 8186). The scent of baked bread and gourmet pizzas fills the air at this ski bum favorite (large pizzas $32; not-so-large $17). Also offers a healthy nightlife scene (beer $5, shots $6) around the bar and pool tables. Open daily 5-11pm or midnight; later in winter. ❸

⌘ CAFES

Cafes cover nearly every block in Dunedin (even the McDonald's has a McCafe).

Arc, 135 High St. (☎474 1135), 1 block from Princes St. Vegetarian, free-trade, and even vegan in a pinch, this bohemian cooperative and iconic Dunedin hangout serves coffee, wines, and beer ($4), as well as baked snacks ($4) and mains ($8-12). 25min. of free Internet. Frequent live music in the back room. Pint night Tu 8pm-midnight ($2 cover; pints $2). Open M-Sa 10am-late. ❶

Modaks Espresso, 339 George St. (☎477 6563). Recover from the previous night's revelry with a strong espresso ($3) at this alternative establishment. Brick walls, dim lighting, and bass-heavy beats contribute to a self-consciously chill atmosphere. Open daily 8am-6pm. ❶

Governors Cafe, 438 George St. (☎477 6871). Midway between the university and downtown, Governor's has been a Dunedin landmark for more than 30 years. Famous banana splits with kiwifruit $7.50. Open M-W 8am-10pm, Th 8am-11pm, F-Sa 8am-midnight; Dec.-Feb. 9am-10pm. ❶

⊙ SIGHTS

SPEIGHT'S BREWERY HERITAGE TOUR AND MUSEUM. A 1½hr. tour takes you through the history of beer-making from Egyptian ales to modern microbrews. Judge the "Pride of the South" for yourself with free samples after the tour. Don't miss the tap outside offering free Speight's spring water from deep underneath the brewery. (☎477 7697. 4-5 tours per day M-Th until 7pm and Sa-Su until 4pm. Extra tours in summer. Bookings essential. $17, students $14.)

CADBURY CHOCOLATE TOURS. The barons of British chocolate have had a strong following in New Zealand for the past century. The 45min. tour ends with a surprise that will leave your inner Willy Wonka hungry for more. (280 Cumberland St., across from Countdown. ☎0800 223 287. Tours every 30min. 9am-7pm; Apr.-Dec. 9am-3:30pm. Bookings essential. $16, students $14.)

OTAGO MUSEUM. This extensive museum takes an in-depth look at the culture and natural history of Otago. The "Southern Lands, Southern People" gallery provides a thorough introduction to the region. Don't miss the giant Maori war canoe on the 2nd fl. (On the green on Great King St. between Albany and Union St. ☎474 7474; www.otagomuseum.govt.nz. Open daily 10am-5pm. Daily tours 11:30am and 3:30pm. Museum free; suggested donation $5. Tours $10.)

OTAGO SETTLERS MUSEUM. This museum is a multicultural tribute to the hardy men and women who tamed New Zealand's frontier. Ride the giant Penny Farthing bicycle inside the Art Deco bus station adjacent to the museum. The brand-new Chinese gardens, located behind the museum, are set to open in mid-2008. (31 Queens Gardens, down Dowling St. ☎477 4000. Open daily 10am-5pm.)

OLVESTON. Built in 1904, this perfectly preserved Edwardian mansion still feels lived-in. The benefactor's will stipulates that anyone may tickle the ivories of the 1906 Steinway grand piano, so feel free to play. (42 Royal Terr. Take George St. to Pitt St., then follow Royal Terr. until you see it on the right. ☎477 3320. Admittance by guided tour only. 1hr. tours at 9:30, 10:45am, noon, 1:30, 2:45, and 4pm. $14.50, students $13.50.)

DUNEDIN PUBLIC ART GALLERY. Dunedin's public gallery is a captivating work of modern art in itself. Rooms showcasing contemporary art open onto a minimalist foyer. The gallery houses a collection of Renaissance and Japanese works, as well as an archive and viewing area for New Zealand films. (In the Octagon. ☎474 3240; www.dunedin.art.museum. Open daily 10am-5pm. Free.)

CHURCHES. The Gothic Revival churches established by early Scottish residents are worth a look, especially the **First Church of Otago**, with its rose window and vaulted wood ceiling. (Down Moray Pl. from Princes St.) **St. Paul's**, in the Octagon, has the only stone-vaulted ceiling in New Zealand and organ with 3500 pipes.

BALDWIN STREET. The steepest street in the world. Stop by the pub at the bottom of the street to "earn" a certificate commemorating your victory in the battle against gravity ($2). The time to beat is about 2min. round-trip, as determined by the annual February "Gutbuster" race. (Take Great King St. north until it becomes North Rd. Baldwin St. is the 10th street on the right. The Normanby bus passes right by it, $2.)

BOTANIC GARDENS. Established in 1863, Dunedin's extensive gardens are arguably the best in the country. The annual **Rhododendron Festival** is world-renowned in botanic circles (usually held in Nov.). picnickers can grab a sandwich ($9.50) or a crepe at **Croque-O-Dile Espresso ❶**, (☎477 5455), in the Gardens. (Take any city bus from the Octagon down George St. or walk from the University on Leith St North. Alternate entrance off Opoho St. ☎477 0026. Information center and cafe open daily 9:30am-4:30pm. Park open dawn to dusk.) **Signal Hill** is a great place to stargaze and admire the lights of the city below. (Accessible off Opoho Rd. on the northern side of the Gardens. Free.)

▟ OUTDOOR ACTIVITIES

BEACHES. One of the best local walks, the track to ▓**Tunnel Beach** is accessible only at low tide. The hike leads through a century-old tunnel onto a secluded beach. The tunnel was built by businessman John Cargill for his young daughter. Legend has it that she drowned on her first trip to the beach. But don't let that stop you. *(Take the Corstophine bus from the Octagon to Stenhope Cres., then walk down Blackhead/Middleton Rd. By car, take Princes St., then make a right on King Edward St. Then turn right on Hillside Rd., left in the roundabout, and then right onto Easther Cres., which becomes Middleton Rd. Tunnel Beach Road is on the left after about 5km. 1hr. round-trip walk from the trailhead.)* **St. Clair Beach,** along with nearby **St. Kilda,** is the city's primary surf spot. *(Take the bus from the Octagon to St. Clair. By car, follow Tunnel Beach directions above until the roundabout. Follow Hillside Rd. as it becomes Forbury Rd., which leads to St. Clair Esplanade.)*

TAIERI GORGE RAILWAY. The railway travels over spectacular gorges, into native forests, through tunnels, and across viaducts en route to Pukerangi. *(☎477 4449; www.taieri.co.nz. Departs from the railway station Oct.-Apr. 9:30am and 2:30pm; May-Sept. 12:30pm. 4hr. Free bike transport. $67, backpackers and students $53.60. AmEx/MC/V.)*

OTAGO CENTRAL RAIL TRAIL. Stretching 152km between Middlemarch and Clyde, this historic trail follows the course of the now-defunct Otago Central Railway. *(The trail takes 2-5 days biking or 5-7 days walking, but can be traveled in segments. Take the Taieri George Railway to Pukerangi, 15km from Middlemarch. $43.)*

WALKS AND RIDES. The 4km track to **Mt. Cargill** opens onto a view of the harbor. Another 1hr. tramp will take you to the spires of the **Organ Pipes.** *(Take Normandy bus to Norwood St. $2. Walk to Bethunes Gully. 3½hr. round-trip.)* A bike path follows **Thomas Burns Street,** intersecting Wharf St. toward the Otago Peninsula—look for blue and white signs. *(To access the path, cross the footbridge to the right of the train station.)* **Hare Hill Horse Treks** offers beach and hillside rides overlooking the harbor. *(Take the city bus from the Octagon to Port Chalmers. $3.40. From there you can call for free pickup. ☎472 8496. Scenic Harbour Ride $50, 3hr. Beach Ride $80, Full-day $120, Overnight Escape $250.)*

🎵 ENTERTAINMENT

Check **The Otago Daily Times** for screenings or check **Fink** online (www.fink.net.nz) for entertainment listings. **The Fortune Theatre Company,** 231 Stuart St., hosts several professional acts throughout the year. *(☎477 8323; www.fortunetheatre.co.nz.)* Box office open M 10:30am-5pm, Tu 10:30am-6pm, W-F 10:30am-8pm, Sa 4:30-8pm, Su 1:30-4pm. Tickets prices vary. The stately **Regent** in the Octagon is home to the **New Zealand International Film Festival** in August; it also hosts several traveling shows throughout the year. *(☎477 8597. Box office open M-F 9am-5:30pm, Sa 10:30am-1pm.)* The **Metro Cinema,** on Moray Pl. behind the municipal chambers, shows foreign and independent films. *(☎474 3350; www.metrocinema.co.nz. $10, students $8.50; matinees $7.)* For a mix of big budget and independent films, head to **Rialto,** 11 Moray Pl. *(☎474 2200. $10-14. M-F $2 student discount.)*

🍸 NIGHTLIFE

Dunedin has its fair share of rocking-until-6am student hangouts, but for a chiller evening, head to one of the many pubs or clubs in the Octagon. Info on Dunedin's nightlife is in **Fink** or **Deadline,** both published weekly.

PUBS

Isis Lounge, 68 Princes St. (☎477 8001), in the Octagon. The house combo at this piano bar dishes out an mix of tunes on most nights. Slide into the suede chairs and enjoy happy hour from 10-11pm (cocktails $6; F also 5:30-6:30pm). House combo Tu, Th and F nights. W jazz. Sa guest artists. Open Tu-Th and Sa 6pm-late, F 5:30pm-late.

Pequeño, in the Savoy on Lower Moray Pl. (☎473 1194), under Etrusco, in the Octagon. Old-fashioned lamps and a brick fireplace lend easy sophistication to a place where many people spend their whole night. Classic mixed drinks $15. Open Tu-Sa 5pm-late.

XIIB (Twelve Below), Lower Moray Pl. (☎474 5055; www.bennu.co.nz), on the corner of Princes St. under Bennu; enter either through Bennu. This chill addition to the scene is an old-school soul lounge inside and out. W Funk, Th Soul and Reggae. Cocktails $14. Open W-Sa 8pm-late.

Captain Cook (☎474 1935), at the corner of Albany and Great King St. Near campus. Even North Islanders have stories about this varsity pub/club with pool tables and throbbing dance music (from 10pm W-Sa nights). Fans watch games on the big screens in the massive, enclosed beer garden. Open M-Sa 11am-late, Su noon-8pm.

CLUBS

Bath St., 1 Bath St. (☎477 6750), across from the Common Room in the Octagon. Alternative types flock here for the leather couches and the best sound system in New Zealand, as do some of the hottest DJs (Tu-Sa). The water gets hot around 1am. Cover $5, $20 for big-name acts. Open Tu-Sa from 10pm.

The Monkey Bar, 65 Hanover St. (☎477 1637), on the corner of Hanover and Great King St. No less than 9 disco balls cast their heavenly light on the organ pipes and high ceilings of this church-turned-nightclub, which can pack in up to 1000 students on particularly sinful evenings. 2-for-1 drink card on entry. Open W-Sa 8pm-late.

10 Bar, 10 the Octagon (☎477 6310; info@10bar.co.nz), underneath Craft. Stairs behind the small entry on the Octagon lead to a 2-level underground lair, replete with pool tables, mod decor, video screens, and thumping beats. Enjoy $7.50 shooters such as "Martian Hard-On" and "Poke Both Holes." Dress to impress, or face rejection at the door. $5 cover on F-Sa after midnight. Open Th 8pm-late, F-Sa 8pm-later.

OTAGO PENINSULA ☎03

Extending 22km from Dunedin, the serene Otago Peninsula leaves the bustling city behind almost immediately. Yellow-eyed penguins, fur seals, sea lions, and royal albatross claim the area. The dramatic tip of the peninsula, **Taiaroa Head,** a 45min. drive from Dunedin, drops off crags and great swaths of billowing kelp.

⊏ TRANSPORTATION. The best way to experience the peninsula is by car, though the flat terrain and harborside travel make for an excellent bike ride although there is no bike lane. **Portobello Road,** the sinuous coastal route along the bay, is full of treacherous curves; the shoreline plays hide-and-seek behind roadside cliffs and is rarely more than a few meters from your car. Exercise caution while driving, and attempt to finish your travels before nightfall. **Citibus** runs daily service to Portobello (and Harrington Point on request) from Cumberland St. (Timetables and route plans can be obtained from the Dunedin i-Site.) **Back to Nature Tours** has intimate tours with knowledgeable guides. Free binoculars allow you to see nature in action. The tour ends at Sandfly Beach, where yellow-eyed penguins waddle up the cliff. (☎0800 477 0484; www.backtonaturetours.co.nz. 5hr. 1 per day. $69, backpackers $59. Free pickup.) **Elm Wildlife Tours** also provides small, in-depth walking wildlife excursions, which lead to a private beach. (☎0800 356 563; www.elmwildlifetours.co.nz. 6½hr. 1 per day, max. 10 people. $75, backpackers/YHA/student $63. Free pickup and binoculars.) **Newton Tours** offers package tours to Larnach Castle. (☎477 5577. Free pickup. $80.)

⌐◪ ACCOMMODATIONS AND FOOD. If you spend the night at the peninsula, **homestays** are a possibility. Costs vary, but the visitors center in Dunedin provides brochures and bookings. One farmstay that beats the cost curve is **McFarmers Backpackers (BBH) ❷,** 774 Portobello Rd., a former pottery studio with views of the harbor, plus bikes ($10) for rent (☎478 0389. Call about closings in June. Dorms $28; singles $38; doubles $52-62; tent sites $15.) **Portobello Village Tourist Park ❶**, in Portobello up Hereweka St., is a retreat midway between Dunedin and the albatross colony. The park is a good starting point for exploring the peninsula by bike. (☎478 0359; portobellopark@xtra.co.nz. Reception 8am-10:30pm. Backpacker rooms $55 for 2, $10 each extra person; 2-person tourist flats $85; tent sites $12, with power $14.) **Penguin Place ❷**, part of the Yellow-Eyed Penguin Reserve, has sparsely furnished rooms with small beds but terrific views of the bay. Ask for a harborside room. (☎478 0286. $20 per person. MC/V.)

Food options on the peninsula are limited, but one reasonable choice is the **1908 Cafe ❸**, 7 Harrington Point Rd., in sleepy Portobello. The cafe offers standard mains in a casual setting (lunch $9-14, dinner $18-26). (☎478 0801. Open daily noon-2pm and 6pm-late; in winter Th-F 11am-2:30pm, Sa-Su 11:30am-2:30pm and 6pm-late.) The **Portobello Store**, on Portobello Rd. at the junction with the road to the aquarium, stocks limited groceries. (☎478 0555. Open M-W 7:30am-7:30pm, Th-F 7:30am-8pm, Sa 8am-8pm, Su 8:30am-7:30am.)

 ALBATROSS IN FLIGHT. Though the Royal Albatross Center is the surest way to see the birds in their home environment, visitors to Taiaroa Head in the early evening can sometimes find albatross circling above the center. There is also a healthy seagull population on the peninsula; binoculars may help distinguish the fake from the flock.

🦅 **WILDLIFE.** At the **Taiaroa Royal Albatross Colony,** you'll learn more than you had previously believed possible about these massive birds. Taiaroa is the only mainland albatross colony on earth; these wanderers fledge and rear their young here, then circumnavigate the globe without landing until they return. Entrance to the **Royal Albatross Centre,** which houses displays and live TV coverage of the birds' activities is by donation, but the educational tour and observatory viewing—your best bets to see a live bird—are costly. (☎478 0499. Open Oct.-Apr. daily 8:30am-8:30pm; May-Sept. daily 9am-5pm. No tours or viewing Sept. 16-Nov. 24 due to hatching season. Observing an albatross in flight is not guaranteed. $30, families $74, children $14.) **Monarch Wildlife Cruises** runs a skiff from Wellers Rock near the head, providing views of massive chimney roosts and rare cormorants. (☎477 4276; www.wildlife.co.nz. Albatross sighting or 2nd trip free. 5 per day in summer, 2 per day in winter. $35, children $10. Binoculars and jackets provided. Transport from Dunedin, some including admission to other Peninsula sights, $75-115.)

Rare yellow-eyed penguins (*hoiho*) have, with a little human assistance, recolonized **Penguin Beach** just beyond Taiaroa Head. Once as scarce as the Giant Panda, the penguins have begun a roaring comeback, boosting the local eco-tourism industry with each new hatching. The Reid family runs 🦩**Nature's Wonders** wildlife tours, a short drive past the Albatross Colony. Led by father Perry, the Reid children whisk guests to remote wildlife sanctuaries on fully amphibious 8WD vehicles called ARGOs. (☎0800 246 446. Guided tours daily at frequent intervals. 10:15am-dusk. Bookings essential. $45, children $40.) At the **Yellow-Eyed Penguin Conservation Reserve,** part of Penguin Place, 5min. before the Albatross Centre, camouflaged trenches affords views of the penguins from just a few meters away. (☎478 0286. 1½hr. tours every 30min. Oct.-Apr. from 10:15am-7:15pm; May-Sept. during the last 3hr. of daylight. $33, children $12. Bookings essential in summer.)

📷 🚣 **SIGHTS AND OUTDOOR ACTIVITIES.** Rent bikes and kayaks from **Peninsula Bike and Kayak,** 13 McCauley Rd., to get up close and personal with Otago's rocky coastline. Coming from Dunedin, turn right at the second Beaconfield Rd. by the playground, and then left onto McCauley Rd. (☎478 0724; 3hr. kayak tours to Taiaroa Head $75. Bikes $25 per half-day; $35 full-day. Call ahead.) About 2.5km up a dirt road from town in Portobello, the University of Otago runs the **New Zealand Marine Studies Centre.** Doubling as a research center for marine biologists and an aquarium open to the public, the small display showcases marine animals and ecosystems. (☎479 5826; www.marine.ac.nz. Open daily noon-4:30pm. Feedings W and Sa 2:30pm. $8, children $4. Guided tour daily 10:30am. $16/8.)

Larnach Castle is a 43-room architectural marvel, though the story behind the castle is even more intriguing. The virile Mr. Larnach, with six children by his first wife alone, eventually married his third wife when he was 57. Upon learning of her reputed affair with his second son, Larnach committed suicide in the Parliament building in Wellington and purportedly haunts it to this day. Take a self-guided tour through the various rooms of the castle, including the inlaid mahogany, teak, and kauri foyer. (☎476 1616. $20, children $8. Gardens $10, children $2.40.) To get there, you can take the Citibus (see p. 367) to McAndrew Bay Stop and hike up a steep trail to High Cliff Rd. Follow this to the left until Camp Rd., which leads to the castle. Halfway down the peninsula and three kilometers up the winding Castlewood Rd., the aptly named **High Cliff Road** is an alternate route with views of the south side of the peninsula. **Broad Bay Equestrian,** based in Broad Bay just before Portobello, embarks on ride through the hillsides and up to the castle. (☎478 0892. Turn right off Portobello Rd. onto Camp St., the driveway is the 2nd on the right. $40 for castle, $35 for other trips. Call ahead, as all tour guides work day jobs.)

OAMARU ☎03

While the rest of the country counts sheep to fall asleep, the folks in Oamaru (OH-ma roo; pop. 12,500) picture the nightly return of their penguins. Known primarily for its blue penguin colony (the smallest penguins in the world), this town can easily entertain visitors who spend a day browsing antiques and collectables in the whitestone historic district or exploring nearby natural attractions.

▤ TRANSPORTATION. Lagonda Coach Travel and Bus Stop, 191 Thames St. (☎434 8716), is the local bus station. The cheapest and fastest bus on SH1, the **Atomic Shuttle** (☎322 8883), goes to Christchurch (3½hr., 2 per day, $30) and Dunedin (1¾hr., 2 per day, $20). **InterCity,** which offers discounted rates for advanced booking, also heads to Christchurch (3½hr., 2 per day, $37; extra late bus on F and Su) and Dunedin (2¼hr., 2 per day, $22). Although *Let's Go* does not recommend hitchhiking, hitchers report heading up Severn St. to the edge of town. The upper end of Thames St. is reportedly the best place for a ride north.

▨ ORIENTATION AND PRACTICAL INFORMATION. SH1 follows **Thames Street** into the heart of downtown Oamaru. The **Oamaru i-Site,** 1 Thames St., is on the left side of Thames St. after the train tracks. By car, continue straight after SH1 veers right onto Severn St.; walking from the bus stop, turn left onto Thames St. and continue 10min. The helpful staff has maps and brochures ($1-2) for nearby DOC attractions. (☎434 1656. Open Nov.-Mar. M-F 9am-6pm, Sa-Su 9:30am-6pm; Apr.-Oct. M-F 9am-5pm, Sa-Su 10am-4pm.) From the visitors center, turn left onto Itchen St. and then follow Tyne St. around to the right to reach the **historic district.** Continue on Tyne St. and turn left on Waterfront Rd. to get to the **Blue Penguin Colony.** The **BNZ,** 149 Thames St. (☎434 3100), one block left from the bus station, has a **24hr. ATM.** (Open M and Th-F 9am-4:30pm, Tu-W 9:30am-4:30pm.) Other services include: the **police station** (☎433 1400), off Severn St.; the **pharmacy,** 171 Thames St. (☎434 8315; open M-F 8am-6pm,

Sa 10am-5pm, Su 11am-12pm and 5-5:30pm); the **hospital,** 8 Steward St. (☎433 0290), two blocks before the visitors center on the right; **Internet** at Small Bytes Computing, 187 Thames St. (☎434 8490; $5 for 1st 30min., $8 per hr.; open M-F 9am-5pm); the **Oamaru Public Library,** 62 Thames St., (☎434 1650; open M-W and F 9:30am-5:30pm, Th 10am-5:30pm, Sa 10am-12:30pm); the **post office,** at Severn and Coquet St. (☎433 1190; open M-F 8:30am-5pm).

⌂ ☂ ACCOMMODATIONS AND CAMPING. While accommodations in Oamaru are near town center, the car-accessible hostels along the coast are some of the finest in the country. Housed in a historic 1867 hotel, ▧**Empire Backpackers (BBH) ❷,** 13 Thames St., combines a convenient location with Victorian charm. Listen for the blue penguins that sometimes roost near the foundation. (☎434 3446; www.empirebackpackersoamaru.co.nz. Free Internet. Dorms $20; singles $33; twins and doubles $50. $3 BBH discount.) Those who make the uphill trek from the Oamaru i-Site to **Swaggers Backpackers (BBH) ❷,** 25 Wansbeck St., at the intersection with Wharfe St., are rewarded with a fine view of the harbor and the warmth of a quiet home. (☎434 9999; swaggers@es.co.nz. Reception 8am-1pm and 4-6pm. Reservations recommended in summer. Dorms $21; singles $31, twins and doubles $45. $3 BBH discount.) The **Red Kettle Hostel (YHA) ❷,** Cross and Reed St., is a simple, seasonal hostel with a large common area. (☎434 5008. Reception 8:30-12:30pm and 4-8:30pm. Closed June-Aug. Dorms $24; twins and doubles $58. $3 YHA discount.) The **Oamaru Top 10 Holiday Park ❶,** up Chelmer St., is within walking distance of the center of town, adjacent to the Botanic Gardens and a small store. (☎434 7666 or 0800 280 202; www.oamarutop10.co.nz. Tent sites $14. Cabins $45 for 1, $20 per extra person; kitchen units $70; self-contained units $90.)

◖◗ FOOD AND NIGHTLIFE. Food in Oamaru gets better and more expensive as you approach the historic district. Those on a budget should stop in at **Countdown** supermarket, at the Thames and Severn St. split. (Open 7am-9pm daily.) **Emma's Cafe ❶,** 30 Thames St., is a homey eatery, where all-day breakfast ($4-15) is served. (☎434 1165. Open M-F 9am-5pm, Sa-Su 9am-4pm.) Oamaru's oldest establishment, the **Star and Garter ❸,** 9 Itchen St., dishes out country mains ($19-27) in giant portions. (☎434 5246. Open M-Sa 6-9:30pm, Su 11:30am-3pm.)

Although Oamaru's nightly post-penguin crowd quickly flocks home, local favorite **The Last Post ❷,** across from Empire Backpackers, is licensed until 3am and is generally open until midnight. Split some nachos ($8.50) with a friend or two, or take your drink to the "Gaming Parlour" in the back. (☎434 8080. Extensive wine list. Open 11am-midnight. Kitchen closes at 9pm.) Rounding out Oamaru's dismal late night offerings is dance club/billiard hall **The Globe,** at Thames and Coquet St.—you'll hear it before you see it. (Open Th-Sa 9pm-around 2am.)

◙ ⚐ SIGHTS AND OUTDOOR ACTIVITIES. You can reach the **Oamaru Blue Penguin Colony** by walking south from the center of town to Waterfront Rd. or via Coastline Tours (see below). Arrive well before dusk to secure a prime seat for the nightly penguin triathlon: penguins swim the waves, climb the rock wall, and scurry to the nest box. Cameras are not permitted, but bring warm clothes and binoculars. (☎433 1195; www.penguins.co.nz. Viewing $17.50, students and BBH/VIP members $15.75, children $6. Call ahead for "Behind the Scenes" daytime tours of nest boxes, $10.) In order to see the larger yellow-eyed penguins, head to **Bushey Beach** around two hours before dusk. This is the northernmost penguin colony in the world. The population in Oamaru is growing slowly, despite strains of avian diphtheria that swept through in recent years, at times killing every chick in the colony. You can drive down Bushey Beach Rd. yourself, or take a tour of both penguin colonies through **Coastline Tours.** (☎434 7744 or 027 256 5651; www.coastline-tours.co.nz. 2½hr. $25; admission to the blue penguin colony included. $3 YHA and BBH discounts.) Former manager of the blue penguin center **Denis Dove** gives 12-person tours coming within five feet of the penguins' nest sites. (Ask at the visitors center for Denis's phone number and times. Oct.-Feb. Tours 45min. $13.)

While Oamaru's attractions center on its smallest feathery inhabitants, there's plenty to do in town until the penguins come home. The **historic district**, with its mix of stately, restored buildings and dilapidated facades, surrounds Harbour and Tyne St. where the **Sunday market** is open 9am-4pm. Harbour St. resembles nothing so much as a Victorian ghost town, complete with employees clad in period garb. One of the newest additions to the historic district is **The Barrel House**, 14-16 Harbour St., which features a general store with local wines, beers, and whiskies and an attached 760-barrel whiskey bar. Guided 30min. tours ($15) of the whiskey aging facility, built from local stones and giant rimu beams, include a few whiskey samples at the end. (☎434 8842. 3- whiskey tasting $5. Open daily 10am-5:30pm.) Browse for second-hand books or relax on one of the tiger-mauled love seats at **Slightly Foxed**, 11 Tyne St., a converted warehouse. (☎434 2155. Open M-Sa 10am-5:30pm, Su 10am-4pm; closes 1hr. earlier in May-September. AmEx/MC/V.) The Oamaru i-Site arranges one hour **historic tours** of the district that peer inside the unrestored structures (ask for times and prices). **North Otago Museum**, 60 Thames St. (☎434 1652; open M-F 10:30am-4:30pm, Sa 10am-1pm, Su 1-4:30pm; free), and the **Forrester Gallery**, 9 Thames St. inside the old "Bank of New South Wales," (☎434 1653; open daily 10:30am-4:30pm; free) make worthwhile rainy-day activities. For the few sunny days, **Oamaru Gardens**, on Severn St., features rhododendron and rose gardens, and no trip to the Gardens should end without a visit to the exotic bird enclosures nestled in the back. (Open dawn to dusk. Free.)

OTAGO COAST ROAD   ☎03

The area surrounding Oamaru offers coastline attractions and plentiful wildlife viewing. Head south toward Dunedin on the **Coast Road**. This scenic route, accessible by following Wharfe St. to Kakanui Beach Rd., winds along the shore through farms and meets SH1 about 30km south of Oamaru. Only 4km south of Oamaru, ▧**Old Bones Backpackers (BBH) ❸**, on Beach Rd. by the moa statue. Named for New Zealand's first archeological dig on the same site, Old Bones may want to make you dig in for a while, too. A total of 16 beds center around a modern kitchen and living room. (☎434 8115; www.oldbones.co.nz. Doubles or twins $60, single $42.50. $2.50 off with BBH. Closed June-Aug. Cash only.) A few kilometers further down the road, you can rest at **Coastal Backpackers (BBH) ❷**, a couple of bunkhouses on a family farm. Choose from free bikes and bodyboards or take a short walk to the deserted beach to see Hector's dolphins. The wee pub pours drafts well into the night for all 9 guests. (☎439 5411; www.coastalbackpacker.co.nz. Reception until 8pm unless arranged by phone. Dorms $25; doubles $46. $2 BBH discount. Cash only.) As the scenic drive returns to SH1, take a right and backtrack less than one kilometer to visit the ▧**Olive Grove Lodge ❷**, New Zealand's only organic hostel. (☎439 5830; www.olivebranch.co.nz. 4-bed dorms $25, doubles $60; tent sites $12 per person. Book ahead. $3 BBH discount.) After returning to SH1, stop in the hilltop town of Hampden for the award-winning fried blue cod and chips ($6) at ▧**Big Ev's Takeaways ❶**, on the highway. Light on the wallet and the waistline, the place has been commended by the Heart Foundation for low-fat frying practices. (☎439 4744. Open Tu-Su 10am-8pm and M on holidays.)

South of Hampden on SH1, the small hamlet of **Moeraki** and the nearby 60 million-year-old **Moeraki Boulders** lie about 40km from Oamaru. The stones are spherical, resembling cast-off marbles from a game between giants. Early European visitors to the famed site snatched up the smaller boulders for themselves; only 1-2m high specimens remain for viewing, preferably done at low tide, lest you lose your marbles. To reach the boulders, follow signs from SH1. (20min. beach walk to the boulders; $2). One of the oldest European settlements in New Zealand, Moeraki itself is a sleepy fishing village just south of the boulders. **Coastline Tours** (see **Sights and Outdoor Activities,** p. 370) runs 3½hr. tours to the boulders from Oamaru ($35). The **Moeraki Village Holiday Park ❶**, in town a 45min. walk from the boulders, has immaculate restrooms, tent sites with a nice (if exposed) harbor view, a market with a wine and beer license, and gas. (☎439 4759; moerakivillageholidaypark@xtra.co.nz. Tent sites $11, with power $22; 2-person cabins $40-45.) Heading sound on Lighthouse Rd. brings you to the historic Moeraki lighthouse at **Kaitiki Point.** Follow trails from the lighthouse to sneak a peek at penguins in a more tranquil setting than Oamaru. The point is also a popular fishing location, with anglers pulling in salmon from surf-cast lines. **Shag Point,** 11km south of Moeraki Boulders off SH1, is home to colonies of the New Zealand fur seal and Stewart Island shag.

WAIMATE   ☎03

Nestled midway between Timaru and Oamaru, the town of Waimate (Why-MATEY; pop. 2,700) lies at the heart of "Wallaby Country" and offers the kind of small-town quirks that lonely drivers on SH1 appreciate. Instead of checking in at the visitor center for info, stop by the "wallaby wander" at **EnkleDooVery Korna,** just north of town on SH82, where affable owner Gwen lets you get up close and personal with her brood of over 40 tame, hand-raised wallabies. Grab a handful of feed and puzzle over the group known as "The Luckless Trifecta." Gwen's other babies include ferrets, enormous rabbits, peacocks, and Muffin—the differently-abled pony. (☎689 7197; cdtaxidermysafari@xtra.co.nz. Open late Sept.-May 10am-5pm, or by appointment.) **Kelcey's Bush Animal Park,** 7km up Mill Rd. from downtown Waimate, displays a wide range of animals in a zoo-like setting. Ask about one-hour guided nighttime bush walks through the habitat of wild wallabies. (☎689 8057; www.kiwicamps.com. Feeding tours daily 9am and 3:30pm. Bush walks limited to 5 people. Admission $5. Tours $12. On-site camping facilities available; call ahead for prices and availability.) Just a few blocks down High St. from the center of town, the **Hollies Heritage Homestead,** 232 High St., provides an out-of-time variation on colonial British culture. Owners Tim and Gail have lovingly refurbished an 1860s farm house, right down to the kitchen stove, upon which they prepare fresh scones and tea. Be sure to ask Poppy the parrot about his independent film career. (☎689 7576. Open daily 10am-6pm or by appointment. $8, under 12 $4; tea $3.50.) Outside of town to the west, Waimate offers a few worthwhile walks and birding opportunities. The **information center** (☎689 7771; www.waimate.org.nz), 75 Queen St., can provide a good map of the area and descriptions of the local walks. (Open M-F 9am-5pm, Sa-Su 10am-2pm.)

Make sure to stop by **The Berry Barn** (☎689 8749) around the corner from Gwen on SH82 for some of Waimate's famous strawberries and fresh fruit ice cream ($3.50; in summer only), mixed as you wait. For a true taste of Waimate, dare to sample a wallaby pie ($3.50) at the **Savoy Tea Rooms**, 59 Queen St., next to the visitor center. (☎689 7147; wallaby pie usually sells out by midday.)

Waimate is best seen from the **White Horse Lookout,** a 60 ft. concrete slab Clydesdale embedded in the hillside commemorating the packhorses which helped to settle the region. The monument can be reached on foot via the steep two and a half hour **Waimate Walkway,** or by car on a seven kilometer unpaved road. (Take a left on Mill Rd. from Queen St. and follow signs to Parkers Rd. and Centrewood Park.) Although much of the native forest around Waimate was wiped out in an 1878 fire, good walks remain. Turn right onto Parsonage Rd. as you come into town on SH82 and follow signs for Methodist Camp to **Gunn's Bush,** a moderately strenuous 1½hr. hike under moss-draped Totara trees. **Kelsey's Bush,** 3km past the Animal Park, offers a 10min. trail to a secluded waterfall overlook, as well as company from the occasional pheasant, escaped from a nearby safari park. Maps for both walks are available at the information center (see above).

THE SOUTHERN LAKES

Among the most beautiful areas of New Zealand, the Southern Lakes region spreads across valleys and lakes carved out ages ago by glaciers. The area seduces travelers to tempt fate in Queenstown, unwind in Wanaka, or tackle nature in sleepy Glenorchy. With summer bringing opportunities for adventure and winter beckoning skiers to the slopes, a visit to the Southern Lakes is never out of season.

QUEENSTOWN ☎03

Arguably the globe's adventure capital, Queenstown (pop. 15,000) has long been the granddaddy of the adrenaline world. Other Kiwis denounce Queenstown's consumerism, but the visitors who pack this outdoor mecca come for good reason; the arresting beauty of the lake and The Remarkables mountain range is undeniable. Linger long enough and the infectious excitement that hangs in the air will entice you to try the unimaginable, the outrageous, and the downright insane. Linger too long, however, and you may need to get a job before your wallet recovers enough to leave again. Whether it's a first time bungy jumper, or an adventure veteran shouting with glee, there's always a faint scream in the air in Queenstown.

⌐ TRANSPORTATION

Flights: The **airport** is 6km east of town in Frankton. **Air New Zealand,** 8 Church St. (☎441 1900 or 0800 737 000) has flights to **Auckland** (1¾hr., 3 per day, from $139), and to **Wellington** (1¾hr., 10 per day, from $149) via **Christchurch** (1hr., 8 per day, from $89). Booking office open M-F 9am-5pm, Sa 10am-1pm. Several airlines do scenic flights to **Milford Sound** (p. 382). To reach the airport, take **Connectabus** (☎441 4471; www.connectabus.com) from the McDonald's on Camp St. (every 20-35min. 7:15am-11:15pm, $6) or **Super Shuttle** (☎442 3639 or 0800 748 885; www.supershuttle.co.nz; $14). Taxis to the airport run approximately $25.

Buses: Buses depart from Camp St. beside the Queenstown i-Site or from "The Station" on Shotover St. **InterCity** (☎442 4922), **Atomic Shuttles** (☎322 8883), and **Southern Link** (☎358 8355) head to **Christchurch** (6-8½hr., 3 per day, $45-50). **Wanaka Connexions** (☎443 9122) goes to **Dunedin,** as do Atomic and InterCity, which have lower fares (4-5hr., 3 per day, $35-45). **Topline Tours** (☎249 8059 or 0508 832 628) offers the cheapest service to **Te Anau** (2¼hr.; 10am; $30). Wanaka Connexions and **Tracknet** (☎249 7777) go to **Invercargill** (2½-3hr., 2 per day, $42-45). Atomic Shuttles, Southern Link, and Wanaka Connexions head frequently to **Wanaka** (1½hr., $25).

Regional Shuttles: The Information and Track Centre, 37 Shotover St. (☎442 9708; www.infotrack.co.nz), books trips through **Backpacker Express** to the **Routeburn, Rees-Dart** and **Greenstone and Caples Tracks** (2hr., 2-3 per day, $36-37; May-Oct. on demand). They also book shuttles returning to Queenstown from **The Divide** (2 per day, $67), including an option to have a **Milford Sound** cruise on the way back (approx. 9hr., 10:45am, $145). Open daily 7am-9pm.

Ski Shuttles: Ski Shuttle (☎442 8106) runs to: **Coronet Peak** (30min., 3 per day, $25); **The Remarkables** (1hr., 3 per day, $25). **Ski Link** (☎441 8395) offers the same service at comparable prices and is the only shuttle that services night skiing. The **Info and Track Centre** (☎442 9708) runs shuttles to Cardrona for $40 and has other options as well. Call ahead for information. **AA Alpine Taxis** (☎442 6666) runs to Coronet Peak (30min., $55 in car; $65 in van) and The Remarkables (45-50min., $85 in car; $100 in van). Their van seats up to 11 people with no change in price.

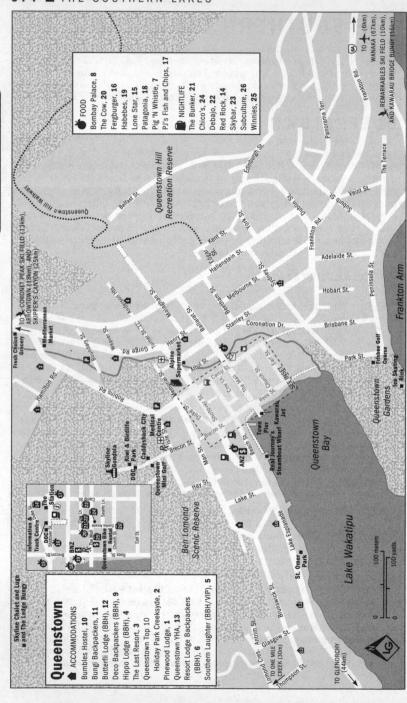

OTAGO

FOOD
Bombay Palace, **8**
The Cow, **20**
Fergburger, **16**
Habebes, **19**
Lone Star, **15**
Patagonia, **18**
Pig 'N Whistle, **7**
PJ's Fish and Chips, **17**

NIGHTLIFE
The Bunker, **21**
Chico's, **24**
Debajo, **22**
Red Rock, **14**
Skybar, **23**
Subculture, **26**
Winnies, **25**

Queenstown

ACCOMMODATIONS
Bumbles Hostel, **10**
Bungi Backpackers, **11**
Butterfli Lodge (BBH), **12**
Deco Backpackers (BBH), **9**
Hippo Lodge (BBH), **4**
The Last Resort, **3**
Queenstown Top 10
   Holiday Park Creeksyde, **2**
Pinewood Lodge, **1**
Queenstown YHA, **13**
Resort Lodge Backpackers
   (BBH), **6**
Southern Laughter (BBH/VIP), **5**

Skyline Chalet and Luge
■ and The Ledge Bungy

TO CORONET PEAK SKI FIELD (13km),
ARROWTOWN (18km) AND
SKIPPER'S CANYON (25km)

Queenstown Hill Walkway

Queenstown Hill
Recreation Reserve

Belfast St.

Edinburgh St.

Panorama Terr.

Frankton Rd.

The Terrace

TO (6km)
WANAKA (67km)
REMARKABLES SKI FIELD (10km),
AND KAWARAU BRIDGE BUNGY(16km),

Veint St.

Suburb St.

Kent St.

Frankton Rd.

Adelaide St.

Peninsula St.

Hallenstein St.

Melbourne St.

Hobart St.

Stanley St.

Brisbane St.

Coronation Dr.

Park St.

Frankton Arm

Fresh Choice
Grocery

Mediterranean
Market

Hamilton Rd.

Robins Rd.

Gorge Rd.

Alpine
Supermarket

Athol St.

Camp St.

The Mall

Cow Ln.

Church St.

Reees St.

Queenstown
Gardens

Frisbee Golf
Course

Ice Skating
Rink

Skyline
Gondola

Kiwi & Birdlife
Park

DOC

Caddyshack City

Queenstown
Mini Golf

Medical
Centre

Isle St.

Brecon St.

Duke St.

Shotover St.

Mall St.

Beach St.

Town
Pier

Real Journey's
Steamboat Wharf
Jet

Kawarau
Jet

Queenstown
Bay

ANZ

Hay St.

Lake St.

Ben Lomond
Scenic Reserve

Lake Esplanade

St. Omer
Park

Lake Wakatipu

100 meters

100 yards

Information &
Track Centre

The
Station

DOC

BNZ

Queenstown Bike
Rental

Brecon St.

Camp St.

Shotover St.

Rees St.

Earl St.

Church St.

Lomond Cres.

Antrim St.

Brunswick St.

Glasgow St.

Thompson St.

TO ONE MILE
CREEK (30km)

TO GLENORCHY
(44km)

Local Buses: Connectabus (☎441 4471; www.connectabus.com) runs to local accommodations, Frankton, the airport and Arrowtown. Maps and schedules are available at the Queenstown i-Site. Single fares range $5-7, daypasses $10-13.

Taxis: AA Alpine Taxis (☎442 6666) and **Queenstown Taxis** (☎442 7788 or 0800 788 294) have 24hr. service.

Bike Rental: Queenstown Bike Hire (☎442 6039), on Marine Pde. near the lake, has a modest but cheap selection of bikes and kayaks. Bikes $10-15 per hr., $30-40 per day. Kayaks $12-20 per hr., $20-35 per 2hr. **Vertigo Bikes,** 4 Brecon St. (☎442 8378 or 0800 837 8446) has a larger selection and also provides helmets, trail maps, and a repair kit. Front suspension $29 per half-day, $45 full-day; high end front suspension $45/69; full suspension $45/69. Open daily 8am-7pm.

Car Rental: Pegasus Rental Cars (☎442 7176), at the top of The Mall, rents cars from $35 per day for reservations over 4 days and includes insurance and unlimited km. Open daily 9am-5:30pm. **Ace Rental Cars,** 35 Camp St. (☎441 3133 or 0800 002 203; www.acerentalcars.co.nz) offers cars from $39 per day for over 4 days with the same benefits. Discounts apply for longer hires. 21+. Open daily 8-5pm. **Queenstown Car Rentals,** 26b Shotover St. (☎442 9220). From $39 per day for rentals over 3 days. Round-trip to Queenstown rentals only. 21+. Open daily 8am-6pm.

Hitchhiking: While *Let's Go* doesn't recommend hitching, hitchers say getting to Glenorchy requires walking along the lake beyond the roundabout at One Mile Creek. Hitching to Milford is an unlikely prospect; it involves taking the Connectabus to Frankton and walking past the airport along the road to Te Anau.

◄█❓ ORIENTATION AND PRACTICAL INFORMATION

Queenstown's satellite towns include **Glenorchy** to the west (45min.) and **Arrowtown** to the northeast (30min.). Queenstown itself is very compact. Booking agencies, bars, and gear rental stores line **Shotover Street.** Shopping boutiques and restaurants are concentrated on **Beach Street** and **The Mall,** both of which run parallel to Shotover St. **Cow Lane,** an alleyway between Beach St. and The Mall, is an often overlooked local secret for late-night nightlife. Beach and **Rees Streets** both lead to the lakefront. The spine of **The Remarkables** mountain range runs south down the east side of **Lake Wakatipu,** and **Coronet Peak** eyes the lake over the town's north shoulder.

Visitors Center: Nearly every shop in town vends its own spin on local info. The official source is the **Queenstown i-Site** (☎442 4100 or 0800 668 888; www.queenstown-vacation.com), at the Clocktower Centre at the corner of Camp and Shotover St. Open daily Nov.-May 7:30am-6:30pm, June-Oct. 7:30am-6pm. The only other independent information centre on Shotover St. is the one inside the **Global Gossip** Internet cafe (see below). Two other good locations to know are the **Information and Track Centre,** 37 Shotover St. (☎442 9708) and **The Station** (☎442 5252), at the corner of Camp and Shotover St., which serve as the departure points for several adventure activities.

Department of Conservation (DOC): 37 Shotover St. (☎442 7935). Open Nov.-Apr. daily 8:30am-5pm. Closed in winter.

Banks and Currency Exchange: The Station (☎442 5252), at Camp and Shotover St., exchanges money. Open daily 10:30am-7:50pm. **BNZ,** 11-13 Rees St. (☎0800 800 468). Open M and Th-F 9am-8pm, Tu-W 9:30am-8pm, Sa-Su 10am-8pm. **ANZ,** 81 Beach St., near the waterfront. Open M-F 9am-4:30pm.

Work Opportunities: Queenstown's bars, restaurants, and accommodations are always looking for staff. The summer season lasts from Oct.-Apr. with high demand. Ski areas post job applications online at www.nzski.com in Feb., though work does not start until mid-June. If you show up in May or June looking for immediate work, you will have poor chances. Watch for help-wanted ads in shop windows. **Addstaff,** 14 The Mall (☎442 4307; www.addstaff.co.nz), is the local employment agency. If you decide to set up an interview, you must have a CV or resume and passport. Addstaff can help with IRD numbers and work permits, though it's best to complete them ahead of time; Queenstown is probably the only place in New Zealand where a standard work permit can be processed in 48 hours. Open M-F 9am-5pm. Two local newspapers, the weekly **Mirror** (W) and **Mountain Scene** (Th), available at kiosks around town, also list job availabilities.

Ski and Snowboard Rental: Browns, 39 Shotover St. and 4 Beach St. (☎442 4003; www.brownsnz.com), has the best skis. Ski, boot, and pole rental $40 per day. Open daily June-Oct. 7:30am-9pm; occupies same storefronts as Alpine Sports and Vertigo Bikes. **Alta,** 45 Camp St. (☎442 9330; www.snowboarder.co.nz), offers the best snowboards. Snowboard and boot rental $45 per day. Open daily 7:30am-9pm. Oct.-May 10am-7pm. **Outside Sports,** 36-38 Shotover St. (☎441 0074; www.outsidesports.co.nz). Ski, boot, and pole rental $52 per day. Snowboard and boot rental same price. Open daily 7:30am-9pm, in summer 8:30am-9pm.

Tramping Gear: Alpine Sports, 39 Shotover St. (☎442 7099; www.alpinesports.co.nz), rents the cheapest tramping gear in town. Tents $15 per day. Packs $5 per day. Sleeping bags $5 per day ($10 cleaning fee). Discounts for long-term rentals. Open daily 9am-8pm, June-Oct. 9am-7pm. The **Information and Track Centre** rents packs and bags for $7, but has no tents (see **Regional Shuttles,** p. 373). **Outside Sports** (see above) stocks an extensive selection of tramping gear with rentals as well. **Small Planet Sports,** 17 Shotover St. (☎442 6393), sells high-quality used tramping gear at bargain prices, plus rock climbing gear. Open daily 9am-7pm, June-Sept. 8am-8pm.

Police: 11 Camp St. (☎441 1600).

Medical Services: Wilkinson's Pharmacy (☎442 7313), at the corner of Rees St. and The Mall. Open daily 8:30am-10pm. May 8:30am-9pm. **Queenstown Medical Centre,** 9 Isle St. (☎441 0500). Open daily 8am-6pm.

Internet Access: Nearly every business in Queenstown has some kind of Internet access. **Cyber Gate,** 53 Shotover St. (☎442 6568), is the largest place in town, with comfy chairs and perks like webcams, free headphones, and Skype. $3 per hr. Same price for laptops. Open daily 9:30am-midnight. The **Internet Depot,** 26 Shotover St. (☎442 8581) $3 per hr. No laptops. Open daily 9am-11pm. **Global Gossip,** 27 Shotover St. (☎441 3018). $3 per hr. Laptops $6 per hr. Open daily 8am-11pm.

Library: Queenstown Public Library, 10 Gorge Rd. (☎441 0600), is the only quiet place in town. Open M-Sa 10am-5pm.

Post Office: (☎442 7670), at the corner of Camp and Ballarat St. Open M-F 8:30am-6pm, Sa 9am-4pm.

ACCOMMODATIONS AND CAMPING

Catering to honeymooners and broke ski bums alike, Queenstown has a wide array of places to stay, with B&Bs and hostels springing up to meet the ever-expanding demand. Even so, book at least a week in advance in summer. While the majority of buspackers stay on Shotover St., the options below offer a bit of removal from the party-all-day-all-night scene without being too far away.

▨ **Butterfli Lodge (BBH),** 67 Thompson St. (☎442 6367; www.butterfli.co.nz), a 10min. walk from Shotover St. Offering peace and quiet with lakeview porches to boot, Butterfli caters to backpacking pairs with scenic double rooms. The lone subterranean dorm lacks windows but allows for use of the spacious common facilities and pleasant company. Dorms $24; doubles $58. $2-3 BBH discount. MC/V. ❷

■ **The Last Resort,** 6 Memorial St. (☎442 4320; www.tlrqtn.com). Though privacy may only be found in the bathroom here, this cozy 18-bed house is superbly set-up for socializing with other residents and manages to be in the center of town without feeling it. Cocco, the resident guard dog, often receives more attention from guests than the endless movie collection. Unlimited Internet, breakfast, and linens included. 6-bed dorms $25, 4-bed $27. $3 BBH discount. MC/V. ❷

Southern Laughter (BBH/VIP), 4 Isle St. (☎441 8828 or 0800 528 4483; www.southernlaughter.co.nz). Far Side cartoons and zany flotsam and jetsam spruce up the walls of these side-by-side houses. Many of the dorm rooms are mini-suites with TVs and kitchenettes, great for groups up to 8. Free vegetable soup from 6pm. Pool table. Key deposit $10. Reception 7:30am-9pm. Dorms $23-26; twins $54; doubles $56, ensuite $64. $2 BBH discount, $1 VIP discount. MC/V. ❷

Deco Backpackers (BBH), 52 Man St. (☎442 7384; www.decobackpackers.co.nz). From the visitors center, walk left up Camp St., and turn left on Man St. This bustling backpackers has a dynamic lounge, filtered tap water, and a scenic backyard picnic area that overlooks the lake. Very ski-friendly, with drying room and long-term stays possible in winter. Free WiFi. Linen $2. Reception 8am-2pm and 4-8pm. Dorms $24; triples $78; twins $54; doubles $54-58; luxury doubles $66. $2-3 BBH discount. MC/V. ❷

Hippo Lodge (BBH), 4 Anderson Heights (☎442 5785; www.hippolodge.co.nz). A 20min. climb leads to this hilltop lodge, with the best view of any backpackers in Queenstown. Free pears in season. WiFi $10 per day. Reception 8:30am-7pm. 5- to 8-bed dorms $25; 3- to 4-bed dorms $26; doubles $65, deluxe $75, ensuite $80. $2-3 BBH discount. MC/V. ❷

Bumbles Hostel, 2 Brunswick St. (☎442 6298 or 0800 428 625). Follow Shotover St. toward the lakefront; Bumbles faces the water at Lake Esplanade. Lakeview balconies, garden barbeque, and bathrooms in each room. Linen included. Key deposit $10. Reception 7:30am-7:30pm. Dorms $27; twins and doubles $60. MC/V. ❸

Bungi Backpackers (BBH), 15 Sydney St. (☎442 8725; www.bungibackpackers.co.nz). From Shotover St., follow Stanley St. uphill for about 10min. until you see the sign. This far-out relative of Southern Laughter has the same decorator, but has a layout much more conducive to socializing, with great outdoor spaces and the cheapest rates in town. Linen, soup, spa, and hammocks included. Reception 8am-10pm. 8- to 4-bed dorms $20-22; triples $69; doubles and twins $49. $3 BBH discount. ❷

Resort Lodge Backpackers (BBH), 6 Henry St. (☎442 4970 or 0800 082 224; www.resortlodge.co.nz). Walk up Shotover St. away from the lake and turn right on Henry St. 2 small, brightly painted kitchens and a balcony make for a pleasant stay. Phones in every room. Free airport pickups. WiFi. Reception 8am-8pm. Dorms $25; singles, twins, and doubles $60. $3 BBH discount. ❷

Pinewood Lodge, 48 Hamilton Rd. (☎442 8273 or 0800 746 396; www.pinewood.co.nz). From the Queenstown i-Site, head left up Camp St., follow Robins Rd. to the right, and then turn left on Hamilton Rd. A separate village within Queenstown. Expansive grounds allow up to 300 guests to gather for socializing and relaxation. Spa, barbeque, trampoline. Ski tuning and drying area. Free pickup. WiFi. Key deposit $10. Reception 7:30am-9pm. Dorms from $21; doubles from $57, ensuite from $85; self-contained 4-6 person units from $130. ❷

Holly's Backpackers (BBH), 71 Upton St. (☎443 8187; hollys@xtra.co.nz). A small, somewhat disorderly home-run hostel with spacious rooms and common areas. Key deposit $10. Bikes half-day $10, full-day $20. Dorms $24-27; twins and doubles $60. $3 BBH discount. Cash only. ❷

Wanaka YHA, 181 Upton St. (☎/fax 443 7405). Located on a quiet side-street, this YHA is composed of several cramped buildings, though it has a pleasant patio. Reception 8am-8pm. Dorms $24-27; twins and doubles $62-72. $3 YHA discount. MC/V. ❷

Queenstown YHA, 88-90 Lake Esplanade (☎442 8413; yhaqutn@yha.org.nz). Head left on Shotover St. along the lakefront, away from town. This flagship YHA is a 147-bed housing machine. If this one is full, YHA enthusiasts can also try the Central YHA on Shotover St., which focuses on private rooms and is slightly more expensive. Reception 6:30am-10pm. Dorms from $26; twins and doubles $74; 3-person family rooms $82; 4-person apartments $152. $3 YHA discount. ❸

Queenstown Top 10 Holiday Park Creeksyde, 54 Robins Rd. (☎442 9447 or 0800 786 222; www.camp.co.nz). Willows surround grassy sites in this eco-friendly campground. Lounges, kitchens, and bathrooms are clean and social. Linen $5. Reception 7am-10pm. July-Aug. 7:30am-9pm. Tent and powered sites $20-25; 2-person sites $38, extra person $15. 2-person cabins $57; 6-person motel apartments from $155. ❷

FOOD

While cheap lunches abound, budget dinners are elusive. The majority of other restaurants are located along **The Mall, Beach Street,** or the waterfront. One notable non-restaurant food option is **Patagonia ❶,** 50 Beach St. (☎442 9066; www.patagoniachocolates.com), on the lakefront, which serves up handmade chocolate bars ($2-3), hot chocolate ($4.50-$5.50), and a wide array of ice creams and sorbets ($3.80), infused with tasty and creative spices, nuts, and fruits. Linger for a while to use their free WiFi. (Open daily 8am-10pm.) **Alpine Supermarket,** at the corner of Shotover and Stanley St., is the most centrally located supermarket (☎442 8961; open M-Sa 8am-9pm, Su 9am-9pm), but **Fresh Choice,** 64 Gorge Rd., has a better selection at lower prices. (☎441 1252. Open 7am-midnight.) The **Mediterranean Market,** 53 Robins Rd., has expensive treats and the best produce in town. (☎442 4161. Open M-Sa 8am-6:30pm, Su 10am-6pm.)

▓ **Fergburger,** 42 Shotover St. (☎441 1232; www.fergburger.com). With gigantic burgers ($8.50-15) smothered in aioli sauce and a population of fans that stretches across New Zealand, "Ferg" always loves you, sober or otherwise. The massive helpings of chips ($4) are better off shared. Open daily 9am-5am. Coffee from 8am. Dining area closes around 11pm. ❷

Habebes (☎442 9861), in the Wakatipu Arcade, accessible from Beach and Rees St. At this popular Lebanese restaurant, add your choice of tabouli and salad to scrumptious lamb, chicken, or falafel ($11.50). The apricot orgasm ($2.50) delivers as promised. Open daily 11am-5pm. Cash only. ❷

Bombay Palace, 66 Shotover St. (☎441 2886). A splendid deal for tasty Indian food (mains; $13-20), with free Bollywood video entertainment. The windows display frequent specials, such as 3-course dinner ($20) and early-bird curry deals (5-6:30pm and W 5-10pm; $14). Open daily 5-10pm. ❸

The Cow (☎442 8588; ww.thecowrestaurant.co.nz), on Cow Ln., off Beach St. This low-beamed pizzeria has wooden, candle-lit booths and tables near a blazing hearth; be prepared to share a table. Enjoy large pizzas ($26-32) and spaghetti ($18-22). Open daily noon-midnight. ❸

P.J.'s Fish & Chips, 37 Camp St. (☎442 6080). This fish 'n chip house specializes in whatever's fresh, available, and cheap, whether it be blue cod and sole or shark and monkfish. Everything comes battered, crumbed, or grilled for $5-6, with a fresh fish meal ($10) adding chips and a side. Occasional seasonal specialties like Bluff Oysters. Open daily noon-3pm and 5pm-9pm. ❶

Lone Star, 14 Brecon St. (☎442 9995). The food comes in anatomically impossible helpings ($29-32), and the chicken in the style of cajun, honky tonk, Dixie, or Johnny Cash. The three-quarter portion ($23) makes mains like the Vegetarian Do-Gooder Burrito more manageable. Open daily 4:30pm-late. Rattlesnakes bar upstairs open 4pm-3:30am. ❸

Pig 'N Whistle (☎442 9055), at the corner of Ballarat and Athol St. Your jolly "Olde English Pub." The outdoor patio kicks back next to a gurgling canal. Meals will leave you and your wallet pleasantly full. Dinner $11-17.50. The bar rocks late into the evening. Open daily 11am-late. ❷

Amigos Cafe, 34 Ardmore St. (☎443 7872). The owner fries his own tortillas and makes his own salsa. Combo platters $16-19.50. Open daily from 5:30pm. ❸

The Doughbin McGregors, (☎443 7290), on Ardmore St. invites those on a budget to "come see their buns." Big cinnamon rolls ($2) and substantial sandwiches (from $4.50). Open daily 6am-6pm. ❶

🎵 🍸 ENTERTAINMENT AND NIGHTLIFE

The disproportionate size of Queenstown's nightlife to its population is overwhelming at first, but the transient nature of most revelers makes wherever your friends are going the best place to start. Two excellent local publications are the **Lakes Weekly Bulletin** and **Source,** which are available at most bars (ask the bartender) and provide handy weekly charts of gigs, DJs, drink specials, and more. For a quieter evening, movies are shown in the **Reading Cinemas,** 11-14 The Mall. (Movieline ☎442 9990. Films $13.50, students $12.50; Tu $9.50.) For those in it to win it, 🍔**Fergburger** caters to the huddled masses outside until 5am nightly (see **Food,** p. 395).

🍸 **Winnie's** (☎442 8635; www.winnies.co.nz), overlooking The Mall from the 2nd fl. of number 7. Pizzeria by day and packed local favorite by night, Winnie's has a balcony and retractable roof to cool off the steaming 20-something crowd. Happy hour 10-11pm; $3 tap beers and $4 house wine. Individual pizzas $14.50. Kitchen closes at 11pm. Open daily noon-2:30am.

🍸 **Subculture,** (☎442 7685; www.subculture.net.nz), under 13-14 Church St. The giant turbine fans the dancefloor of this underground late-night hip-hop and drum and bass club. If you're there early, enjoy the pool table or relax by the virtual fire, but things heat up for real after 2am with the best guest DJs in town. Mixed drinks $16, in mini versions $9. Open Tu-Su 10pm-6am, in May-June Th-Sa. Occasional cover $5 and up.

Chico's (☎442 8439), on the 2nd fl. of the Mall at the corner of Eureka Arcade. Chico's offers a relaxed and popular classic bar setting that really rocks when the house cover band plays on the weekend. Happy hour 10:30pm-11:30pm; $2 off drinks. Open daily 10pm-3:30am.

Skybar, 26 Camp St. (☎442 4283; www.goodbars.co.nz), above Betty's Liquor Store. The Magritte-inspired blue sky elevates the mood of the clientele at this chic cocktail bar, but things really get exciting when the bartenders light the bar on fire. Specialty mixed drinks $16. Wine $8-9. Open daily 5pm-4am.

Red Rock (☎442 6850), at the corner of Camp and Man St. Younger backpackers pre-party here before hitting The World, while others stay to watch the giant TV over a few more beers. Frequent adventure activity giveaways at 10:30pm. Happy hour nightly 5-6pm and 7-8pm. DJs W-F. Open daily 10am-late.

The Bunker (☎441 8030; www.thebunker.co.nz), on Cow Ln. Nightlife survivors hunker down at this barrel-lined 2nd fl. bar, named after the expensive restaurant below. Cocktails $16, wine $10-16. DJs on F. Open daily 5pm-5am.

Debajo (☎442 6099), on Cow Ln. House beats rattle the door of this tucked-away bar, where the crowd comes in late and stays until sunrise. Happy hour 9-11pm. DJs nightly from midnight. Bottled beers $6-7.50. Open daily 9pm-5am.

Minibar (☎441 3212; www.goodbars.co.nz), on Eureka Arcade off the Mall. The smallest member of the Goodbars family (Barup, Barmuda, Bardeaux, and Skybar), Minibar packs a surprise in its huge selection of imported beers from $5-100 per bottle. Open daily 4pm-4am.

The World, 27 Shotover St. (☎442 6757; www.theworldbar.com/queenstown.html). A perennial favorite among backpackers, The World spins hard every night of the week. Shakers served in teapots ($15-20) are the best deal. Frequent activity giveaways are often promoted in the hostels earlier in the day. Open daily 4pm-4am. DJs from 10:30pm. Su teapot happy hour all night.

OUTDOOR ADVENTURE ACTIVITIES

Queenstown has a little bit of everything, and a lot of the outdoors. With its heart-stopping thrills and breathtaking scenery, the area lets you dive, ride, jump, saunter, float, dart, or glide through a spectacular setting. Budgeting for Queenstown activities requires a magically expanding bank account or the mental resolve to watch your savings dwindle. The multitude of booking agents can be overwhelming, and hostel owners and fellow travelers will often be your best source of advice. To maximize your money, consider buying a **pre-packaged combo,** which can save you up to $100. Combos include anywhere from two to five activities, including helicopter flights, bungy jumps, jetboat rides, 4WD tours, and rafting trips. One of the best deals for tireless adrenaline junkies is the all-day **Awesome Foursome** ($495), which combines bungy, jet-boats, helicopters, and rafts. There are many other combos available at booking agencies, and sometimes special deals are posted near the reception desk at many hostels. You can book most at the **Queenstown Combos** (☎442 7318 or 0800 423 836) section of the Challenge Rafting desk inside The Station. Nearly all activities offer some kind of pickup or transport from town (though some charge for it), so far-off locations should not seem daunting. Many activities depart from **The Station,** at Shotover and Camp St. (☎442 5252. Open daily 7:30am-8:30pm. In winter 8am-8pm.) **The Information and Track Centre** (p. 373) is geared toward backpackers and offers info on transport to local tracks and ski fields, tramping conditions, and outfitting.

BUNGY JUMPING

AJ HACKETT. Brought to you by the man who got arrested after jumping off the Eiffel Tower in 1987, completely failed to learn his lesson, and immediately built the world's first commercial jump, AJ Hackett's three Queenstown jump sites constitute the region's single biggest adventure draw. Each offers its own twist on the same killer freefall and ground rush, with the main challenge being your own willingness to let yourself jump. The **Kawarau Bungy Centre,** a 20min. drive from Queenstown on SH6, offers the chance for curious visitors to freely gawk at people jumping off the **Kawarau Bridge** (43m), the world's first commercial bungy. If you choose to take the plunge yourself, the jumpmaster can calibrate just how much "water touch" you'll get from the river below. The most terrifying site is the **Nevis Highwire,** which suspends jumpers from a glass-bottomed gondola above a wide canyon and is Australasia's highest fixed jump at 134m. **The Ledge** makes the most of its above-town location; a specialized harness allows jumpers to get a running start and hurtle themselves 47m down in any position; the **Ledge Sky Swing** offers the same location but takes away the fear of the running start. For those who are terrified yet curious about how it all works, the **Secrets of Bungy** tour at the Kawarau Bungy Centre lets guests get all strapped up, see how the cords are made, and experience the "world's shortest bungy" (1ft.). *(Office in The Station. ☎442 4007 or 0800 286 495; www.ajhackett.com. Open daily 8am-8pm. All jumps include transport. Kawarau Bridge $150. Nevis Highwire $210. The Ledge $150. Ledge Sky Swing $99. Thrillogy, all 3 jumps, $350. Secrets of Bungy tour $20, children $10. Transport to Kawarau Bungy Centre from Queenstown $20 return.)*

OTAGO

CANYON SWING. AJ Hackett may have written the book on bungy jumping, but he won't play you Barry White, stick a bucket on your head, and strap you upside down 109m over Shotover Canyon. The merry pranksters at ◪**Shotover Canyon Swing** offer all this and more, and even the most jaded adventurer will have cause to soil his knickers. There are 10 different advertised jumps—Gimp Boy Goes to Hollywood and the Elvis Cutaway are among the more popular—but Jumpmaster's Choice inevitably yields the most creative and terrifying results. *(Bookings and departures from the Information and Track Centre, 37 Shotover St. ☎442 6990 or 0800 279 464. 2½hr., 8 per day 8:30am-5:30pm. $169. $39 for repeat jumps. Accompanying spectators cost $29, but the hilarious antics involved make it worth the money.)*

ON THE WATER

JETBOATING. ◪**Dart River Jet Safaris** offers two fantastic trips through the remote river valleys north of Glenorchy. *(27 Shotover St. ☎442 9992 or 0800 327 853; www.dartriver.co.nz. Half-day, including transport from Queenstown and nature walk $209. Full-day with funyak trip $285.)* Less personal but more action-packed, **Shotover Jet** is the only company with the rights to the deepest and rockiest stretch of canyon. Skimming impossibly close to the rock walls and over waters as shallow as 10cm, the speedboats swivel and twist at 70kph and have awed nearly two million customers with their trademark 360° spin. *(☎0800 802 804; www.shotover-jet.co.nz. Pickup from The Station every 15min. $109, children $69. Several trip combinations exist from $205.)* **Kawarau Jet** initiated the jetboating craze in 1960, speeding eager vacationers down the Kawarau River. Their scenic 43km two-river trips last twice as long as some other operators, but are restricted to the lower reaches of the Shotover River and lack the narrow-canyon thrill. Since the trips depart directly from town, however, you don't waste any time in transport and get more bang for your buck. *(On the lakefront at the base of Rees St. ☎442 6142 or 0800 529 272. Trips depart from bottom of The Mall every hr. $89, children $49, 4-person family $225; includes entrance to underwater observatory.)* **Skippers Canyon Jet** offers a combination 30min. jetboating trip in the rocky stretches of the Shotover River and historic gold-mining tour of Winky's Museum, which has been in the family for 5 generations. *(☎442 9434 or 0800 226 966; www.fourwheeldrive.co.nz. 4-4½hr. $149, children $79. Departs 8am and 1pm daily. Free pickup from town. Jetboating without tour 2½hr. $95/48.)*

RAFTING. While Queenstown isn't known for world-class rapids, novice rafters will certainly be thrilled. The Shotover River has more consistent Class IV rapids and rides through the 170m Oxenbridge Tunnel, while the Kawarau River offers more in the way of scenery than it does in screams. **Queenstown Rafting, Extreme Green Rafting,** and **Challenge Rafting** all share boats, guides, and river space, and run half-day trips on the Shotover and Kawarau. *(QR ☎442 9792 or 0800 723 846; www.rafting.co.nz. EGR ☎442 8517; www.nzraft.com. CR ☎442 7318 or 0800 423 836; www.raft.co.nz; $149-159.)* River boarding in Queenstown allows the audacious to boogie over the rapids on the Kawarau River. Advance instruction provides basic technique, but once you hit the rapids, you're on your own. **Mad Dog River Boarding** *(☎442 7797 or 0508 623 364; www.maddogriverboarding.co.nz)* leads 5hr. trips, which include extensive time on the river and access to their extreme aquatic "playground" at the Goldfields Mining Centre. *($129).* **Serious Fun River Surfing** *(☎442 5262 or 0800 737 4687; www.riversurfing.co.nz)* has 4hr. trips which cover among other things, the "Dogleg," an 800m whitewater stretch. *($139).* Quality and availability of all trips depends on water levels.

CANYONING. For those who find jumping off bridges and riding through rapids entirely too passive, canyoning is the harrowing answer to your hardcore prayer. ◪**Routeburn Canyoning Limited** and **Queenstown Canyoning** lead canyoning trips that plunge into pools, rappel into ravines, and slide down chutes (not for those with fears of heights, water, or very hard rocks). The two companies share the same owners but run separately, leading two trips: a shorter, less expensive adventure at **12-Mile Delta** and a longer journey down scenic **Routeburn Canyon.** *(☎441 4468 or 441 4386; www.xiimile.co.nz or www.gycanyoning.co.nz. 12-Mile Delta $145, 10+; Routeburn Canyon $195 from Glenorchy, $215 with transport from Queenstown; 16+. Oct.-Apr.)*

LAKE WAKATIPU. Steamships were once the sole form of transport across the lake to Glenorchy and to the area's various sheep stations. Today, only the revamped **T.S.S. Earnslaw** remains. The 3½hr. **▧farm cruise to Walter Peak** with afternoon tea is a highlight. Once there, watch sheep shearing and a sheep dog demonstration or enjoy a horse trek. The dinner cruise involves a posh buffet dinner followed by a rollicking farm show. 1½hr. cruises on the Earnslaw with no extra stops are also available. *(Cruises depart from the Steamer Wharf at the end of Shotover St. ☎0800 656 503; www.realjourneys.co.nz. Departs Oct. to mid-Apr. up to 6 times daily. $60, children $15. Dinner cruise 6pm; $99/49.50. Horse treks $99. Earnslaw cruise only $40/15.)*

IN THE AIR

SKYDIVING. If the scenery looks beautiful from the waterfront, imagine it looks like from 12,000 ft. and falling. The only thing not reassuring about the extremely professional crew at **NZONE** is the uneasy truce the company's grassy runway has with nearby sheep. Before the plane lands between drops, a van drives through honking to clear a path. Their spacious dropzone complex allows you to relax before your dive by watching your fellow divers whoosh in from above every few minutes. *(☎442 5867 or 0800 376 796; www.nzone.biz. 9000 ft. $245, 12,000 ft. $295, 15,000 ft. $395. Discounts for repeat jumpers. 3½hr. Complete photo and DVD package costs a hefty $209.)* **NZSKYDIVE** operates out of Glenorchy and offers smaller and more personal trips; the 30min. scenic drive to Glenorchy is a bonus. *(☎409 0363 or 0800 586 749; www.nzskydive.com. 9000 ft. $245, 12000 ft. $295, 15000 ft. $395. DVD $175. Four trips daily from 8:30am to 2:30pm. Free pickup from Queenstown.)*

FLIGHTS. Offering the country's only acrobatic flight, **Actionflite** customizes their pricey 15min. flight to your tolerance for swoops and radical shifts. *(☎441 4413; www.actionflite.co.nz. $329, $395 per 25min.)* **The Helicopter Line** has 20min. trips to The Remarkables with a landing at 1538m. *(☎442 3034 or 0800 500 575; www.helicopter.co.nz. $180 per 20min., $250 per 30min. 2- to 3-person min.)* **Over The Top** has 30min. flights over the Remarkables and 45min. alpine landing flights; longer flights to Milford Sound are expensive but beautiful. *(☎442 2233 or 0800 123 359; www.flynz.co.nz. 30min. from $195, 45min. from $385, Milford from $770 with 3-person min.)* Several airlines do scenic flights to **Milford Sound** *(70min.),* including **Air Fiordland** *(☎442 3404 or 0800 103 404; www.airfiordland.co.nz; $299),* **Milford Sound Scenic Flights** *(☎442 3065 or 0800 207 206; www.milfordflights.co.nz; $295),* and **Glenorchy Air.** *(☎442 2207 or 0800 676 264; www.glenorchy.net.nz. $315, with landing $325.)* 4hr. fly-cruise-fly options are available ($355-385).

PILOTING. For those who've always dreamed of being a pilot, **Air Wakatipu** actually lets you get behind the wheel. They run 20 and 40min. "trial flights" in their 2-seater planes, and for less hands-on types, 30min. scenic flights through Skippers Canyon and Arrowtown. *(☎442 3148 or 0508 645 367; www.flying.co.nz. 20min. trial flight $139, 40min. $209; spectators $30 per person extra with upgrade to larger plane. 30min. scenic flights $150 per person up to 6 people.)* For a piloting option with a bit more of a restricted flight-path, **Fly By Wire** straps customers into a 60 horsepower aircraft that acts like a pendulum with a throttle and lets them loop around their 400m wide canyon at up to 170kph. The flight lasts only 5min., but you can press the "extra fun" button to keep going for another 2. (☎442 2116 or 0800 359 299; www.fly-bywire-queenstown.co.nz. 2½hr. $139, extra fun $29. Spectators $29.)

For a virtual piloting experience, check out **Flight Experience** (☎442 8878 or 0800 746 852; www.flightexperience.co.nz), in front of the Crowne Plaza Hotel on Beach St., which uses a Boeing 737-800 cockpit and a database of 24,000 world airports to offer professional-level flight training without leaving the ground. Novices can try 30min. scenic flights over Queenstown or simulated flights from 1hr. and up. (30min. flights $125; 1hr. simulator $225. All flights accompanied by trained pilot. Open daily 9am-7pm.)

OTHER AIRBORNE ACTIVITIES. Sunrise Balloons takes passengers up to 5000 ft. in true style, then lands for a champagne breakfast. (☎442 0781 or 0800 468 247; www.ballooningnz.com. 3½hr. $345.) Aerophiles should try **paragliding**—an exhilarating tandem ride from above the Skyline Gondola over Queenstown and Lake Wakatipu. **Tandem Paragliding** cruises down from the gondola amid scenic splendor with an immediate 400m vertical drop. (☎441 8581 or 0800 759 688; www.para-glide.net.nz. 1hr. Approximately 10min. in the air. $185; includes free ride back to the top, a roll of film, and a free beer.) Offering more in the way of acrobatics, **Sky Trek Tandem Hang Gliding** offers a 10-20min. flight from Coronet Peak or The Remarkables. (Book through NZSHRED at 19 Shotover St. ☎442 6311 or 0800 759 8735; www.skytrek.co.nz. $185.) **Queenstown Paraflights** lifts riders gently up over the waters of Lake Wakatipu with their smiling parachutes for 10-15min. rides. (Trips depart from the wharf in Queenstown. ☎441 2242; www.paraflights.co.nz. $95, children $80; $85/65 per person tandem or triple. Min. combined weight 35kg, max. 200kg. Spectators on boat $25.)

ON THE SLOPES

From June to early October, **skiing** and **snowboarding** take over Queenstown as enthusiasts flock to **Coronet Peak** and **The Remarkables**. Lift passes and transport are cheaper in town, particularly when part of a package. An ISIC card is not valid for student deals; another **student ID** is necessary. While the road to Coronet Peak is paved, the road to the Remarkables is not and will require chains; shuttles are a safer option for those unsure of their vehicle's gumption (see **Transportation,** p. 373). Those skiing for a number of days or in a number of locations may wish to consider the **NZ Superpass** (p. 321). If you're planning in advance to spend a ski season in Queenstown, consider purchasing a **Season Ski Pass** early—buying passes before March can save an enormous amounts. For more details, check www.nzski.com or stop by the ski desk in The Station. Although Wanaka makes a more convenient base, skiers and snowboarders frequently stay in Queenstown and catch morning shuttles to **Cardrona** or make the longer drive to **Treble Cone.** (For more information on both ski fields, see **Wanaka: Outdoor Activities,** p. 397.)

THE REMARKABLES. The Remarkables ski field (1943m; vertical rise 321m) tries to resist the commercialization of the Queenstown area but is still hugely popular. It usually has better snow conditions than Coronet Peak, a wider beginners' area, a greater range of off-trail extreme terrain, and more sun. Its slopes cater to skiers and snowboarders of all skill levels as well as to cross-country skiers. (Office in The Station. ☎442 4615. Lift pass $84, students $61, children $45. Half-day pass $55/41/32.)

CORONET PEAK. New Zealand's first commercial ski area (est. 1947), Coronet Peak (1649m; vertical rise 481m) is still popular today—in fact, the slopes are often uncomfortably crowded on weekends. However, due to new snow guns (now totaling 105), former problems with icing from overuse are a thing of the past. Bigger and closer to Queenstown, Coronet has a longer season than The Remarkables, opens earlier in the day and offers weekend night skiing, and contains a half-pipe and a terrain park with jumps and tabletops. Its slopes are suitable for all levels of skiers and boarders, particularly intermediate skiers,

OTAGO

though the expanded beginners area is a great boon. *(Office in The Station. ☎442 4620. Lift pass $89, students $68. Night skiing lift pass valid F-Sa 4-9pm. $30. "First Tracks" 8am-9am pass $30. Half-day pass $57/47/34.)*

OFF-ROAD

4WD TOURS. The rock walls and precipitous roads through **Skipper's Canyon,** constructed during gold-rush days, now attract 4WD tours that give the fantastic drive a historical perspective. **NOMAD Safaris** guides morning and afternoon tours up the rugged, winding road into Skippers Canyon and up to the mining settlement of Macetown. They also run a scenic "Safari of the Rings" which visits filming locations of the *Lord of the Rings* trilogy. Tours include a light tea and gold panning. NOMAD runs "4WD Experience" tours that allow you to get behind the wheel with a guide. *(19 Shotover St. ☎442 6699 or 0800 688 222; www.nomadsafaris.co.nz. All 4WD tours $130 and 4-4½hr. 4WD Experience $230 for driver, $130 per passenger; 2 person min.)* **Offroad Adventures** (see below) offers two 4hr. LOTR-themed 4WD tours in the Wakatipu area. *("One 4WD Tour to Rule them All" $139.)*

BIKING. Off-road motorbike and ATV treks through the canyon and anywhere else you want are available through **Offroad Adventures.** *(61a Shotover St. ☎442 7858; www.offroad.co.nz. 3hr. 9am and 1pm. $199-239.)* One especially good trip on your own is the 20km ride past Lake Hayes to **Arrowtown,** where you can stop to check out the historic Chinese settlement, pan for gold, or continue up the 13km 4WD track to Macetown, where river crossings are not uncommon. *(Rides start 25min. out of Queenstown toward Gibbston Valley.)* **NOMAD Safaris** (see p. 384) runs very popular 3½hr. quad bike excursions around Queenstown Hill *($185 per person)*. In the summer, **Gravity Action** runs half-day **mountain biking trips** to the canyon three times daily; they drive you—or take you in a helicopter for $80 more—up to Skipper's Saddle and Coronet Peak, let you coast 10km down through creeks and over gravel, and top it off with a beer and a meal on the way home. *(19 Shotover St. ☎442 5277; www.gravityaction.com. 3½hr. $139, 8am early bird tour $119. Additional combos available.)* **Vertigo Bikes** runs two downhill tracks to choose from, with a Heli-Bike on the Remarkables featuring a 2000m-high drop point and a downhill track on the Gondola hill in town. *(4 Brecon St. ☎442 8378 or 0800 837 8446; www.vertigobikes.co.nz. Heli-Bike trip 4hr., $314. Gondola downhill 2½hr., $149. Gondola downhill involves two runs.)*

HIKING. The DOC office and the Information and Track Centre next door offer a *Queenstown Walks and Trails* guide ($1), which details walks in and around the area. For those with a car, *Lake Wakatipu Walks and Trails* ($1) is also helpful. Shorter tracks on the way to Glenorchy offer less-trodden native forest experiences (some suitable for mountain biking or trail running). Trailheads are clearly marked along the road. One of the most difficult and rewarding treks scales the steep sides of ■**Ben Lomond.** Mt. Aspiring and a panorama of peaks can be seen from the summit (1748m) on a clear day. *(Trail accessible from the top of the Gondola or by taking the Skyline Access Rd. from the end of Thompson St. or One Mile Creek Walk from the Fernhill roundabout on the road to Glenorchy; see DOC map. Check weather conditions with the DOC before tramping. 6-8hr. round-trip to the summit; 3-4hr. to the saddle.)* The **Queenstown Hill Time Walk** is a less arduous climb that leads through thick forest to the peak of **Te Tapunui,** with a 360° view of The Remarkables, Cecil Peak, and Lake Wakatipu. The climb is particularly beautiful around sunset. *(Walk up Mallaghan St. and use the walkway to connect with the end of Belfast Tce., where the trail begins. 2-3hr. round-trip.)*

CLIMBING. The **Rung Way** runs a series of personalized rock-climbing and abseiling adventures on the cliffs of nearby Queenstown Hill, including a via ferrata course of permanently fixed rungs, pegs, rails, ladders, and cables. Enthusiastic guides cater to any level of experience and will provide basic training for newcomers to rock climbing. In winter, additional courses in mountaineering and avalanche training are available. *(Trips depart from Outside Sports. ☎450 2119 or 0800 786 4929; www.rungway.co.nz. Rock climbing and via ferrata trips 4hr., $149. Abseiling 2hr., $99. Trips depart daily at 1:30pm. Book ahead.)* **Independent Mountain Guides** offers instruction in rock and ice climbing and can lead you on a full-day trip around the area, with the option of climbing **Single Cone**, the highest of The Remarkables at 2319m. *(☎442 3381 or 027 414 0544; www.independentmountainguides.co.nz. Full-day trips $350, for 2 $175 each. Single Cone $425/350.)*

HORSE TREKS. A few stables operate in the valleys surrounding Queenstown and include trips through farmland, foothills, and mountain tracks. **Moonlight Stables** heads out daily through the family-owned 700-acre deer farm 15min. from Queenstown. Afternoon fishing is possible for mid-sized groups with advance notice, but a free post-ride cuppa and relaxed company comes standard. *(☎442 1229 or 0800 581 111; www.moonlightcountry.co.nz. 1½hr. Departures at 9:30am, 1:30 and 4:30pm. Late departure not available in winter. $95.)* **Shotover Stables** offers 1hr. rides through fields downhill to the Shotover River and back, with some opportunity for trotting and cantering as ability allows. *(☎442 7486; www.shotoverstables.net. Pickup from town included. Trips depart 9:30am, 1:30pm, 3:30pm. $65, children $40.)*

OTHER SIGHTS AND ACTIVITIES

ABOVE QUEENSTOWN. The **Skyline Gondola** runs up to the Skyline restaurant and expensive bar for panoramas of the lake and mountains. The buffet is often swamped with the older tour bus crowd but makes extensive use of local seafood. *(☎441 0101; www.skyline.co.nz. Open daily 9am-late. $20 round-trip, down only $10. No one-way fare from base. Dinner buffet from 6pm. $67 including gondola Lunch buffet noon-2pm in summer only; $43 with gondola. Meal reservations essential.)* Better yet, walk the uphill **One Mile Creek Trail**, which passes through a canyon and pine forest to Skyline, where you can catch the gondola down. *(Walk along the lakefront toward Glenorchy, turn right onto Brunswick St. and continue as it bears to the right, becoming Thompson St. The trailhead is in a cul-de-sac at the end of the street. 1hr. one-way.)* By the top of the gondola, the **Skyline Luge** may look tame, but its 800m of sharp turns and steep straightaways are exciting when you're racing in a three-wheeled plastic cart. *(Open daily 9:30am-dusk. $7 for 1 ride, $12 for 2, $16 for 3, and $22 for 5. Discounts with round-trip gondola purchase.)* The 30min. **Kiwi Haka** Maori cultural show *($30; cheaper with gondola purchase.)* at the top of the gondola provides additional entertainment, but watching jumpers hurl themselves from the **Ledge Bungy** is free.

KIWI AND BIRDLIFE PARK. The five-acre complex includes a nocturnal kiwi house with guaranteed sightings though no photography, a range of native parakeets and ducks, and two of the world's rarest birds—the **black stilt** (kaki) wading bird and the **brown teal.** Walk-in kea and weka enclosures and feeding opportunities for more common ducks round out the highlights. An audio tour headset is included with the price of admission. Proceeds support captive breeding programs. *(At the base of the gondola. ☎442 8059; www.kiwibird.co.nz. $30, children $15. Open daily Oct.-Mar. 9am-7pm, Mar.-Oct. until 6pm.)*

WINE TOURS. The dry mountainous terrain surrounding Queenstown produces some hardy varieties of grapes (pinot noir is the stand-out). A number of tour operators offer trips to local wineries as a sophisticated alternative to adventure offerings (though wine and jetboat and wine and bungy packages are available for the devoted). The **Queenstown Wine Trail** is the established front-runner in town, with informative and entertaining commentary along the way. The Original Tour visits four local wineries with the option of purchasing lunch along the way, while the Summer Sampler is shorter, includes lunch, and tours a cheese factory. (☎ 442 3799 or 0800 827 8464; www.queenstownwinetrail.co.nz. Original Tour 5hr., $106 with $10-20 lunch option. Summer Sampler 3½hr., $126. Tours depart at 12:30pm from the Station. Garden tours also available. Book ahead.) **It's Wine Time** also guides small group tours of the area's wineries. (☎ 442 1895 or 0508 946 384; www.winetime.co.nz. 2-winery morning tour $115 including lunch, full-day 5-winery tour $158. 3-winery short afternoon tour $99.) Drop-in visits to wineries are welcome. The majority of nearby wineries lie along SH6 as it heads into the Gibbston Valley and through to Cromwell, the capital of Central Otago wines. Remember to appoint a designated driver if you plan an extensive tour. The **Amisfield Winery & Bistro** ❸, is the closest to town and features gourmet family-style mains. (10 Lake Hayes Rd. ☎ 442 0556; www.amisfield.co.nz. Mains $16.50-27. Tasting $5 for 4 wines. Bistro open Tu-Su 11:30am-8pm. Cellar door open daily 10am-6pm.) The **Gibbston Valley Winery,** just a bit farther down the highway, was the first in the area and features a wine cave, cheesery, and lunchtime fare. (☎ 442 6910; www.gvwines.com. Tastings from $5. Cave tour $9.50, $7.50 with lunch purhcase. Open daily 10am-5pm.)

OTHER ACTIVITIES. At the end of Beach St. near the Lake, a small archway and path leads to the **Queenstown Gardens.** With a track looping out onto the peninsula and an excellent ◙frisbee golf course that starts near Park St., the gardens are an excellent place to feed the ducks, stretch out on a bench, and not jump off anything for a while. (Bring your own frisbee or purchase one from a local outdoors store, where course maps are also available.) Within putting distance of the Kiwi and Birdlife Park, **Queenstown Mini Golf** has a rudimentary, but well-kept course. Play your best to vie for a spot on the chalkboard tally of top scores from different nations. (34 Brecon St. ☎ 442 7652. Open daily 9:30am-dusk. $10, children $8, family of 5 $40.) Across the street, Caddyshack City offers indoor mini-golf with so many automated doohickeys, strategy is hardly relevant. Price of admission comes with a free drink. (☎ 442 6642. $17, children $12, 4-person family $48. Open daily 10am-7pm. In winter until 8pm.) Last but not least, blur the line between nightlife and sightseeing with **Minus 5°,** a chill bar where everything is made out of ice, including your glass. Admission includes use of a stylish parka, boots, and gloves, as well as a free vodka cocktail. Trips are limited to 30min., but considering how cold it is in there, you won't be tempted to linger much longer. (On Steamers Wharf. ☎ 442 6050; www.minus5.co.nz. $25. Free vodka cocktail can be subsituted for 2 non-alcoholic drinks. Open daily 3pm-11pm.)

🔢 DAYTRIP FROM QUEENSTOWN

ARROWTOWN

Arrowtown lies 20km northeast of Queenstown, accessible either by following the signs east through Frankton on SH6a or via the scenic route north on Gorge Rd. Arrowtown Bus Tours (☎ 442 1900; www.arrowtownbus.com) runs from the McCafe on Camp St. in Queenstown to the Lakes District Museum in Arrowtown. (25min.; 5 per day; round-trip $25, children $10). The Double Decker Bus (☎ 441 4421; www.double-deckerbus.co.nz) also runs jolly red vehicles on 3hr. sightseeing tours from the top of The Mall in Queenstown via Lake Hayes and the Bungy Bridge, including 50min. in Arrowtown (departs 9:30am, 1:30pm; $38 round-trip, children $17).

William Fox and a small group of miners pulled 230 lb. of gold from the Arrow River in 1862, sparking one of the region's gold rushes. Today, Arrowtown draws a middle-aged crowd looking for a historical diversion from Queenstown. The **Lakes District Museum,** at the end of Buckingham St., reacquaints adventurous travelers with the area's frontier spirit with hands-on gizmos and a recreated 1860s Arrowtown street. The museum also serves as a **visitors center** for local information and bookings. Pick up brochures and local trail maps ($3 or less) here. (☎442 1824; www.museumqueenstown.com. Open daily 8:30am-5pm. $6, children $1.)

Branching off from the main parking area, the historic **Chinese Settlement** features a series of mud-walled huts and tales of harsh living conditions Chinese laborers faced during the gold rush. If you fancy striking it rich, the Lakes District Museum will rent you a pan ($3 with $10 deposit) and let you have at it. Otherwise, a 14-ouncer and other special nuggets sit in a case at **The Gold Shop**, 29 Buckingham St. (☎442 1319. Open daily 8:30am-5:30pm.) Arrowtown comes alive in April with the annual **Autumn Festival** (www.arrowtown.com), complete with a parade, live music, and street performers. Several walking and biking **tracks** depart from the settlement, though they are slippery in winter. **Macetown Road** is a rigorous 13km 4WD track upriver and across a number of easily flooded streams to the Arrowtown **ghost town.** The visitors center can provide a map ($10) for the well-prepared, but a 4WD tour with **NOMAD Safaris** is the safest and most fun way to go. (☎442 6699 or 0800 688 222; www.nomadsafaris.co.nz. 4-4½hr. $130.) Biking trips down Macetown Road are also available. "Pink" and "Fabulous" seem to be the design inspiration for **Dorothy Browns Cinema,** through the alley next to the pharmacy on Buckingham St., where moviegoers can select between the chandeliered elegance of the main theatre or the gilded high-backed chairs in "The Den." Tickets may be pricey but cheap bottled drinks ($3-6) make up some of the difference. (☎442 1964; www.dorothybrowns.com. Mainstream and foreign films $18, before 5pm weekdays $15. Films in the Den $15.)

As a peaceful alternative from the never-stop mentality of Queenstown, the **Riverdown Guesthouse (BBH) ❷,** 7 Bedford St., has a quiet riverside garden and cozy communal kitchen. Head left out of the museum, turn left on Merioneth St., and right on Bedford St. (☎409 8499. Linen $3. Check-in after 4pm. Dorms $27; doubles and twins $60, with bath $80. $3 BBH discount.) Upscale cafes line **Buckingham Street,** offering many dining options. The goodies in the case at **Cafe Mondo ❷,** near the parking lot, are substantial, tasty, and cheap ($3-10). Linger with coffee and watch bemused as the friendly waitstaff fend off scavenging birds. (☎442 0227. Open daily 8am-5pm, also W-Su 5pm-late.)

GLENORCHY
☎03

The cinematic drama of Glenorchy's frosty mountain setting has been captured countless times on film, everywhere from Middle Earth to middle America—take a good look at the "Rocky Mountains" on your next case of Coors Light. This small town (pop. 300), just 48km north of Queenstown, lies at the intersection of Fiordland and Mt. Aspiring National Parks and fills its sleepy role as gateway to self-made adventure in the heart of South Island. Though a few of Queenstown's farther-flung activity providers call the town home, trampers flock to Glenorchy mainly for access to the Routeburn Track (p. 389), Greenstone and Caples Tracks (p. 391), Rees-Dart Track (p. 403), and a number of shorter but still impressive valley walks in the area.

◖◪ TRANSPORTATION AND PRACTICAL INFORMATION. Backpacker Express (☎442 9939) has shuttles to and from Queenstown (Nov.-Apr. 2 per day, May-Oct. on demand; $18). The road to Glenorchy is a winding 45min. along Lake Wakatipu; some choose to hitch (not recommended by *Let's Go*), although the road is sparsely traveled.

The **Glenorchy Store,** which runs the Holiday Park on the way into town, is also the **information center.** (☎441 0303. Open daily 8am-6:30pm, in winter 8am-5:30pm.) The **DOC,** at the end of Main Rd., has up-to-date weather, hut, and trail condition reports. (☎442 9937. Open daily 8:30am-4:30pm. Closed late Apr.-Sept.) The **post office** is in the **gas station** at the end of town. (☎442 9913. Open M-F 8am-6pm, Sa-Su 9am-6pm. In winter until 5pm.) **Internet access** is available at either the Glenorchy Hotel ($6 per hr.) or Glenorchy Store ($4 per hr.). There are **no banks or ATMs** in Glenorchy, but luckily, also relatively few places in which to exchange money for goods and services. Stock up in Queenstown with everything you need including groceries before heading over.

┏╋┗ ACCOMMODATIONS AND FOOD. The **Glenorchy Hotel ❷**, on Mull St., embodies the good vibes of its enthusiastic proprietors. Beds in the bunkhouse share space with a woodstove, a canary-yellow kitchen, and a cat named Todd. (☎442 9902 or 0800 453 667; relax@glenorchy.org.nz. Dorms $20; doubles $50; motel units from $75. MC/V.) The **Glenorchy Holiday Park ❶**, to your right as you enter town, has an array of worn but cheap options. (☎441 0303. Reception at Glenorchy Store 8am-6:30pm, after hours at the back of the building. Free car storage for guests and Backpacker Express customers. Tent sites $10, powered $15. Dorms $16 per person. Cabins $40 for 2, $14 per extra person up to 4. MC/V.)

At the bar and restaurant of the **Glenorchy Hotel ❷**, filling mains ($9.50-18.50) satisfy post-tramp cravings. The stonegrill self-cooking entrees ($26-28.50) are a sizzling carnivorous option. (Open daily 8am-9pm. Bar open late. MC/V.) **The Glenorchy Cafe ❷**, opposite the gas station, serves pastries and light meals ($7.50-16.50), with ample outdoor seating in back. (☎442 9978. Open Su-Th 8am-5pm, F-Sa 8am-8:30pm with pizza after 5pm. Cash only.)

▐▞ OUTDOOR ACTIVITIES. ▨**Dart River Safaris** is a fast-paced foray up the Dart River, past **Mt. Earnslaw,** and into the heart of **Mt. Aspiring National Park.** The trip enters the **UNESCO South West New Zealand World Heritage Area,** where ancient forests and ethereal fields blanket the bases of rugged mountains. The jetboats spin, grind, and fly up the pebbled braids of the river, stopping at scenic **Routeburn Valley.** A unique combination of speed and scenery, the 3hr. safari astounds with its views and hits the spot for jetboat enthusiasts. Also run by Dart River Safaris, half-day **Funyak** trips take passengers upriver, letting them loose in three-person inflatable canoes. (☎442 9992 or 0800 327 853; www.dartriver.co.nz. Lunch, wetsuits, and gear provided, but bring a swimsuit. Safaris runs daily 9am, 1pm. $179, children $89.50. Funyak trips 6hr. $255/192. Both trips depart 1hr. earlier and cost $30 more from Queenstown.) Horse rides through the Glenorchy area make for a relaxing way to explore the area. **Dart Stables** (☎442 5688 or 0800 474 3464; www.dartstables.com) offers two shorter rides through local Glenorchy scenery, in addition to daytrips and overnight trips through the beech forests of the Paradise estate. (2hr. "River Wild" $105, $125 from Queenstown; full-day $215/235. Rides depart Glenorchy at 9:15am and 2:15pm.) **High Country Horses** (☎442 9915 or 0508 595 959; www.high-country.horses.co.nz) depart from the Paradise Rd. 5.5km outside of Glenorchy, and offer rides similar to Dart Stables. (2hr. ride $105, full-day $205, overnight $525. Multi-day trips to Arthur's Creek and Lennox Falls available. Add $20 for transport from Queenstown.) **Mountainland Rovers** leads scenic 4WD tours from Glenorchy up the Rees River toward Lennox Falls, with time to explore the falls over tea. (☎441 1323 or 0800 246 494; www.mountainlandrovers.co.nz. 3hr. Trips depart Glenorchy at 9:15am and 2:15pm, $139. 4½-5hr. Trips from Queenstown depart 8am and 1:30pm, $159.)

Free, self-guided walks around Glenorchy have maximum scenic impact and relatively low time commitment; the DOC office has maps. Many daytrippers hike the first leg of the Routeburn Track (p. 389) for an afternoon glimpse of its legendary scenery. Walkers really in a pinch can tackle the **Glenorchy Walkway,** a tame 45min. stroll across mostly boardwalked and spongy terrain that affords unobstructed mountain views and a few picnic spots. The walk begins at the far end of Mull St. Other walks in the area require a car to reach the trailheads. The **Invincible Gold Mine Walk** (3hr. round-trip) goes to an abandoned mine and offers views of Mt. Earnslaw and the Rees Valley. The trail starts 16km north of town; follow Paradise Rd. north for 7km, then turn right at the sign for the mine on Rees Valley Rd. just before the Rees River. The track to **Lake Sylvan**, (2hr. round-trip, includes a tame but bridgeless stream crossing), is another popular day-hike. The trailhead is 22km from Glenorchy, reached by following signs for the Routeburn and traveling 5km north of the Dart River Bridge.

🖾 ROUTEBURN TRACK

Lying half within Fiordland National Park (p. 365) and half within Mt. Aspiring National Park (p. 401), Routeburn is the shortest of the Great Walks (33km) but among the most spectacular. The track climbs gently through the idyllic Routeburn Valley, passing the Harris Saddle and then ambling high above the treeline on the Serpentine Range. On clear days, the dramatic views approach the sublime; trampers gaze across the Hollyford Valley to the snow-capped peaks of the towering Darren Range.

Length: 33km, 2-4 days.

Trailheads: The Mt. Aspiring side of the track begins at **Routeburn Shelter,** 24km north of Glenorchy. The Fiordland side begins at **The Divide,** on Milford Rd., 84km north of Te Anau. Trampers can walk the track in either direction, and many combine the track with either the **Caples** or **Greenstone** walks to create a loop.

Transportation: Both **Backpacker Express** (☎442 9939) runs between **Routeburn Shelter** and **Glenorchy** (30min., 2-3 per day, $18) and then on to **Queenstown** (1¼hr., $37). **Tracknet** (☎249 7777 or 0800 483 262) makes the most frequent trips to **The Divide** (from **Te Anau** 1½hr., $32; from **Milford Sound** 30min., $27; from **Queenstown** 4hr., $67). **Buckley Transport** (☎442 8215; www.buckleytranport.co.nz) offers on-demand transport from Glenorchy to the Routeburn Shelter generally for a bit cheaper than Backpacker Express. Book ahead. Although one should always consider the risks, patient **hitchhikers** report success getting to The Divide; those who've tried to hitch to Routeburn Shelter say it is quite difficult. Day hikers populate the lower stretches of the track in summer months; many trampers ask them for a ride while on the track.

Seasonality: Year-round, but winter trips in the avalanche-prone Fiordland/Mt. Aspiring area are only for experienced alpinists. May-Nov. are very dangerous. Throughout the year, there is plentiful rain and the possibility of freak snow storms.

Huts and Campsites: Late Oct. to late Apr., the 4 huts and 2 campsites operate on a booking system. In summer, all huts have gas cookers, taps, and flush toilets ($40 per night). Camping is allowed only at the MacKenzie and the Routeburn Flats Huts. These campsites have toilets and cooking shelters, but no stoves ($10 per night). Trampers must pick up their hut and campsite passes from a DOC office either the day before or by 2pm the day they start the track. In winter (late Apr. to late Oct.), the gas is removed from the huts, hut fees revert to the backcountry ticket system ($10 per night), and camping is free, but not recommended.

Bookings: The Routeburn fills up fast; spots at MacKenzie and Routeburn Falls Huts are the first to go. Dec. and Jan. are busiest. Nearly everyone books on the DOC web-site (www.doc.govt.nz), which lists the availability of each hut for each night of the season. Applications to walk the Routeburn are first come, first served, starting on July 1 for the following season (late Oct. to late Apr.). The DOC does not keep a wait-ing list. Couples and solo trampers have the best chances. Guided walks of the

Routeburn are also available starting from $1050; call **Ultimate Hikes** (☎441 1138 or 0800 659 255; www.ultimatehikes.co.nz).

Storage: Most accommodations will oblige free of charge. **Topline Tours** (☎0508 832 628) transports extra gear between Te Anau and Queenstown ($10 per bag up to 15kg, $15 after that). Pick-up or drop-off from any hostel in Te Anau and the Info and Track Centre in Queenstown.

Parking: Parking at the Routeburn Shelter carpark is generally considered to be safe, though those wishing to take arranged transport to the trailhead can leave their cars at the Glenorchy Holiday Park if traveling with Backpacker Express.

ROUTEBURN SHELTER TO ROUTEBURN FALLS HUT. *8.8km, 3-4½hr.* From **Routeburn Shelter**, a gradual ascent (2-3hr.) through an ancient beech forest winds over and along various charging blue streams before reaching the turn-off (10min. round-trip) for **Routeburn Flats Hut** (20 bunks), which fronts a broad tussocked valley and the gentle Routeburn River. About 15 campsites lie secluded amid tall grasses, 200m away from the hut. On the way to the Route-burn Flats Hut is a side-trip to **Forge Flat,** an old blacksmith camp (5-10min. return), which should not be mistaken for the main track. Ideal for those frustrated by heavy traffic on the main track, The **North Branch Routeburn** side-trip (4-5hr. round-trip) explores the narrowing valley between Mt. Somnos and Mt. Erebus. The path begins at the orange pole directly across the unbridged river from the hut; it is only lightly marked with poles and rock cairns and can become boggy after rain. Back on the main track, the gradually steepening trail climbs through the ferned and forested flanks of the Routeburn Valley's southern side. The track crosses the scars of several slips during the ascent—stony proof of the power of snow and rain to move mountains. Just at the edge of the treeline perches **Routeburn Falls Hut** (48 bunks), a wood-paneled palace with two separate bunkrooms and a balcony overlooking the valley.

ROUTEBURN FALLS HUT TO LAKE MACKENZIE HUT AND CAMPSITE. *11.3km, 4½hr.* This is the Routeburn's most awesome stretch and its most exposed; be prepared for intense, unpredictable sun, wind, rain, or snow at any time of the year. Parts of the track are solid rock and slippery when wet, while most of the rest is strewn with ankle-busting rocks; watch your step. Initially very steep, the track passes the neighboring guided walkers' hut and roaring **Routeburn Falls** before leveling out in a wide glacial bowl—the valley below looks like it has been untouched since the last ice age. The path winds under craggy, moss-encrusted peaks, then edges above **Lake Harris.** Just through the saddle from the lake, the **Harris Saddle Shelter** contains toilets and emergency equipment—be warned that the saddle shelter is an emergency shelter only and carries a $500 fine for overnight use. From here, a steep and rewarding side trip leads to the top of ▓**Conical Hill** (1-1½hr. round-trip), where, on a clear day, the 360° panorama encompasses crinkly ridges, unnamed glaciers, and the Hollyford Valley's stretch to the Tasman Sea. The main track sidles along the mountainside above the **Hollyford Valley,** traversing the treeless Serpentine Range and exposing greater views with every step. Once the emerald green **Lake MacKenzie** comes into sight, the trail drops steeply to **Lake MacKenzie Hut** (48 bunks), another backcountry grand hotel. Arrive early if you want to avoid the communal bunkroom. Outside, **Emily Peak** is reflected in the lake, and dozens of trampers sunbathe on boulders or take a limb-numbing swim. The **camp-site**—nine sites ringed by trees—lies 400m farther.

LAKE MACKENZIE HUT AND CAMPSITE TO THE DIVIDE. *12km, 4-5½hr.* A steep ascent brings trampers to the bushline. Easing back down, the track weaves through the **Orchard,** a patch of native ribbonwood trees, in the midst of a silver beech forest. The thundering 80m **Earland Falls** makes for a good water break nearly an hour later. **Lake Howden Hut** (28 bunks) sits on the shores of its namesake; the junction for the **Greenstone Track** is right outside. A 20min. hike along the Greenstone leads to the free **Greenstone Saddle Campsite,** which sports a pit toilet but no shelter or water. Back at the Lake Howden junction, the track ascends to the turn-off for **Key Summit** (1hr. round-trip), a popular dayhike for those cruising the Milford Rd. If cloud cover ruined the view from Conical Hill, Key Summit's slightly less spectacular panorama makes a good substitute. The main track switchbacks down to **The Divide,** where there are toilets and shelter to freshen up and wait for a ride out.

⑨ GREENSTONE AND CAPLES TRACKS

A graceful and pastoral pair, the Greenstone and Caples Tracks stretch around impressive mountain peaks and through cow-filled river valleys. While a tiny corner of the loop lies inside Mt. Aspiring and Fiordland National Park (p. 401), most of it falls within the Wakatipu Recreational Hunting Area. Trout fishing is very popular in the Greenstone Valley, but a back country fishing license, controlled fishery license, and didymo permit are required. The fishing season usually lasts from November to May—for more information check www.fishandgame.co.nz. Deer hunting is also possible between April and September, but only with a license from the DOC, who also provides info on local pesticide use. Licenses are granted via a balloting process. Contact the DOC for more information.

Length: 50km, 4-5 days.

Trailheads: The 2 tracks loop between Fiordland National Park and Glenorchy, which can be entered from the eastern **Greenstone Station** road-end (42km from Glenorchy) or from the western **Divide,** midway between Milford and Te Anau. Tramping in either direction is generally the same difficulty, though the descent from Upper Caples Hut to Lake McKellar (as published below) can be quite difficult in inclement weather.

Transportation: Backpacker Express (☎442 9939) runs from the motor park in Glenorchy across Lake Wakatipu to the Greenstone Station road-end (30min.; departs Glenorchy Nov.-Apr. daily 9:30am, 1:30pm, departs trailhead 10am, 2pm; on demand in winter; $19). They also travel to Queenstown ($18). **Buckley Transport** (☎442 8215; www.buckleytranport.co.nz) offers on-demand transport from Glenorchy to the trailhead for a bit cheaper than Backpacker Express. Book ahead.

Seasonality: Thick snow and a lack of hut wardens make the winter season more challenging, but the track is considered reasonably safe year-round.

Huts and Campsites: All of the huts ($10 per night) provide coal stoves, water taps, outhouses, and a weather report; none offer gas cookers. **Mid Caples** and **Greenstone Huts** have 2 bunkrooms flanking a small, central kitchen; **Upper Caples** and **McKellar Huts** are identical 1-room shelters. Camping is free but use of any hut facilities costs $5 per night; DOC prefers that campers choose sites at the huts rather than camping along the trail.

Special Gear: Chlorine, iodine tablets, or other water purification measures are advisable; gut-wrenching giardia has been detected on the track, although not for several years. Trampers frequently drink the water in the huts untreated.

Storage: Most hostels will oblige. **Topline Tours** (☎0508 832 628) transports extra gear between Te Anau and Queenstown ($10 per bag up to 15kg, $15 after that). Pick-up or drop-off from any hostel in Te Anau and the Info and Track Centre in Queenstown.

Parking: Parking at the road end carpark at the junction of the Greenstone and Caples Tracks is generally considered to be safe; however, those wishing to take arranged transport to the trailhead can use the carpark at the Glenorchy Holiday Park if traveling with Backpacker Express.

ROAD-END TO MID CAPLES HUT. *7.5km, 2-3hr.* From the parking lot at the end of the road, the track leads past the confluence of the Greenstone and Caples Rivers. Do not cross the river at the bridge for the Lake Rere Track; keep to the downstream left bank until you reach the swing bridge posted for the Greenstone Track. The Caples Track branches off to the right alongside the river through beech forest until crossing a narrow gorge before **Mid Caples Hut** (12 bunks). This two-wing hut has great views of fields, streams, and distant peaks.

MID CAPLES HUT TO UPPER CAPLES HUT. *7.5km, 1½-2½hr.* The track weaves between beech forests and grassland replete with sublime mountain and river views before reaching the **Upper Caples Hut** (12 bunks). The rugged **Steele Creek Route,** which essentially bisects the Greenstone and Caples loop, is accessible from the hut 20min. back up the track, and is an unmarked, unforgiving path (10-12hr., for experienced trampers only) to **Greenstone Hut** (see below).

UPPER CAPLES HUT TO LAKE MCKELLAR JUNCTION. *7.5km, 4-6hr.* Along the glacial blue vein of the Caples River, the track climbs through thick mossy bush, which becomes full of slick roots underfoot. The uphill going is tough in good weather, and heavy rain can cause hazardous stream crossings along the way. Within 3hr. the track breaks onto the grasslands and misty mountain vistas of McKellar Saddle. Jagged Mt. Christina and the Darren Mountains beckon on the horizon. The brutal drop-off descent to the junction at **Lake McKellar** is the steepest on the Greenstone and Caples Tracks, but trusty roots offer good footholds. While generally traversible in clear weather, any rain can cause it to be too slick to be safe; waiting for better conditions is advisable. After a valley crossing to the junction, trampers have the choice of exiting to the Divide or continuing along the Greenstone Valley via McKellar Hut.

LAKE MCKELLAR JUNCTION TO THE DIVIDE. *6km, 1-2hr.* The northbound fork leads across a stretch of soggy grassland and past the stream-fed, rocky, and free **Lake Howden Campsite** (toilet, no tap) before joining the Routeburn Track at **Lake Howden Hut.** From here, you can head up a 15min. climb, then down for 45min. to the **Milford Road** (p. 416), or set off along the Routeburn Track. Note that staying at the Lake Howden Hut requires booking a spot on the Routeburn Track.

LAKE MCKELLAR JUNCTION TO MCKELLAR HUT. *3km, 1-1½hr.* From the junction, the track follows the lake past lichen-encrusted beeches along the loamy side of Lake McKellar and out of Fiordland National Park to **McKellar Hut** (12 bunks), a one-roomer in the shadow of McKellar Saddle.

MCKELLAR HUT TO GREENSTONE HUT. *19km, 4½-6½hr.* Through the forest, meadows, and cow herds, the track opens out within 1hr. to meander along the leafy edge and across the gold tussocks of the Greenstone Valley. The track crosses a swing bridge over the Steele River, followed by a 1-2hr. walk along the river through an open valley before the **Greenstone Hut** (20 bunks). The 10min. side-trail to the hut bridges a deep chasm and then ascends briefly before arriving at the tent-friendly fields surrounding this backcountry commode.

GREENSTONE HUT TO ROAD-END. *8km, 3-5hr.* The Greenstone Hut is one end of the **Mavora-Greenstone Walkway** (51km, 4 days), which leads south to an unpaved offshoot of SH94. Back on the track, however, it's another rolling, blue-pooled riverside stretch back to the Caples junction and the parking lot. Excellent fishing spots abound on the river about halfway to the end, just as the track crosses open fields before entering the narrow gorge it follows back toward Lake Wakatipu. Fishing permits are required.

WANAKA   ☎03

Surrounded by the glassy waters of Lake Wanaka and the peaks of Mt. Aspiring National Park, Wanaka has become a destination for those seeking adventure in the great outdoors. With some of South Island's top rock climbing, hiking, mountain biking, and skiing, the town has boomed in recent years. Even with the increasing numbers of people, Wanaka retains its local character in funky cafes and lively nightlife venues and seals its reputation as an alternative to the flashiness and commercialism of a certain neighbor (ahem, Queenstown) to the south.

▐▘ TRANSPORTATION

Flights: The airport is 9km east of town on SH89. **Aspiring Air/Air New Zealand** (ANZ ☎0800 737 000; Aspiring: ☎0800 100 943 or 443 7943; www.aspiringair.com) flies daily to **Christchurch** (1hr., $160) and on demand to **Queenstown** ($135; Min. 2 people). **Taxis** to downtown Wanaka around $45. **Shuttle service** is available for $10.

Buses: Booking agencies will eagerly arrange your transport. Most buses and shuttles leave from the Information Centre (which can book tickets throughout Otago) or across from the log cabin. **InterCity** (☎474 9600) runs to: **Christchurch** (7¼hr., 8am, $63) via **Aoraki/Mt. Cook** (4hr., $46); **Franz Josef Glacier** (6½hr., 9:45am, $74) via **Fox Glacier** (5¾hr., $70); **Queenstown** (1½hr., 2:35pm, $31) **Southern Link** (☎0800 881 188 or 0508 458 835) goes to **Christchurch** (6½hr., 10:15am, $45) and **Queenstown** (1½hr., 4:35pm, $25). **Wanaka Connexions** (☎443 9122; www.wanakashuttles.co.nz) shuttles to **Queenstown** (1½hr., 4 per day, $25) and on to **Invercargill** (4½hr., 7am, $60) and **Te Anau** (6¼hr., 10:30am, $50). **Catch-A-Bus** (☎479 9960) is bike-friendly ($10 extra) and serves **Dunedin** (4hr., 3 per day, $48). **Atomic Shuttles** (☎0508 108 359) goes to the **Greymouth** (8¾hr., daily 9:15am, $80) via **Fox Glacier** (5¼hr., $45) and **Franz Josef** (5¾hr., $50); **Christchurch** (6½hr., 3pm, $50); **Dunedin** (4hr., 3pm, $40); **Queenstown** (1½hr., 2 per day, $25); **Te Anau** (4¼hr., 8:15am, $45).

Shuttles: Door-to-door shuttles run frequently from Wanaka to the slopes and to Mt. Aspiring trailheads. **Alpine Shuttles** (☎443 7966) and **A Class Shuttles** (☎0800 186 754) make trailhead runs to the Mt. Roy tramp (from $10), Diamond Lake ($15) and to Mt. Aspiring National Park ($30, return $55). Both companies also shuttle to the slopes in winter as does **Wanaka Connections** (see **Buses,** above). All shuttles have comparable prices, usually $25-28 round-trip.

Taxis: Wan A Cab ☎443 5555.

Car Rental: Wanaka Rentacar, 2 Brownston St. (☎443 6641); **Ace Rental Cars** (☎0800 330 111), next to Caltex Garage; **Alpine Rentals** (☎443 7966), in Good Sports; **Adventure Rentals** (☎443 6050), 20 Ardmore St.; **Aspiring Rentals** (☎443 7883), Lakeview Holiday Park all have good deals on rentals.

Hitchhiking: Although *Let's Go* does not recommend hitchhiking, hitchers report finding rides out to the slopes easily, though shuttles are a must for Mt. Aspiring. At the western edge of town, the Cardrona/Queenstown-bound gather at the corner of Brownston and McDougall St.; those going to Treble Cone assemble at the corner of Ardmore and McDougall St. Hitchers heading up the coast wait past the DOC office on Ardmore St.

◼✦ ⊠ ORIENTATION AND PRACTICAL INFORMATION

Wanaka is extremely compact, with most shops and services occupying **Helwick** and **Ardmore Street (SH89).** SH89 traces the shore of Lake Wanaka, becoming **Mt. Aspiring Road** south of town and offering access to the National Park. The **Cardrona Road** is the fastest way to Queenstown and begins in the south as **McDougall Street.**

Visitors Center: Lake Wanaka Information Centre, 100 Ardmore St. (☎443 1233; www.lakewanaka.co.nz), in the log cabin. Open daily in summer 8:30am-6:30pm, in winter 8:30am-5:30pm.

Department of Conservation (DOC): The **DOC** (☎443 7660) is at the top of Ardmore St. Open daily 8am-5pm. May-Oct. M-F 8am-4:45pm, Sa 9:30am-3:45pm reduced weekend hours.

Booking Agents: Deep Canyon, (☎443 7922), in the Good Sports building, has a comprehensive list of Wanaka activities, accommodation and transportation and does bookings. Open daily 8am-6pm.

Banks: Various banks can be found on Ardmore and Helwick St.; most with 24hr. **ATMs.**

Gear Rental:

▨ **Good Sports,** 23 Dunmore St. (☎443 7966 or 0800 754 926; www.good-sports.co.nz). A wide selection of tramping and climbing toys, as well as skis, boots, and poles from $32 per day; snowboards from $35. Fishing rods and reels from $10 per day. Sleeping bags $7.50. Tents $10. Bikes from $20. Open daily July-Sept. 7am-8pm; Oct.-June 8am-7pm.

Base, 39 Helwick St. (☎443 2290; www.base.net.nz). High-quality equipment and a knowledgeable staff. Skis, boots, and poles from $32 per day. Snowboard and boots $39. Open June-Sept. daily 7am-7pm.

Sun and Snowbusiness, 103 Ardmore St. (☎443 8855; www.sunandsnow.col.nz), rents a variety of carver skis, boots, and poles for $30 per day. Snowboards and boots for $35. In summer, waterskis from $25 per day. Kayaks $25 per day. Fishing rods $15. Fly fishing equipment $20. 1-day license $18.50. Open daily June-Oct. 7:30am-8:30pm; Nov.-May 9am-5:30pm.

Thunderbikes, 48 Helwick St. (☎443 2558; www.thunderbikes.co.nz), has a range of mountain bikes and detailed trail information. Half-day rental from $20; full-day from $30. Full suspension bikes $40/55. Downhill bikes $50/75.

Police: 28 Helwick St. (☎443 7272).

Medical Services: Wanaka Pharmacy, 41-43 Helwick St. (☎443 8000). Open M-Sa 8:30am-7pm, Su 10am-7pm. **Aspiring Medical Centre,** 28 Dunvargon St. (☎443 1226), and **Wanaka Medical Centre,** 21 Russell St. (☎443 7811), have 24hr. emergency call service.

Internet Access: Wanaka Web, 3 Helwick St. (☎443 7429; wanakaweb@netspeed.net.nz), has high-speed Internet wireless and laptop hookups. Internet $6 per hr. $20 per 5hr. Open daily 10am-9pm; later when busy.

Post Office: 39 Ardmore St. (☎443 8211). Poste Restante. Open M-F 8:30am-5:30pm, Sa 9am-noon.

⋔ ⛰ ACCOMMODATIONS AND CAMPING

In winter, the long-term ski and snowboard bunnies move in, often filling more than half of the hostel beds for weeks and months at a time; it is essential to book ahead. Though summer is not as busy as winter, it is still advisable to book ahead.

The Purple Cow (BBH), 94 Brownston St. (☎443 1880 or 0800 772 277; www.purplecow.co.nz). This large lodge gives guests a touch of luxury with sunny common spaces, a helpful staff, brand new kitchen, and nightly movies on the big-screen TV. Bike rental $9 per hr.; $25 per day. Linen $2. Key deposit $10. Reception 8am-8pm. Dorms $24-28; twins and doubles $69, with lakeview $75. $3 BBH discount. MC/V. ❸

Altamont Lodge, 121 Mt. Aspiring Rd. (☎443 8864; altamontlodge@xtra.co.nz), 2km from town. Pine-paneled walls, free spa, ski-tuning room, and a welcoming hearth achieve a classic ski-lodge feel. Their rooms are one of the best deals in town and an excellent choice for couples with cars. Linen $5. Reception 8am-9pm. Book ahead. Singles $40; doubles $60. $15 per extra person. MC/V. ❸

Mountain View Backpackers (BBH), 7 Russell St. (☎443 9010 or 0800 112 201; www.mtnview.co.nz). The thick mattresses, outdoor courtyard, and quiet but convenient location near town make up for the "cosy" indoor common facilities. No Inter-

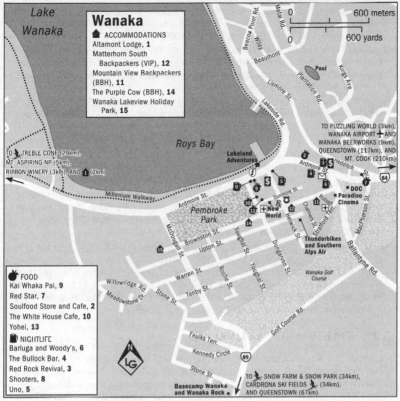

Wanaka

⌂ ACCOMMODATIONS
Altamont Lodge, **1**
Matterhorn South
  Backpackers (VIP), **12**
Mountain View Backpackers
  (BBH), **11**
The Purple Cow (BBH), **14**
Wanaka Lakeview Holiday
  Park, **15**

🍴 FOOD
Kai Whaka Pai, **9**
Red Star, **7**
Soulfood Store and Cafe, **2**
The White House Cafe, **10**
Yohei, **13**

🍸 NIGHTLIFE
Barluga and Woody's, **6**
The Bullock Bar, **4**
Red Rock Revival, **3**
Shooters, **8**
Uno, **5**

Lake Wanaka

Roys Bay

Pembroke Park

Wanaka Golf Course

TO TREBLE CONE (29km), MT. ASPIRING NP (5km), RIPPON WINERY (3km), AND **1** (2km)

TO PUZZLING WORLD (3km), WANAKA AIRPORT ✈ AND WANAKA BEERWORKS (9km), QUEENSTOWN (117km), AND MT. COOK (210km).

■ DOC
■ Paradiso Cinema

Thunderbikes and Southern Alps Air

Basecamp Wanaka and Wanaka Rock ■

TO SNOW FARM & SNOW PARK (34km), CARDRONA SKI FIELDS (34km), AND QUEENSTOWN (67km)

Lakeland Adventures

0 600 meters
0 600 yards

OTAGO

net. Key deposit $10. Reception 8:30am-12:30pm, 3:30-8:30pm. Dorms $24-27; doubles $59. $3 BBH discount. MC/V. ❷

Matterhorn South Backpackers (VIP), 56 Brownston St. (☎443 1119; www.matter-hornsouth.co.nz), at the corner of Helwick St. This central backpackers offers plush seating around a wood-burning stove and a chalet-style dorm. Next door, the sparkling lodge units share a modern kitchen and a quiet lounge. Reception 8am-8pm. Dorms $24; twins and doubles $54. $1 VIP discount. MC/V. ❷

Wanaka Bakpaka (BBH), 117 Lakeside Rd. (☎443 7837; www.wanakabakpaka.co.nz), perched on a hill 5min. from town, they have the best view in town, and very relaxed management. Bikes $24 per day. Reception 8:30am-7pm. 3- to 5-bed dorms $24; twins $56; doubles $60. $3 BBH discount. MC/V. ❷

Wanaka Lakeview Holiday Park, 212 Brownston St. (☎443 7883), past Pembroke Park. Built like a military installation, this camp is large and near town. Softer ground for tents is past the entrance on the right. Linen $3-5. Reception 8am-9pm. Tent and powered sites $13. Dorms $18; 2-person cabins $40; 2-person flats $79. MC/V. ❶

🍴 FOOD

Groceries are at **New World,** 20 Dunmore St. (☎443 0048. Open daily 8am-8pm.)

🍔 **Red Star Luxury Burgers,** 26 Ardmore St. (☎443 9322). The only downside to eating at Red Burger is picking just one thing from the menu. All burgers ($9-14) are overflowing combos of ingredients, such as spicy lentil with sundried tomato hummus, sweet chili and minted yogurt, that you're unlikely to find anywhere else. Open daily in summer and winter midnight-late; in spring and fall 3pm-late. ❷

▨ Soulfood Store and Cafe, 74 Ardmore St. (☎443 7885) has all-natural baked goods and smoothies ($7). Enjoy one of their freshly brewed coffees or teas in the courtyard and discover how easy it is to lose an afternoon. Small organic grocery store attached. Open M-F 8am-6pm, Sa-Su 8am-4pm. ❶

Yohei, Spencer Mall, Dunmore St. (☎443 4222), rolls up sushi ($1.90 per pc.) with a twist, only using local ingredients. Fresh juices and smoothies $6.50-7. Open M-F 8am-4pm, Sa-Su 10am-3pm; in winter open evenings as well. ❶

Kai Whaka Pai (☎443 7795; www.kaiwanaka.co.nz), Ardmore and Helwick St., bustles with cafegoers enjoying the lakefront location. Enormous sandwiches ($6) and quiche ($6; with salad, $12) served all day. Local beers on tap, pints $6. Open in summer and winter daily 7am-10pm; in fall and spring W-Sa 8am-10pm, Su-Tu 8am-6pm. ❶

The White House Cafe, 33 Dunmore St. (☎443 9595), at the corner of Dungarvon St. Set in a stuccoed 1933 Art Deco palace, White House serves a North African and Mediterranean-influenced menu (mains $20-35) in a wooded courtyard. Open daily 5pm-late. Reservations recommended in summer. ❺

Dirty Mary's ❶, 198 Palmerston St., has all-day breakfast ($10), hearty burgers ($11), and fresh smoothies ($4.50). (☎789 6648. Hours vary, but usually open M-F 8am-late, Sa 9am-late, Su 9am-3pm.) Right beside the ocean 34km north of Westport in Hector, **Imagine Cafe ❷,** 37 Main Rd., is full of local character, and local characters. Run by an artist who lives next door, the small thatched roof hut cranks out heaping souvlaki ($9) and strong coffee.

◎ ▨ SIGHTS AND FESTIVALS

Though most of Wanaka's attractions are outdoor activities, there are a few places to visit on a rainy day. Boggle your mind at **Puzzling World,** 3km out of town, opposite Mt. Iron. In the world's first **two-story maze,** you may get lost and never leave. Bring a camera along to capture the special effect of the four illusion rooms. (☎443 7489; www.puzzlingworld.co.nz. Open daily Nov. to mid-Apr. 8:30am-6pm. Mid-Apr. to Oct. 8:30am-5:30pm. Last admission 30min. before closing. Illusion rooms or the maze $7, children $5. Combo $10/7; prices expected to increase with upcoming expansions.) Alternatively, down a pint of **Wanaka Beerworks** brews. The two-person micro-brewery next to the airport in the Wanaka Transport Museum has produced top-prize winners (Brewski, Cordona Gold, and Tall Black) at the New Zealand and Australian International Beer Awards. Though the tour is only 30min., the buzz from the sample brews keeps you happy longer. (☎443 1865; www.wanakabeerworks.co.nz. Tours daily 2pm. Open M-Sa 8am-3pm. $5.) The four warehouses surrounding the brewery are home to the eclectic **Wanaka Transport and Toy Museum.** The seemingly random but always entertaining pairing of toys and transport becomes no more logical after a run through the packed warehouses. (☎443 8765; www.wanakatransportandtoymuseum.com. Open 8:30am-5pm; more in summer. $8, children $4.) To get to the airport, brewery, and museums, take the airport shuttle (see p. 359).

In even numbered years, the New Zealand Fighter Pilots Museum hosts **Warbirds Over Wanaka** (www.warbirdsoverwanaka.com), a flight show featuring WWII-era fighter planes. The next show will occur Easter, 2008. Tickets available through the New Zealand Fighter Pilots Museum. In late April of odd-numbered years, Wanaka is home to world-class art exhibits and theater, dance, and music during the **Festival of Colour** (www.festivalofcolour.co.nz). The annual **Race to the Sky Motor Rally** (www.racetothesky.com) takes place over Easter weekend.

🎵 🎬 ENTERTAINMENT AND NIGHTLIFE

Wanaka's bars fill with travelers fresh from a day's adventure and looking to tell a tale or pick up another one. A staple of Wanaka nightlife and a legendary South Island establishment, ▓**Paradiso Cinema,** 1 Ardmore St., is a quirky theater that doubles as a cafe, serving the best fresh-baked cookies ($3) you'll ever have during an intermission, homemade ice cream ($3.50), and an eclectic menu of mains ($16-19). Watch a flick on the cushy sofas or snag a seat in the vintage car. (☎443 1505; www.paradiso.net.nz. Cafe opens 30min. before 1st screening. Schedules posted in hostels and the visitors center. Internet $2 per 15min. Films $13, children $8.)

Barluga and **Woody's,** Post Office Lane (Barluga ☎443 5400; Woody's ☎443 5551), behind the post office off Ardmore St. Wanaka's two newest bars have been a smashing success. When everywhere else closes for the night, you'll find locals queuing to get in here. Barluga's is the swankier of the two; smart dress required. Woody's is a more relaxed pub; smart casual. Live music every F night. Both open daily 4pm-2:30am.

Shooters, 145 Ardmore St. (☎443 4345). Consistently brings in a young, party-hard crowd of travelers and skiers eager to guzzle, mingle, and bust a move. DJs F-Sa. W is the popular karaoke and pool comp night. Thirsty Th $4 drinks 9pm-midnight and a free barbeque. Open daily 11am-as late as 2:30am.

Red Rock Revival, 68 Ardmore St. (☎443 5545). More casual than Post Office Lane and with cheaper drinks. Plush couches and deck seating in a cool red-and-black theme. Happy hour 5-6pm and 8-9pm $3.50 handles, $8 jugs. Open daily in winter 11am-1am, summer 4pm-1:30am.

Uno, 99 Ardmore St. (☎443 4911), behind the Adventure Centre on the 2nd fl. The polished, unpretentious atmosphere of Wanaka's only wine bar has a selection of Kiwi wines (wine by the glass $7-12). Dress smart; act drunk and you are likely to be turned away. Open daily 4pm-2:30am; doors close at midnight, but you can ring the bell.

The Bullock Bar, 71 Ardmore St. (☎443 7148), is the only place to watch Rugby Union. Try your luck on the gambling machines. Th night in winter, they put huge ice blocks in front of the bar for curling. W Happy hour 5-7pm jugs $6. Open in winter daily 11am-late. In summer M-Sa 10am-2:30am; Su 11am-8pm.

🏔 OUTDOOR ACTIVITIES

SKI FIELDS

Two major downhill ski fields, a terrain park, and cross country tracks are accessible from Wanaka. Ask around to score some sweet specials on transport, tickets, and rentals. A New Zealand student ID are necessary for student deals. Serious ski bums should buy season tickets as early as February for incredible savings. Conditions between the ski fields vary, and snow reports are posted at accommodations in town in the morning. On mountain accommodations can be found on Cardrona, Snow Farm and Snow Park; expect to pay higher rates. Those who want to speed down the slopes in summer, should get a mountain bike, as both Treble Cone and Snow Farm have mountain biking trails in summer.

CARDRONA. Cardrona (1670m; vertical rise 390m) is a more family-oriented field, with wide, gentle slopes perfect for learning. They have predictably good, natural snow and varied terrain for all abilities (25% beginner, 55% intermediate, 20% advanced). Four half-pipes draw snowboarders. *(Ski field: 34km away on Cardrona Rd. ☎443 7411; www.cardrona.com. Wanaka office: 18 Dunmore St., just west of Helwick St. Open in ski season daily 8:45am-4pm. Lift pass $77, student $62, children $39; half-day $56/50/30. 1-day lift and ski/snowboard rental pack $110/70.)*

TREBLE CONE. Treble Cone (2090m) has the highest vertical rise (660m) in the Southern Lakes and contains more skiable terrain than anywhere else on South Island. Runs are generally steeper and more difficult than at Cardrona and better for intermediate and advanced skiers—novices will have bruised bums. *(26km from Wanaka. Wanaka office at 99 Ardmore St. ☎ 443 7443; www.treblecone.com. Lift pass $99, student $69, children $39; half-day $75/55/40. Mountain biking single ride $15, day pass $30.)*

SNOW FARM. New Zealand's only cross-country ski area, the Snow Farm has 55km of impressive trails and views of Cardrona Valley. Wide, well-groomed trails, open night and day, swoop across the hills and into valleys, following ridgelines and rivers. Toyota and Subaru even use the legendary snows to test their tires. In late August, the Snow Farm plays host to international ski races and the famous "Merino Muster" community race. In summer, they open their trails to mountain bikers and trampers. *(34km from Wanaka along the Cardrona Rd. ☎ 443 0300; www.snowfarmnz.com. Equipment rental from $25 per day, $20 for night. Entry $30, night $20; New Zealand students $25/20; children $15/10. Mountain biking $10, with bike hire $20.)*

SNOW PARK. Opened in 2002, this terrain park is now a favorite for skiers and snowboarders. Recent expansions have created terrain options to suit and challenge all ability levels. *(Off the Snow Farm access road. ☎ 443 9991; www.snowparknz.com. Day pass $55-75, student $42-57, children $29-40; half-day $49-67/37-51/26-36.)*

ON THE WATER

Beautiful Lake Wanaka and the rivers that feed it are fished and played upon in every way imaginable. While there are plenty of adrenaline outlets, numerous relaxed lake activities are also available. **Lakeland Adventures,** based in the information center, runs lake cruises (see below) and rents everything you need for a calm morning on the lake. *(☎ 443 7495 or 0508 525 352; www.lakelandadventures.co.nz. Kayaks single $10 per hr., 3km. restriction; doubles $20 per hr., $80 per full-day. Dinghies $20 per hr. Mountain bikes $10 per hr., $35 per full day.)* **Alpine Kayak Guides** (see below) also rents high-quality kayaks.

 WANAKA FOR POCKET CHANGE. Summertime tours on the lake are Wanaka's main draw, but those running short on funds can still explore its waters under the power of two sturdy legs. Rent a bike (p. 394) and hit the lakeside trails followed by a swim or a paddle (p. 394). Fresh baked cookies at Paradiso Cinema (p. 397) are a sweet treat to the end of a hard day's work.

KAYAKING. Alpine Kayak Guides runs instructional courses, as well as scenic day trips with Class II rapids for novice and experienced paddlers. *(☎ 443 9023; www.alpinekayaks.co.nz. 2-person min. 4-5hr. relaxed float $110, children $79. Half-day adventure on Class II rapids $129, full-day $180, full-day instructional $250. Kayak rentals from $25 for half-day, $70 for full-day.)*

SLEDGING. Challenging the dominance of whitewater rafting and boogie-board river surfing, **Frogz Have More Fun** has an alternative. Careening through the Class III-IV rapids on your own, buoyant personal "sledge" (a cross between a personal raft and a sled) is the most in-your-face way to conquer the river. *(☎ 443 9130 or 0800 437 649; www.frogz.co.nz. 4-5hr. Oct.-May 2 per day. Half-day $135, full-day $285.)*

JETBOATING. It wouldn't be the Southern Lakes region without a chance to rip through water only a few centimeters deep. Though big-rapid thrills are tough to find, **Clutha River Jet** runs fast rides on Lake Wanaka and the Clutha River. *(100 Ardmore St. ☎ 443 7495; www.lakelandadventures.co.nz. 1hr. $75, children $35.)* **Wanaka River Journeys** and **Wilkin River Jets** both run heli-jetboating trips as well as combo jetboat-hike tours. *(Wanaka: ☎ 443 4416 or 0800 544 555; www.wanakariver-*

*journeys.co.nz. Jetboating and forest walk $175, children $85; heli-jetboating from $455. Wilkin:
☎ 443 8351 or 0800 538 945; www.wilkinriverjets.co.nz.)*

SAILING. For groups looking to sail to uninhabited islands, **Lake Wanaka Yacht Charters** lets you take the 25 ft. *Astrolabe* for the day. *(☎ 027 240 4045; www.sailwanaka.co.nz. Half-day from $150, skippered charter from $250.)*

FISHING. Lakeland Adventures, located at the wharf, runs 3hr. fishing trips, rents gear, and sells licenses. *(☎ 443 7495; www.lakelandadventures.co.nz. 3hr. trip $285 for 3. Fishing rods $20 per day. 1-day license $18.50.)* Angling supplies are also available from **Good Sports** (p. 394). If you're planning on fishing for multiple days, the multi-day licenses are the best deal. Inquire at the visitors center for a list of local trout and fly fishing guides, but be prepared to pay at least $300 for a half day of fishing. **Eco Wanaka Adventures** (see p. 399) runs boat fishing trips.

WAKEBOARDING. For those wishing to play in the wake of a speed boat, **Watersports Wanaka** is the one to call. Their drivers provide lessons and gear along with hourly boat charters for wakeboarding and waterskiing. *(☎ 021 926 252 or 0800 925 326. Oct.-June only. $150 per hr., $425 per half-day, $725 per full-day. Up to 4 people.)*

SCENIC CRUISES. Lake Wanaka Cruises, run by Lakeland Adventures in the visitors centre, cruises to Stevenson's Island or Mou Waho and allows time for guided bushwalks and afternoon tea. *(☎ 443 1236 or 027 222 4426; www.wanakacruises.co.nz. 2-2½hr. cruise $70, children $35. 3-3½hr. cruise $90/35.)* **Eco Wanaka Adventures** has lake cruises and nature walks as well as boat fishing. *(☎ 443 2869; www.ecowanaka.co.nz. 4hr. cruise and walk on Mou Waho daily 9am and 1:30pm. $135, children $85. Boat fishing 3hr. $270 for 1-2 people; $30 per extra person. Equipment included.)*

IN THE AIR

SKYDIVING. If you're into tempting fate at 15,000 ft. with a jumpmaster strapped to your back, ◾**Tandem Skydive Wanaka** is happy to oblige. The alpine views of Mt. Aspiring and Aoraki/Mt. Cook National Parks, family-run company, and personal instruction make Wanaka an excellent choice for a big fall. *(☎ 443 7207 or 0800 786 877; www.skydivenz.com. Based at the Wanaka airport. Includes 15min. scenic flight. 9000 ft. $229; 12,000 ft. $279; 15,000 ft. $369. DVD and photos $189, just photos $109.)*

PARAGLIDING. With 800m of descent, **Wanaka Paragliding's** Big Mountain flight takes in the terrific scenery of Treble Cone from top to bottom. *(☎ 0800 359 754 or 443 9193; www.wanakaparagliding.co.nz. All trips 1½-2½hr. Big Mountain $170. Return transport to Treble Cone $28.)*

HELICOPTER FLIGHTS. Helicopter flights from Wanaka are generally less expensive than those from Queenstown and just as scenic. The companies below are available for heli-skiing charter in winter. **Wanaka Helicopters** whirs around Wanaka Lake from as little as $160. A 45min. trip that offers close-up views of Mt. Aspiring and a snow landing ($435), or go all the way to Milford Sound ($795). All four pilots at Wanaka Helicopters are trained instructors and offer "do it yourself" scenic flights. *(☎ 443 1085 or 0800 463 626; www.heliflights.co.nz.)* **Alpine Helicopters** and **Aspiring Helicopters** have similar trips. *(Alpine: ☎ 443 4000 or 021 395 737; www.alpineheli.co.nz. 20min. scenic Wanaka trip $150. Aspiring: ☎ 443 7152 or 027 437 3571; www.aspiringhelicopters.co.nz. 25min. scenic flight $155.)*

OTHER SCENIC FLIGHTS. Classic Flights flies in a vintage Tigermoth plane. No cabin means open-air flying complete with fashionable goggles. *(☎ 027 220 9277; www.classicflights.co.nz. 20min. scenic flight over the Clutha River $175, 30min. acrobatic flight $225.)* One of the longest-running flight companies in Wanaka, **Southern Alps Air and Siberia Experience** has scenic flights in the famous yellow plane as well as combo options. *(Office 48 Helwick St. ☎ 0800 345 666; www.siberiaexperience.co.nz. Flights from $230. Milford Sound from $395. Half day flight-hike-jetboat combo $270, children $213.)*

OTHER ACTIVITIES

CANYONING. Not for the armchair adventurer, ▨**Deep Canyon Experience** entices the bold to plunge 25 ft. into narrow pools, coaxes the timid to abseil slippery overhanging faces, and tempts thrill-seekers to slip down slick rock slides. After a day of "tangoing with your fears," the canyon spits you out just in time for a proper afternoon repast. (☎443 7922; www.deepcanyon.co.nz. Nov.-Mar. only. Beginner Niger trip $215. Big Niger $280. All trips include lunch but a big breakfast is advisable.)

MOUNTAIN BIKING. Wanaka's mountain biking is renowned throughout New Zealand as the country's best. Both Treble Cone and Snow Farm open their trails to bikers outside of ski season (see p. 398). Otherwise, beginners should try the **Outlet Track** (18km loop, 1-2hr.) or the **Minaret Burn Track** (3-4hr. one-way) in West Wanaka. Experienced riders should head to **the Plantation,** where 30-40km of single track awaits, including the popular **Sticky Forest. Tuohy's Gully,** near Snow Park, has a mean climb and serious downhill. Most cyclists opt to rent a bike and hit the trails on their own. Quality rentals are available from Thunderbikes (see 375). Those who want guidance should contact **Freeride NZ.** (☎0800 743 469; www.freerideNZ.com. Daytrips from $70. Heli-biking $280-300. Trips only operate in the summer.)

MOTOR SPORTS. If you've ever wanted to drive over cars, head to **Cardrona Adventure Park,** 2km before Cardrona, Cardrona Valley Rd. (SH89). They will put you at the helm of a school bus on steroids. (☎443 6363; www.adventurepark.co.nz. Open daily 10am-5pm, sometimes later. 15min. monster truck drive from $250, school bus from $140. Argo 8 wheeler $30 per person. Min. 3 people; max. 6. Off-road race car 10 laps $135, with passenger $135.)

ROCK CLIMBING. Basecamp Wanaka, 50 Cardrona Valley Rd., just out of town, is a brand-new rockclimbing facility with 300 sq. m of indoor and 400 sq. m of outdoor climbing. **Wanaka Rock,** based in the Basecamp building, tailors half- or full-day courses to ability level and scales some of New Zealand's finest rock. (Basecamp: ☎443 1110; www.basecampwanaka.co.nz. Unlimited day of climbing from $15, students $12, children $9; gear hire $10. 1hr. guided adventure $17. Open daily 9am-9pm, sometimes later. Wanaka Rock: ☎443 6411; www.wanakarock.co.nz. Half-day $110, children $75; full-day $185. Full-day course includes lunch.)

GOLFCROSS AND WINE TASTING. Unable to escape a vicious slice that's ruining your golf game? The rugby-ball shaped golf balls at the Rippon Winery's GolfCross course fly truer than normal balls. What's more, wide goal-posts replace holes, meaning you can still slide in below par after a few free tastings. The winery itself is Central Otago's oldest, and hosts Rippon, a biennial festival of New Zealand music held on the first Saturday in February. The next festival is in 2008. (246 Mt. Aspiring Rd., 4km from Wanaka. ☎443 8084; www.rippon.co.nz. Open daily Dec.-Apr. 11am-5pm; July-Nov. 1:30-4:30pm. Closed May-June. GolfCross $25. Set of clubs $15. Tastings free.)

HORSE TREKS. New Zealand Backcountry Saddle Expeditions has 2hr. Apaloosa horse runs daily in the Cardrona Valley as well as full-day excursions. (25km south of Wanaka on SH89. ☎443 8151; backcountry.saddle.expeditions@xtra.co.nz. Apaloosa horse 2hr. run $70, children $50. Full-day excursions $210, including lunch. Transport $10.)

HIKING AND MOUNTAINEERING

Tramping abounds around Lake Wanaka and the surrounding mountains. Several walks begin right inside town, tracing the scenic lakeshore, although the more scenic tracks require either transport or very hardy legs. Most of the trails along the lake allow bikes. **Alpine Shuttles** and **A Class Shuttles** run daily from October to May. (Alpine: 9:15am. Express: 9:30am. Diamond Lake $15, return $20; Mt. Roy $10, 15 return.)

HIKES. The **Diamond Lake Track,** through glacially carved terrain, is one of the prettiest short hikes in New Zealand. The track takes 2hr. for the lower circuit and 3hr. if you opt to climb Rocky Mountain, where the best views are. *(Trailhead is signposted from Mt. Aspiring Rd., 12km and 25min. west of Wanaka on Ardmore St. Bikes prohibited. Not recommended July-Sept.)* Beginning along the south side of Roy's Bay, the **Waterfall Creek Track** also called the **Millenium Walkway**, is ideal for those looking for quiet views of Lake Wanaka. *(1½hr. round-trip; with Millennium extension 4hr.)* Just 1km outside Wanaka on SH6 is the trailhead for a short hike that ascends **Mt. Iron** (240m) and offers panoramic vistas of Lake Wanaka and the Clutha River Valley. *(2km from Wanaka. 2hr. round-trip.* The tramp up **Roy's Peak** delivers views of Mt. Aspiring National Park, including the park's namesake, also known as the Matterhorn of the South. In good weather, hikers opt to continue over Mt. Alpha and through the tussock down to Cardrona Rd./SH89. *(The marked trailhead is off Mt. Aspiring Rd. about 6km from Wanaka. 11km and 5-6hr. round-trip. Walkers only. Closed Oct. for lambing.)*

MOUNTAINEERING. Various mountaineering companies lead guided treks into Mt. Aspiring NP and the Southern Alps. **Mountain Recreation Ltd.** summits Mt. Aspiring (3033m) in 3-4 days with larger groups and lower rates than the other companies. *(☎ 443 7330; www.mountainrec.co.nz. 3-day $595, 4-day $695. Prices are all inclusive.)* **Alpinism Ski** does guided treks by summer and ski and snowboard touring by winter. *(☎ 443 6593; www.alpinismski.co.nz. 5-day Mt. Aspiring trip from $2180. 6-day backcountry ski or snowboard touring from $1540, all inclusive.)*

MT. ASPIRING NATIONAL PARK ☎ 03

The craggy, snow-covered peaks of Mt. Aspiring National Park are the center of the Te Wahipounamu South West New Zealand World Heritage Area. Of the park's 100 odd glaciers and 13 peaks over 2500m, Mt. Aspiring (3027m) is the highest. The varied regional terrain has been featured in films and television commercials.

Most activities, hikes, and scenic flights begin in the gateway towns of **Glenorchy** (p. 387), **Queenstown** (p. 373), and **Wanaka** (p. 393). Even far-off **Te Anau** (p. 406) takes part, as an access point for Fiordland and Mt. Aspiring's shared **Routeburn Track** (p. 389). Shorter tracks depart from both the Glenorchy and Wanaka areas, including the popular **Rob Roy Valley Track** (3hr. round-trip), which features dramatic views of the Rob Roy glacier. The understandably popular track covers alpine terrain. (Trailhead 54km from Wanaka at Raspberry Creek. Shuttle 3-4hr., $55 return.) A challenging summertime route in the Wanaka area climbs from the end of Mt. Aspiring Rd. to a point near the ◪**Cascade Saddle,** one of the most acclaimed vantages in the Southern Alps. The route is a multi-day trip for experienced hikers, with overnight options at the Aspiring and Dart Huts. It connects with the Rees-Dart Track (p. 403) on the far side of the saddle. Before attempting the climb, consult the Wanaka DOC office.

AT A GLANCE	
AREA: 355,543 hectares.	**GATEWAYS:** Wanaka, Queenstown, Glenorchy, Te Anau.
CLIMATE: Pleasant, although occasionally very wet climate in summer; dangerous conditions in winter.	**CAMPING:** Established camping areas, as well as backcountry huts and camping.
FEATURES: Haast River, Humbolt Mountains, Red Hills "mineral belt."	**FEES AND RESERVATIONS:** Backcountry huts cost $10 per night, though the $90 Annual Hut Pass from DOC covers all huts in the park except for Routeburn Great Walks Huts.
HIGHLIGHTS: Superb views and extreme terrain.	

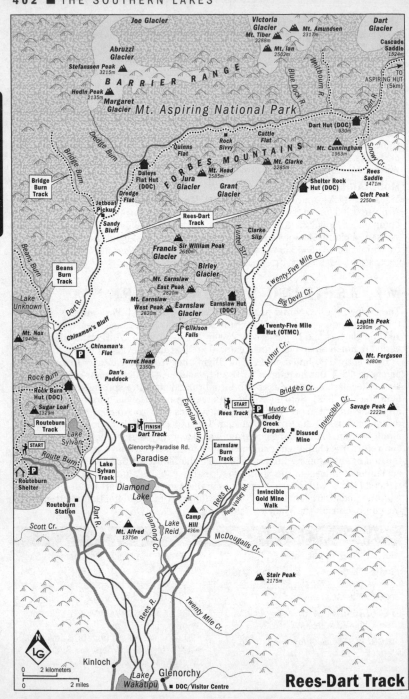

OTAGO

Joe Glacier

Victoria Glacier
Mt. Tiber
2288m

Mt. Amundsen
2317m

Dart Glacier

Mt. Ian
2502m

Cascade Saddle
1524m

TO ASPIRING HUT
(5km)

Abruzzi Glacier

Stefanssen Peak
3215m

Blue Duck R.

Whitbourn R.

Dart R.

BARRIER RANGE

Hedin Peak
2135m

Margaret Glacier

Mt. Aspiring National Park

Dredge Burn

Dart Hut (DOC)
930m

Bridge Burn

Quinns Flat

Rock Bivvy

Cattle Flat

FORBES MOUNTAINS

Mt. Cunningham
1963m

Snowy Cr.

Bridge Burn Track

Daleys Flat Hut (DOC)

Jura Glacier

Mt. Head
2585m

Mt. Clarke
2285m

Shelter Rock Hut (DOC)

Rees Saddle
1471m

Dredge Flat

Grant Glacier

Cleft Peak
2250m

Jetboat Pickup

Beans Burn

Sandy Bluff

Rees-Dart Track

Clarke Slip

Beans Burn Track

Dart R.

Francis Glacier

Sir William Peak
2610m

Hunter Str.

Lake Unknown

Birley Glacier

Twenty-Five Mile Cr.

Mt. Nox
1940m

Chinaman's Bluff

Mt. Earnslaw East Peak
2820m

Mt. Earnslaw West Peak
2820m

Earnslaw Glacier

Earnslaw Hut (DOC)

Big Devil Cr.

Lapith Peak
2280m

Chinaman's Flat

Gilkison Falls

Twenty-Five Mile Hut (OTMC)

Mt. Ferguson
2480m

Rock Burn

Dan's Paddock

Turret Head
2350m

Arthur Cr.

Rock Burn Hut (DOC)

Sugar Loaf
1329m

Earnslaw Burn

Bridges Cr.

Savage Peak
2222m

Routeburn Track

START

Route Burn

Lake Sylvan

Rees Track

START

Muddy Cr.

Muddy Creek Carpark

Invincible Cr.

Routeburn Shelter

FINISH

Dart Track

Disused Mine

Routeburn Station

Glenorchy-Paradise Rd.

Paradise

Lake Sylvan Track

Earnslaw Burn Track

Rees R.

Rees Valley Rd.

Invincible Gold Mine Walk

Scott Cr.

Dart R.

Diamond Lake

Diamond Cr.

Lake Reid

Camp Hill
436m

McDougalls Cr.

Mt. Alfred
1375m

Stair Peak
2175m

Rees R.

Twenty Mile Cr.

N
LG

0   2 kilometers
0   2 miles

Kinloch

Lake Wakatipu

Glenorchy

DOC Visitor Centre

Rees-Dart Track

REES-DART TRACK

Highly challenging and never monotonous, the Rees-Dart Track traces a glorious arc through two river valleys lined with living glaciers. Trampers pass through a variety of landscapes, including beech forests, subalpine herb fields, grassy flats, and manmade pastures. The walk is one of the most difficult major hikes on South Island; many streams are unbridged and much of the path is subtly marked—poles and cairns make better friends than often misguided footprints. With two stunning daytrips beyond the main loop, including the ascent up the jaw-dropping ◪**Cascade Saddle,** the track is well worth the effort for those who make the trip.

 WHEN TO GO. The park is much safer in the summer months—the winter can get extremely cold in the high altitudes. Many trails lack hut wardens, and weather conditions can make trekking an expert-only activity.

Length: 72km, 4-5 days.

Trailheads: The track is most commonly walked, and is described below, starting in the Rees Valley at **Muddy Creek Carpark.** The Dart end of the track is accessible at the **Paradise Carpark,** although major transport services pick up and drop off at the **Chinaman's Bluff** shelter, a few kilometers from Paradise along a 4x2 only stretch of road. It is also possible to access the trail via the **Cascade Saddle** from Aspiring Hut; see DOC for information.

Transportation: Backpacker Express (☎442 9939) runs from **Glenorchy** to the **Rees-Dart Track Trailhead** at Muddy Creek Carpark (30min., in summer daily 9:30am, $19) and from Glenorchy to Queenstown (1hr., $18). Backpacker Express also departs from the **Rees-Dart Track trailhead** at Chinaman's Bluff (30min., departs Chinaman's Bluff 2pm). **Dart River Safaris** (☎0800 327 853) can arrange jetboat pickup from **Sandy Bluff** ($179) on request, though availability is not guaranteed. **Buckley Transport** (☎442 8215; www.buckleytranport.co.nz) offers on-demand transport from Glenorchy to both trailheads for a bit cheaper than Backpacker Express. Book ahead. Buses often run a few minutes behind, so don't fret if you arrive on time and don't see a shuttle.

Seasonality: Mar.-Nov. is dangerous. Avalanches and heavy snowfall make conditions treacherous, and the Upper Snowy Creek swing bridge is removed to avoid avalanche damage. Those attempting the track in winter must have alpine experience. However, alpine conditions should be expected at any time of year.

Huts and Campsites: Huts $10 per night. Huts include heating, taps, and flush toilets; none have cooking stoves. In summer, there are live-in wardens. Often there are additional mattresses in storage, allowing latecomers to sleep on the floor of the common room. 25 Mile Hut has no such amenities. Camping is restricted to the areas surrounding the huts only. Campers using hut facilities are asked to pay a $5 fee, but camping is otherwise free. There is trail-end camping at the Muddy Creek Carpark.

Special Gear: Chlorine, iodine tablets, or other **water purification** measures are advisable; giardia has been detected on the track, albeit not for a few years. Trampers and hut wardens frequently drink the water in the huts untreated.

Storage: See **Greenstone and Caples Tracks: Storage,** p. 391.

Maps: Subtly marked trails and plentiful sights make a good topographical map a necessity for the Rees-Dart ($19, available from DOC).

Parking: Parking at the Muddy Creek carpark is not recommended, not for theft concerns, but because it can be difficult to get your car back out again in wet conditions. Parking is available at the Glenorchy Holiday Park for those with arranged transport.

MUDDY CREEK CARPARK TO 25 MILE HUT. *6km, 2-3hr.* This stretch of the Rees Valley can be a swampy walk along a faintly marked track. If the mud is getting the best of you, head for the streambed and walk on the rocks to keep your feet dry. The ramshackle **25 Mile Hut** (5 bunks; free), maintained by the Otago Tramping and Mountaineering Club (OTMC) as a base camp for Mt. Earnslaw—which you'll spend the next few days walking around—can provide a (leaky) roof during severe weather, but little else.

25 MILE HUT TO SHELTER ROCK HUT. *10.5km, 4-5hr.* Take care crossing 25 Mile Creek, as it can become deep and swift during and after rain. The lovely **Lennox Falls** quickly come into view across the valley; about 2hr. later, a swing bridge leads into Mt. Aspiring National Park proper. Winding in and out of beech forest and grassy slip sites, the track crosses a swing bridge to bring you to **Shelter Rock Hut** (20 bunks), a well-maintained, two-building abode on the east side of the river.

SHELTER ROCK HUT TO DART HUT. *9km, 4-6hr.* This is the main track's most challenging stretch, with steep inclines and faint markings. The track climbs steadily through alpine vegetation until it hugs a bluff for the extremely steep (but brief) 1hr. ascent to the Rees Saddle. The track then makes a tricky descent. Just across the Snowy Creek swing bridge is the new **Dart Hut** (32 bunks), with a shiny kitchen that rivals that of many hostels. Note that the Snowy Creek swing bridge is removed in winter and that the resultant river crossing can be very tricky.

DAYTRIP: DART HUT TO CASCADE SADDLE. *8km, 4-5hr. one-way.* Dart Hut is a popular base for daytrips up to the spectacular ◼**Cascade Saddle.** Side-creeks overflow and the path becomes treacherous. The track to the saddle begins across the swing bridge at the campsite past Snowy Creek. As you follow the Dart River upstream, it disappears into an irregular hill—the terminal moraine that marks the glacier's farthest advance. Beyond is the Dart Glacier itself, mostly covered with rock and dirt, which becomes a brilliant river of crevassed, white snow high in the valley. The track runs high above the glacier's current melted level along the lateral moraine (which marks the glacier's widest width) before climbing to the prize: Cascade Saddle. Don't mistake it for the sandy, gray plateau you'll see first; the actual saddle is the ridge 20min. beyond. On the far side, Cascade Creek plunges into the forests of the Matukituki Valley. On the near side, **Dart Glacier** tumbles down blue ice falls from an amphitheater of rock. If you intend to cross to **Aspiring Hut** (8-10hr. from Dart Hut), don't do it. The steep descent on the other side of the saddle is for highly experienced alpinists with route-finding experience only. Traveling in the reverse direction (from Aspiring Hut to Dart Hut) is the recommended route; consult the DOC for track details.

DART HUT TO DALEYS FLAT HUT. *15.5km, 5-7hr.* After an initial steep section, the main track becomes less strenuous across the wide Cattle Flat, where grassy terraces are framed by legions of glaciers. The DOC has made improvements to this section, including railings, boardwalks, and footbridges—much to the outrage of some hikers. **Daleys Flat Hut** (20 bunks) is very spacious, occupying an idyllic riverside setting marred only by many, many sandflies. Those with the energy for a detour can take a seldom-traveled spur across some difficult but beautiful country to the **Whitbourn Glacier** (2-4hr. one-way). Beginning 30-45min. beyond Dart Hut, the path drops steeply to the Dart River, crosses a swing bridge, and scrambles through grass and forest to thick subalpine scrub. Eventually the track hits open flats, where a profusion of tiny plants flourish alongside the frothing Whitbourn River. Snowfields and waterfalls ring the lonely valley, which leads up to the gritty snout of the Whitbourn Glacier itself, along the Whitbourn Track.

DALEYS FLAT HUT TO CHINAMAN'S BLUFF. *14.5km, 4-5hr.* The final day's tramping is largely a breeze, hugging the Dart River as the well-marked path runs through beech forest to Sandy Bluff. The only moderately harrowing portion of this section comes on the bluff itself, with 200m of steep ascent along a sheer drop-off. Beyond the signs for jetboat pickup, about 2hr. from the hut, the speeding watercrafts zoom up and down the otherwise tranquil river. Beyond a shelter at Chinaman's Bluff, complete with sink and toilets, lies the road to Paradise Carpark, an additional 2-2½hr. walk along a fair weather 4x2 road. Note that while staunch 4WD vehicles can make it to Chinaman's Bluff, the many river crossings may require that you leave your car along the road in high flood.

FIORDLAND

A series of rugged ranges and valleys, green with beech trees and brimming with waterfalls, Fiordland is New Zealand's largest national park. Home to iconic Milford Sound, tranquil Doubtful Sound, more than 500km of trails, and three Great Walks, the region delights kayakers and trampers alike. Fiordland's tireless forces of nature—frequent avalanches and persistent rainfalls—complement a majestic terrain. Manapouri, Tuatapere, and Queenstown can serve as bases for an assault on the park, but Te Anau rightfully lays claim to the role of regional gateway.

◾ FIORDLAND HIGHLIGHTS

STRIDE past two glacial valleys and countless cascades on the **Milford Track** (p. 418), heralded as "the finest walk in the world."

GLIDE past pods of dolphins and Fiordland crested penguins while sea kayaking in **Doubtful Sound** (p. 423).

TE ANAU ☎ 03

The "walking capital of the world," Te Anau (tee-uh-NOW; pop. 4000) draws countless trampers each year. A compromise between the secluded expanse of Fiordland and the commercial buzz of Queenstown, the town is a slow-paced base for forays into the wilderness. The scenery is enough recommendation: beyond the glacial calm of Lake Te Anau, green mountain ranges soar to alpine heights and beckon newcomers to experience the terrain that put New Zealand on the map.

▆ TRANSPORTATION

Buses: Book at Te Anau's booking agencies. Most buses stop at the **Pop Inn Cafe** beside the roundabout on the lake. **Atomic Shuttles** (☎322 8883) goes to **Wanaka** (3½hr., 1:15pm, $45) via **Queenstown** (2¼hr., $35). **InterCity** (☎474 9600) runs daily to **Invercargill** (2¼hr., 8am, $46.) and **Queenstown** (2¼hr., 5:30pm, $43). **Scenic Shuttle** (☎249 7654) heads daily to **Invercargill** (2½hr., 8:15am, $40). **Topline Tours** (☎249 8059) heads daily to **Wanaka** (3½hr., 10am, $50) via **Queenstown** (2½hr., $30). For transport to **Milford Sound**, see p. 416.

Taxis: Tracknet (☎249 7777). Taxis run regularly from 7am-11pm daily. Book ahead for after-hours travel.

Car Rental: The **Caltex gas station** (☎249 7140), next to Subway on Luxmore Dr., rents cars for $89 per day with unlimited km through First Choice. Open daily 7am-10pm.

Bike and Kayak Rental: Te Anau Minigolf, Quadricycle, and Bike Hire, 7 Mokonui St. (☎249 7211). Mountain bikes $10 per hr., $20 per half-day, $25 per full-day. Mini-Golf $6. Open daily Sept.-Apr. 10am-7:30pm. **Fiordland Wilderness Experiences,** 66 Quintin Dr. (☎249 7700 or 0800 200 434; www.fiordlandseakayak.co.nz). Kayaks from $55 per day. **Watercycles** (☎027 332 8505 or 0800 310 415; www.seacycle.co.nz) rents ingenious sea cycles across from Lakefront Backpackers. These contraptions are pedaled like a bicycle and are steered by leaning. Call ahead for nighttime trips on Lake Te Anau. Open daily 11am-dusk, weather permitting. Call if you can't find them, as locations are expected to vary in the future. $10 per 20min., $20 per hr.

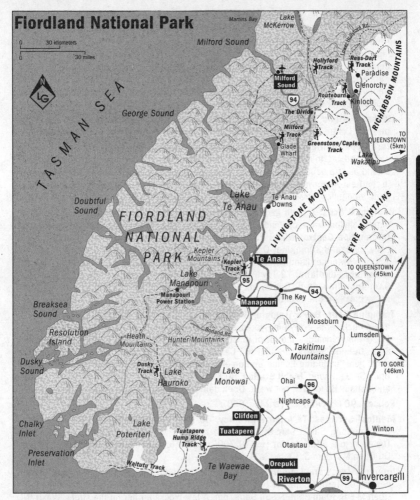

Fiordland National Park

FIORDLAND

Hitchhiking: While *Let's Go* does not recommend hitching, Milford hitchers catch rides at the school at the north end of town in the early morning. Hitching is nearly impossible in winter. Getting to Manapouri or Queenstown is easy in summer and more difficult in winter; most hitchhikers try where the Southern Scenic Rte. splits from Lakefront Dr.

✦🛈 ORIENTATION AND PRACTICAL INFORMATION

The short main drag of the town center is called **Town Centre** and runs perpendicular to the lake and **Lake Front Drive**. The **Southern Scenic Route (SH95)** runs west beyond the DOC office (left as you face the water) toward **Manapouri** (20km), while **SH94** runs inland east toward **Mossburn**. The **Milford Road** branches off from Town Centre and away from the lake to **Milford Sound** (120km). Shops are concentrated on Town Centre, while booking agencies are largely on Lakefront Dr.

Visitors Center: The **Fiordland i-Site** (☎249 8900; fiordland-iSITE@realjourneys.co.nz), located on the waterfront at the end of Town Centre, in the same building as **Real Journeys** (see **Booking Offices,** below). Open daily 8:30am-6pm; in winter 8:30am-5pm.

Department of Conservation (DOC): (☎249 7924; fiordlandvc@doc.govt.nz), at the corner of Lakefront Dr. and the Manapouri-Te Anau Rd., services Fiordland National Park and the Milford Rd. Regional office for **Great Walks** (☎249 8514; greatwalks-booking@doc.govt.nz). Open daily 8:30am-6pm; Apr.-Oct. 8:30am-4:30pm; Great Walks booking desk closes on weekends.

Banks: Westpac Trust (☎249 8600 or 0800 400 600) and **BNZ** (☎249 9250), both on Town Centre, have 24hr. **ATMs** and offer **currency exchange.**

Work Opportunities: Help is always needed in Te Anau during the summer; hostels, cafes, and big tour operators are the best bets. The season begins in Aug. and can extend as late as Apr.; late arrivals often have good luck, too. **Fiordland Employment,** in the Real Journeys Fiordland Community Event Centre on Luxmore Dr. (☎249 7754; fiordlandemploy@xtra.co.nz). Open M-F 8:30am-4:30pm. Small registration fee.

Booking Offices: Though generally sponsored by a certain company, these will book almost anything. The only independently run booking office is the **Te Anau Travel and Information Centre** (☎249 7516; teanau.travel@xtra.co.nz), on the lakefront. Open daily 7:30am-8:30pm; May-Oct. 8am-5:30pm. **Air Fiordland,** 70 Town Centre (☎249 7505; www.airfiordland.co.nz). Open daily 8am-6:30pm, May-Sept. 8:30am-5:30pm. **Adventure Fiordland,** 72 Town Centre (☎0800 476 726 or 249 8500). Open daily 9am-9pm, in winter 10am-5pm. **Real Journeys** (☎0800 656 501; www.realjourneys.co.nz), on the lakefront. Open daily 8:30am-6pm, in winter 8:30am-5pm.

Tramping Gear: Bev's Tramping Gear Hire, 16 Homer St. (☎249 7389; www.bevshire.co.nz), rents everything you'd ever need, and offers a Great Walks Package for $120 which includes the lot of it. Boots cost extra. Open daily 9am-noon and 6:30-8pm. **Outside Sports,** 38-40 Town Centre (☎249 8195), sells and rents a variety of sport gear, including fishing equipment. Open daily 9am-9pm; May-Sept. M-F 9am-6pm, Sa 9am-noon. **Mobil Station,** 80 Town Centre (☎249 7247), provides **AA** service and rents PLBs for $25 per week. Open daily 7am-9pm.

Police: 196 Milford Road (☎249 7600).

Medical Services: Te Anau Pharmacy, 60 Town Centre (☎249 7134). Open M-F 8:30am-9pm, Sa-Su 9am-9pm; June to mid-Oct. M-F 8:30am-6pm, Sa 9am-noon. There's also a 24hr. **doctor** (☎249 7007) at the Te Anau Medical Centre on Luxmore Dr. Open M-F 8am-5:30pm, Sa 9am-noon.

Internet Access and Laundry: Log on early to avoid the afternoon rush. **Te Anau Photocentre,** 62 Town Centre (☎249 7620). $1 per 10min. Laptop connections available. Open M-F 8:30am-8pm, Sa-Su 9am-7pm. A few blocks farther up the street, **Wash 'N' Surf** has terminals, washers, and dryers, all coin-op. $1 per 10min. Wash $4 includes detergent; dry $1 per 10min. Open daily 9am-9pm.

Post Office: 102-104 Town Centre (☎249 7348), at Paper Plus. Poste Restante. Open M-F 8:30am-7pm, Sa 9:30am-6pm, Su 10am-4pm.

⌂ 🏠 ACCOMMODATIONS AND CAMPING

In summer, be prepared to either book ahead or face paying outside of your price range. For those with transportation, bunking in Manapouri (see p. 422) is an bad option. In winter, call ahead as many hostels close for the season.

▨ **Rosie's Backpackers (BBH),** 23 Tom Plato Dr. (☎249 8431; backpack@paradise.net.nz). Head up Milford Rd., turn left on Howden St., and right on Tom Plato Dr. A

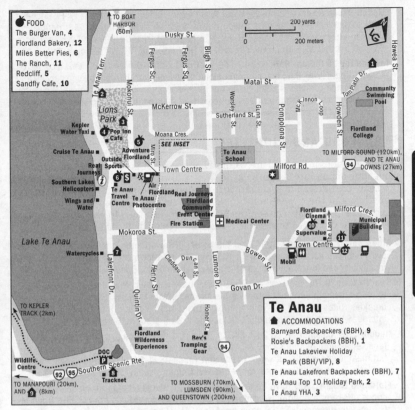

FOOD
The Burger Van, **4**
Fiordland Bakery, **12**
Miles Better Pies, **6**
The Ranch, **11**
Redcliff, **5**
Sandfly Cafe, **10**

TO BOAT
HARBOR
(50m)

Dusky St.

0   200 yards
0   200 meters

Hawea St.

Matai St.

Fergus Sc.
Fergus Sq.
Bligh St.

Te Anau Terr.
Mokonui St.

Community
Swimming
Pool

Lions
Park
McKerrow St.

Worsley St.
Sutherland St.
Gunn St.
Pompolona St.
McKinnon Loop
Howden St.
Tompato Dr.

Kepler
Water Taxi ■

Pop Inn
Cafe
Moana Cres.

Fiordland
College

Cruise Te Anau ■

Adventure
Outside
Fiordland
Real
Sports
SEE INSET

Te Anau
School

TO MILFORD SOUND (120km),
AND TE ANAU
DOWNS (27km)

Mira St.

Milford Rd.

94

Real
Journeys
Southern Lakes
Helicopters ■

Town Centre

Wings and ■
Water

Te Anau
Travel
Centre

Air
Fiordland
Te Anau
Photocentre

Real Journeys
Fiordland
Community
Event Center
Fire Station

Fiordland
Cinema

Milford Cres.

Municipal
Building

Flordland
Event Center

Medical Center

Supervalue

Town Centre

Municipal
Building

Lake Te Anau

Mokoroa St.

Henry St.

Cleddau St.

Duncan St.

Luxmore Dr.

Bowen St.

Mobil

Watercycles ■

Lakefront Dr.

TO KEPLER
TRACK (2km)

Quintin Dr.

Fiordland
Wilderness
Experiences

Rev's
Tramping
Gear

Homer St.

Govan Dr.

94

Wildlife
Centre

92   95

DOC

Southern Scenic Rte.

Tracknet

TO MANAPOURI (20km),
AND ❾ (8km)

TO MOSSBURN (70km),
LUMSDEN (90km),
AND QUEENSTOWN (200km)

Te Anau
ACCOMMODATIONS
Barnyard Backpackers (BBH), **9**
Rosie's Backpackers (BBH), **1**
Te Anau Lakeview Holiday
  Park (BBH/VIP), **8**
Te Anau Lakefront Backpackers (BBH), **7**
Te Anau Top 10 Holiday Park, **2**
Te Anau YHA, **3**

FIORDLAND

peaceful home with only sheep between you and Lake Te Anau. Free pickup. Reception 3-8pm. Book ahead. Dorms $26; doubles $62. $4 BBH discount. MC/V. ❸

▧ **Barnyard Backpackers (BBH)**, 80 Mt. York Rd. (☎249 8006; rainbow-downs@xtra.co.nz), 8km from Te Anau toward Manapouri. Hillside cottages overlook pasture land and the Kepler Mountains in the distance. Free Kepler Track shuttles. Discounts on horse treks. Reception 8:30am-8pm; mid-Apr. to Oct. 9am-8pm. Dorms $24; twins and doubles $62. Tent sites $16. $3 BBH discount. MC/V. ❷

Te Anau YHA, 29 Mokonui St. (☎249 7847; yha.teanau@yha.co.nz). This clean haven has a knowledgeable staff and the honor of being the longest-running hostel in town. Reception 8am-8:30pm; May-Sept. 8:30am-8pm; occasionally closed in the afternoon. Dorms $27; doubles $68, with bath $82. $3 YHA discount. MC/V. ❸

Te Anau Lakefront Backpackers (BBH), 48 Lakefront Dr. (☎249 7713; www.teanaubackpackers.co.nz). Lively common areas. Bathrooms and kitchenettes in every room and ample outdoor deck space offer privacy. Bike rental. Movie room. Reception 7:30am-7:30pm; June-Sept. from 8am. Dorms $26; twins and doubles $60-64; quads $108. $3 BBH discount. ❷

Te Anau Lakeview Holiday Park (BBH/VIP) (☎249 7457 or 0800 483 2628), at the junction of SH94 and 95 across from the DOC office. A well-kept variety of indoor and outdoor accommodations with common facilities. Includes the sociable **Steamer's**

Beach Backpackers and private **West Arm Lodge**, perfect for trampers. Wi-Fi. Kitchens and storage lockers. Steamers Beach dorms $25; West Arm singles $32; doubles or twins in either $60. Standard cabins $60 for up to 2, extra person $20. Tent sites $14.50 per person, with power $16.50. $3 BBH discount; $1 VIP discount. MC/V. ❷

Te Anau Top 10 Holiday Park (☎249 7462 or 0800 249 746; www.teanautop10.co.nz), on Te Anau Terr. Facing the lake, turn right along the waterfront. This central, campervan- and family-oriented complex is nothing short of luxurious with fabulous bathrooms. Bike rental. Spa. Reception 8am-9pm. Tent and powered sites $18 per person. 2-person cabins $63, extra person $16; 2-person self-contained cabins $125. Prices lower in winter. MC/V. ❷

📱🎵 FOOD AND NIGHTLIFE

All dining options in Te Anau are within a 5min. walk of Town Centre, and virtually all nightlife options are 200km away in Queenstown. The sleek **Fiordland Cinema**, 7 The Lane, provides an upscale moviegoing experience, showing mostly independent films and the occasional blockbuster. (☎249 8844; www.fiordlandcinema.co.nz. $15, students and seniors $12.) For groceries and freeze-dried tramping food, head next door to **Supervalue**, 1 The Lane. (Open daily 8am-8pm.)

▨ **Miles Better Pies** (☎249 9044), on the corner of Town Centre and Lake Front Dr., has every claim to its name, serving up flaky, tender pies for mere tuppence ($4.50). The freshly blended fruit ice cream ($4) is reason alone to go. Open daily 6am-4:30pm. ❶

▨ **Sandfly Cafe**, 9 The Lane (☎249 9529). This tucked-away cafe makes for a great place to devour items from their tantalizing display case. With toasties ($5-6.50) and several breakfast bites under $10, your tramping plans will be a lazy afterthought. Fur-lined Internet $1 per 10min. No sandflies. Open daily 8am-4:30pm. Breakfast until 11am. ❶

Redcliff, 12 Mokonui St. (☎249 7431; Redcliff_Cafe@xtra.co.nz). This weathered cottage serves unpretentious New Zealand fare with style and flavor. It may be expensive, but meat lovers will find it worth every cent (mains $21-34). Locals congregate at the bar later. Open daily 5pm-late; dinner served 6-9pm. Usually closed June-Aug. ❹

Fiordland Bakery, 106 Town Centre (☎249 8899), is a great stop for on-the-run baked goods ($3-5) or a bottomless coffee ($2.50). Several breakfasts from $6.50. Open M-F 7am-early afternoon, Sa-Su open from 8am; May-Sept. reduced hours. Cash only. ❶

The Burger Van, on the lakefront in front of the Pop Inn Cafe, appears out of the evening mists to offer well-stacked burgers for decent prices. Burgers $7-9. Chips $1.50. Open Oct-Apr. W-Su 6:30pm-10:30pm. In winter only Sa-Su. ❶

🏔 OUTDOOR ACTIVITIES

As epicenter of activity planning for Fiordland National Park, Te Anau has infinite options for getting in touch with nature. Though most can be booked through Te Anau and most companies tend to headquarter in town, the coverage in this chapter has been split to help clarify things. For trips in Manapouri and Doubtful Sound, see p. 422; for trips to the Milford Road and Milford Sound, see p. 416.

WALKS AND TRAMPS. A starting point for three of New Zealand's **Great Walks** and a gateway to the Fiordland wilderness, Te Anau could entertain outdoor enthusiasts for months. Detailed coverage of the following Fiordland multi-day tramps can be found elsewhere in the book: Dusky Track on p. 424, Greenstone and Caples Tracks on p. 391, Kepler Track on p. 412, Milford Track on p. 418, and the Routeburn Track on p. 389. A popular daytrip hike is the **Mt. Luxmoore Track** (8-10hr. round-trip), which travels part of the Kepler Track. Accessible by walking from the DOC office around the lake or by taking a shuttle with **Tracknet** (☎249

7777; $6, with pickup from swing bridge $9), this track offers fabulous lake and mountain views and sore legs at the day's end. Check at the DOC office for a Mt. Luxmoore Hut weather forecast. **Kepler Water Taxi** (see **Kepler Track**, p. 412) offers transportation to Brod Bay for Mt. Luxmoore trekkers as well ($20 one-way). Pick up an infosheet on **Te Anau walks** at the DOC office. **Upland Journeys** (☎0800 486 774; www.upland.co.nz), offers a variety of one-day guided hikes in Fiordland National Park, through many less-touristed trails ($200 per person per day for 2 people, $100 for 4 people). **Real Journeys** (see **Booking Offices,** p. 417) offers one-day guided walks on the Milford Track, including boat connections (from $150). **HikeSouth** (☎226 6739; www.hikesouth.com) organizes multi-day guided walks of the full great walks in the area and other long treks in Southland (Milford Track from $1590; Routeburn from $950).

WATER ACTIVITIES. Te Anau's name comes from the **Te Ana-au** (Maori for "caves of rushing water") **Glowworm Caves.** Limestone walls worn away by 15,000 years of running waters have formed impressive caverns housing a glowworm grotto. **Real Journeys** (see p. 417) runs to the cave up to seven times daily. (2½hr. $54, children $15.). The scenic surroundings of Lake Te Anau make for fun times without the glowing fly larvae poo. **Cruise Te Anau** (☎249 7593; www.cruiseteanau.co.nz), on the pier next to Real Journeys, offers 2½hr. cruises aboard the Carousel to the lake's South Fjord, which include an easy walk to the hidden lakes area. Trout fishing and hunting trips are also available. (Tours $67 per person; trout fishing from $125 per hr.) **Luxmore Jet** (☎0800 253 826; www.luxmorejet.co.nz) offers 1hr. rides along the Waiau River, which connects Lakes Te Anau and Manapouri. They also offer fly and boat combinations with Wings and Water and Southern Lakes Helicopters (1hr. trip $85, children $40; combos from $205). **Fiordland Wilderness Experiences** (see gear rentals, above) rents kayaks for use in the lake.

AIRBORNE ACTIVITIES. Sometimes the best way to experience New Zealand's largest national park is by seeing all of it at once from the air, just like Peter Jackson. **Southern Lakes Helicopters** (☎249 7167 or 0508 249 7167; www.southern-lakeshelicopters.co.nz), offers flyovers of the area, with the ability to land at some of the least accessible locations in Fiordland. (25min. "Scenic Te Anau" $170 per person, 1hr. Doubtful Sound $470 per person. Other trips including heli-hiking from Mt. Luxmoore available.) **Wings and Water,** also on the waterfront, runs float-plane flights including a 10min. flyover of Lake Te Anau for only $75 per person. (☎249 7405; wingsandwater@xtra.co.nz. 20min. Kepler Track Overfly $175, 40min. Doubtful Sound Overfly $265. Minimum numbers apply. Charters available.) **Air Fiordland** (☎249 7505 or 0800 107 505; www.airfiordland.co.nz) offers several superb scenic flight options (from $250) as well. For a 20min. scenic flight with excellent door-to-ground service, call **Skydive Fiordland** (☎0800 746 754; www.simplifly.co.nz), whose sunset jumps are unique. (9000 ft. $245; 12500 ft. $295.)

GROUNDED ACTIVITIES. High Ride (☎0800 822 882 or 249 8591; www.high-ride.co.nz), located 17km out of town toward Mossburn, runs horse treks (3-3½hr., $80) through surrounding farmland and river valley and 4WD ATV tours of the Danby Hills east of Te Anau. (3hr.; 9:30am, 2pm, in summer also 6pm; $145. Pickup from Te Anau included.) **Westray Horse Treks** (☎0800 148 735 or 249 9079; www.fiordlandhorsetreks.com), also toward Mossburn, offers cheaper but shorter trips. (1½-2hr., $60. Trips daily at 9:30am and 2pm. Bookings essential.)

OTHER ACTIVITIES. Walk along the shore away from town (15min.) and past the DOC office to reach the ■**Wildlife Centre,** home to some of the earth's rarest birds. The perilously endangered takahe is the center's hallmark, and is well worth seeing. The Murchison Mountains, one of the few remaining natural habitats for the birds, loom in the background. (Donations appreciated. Open dawn-dusk.)

⬛ KEPLER TRACK

Officially opened in 1988 to commemorate New Zealand's National Parks Centennial, the Kepler Track has become nearly as popular as its historic neighbors, the Milford and Routeburn Tracks. Beginning on the sun-dappled shores of Lake Te Anau, the track climbs Mt. Luxmoore for a breath catching ridge walk before descending through beech and podocarp forests to the shores of Lake Manapouri. With frequent openings, the Kepler remains the most accessible Great Walk, allowing trampers to set out on foot from Te Anau without transport costs.

Length: 60km, 3-4 days.

Trailheads: The track forms a loop, beginning and ending at the **Control Gates** at the southern end of Lake Te Anau. The Control Gates can be reached from the DOC office via a 50min. walk through the Te Anau Wildlife Centre. Most walk the track in a counterclockwise direction, heading first toward Mt. Luxmoore Hut.

Transportation: Although no transportation is needed beyond two strong legs, some trampers choose to shorten the duration of their walk by shuttling to or from the Control Gates or Rainbow Reach. **Fiordland TrackNet** (☎249 7777) runs from **Te Anau Lakeview Holiday Park** (p. 409) to the **Control Gates** and **Rainbow Reach.** (Control Gates: 10-15min. Oct.-Apr. 8:30, 9:30am; in winter on demand; $6. Rainbow Reach: 10-15min.; 10am, 3, 5pm; $9.) **Kepler Water Taxi** (☎249 8364) departs at 8:30 and 9:30am. ($20 one-way. Group charters available.)

Seasonality: Year-round, but winter trips in the avalanche-prone Fiordland area are only for experienced alpinists. May-Nov. are very dangerous. Throughout the year, there is plentiful rain and the possibility of freak snow storms, so be prepared for at least one day of heavy rain and extreme weather variation.

Huts and Campsites: Huts have gas cookers and live-in wardens during the summer ($40 per night); tent site quality varies ($10). Camping elsewhere on the track is prohibited. In winter, when gas and wardens are removed, the huts revert to the backcountry system ($10 per night). Huts can be booked online at www.doc.govt.nz.

Storage: Most accommodations store bags for free.

Parking: The DOC visitors center has a free long-term parking lot. Safer Parking, 48 Caswell Rd. in the industrial area (☎249 7198; www.saferparking.co.nz; $8). Parking at Rainbow Beach or the Control Gates is not recommended.

CONTROL GATES TO BROD BAY CAMPSITE. *5.6km, 1½hr.* From the Control Gates, which regulate the level of Lake Te Anau for the greater glory of hydroelectric power, the track edges into swim-worthy **Dock Bay.** Farther along, the long beach of **Brod Bay** has a toilet, several sheltered campsites, unpurified lake water, and the opportunity to start day two by watching the sun rise over Lake Te Anau.

BROD BAY CAMPSITE TO MT. LUXMOORE HUT. *8.2km, 3½-4½hr.* From Brod Bay, the track steadily climbs a series of long, gradual switchbacks past limestone bluffs, through a forest of lichen-covered beech trees, before suddenly breaking onto golden alpine tussocks with expansive views. Forty-five minutes farther, ⬛**Mt. Luxmoore Hut** (50 bunks) is a veritable mountain chalet with arguably the best view of any hut in the Great Walks system. The South Arm of Lake Te Anau and the Hidden Lakes twinkle far below, while in the distance loom the Murchison Mountains, the last natural habitat of the takahe. Nearby are the **Luxmoore Caves,** where two flashlights per person, an intrepid spirit, and a slim waist are requirements for entry. Mt. Luxmoore Hut is a fine dayhike destination and an ideal waiting place for when inclement weather postpones plans for the next stretch.

Kepler Track

MT. LUXMOORE HUT TO IRIS BURN HUT. *14.6km, 5-6hr.* Alpine weather shifts are no joke, and if they were the punchline could be fatal; the DOC recommends checking the updated morning forecast at the hut before continuing on. In this exposed alpine section, the track steeply ascends for about an hour until crossing the Luxmoore Saddle, just below the summit of **Mt. Luxmoore** (1472m). A 10min. scramble brings you to the top for a 360° panoramic view of the region, with sweeping terrain unfolding in every direction. The track then descends, but remains above the treeline, to **Forest Burn Shelter,** the first of two emergency over night only shelters. The path to the second of these shelters, the **Hanging Valley Shelter,** is a prize in itself; the track follows the crest of several humped ridges. A steep series of switchbacks plunging into the beeches follows a worthwhile look-out (5min. round-trip) over a panorama of hanging valleys. **Iris Burn Hut** (50 bunks) overlooks a meadow, with serviceable tent sites about 200m away. From the hut, a 1.5km side trip leads to the **Iris Burn Waterfall.** The area around the hut is frequented by kiwi; light sleepers are awoken by their distinctive hooting.

IRIS BURN HUT TO MOTURAU HUT. *16.2km, 5-6hr.* Days one and two are quickly forgotten on the easy, pleasant stretch from Iris Burn Hut to the Control Gates. The track briefly ascends past the hut, before opening into the **Big Slip,** a testament to the erosive powers of water: the mountains are literally falling down.

Back in the intact forest, the track provides a reasonably level walk to **Moturau Hut** (40 bunks) by the shores of Lake Manapouri, which features a large communal area, a spiral staircase, and great sunsets. Trampers who complete the walk in three days often get an early start from Iris Burn and bypass Moturau by lunchtime en route to the afternoon Tracknet Shuttle from Rainbow Reach.

MOTURAU HUT TO RAINBOW REACH. *6km, 1½-2hr.* Beyond Moturau Hut lies the turn-off to **Shallow Bay Hut** (6 bunks), a small, unserviced hut with a toilet and a shore of free camping. Not part of the Great Walks, this hut is cheap ($5). From the turn-off, the Kepler winds through boglands, crosses the Forest Burn River, and then reaches the swing bridge that leads to Rainbow Reach and its shuttles.

RAINBOW REACH TO THE CONTROL GATES. *9.5km, 2½hr.* This less-traveled but beautiful stretch closes the loop back to the Control Gates. The track lies sandwiched between the fast-flowing Waiau River and Fiordland's forested border, promising a variety of views and a good chance to fish for trout or see parakeets.

THE MILFORD ROAD

For those traveling to Milford Sound, getting there is half of the experience. From Te Anau to the sound, the 119km Milford Rd. (2hr. without stops and depending on bus traffic) climbs through Fiordland National Park. Pick up a guide to the sights for $1 at the **DOC office.** In winter, make sure to stop at the DOC office in Te Anau to see if the road is passable or if tire chains are required (chains can be rented from the Te Anau Mobil station; when required, vehicles without them are subject to fines). Te Anau provides the only reliable services for Milford Sound and the Milford Rd. There are **no gas stations** along the way. Droves of tour bus operators clog the length of the narrow road on their way to and from Milford Sound (see **Transportation,** p. 418). To avoid most of the tour bus traffic in the summer, try leaving before 7:30am or after 11am. Most buses return to Te Anau by 5pm. There are 10 **DOC campsites,** most with pit toilets, picnic tables, fire pits, and fresh water access, along the route ($5 per person; self-register).

TE ANAU TO LAKE GUNN. From Te Anau, the road runs beside Lake Te Anau for 30min. until reaching the wharf at **Te Anau Downs,** the departure point for the Milford Track. After this last outpost of Te Anau, the road enters the red and silver beech forest of Fiordland National Park. Traversing the glacial U-shaped **Eglinton Valley,** the road runs through wide expanses of grassland beneath the backdrop of the Earl and Livingstone Ranges. The short walk to **Mirror Lakes** allows a moment to reflect on one of the DOC's most clever signs, particularly when the winds are calm. Just up the road in **Knob's Flat,** displays on avalanches and native bats occupy the people who didn't have to use one of the many toilets on site. **Lake Gunn,** farther down the road, harbors a 45min., wheelchair-accessible walk through the moss-covered glory of the forest. Beaches and fishing spots abound.

THE DIVIDE AND HOLLYFORD ROAD. A shelter at **The Divide** marks the starting point for the **Routeburn Track** (p. 389) and the **Greenstone** and **Caples Tracks** (p. 391). From here, enter the Routeburn Track trailhead to reach the **Key Summit** (3hr. round-trip), which makes for a great dayhike with wonderful valley views perfect for those short on time. From the Divide, turn right onto **Lower Hollyford Road** for 1km to reach the track to **Lake Marian** (3hr. round-trip), which threads through lush rainforest and past waterfalls to an idyllic picnic spot in a hanging glacial valley. Just 7km farther down the Hollyford Rd. is **Gunn's Camp ❶** (gunnscamp@ruralinzone.net), an isolated, quirky campground straight out of the 1930s, with stream-cooled refrigeration, coal-heated showers, and hand-pumped gas. The camp store

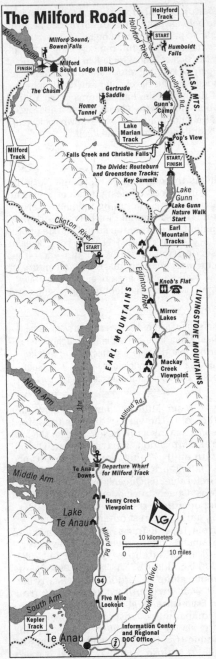

The Milford Road

Hollyford Track

Milford Sound, Bowen Falls

Milford Sound
START
Humboldt Falls

Milford Sound Lodge (BBH)

FINISH

Milford Sound

Hollyford River

Lower Hollyford Rd.

AILSA MTS.

The Chasm

Gertrude Saddle

Homer Tunnel

Gunn's Camp

Milford Track

Lake Marian Track

Pop's View

Falls Creek and Christie Falls

The Divide: Routeburn and Greenstone Tracks; Key Summit

START/FINISH

Lake Gunn

Lake Gunn Nature Walk Start

Clinton River

Earl Mountain Tracks

START

Eglinton River

Knob's Flat

Mirror Lakes

EARL MOUNTAINS

LIVINGSTONE MOUNTAINS

Mackay Creek Viewpoint

North Arm

Milford Rd.

Middle Arm

Te Anau Downs

Departure Wharf for Milford Track

Henry Creek Viewpoint

Lake Te Anau

Milford Rd.

VG

0   10 kilometers
0   10 miles

94

Five Mile Lookout

South Arm

Kepler Track

Te Anau

Upukerora River

Information Center and Regional DOC Office

FIORDLAND

features a small selection of reasonably priced snacks and drinks, as well as the only concession for Milford teardrop greenstone, a translucent stone that features flecked white "tears" throughout. (Dorms $20; cabins $45 for 2, $10 per extra person up to 6; tent sites $10. Linens $5. Power for charging appliances available. Store open daily 8:30am-8pm. MC/V.)

Farther down Hollyford Rd. is the **Hollyford Track** (56km, 4 days one-way), which penetrates lowland forest before reaching the sea at Martin's Bay. The route's low altitude makes it less scenic than other tracks, but it is one of few hikes in Fiordland accessible year-round. A few hundred meters up from the Hollyford Trailhead is the 30min. side trail to excellent views of the distant **Humboldt Falls. Fiordland Tracknet** (☎ 249 7777 or 0800 483 2628) runs to the roadside trailhead from Te Anau (Oct.-May daily; in winter on demand; $42). Both **Air Fiordland** (see p. 408) and **Milford Sound Helicopters** (see p. 411) run flights to Martins Bay and Big Bay at the other end. Call ahead for availability and prices. **Huts** along the Hollyford cost $10 per night year-round; they have tank water and pit toilets, but no stoves.

Meanwhile, back on the Milford Road, the journey continues past **Pop's View,** a lookout named for a bulldozer operator killed in an avalanche, and over **Falls Creek,** where **Christie Falls** is visible from the roadside.

HOMER TUNNEL AND BEYOND. The final major landmark on the Milford Road is the **Homer Tunnel;** "completed" in 1953 after decades of work, the rough-hewn tunnel drips disconcertingly on your windshield and still has no internal lighting. Turn on your headlights to navigate the 1km of darkness. Traffic signals control the tunnel 9am-6pm, often causing delays of 15min. or more. A waiting area before the tunnel provides views of the MacPherson Glacier and curious keas. The trail leading to **Gertrude Saddle** (4hr. round-trip) is just before the tunnel; experience alpine territory, but bring a topo map to help navigate. The stretch of road near the Homer Tunnel is one of the more avalanche-prone pieces of highway on earth—an average of one avalanche per day in winter keeps a full-time clearing crew stationed nearby very busy. On April 1st, the **Homer Tunnel Nude Run** blocks traffic at night; contestants are allowed only a pair of running shoes and a headlamp, and the female and male winners are awarded a naked Barbie and Ken doll trophy.

After emerging on the other side of the mountain, hairpin turns down Milford Valley—pray not to get stuck behind a bus—lead to the **Chasm,** where a boardwalk (10min. round-trip) spans the **Cleddau River** and its surreal, water-hewn rock sculptures. Just beyond the Chasm lies the haunting Milford Sound itself.

MILFORD SOUND ☎03

Dramatic Milford Sound (Piopiotahi) is the emblem of Fiordland National Park. In 1993, the sound (actually a fjord) received designation as a marine reserve in recognition of its abundant sea-life, including unique waterline flora, bottlenose dolphins, fur seals, and the occasional Fiordland crested penguin. Sheer cliffs and snow-capped summits rise from the sound and its photogenic focal point, the rugged Mitre Peak (1482m), while trees grip rock faces in defiance of gravity. Waterfalls cascade from dizzying heights—at 146m, Stirling Falls is among the most spectacular. Scarcely marred by a century of eager tourist eyes (commercial guided walks to the area began in the 1890s), Milford Sound retains its majesty despite the droning fleet of cruise ships and the buzzing swarm of scenic flights.

THE KEA TO SUCCESS. The abundance of keas—Fiordland's "mountain parrot"—in the area may make them seem little more than a naughty street pigeon, but it's important to remember that they are a protected bird with limited alpine habitat. **Do not feed the kea** under any circumstances. Watch out: they prey on windshield wipers, packs, and boots of the unsuspecting travelers.

█ TRANSPORTATION. The best way to reach Milford Sound is to drive, but those without cars won't be left in the cold. The variety of tours to Milford Sound is overwhelming—in peak season, as many as 70 buses head up the Milford Rd. in the morning and back in the afternoon. Daytrips depart Queenstown or Te Anau early and don't return until evening; book well in advance and bring lunch with you—or prepare for high-priced mediocrity. Leaving from Te Anau rather than Queenstown is preferable, as Queenstown Trips take up to 12 hours with six hours of driving. Most Queenstown operators pick up from Te Anau along the way. The following operators run daily in summer (Oct.-Apr.) and at least a few times per week during the rest of the year.

The tongue-in-cheek local guides from **Trips 'n Tramps** run small (max. 12 people) and unhurried tours from Te Anau; some of their trips allow several hours for tramping along the Milford and Routeburn Track. (☎249 7081; www.milfordtourswalks.co.nz. From $136, children $75.) The **BBQ Bus,** flavors its commentary with optional bushwalking along Milford Rd. and a hearty barbeque lunch. (☎442 1045 or 0800 421 045; www.milford.net.nz. $189 from Queenstown, $145 from Te Anau.) **Kiwi Experience** (☎442 9708) and Magic partner **Kiwi Discovery** (☎442 7340) offer comparable daytrips from Queenstown ($159). Kiwi Experience allows one-way sector fares with unlimited stopping time along the course of the Milford Sound trip. (Queenstown to Te Anau $40, Te Anau to The Divide $20, The Divide to Milford Sound $15.) **Real Journeys** also offers large capacity coach-cruise-coach excursions. (☎249 7416 or 0800 656 501. From Te Anau $127-147, children $63-73.) **Milford Wilderness Explorer** runs a similar coach-cruise-coach service. (☎249 7505. Book through Air Fiordland in Te Anau. From Te Anau $125, children $80. Max. 8 people.) **Rosco's Sea Kayaks, Fiordland Wilderness Experience, Tawaki Dive,** and some of the scenic flight operators also offer packages that include transport to and from Te Anau; see **Outdoor Activities,** p. 410. Although *Let's Go* doesn't recommend it, **hitchhikers** claim that standing on Milford Rd. just past town is the best way to catch a ride to Milford Sound.

⌐☐ ACCOMMODATIONS AND FOOD. Due to Milford Sound's hit-and-run brand of tourism and the DOC's control of real estate, there aren't many lodging and dining choices around the sound. However, the few places in town carry off their duties with admirable charm, making an overnight stay in the sound a pleasure. About 1km before the sound, the ▨**Milford Sound Lodge (BBH) ❸,** is luxury incarnate for weary trampers with a toasty gear drying room, free shuttles to the wharf and pub, and modern bathrooms, and comfortable beds. The massive lounge offers free board games and a giant Fiordland track map for geographical brush-ups. (☎249 8071; www.milfordlodge.com. Breakfast bar. Unlimited wireless Internet $20. Dorms $28; twins and doubles $70. Tent sites $15. $3 BBH discount. MC/V.) The **Blue Duck Cafe ❶** and **Bar ❸,** (☎249 7982), just before the wharf on the main road, has reasonably priced food. The cafe features a lunch buffet ($15-19). The bar serves mains ($21-28) and local brews. (Internet in Cafe $1 per 10min. Cafe open daily 8:30am-4pm. Bar open 4:30pm-late. Dinner closes at 9pm. Cash only.)

⚠ OUTDOOR ACTIVITIES

BY BOAT. Boat tours are the most popular way to see the sound and the only way to view its entirety. Most trips depart 9am-5pm and last 1-3hr. If possible, take advantage of early morning cruises; they're often cheaper than those offered once the buses start rolling in. Most boat companies offer a trip to **Milford Deep,** the world's deepest **underwater observatory,** which floats more than 8m below the surface of the sound. The observatory allows visitors a peek at cool critters like black coral and snake stars, which grow close to the surface, thanks to the light-repelling layer of fresh water that Fiordland's heavy rainfall deposits on the sound. Milford Deep cannot be visited independently, so check with boat operators for package prices. **Cruising Milford Sound** is the newest, cheapest company on the wharf. (☎249 7735 or 0800 500 121; www.cruisingms.co.nz. 4 per day, 9:30am-3:15pm. $50-65, children $15.) **Real Journeys** sends out 1¾hr. scenic cruises and 2½hr. nature cruises daily. The tugboat-like *Mariner* and the *Milford Wanderer,* as well as the *Friendship,* offer relaxed overnight trips that include a hearty dinner, breakfast, and kayaking. (☎249 7419 or 0800 656 501; www.realjourneys.co.nz. Nov.-Mar. 8 per day. Apr.-Oct. at least 3 per day. $55-80, children $15. Overnight trips from $205, children $102.50.) **Red Boat Cruises** runs a fleet of modern cruise boats decked out in their namesake color, offering an additional "encounter" cruise that uses smaller boats to get closer to the wildlife. (☎441 1137 or 0800 264 536; www.redboats.co.nz. Oct.-Apr. 11 per day 9am-3:45pm. May-Sept. 4 per day 9:30am-1:30pm. Regular cruises $55-75; Encounter cruises $65-80; children $15.) **Mitre Peak Cruises'** boats carry 75 passengers, keeping things cozier. (☎249 8110; www.mitrepeak.com. 7 per day in summer 8:55am-4:30pm, 3 per day in winter 9:55am-2:45pm. $56-68, children $25.)

OTHER AQUATIC ACTIVITIES. Kayaking may be the best way to comprehend the Milford Sound's vast scale, too great to see in a single day's paddle. **Rosco's Sea**

Kayaks, which meets at the Milford Sound Lodge, runs half-day "sunriser" and "twi-lighter" kayak tours; the sunriser can be paired with a short Milford Track walk or transport to and from Te Anau. (☎ *249 8500 or 0800 476 726; www.kayakmilford.co.nz. Sunriser $105, from Te Anau $135; twilighter $149; sunriser plus Milford Track combo $159.)* Operating out of Te Anau, **Fiordland Wilderness Experiences** offers coach-kayak-coach tours. (☎*249 7700 or 0800 200 434; www.fiordlandseakayak.co.nz. $130. From Mil-ford Sound $100. Not always available in winter.)* Meanwhile, **diving** in the sound allows firsthand encounters with black coral and other creatures of the deep; **Tawaki Dive** runs great personalized excursions from Te Anau and comparable snorkeling trips for those without certification. (☎*249 9006; www.tawakidive.co.nz. 12hr. trip with a 5hr. cruise and 2 dives $274, from Milford Sound $244. $75 less without gear rental. Snorkeling $69. 6-person max. 4-day PADI scuba certification classes available for $525.)*

AIRBORNE ACTIVITIES.
Helicopter and flight tours are dazzling but expensive. **Wings and Water** runs floatplanes from Te Anau over the sound. (☎*249 7405; wing-sandwater@xtra.co.nz. 1hr. $395. 3-person min.)* **Air Fiordland** features similar trips, as well as a posh flight-cruise-flight combo from Queenstown or Te Anau. (☎*249 7505 or 800 107 505; www.airfiordland.co.nz. Milford Sound Overflight $315. 2-person min. Combos $375-415.)* **Milford Sound Helicopters** (☎*249 8384; milford.helicopters@xtra.co.nz)* take off straight from the sound; trips range from a 10min. flight to Mitre Peak *($130)* to flights landing on the Tutoko Glacier *(22min.; $205).* You can even coach, cruise, and then meet your bus via helicopter *(25min.; $250)* along the return trip. *(3 person min. Landings subject to weather.)* **Southern Lakes Helicopters** (p. 411) also runs 80min. trips to Milford Sound from Te Anau, with free bubbly along the way *($670).*

▶ MILFORD TRACK

Despite the generations of trampers, the ■**Milford Track,** has lost none of its charm and grandeur. Over four days, the walk leads those lucky enough to garner a ticket through waterfall-laden valleys, up a blustery alpine pass, and along crashing mountain rivers, from Lake Te Anau to the Milford Sound. The track itself is not complete without its annual 8m of rainfall, and few escape without a damp day or two. However, with tightly regimented scheduling and over 12,000 walkers per year, choice in weather is not an option. Rest assured that no matter when you go, it will be well worth it. Anyone who tries to convince you otherwise is just jealous that they couldn't get a ticket.

Length: 54km, 4 days. The track is traditionally measured in miles, of which there are 33½.

Trailheads: The track begins at **Glade Wharf** at the northern tip of Lake Te Anau and ends at **Sandfly Point** near Milford Sound. Both are accessible only by boat.

Transportation: Book all transport ahead. **Tracknet** (☎ 249 7777) runs from the DOC in Te Anau to the boat launch at **Te Anau Downs** (25min.; 9:30am, 1:15pm; $19, under 14 $12), connecting to the cruiseboat run by **Real Journeys** (☎ 249 7419 or 0800 656 501) that heads across Lake Te Anau to **Glade Wharf** (1½hr.; 10:30am, 2pm; $57, under 14 $15). **Red Boat Cruises** (☎ 441 1137 or 0800 264 536) runs boats from Sandfly Point to Milford Sound on the other end of the trail (20min.; 2pm and 3:15pm; $28.20, children $16.70). From Sandfly Point, Tracknet also runs a bus from Milford to **Te Anau** (2hr.; 9:30am, 3pm, 5pm; $42, under 14 $28) and Queenstown (4¼hr.; 9:30am, 2:30pm; $77, under 14 $50). The **Great Walks Booking Desk** (p. 67) can arrange all transportation when you book your trip. **Cruise Te Anau** (☎ 249 7593; www.cruiseteanau.co.nz) runs bus-boat-hike-bus package trips for Milford Hikers, including a bus to Te Anau Downs, boat to Glade Wharf, and transportation back from Milford Sound ($150 per person. Book ahead.) Though *Let's Go* does not recommend **hitchhiking,** hitchers set out very early or try to catch rides the day before in order to

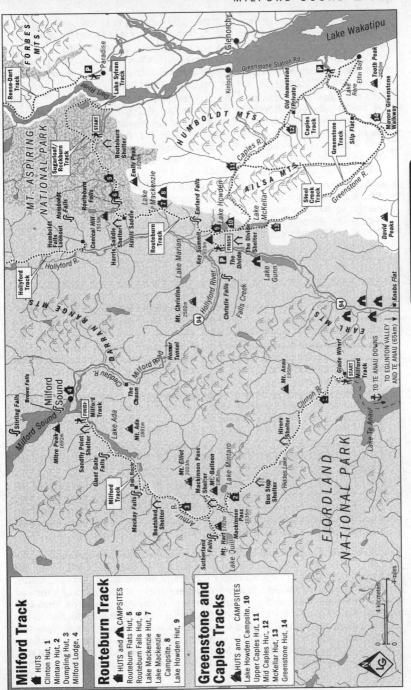

FIORDLAND

Milford Track

▲ HUTS
Clinton Hut, **1**
Mintaro Hut, **2**
Dumpling Hut, **3**
Milford Lodge, **4**

Routeburn Track

▲ HUTS and ⛺ CAMPSITES
Routeburn Flats Hut, **5**
Routeburn Falls Hut, **6**
Lake Mackenzie Hut, **7**
Lake Mackenzie Campsite, **8**
Lake Howden Hut, **9**

Greenstone and Caples Tracks

▲ HUTS and ⛺ CAMPSITES
Lake Howden Campsite, **10**
Upper Caples Hut, **11**
Mid Caples Hut, **12**
McKellar Hut, **13**
Greenstone Hut, **14**

make the early boat the first morning of the tramp; returning to Te Anau, most summertime hitchers report success when hitching from near the exit to Milford Sound Lodge.

Seasonality: Year-round but winter trips in the avalanche-prone Fiordland area are only for experienced and committed alpinists. May-Nov. are very dangerous. Throughout the year, there is plentiful rain and the possibility of freak snow storms, so be prepared for at least one day of heavy rain and extreme weather changes.

Huts and Campsites: 3 huts along the track for independent walkers; the other 3 huts for guided walkers are off-limits. Huts are expensive—$120 total for 3 nights—with spacious common areas, flush toilets, and rows of gas cookers (bring matches). Each independent hut has its own DOC warden. Late Apr.-Oct., fees revert to the backcountry hut system ($10 per night) with pit toilets and fuel for fires. Trampers must collect their hut passes from a DOC office either the day before or by 11am on the day they start the track. Camping is not permitted.

Bookings: Bookings are handled by the **Te Anau DOC Great Walks Booking Desk**. See **Practical Information,** p. 407. Unlike any other track in New Zealand, the Milford is entirely scripted: you must book in advance and you must stay in a designated hut each night. This policy precludes waiting out the weather in hopes of better views. The DOC allows 40 independent trampers to start the track each day. It's possible to do dayhikes from Te Anau and Milford Sound, but you won't reach the best scenery in such a short time. **Ultimate Hikes** (☎441 1138; www.ultimatehikes.co.nz) charges a minimum of $1690 per head for the privileges of cooks, portered gear, and hot showers in upscale accommodations. Applications to walk the Milford independently are first come, first served, available from July 1 for the following season (late Oct.-Apr. fills up fast). If full, don't despair; stopping by or calling the Booking Desk to inquire about cancellations can sometimes yield a last-minute spot for those with flexible dates. Solo trampers and flexible couples have the best chances.

Recommended Gear: Milford trampers need to be prepared for heavy rain and very cold weather at all times of year. A nice tramping day could turn into a freezing trip over MacKinnon's pass, and unprepared trampers have been caught huddling from overexposure more than once. Bring a hat and gloves, polypropylene clothing layers, gaiters, and sturdy rain-proof wind-proof clothing for you and your pack. Two walking poles can be a great help on the downhill sections. Yellow pack liners can be bought from the DOC for only $5 and will ensure that you always have a dry set of clothes and a dry sleeping bag to crawl into at night. All of the above gear can be rented from Te Anau (see p. 406).

Storage: Tracknet (☎249 7777) shuttles extra gear from Te Anau to Milford Sound ($5 per bag). Most accommodations will store. The West Arm Lodge in Te Anau (see **Accommodations,** p. 408) has ample storage lockers.

Parking: The DOC visitors center has a free long-term parking lot. **Safer Parking,** 48 Caswell Rd. in the industrial area (☎249 7198; www.saferparking.co.nz; $8). Those who want to drive themselves to Te Anau Downs can use the parking lot at **Te Anau Downs Motor Inn** (☎249 7811; cars $15, campervans $20). Allow 10min. for walking from the motor inn to the wharf. Parking at the wharf is not recommended.

GLADE WHARF TO CLINTON HUT. *5km, 1hr.* On the boat over to Glade Wharf on Lake Te Anau, don't miss the eerie memorial to Quintin MacKinnon, the founder of the Milford Track who later was shipwrecked and never seen again. With that disquieting thought in mind, trampers arrive at the grand entrance of the Milford Track, surrounded by tall, slender beeches and the occasional totara. The width of the track at this point may make things as difficult as following the Yellow Brick Road toward Oz, but don't worry Dorothy, just enjoy the forest scenery and ever-twittering birdsong on this short leg. Just shy of the hut, the boardwalk **Wetlands Walk** (5min. round-trip) provides educational displays on multi-colored mosses and a bizarre array of carnivorous plants. **Clin-**

ton Hut (40 bunks) is a corrugated outdoor mansion near the clear Clinton River. Those on the morning boat generally reach the hut very early in the afternoon and have time for a dip in some nearby frosty swimming holes.

CLINTON HUT TO MINTARO HUT. *16.5km, 6hr.* The second day starts off relatively flat through more beech forest and groves of bizarre lancewoods as trampers follow the Clinton River toward Lake Mintaro. This track crosses several small streams along the way, which in very wet conditions can become a challenge to ford. After a few hours, the track opens up dramatically, allowing views of the surrounding rocky valley and even a far-off look at MacKinnon Pass. Waterfalls spill over the edges of the valley in several locations, offering several small lakes for swimming or a snack break. The alternate track via **Hidden Lake** is worth taking, but its resident eels may make a swim at forthcoming **Prairie Lake** a better choice. Ask the sandflies in which location they'd prefer to devour you. Many walkers along this open stretch may wonder why the DOC has marked the trail so frequently with large posts; walkers in heavy rain won't. As the track meanders back into the bush, it starts climbing uphill and passes **Hirere Falls,** a lunch stop for the guided walkers. Feel free to use the water tap out back, and enjoy the first of what will be many encounters with local keas. The way gets rougher and steeper just before passing the dank **Bus Stop** shelter and remains so as it approaches **Mintaro Hut** (40 bunks). A cozy, two-story affair, Mintaro offers the best accommodation on the track and access to a great swimming hole a few minutes down the track by the helicopter pad (past the sign marking Lake Mintaro). Use the provided ladder to climb back out, but keep the helipad clear for rangers to come and go.

MINTARO HUT TO DUMPLING HUT. *14km, 6-7hr.* This stretch is the most taxing and most incredible, and inclement weather can make it even more so. Twenty minutes after departing Mintaro Hut, the track begins a switchback ascent, which runs about 2hr. to the top of the pass. The Mile 15 marker indicates the halfway point to **MacKinnon Pass,** where spectacular panoramic views and a cliff with a 12sec. drop make the climb a hazy memory. An army of keas protect the imposing monument to Quintin MacKinnon, the Scotsman who discovered and first guided people over the pass. Before continuing over the pass for the 20min. journey to the shelter, be sure to pile on your warm gear and steel

FROM THE ROAD

IT'S RAINING MILFORD

In the MacKinnon Pass shelter on a very rainy day, the women next to me were bemoaning the wet state of their feet and gesturing to the rest of our rain-stung lot. Proud of my full-body Gore-Tex lining, I declared, "well, my feet are dry!"

Oh, if I only knew what was to come. When it rains in Fiordland, the water doesn't have anywhere to go but down. Glacially carved peaks are not rich in topsoil, and waterfalls spring out of nowhere in order to funnel all the extra moisture into tributary streams and roaring rivers.

The next day, I found a friendly DOC orange triangle directing me into a river. From then on, I was carrying enough water around in my boots to bring rainforests to Tunisia. I'd pass cliff ledges dumping their loads onto the track and trudge dilligently through.

The track was under thigh-deep waters, and all the trampers started feeling giddy, helping each other through puddles the size of lakes, and snapping embarrassing photos. And hallelujah, I actually started to enjoy myself. I was in the water, of the water, living and breathing the water.

—Richard Lonsdorf

yourself against strong winds. The **MacKinnon Pass Shelter,** a cheerless but safe place sheltering gas cookers, is a welcome retreat from the elements, featuring a pit toilet with 2-ply toilet paper and the best view you've ever seen with your pants down. Heading back down, the track winds beneath a cliff topped by the **Jervois Glacier,** where wispy waterfalls are but a prelude to the crashing waters to come. This downhill stretch is the most difficult, punishing part of the walk, descending 970m over several hours to the Dumpling Hut. Once the trail enters the trees, the **Arthur River** makes a powerful entrance, fueled by several crashing waterfalls that cross your path and make dryness a faint memory. Further down the way, a series of solid staircases travel along the cliff-side river banks until reaching **Quintin Hut,** the next guided walkers' accommodation. At the junction with Quintin Hut, independent trampers can stash their packs in the kea-proof day-shelter while they wander down the 1½hr. round-trip side trail to the three-tiered, 580m ▧**Sutherland Falls,** the highest waterfall in New Zealand and the fifth highest in the world. The crashing waters blow out enough mist to drench anyone within 10m, to say nothing of those who make the chilling and slippery venture behind the torrent. One more hour along a muddy riverside detour, which may become permanent due to recent rockfalls on the main trail, leads down to **Dumpling Hut** (40 bunks). While the indoor/outdoor design is baffling, the Dumpling Hut does feature a lovely swimming hole perfect for icing sore knees.

DUMPLING HUT TO SANDFLY POINT. *18km, 5-6hr.* This final leg of the Milford Track is relatively straightforward in sunshine, though it is particularly prone to flooding in wet weather. Additionally, since the boats at the end depart precisely at 2pm and 3:15pm, speedy trampers will need to space out their walking in order not to end up waiting around at Sandfly Point. An excellent landmark timing guide is posted on the wall of Dumpling Hut for this purpose. Fairly flat, the home stretch passes the historic **boatshed shelter** (for guided walkers) after 1½hr. 20min. past the shelter, trampers reach **Mackay Falls** and **Bell Rock,** the latter of which can be easily explored with a flashlight to see the water-carved interior. The next two hours of tramping cross low and close to the **Arthur River.** The track ascends over a series of cliff-side rock carvings blasted out by prison gangs and contracted workers in the early days of the track. Other than the path to Sutherland Falls, these cliffs are the only remaining original stretch of trail. The shelter near **Giant Gate Falls** is a welcome toilet stop, but the swarms of sandflies may demand skipping lunch until the enclosed shelter at the track's end. From the falls, the track traces the Arthur River, becoming rocky while navigating the shoreline of Lake Ada. The final stretch of trail widens considerably to become as comfortable as the beginning, while the proverbial finish line at **Sandfly Point** glitters in front of you. Although the glittering may actually be caused by the swarms of namesake residents awaiting your arrival. Here, a stout shelter protects trampers as they await transport to Milford Sound and fresh food. Upon reaching the wharf at Milford Sound, yellow and blue free shuttles lead you to the carpark and airport, and the Milford Lodge shuttle will take you to the Blue Duck Cafe and Bar and the lodge itself. Pre-arranged bus connections await out front at the appointed time.

MANAPOURI ☎03

The fog-shrouded peaks of the Hunter and Kepler mountain ranges preside over the quiet town of Manapouri, nestled on the beech-lined banks of Lake Manapouri. Rain forests and rugged, snow-capped peaks reflect in the cool waters of this stunning "lake of the sorrowing heart," widely regarded as the most beautiful in New Zealand. Although tourist ventures have a small foothold, Manapouri remains a pleasant gateway to the remote and serene Doubtful Sound.

⎗ TRANSPORTATION. Scenic Shuttle (☎249 7654) leaves for Invercargill (2¼hr.; 8:30am; $35) via Tuatapere (1¼hr., $25), Riverton (1¾hr., $30), and Te Anau (15min.; 8:15am; $15). While *Let's Go* doesn't recommend it, **hitchhikers** report that getting a ride to Te Anau is easy, though buses are better for getting back to Manapouri again.

▰⁊ ORIENTATION AND PRACTICAL INFORMATION. The town lies at the junction of the Southern Scenic Rte. and SH95, 20km south of Te Anau (p. 406), where you'll find the nearest **police station, doctor, bank,** and **DOC office.** Limited visitor information, largely in the form of brochures, is provided by both **Real Journeys** and **Adventure Kayak and Cruises** (p. 425). The Manapouri Motors **gas station** is on Waiau St. (☎249 6644. Open M-F 8am-6pm, Sa-Su 9am-5:30pm.) The **Lakeview Cafe and Bar** (see below) has **Internet** for $1.50 per 10min. The **post office** is inside the **Manapouri Store** (see below).

▰⚆ ACCOMMODATIONS AND FOOD. **▰Freestone Backpackers (BBH) ❷,** on the Scenic Route 2.5km south of Manapouri, is perfectly situated for sunset views. Relax on the porches attached to five solar-powered cabins built by owner Jimmy. Each has its own kitchen, pot-bellied stove, and hand-crafted furniture. (☎249 6893. Book ahead. Cabin as dorm $23 per person; as single or double $56. Ensuite cabin $76 for 2. $3 BBH discount. MC/V.) The tri-lingual, Swiss-themed **Manapouri Lake View Chalets and Camp ❷,** on Cathedral Dr. toward Te Anau, entertains campers with ecclectic collections, vintage pinball machines, and comics taped to the walls of the loo. (☎249 6624; manapouri@xtra.co.nz. Basic cabins $28; $45 for 2, cabins with kitchen $55. Tent sites $13 per person; 2-person powered sites $26. MC/V.) For a more cozy campground setting, try the **Possum Lodge (BBH) ❷,** 13 Murrell Ave., off of Waiau St. Backpackers in search of an upgrade should spring for one of the rooms in the house with separate shared kitchen and bath. (☎249 6623; possumlodge@xtra.co.nz. Dorms $21; cabins $46 for 2; house doubles $59, triples $79; powered sites $14 per person. MC/V.) The **Lakeview Motor Inn ❸,** next to the Lake View Chalets and Camp, offers heaps of rooms with superb views in a backpacker-friendly setting. (☎249 6652; www.manapouri.com. Reception 8am-7:30pm, after hours at the cafe next door. Budget rooms $35 per person for 2-3 people, $50 as a single. Deluxe rooms available. MC/V.)

The **Lakeview Cafe and Bar ❷,** run by Lakeview Motor Inn, has cheap espresso and expensive everything else, but it's the only restaurant in town. (Lunch $15. Dinner $25. Open daily 11am-9:30pm; May-Oct. 2pm-9:30pm. Bar closes late.) The upper deck at **Cafe 23 ❶,** next to the Cathedral Cafe, makes for a nice setting to enjoy wraps and panini ($5.50-7) at lunch time. (☎249 6988. Open daily 7:30am-8:30pm, in winter 8:30am-5pm.) On Waiau St., the bright **Cathedral Cafe ❷** has a lake view, assorted baked goods, cheap takeaways ($2-4), and tasty mains from $15. In the same building, the **Manapouri Store** has basic items. (☎249 6619. Store and cafe open daily 7am-7pm, mid-Apr. to Sept. 8am-6pm.)

◨⚠ SIGHTS AND OUTDOOR ACTIVITIES. Captain Cook was skeptical that there would be wind to return his ship to sea, so he skipped over **Doubtful Sound** in 1770, leaving the name as his only legacy. Rounded ranges carved by ancient glaciers mark the entrances to over 100km of waterways. Inaccessible by road, Doubtful Sound leaves its serenity to the pods of dolphins and New Zealand fur seals. **Boat tours** of the pristine sound leave from Pearl Harbour in Manapouri, at the Waiau River outlet, crossing Lake Manapouri to the West Arm. From the West Arm, land shuttles transport tourists over Wilmont Pass Rd. to Deep Cove in Doubtful Sound. Because Doubtful Sound doesn't draw as many tourists as Milford Sound to the north, tours from Manapouri often feel much more relaxed. All tours that leave from Manapouri can also be booked from Te Anau.

Guided kayak tours can be the best way to see the sound up close. ◪**Fiordland Wilderness Experiences,** in Te Anau, (see p. 406) offers acclaimed two-day sea kayaking excursions. The trips explore a peaceful arm of the sound and include a night of camping in the Fiordland wilderness. (☎249 7700 or 0800 200 434; www.fiordlandseakayak.co.nz. Book ahead. Bring food and a sleeping bag. Supplies and transport from Te Anau included. 2-day tours $310; 3-day tours $425.) **Adventure Kayak and Cruise,** next to the Manapouri Store, runs a 10hr. cruise and kayak tour of Doubtful Sound ($195, overnight $309) and offers kayak rentals ($45 per day) on Lake Manapouri. Transport for guided tours ($10) is available from Te Anau, but book ahead. (☎249 6626 or 0800 324 966; www.fiordlandadventure.co.nz. Office open daily Oct. to mid-May 9am-noon and 1-5pm.)

Boat cruises of the sound often include a tour of the **Manapouri Power Station,** one of the world's most environmentally benign hydroplants. Turbines at the end of a 2km underground tunnel generate power from plummeting lake waters; its costly construction explains the reliable road connecting Lake Manapouri to Deep Cove. The least expensive, most intimate Doubtful Sound trip is run by **Fiordland Explorer Charters.** Their 8hr. journeys include 3hr. on the sound with a trip to the Power Station. (☎0800 434 673; www.doubtfulsoundcruise.com. 20-person max.; $200. Ask about winter specials May-Sept.) **Real Journeys,** from their location on Pearl Harbour, offers extensive, full-day trips around Doubtful Sound. After a lake cruise, a visit to the power station, and an overland bus ride with ecological commentary, the tour heads through 40km of Doubtful Sound to the seal colonies on the Tasman Sea before returning to Manapouri. DVD, live commentary, and on-board bar are luxurious perks. Transport from Te Anau costs $18. Bring your own lunch or pay for the expensive alternative. (☎249 6602 or 0800 656 502; www.realjourneys.co.nz. Oct.-Apr. up to 3 tours per day. May-Sept. at 9:45am. $230, children $55. Overnight cruises from $325; includes meals and kayaking.)

Fishing opportunities abound in Fiordland's fertile waters, and Deep Cove Charters (☎249 6828 or 021 396 535; www.doubtful-sound.com) combines an intimate scenic cruise with mouth-watering fresh seafood. Up to six guests travel overnight aboard the "Flyer" through Doubtful Sound, with skipper and chef Chris cooking and eating the day's catch. Fiordland crayfish are included as part of three full meals on board. Chris requests that all guests bring their own wine and beer. ($360 per person. Trips go from 9am in Manapouri to 11:15am the next day. Fishing equipment provied.) Mike Molineux of Adventure Manapouri (☎249 8070; www.adventuremanapouri.co.nz) leads intimate one- or two-person trout fishing tours in the Lake Manapouri area starting from $75 per hour. (Fishing license required. Assistance can be provided. Refreshments and all gear included.) A variety of one- to three-day tracks in the area offer an inexpensive immersion in the grandeur of Fiordland. Longer tracks begin at the orange marker 200m downstream across the Waiau River from Pearl Harbour. Rent a boat or hire a water taxi. The Circle Track (3hr. round-trip) promises excellent lookouts over the Hope Arm of the lake, Mt. Titiroa, Manapouri, and Te Anau. Two **huts** ($10) are also available for longer hikes; pick up a pamphlet from the DOC office in Te Anau.

🟦 DUSKY TRACK

The cardinal rule of walking the Dusky Track—one of New Zealand's more demanding walks—is simple: unless some fortuitous Fiordland weather brings eight days of sunshine, it will take longer than you think. The Dusky is infamous for gnarled-root and mossy-rock footpaths, waist-deep mud, snow-covered alpine passes, and swims through flooded river backwaters. Bring a topo map, and have a chat with the DOC about weather conditions and equipment before you go.

WHERE YOU AT. Due to the particularly challenging, isolated, and unpredictable nature of the Dusky Track, the DOC strongly recommends that all trampers travel with a **Personal Locator Beacon (PLB)** or **mountain radio.** See **What to Buy,** p. 70 for more information.

Length: 84km, 8-10+ days.

Trailheads: Lake Hauroko (Tuatapere), **Supper Cove** (Dusky Sound), and **Lake Manapouri** (Manapouri) are all access points for the Dusky Track. All 3 can be reached by boat, floatplane, or a murderous scramble through days of Fiordland bush.

Transportation: Lake Hauroko Tours (☎226 6681; www.duskytrack.co.nz) offers service from Tuatapere to the Hauroko Hut (M and Th $70 per person; charter up to 6 people $450). **Real Journeys** (☎249 6602 or 0800 434 673) services the West Arm of Lake Manapouri several times daily ($30). Advance booking required if beginning the track from the West Arm; if exiting from the West Arm, transport from the wharf is available without a booking. From the drop-off, the track begins a 45min. walk down Wilmot Pass Rd. **Fiordland Explorer Charters** (☎249 6616 or 0800 434 673) offers less expensive, less frequent service to the West Arm. They also include shuttle service on Wilmot Pass Rd. to the trailhead ($30; advance booking required). Flag the bus on Wilmot Pass Rd. for the once daily departure back to town at 5:30pm. **Scenic Shuttle** (☎249 7654 or 0800 277 483) runs door-to-door between Te Anau, Manapouri, and Tuatapere ($17-27). **Wings and Water** (☎249 7405) flies from Te Anau to Supper Cove at 9am with return flights on demand ($270 per person for 2-4 people). **Parking** is available in Tuatapere and at the View St. lot in Manapouri. Though *Let's Go* doesn't recommend **hitchhiking,** trampers report summertime success along the Southern Scenic Route; winter traffic is sparse.

Seasonality: The track becomes impassable after a bout of rain. Winter is dangerous, as avalanche conditions on the track's alpine sections pose extreme risks. Most non-Manapouri transport does not operate in winter.

Huts and Campsites: Eight **huts** service the Dusky Track ($10 per night). All come with fireplaces or pot-bellied stoves, with the exception of the West Arm Hut. With average tramping time exceeding 8 days, doing the Dusky makes an **Annual Hut Pass** ($95) an attractive option. Camping is permitted but strongly discouraged along the track.

Storage: Accommodations in Tuatapere, Manapouri, and Te Anau will oblige.

THE WEST ARM TO UPPER SPEY HUT. *13km, 4½-6hr.* Beginning at the DOC West Arm visitors center, the track follows Wilmot Pass Rd. to a signpost indicating the start of the track. The **West Arm Hut,** 200m from the visitors center, is a sparse affair with no heat but plenty of screeching keas. Descending to the Spey River, the track follows the river valley through beech forests. The first hour of the track is uncharacteristic; don't worry, the gravel ends soon and there are plenty of muddy bogs. **Upper Spey Hut** (12 bunks) sits in the middle of a swampy clearing.

UPPER SPEY HUT TO KINTAIL HUT. *6km, 5-7hr.* After the hut, the track climbs abruptly and then flattens to a gradual incline as it approaches the **Warren Burn.** Be sure to watch for the elusive orange markers along this section of the track. Climbing through tussocks of snowgrass, the track reaches **Centre Pass,** affording arresting views of Tripod Hill, Gair Loch, and the distant Seaforth Valley. Don't stay long, as the winds are fierce; instead, follow the track along the ridge for more impressive views. The descent from the pass to the Kintail Stream is precipitous. **Kintail Hut** (12 bunks) lies sheltered against a hill with a bubbling stream out front.

KINTAIL HUT TO LOCH MAREE HUT. *9km, 6-8hr.* Depending on weather conditions, this section of the track can be one of the most demanding. When rain has been constant and heavy, the lower section of the track is impassable. Following the shores of **Gair Loch,** the track passes over rough terrain when descending the gorge, and emerges near the head of an enormous slip. After crossing the Kenneth Burn walkwire, the track flattens out and passes easily underfoot for several kilometers, occasionally forcing trampers to wade across backwaters of the Seaforth River when it's been raining. The last several kilometers between the Deadwood Creek and Loch Maree are tricky and can be entirely flooded when the Seaforth is high. **Loch Maree Hut** (12 bunks; pot-bellied stove) provides a welcome respite from a long day of sludging through the muck.

LOCH MAREE HUT TO SUPPER COVE. *13km, 6-8hr.* Many trampers have spent a day, or two, or five, stranded at Loch Maree due to high flows of the Seaforth. The best indicators of whether or not the river is low enough to proceed are the tree trunks in the lake: when the trunks are completely submerged, sit it out or be prepared to swim for your life. The track to **Supper Cove** follows an old miners' road and can be easy going when not flooded. The last leg of the track after the Henry Burn can be rough, but trampers who have planned the tides right (there's a tide chart in Loch Maree Hut) can avoid this section by cutting across at low tide. **Supper Cove** (12 bunks) sits on the shores of the track's namesake, the Dusky Sound, and, as the name of the cove implies, those who have lugged fishing line into the woods will be rewarded with fresh trout. For those continuing to Lake Ha[u]roko, the next stage is a return to Loch Maree Hut before proceeding south.

LOCH MAREE HUT TO LAKE ROE HUT. *8km, 5-7hr.* After leaving the hut, the track quickly approaches the most unpredictable obstacle on the Dusky Track: the walkwire crossing of the Seaforth. In foul weather, the entire far side of the crossing can be submerged by the engorged river, making it impassable. There's a three-wall shelter on the far side above flood level to harbor trampers coming from Lake Roe. Across the walkwire begins the steepest ascent on the Dusky, a 600m vertical scramble spread over only 1km of horizontal distance. The top rewards with exceptional views of Dusky Sound, the surrounding mountains, and the Tasman Sea. From here, the track traverses the Pleasant Range, achieving a series of alpine vistas as it travels to **Lake Roe Hut** (12 bunks; pot-bellied stove).

LAKE ROE HUT TO HALFWAY HUT. *7.5km, 3-5hr.* After about 45min. of tramping, the track dips below treeline, following the Hauroko Burn as it descends rapidly. After crossing two walkwires, the track flattens a bit, following the burn through native beech forest. **Halfway Hut** (16 bunks) has an open fireplace.

HALFWAY HUT TO HAUROKO HUT. *9km, 4-6hr.* Similar to the previous day's tramp, the track winds through lush forests, occasionally offering scenic views of the Hauroko Burn. Once at **Hauroko Hut** (10 bunks), break out the bug spray and prepare to battle the sandflies as you wait for your boat out.

SOUTHERN SCENIC ROUTE

When heading to or from Te Anau and Invercargill, consider taking the **Southern Scenic Route.** While the inland route passes through the service towns of Lumsden and

Mossburn, the Scenic Route takes an equally efficient, more enjoyable path, skirting ocean vistas and mountain panoramas before heading inland and upland to Te Anau. The stretch of road from Tuatapere to Riverton is dotted with small towns, a handful of motor parks and taverns, and innumerable bays and inlets with great surfing and paua shells.

The **Kiwi Experience Bottom Bus** runs from Invercargill to Te Anau with an overnight in Riverton. (☎442 9708. Daily 5:30pm, $55.) **Scenic Shuttle** runs in both directions. (☎249 7654. May-Oct., 1pm; Nov.-Apr., 2pm. Invercargill to Te Anau $40; Te Anau to Tuatapere or Tuatapere to Invercargill $25. Book ahead.) While **gas stations** are abundant, there are **no ATMs** between Te Anau and Invercargill. Though *Let's Go* doesn't recommend it, **hitchhiking** along the Scenic Route is reportedly a good prospect in summer, but uncertain in winter.

BORLAND ROAD ☎03

Thirty-four kilometers south of Manapouri and 49km north of Tuatapere on SH92, the unpaved ⊠**Borland Road** veers west toward the untouristed mid-section of Fiordland National Park. To reach it, follow the turn-off for Lake Monowai. After 10km, the road splits, with the right fork going 4km to the **Borland Lodge ❷**. Set on the edge of rising mountains, this educational center hosts numerous school groups and rents two- to five-person cabins to backpackers. (☎225 5464; www.borland.co.nz. Book ahead year-round. Cabins $25 per person.) From a free parking area near the lodge, several hiking trails range out into the park (20min. round-trip to multi-day DOC tramps). The Borland Lodge does not sell DOC hut passes, but they rent camping equipment, as well as kayaks (half-day $25, full-day $40) and battered mountain bikes (half-day $15, full-day $25).

It's possible to drive 23km farther along the Borland Rd., which follows power pylons deep into Fiordland on the way to the Power Station at Lake Manapouri. After about 17km from the Borland Lodge, you reach **Borland Saddle** (982m), which has cinematic views of the Hunter and Kaherekoau Mountains. About 6km after the saddle, all but the heartiest of off-road vehicles will have to stop at the **Grebe Valley Lookout,** which sits on a bluff surrounded by the vast Grebe River Valley and snow-capped peaks. Borland Rd. is unpaved and subject to slips and washouts; at the very least, it contains frequent, large potholes. Four-wheel drive is recommended, but some non-SUVs make the trip in dry weather. The entire trip to Grebe Valley Lookout and back takes about 1½-2hr., so check the weather report before

UH OH DIDYMO: IT'S SNOT FUNNY

New Zealand faces a constant battle to ensure that its ecosystems are free of foreign species. The latest front has emerged in its rivers and streams, the culprit being *didymosphenia germinata.* Didymo for short, or "rock snot" as it is contemptuously known, the freshwater algae forms mats on rocks that can become thick enough to compromise the health of other plant and animal species living in the water.

First spotted in the Lower Waiau River in 2004, didymo has since spread to other waterways in South Island. It has yet to make it to North Island. The main source of spreading is thought to be humans moving wet boats and other gear between waterways. To knowingly spread didymo is an offense punishable with up to five years in prison and NZ$100,000 in fines.

To combat the onslaught of the dangerous algae, Biosecurity New Zeland has mounted a massive public awareness campain that targets tourists and would-be-trampers with large black and yellow "Check, Clean, Dry" signs. After time spent in the wild, check all gear (including fishing poles and boots) for clumps of didymo, clean with a strong solution, and dry gear for at least 48hr. For more information on the spread of didymo, visit www.biosecurity.govt.nz.

setting out. Be sure to call the lodge for road conditions before making the drive, and use good judgment when driving; if an obstruction looks like it could rip out your undercarriage, it probably can. (Closed in winter.)

Back at the fork before the Borland Lodge, the road to the left runs 6km to secluded **Lake Monowai,** where tent and caravan sites are $2 in the self-registration box. The lake curves away from the camping area and disappears into the park. Hiking trails begin at the lake 200m before the parking lot.

CLIFDEN ☎03

South of Manapouri and 14km north of Tuatapere, the hamlet of Clifden is known for its **limestone caves,** located 1km up Clifden Gorge Rd. after the limeworks en route to Winton. Spelunkers need to get a map in Tuatapere and bring two light sources, including a headlamp, before venturing inside (300m, 1½-2hr. return via roadway). The caves are cramped and flood after rain, so if you decide to go, be extremely careful, and travel with a buddy. Take a moment to walk the **suspension bridge,** completed in 1899. Downstream, the protruding cliff face is said to resemble the profile of a legendary Maori maiden whose broken heart drove her to leap off the precipice. **Free camping** is allowed next to the bridge, where there is a rudimentary toilet. From Clifden, the road runs through the Waiau River Valley.

TUATAPERE ☎03

Thanks to the creation of the Tuatapere Hump Ridge Track in 2001, Tuatapere (tu-a-TAP-ery), situated halfway between Invercargill and Te Anau, has gone from a small logging town (pop. 650) to a destination in its own right. While the track has yet to draw Great Walk-level traffic and the town is still adjusting to its newfound tourist status, the top-notch tramping and expanding jetboat options hint at a more adventurous future for a town previously renowned for its sausage. The sausage is still good, too.

SHEAR MAGIC. 7 former and 1 current world-record holding sheep shearers live within 70km of Tuatapere. Tuatapere is the place to take up the clippers.

TRANSPORTATION AND PRACTICAL INFORMATION. Tuatapere lies along the Southern Scenic Route with most shops clustered south of where SH99 crosses the Waiau River. **Scenic Shuttle** (☎249 7654 or 0800 277 483) goes to **Invercargill** and **Te Anau** (1 per day, $30). The **Tuatapere Information Centre,** south of the bridge where SH99 turns, is also the **Hump Ridge Track Office** and **Bushman's Museum** and sells **hut passes** for DOC tramps. (☎226 6399. Open Nov.-Mar. daily 7:30am-7:30pm. Apr.-Oct. W-Su 10:30am-3:30pm. Museum entrance with donation.) There are **no banks** or ATMs in Tuatapere. Local services include: the **police,** 16 Orawia Rd. (☎226 9020), across from the **Mobil gas station,** 20 Orawia Rd. (☎226 6475); the **Medical Center,** 69 Orawia Rd. (☎226 6123); **Internet** at the visitors center ($2 per 10min.). **Tuatapere Health and Gift,** 16 Orawia Rd., doubles as the **post office.** (☎226 6999. Open M-F 9:30am-5:30pm.)

ACCOMMODATIONS AND FOOD. The best budget option in town is the two-story **Shooters Backpackers Holiday Park ❷,** with modern, spacious facilities frequented by buspackers. (☎226 6250; shooters.backpackers@xtra.co.nz. Reception across the street at Highway 99 Cafe. Dorms $24; doubles and twins $55; singles $35. Tent sites $10 per person, campervans $30. $5-6 BBH discount. More expensive motel units next door: singles $60; doubles $90, extra person $20. MC/V.) **Five Mountains Holiday Park and Hump Track Backpackers ❶,** 800m north of the bridge, has clean, crowded dorm rooms, as well as cheap two-room twins with kitchenettes. (☎226 6667. Linen $5. Reception 8am-8pm daily in the on-site Cookhouse Cafe; takeaways under $5. Dorms $10; twins $40. Tent sites $10; powered caravan sites $15. Cash only.) The historic **Waiau Hotel ❸**, 47 Main St., offers well-appointed rooms for reasonable, breakfast-inclusive prices. For free entertainment, try the sheep-adjacent suites, but there's also TV in every room. (☎226 6409; www.waiauhotel.co.nz. Wi-Fi. $35-45 per person with shared facilities, $50-55 ensuite. MC/V.) For a wee bit of homespun luxury, try the **Kiwi Haven B&B ❹**, 58 Clifden Hwy., just as you start heading out of town. The homestead sits on 5 acres with connection to DOC short walks. (☎226 6244 or 027 625 4533; kiwihaven@paradise.net.nz. Single $60; doubles $110. Cash only.)

The restaurant at the **Waiau Hotel ❷**, see above, has meals from $14. (Open daily 6:30am-8pm. Bistro open from 5:30pm.) In the same building, **4 Square** has groceries. (Open M-F 7am-8:30pm, Sa-Su 8am-8:30pm, Apr.-Nov. until 7:30pm.) The **Highway 99 Cafe and Bar ❷**, across the street from Shooters, grills country meals ($15-22) as well as burgers ($5). (Open Dec.-Mar. daily 7am-8:30pm.) The **Western Foodmarket**, north of the river, has a smaller selection. (Open M-F 7am-6pm, Sa 8am-4pm, Su 9am-4pm.)

🔲 🏔 **SIGHTS AND OUTDOOR ACTIVITIES.** Though the **Tuatapere Scenic Reserve** no longer shelters ancient tuataras, it's now home to towering beeches. Ask the visitors center for information on the DOC walks in the area. Mountain biking along the old logging roads allows access to the lakes of eastern Fiordland; bikes can be rented in Te Anau or Manapouri. Fourteen kilometers north of Tuatapere, follow signs for **Lake Hauroko** from SH99 for the dirt roads leading 32km to the water's edge. There are **toilets** and a **DOC campsite** ($10 honesty box). Farther north, Borland Rd. (see p. 427) leaves SH99 halfway to **Manapouri** and brings cyclists to hiking trails and **Lake Monowai**. The **Giant Totara Tree Loop** (15min. round-trip), 37km northwest of Tuatapere on the edge of Dean Forest, hosts a 1000-year-old tree. Take Clifden Lake Hauroko Rd. via Motu Bush Rd.

Jetboat companies fly over Lake Hauroko and down the rapids of the **Wairaura-hiri River**. The river drops more rapidly than any other jetboat-accessible river in New Zealand. Some people love to claim that it's New Zealand's "longest" waterfall, making the high-speed rush all the more intense. Full-day tours generally include extensive time on the river, nature walks, and pickup from Tuatapere. **Wairaurahiri Jet** (☎226 6845 or 0800 376 174; www.wjet.co.nz) has full-day trips with lunch included for $199. **Hump Ridge Jet** (☎225 8174 or 0800 270 556; www.humpridgejet.com) offers full-day tours without lunch for $180 (lunch $15). **South Coast Jet** (☎226 6328; www.southcoastjet.co.nz), offers custom fishing, hunting, and wilderness exploration that extend beyond the river and along the coastline. Daytrips from $250. Book ahead. Jetboats are also an option for combining tramping on the Tuatapere Hump Ridge Track with more aquatic activities. Call for details. For those who'd rather experience the thrills and spills of an active sheep farm, the 🔳**Waiau Downs Sheep Shearing and Farm Tours**, on SH99 just to the south of Tuatapere toward Riverton, is the best opportunity you'll find in all of New Zealand. Farmer Ray Horrell and his trusty team lead clumsy novices through the fast-paced process of working the farm dogs, sheep shearing, and throwing a fleece of wool. The full farm tour also includes a 4WD tour of the sheep paddocks, as well as a visit to a dairy farm and hosts of other animals. (☎0508 226 662; www.farmadventures.co.nz. 1hr. tour $20, children $5; 2hr. tour $45/10. Overalls and boots provided. Call ahead.)

Tuatapere is a gateway to the rugged forests of southern Fiordland. In addition to the **Hump Ridge Track** (see p. 430) and **Dusky Track** (p. 424), the **South Coast Track** offers a path into the Fiordland wildlands. It begins at **Bluecliffs**

Beach, 19km south of town along Papatotara Rd., and follows the same coastal route as the Hump Ridge Track (in the opposite direction) to the **Percy Burn Viaduct,** the largest of its kind in the world. Reaching this feat of engineering requires a two-day walk. Two hours before the viaduct, the Old Port Craig Schoolhouse (now a DOC hut) makes for a pleasant place to stay both nights on this trip. Trampers wishing to continue further on the track should note that it becomes extremely challenging and muddy after its departure from the Hump Ridge track, and it's best to speak to someone at the Tuatapere visitor center or a local DOC office before traveling further.

◪ TUATAPERE HUMP RIDGE TRACK

Completed in 2001, the track traces its namesake, the Hump Ridge, from sea level to subalpine terrain along the untamed border of southern Fiordland, returning to its starting point via a coastline walk of railroad beds and paths over towering wooden viaducts. Privately built by a local foundation, the Hump Ridge Track is the only major tramping experience not run by the DOC. And though it lacks the celebrity flash of other Fiordland tracks, its variety of environments and views make it well worth a visit.

Length: 53km, 3 days.

Trailheads: The track is hiked as a loop, beginning and ending at Rarakau Carpark above Bluecliffs Beach. The trailhead and parking lot are about 19km southwest of Tuatapere, along Papatotara Rd.

Transportation: The **Tuatapere Information Centre** (p. 428) runs a shuttle to the trailhead (Nov.-Apr. daily 7:30am; round-trip $40). The shuttle also runs to the Track Burn, cutting 6km from the hike (Tuatapere to Track Burn round-trip $80). **South-West Helicopters** (☎226 6206) provides helicopter lifts for hikers who don't want to make the climb with their packs, an especially popular option for the first day's steep ascent ($135 or $50 per sector of the 3-day trip).

Seasonality: The track is open year-round; however, May-Oct. the huts are stripped of all amenities and prices are halved. The South Coast Track (see above) to the DOC Port Craig Hut is open year-round.

Huts: The Hump Ridge Track Trust maintains 2 well-stocked huts ($45, children $22.50) with live-in wardens, gas cookers, flush toilets, tables, and 6-bed dorms. Showers $10. Morning porridge free. Bush camping is permitted—but strongly discouraged—200m away from the track.

Bookings: Bookings are required and should be made in advance; call the **Tuatapere Information Centre** or check www.humpridgetrack.co.nz (p. 428). Track briefing 5:30pm the day before hiking.

Storage: Local accommodations are very track-friendly and will store gear for trampers.

Parking: An unattended parking lot is located just past Bluecliffs Beach.

BLUECLIFFS BEACH TO FLAT CREEK. *8km, 2½-3½hr.* From the parking lot, the track begins with a nature walk, complete with labeled flora, before descending a staircase to the beach. Trampers have the option of continuing along the beach for 3km or staying on firmer ground along an old coastal road. Crossing several streams on swing bridges, including the Track Burn, follow signs for the Hump Ridge Track and, after crossing Flat Creek, for Okaka Hut.

FLAT CREEK TO OKAKA HUT. *11km, 5-6hr.* The first hour or so after the Okaka Hut turn-off consists of a gradual inland ascent that takes you over three bridges. Be sure to make use of the helpfully labeled "water" jug at the last creek, as the climb from here to the top of the ridge is truly brutal, covering the better part of a vertical kilometer in a few hours. The fascinating shift from fern-drenched coastal forest to subalpine moss, fairy-land mountain daisies, and a view of the still-distant hut is a good excuse to stop and tend to the crippling pain in your lungs at Stag Point. Thirty minutes of relatively easy climbing leads to a junction to day two's track to Port Craig; veer right for another 30min. to reach the well-provisioned **Okaka Hut** (40 bunks) and a welcome cuppa. At sunset or sunrise the next day, be sure to make the easy 1hr. **⧉Summit Loop,** a boardwalk through strange rock formations and nonstop panoramic views.

OKAKA HUT TO LUNCHEON ROCK. *6km, 2-3hr.* The excellent facilities at Okaka rest on a perch often called the "Gateway to Heaven," which affords arresting views of both the tumultuous South Pacific and the southern boundary of Fiordland National Park. The trail toward Port Craig follows the Hump Ridge and the trail to **Luncheon Rock** lies above the treeline, featuring stupendous views but also weather exposure. Perhaps better situated along the trail for a mid-morning snack, Luncheon Rock has toilets, water, and a view of the Percy Burn Viaduct.

LUNCHEON ROCK TO PERCY BURN VIADUCT. *6.5km, 3-4hr.* Past Luncheon Rock, the track gradually drops below the treeline. At the Edwin Burn Viaduct, the track splits, heading east (over the viaduct) toward the Port Craig Hut, and west to the South Coast Track. Following the old railway line, the track soon reaches the **Percy Burn Viaduct,** the world's largest still-standing wooden viaduct.

PERCY BURN VIADUCT TO PORT CRAIG HUT. *6.5km, 2-2½hr.* After crossing the valley on this historic walkway, the track crosses a third viaduct and changes from a promenade across soaring architectural wonders to a long, straight, and uneventful slog. After what seems like hours of plodding, the track enters the historic sawmill town of **Port Craig Village.** Home to over 200 people and New Zealand's largest sawmill before succumbing to its isolation and a plague of fatal accidents, it is now a welcome stop for weary backpackers. The DOC-run **Port Craig Hut** has 40 bunks; the **Hump Track Hut** lies 50m beyond. Beyond both buildings is an excellent beach, occasionally rewarding visitors with dolphin encounters.

PORT CRAIG HUT TO PARKING LOT. *17km, 5-7hr.* The hike out barely rises above sea level, shadowing the coast back to the trail beginning. The track splits between an inland route and a rocky coastal path only accessible at low tide. Due to the relatively high danger of getting stuck when the tide comes back in, the Hump Track Foundation no longer recommends taking the low road. The track then runs across three more beaches. On the way, keep an eye out for artifacts of a 1920s settlement, Hector's dolphins, and tidal blow holes. Shortly before the creek, the path re-enters the bush and backtracks along the first part of the tramp.

FROM TUATAPERE TO RIVERTON   ☎ 03

From Tuatapere, SH92 runs past the Longwood Range to Riverton. Not long after leaving Tuatapere, you are greeted by the misty shores of Tae Waewae Bay, where you can sometimes see whales or Hector's dolphins from McCracken's Rest. Yes, it's actually called that. Look for the turn-off as you approach Orepuki (pop. 150). Originally located farther down the road at Monkey Island (or *Te Puka a Taka-timu,* meaning "anchor stone of Tatuatea's great canoe"), this mining town was relocated three times to satisfy prospectors. Nearby at Orepuki's Gemstone Beach you may find tiny low-grade gemstones amid the sand; hopefuls still pan for gold.

After Orepuki, take a quick stop at **Cosy Nook,** just off the highway, where five fisherman's cottages built in the 1960s without regard to local regulations have been preserved through a strange legal loophole, wherein they have no land deeds

F I O R D L A N D

but cannot be sold or enlarged. Talk about keeping property in the family! Just 10km before Riverton, **Colac Bay,** once a Maori settlement, is a surfing beach popular for its long, shallow stretch of sand and consistent surf. Just before the bay, you'll find **Colac Bay Tavern and Dustez Bakpakas (BBH) ❷,** 15 Colac Bay Rd. (☎234 8399; www.dustezbakpakas.co.nz. Reception at Tavern noon-late. Cabins $24 per person; tent sites $12 per person. $3 off with BBH.)

RIVERTON   ☎03

One of New Zealand's oldest towns, Riverton (pop. 2000) is a modest seaside retreat where backpackers can relax before heading north to the mountains or south to the sea. From the bridge on the north end of town, **Rocks Highway** follows an increasingly beautiful coastline 6km out of Riverton along **Riverton Rocks.** Riverton Rocks, the area's main attraction, is a pebbly beach with a cluster of unusual rock formations. The **Mores Scenic Reserve** sits above the town and is well marked from Rocks Hwy. up Richard St. Several easy walks, including the 2hr. round-trip **Mores Coastal Loop Track,** leave from the top of this excellent vantage point, which overlooks the Southland plains, Stewart Island, and Te Waewae Bay. The **Maori Craft Studio,** 130 Palmerston St., displays unique mementos including handwoven bulrush and flax creations. (☎234 9965. Open M-Sa 9am-5pm, Su noon-5pm. AmEx/MC/V.) The brand-new **Te Hikoi–Southern Journey,** 170-174 Palmerston St. (nearing completion at press time) presents the social history of the southern coast. The attached **visitors center** is the town's best source of information.

The **Globe Backpackers ❷,** 144 Palmerston St., is a friendly, fun-loving hostel equipped with Sky TV, a pizzeria, and a bar. Pizza $9-16. (☎234 8527 or 0800 843 456; www.theglobe.co.nz. Breakfast $5. Linen $2. Reception 4pm-late at the bar. Dorms $20; doubles from $50. Cash only.) Each room at the **Riverton Rock Guesthouse ❹,** 136 Palmerston St., has a homey feel. A cozy lounge with a wood stove adjoins a modern kitchen. (☎234 8886. Breakfast $12-20. Singles $55; doubles $95-145. MC/V.) **Longwood Lodge Caravan Park ❶,** between Mores Scenic Reserve and town, offers quiet tent sites with ocean views, a large indoor lounge, and a fully equipped kitchen. (☎234 8132. Free laundry. Tent sites $10; dorms $25. Cash only.) The **Aparima Tavern ❷,** 17 Orepuki-Riverton Hwy. (☎234 8502), on the north side of the river, serves up an extensive $10 snack menu. An outdoor patio, pool table, and occasional music entertain guests well into the night. (Mains around $20. Kayak rental $20 per hr. Takeaways. Open daily 10am-late.)

There are **no ATMs** in Riverton, and the nearest ones are in either Invercargill or Te Anau. The **National Bank** on Palmerston St. (☎234 7121; open M-F 9am-4:30pm) can give cash advances on credit cards in a pinch. The **Fiordland Gift Studio,** on Palmerston St., has **Internet** and laptop connections ($5 per hr.), as well as coffee and a selection of souvenirs. (☎234 8153. Open daily 9am-5pm.) Other services along Palmerston St. include: the **Riverton Pharmacy** (☎234 9999; open M-F 9am-5:30pm, Sa 10:30am-noon); a **medical center** (☎234 8290; open M-F 9am-4:30pm); and the **post office** in the **Supervalue Supermarket.** (☎234 8541. Open M-F 7:45am-7pm, Sa 9am-7pm, Su 9am-6pm.) And finally, for a little bit of Riverton trivia, the town pharmacist is the man behind the creation of the Southern Scenic Route. As you pass through, feel free to tell him if you enjoyed your trip.

SOUTHLAND

Southlanders ardently claim that the bottom of New Zealand should be at the top of any visitor's destination list. What the region lacks in tourist infrastructure and sensational urban centers, it makes up for with a down-to-earth approach to its own rugged beauty. From the slow-paced, inviting Catlins to the wild, untouched beauty of Stewart Island—as of 2002 New Zealand's newest national park—Southland delivers intriguing views of off-the-beaten-path New Zealand.

◪ SOUTHLAND HIGHLIGHTS

PRAY for a low tide to access the awe-inspiring **Cathedral Caves** (p. 437).

TAME the wild as you wander amid Stewart Island's **Northwest Circuit** (p. 449).

CHARGE the freezing surf at **Slope Point,** South Island's southernmost point (p. 442).

INVERCARGILL ☎ 03

Perpetually picked on by its northern rivals Christchurch and Dunedin, Invercargill (pop. 53,000) kind of deserves it. Although students rush here to enroll at the tuition-free Southern Institute of Technology, nights on Dee St. are still characterized by aimless local youth ("bogans") revving up their hot-rods and drinking themselves into a fever. Invercargill can provide an afternoon's worth of entertainment, but most travelers prefer to prepare for their next southern adventure.

▇ TRANSPORTATION

Flights: The **airport** is 2.5km west of the city. **Air New Zealand** (☎0800 737 767), 46 Esk St., flies frequently to **Auckland** (one-way from $150, round-trip from $300), **Christchurch** (one-way from $89, round-trip from $178) and Wellington (one-way from $134, round-trip from $268). Take Dee St. south as it becomes Clyde St. and follow the signs on the roundabout to the airport. Or, take the door-to-door **Invercargill Airport Shuttle** (☎214 3434 or 027 221 6259; $10). A **taxi** to the airport costs $10-12.

Buses: From the visitors center or the Tuatara Lodge, **Atomic Shuttles** (☎322 8883) go daily to **Christchurch** (9-10hr., 10:30am, $70) via **Dunedin** (3hr., $35). **InterCity** (☎214 6243) has student fares to **Christchurch** (8:45am, $54-67) via **Dunedin** ($33-41). **Scenic Shuttle** (☎0800 277 483) goes to **Te Anau** (3hr., 2pm, $40). **Wanaka Connections** (☎443 9122) goes daily to **Queenstown** (3hr., 1pm, $45). Call for booking and pickup. **Stewart Island Experience** (☎212 7660) runs to **Bluff** (5 per day, $16).

Public Transportation: Buses (☎218 7170) serve the suburbs M-F every hr. ($2). There's also a free bus that services the downtown area (M-Sa 10am-2:30pm), and departs from Dee St. near the library; the visitors center has schedules.

Taxis: Blue Star (☎218 6079 or 217 7777) runs 24hr.

Car Rental: Pegasus, 76 Clyde St. (☎214 3210 or 0800 803 580). From $39 per day. Long-term rates. 10% off with YHA. **Rent-A-Dent** (☎214 4820) is also in budget range.

Automobile Clubs: Automobile Association, 47-51 Gala St. (☎218 9033). M and W-F 8:30am-5pm, Tu 9am-5pm.

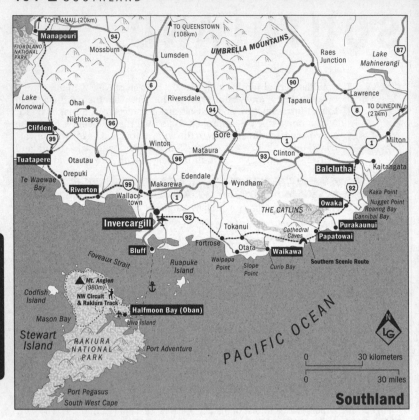

TO TE ANAU (20km)

Manapouri

Mossburn

FIORDLAND
NATIONAL
PARK

TO QUEENSTOWN
(108km)

Lumsden

UMBRELLA MOUNTAINS

Raes
Junction

Lake
Mahinerangi

94

87

Lake
Monowai

Ohai

Nightcaps

6

Riversdale

94

Tapanui

Lawrence

TO DUNEDIN
(27km)

8

Clifden

96

99

Tuatapere

Otautau

Orepuki

Winton

Gore

Mataura

96

1

Clinton

93

Milton

1

Te Waewae
Bay

Riverton

Wallace-
town

99

Makarewa

Edendale

1

Wyndham

Balclutha

92

Kaitangata

Kaka Point

Nugget Point

Invercargill

92

Tokanui

THE CATLINS

Cathedral
Caves

Owaka

Purakaunui

Roaring Bay
Cannibal Bay

Papatowai

Bluff

Foveaux Strait

Fortrose

Otara

Waikawa

Southern Scenic Route

Ruapuke
Island

Waipapa
Point

Slope
Point

Curio Bay

Codfish
Island

Mt. Anglem
(980m)

NW Circuit
& Rakiura Track

Halfmoon Bay (Oban)

Mason Bay

Ulva Island

Stewart
Island

RAKIURA
NATIONAL
PARK

Port Adventure

PACIFIC OCEAN

0   30 kilometers

0   30 miles

Port Pegasus

South West Cape

Southland

Bike Rental: Wensley's Cycle Centre, 53 Tay St. (☎218 6206). Mountain bikes $20 per day, $35 for off-road. Open M-Th 8am-5:30pm, F 8am-7pm, Sa 9:30am-12:30pm.

Hitchhiking: Hitchers heading toward Queenstown are said to take the Waikiwi bus from the library up North Rd. as far as possible to Westlans Rd. For rides to Dunedin, they take the Hawthornedale bus from Tay and Lithgow St. as far as it goes. The Clifden bus is commonly used by travelers heading towards Bluff and the Catlins. *Let's Go* does not recommend hitchhiking.

✦ 🄷 ORIENTATION AND PRACTICAL INFORMATION

To get downtown from the visitors center, turn right onto **Victoria Avenue** and then left onto **Dee Street,** Invercargill's main drag. Dee St. runs southeast toward Bluff and the Catlins, and north toward Queenstown as SH6. North of the city, it becomes **North Road.** South of **Wachner Place,** it becomes **Clyde Street.** Across from the clock tower, **Esk Street** is the main shopping area. **SH1** from Dunedin cuts through the city as **Tay Street,** hosting larger shops before turning toward Bluff.

Visitors Center: The Invercargill i-Site (☎214 6243, fax 218 4415; www.visitinvercargillnz.com), on Gala St. off Victoria Ave., inside the massive white pyramid. Internet $4 per hr. Open daily Dec.-Mar. 8am-6pm; Apr.-Nov. 8am-5pm.

Invercargill

⌂ ACCOMMODATIONS
Invercargill Top 10 Holiday
Park, **2**
Kackling Kea Backpackers
(BBH), **13**
Living Space, **11**
Southern Comfort
Backpackers (BBH), **1**
Tuatara Lodge (VIP/YHA), **6**

🍴 FOOD
Fat Indian Curryhouse, **3**
Turkish Kebabs, **8**
Ziffs Cafe and Bar, **12**
The Zookeepers Cafe, **10**

🍺 NIGHTLIFE
Frog 'N Firkin, **9**
One Blue Dog, **7**
Speight's Ale House, **5**
The Sugar Shack, **4**

SOUTHLAND

Department of Conservation (DOC): 33 Don St. (☎211 2400), on the 7th fl. of the TV Tower Bldg. Open M-F 8am-4:30pm.

Outdoor Gear: A few good places line Tay St., with the best for tramping being locally owned **Southern Adventure,** 31 Tay St. (☎218 3239). Open M-F 8:30am-5:30pm, Sa 10am-3pm. For fuel, head to **E. Hayes and Sons,** 168 Dee St. (☎218 2059; www.ehayes.co.nz. Open M-Th 7:30am-5:30pm, F 7:30am-7pm, Sa 9am-4pm, Su 10am-4pm.)

Currency Exchange: Worldwide Money (Travelex), 60 Tay St. (☎214 4119). Open M-F 8:30m-5pm, Sa 10am-noon. 24hr. **ATMs** are on Dee and Kelvin St.

Library: (☎211 1444), 50 Dee St., near Wachner Pl. Internet $4 per hr. Open M-F 9am-8pm, Sa 10am-1pm, Su 1-4pm.

Police: 117 Don St. (☎211 0400).

Medical Services: Mills Pharmacy (☎214 4249), at the corner of Don and Kelvin St. Open M-Th 8:30am-5:30pm, F 8:30am-6pm, Sa 9:30am-1pm. **Urgent Doctor,** 103 Don St. (☎218 8821, after hours 027 424 6423). Open M-F 5-10pm, Sa-Su 8am-10pm. The **Southland Hospital** (☎218 1949) is on Kew Rd. 3km south of the city along Clyde St.

Internet Access: Comzone.net, 45 Dee St. (☎214 0007). $5 per hr. Laptop stations available. Free coffee. Open daily 10am-midnight. Access also available at the Invercargill i-Site and library (see above).

Post Office: 51 Don St. (☎214 7700). Poste Restante. Open M-F 8:30am-5pm, Sa 10am-12:30pm.

▶ ▶ ACCOMMODATIONS AND CAMPING

▨ **Southern Comfort Backpackers (BBH),** 30 Thomson St. (☎218 3838). From the visitors center, turn right on Victoria Ave., then right on Thomson St. Two rambling houses and fine china lend an air of gentility. Linen $2. Reception 8am-8pm. Book ahead. Dorms $23; singles $42; twins and doubles $52. $3 BBH discount. MC/V. ❷

▨ **Kackling Kea Backpackers (BBH),** 225 Tweed St. (☎214 7950). The lack of a TV greatly enhances the social dynamic in this cozy, modern hostel, and the friendly hosts gets you going every morning with freshly baked bread. Includes linens. 6-bed dorms $23, 4-bed dorms $24; doubles $54. $2 BBH discount. MC/V. ❷

Tuatara Lodge (VIP/YHA), 30-32 Dee St. (☎214 0954 or 0800 488 282), next to Wachner Pl. A spotless backpackers in the heart of the city whose potential for personality is stifled by its large size (100 beds). Reception 7am-8pm. $10 key deposit. Dorms $25; twins and doubles $60, with bath $80. $1-3 VIP/YHA discount. MC/V. ❷

Living Space, 15 Tay St. (☎211 3800; www.livingspace.net). If nothing compels you to leave your room, why bother? 2-person studio is a bargain with the kitchenette, ethernet, bathroom, and common facilities and DVD surround-sound. Studio $89; duplex studio for 4 $109; 2-bedroom apartment $119; 3-bedroom apartment $149. MC/V. ❹

Invercargill Top 10 Holiday Park, 77 McIvor Rd. (☎215 9032; www.invercargilltop10.co.nz) Drive 5km north of the city on Dee St. and turn right onto McIvor Rd., or take the Purple Route bus north to the Woolworth's carpark and continue about 1km further up North Rd. In contrast to campsites in town, this has modern facilities and birdsong. Proximity to Anderson Park is a plus. Powered sites $14 per person; standard cabins $85, self-contained $95. MC/V. ❶

◖ FOOD

Restaurants are scattered in the city near **Dee Street,** and many double as bars. The **Pak 'N Save** supermarket is at 95 Tay St. (☎214 4864. Open daily 8am-9pm.) The **Countdown** supermarket is also on Tay St. (☎218 6716. Open daily 8am-midnight.)

▨ **Fat Indian Curryhouse,** 38 Piccadilly Ln. (☎218 9933), off Dee St. Follow your nose to this back-alley hideaway for delicious food in a welcoming outpost. Mains $15-16. Vegetarian delights $12.50-14. Open daily noon-2pm and 4:30pm-late. AmEx/MC/V. ❷

The Zookeepers Cafe, 50 Tay St. (☎218 3373). Graze with the cool cats downstairs or flit up to a perch on the upper level of this colorful, chic cafe. Beers on tap $3.60. Snacks and light meals $9-25. Open daily 10am-late. Cash only. ❶

Turkish Kebabs, 29 Esk St. (☎218 3399). Good, cheap meals and more atmosphere than its unassuming name suggests. Massive kebabs $9.50. Vegetarian falafel plate $13.50. Open daily 10am-10pm. Cash only. ❷

Ziffs Cafe and Bar, 141-143 Dunns Rd. (☎213 0501; www.ziffs.co.nz), 5min. past the airport in Otatara. Too hip for Invercargill proper, Ziffs dishes up upscale, exquisitely prepared mains and pricey desserts ($10.50) worth every penny. Bo Didley's squid $16.50. Open daily 10:30am-late. AmEx/MC/V. ❸

◉ SIGHTS

The **Southland Museum and Art Gallery,** at the end of Queen's Park, is in the same white pyramid as the visitors center. The tuatarium features a live exhibit on the ancient nocturnal reptiles that once roamed New Zealand, while the Roaring 40° gallery provides an explanation of New Zealand's subantarctic satellite islands. On a clear, cool night, hunt for shooting stars at the **observatory** next to the visitors center. (☎219 9069. Museum open M-F 9am-5pm, Sa-Su 10am-5pm. Observatory open Apr.-Oct. W 7-9pm. $2 donation.) For a different taste of Kiwi culture, the **Invercargill Brewery**, 8 Wood St., (☎214 5070; www.invercargillbrewery.co.nz), between Liddel and Clyde St., churns out four delicious microbrews and a cider. Brewmaster Steve fields questions from beer enthusiasts during free informal tours and tastings. The bottle shop offers "fill-your-own" specials ($9), providing 4L bottles for you to bring to the tap. (1½hr. detailed tours available at $5 per person. Call ahead. Open M-Th, Sa 11am-6pm, F 11am-7pm.) **Queen's Park** is worth a visit and displays New Dawn and Madame de Por roses, as well containing a running track and a small zoo. Just north of the city, down McIvor Rd. from the Top 10 park, **Anderson Park and Gallery** houses a collection of Kiwi art in a Georgian manor, but the main attraction is the surrounding lawn and gardens. (☎215 7432; andersonparkgallery@xtra.co.nz. Free coffee and tea. Gallery open 10:30am-5pm daily.)

🎵 🎭 ENTERTAINMENT AND NIGHTLIFE

Nightly entertainment in Invercargill is limited, though a few theatres host touring acts. Check with the visitors center or **The Plot**, a weekly music calendar, to see what's on during your stay. **Reading Cinemas**, 29 Dee St., is the only place within 100km to catch a flick. (☎211 1555. Films $12.50, Tu $9.) The streets in Invercargill are bright after dark and serve as a forum for drag-racing. Nightlife in Invercargill hops Thursday through Saturday and flops during the rest of the week. Non-Kiwis should remember to bring their passports, as even quieter bars card at the door.

The Sugar Shack, 77 Don St. (☎218 6125; www.sugarshack.co.nz). This popular dance club provides shack ambience after 2am. The sugar is left up to the guests. Free membership card for half-off drinks (valid until 1am Th-Sa). Open Th-Sa 10pm-late.

Frog 'N Firkin (☎214 4001), next to the movie theater on Dee St. The place students go to begin their evening, the Frog 'N Firkin packs them in with $5 pints and hopping dance music. Open M-Tu 4pm-10pm, W 4pm-midnight, Th-Sa noon-3am.

Speight's Ale House, 38 Dee St. (☎214 5333). This new addition to the scene in Invercargill is generally the place where the older "kids" go to have a responsible night of fun. $5 pints. Open daily 11am-late.

One Blue Dog, 34 Esk St. (☎214 6970). A large seating area with pool table behind the bar provides a balance to the small dance floor in front. Bar snacks $3-5. Shakers $12, bottled beers $4. Open Th-Sa 10pm-4:30am.

THE CATLINS ☎03

The Catlins are hidden, even from the scenic highway that serves as the region's main thoroughfare, hiding their best offerings down numerous unpaved side roads. Those who take time to explore are rewarded with secluded cliffs dotted with natural bush, antarctic waters populated by a host of exotic and rare fauna, and some of the best surfing beaches South Island has to offer. While no longer New Zealand's best-kept secret, the Catlins remain worthy of the detour.

THE REAL DEAL. While many national tour bus companies favor a whirlwind 10hr. tour, this region is much more satisfying when seen slowly over the course of three or more days. Since the area is relatively small, book a hostel that suits your tastes and use it as your base of operations. *—Richard Lonsdorf*

⊏ TRANSPORTATION IN THE CATLINS

The **Southern Scenic Route** (**SH92**; p. 426) runs 162km through the Catlins from Balclutha to Invercargill, winding through hills only a few kilometers away from the region's renowned coastline. Many side roads are unpaved but signposts lead the way to everything from whole towns to hostels. A car or mountain bike (and strong lungs) are the best ways to take in the coast at your own pace. Backpackers in a hurry use **Kiwi Experience's Bottom Bus,** which makes frequent guided trips from Dunedin to Invercargill, shuttling travelers along the whole trip in one 10hr. day. (☎442 9708; www.BottomBus.co.nz. Runs M, W, F-Sa 7:30-8am. Free pickup. $135.) Although *Let's Go* does not recommend it, **hitchhiking** through the Catlins is said to be feasible in summer, but more difficult in winter due to decreased traffic.

⚡ PRACTICAL INFORMATION

There are **no banks** between Balclutha and Invercargill, though some establishments may be willing to give cash back on debit cards. There are plenty of campsites, but the Catlins' top-notch backpackers should not be missed. Free camping is permitted on public land and beaches except where posted. Most of the region's accommodations have very few beds, making advance booking essential.

BALCLUTHA   ☎03

Balclutha (pop. 4100) is the "largest city" of the Catlins, and is the best place to stock up on groceries and withdraw funds. Located at the junction of SH1 and SH92, 30km from Owaka and 60km from Papatowai, Balclutha has resources for Catlins-bound travelers, but little else of interest. The **Balclutha i-Site,** 4 Clyde St., has maps. (☎418 0388; clutha.vin@cluthadc.govt.nz. Open M-F 8:30am-5pm, Sa-Su 9:30am-3pm. Weekends in winter 10am-2pm.) Get your fill of trail mix and groceries at the **New World** down Lanark St., a block after the bridge. (☎418 2850. Open daily 8am-8pm.) Other Balclutha services include: **banks** with **24hr. ATMs** along Clyde St.; a BP **gas station** (☎418 0034), 79 Clyde St.; the **police,** 7 Renfrew St., two blocks down from Clyde St. (☎418 0203); **Clutha Health First,** 3-7 Charlotte St. (☎418 0500), also accessible from Clyde St., which serves as the region's hospital. For a quick bite before plunging into the Catlins, stop off at **The Captain's ❷,** 13 Clyde St., in the hotel between the bridge and the turnoff to SH92. (☎418 2100. Mains $14-24.50. Open daily 11am-9pm. Cash only.)

KAKA POINT, NUGGET POINT, AND ROARING BAY   ☎03

The Catlins' claim to fame is their coastline, with fine sand beaches and jutting headlands where sea lions bask amid colonies of birds. Start exploring at **Kaka Point,** 18km north of Owaka on a well-marked road off SH92. Kaka Point is a tiny beach retreat town. The beach at Kaka arcs toward ◙**Nugget Point,** 8km south down a gravel road. The lighthouse (the southernmost in the world) is a 10min. jaunt along a rock ledge that towers over the sea, bending toward the islets that give the point its name. Fur seals, elephant seals, and hooker sea lions frolic on the waterlogged crags—the only place in New Zealand that these creatures coexist—but you'll need a pair of binoculars to see them from the lighthouse. Straight ahead from the parking lot at the end of the road to Nugget Point, **Roaring Bay** is home to yellow-eyed penguins that hop up the cliffs in the two hours before sunset.

The town clusters around **Kaka Point Stores,** which has groceries, takeaways, a bar, and postal services. **The Point Cafe ❸,** in the same complex, has the ocean

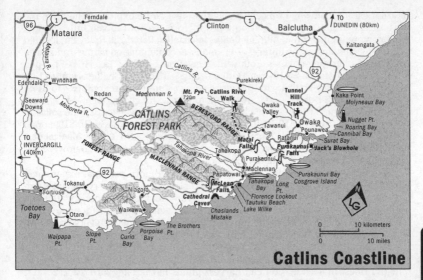

Catlins Coastline

vistas, pleasant ambiance, and expensive meals (lunch $11-19; dinner $25-29) expected of a beach resort bar. (☎412 8800; www.kakapoint.co.nz. Open daily noon-3pm and 6-7:30pm. Bar open daily 10am-late. Cash only.) A public phone is outside the store. A path up the leafy hillside leads to the **Fernlea Backpackers ❶**, off Moana St. directly beyond the Kaka Point Stores. Overlooking the bay, this well-loved bungalow is maintained by resident hosts. (☎412 8834 or 418 0117. Linen $2. Reception 9am-10pm. Dorms $20; alcove doubles $40.) **Nugget View and Kaka Point Motels ❹**, 11 Rata St., offers self-contained multi-room units with ocean views. (☎0800 525 278 or 412 8602; www.catlins.co.nz. Reception 8:30am-10pm. Rooms from $75. Cash only.) **Kaka Point Camping Ground ❶** is above the town but trees block any possible ocean view. (☎412 8818. Self-registration. Caravan and tent sites $10 per person, power $5. Cabins $20 per person. Cash only.)

FROM KAKA POINT TO OWAKA   ☎03

From Kaka Point, follow signs for Owaka along the unpaved roads to return to SH92. Soon after rejoining it, **Tunnel Hill** lies just a 10min. walk off the main road. Turn off your flashlight for an eerie experience crossing through this abandoned railway tunnel. Farther along SH92, fur seals and sea lions congregate on the beach at **Cannibal Bay** or on the dunes at **Surat Bay** (p. 439). The road from SH92 to Cannibal Bay, however, is windy and dangerous, having been the site of many recent campervan collisions. A better option is to walk from Surat Bay. A rocky walking path connects the two (30min.). Although human bones were once discovered at Cannibal Bay, it's more likely that the unlucky man was killed in a battle than eaten alive. Just north of Owaka, signs point the way to **Jack's Blowhole.** More accurately a slurp hole, the deep depression is connected to the ocean (200m away) by caves. To reach the blowhole, walk the 30min. track; visit at high tide for the most dramatic view.

OWAKA   ☎03

Thirty kilometers south of Balclutha, Owaka (pop. 400) consists of a couple of restaurants, a couple of backpackers, a grocery store, an information center, and an

Internet cafe. A convenient place to stay the night while exploring the area, the town offers little other than charming proprietors, except the last fully stocked grocery store until Invercargill. The **Catlins Information Centre**, 20 Ryley St., located in the same building as the library, offers maps, accommodation listings, and farmstay information and bookings. Follow the signs from SH92. (☎/fax 415 8371. Open M-F 9:30am-4:30pm, Sa-Su 10-4pm.) Other services include: a Shell **gas station** that is also an **AA service station** with the last cheap gas until Invercargill (☎ 415 8179, afterhours 415 8311 or 415 8362; owaka.motors.ltd@xtra.co.nz; open M-F 7:30am-6pm, Sa 9am-4pm, Su 10am-4pm; closes at 2pm on winter weekends); the **police** at the west end of town (☎ 419 1070); a **pharmacy**, 26 Waikowa Rd. (☎ 415 8109; open M-Tu, Th 10:30am-5:30pm, F 11am-5pm. No pharmacist F); the **Catlins Medical Centre**, 29 Main Rd. (☎ 415 8006); **Internet** access at Sue's Shed (see **Food**, below; $2 per 15min.); **postal service** at 4 Square (see below).

The smaller hostels outside of town provide for a more personal experience, but for those interested in an amusing use of reclaimed property, try **Thomas's Catlins Lodge & Holiday Park ❷**, at the corner of Ryley and Clark Streets, located in a rambling converted hospital. The facilities have been given colorful makeovers, but the small touches such as the red emergency buttons outside every room preserve the charming institutional feel. (☎ 415 8333; www.thomascatlins.co.nz. Dorms $25; twins $55, ensuite $90; tent sites $7 per person, with power $12.)

Just before town, **Blowhole Backpackers (BBH) ❷**, 24 Main Rd., has soft beds at budget prices. In season, you can harvest plums in the backyard. (☎ 412 8111. Dorms $26; singles $33; doubles $58. $3 BBH discount. Cash only.) Follow the signs as you head into Owaka from the north to reach the sunny **Pounawea Motor Camp ❶**, with its changing view of the estuary on the Catlins River. The Pounawea Bush Walk begins from the campground, and the trills of songbirds will greet you in the morning. You can also rent canoes and kayaks ($5 per hr., $10 per day) to explore the birdlife along the waterway. (☎ 415 8483. Reception 24hr. Tent and caravan sites $10; cabins $19 per person. Cash only.)

There are several food options in town, although the grocery at **4 Square**, on Overden St., has cheap provisions for roadtrippers. (☎ 415 8201. Open daily 8am-7pm.) **Sue's Shed ❷**, 3-5 Main Rd. (☎ 415 8392), before the visitor's center, dishes up burgers ($4.50-7), creative mains ($12.50-18), and organic fair-trade coffee ($3-5). The attached gallery functions occasionally as an evening concert space or dining room. (Open M-F 7am-8pm. MC/V.) The **restaurant ❷**, adjoining the Catlins Inn serves up assorted pub fare ($11-16) and popular takeaways. (Open M-Sa 11am-late, Su 11am-8pm.) The adjacent **pub** has pool, darts, a big-screen TV, and lots of cheap beer ($3.50), making it popular with locals.

Ten minutes from town, New Zealand sea lions bray, and butt heads along the beach in **Surat Bay**. The colony, numbering 40 in winter, makes up a substantial percentage of a "mainland" sea lion population of 100; the rest are chilling in Antarctica. **Surat Bay Lodge (BBH) ❷**, (☎ 415 8099; www.suratbay.co.nz), is just a few hundred meters from the lions and rents canoes to explore the estuary. (Canoes $5 per hr., $35 per day. Dorms $25, doubles $60. $3 off with BBH. Cash only.)

FROM OWAKA TO PURAKAUNUI   ☎ 03

Back on the highway after Owaka, an unpaved road to the right leads 11.5km up the Owaka Valley through forests along the **Catlins River Gorge**. Get a ride to the top of the **Catlins River Walk** (5hr. one-way), a well-maintained tramp through unspoiled beech forest and over four suspension bridges. When the trout are biting, this is the place to catch them; you may even see the yellowhead or Mohua bird along the way. Ask at the visitors center in Owaka about rides to the trailhead. There is no camping or facilities at the top of the track; the only four-walled toilets along the way are at the **Tawanui DOC campsite ①** ($6 per person) near the track's base. Look for the trailhead at the far end of the large grassy campsite. About three and a half kilometers along the River Walk Drive, you'll see the giant guitar that heralds the ▓**Catlins Woodstock Lodge & Camp ①**, (☎415 8583), home of the annual Catlins Woodstock music festival (3rd week in Jan.). Even when Southland hippies haven't descended upon the place, you'll still find modern accommodation in a lush river valley. The luxury suites ($195 for 6, $20 per extra person up to 10) are an excellent group splurge. (2-bed "dorms" $25; double $50; 2-person self-contained $90; family room for 4 $100; tent sites $10 per person, with power $15.)

PURAKAUNUI BAY AND FALLS ☎03

Local beach cows munch kelp on the sand of **Purakaunui Bay,** a surfing beach for the brave-hearted. The mist from crashing waves creates a dense spray which can be seen from the popular **DOC campsite ①** ($6). To reach it, take the rough road south from SH92. Several well-marked routes south of SH92 climb to **Purakaunui Falls.** The 20min. return walk from the parking lot meanders through a dense rain forest down to the multi-tiered, cascading falls. These are probably the best falls in the Catlins, made even more lovely at night with the arrival of glowworms. On the road to the falls, stop for a night's rest at the ▓**Falls Backpackers (BBH) ②.** The snug farmhouse was transported by truck to its hillside locale amid the sheep, and the cozy family environment it fosters cannot be beat. Everyone gets an electric blanket and a farm egg for breakfast, provided the hens are laying. (☎415 8724. Dorms $25; twins and doubles $62. Bookings essential. $3 BBH discount.) On your way toward Papatowai, **Matai Falls** offers a brief 10min. detour from the main road and a chance to stretch your legs.

PAPATOWAI ☎03

Papatowai Beach is impressive—crashing waves, mist rising off the sand, cliffs visible farther down the coast, and an estuary flowing through the dune forest. Accessible from SH92 just north of Papatowai and offering commanding views of the sea, the fabulous accommodations at ▓**Hilltop Backpackers ②** initiated the trend toward luxurious budget quarters that makes backpacking in the Catlins a five-star affair. (☎415 8028; hilltop@ihug.co.nz. Reservations recommended. Dorms $25; twins $60; doubles $65, ensuite $75. MC/V.) In Papatowai proper, the **Southern Secret Motel ⑤** has opulent one-room apartments from which to explore the area. At press time, the owner was putting the finishing touches on either a vacation home or an upscale backpackers next door; if it becomes the latter, it will be well worth checking out. (☎415 8600; http://homepages.ihug.co.nz/~aikman. Reception 24hr. Rooms $95.) The **Papatowai Motels and Store ④** has expensive gas, postal services, groceries, and spacious rooms behind the store. (☎/fax 415 8147. Reception and store open Dec. to mid-Apr. daily 9am-7pm; mid-Apr. to Nov. Su-Th 9am-6pm, F-Sa 9am-7pm. Doubles $85. $15 per extra adult, $10 per extra child. Cash only.) Hit the trampoline at the **Papatowai Motor Park ①,** behind the store in a bushy area. (☎415 8565. Reception 8:30am-9:30pm. Tent sites $6; caravan sites $7. Dorms $12; 2-person cabins $20-30. MC/V.)

Before leaving Papatowai, take a moment to follow the "Curios" sign off the main road to the ▓**Lost Gypsy Gallery,** located in a big green bus. It would be terrible to ruin the surprise here, but you'll enjoy playing with Blair's contraptions. Just beware of the temptation button. (☎415 8908. Open M-Tu, Th-Su 9am-6pmish. Mostly closed over winter.) For travelers seeking to stroll the coast, the **Catlins Wildlife Trackers** (☎0800 228 546 or 415 8613; www.catlins-ecotours.co.nz) traces the shoreline on lonely beaches and towering cliffs over a two-day self-guided romp. The **Top Track** (22km., 12hr.) crosses private farmland and costs

$35 for overnight or $15 for the day. South of Papatowai, the road winds to **Florence Lookout** and a spectacular view of **Tautuku Beach**. Backed by the rusty hues of the native forest, Tautuku may be the best of the Catlins' remarkable beaches. Turn off for **Lake Wilkie** and its 20min. boardwalk a bit farther down the hill. Don't miss the ◙**Cathedral Caves** turn-off, 16km from Papatowai. The two 30m mouths of the caves are only accessible at low tide, and even then you'll probably be doing some wading; check a tide table at the visitors center or your hostel before making the 30min. trek to **Waipati Beach** and the caves. (Gates open 2hr. before and after low tide. $3 per person.) Just after the caves, turn onto Rewcastle Rd. for the 30min. walk through the beech forest to **McLean Falls**.

WAIKAWA, CURIO BAY, AND SLOPE POINT ☎03

Continue on the main road toward Invercargill via **Tokanui,** which has both gas and a public phone, or turn off toward **Waikawa** some 20km beyond the Cathedral Caves. Either way, make sure to stop for a warming bowl of chowder ($11.50), a slice of carrot cake ($4), or the enormous "All Day" Breakfast ($15.50) at the ◙**Niagara Falls Cafe ❷**, about one kilometer toward Waikawa. (☎246 8577. Open daily 9am-5:30pm, 5:30pm-7:30pm with dinner menu. In winter open at 10am. Later dinners possible with advance booking.) Once you're in Waikawa, the **Waikawa Museum and Information Centre** (☎246 8464), provides postal services, a small collection of local artifacts, and bookings for farmstays and accommodations. (Open daily 10am-5pm.) Next to the visitors center, **Waikawa Holiday Lodge (BBH) ❷** provides spartan rooms with metal-frame bunks and free local phone calls. (☎/fax 246 8552. Reception 24hr. Dorms $25; twins $50; doubles $54. Cash only.)

Porpoise and **Curio Bays** are each a 10min. drive from Waikawa, with Porpoise Bay providing ample surfing opportunity. Located about 1km before Curio Bay itself, ◙**Curio Bay Backpackers (BBH) ❷** has all the advantages of a laid-back beach house with a wall of windows to watch Hector's dolphins in Porpoise Bay. (☎246 8797; www.curiobay.com. Dorms $25; doubles $58, with bath $78. $3 BBH discount. Cash only.) At the point of a craggy coastal peninsula, the **Curio Bay Campground ❶** has extremely basic facilities, but beach access and fishing spots. (☎246 8897. Office and essentials shop open daily 8:30am-8pm, in winter 9am-6pm. Tent sites $15, with power $25. Cash only.) The campground is also a good spot to spy a small colony of yellow-eyed penguins, as well as occasional Hector's dolphins.

On the other side of the point lie **Curio Bay** and a 180-million-year-old **petrified forest,** visible on the rocky coast at low tide. Amid pools of bead-like seaweed and unhinged bull kelp lie the mineralized trunks of ancient trees.

From the turn-off at Porpoise Bay, past Waikawa, follow signs to **Slope Point,** the southernmost tip of South Island. The lonely light signal is a windy 10min. walk from the road markers; beware of gusts at the cliff's edge. Four kilometers before the Point you'll pass **Slope Point Backpackers ❶**. This sheep farm and friendly hostel sports gardens and a new building on the way. (☎/fax 246 8420. Linen $2. Reception 24hr. Book ahead. Dorms $18; doubles $40, ensuite $44. Tent sites $10.)

The lighthouse at **Waipapa Point** is the site of the worst maritime disaster in New Zealand history (the wreck of the *SS Tararua* in 1881), 2km from Slope Point past Otara toward Invercargill. Divers blew up the wreckage a while ago, but the visitors center details the tragedy. The remains of the similarly unlucky *Ino* can still be seen at low tide from a lookout point in Fortrose, on the way to Invercargill.

BLUFF ☎03

As the departure point for the ferry to Stewart Island, seaside Bluff (Invercargill's port town, 27km south of the city) also marks the terminus of SH1. Bluff is known for its world-famous oysters, but there's not much else in this industrial town aside from a handful of local sights. The **Bluff Maritime Museum,** on the pier, features a decommissioned oyster ship for visitors to climb on. (☎212 7534. Open M-F 10am-4:30pm, Sa-Su 1-5pm. $2.) SH1 ends—or begins, depending on who you ask—a kilometer from town at **Stirling Point,** the trailhead for a number of short walks. The multidirectional signpost there makes for an obligatory photo op and serves two purposes: to remind you just how far you are from New York City (15,008km) and to encourage the local belief that Bluff is the southernmost point on the South Island despite the fact that Slope Point (see p. 442) holds the prestigious honor. The only attraction in Bluff bordering on scenic is the lookout from **Bluff Hill,** a view extending to Stewart Island and over Invercargill to the southern corner of Fiordland National Park. Follow the brown signs from Gore St.

If you can't make it back to Invercargill, try harder. Still here? **Bluff Lodge ❶,** at the corner of Gore and Lee St., is dilapidated, friendly, and cheap. (☎212 7106. Internet free for first 15min. Dorms $15, doubles $40, triples $60. MC/V.) The **Bay View Hotel ❷,** 48 Gore St., has a few more frills, with Sky TV and continental breakfast. (☎212 8615. Singles $35; twins and doubles $70. MC/V.) A good option for large groups planning in advance is the cute and comfortable **Lazy Fish ❷,** up Burrows St. from Gore as you head south from town. (☎212 7245. 4-person unit $95. MC/V.) Follow signs from Marine Pde. to the basic **Bluff Camping Ground ❶.** Pay by the honor system—there is no attendant. (☎212 8774. Call ahead before 8pm. Tent sites $8 per person; caravans and cabins $10 plus $5 per person. Cash only.) Groceries are available at **4 Square,** 54 Gore St., across from the Bay View Hotel. (☎212 8179. Open M-W 7am-7pm, Th-Sa 7am-8:30pm, Su 9am-7pm.)

The **Stewart Island Experience** runs coaches between Bluff and Invercargill. (☎212 7660. Departs Invercargill i-Site, Tuatara Lodge, and airport 1hr. before ferry departure. 30min.; $16. Bookings required.) With **no bank, ATM,** or **visitors center,** outlets of information are limited to a display board located at the corner of Gore and Onslow St. Some local establishments will accept major credit cards for payments but not for cash withdrawals, making it necessary to get money while in Invercargill. The **Medical Centre** is located on Tone St. behind the campground. (☎212 7337. Open M-F 8:30am-5pm.) The **post office** is at 98 Gore St. (☎212 8759. Open M-Tu and Th-F 8:30am-5pm, W 9am-6pm, Sa 10am-1:30pm.)

STEWART ISLAND ☎03

Maori legend holds that when Maui fished up North Island from his South Island canoe, Stewart Island was his anchor stone. Named Rakiura in Maori for "the place of glowing skies," the island sees red sunsets and the aurora australis in winter. Most of the time, the muddy tracks and remote beaches are what visitors find on the island where kiwis still vastly outnumber Kiwis. Celebrating this untouched splendor, Stewart Island became New Zealand's newest national park in 2002. Birdlife abounds, with rare birds thriving on Ulva Island, and droves of penguins crowding the beaches. The island's 400 or so residents cluster in the fishing village by Halfmoon Bay, weathering over 275 days of rain per year. They insist, with good reason, that you haven't seen New Zealand until you've seen the pristine beaches and primeval bush of this unique habitat.

▐ TRANSPORTATION

Flights: Stewart Island Flights (Invercargill for bookings ☎218 9129, Oban 219 1090) flies 9-seat prop planes to and from **Invercargill** (30min.; 3 per day; $90, round-trip $155; standby $60, round-trip $105). Only 15kg of baggage per person; extra luggage will come on the next flight. Call the night before for standby flights. Stewart Island Flights runs a free shuttle from their Stewart Island airstrip to **Halfmoon Bay.**

Ferries: Stewart Island Experience runs the **Foveaux Express** (☎212 7660 or 0800 000 511; www.stewartislandexperience.co.nz) between **Bluff** and **Halfmoon Bay** (1hr.; 2-3 per day; $51, children half-price). The Foveaux Straight is notoriously rough even on good days. Alternatively, the record for swimming the strait is 9hr. and 41min. Car storage around the ferry terminal in Bluff costs $7.50 per night, with discounts for long-term stays; ask at the Foveaux Express ticket desk. Parking on the street is free and common, though at your own risk.

Shuttles and Rentals: Stewart Island Experience on Main Rd. in the "Oban Visitor Centre" (☎219 0056) rents **mountain bikes** ($26 per 4hr., $36 per 8hr.), **mopeds** ($50 per 4hr., $60 per 8hr.) and **cars** ($80 per day, $60 per half-day), and runs a **shuttle** service mainly for ferry transfers, but on demand if available (on-call daily 7am-6pm). Open daily 9am-6pm; reduced hours mid-Apr. to Nov.

Water Taxis: Several companies on the island offer similar services to the nearer backcountry huts, Ulva Island, and other locations. Your best bet is usually to book through the i-Site. Most trips require a 2-3 person min. (or charge extra for only one passenger). Companies include **Seaview Enterprises** (☎219 1014), **Stewart Island Water Taxi** (☎219 1394), **Rakiura Adventure** (☎219 1013), and **Seabuzzz** (☎219 1282).

■ ? ORIENTATION AND PRACTICAL INFORMATION

Stewart Island lies 35km across the **Foveaux Strait** from Bluff, the nearest mainland town. The island's primary human settlement is tiny **Oban** (oh-BAN), also known by its location as **Halfmoon Bay. Elgin Terrace** curves along the bay, while **Ayr Street, Main Road,** and **Horseshoe Bay Road** branch inland. Nothing in town is farther than a 15min. walk. **Golden Bay Road** crosses to **Paterson Inlet** in the south (10min.), and Horseshoe Bay Rd. and Elgin Terr. lead along the water to quiet beaches and coves. Travelers should be aware that there are **no banks or ATMs** on the island, and though credit cards are accepted at many places, a pocketful of cash is a must.

Visitors Center: Stewart Island i-Site (☎219 1400; www.stewartisland.co.nz), near the wharf in the "Red Shed," arranges bookings for transportation, accommodations, and activities on the island.

DOC Office: Rakiura National Park Visitor Centre (☎219 0002; stewartislandfc@doc.govt.nz), on Main Rd., provides official information on Rakiura National Park and sells hut passes. Trampers are required to check in and check out for longer tramps. Luggage storage (small lockers $2.50, large $5). Open M-F 8am-5pm, with decreased weekend hours in winter.

Outdoor Equipment Rental: Trampers should call **Ruggedy Range** (☎219 1066; www.ruggedyrange.com), 170 Horseshoe Bay Rd., for gaiters, walking poles, fuel canisters, and a variety of other useful items. Advance reservations recommended, as supplies are limited. **Stewart Island Adventures** (☎219 1439) can provide kayaks (single $40 per day, double $50) and diving gear (full outfitting with tank $113 per day) from their Island/Outdoors Adventure Center in the "Red Shed" by the wharf.

Police: (☎219 0020), on Golden Bay Rd.

Medical Services: 24 hr. district nurse (☎219 1098 or 0800 100 776), on Argyle St. Clinic open daily 10am-12:30pm.

Internet Access: Justcafé, South Sea Hotel Restaurant and Pub, and **Stewart Island Backpackers** all have Internet connections; see below.

Telephones: Card phones outside Stewart Island Backpackers and Crazy Fish; **coin phones** at the South Sea Hotel and DOC Office. **Cellular phone** service is limited to Telecomm 027 customers.

Post Office: Run by **Stewart Island Flights** (☎219 1090), on Elgin Terr. Open Oct.-Apr. M-F 7:30am-5:45pm, Sa-Su 8:30am-5pm; May-Sept. daily 8:30am-4:45pm.

ACCOMMODATIONS AND CAMPING

The influx of non-budget visitors to the island in recent years has caused the hostel scene to shrink, creating a crunch during peak times (or whenever the Stray Bus shows up). Booking ahead is crucial, but if you find yourself with no place to stay, contact the Stewart Island i-Site, as there are several small places that may have room. At the centrally located **Stewart Island Backpackers ❷**, 18 Ayr St., the rooms and enormous lounge are connected by covered boardwalks. (☎219 1114. Reception 7:30am-noon and 1-7pm. Dorms $24; singles $30; doubles $50. Tent sites $10. MC/V.) For a more intimate experience and a home-cooked breakfast to boot, stay at **Jo and Andy's B&B ❸**, at the corner of Main Rd. and Morris St. (☎219 1230. Singles $35, doubles $45. Cash only.) Two spacious decks allow **The View ❷**, 18 Nichol Rd., to live up to its name. (☎219 1328. Linen $5. Dorms $25; doubles $70. Cash only.) **Deep Bay Cabin ❸**, 22 Deep Bay, is a 25min. walk from town. Call for a pickup to enjoy the outdoor toilet and the birdsong in this isolated cabin. (☎219 1219. $50 for 2; $10 per extra person. Sleeps up to 4. Cash only.)

FOOD

Dr. Britt's Swedish-themed **Justcafé ❶**, on Main Rd., is a mellow place to plan adventures and savor one of the southernmost cappuccinos New Zealand has to offer ($4). Don't let the name fool you—homemade sandwiches ($7-9) and baked goods ($2-4.50) are available, too. (☎219 1422. Mac-based Internet $2.50 per 15min. Open Oct.-June daily 9am-5pm. Cash only.) After the half-pipe, the **Kai Kart ❶**, set in an old trailer on Ayr St., serves up fresh local seafood at rock-bottom prices. (☎219 1225. Takeaways from $3. Dinner mains from $15. Open 11:30am-2:30pm and 5-9pm. Cash only.) The only pub in town is the comfortable **South Sea Hotel Restaurant and Pub ❸**, at the corner of Main Rd. and Elgin Terr., where locals mingle to tell stories about, and drink like, fish. (☎219 1059. Mains from $14. Internet $2 per 15min. Open daily Dec. to mid-Apr. 7-10am, 11:30am-2pm, and 6-9pm; mid-Apr. to Nov. 8am-8pm. Pub open from 11am until "as late as necessary." Cash only.) The **Crazy Fish ❸**, on Main Rd. next to Justcafé, offers wood-fired pizzas ($16-30) and drinks (beer and wine $5-12). You can also catch a screening of various independent and foreign films ($18) in the adjoining movie theater. (☎219 1429; www.thecrazyfish.co.nz. Open daily 5pm-9pm. Cash only.) **Ship to Shore (4 Square)**, on Elgin Terr., sells vitals. (☎219 1069. Open Oct. to mid-Apr. daily 7:30am-7:30pm; mid-Apr. to Sept. daily 7:30am-6:30pm.)

OUTDOOR ACTIVITIES

Stewart Island's star is the elusive brown kiwi, and those who venture into the wilderness won't come away disappointed.

HIKING

Stewart Island is famous for its long, muddy hikes, but an interconnected network of easy dayhikes start in Halfmoon Bay; the DOC office can help you to plan an itinerary. **Observation Rock**, a 15min. walk beyond Ayr St., affords prime sunset views over Paterson Inlet. The 3hr. round-trip walk to **Ackers Point**, east of town, is a great option for dusk, as muttonbirds nest there. Quiet, sandy beaches are close to town along any coastal road. The **Golden Bay/Deep Bay** walk (2hr. round-trip) affords forest-framed views of the striking Patterson Inlet. Follow Ayr Rd., then Golden Bay Rd., and look for signs. For a brief glimpse of native bush, try the **Fern Gully** walk (2hr. round-trip). Take Main Rd. onto Kaipipi Rd. and follow track signs. The **Garden Mound/Little River/Lee Bay** walk (4-5hr. round-trip) climbs to a lookout at Garden Mound and then emerges from the bush where the Little River meets the sea at Lee Bay. Walk along Horseshoe Bay Rd. for nearly 1hr., then turn left on Lee Bay Rd. and look for track signs.

BIRDWATCHING AND GUIDED WALKS

The astounding diversity of birdlife on both Stewart and Ulva Islands makes for fascinating, accessible birdwatching that will charm even the most adrenaline-hungry naysayers. The avian superstar of New Zealand is the **kiwi,** and the Stewart Island variety has the distinction of being common and visible. Trampers on the Northwest Circuit (see p. 449) have the best chances for kiwi spotting, but short trips to scenic **Mason Bay** by boat or plane are a good alternative to spending 10 days in the backcountry. The multi-talented Furhana of ▧**Ruggedy Range** (☎219 1066; www.ruggedyrange.com) leads overnight kiwi-spotting trips from Freshwater Landing to Mason Bay. (4-6 people. $385 per person. Price includes all meals, DOC fees, water transport, and cooking gear. Booking essential.) For travelers who don't want to stay overnight, **Bravo Adventure Cruises** (☎219 1144; philldismith@xtra.co.nz) leads twilight boat cruises to Mason Bay with flashlight-guided 4hr. kiwi walks. **Independent trips** to Mason Bay are possible, either by arranging a water taxi to Freshwater Landing Hut ($50 one-way) or by taking a charter flight from Stewart Island flights (see p. 447). Flights can depart from either Invercargill or Oban. If you intend to stay the night in the Mason Bay hut, be sure to book through the DOC before departing.

While kiwi-spotting can make for an excellent excursion, thousands of exotic birds inhabit the area. ▧**Ulva Island,** just a quick (6-8min.) boat ride from Golden Bay wharf (a 10min. walk from town over Golden Bay Rd.), has the distinction of being one of the largest predator-free sanctuaries in the world. Several rare and endangered bird species have been reintroduced onto the island after rodent eradication was completed in 1997. Several water taxi companies travel to Ulva Island ($20-25 per person; book at the Stewart Island i-Site), but the best way to get the most out of the island is to take a guided walk with a trained bird-spotter. **Ruggedy Range** leads small, species-counting parties on half- or full-day walks. (4-12 people. Half-day $85 per person, full-day $135. Price includes water transport, DOC fees, and meal for full-day trips. Booking essential.) In a line of work that may well have been named for her, Ulva Goodwillie of **Ulva's Guided Walks** (☎219 1216; www.ulva.co.nz) does half-day and full-day trips as well, drawing from her local knowledge. (Half-day trips $95, full-day with included lunch $160. Price includes transportation and DOC fees. Booking essential.) The **DOC Summer Visitor Programme** has periodic guided half-day trips to Ulva Island during January and February ($65, children $35; 4-8 people. Book ahead.)

WATER ACTIVITIES

Stewart Island's fishy beginnings (see **Stewart Island,** p. 443) have led to a lot of ways to enjoy the surrounding waterways. **Chartered trips** are great way to see the area, and most companies offer fishing and hunting options, as well as guided walks. Contact the following companies directly, or talk to the Stewart Island i-Site to see who's free: **Aurora Charters** (☎219 1126; www.auroracharters.co.nz), **Bravo Adventure Cruises** (☎219 1144; philldismith@xtra.co.nz), **Lo Loma** (☎219 1141; info@seabuzzz.co.nz), **Rawhiti Excursions** (☎219 1023), **Southern Isle Charters** (☎219 1133; lhhansen@xtra.co.nz), and **Takaroa 2 Cruises** (☎212 8170;

takaroa@ihug.co.nz). For those who want to see what lies under the water, **Seabuzzz** (☎219 1282; www.seabuzzz.co.nz), offers 2hr. trips into Big Glory Bay to see the salmon and mussel farms through their glass-bottomed boat ($60, min. 2 people). The **Underwater Explorer,** run by Stewart Island Experience (☎212 7660; www.stewartislandexperience.co.nz), offers 45min. semi-submersible tours of Halfmoon Bay, through forests of bladder kelp (1-3 tours daily. $35 per person).

Stewart Island Adventures (☎219 1429; www.stewartislandadventures.co.nz), from their location in the "Red Shed" on the wharf, organizes morning and overnight cruises (2½hr. morning cruise to Ulva and beyond, $59. Call ahead for overnight prices and availability.), however, their **Rakiura Yak About** 4hr. adventure cruise is the most wet and wild of their offerings, with a cruise to a remote location and included kayaks and wet suits. ($98 per person. Lunch and snorkel or fishing gear available onboard for extra cost. Departs daily at 2pm.). For a self-made adventure, Liz at **Rakiura Kayaks** (☎219 1160; www.rakiura.co.nz) offers multi-day kayak rentals ($40 per day, discounts with longer rentals).

OFF YOUR FEET

For those who prefer to see nature from a safe distance, **Stewart Island Flights** (☎218 9129; www.stewartislandflights.com) offers a variety of scenic flight options over and around the surrounding territory, offering a chance to see many of the places usually accessible only by days of muddy tramping. (30min. Departs from Halfmoon Bay. $275 per plane, up to 5 people.) **Stewart Island Helicopters** (☎219 1429; www.stewartislandadventures.co.nz) offers the same luxury, but in a helicopter (Heli-flightseeing from $155). Several road tours of the island's history and scenery are available, from **Stewart Island Experience** (☎212 7660; 1½hr. $35) and **Ruggedy Range** (☎219 1066; 2hr. $35.) After all your adventures, the serene **Stewart Island Spa,** run by Dr. Britt Moore of Justcafé, offers myriad relaxation options from its scenic perch high in the hills above town. The outdoor bush bath ($95 for 1 or 2 intimately acquainted people) is the epitome of relaxation, with exotic birds flitting about your lavender-scented toes. (Reiki, hot stone, and Thai massage from $95. To book, call or drop by Justcafé; see **Food,** above. MC/V.)

◪ THE RAKIURA TRACK

An occasionally monotonous boardwalk below the bushline, the Rakiura Track lacks the flash of more scenic Great Walks. There's plenty to delight bird-

MORE PAUA TO YOU

Paua, otherwise known as abalone in the US, are fairly common in Stewart Island waters and can make for a great meal while tramping. However, as they are highly prized for their shells and meat, strict rules apply to harvesting them to prevent depopulation.

The recreational daily limit for paua fishing is 10 per person, and you can only legally harvest them through surface diving (read: without scuba gear). Any paua shorter than 125mm are considered undersized and must be left alone or tosed back. Do take special care when replacing undersized paua, as paua blood does not clot and the tiniest cut can be fatal for the little guys.

Once you are ready to cook your paua, slice it from the shell using a quick circular motion. Remove the long white flat part (the tongue), and then give the meat a resounding whack or two with a hammmer (or any handy blunt object) to split the foot and tenderize the meat. Don't beat your paua to a pulp! Sauteeing the meat with a few spices in your billy pot may be the way to best cook it, but it is really up to you to see what works best in the bush. Finally, sit back and enjoy one of New Zeland's finest delicacies.

watchers and botanists, from silver-throated tui to exquisite hanging orchids. The track is too close to the development of Halfmoon Bay to support many kiwi, but the alternation between beach and forest makes for an enjoyable tramp nonetheless.

 WATER, WATER EVERYWHERE! Stewart Island's freshwater supplies come entirely from rain collection, and the absence of many large mammals makes giardia a largely non-existent threat. Therefore, hut water supplies and those from fast-moving streams are considered safe to drink by the DOC.

Length: 36km, 2-3 days.

Trailheads: The DOC office is at the center of the loop. The proper trailhead is at **Lee Bay,** about 5km from town. Just across from the wharf, Horseshoe Bay Rd. runs north 1km to Lee Bay Rd., which dead-ends at this trailhead. From the office, Main Rd. leads west about 2.5km to the other **North Arm** trailhead.

Transportation: It's an easy walk, but Stewart Island Experience (☎219 0034) offers a shuttle service. $24.

Seasonality: Year-round, though the island's southern location means limited winter daylight. Light but constant rain is never out of season, so expect at least ankle-deep mud.

Huts and Campsites: 2 huts have running water and pit toilets but no cooking facilities. 3 camping areas have similar amenities. **Hut** and **Camping Passes** (huts $10; camping $2.50) can only be bought at the Oban DOC office. Advance booking is not necessary.

Storage: Most accommodations store for free. The DOC office has large and small lockers ($5/2.50 per day).

HALFMOON BAY TO PORT WILLIAM HUT. *12km, 4-5hr.* This stretch is easily Rakiura Track's most scenic; many hikers attempting the trail in two days opt to linger for most of day one on this leg. The leg also makes for a popular dayhike or overnight stay. Skirting the coastline from Lee Bay, the track soon reaches **Little River,** a sandy inlet surrounded by dense brush. Farther on, **Maori Beach,** a popular dayhike from Halfmoon Bay, serves as a good rest spot before the final hour's walk to the hut. The bug-filled campsite features several sites amid the tall dune grass, a basic shelter, water, and an outhouse. The trail follows Maori Beach, where, at its end, a swing bridge crosses a wide tidal estuary. From there the path turns inland and uphill before splitting. The north fork leads 45min. to **Port William Hut** (20 bunks). The hut area is a laid-back place, with a nearby campsite and picnic tables sheltered under gum trees. Five minutes before the hut, just before the wharf, is the junction for the **Northwest Circuit** (p. 449).

PORT WILLIAM HUT TO NORTH ARM HUT. *12km, 5-6hr.* Back at the track junction, the westward fork steadily ascends over an extensive boardwalk and two swing bridges, eventually reaching the spectacular **Lookout Tower.** It's amazing what a difference five kilometers can make; a lush canopy of rata, rimu, and spindly inaka extends down to Patterson Inlet, with mountains looming in the distance. Past the tower, the track continues to climb, reaching an elevation of 305m before beginning a steep, undulating descent. About halfway to the hut, a junction branches off to the other side of the **Northwest Circuit.** The **North Arm Hut** (24 bunks) is set above a rocky shore; camping is not permitted.

NORTH ARM HUT TO TOWN. *12km, 4-5hr.* This lackluster section of graveled track has some elevation change along the way to **Sawdust Bay Campsite,** a simple shelter with scraggly trees and a bayside location. After passing a small spur to the lovely **Kaipipi Bay,** the track follows a steady grade, trading boardwalk for faster walking on a long-abandoned logging road, which leads out of the forest along roadways 2.5km back into town.

🔖 THE NORTHWEST CIRCUIT

Announce that you are planning to hike the Northwest Circuit on Stewart Island, and the average Kiwi's eyes will either glaze over in awe or narrow in criticism of your sanity. After all, ten days in the backcountry is one of the longest DOC treks possible, and most New Zealanders "couldn't be bothered." And effort it *does* require—the knee-to-thigh-deep mud is legendary, but what doesn't get talked up as much is the frequent scramble on all fours up steep hillsides and the ballet of tree-root jumping. However, tramp and ye shall receive isolated beaches, unparalleled wildlife viewing, and permanently discolored boots.

 WERE YOUR BOOTS MADE FOR WALKIN'? That prized photo with a kiwi bird isn't worth a thing if you end up hurt. The terrain of the Northwest Circuit is physically demanding. Only experienced trampers should tramp it in its entirety.

Length: 125km, 9-11 days.

Trailheads: The circuit can be tramped in either direction, but counterclockwise is the direction of choice, beginning at Port William Hut and ending at North Arm Hut, both on the Rakiura Track (p. 447).

Transportation: See **The Rakiura Track,** p. 447. For those wishing to shorten their tramp, several alternate start- and endpoints are available by water taxi, usually for a min. of 2 people (Port William $40-50, Bungaree Hut $50-60, Christmas Village Hut $70-90, Yankee River Hut $100, and Freshwater Landing Hut $50). Flights from Stewart Island Flights or Stewart Island Helicopters (see Off Your Feet, above) are also possible for a higher price, with the advantage of getting dropped farther along the track. Flights available to Smoky Beach, East Ruggedy Beach, West Ruggedy Beach, Little Hellfire Beach, Mason Bay, and Doughboy Bay on the Southern Circuit. Call ahead for prices and availability, as flights are tide and weather dependent.

Seasonality: Year-round, though the island's southern location means limited winter daylight. Light but constant rain is never out of season, so expect at least knee-deep mud at various points.

Huts and Campsites: 8 backcountry huts have running water and pit toilets but no cooking stoves. Camping in the overgrown bush is allowed. The Northwest Circuit Pass ($45), available from the DOC, buys you 10 nights of huts along the Northwest Circuit and the Rakiura Track. Otherwise, backcountry huts cost $5 per night, and great walk huts cost $10. Camping is free, but you must pay for a hut if you intend to use its facilities. Only Port William Hut, North Arm Hut, and Mason Bay Hut are staffed with full-time wardens during the summer.

Equipment: The 1:50,000 Halfmoon Bay topographic map ($12.50 from the DOC) is the best reference, though the trail is generally well-marked. *Let's Go* recommends renting an emergency personal locator beacon ($40) from the DOC office.

Storage: See **The Rakiura Track,** p. 447.

Registration: Check-in and check-out with the DOC is essential, lest a search-and-rescue be started on your behalf while you sip mocchachinos from Dunedin.

HALFMOON BAY TO PORT WILLIAM HUT. *12km, 4-5hr.* See **The Rakiura Track,** p. 447. Leaving early in the morning from town, stopping for lunch at Port William Hut, and then reaching Bungaree Hut by the afternoon is a popular first tramping day, though there is no need to rush, and you might appreciate the chance to eat off a bit of your pack weight by stopping here for the night.

PORT WILLIAM TO BUNGAREE HUT. *6km, 3-4hr.* Though the beginning parts of this leg are well-planked, this quickly disappears as you cross the first big saddle, where your torrid love affair with the island's mud begins. After several undulating hills through dense bush, the track descends first to a swing bridge by Little Bungaree Beach, and then over a smaller headland to the calm 1km sweep of Big Bungaree Beach. **Bungaree Hut** (16 bunks) occupies a scenic perch at the far end and is a comfortable spot for a little fishing and paua diving. This stretch also makes for an excellent short overnight tramp from town for the curious.

BUNGAREE TO CHRISTMAS VILLAGE HUT. *11.5km, 6hr.* The tramping begins here in earnest as you head inland past Gull Rock Point. After roughly 3km of up and down, the track reaches Murray Beach for a lovely 2km beach walk before crossing the Murray River over a swingbridge and heading back into the bush. The track travels about 5km through more unrelenting, undulating bush before reaching **Christmas Village Hut** (12 bunks), less than a kilometer past Christmas Village Bay. Just past the hut, a well-defined path leads up to **Mt. Anglem/Hananui** (11km, 6hr. round-trip), the island's highest point at 980m. If it's a nice day, the views from the top can justify the extra day spent getting there and back.

CHRISTMAS VILLAGE TO YANKEE RIVER HUT. *12km, 6hr.* Regardless of whether they've been naughty or nice this year, trampers awake in Christmas Village to face another day of bush tramping and, say it with us, *undulating terrain.* The positive thing about it, however, is that the first 5.5km until Lucky Beach follow higher ground and are generally dry. After the swingbridge into Lucky Beach, sandflies will cause you to curse your luck and send you back up into the forest, where you'll need to pay attention as you look for the continuing trail. A solid 4km later, you'll descend to the **Yankee River Hut** (16 bunks), located a few minutes downstream from its namesake river.

YANKEE RIVER TO LONG HARRY HUT. *8.5km, 5hr.* After crossing the Yankee River via swingbridge, the trail ascends steeply over Black Rock Point and down onto hilly Smoky Beach, which is a welcome sight for sore legs. After 2km of beach walking, the track crosses the Smoky River, and though another swingbridge is ready to assist, the river can be waded easily unless flooded or during peak high tide. After the crossing, the trip to the hut can be a hairy one, but you can rejoice in the fact that the DOC moved **Long Harry Hut** (12 bunks) to a more scenic location 1.5km to Yankee River.

LONG HARRY TO EAST RUGGEDY HUT. *9.5km, 5-6hr.* This scenic stretch of the trek often ranks among trampers' favorites, mainly for the penguin-viewing and fishing opportunities in Long Harry Bay and the lookout over East Ruggedy Beach. The track starts with a short 1.5km of forest walking to Long Harry Bay. Afterward, the trail climbs over Cave Point to follow a ridge before descending back down 30min. to rocky coastline; follow the coastline until the sign directs you back into the scrub. The track ascends steeply once again until the panoramic lookout over East Ruggedy Beach and the Rugged Islands. The subsequent descent to the beach involves crossing soggy sand, but don't worry, there's little danger of being swallowed. **East Ruggedy Hut** (12 bunks) is reached after 15min. of walking along the poles marking the track in the sand dunes.

EAST RUGGEDY TO HELLFIRE PASS HUT. *14km., 7-8hr.* This long, difficult stretch can try the patience of even fit trampers, but the views at the end are worth it. From East Ruggedy Hut, the track descends onto West Ruggedy Beach (make

Northwest Circuit and Rakiura Track

Foveaux Strait

TO BLUFF (30min)

SOUTHLAND

Stewart Island

RAKIURA NATIONAL PARK

SEE NORTHWEST CIRCUIT AND RAKIURA TRACK ENLARGEMENT

Foveaux Strait

Halfmoon Bay

Paterson Inlet

Mason Bay

Doughboy Bay

Codfish Island

Ruggedy Mountains

Toitoi Flat

Deceit Peaks

Tin Range

Pearl Island

Fraser Peaks

Big South Cape Island

South Cape

Ocean Beach

Oban

The Neck

Glory Cove

Ocean Beach

Ackers Point

Native Island

Ulva Island

Big Glory Bay

Golden Bay Wharf

Prices Inlet

Paterson Inlet

Kaipipi Walk

North Arm Hut

Pryse Peak 352m

South West Arm

Freds Camp Hut

Mt. Rakeahua 681m

Rakeahua Hut

Southern Circuit

TO DOUGHBOY BAY HUT (15km)

Trails Hill 431m

Mason Bay Hut

Homestead

Big Sandhill 156m

Lower Island Hill 137m

Island Hill

Scott Burn

Duck Cr.

Tolson Cr.

Rocky Mt. 549m

Freshwater Landing

Freshwater R. Hut

Freshwater R.

THOMSON RIDGE

The Paps 610m

Little Mt. Anglem 738m

Mt. Anglem / Hananui 980m

Murray R.

Lake Shella

Ruggedy Flat

Forkes Cr.

Upper Island Hill 62m

Benson Peak 360m

Hellfire Pass

Big Hellfire Hut

Little Hellfire Beach

Mason Head

Richards Point

Shark Island

RUGGEDY MOUNTAINS

Red Head Peak 510m

North Red Head

West Ruggedy Beach

Rugged Islands

East Ruggedy Beach

East Ruggedy Hut

Cave Point

Long Harry Bay

Long Harry Hut

Smoky Beach

Smoky Cr.

Black Rock Point

Yankee River Hut

Yankee R.

White Rock Point

Lucky Beach

Lucky Point

Saddle Point

Christmas Village Bay

Garden Point

Poliers Beach

Murray Beach

Gull Rock Point

Big Bungaree Beach

Bungaree Hut

Sawyers Beach

Port William Hut

Magnetic Beach

Lee Bay

Maori Beach

Garden Mound 164m

Rakiura Track

Northwest Circuit Track

Codfish Island

Waituna Bay

Mason Bay

Cavalier Cr.

Double Cr.

Wreck Cr.

Duck Cr.

Rakeahua R.

Kaipipi R.

Horseshoe Bay

Halfmoon Bay

Bobs Point

Mamaku Point

North Arm

0 2 4 kilometers
0   4 miles

0 5 10 kilometers
0   10 miles

sure you get the route correction from the DOC, as the topographic map has yet to be updated), following the beach for 2km. Check on the tide level before setting out on the beach. The track then re-enters the bush and climbs over the Ruggedy Mountains (yes, over them) before descending into Waituna Bay. The track climbs back up through mind-boggling mud and continues along a ridge for 3km until Hellfire Pass, location of the **Hellfire Pass Hut** (12 bunks).

HELLFIRE PASS TO MASON BAY HUT. *15km, 7hr.* This last push before Mason Bay is one of the most down and dirty, ascending from Hellfire Pass up to follow a ridge for about 2km before gradually descending into Little Hellfire Beach for 1km. Afterward, the track climbs over Mason Head and descends finally into Mason Bay, where you are likely to find many other people who haven't expended nearly as much energy to get there. If you arrive during high tide, the first stretch of beach can be difficult to navigate. It may be best to wait and walk on the hard-packed low-tide sand. The **Mason Bay Hut** (20 bunks) is located a few minutes up Duck Creek and is well-marked by a large pole. Early evening is the best time to go out looking for kiwis, but remember not to shine your flashlight directly at any you may find, as their eyes are incredibly sensitive. One of the entrances to the **Southern Circuit** (toward Doughboy Bay Hut) can be found by following the beach south from Duck Creek and looking for the bouys.

MASON BAY TO FRESHWATER LANDING HUT. *15.5km, 3-4hr.* This stretch of the track is blissfully flat and quick. However, in times of flood or heavy rain, allow extra time to get through. The track advances to the Island Hill Homestead just after Mason Bay Hut, and after 2km, you'll pass around Lower Island Hill. Beyond the hill, you'll cross a marshy, boardwalked area along and finally across Scott Burn, but beware of the so-called Chocolate Swamp. The **Freshwater Landing Hut** (16 bunks) is just over the swingbridge on the other side of the Freshwater River. There is an optional side-trip from the hut to **Rocky Mountain** (5km, 3hr. return), which affords decent panoramic views of the area. One of the entrances to the **Southern Circuit** (toward Fred's Camp Hut) begins directly opposite the hut.

FRESHWATER LANDING TO NORTH ARM HUT. *11km, 6-7hr.* The difficulty of this stretch of track often tempts trampers to book a water taxi back to town from Freshwater Landing. Simply put, you spend the majority of your time climbing inland up slippery slopes but without the bonus of scenery and wildlife. Start by following the Freshwater River and then go up and over Thompson Ridge. Several of the small rivers in this stretch can become impassible in heavy rain. The ridge descends steeply over a swingbridge onto the Rakiura Track, where you'll arrive dazed and exhausted, but only 45min. from the **North Arm Hut** (24 bunks).

NORTH ARM HUT TO TOWN. *12km, 4hr.* See **The Rakiura Track,** p. 447. Follow the former Kaipipi Rd. as it becomes Main Rd. into town, terminating at the South Sea Hotel for a well-earned beer. Don't forget to sign-out at the DOC before you leave!

APPENDIX

MEASUREMENTS

CLIMATE

The climate of New Zealand is generally temperate, with sharp regional contrasts. Glaciers, rain forests, and everything in between coexist in New Zealand.

Av. Temp. and Precipitation	January			April			July			October		
	°C	°F	mm	°C	°F	mm	°C	°F	mm	°C	°F	mm
Auckland	16/23	61/73	79	13/19	55/66	97	8/13	46/55	145	11/17	52/63	102
Christchurch	12/21	54/70	56	7/17	45/63	482	2/10	36/50	69	7/17	45/63	56
Dunedin	10/19	50/66	86	7/15	45/59	71	3/9	37/48	79	6/15	43/59	89
Napier	14/24	57/75	74	10/19	50/66	76	5/13	41/55	102	9/19	48/66	56
Nelson	13/22	55/72	73	8/18	46/64	81	3/13	37/55	89	7/17	45/63	78
Queenstown	10/22	50/72	82	6/16	43/61	71	1/10	34/50	78	5/16	41/61	88
Rotorua	12/24	54/75	90	9/18	48/64	119	4/13	39/55	145	7/17	45/63	116
Wellington	13/21	55/70	81	11/17	52/63	97	6/12	43/54	137	9/16	48/61	102

New Zealand uses the metric system. The basic unit of length is the **meter (m)** which is divided into 100 **centimeters (cm)**, or 1000 **millimeters (mm)**. One thousand meters make up one **kilometer (km)**. Fluids are measured in **liters (L)**, each divided into 1000 **milliliters (ml)**. A liter of pure water weighs one **kilogram (kg)**, divided into 1000 **grams (g)**, while 1000kg make up one metric **ton**.

1 inch (in.) = 2.54cm	1 centimeter (cm) = 0.39 in.
1 foot (ft.) = 0.30m	1 meter (m) = 3.28 ft.
1 mile (mi.) = 1.61km	1 kilometer (km) = 0.62 mi.
1 ounce (oz.) = 28.35g	1 gram (g) = 0.035 oz.
1 pound (lb.) – 0.454kg	1 kilogram (kg) = 2.202 lb.
1 fluid ounce (fl. oz.) = 29.57ml	1 milliliter (ml) = 0.034 fl. oz.
1 gallon (gal.) = 3.785L	1 liter (L) = 0.264 gal.
1 square mile (sq. mi.) = 2.59 sq. km	1 square kilometer (sq. km) = 0.386 sq. mi.

KIWI ENGLISH GLOSSARY

All Blacks: the national rugby team; never let on that you don't know what this is

ANZAC: Australia New Zealand Army Corps (p. 44); ANZAC Day is a national holiday (Apr. 25)

Aotearoa: "Land of the long white cloud"; the Maori name for New Zealand

ap-jump: to abseil face-first down a building

bach ("BATCH"): beachside holiday house; called a "crib" on South Island

backpackers: hostel

bathroom: room with a bath; not necessarily with a toilet

big bikkies: big bucks

bikkies: cookies, crackers

billy: backcountry cooking pot

biscuit: cookie

bloody: all-purpose curse

bogan: hooligan

bonnet: hood of a car

boot: trunk of a car

bottle shop: liquor store

capsicum: green, red, or yellow bell peppers

cashpoint: ATM

cheers: pardon; bye; thanks

chemist: drugstore, pharmacy

chips: french fries

chockers, chockablock: packed, crowded, busy, full

college: secondary school

concessions: senior citizens

crib: see "bach"

crisps: potato chips

cruisy: mellow, no worries

cuppa: cup of tea or coffee

dag: good guy; joker

dairy: convenience store

dear: expensive

DOC ("DOCK"): Department of Conservation

flash: glam, upscale, trendy

flat white: coffee; a long black with a dollop of milk

footie: soccer

French letter, frenchie: condom

get on the piss: to get drunk

Godzone: New Zealand (from "God's own")

good as gold: fine, sure, great

good on ya: good for you

gridiron: American football

grotty: dirty, run-down

gumboots: rubber boots

handle: a glass of beer smaller than a pint

hoe: to eat quickly

hokey pokey: NZ's favorite ice cream

hoon: slob, jerk

hoover: to vacuum or eat quickly

hottie: hot water bottle

hundreds and thousands: sprinkles

jandals: flip-flops

jersey, jumper: sweater

judder bar: speed bump

jugger: bloke, man

Kiwi: New Zealander; of or relating to New Zealand

kiwi: small flightless bird; the national symbol

kiwifruit: a furry greenish-brown fruit

knackered: very tired

L&P: soda

lift: elevator

long black: espresso with hot water

long drop: outhouse

main: main course of a meal

Mainland: South Island

Marmite: yeast spread

metal road: gravel road

milk bar: convenience store

no joy: no luck

ocker: over the top Kiwis

Pakeha: person of European descent; Caucasion foreigner

paper (university): class, course

paua: abalone, type of shellfish

pavlova: creamy, fruity meringue dessert

pipi: clam-like shellfish

piss down: to rain hard

plate: potluck dinner

Pom: Englishman (derisive)

pot plant: house plant

powerpoints: electrical hook-ups for tents or caravans

punting: any water activity in a boat

push bike: bicycle

quay ("KEY"): pier

rag: local newspaper

rattle your dags: to hurry up

rockmelon: cantaloupe

rubber: eraser

salad: cucumber, carrots, beetroot; "with salad" means these items come on a sandwich

scroggin: trail mix, gorp

sealed road: paved road

short black: between an espresso and a long black

Shortland Street: New Zealand soap opera; constant hostel entertainment

shout: to buy for someone

skull: to chug (beer)

Sky TV: satellite television

snog: to kiss or make out

snooker: pool-like game; to take a person's money usually in a game of snooker

spit the dummy: a diva-worthy temper tantrum

spinner: jerk

stubby: small bottle of beer

sweet as: great, cool

ta: thanks

TAB: shop to place bets without going to the tracks

take the piss/mickey out of: to mock; ridicule

tariff: price

tinny: lucky

ute: pickup truck ("utility vehicle")

Vegemite: yeast spread

wanker: jerk

woolies: winter clothes; long underwear

yob: see "hoon"

yonks: forever

MAORI-ENGLISH GLOSSARY

ao: cloud

Aotearoa: Maori name for New Zealand

e noho ra: goodbye (said by the person leaving)

haere mai: welcome

haere ra: goodbye, farewell (said by the person staying)

haka: war dance

hangi: underground Maori oven; also the meal cooked in said oven

hapu: regional community

hoa: friend

hongi: "sharing of breath"; Maori welcome expressed by touching together of noses

iwi: tribe, people, nation

ka pai: thank you; excellent

kai: food

kei te pehea koe: how are you? (singular)

kia ora: hello; health; luck

koe: you (singular)

koutou: you (plural)

kumara: sweet potato

mana: prestige, power

manaia: bird men

Maoritanga: Maori culture

marae: meeting place; sacred ground

moana: sea, lake

moko: traditional facial tattoo

motu: island

ngai, ngati: prefix indicating tribe, people, or clan

noa: counterpart to tapu

ora: life; alive, healthy, safe

pa: fortified Maori village

Pakeha: person of European descent; foreigner

patu: club (weapon)

poi: dance involving twirling balls on the ends of strings

pounamu: greenstone

powhiri: formal welcome

roto: lake

tane: man

tangata: humans, people

tangata whenua: "people of the land"; local Maori people

tapu: taboo, holy

tena-koe: hello (singular)

tukutuku: woven reed panels frequently found in marae

tupuna: ancestors

waka: canoe

whaikorero: welcome speech

whanga: bay, body of water

whanau: family

where: house

whenua: ground, land

INDEX

INDEX

GET CONNECTED & SAVE WITH THE HI CARD

An HI card gives you access to friendly and affordable accommodations at over 4,000 hostels in over 60 countries, including across Australia and New Zealand. Members also receive complementary travel insurance, members-only airfare deals, and thousands of discounts on everything from tours and dining to shopping, communications and transportation.

Join millions of HI members worldwide who save money and have more fun every time they travel.

 Hostelling International USA

ABOUT LET'S GO

NOT YOUR PARENTS' TRAVEL GUIDE

At Let's Go, we see every trip as the chance of a lifetime. If your dream is to grab a machete and forge through the jungles of Costa Rica, we can take you there. If you'd rather bask in the Riviera sun at a beachside cafe, we'll set you a table. We write for readers who know that there's more to travel than sharing double deckers with tourists and who believe that travel can change both themselves and the world—whether they plan to spend six days in Mexico City or six months in Europe. We'll show you just how far your money can go, and prove that the greatest limitation on your adventures is not your wallet, but your imagination.

BEYOND THE TOURIST EXPERIENCE

To help you gain a deeper connection with the places you travel, our fearless researchers scour the globe to give you the heads-up on both world-renowned and off-the-beaten-track attractions, sights, and destinations. They engage with the local culture only to emerge with the freshest insights on everything from local festivals to regional cuisine. We've also opened our pages to respected writers and scholars to hear their takes on the countries and regions we cover, and asked travelers who have worked, studied, or volunteered abroad to contribute first-person accounts of their experiences. In addition, we increased our coverage of responsible travel and expanded each guide's Beyond Tourism chapter to share more ideas about how to give back while on the road.

FORTY-EIGHT YEARS OF WISDOM

Let's Go got its start in 1960, when a group of creative and well-traveled students compiled their experience and advice into a 20-page mimeographed pamphlet, which they gave to travelers on charter flights to Europe. Four and a half decades later, we've expanded to cover six continents and all kinds of travel—while retaining our founders' adventurous attitude toward the world. Laced with witty prose and total candor, our guides are still researched and written entirely by students on shoestring budgets, experienced travelers who know that train strikes, stolen luggage, food poisoning, and marriage proposals are all part of a day's work.

THE LET'S GO COMMUNITY

More than just a travel guide company, Let's Go is a community. Our small staff comes together because of our shared passion for travel and our desire to help other travelers see the world the way it was meant to be seen. We love it when our readers become part of the Let's Go community as well—when you travel, drop us a postcard (67 Mt. Auburn St., Cambridge, MA 02138, USA), send us an e-mail (feedback@letsgo.com), or post on our forum (http://www.letsgo.com/connect/forum) to tell us about your adventures and discoveries.

For more information, visit us online: www.letsgo.com.

MAP INDEX

MAP LEGEND

✈	Airport
🚌	Bus Station
🚆	Train Station
⚓	Ferry Landing/Line
⛪	Church
⛷	Ski Area
🚶	Trailhead
⌒	Waterfall
)(	Pass
▲	Mountain Range
▲	Mountain Peak

✚	Hospital
✪	Police
✉	Post Office
ⓘ	Tourist Office
⑤	Bank
⚑	Embassy/Consulate
■	Site or Service
☻	Theater
▮	Library
℞	Pharmacy

🏛	Museum
🏨	Hotel/Hostel
⛺	Camping
🍴	Food
◗	Nightlife
★	Entertainment & Clubs
☕	Cafe
🏠	Hut
⌂	Shelter
💻	Internet
🏄	Surfing

	Park
	Water
	Beach
∿	Sealed Road
⋯	Unsealed Roads
⋯	Trail or Track
-----	Pedestrian Zone

R.C.L.

The Let's Go compass always points NORTH.

MARS 2008